D1349786

LOCOMOTIVES
WE HAVE LOST

Will Adams

An imprint of
Ian Allan Publishing

First published 2015

ISBN 978 086093 667 1

© Ian Allan Publishing 2015

Published by Oxford Publishing Co

an imprint of Ian Allan Publishing Ltd, Addlestone, Surrey KT15 2SF

Printed in the Czech Republic.

Visit the Ian Allan Publishing website at www.ianallanpublishing.com

Contents

FRONT COVER
Main picture: Ex-LMS 'Patriot' 4-6-0 No 45519 *Lady Godiva* passes through Longsight, Manchester, in June 1957; withdrawals of these unrebuilt members of the class began in 1960, and all had gone by the end of 1962. *W. Oliver, Colour-Rail*

Top left: Another unrebuilt 'Patriot', No 45518 *Bradshaw*, heads the up 'Mancunian' on Castlethorpe troughs in August 1958. *T. B. Owen, Colour-Rail*

Top middle: One of the last seven ex-NER 'D20' 4-4-0s stands at York during 1956, it was taken out of service in November. *Dave Cobbe, railphotoprints collection*

Top right: 'Saint' Class 4-6-0 No 2920 *Saint David* is seen at Banbury on 15 June 1952 during an SLS 'Saints' farewell tour. This was the last of its class, withdrawn and scrapped at the end of the following year. *K. Cooper, Colour-Rail*

BACK COVER
Top: Work-worn 'N1' 'Mogul' No 31878 passes through Ashford on an unknown date. It was one of six inherited by BR, and all were withdrawn in November 1962. *Colour-Rail collection*

Bottom: On 11 April 1962 Vulcan-built 'WD' 2-8-0 No 90672 enters the former Stratford-upon-Avon & Midland Junction station at Fenny Compton. All 733 locomotives purchased from the War Department by the LNER and BR were scrapped; this example was withdrawn from its home shed of Woodford Halse two years after the date of this photograph. *Rob Tibbits, Colour-Rail*

Introduction

'DON'T IT ALWAYS SEEM TO GO

THAT YOU DON'T KNOW WHAT YOU'VE GOT TILL IT'S GONE.'

Joni Mitchell, *Big Yellow Taxi*, 1970

'Most of these engines did the work for which they were designed in a more or less satisfactory and unobtrusive manner and then in the way of all locomotives, good and bad, went to the scrapyard when it was done, with no record of their passing but a routine entry in the book of the mechanical department.' So wrote one of the contributors to *London Midland and Scottish Railway Centenary*, published by *The Times* newspaper in 1938. He goes on to say, 'Mr W. A. Stanier came from the Great Western Railway … bringing some degree of uniformity into the L.M.S. locomotive stud which became essential on the formation of the company. By a drastic scrapping of obsolete, inefficient and small miscellaneous classes of engines to which the company had fallen heir in 1923, hundreds of locomotives disappeared.'

There is no sense of loss or nostalgia in these words. Indeed, the disposal of 'obsolete, inefficient and small miscellaneous classes' is seen as a good thing, a necessary move towards modernity and progress. For despite how we might view it otherwise, the British steam railway was not created for the delight of the railway enthusiast, but as a vast and complex multi-million-pound industry where shareholders had to be satisfied, dividends paid, and rivals overcome. Yesterday's steam locomotive, once it became inefficient and worn out, was a poor advertisement for any railway company.

In a 2011 article in *Railway Heritage* magazine, editor Robin Jones drew a telling analogy between the technological development of steam power in the 19th and early 20th centuries and today's fast-moving digital age. 'There would be little sentimentality for a machine which did a job far less efficiently than one which had replaced it,' he wrote. 'The emphasis was on the future, not the past, and in the booming railway sector there was so much that was new to generate excitement. In the same way, a state of-the-art laptop of 2003 which has only a small hard drive and a comparatively slow processor, is big and bulky, and does not have wi-fi access may well end up in the landfill site. Who would want to give it shelf space when they have the latest all-singing, all-dancing model?'

Of course, if that philosophy had been adopted by our private railway industry, there would be no railway heritage movement today. What might be called 'corporate' railway preservation goes back to the very earliest days. In 1829 the Robert Stephenson locomotive *Invicta* was built for the Canterbury & Whitstable

Railway. Never a great success, it was offered for sale in 1839, but there were no takers and it duly became South Eastern Railway property. It was later given to Canterbury City Corporation as a museum artefact, thus becoming the first locomotive to be preserved. The famous *Rocket*, albeit much modified, followed in the early 1860s.

By that time there was an increasing sense of the historical value of the earliest engines, especially with the establishment of the Patent Office Museum in London, which later became the Science Museum. The Commissioners of Patents acquired several significant exhibits, including *Sans Pareil*, sans wheels, and *Locomotion No 1*, much rebuilt. *Puffing Billy* of 1813, also much rebuilt, went to the Patent Museum at the same time.

The railway companies themselves were not unaware of the historical significance of some of their products. In 1875 the 50th anniversary of the Stockton & Darlington Railway was celebrated by the North Eastern Railway with a major exhibition of historical locomotives at Darlington. In 1881 a similar event marked the centenary of George Stephenson's birth. Even then there was clearly a growing awareness of the significance – and publicity value – of our railway heritage. A few years later the Great Northern Railway's former Locomotive Superintendent Archibald Sturrock suggested the formation of a national collection of historic locomotives, but nothing came of the idea.

Of course, the only option for preservation in those days was for the engines to be 'stuffed and mounted' for display – 'heritage railways' were still more than seven decades in the future. Timothy Hackworth's 0-6-0 *Derwent* of the Stockton & Darlington Railway was mounted on a plinth at Darlington Bank Top station; the Furness Railway's Bury 0-4-0 *Coppernob* of 1846 was placed in a large glass case outside Barrow-in-Furness station in 1900; and South Devon Railway 0-4-0 *Tiny* of 1868 was put on display by the GWR at Newton Abbot station in 1927. Space has always been one of the major problems associated with the preservation of locomotives, which are, by their very nature, large and heavy. The GWR put aside two broad gauge engines, *North Star* and *Lord of the Isles*, upon withdrawal in the 1870s with a view to their preservation. However, Churchward was coldly unsentimental when he wrote to the Board at the end of 1905: 'These engines are occupying valuable space in our Shops at Swindon. They have been offered to several Institutions without success, and I beg to recommend that authority be given for them to be destroyed.' They were duly scrapped, demonstrating that the future of even the most valuable items cannot be assured. Twenty years later a replica of *North Star* was built (some of the parts of the original having magically reappeared), and displayed on a plinth in the Works' Locomotive Shop – the first 'new-build' project?

Britain's awareness of its contribution to railway technology was given a boost when the British Empire Exhibition was held at Wembley in 1924. Alongside the latest products of the newly formed 'Big Four' companies was *Locomotion No 1*. In 1925 the centenary of the Stockton & Darlington Railway was marked by the LNER with what was then the largest cavalcade of historic and modern locomotives, watched by 250,000 spectators and members of the Royal Family.

This event, as well as perhaps a desire to commemorate the many old companies so recently absorbed into the 'Big Four', led to the creation of Britain's first railway museum, set up at York under the auspices of the LNER in 1927. (This was quite late in the day compared with overseas, where railway museums had been long established in Norway since 1895 and Germany since 1899.) The museum occupied the old station buildings and former locomotive erecting and repair shops of the York & North Midland Railway, and at first the collection principally consisted of items from the North Eastern and Great Northern companies. Nevertheless, it became in effect a 'national' railway museum, and engines from other companies gravitated towards it, including the GWR treasure *City of Truro*, withdrawn from regular service in 1931.

Meanwhile the LMS was following the lead established by the LNWR by setting aside important engines for preservation. Sadly, when Stanier joined the company from Swindon some of the engines supposedly safeguarded were scrapped in 1932. Happily, LNWR 'Precursor' *Hardwicke*, the unique Caledonian Railway 4-2-2 No 123 and Highland Railway 'Jones Goods' were secure by 1935, as well as the well-known Liverpool & Manchester 0-4-2 *Lion* of 1838.

However, as the *Oxford Companion to British Railway History* points out, 'The conflict between the business interest of railway management and preservation in museums is a recurrent theme.' This would become even more so when Britain's railways were nationalised in 1948, and preservation became a public matter, maintained by the taxpayer.

A 1951 report 'The Preservation of Relics and Records' proposed a truly national railway museum, but its rather lesser achievement was the Museum of British Transport, established in a former bus garage in Clapham, south London, in 1961, together with the local-authority-operated museums at Swindon (1962) and Glasgow (1964). Other smaller local museums had been set up in Hull (destroyed during the war), Birmingham, Bristol, Leeds, Leicester and Liverpool, tending to concentrate on local railway artefacts or industrial railways.

British Railways continued to add to the list of 'locomotives scheduled for preservation', placing them in store at various works. Ex-GWR 'Star' 4-6-0 No 4003 *Lode Star* and 'Dean Goods' 0-6-0 No 2516 were two such. However, other important early types – the LNWR 'Claughtons', for example

– were not considered, and were lost, as we shall discover many times in these pages.

In the mid-1960s the British Transport Commission decided it no longer wanted to be responsible for these collections, and under the Transport Act of 1968 they passed to the Department of Education and Science – in effect, the Science Museum. Space to house the collection was now needed, and the former steam shed roundhouse at York was eventually chosen. Work on the building began in 1973, and it opened in 1975, exactly 150 years since the opening of the Stockton & Darlington Railway.

Thus far the locomotive preservation movement had been official and corporate, but the 1950s saw a huge sea change. In 1950 the narrow gauge Talyllyn Railway in Wales was taken over by a preservation society, and volunteers operated the first public trains the following year. It was the first railway preserved in this way anywhere in the world, and was run by volunteers and enthusiasts with no direct connection with the railway industry. Railway preservation was becoming increasingly led by individuals and groups of individuals, but was also increasingly governed by available funds and available space.

As far as individual locomotives were concerned, the Stephenson Locomotive Society had achieved a first in 1927 when it saved LB&SCR 0-4-2 No 214 *Gladstone*, and placed it in the York Museum. Then in 1955 the British Transport Commission published its report, *The Modernisation and Re-equipment of British Railways*, whereby £1,240 million was to be made available to, among other matters, accelerate the move to diesel and electric traction, and the total elimination of steam. When the railways had been nationalised in 1948, BR had inherited about 20,000 steam locomotives of all ages, types and conditions and, as with the situation on the LMS ten years earlier (outlined at the beginning of this Introduction), rationalisation was essential. It is perhaps less well known that more than 600 engines had already been withdrawn and scrapped by the 'Big Four' in 1947. More than one-third of the 20,000 that remained (7,440) was made up of 0-6-0 tender and tank locomotives, together with just over 2,500 4-6-0 types. However, by the time of the report only about 1,000 locos had been dispensed with, and many were still being built to pre-nationalisation designs and to the brand-new Standard designs.

In 1958 the position was reviewed again, and the disposal of the steam fleet was to be accelerated. There were still some 16,000 steam engines on BR's books at this time, and they all had to go. As Robert Adley wrote (in *Out of Steam*), 'Heretofore, scrapping had been a task undertaken as an orderly part of the railway's process of renewal... But the laying waste of over 16,000 working locomotives in ten years was a task of a totally different magnitude from anything seen before.'

In 1959 a landmark was established when Captain Bill Smith RNR became the first private individual to buy for preservation a locomotive from British Railways. The engine was former GNR 'J52' 0-6-0ST No 1247 (BR No 68846), and in his book *1247: Preservation Pioneer* (Silver Link Publishing, 1991) he recalls the bemused phone call from an official at Great Northern House following his letter suggesting the purchase: 'It has caused a bit of a stir here and has been passed from one to another round the office because, you see, BR have never sold an engine before, and no one knows how to go about it!' Nonetheless, the purchase went through (for a never-disclosed sum), and No 1247 became a popular engine at exhibitions and hauling rail tours until it was eventually donated to the NRM at York, in working order, in 1980.

The same year the last LNWR 'Coal Tank' No 58926, withdrawn in 1957, was purchased by a group of enthusiasts led by former shedmaster Max Dunn. He was told, delightfully, 'The British Transport Commission require £666 for this engine in order to satisfy their auditors, and are pressing for a substantial remittance on account. Please send what you can afford to save this gentle and homely relic of a more tranquil age from the oxyacetylene cutting apparatus.'

In 1963 businessman Alan Pegler bought the world-famous 'Pacific' *Flying Scotsman* for its scrap value of £3,000. This may seem an insignificant sum, but at that time it was about three times the average annual salary, and at today's values would equate to more than £57,000. Yet that was still a tiny fraction of the cost of recreating a similar engine from scratch today in order to fill a preservation gap – 'new-build' 'A1' *Tornado* came in at £3 million! The subsequent turbulent history of *Flying Scotsman* is a sobering tale of pouring money into a seemingly bottomless pit to keep a famous engine operational.

Another example is graphically illustrated by David Shepherd, the wildlife artist who used the income from a very successful art exhibition in New York to 'invest' in two redundant BR engines. 'My life changed in many ways when I made that telephone call to British Rail in 1967,' he wrote. 'Helplessly caught up in the great buying mania when enthusiasts all over the country were feverishly trying to raise the funds to buy "their" favourite locomotive, I picked up the telephone and bought two. For just £3,000 [about £50,000 at today's values], No 92203, a British Railways Standard class 9F 2-10-0, just eight years old, was mine… For a further £2,000 I also purchased 75029, a Standard class 4-6-0, just a few years older. I had purchased two almost brand-new locomotives weighing collectively 275 tons, and they were both taken out of service for me shortly after that phone call.' His subsequent involvement with the engines was 'fraught so often with drama, despair, humour, frustration, not to mention near financial bankruptcy caused by my "hobby".' And where do you put 275 tons of steam locomotive? After looking at more than 30 potential sites across the South of England, he eventually found a home for them on what was to become the East Somerset Railway.

So, just because there were suddenly 16,000 steam locos available to be bought either 'off the track' or from a scrapyard, it was a far from easy or inexpensive process, and there was the continual problem of where to house them, private or BR sidings being about the only option; initially Shepherd was paying BR £20 a week to rent a siding near Southampton. The country's first preserved standard-gauge line, the Bluebell Railway, was not opened until 1960, and was having its own problems in acquiring motive power. Being an ex-LB&SCR line it wanted to concentrate on rescuing as much of that company's stock as possible; one choice was a Stroudley 'D1' Class 0-4-2T, but it was found that the last one had been scrapped 18 months earlier! Next choice was a Stroudley 'Terrier' 0-6-0T, and happily BR had a surplus one and sold it to the railway, together with a couple of coaches, for just £750 (nearly £16,000 today). Other engines on the 'wish list' simply could not be afforded, as the Bluebell's finances were principally tied up in purchasing the freehold of the line. Thus several locos it would like to have saved were lost for ever.

Sometimes sheer serendipity played a part in deciding which of those 16,000 engines were spared the cutter's torch. Patrick Whitehouse, of Tyseley fame, nearly chose ex-GWR 'Grange' Class 4-6-0 No 6853 *Morehampton Grange* for just £1,200 instead of a 'Castle', but it was found to have a cracked steam manifold. By 1965 the 'Granges' were extinct, and the cost of recreating 'the 81st Grange', No 6880 *Betton Grange*, is quoted as £350,000 – and that is using a number of major 'second-hand' parts. As Patrick said, 'We have kicked ourselves ever since.' Likewise, the Great Western Society at Didcot was faced with a choice between a 'Grange' and a 'Hall' – the former had a higher scrap value, so was rejected.

Another potential purchaser was offered a virtually brand new '82xxx' Standard 3MT 2-6-2T but was unable to raise the money, acquiring 'Jinty' 0-6-0T No 47383 instead. The subject of yet another 'new-build' project, No '82045' is expected to cost well over £1 million.

When one considers the turnovers of today's heritage railways, and the enormous sums that can seemingly be readily raised for restoration or building from scratch, it is galling that so many rare and desirable engines were lost in the 1960s for the sake of a few thousand pounds. Nonetheless, we are still fortunate to have well over 400 preserved steam locomotives in Britain, ranging from historic museum-pieces to BR Standard classes that had hardly been run in, and from rusting 'kits of parts' optimistically stored in the far corners of heritage sites to gleaming fully operational types, altogether representing some 150 different classes (and more than 50 of these locomotives had main-line certification in 2014).

But that total would have been much smaller had it not been for one remarkable scrapyard story. Between 1960 and 1963 more than 6,000 steam locomotives were withdrawn (just under half of all those than remained), and soon BR's works were overwhelmed by the work of cutting. For example, only a couple of dozen of the nearly 1,000 BR Standard locomotives were scrapped at BR works. The business was therefore put out to tender, and numerous scrapyards up and down the country were soon receiving sad cavalcades of dead engines, sometimes hauled by an engine in steam that was also making its last journey – driving itself to its own funeral. The yards in South Wales – Buttigieg and Cashmore of Newport, Hayes of Bridgend, Bird of Risca, Ward of Briton Ferry and Cohen of Morriston – were ideal destinations, being close to the steel furnaces where the scrap could be recycled using the new Electric Arc Furnaces, developed commercially for the melting of iron and steel scrap in the mid-1960s.

The scrap merchants bid for withdrawn locos on a 'per ton' basis, and acquired them with strict conditions imposed by BR, including a prohibition on selling them on to private buyers, including preservation groups. Perhaps this was to prevent profiteering, or because BR was selling some engines for further industrial use, and did not want to be undercut by the scrappers.

Once they made the journey to the scrapyards, there was really no way back for most of the engines; Cashmore, for example, which had yards at Newport and Great Bridge, Birmingham, cut most of its acquisitions within days of receiving them. At that time the company had a 20-strong team cutting up around six locomotives a week. It would take two men around a week to entirely dismantle an engine; protected only by goggles, gauntlets and heavy overalls, it could be dangerous work, their torches sometimes igniting the grease that had lubricated the wheels. Some individual bits were sold on – chimneys became flowerpots – and at one time Cashmore's Tipton yard offered conducted tours for enthusiasts, but these had to be stopped when the coach-loads of schoolboys became difficult to manage. All told, Cashmore disposed of more than 2,150 steam locomotives.

The unique 'Pacific' No 71000 *Duke of Gloucester*, already shorn of its cylinders, was sent to Cashmore's Newport yard in error. Happily for posterity, it was redirected to Woodham Brothers' yard at Barry – otherwise it would likely not have survived. Woodhams' became the most famous of all the South Wales yards, and since the mid-1950s had been producing high-quality scrap metal for the newly nationalised steel industry. In 1957 Dai Woodham negotiated a contract with BR to scrap rails and rolling stock, mostly from the Western Region. Part of the Modernisation Plan was to reduce the goods wagon fleet from 1¼ million to 600,000. Each lot of metal was bought at an auction, with a priority for scrapping detailed by BR. Woodhams' took a lease on the former marshalling yard at Barry Docks to accommodate the acquired stock (and had to pay a per-engine rental charge to Associated British Ports thereafter).

In 1958 the company won a tender to scrap locomotives, and in 1959 Dai spent a week at Swindon Works learning how to do this hitherto unfamiliar job. On 25 March of that year the first batch of engines left Swindon for Barry. However, Woodhams' found the scrapping of rails and wagons easier and more profitable; also, the wagons were taking up an enormous amount of space that could be used to store more engines, so the wagons were disposed of first. From mid-1964 the yard won additional contracts to scrap Southern Region stock, and the yard was increased in size again. In 1965 65 locomotives had arrived, and 28 were scrapped, but thereafter wagons and rails took priority and the mass scrapping of engines ceased. By the end of steam on BR in August 1968, Dai had bought 297 locomotives, and 217 were still in the yard.

The yard duly became a Mecca for steam-starved enthusiasts, and the story of how these engines were preserved and, in many cases, restored to working order is well known. The first engine was bought and towed away as early as September 1968. However, as mentioned above, the company was contractually prevented from selling complete locomotives that had been sold to them for scrap unless payment of a levy was made (this was later discontinued). Woodhams' set the price for each locomotive at its exact scrap value – there was apparently no haggling! – plus the BR levy, plus VAT. In most cases the preservation group paid a deposit for a particular locomotive to reserve it. The new owners were also allowed to remove components from similar loco types as spare parts; sadly this developed into widespread pilfering, and security guards had to be employed by the early 1980s. By this time the supply of wagons was diminishing, so two steam locos were scrapped – but they were the last to suffer that fate.

When Dai Woodham announced his retirement, a concerted effort was made to clear the remaining hulks, and the last steam engine to leave the Barry yard did so in January 1990. An amazing total of 213 locomotives were 'rescued' from Woodhams' yard ('steam's Dunkirk', as Robert Adley termed it), and more than 100 have been restored to working order. Had it not been for Dai Woodham's perceptive entrepreneurship, some might well have ended up in these pages, and the preservation movement would have been very much the poorer.

By that fateful day in August 1968 BR's standard-gauge main-line steam fleet, having numbered 16,099 locomotives just ten years earlier, had been reduced to zero, leaving just three narrow-gauge engines on the Vale of Rheidol Railway in mid-Wales, still at that time owned and operated by BR. Some engines lingered in scrapyards for another year or so before being cut up, but thereafter it was a case of 'when they're gone, they're gone'.

This book provides details of almost 350 classes of engines – a total of 10,252 machines – that were lost for ever as a result of the 'Modernisation' process, because not a single example was preserved. Some were as much as 80 years old, others not much more than five years old. If one takes an arbitrary figure of, say, 50 tons as the weight of an average six-coupled tender engine, and uses that figure as the average weight of each scrapped locomotive (many were lighter, some much heavier), it amounts to maybe half a million tons of scrap metal to be turned into the proverbial razor blades and cookers.

It is heartening, perhaps remarkable, that so many engines live on in preservation, even though they represent a minute proportion of the former total. The majority of those scrapped were workaday, unremarkable goods engines – the 'obsolete, inefficient and small miscellaneous classes' referred at the beginning – and, with the hardest of noses, their loss would not have occasioned the shedding of a tear. But it is the rare, historically significant engines that were lost by chance, by lack of money, by oversight, that are most missed. And so many of the smaller examples – the quaint, the quirky and the unique – would have been invaluable and economical additions to the stock of especially the smaller heritage lines. But where would the larger engines have been accommodated? How would they have been financed – maintenance, overhaul, accommodation, coal? When BR Standard 4MT 4-6-0 No 75027 arrived at the Bluebell Railway in working order, having been purchased and donated by a member, it was thought ridiculously large for the line, even though in time it proved to be ideally suited. There were no main-line steam rail tours from 1968 until grudgingly allowed by BR some years later, so where would the main-line 'racehorses' have been allowed to gallop if rescued in the early 1960s? Many claim that there are already too many preserved engines in operation or still under restoration, that the pot of preservation money is being spread too thinly.

Yet our appetite for the steam locomotives of the past seems insatiable. Buoyed by the conspicuous success of 'new-build' 'A1' No 60163 *Tornado*, there are currently some two dozen schemes to bring back long-lost classes (outlined in the appropriate sections of this book) – the so-called 'Lazarus locomotives'. So let us celebrate what we have, and what we will be able to enjoy anew in the future, for clearly all is *not* lost!

Acknowledgements

I must stress at the outset that this is not a work of original scholarship, but rather a compilation of information marshalled from many different sources. I am therefore primarily indebted to the many knowledgeable authors on whose works I have drawn.

First and foremost among them is Hugh Longworth, whose monumental, authoritative and comprehensive books – *British Railways Steam Locomotives 1948-1968* and *BR Steam Locomotives: Complete Allocations History, 1948-1968*, both published by Ian Allan – provided the inspiration and springboard for the present project. I must also thank Nick Grant, Publishing Manager at Ian Allan, for inviting me to compile this record.

The authors of the books and websites consulted, where known, as listed in the Sources. As far as the illustrations are concerned, my thanks go to Richard Casserley for supplying so many images from his and his father's vast collection. He seemed to be able to find a photograph of even the most obscure locomotives! My thanks also go to Paul Chancellor of Colour-Rail, whose comprehensive, well-ordered and easily accessed website made choosing the colour images straightforward, readily assisted by Paul himself. The other photographers and collectors who have provided pictures are credited individually, and I am grateful to them, too, for their foresight in recording often rare and threatened locomotive classes, and for their general assistance.

I have been interested in railways all my life, and have been involved in railway publishing as an editor and occasional author for some 30 years, but I have still managed to glean a great deal of fascinating new information during the course of writing this book. I hope the reader will take as much pleasure in reading or dipping into it as I have found in researching it. Although every care has been taken to verify and double-check the information it contains, I must take responsibility for errors of fact or interpretation.

Will Adams
Denford, Northants

Note Unless otherwise stated, the locomotive numbers listed in the heading of each class are the numbers actually carried by those locos that entered BR ownership. In some cases locomotives retained their pre-nationalisation number until scrapped, without ever carrying their allocated BR number.

1

Locomotives of the former Great Western Railway and its constituents

'YTW' 0-4-0ST

No 1

British Railways' only 'No 1' locomotive was an 0-4-0 saddle tank built in 1900 for the Ystalyfera Tinplate Works in 1900. Ystalyfera is a village on the River Tawe, about 13 miles (21km) north-east of Swansea.

In 1838 a furnace was built by James Palmer Budd at Ystalyfera, and from this grew the iron and tinplate works that by 1863 was described as 'the largest tinplate manufactory in the world'. Tinplate sheets of approximately 3 feet by 2 feet were dispatched in packages or bound bundles by rail via the Swansea Vale/Midland/LMS line to Swansea, where they were sent to various ports to be shipped around the world, as well as to large British companies such as ICI, Cadbury's and Colman's.

In 1908 an engine driver earned 5s 9d per day for a six-day week, and a fireman 4s 7d a day.

Before the Second World War the works had four mills and employed 300 workers; during the war one mill closed because so many young men had joined the armed forces.

The plant was dismantled under the Tinplate Redundancy Scheme in March 1946, having closed due to the high cost of materials and the out-of-date machinery; the company was

Introduced 1900
Designed by Peckett
Built by Peckett
Number built 1
Number inherited by BR 1
Last example withdrawn January 1954

No 1, with its Peckett works plate prominent, stands at Danygraig shed on 27 August 1948. *H. C. Casserley*

voluntarily wound up in April 1947. The saddle tank, built by Peckett of Bristol and named *Hercules*, was acquired by BR in July 1948 and entered stock as a service locomotive in South Wales, allocated to Danygraig shed, Swansea, until withdrawn there in January 1954, and scrapped in March.

Weston, Clevedon & Portishead Railway 0-6-0T 'Terrier'

Nos 5, 6

The Weston, Clevedon & Portishead Railway opened in 1897 between Weston and Clevedon, and was extended to Portishead in 1907. Always an impecunious concern, it entered receivership in 1909 and was to spend 31 of its 43 years in the hands of receivers. The famous 'Light Railway King' Col H. F. Stephens took over the running in 1911, but when he died in 1931 the railway continued its decline. Eventually the company applied for a Court Order to close the line and the last train ran on 18 May 1940.

The sole creditor sold the line to the GWR (but not the land) for use as storage of redundant coal wagons. Meanwhile the WC&PR stock was removed to Swindon and mostly scrapped, and the track was later removed for use in the war effort.

The two last locomotives bought by the company were two LBSCR 'A1X' Class 'Terriers', built for London suburban traffic and country branches, small but surprisingly powerful engines. No 43 *Gipsyhill* (built in 1877) and No 53 *Ashtead* (1875) were acquired from the Southern Railway in 1925 and 1937 respectively. No 43 became No 2 *Portishead* and No 53 was the new No 4.

When acquired by the GWR in 1940 No 2 was repainted in GWR livery and renumbered No 5, retaining its name. It was allocated to St Philip's Marsh, Bristol, for shunting and harbour duties. Passing to BR, it was moved to Taunton for shunting at Bridgwater docks. In January 1950 it briefly became shed pilot at Newton Abbot, but then went into store at Swindon. Attempts to have the loco preserved failed and it was broken up in March 1954.

No 4 hauled the very last train on the WC&PR, then as the

Ex-WC&PR No 2 *Portishead*, as ex-GWR No 5, languishes in Swindon Stock Shed on 2 March 1952.
A. J. Pike, Frank Hornby collection

Introduced 1872
Designed by William Stroudley
Built by LBSCR, Brighton Works
Number built 50
Number inherited by BR (from WC&PR) 2
Last example withdrawn March 1954

GWR's No 6 it too went to St Philip's Marsh for shunting and harbour duties. After helping to lift the rails from the WC&PR, it went to Nottingham, but was little used and was returned to Bristol and scrapped in July 1948.

Interestingly, of the 21 'Terriers' that passed in BR ownership, 10 have been preserved.

Brecon & Merthyr Railway '36' Class 0-6-2T

Nos 421-426, 428

The Brecon & Merthyr Tydfil Railway was authorised in 1859 and the full 61½-mile line was completed ten years later, pursuing a difficult and steeply graded course between the two places in its name. Like many railways of South Wales is life blood was coal traffic, and like the others it favoured the 0-6-2T wheel arrangement. Such an arrangement gave high adhesive weight and plenty of power with good braking ability, essential for coal trains on steep routes. Speed was not a requirement, nor were large tanks or bunkers as the distances covered were generally short. The locomotives would blast their way up the valleys chimney-first, then return with loaded trains more quickly bunker-first, the pony truck providing useful guidance on the curves.

The B&M '36' Class of 0-6-2Ts was based on the Rhymney Railway's 'R' Class, but with round-topped fireboxes. They were designed by James Dunbar, Locomotive Superintendent of the B&M from 1909 until his death on 26 February 1922. The initial four locos were augmented with four more in 1914, and carried an assortment of numbers until they were absorbed by the GWR at the Grouping, when they became Nos 421-428 in the 1946 renumbering scheme, although only four got to carry the new numbers prior to withdrawal. Some were rebuilt with GWR taper boilers.

Introduced 1909
Designed by James Dunbar
Built by Robert Stephenson
Number built 8
Number inherited by BR 7
Last example withdrawn March 1951

No 11, which would have become GWR/BR No 421, is seen here circa 1949, after rebuilding with a GWR taper boiler. Allocated to Newport Pill shed, it was withdrawn and scrapped in the early part of that year. *R. M. Casserley collection*

They were described by O. S. Nock as 'massive looking, very handsome … with the kind of proportions one would expect for a mountain climbing engine.'

Cleobury Mortimer & Ditton Priors Light Railway 0-6-0PT

Nos 28, 29

The Cleobury Mortimer & Ditton Priors Light Railway, which ran parallel to the Severn Valley line in south Shropshire, but some miles to the west, was authorised in 1901, and took seven years to built, opening for goods on 19 July 1908 and to passengers on 20 November. Its main freight traffic was stone from the quarries in this part of the Clee Hills. The line was absorbed into the GWR at the Grouping in 1923, and passenger traffic ceased in 1938, goods following in 1939. However, the railway was not yet finished, for following the outbreak of the Second World War a Royal Naval Armament Depot was opened at Ditton Priors in 1941, ensuring the line's survival into the 1960s. The depot had 25 magazines and four stores for naval mines around Brown Clee Hill. The buildings were camouflaged and served by rail sidings, and the trains and their dangerous cargo were loaded and unloaded inside.

The line had two locomotives, both 0-6-0 saddle tanks built by Manning Wardle in 1908, and named *Burwarton* and *Cleobury*. Under GWR ownership they became Nos 28 and 29. In 1931 and 1924 respectively they were rebuilt by the GWR with new boilers and pannier tanks, losing their names in the process, after which they bore a strong resemblance to the GWR '1366' Class.

Following the opening of the RNAD the two locomotives were fitted with 'balloon stack' spark arrestors. Then between 1952 and 1955 three Ruston & Hornsby 'flameproof' diesel locomotives were acquired, and thereafter the steam

No 29, with its distinctive spark-arresting chimney, was photographed on 10 September 1949. *H. C. Casserley*

Introduced 1908
Designed by Manning Wardle
Built by Manning Wardle
Number built (for CM&DPR) 2
Number inherited by BR 2
Last example withdrawn February 1954

locomotives did not enter the armaments depot. They were taken off the train at Cleobury North (just south of Ditton Priors) and the wagons were drawn into the depot by a diesel.

The railway line closed in 1960, but the Royal Navy continued to use Ditton Priors until 1965. The following year the depot was taken over by US forces that had left France following the French withdrawal from NATO's military structure. The depot finally closed in 1968.

Meanwhile, Nos 28 and 29 were withdrawn in 1953-54 and scrapped.

Rhymney Railway 'M' Class 0-6-2T

> **Note** The following former Rhymney Railway classes are included in order of development and building rather than their subsequent GWR numerical order, to give a clearer idea of their evolution.

Nos 33, 47, 51

Introduced 1904
Designed by Richard Jenkins
Built by Robert Stephenson
Number built 6
Number inherited by BR 3
Last example withdrawn November 1949

No 47, with 'GWR' still faintly visible on its tank side, stands on the scrap line, possibly at Cardiff East Dock, and probably in 1949. *R. K. Collins/transporttreasury.co.uk*

The 0-6-2T wheel arrangement was a departure for the Rhymney Railway when introduced by Jenkins in 1904. These were substantial tank engines with Belpaire fireboxes, and are sometimes referred to as the 'Rhymney Stephensons', even though Hudswell Clarke and Beyer Peacock built later derivations of the design.

Jenkins's engines had relatively large grates, which led to high coal consumption as the heaviest work done by these engines was working empty trains, uphill back to the collieries or ironworks – the loading was 50-55 wagons, to be hauled at 17-20mph. When working downhill the engines did a good deal of coasting, so a large grate was' not necessary. When Riches introduced his development of the design, the 'R' Class (see below), although outwardly they were very similar, he made the grate area smaller.

The locomotives were Rhymney Railway Nos 16 and 106-110; all passed to the GWR and were renumbered 33 and 47-51 respectively. Three locomotives, Nos 33, 47 and 51, were taken into British Railways stock in 1948, and spent what remained of their working lives allocated to Cardiff East Dock shed. No 51 was cut up within a year, No 47 followed in 1949, and No 33 just made it into 1951.

Rhymney Railway 'R' Class 0-6-2T

Nos 30-32, 34, 46

Introduced 1907
Designed by Charles T. Hurry Riches
Built by Robert Stephenson
Number built 5
Number inherited by BR 5
Last example withdrawn February 1951

'R' Class 0-6-2T No 46 was withdrawn in July 1950. It is seen here at Swindon Works on 8 October of that year, four months before it was scrapped. *W. G. Boyden, Frank Hornby collection*

Initially the Rhymney Railway connected the Rhymney Ironworks with Bute East Dock in Cardiff by its own lines and that of the Taff Vale Railway. However, when there was disagreement between the companies, the RR obtained powers to build its own direct line from Caerphilly to Cardiff, with running powers granted to the London & North Western Railway; this opened in 1871. The RR's first Locomotive

Engineer, Cornelius Lundie, was in the post for 42 years (retiring at the age of 89!), and provided this very prosperous railway with saddle tanks. His short-lived successor, Richard Jenkins, introduced a more powerful design of 0-6-2 tank (the 'M' Class – see above), and Charles Riches (son of the Taff Vale's Locomotive Superintendent, Tom Hurry Riches, who designed many 0-6-2Ts for that railway) followed these with his own substantially sized 'R' Class in 1907.

The first three, RR Nos 1-3, were built by Robert Stephenson in 1907, and two more (Nos 17 and 97) followed in 1909. When the Rhymney Railway became part of the GWR in 1923, the engines were renumbered 30-32, 34 and 46 respectively, and two were rebuilt with GWR superheated boilers and GWR bunkers in 1930. Being only relatively young, these modern 0-6-2Ts were in generally good order and had proved successful on the RR. Collectively the 'Rs' and related classes became the model for the 200-strong GWR '5600' Class, several of which are preserved.

All five made it into BR ownership, but Nos 30 and 34 were withdrawn in 1949, and the rest in 1950-51.

Rhymney Railway 'P' Class 0-6-2T

Nos 82, 83

This next version of the 0-6-2T design was intended for passenger work, and the locomotives had larger driving wheels, of 5-foot diameter. They were also fitted with vacuum brakes.

Passenger services on the RR had begun on 3 April 1858, and initially there were two trains a day, using running powers over the Taff Vale Railway. Passenger services over the RR's own direct line to Cardiff began on 1 April 1871, when an iron train and a coal train travelled from Rhymney to Cardiff, decorated with flags and evergreens. Over the years several branches were built and links with other lines, including running powers over GWR and LNWR tracks. The Taff Vale tried to absorb the RR in 1909-10, but Parliament denied the application. However, in 1917 the TVR and Cardiff Railway accepted the RR's manager as theirs also, and from then until absorption into the GWR at the Grouping the three railways were run as one.

The three 'P' Class locos were numbered 4 to 6. No 5 was rebuilt in 1915 to become a 'P1' (see below). The other two became Nos 82 and 83 under the GWR and were rebuilt with GWR superheated boilers, thus becoming identical to the 'P1' version. They both became BR engines, and were withdrawn and scrapped in 1954-55.

No 83, looking very smart with its GWR boiler and BR livery (including the pre-1956 'cycling lion' logo), works at Radyr on 14 September 1951. Shedded at Rhymney at this time, it was withdrawn from Cardiff East Dock in May 1955 and scrapped. *H. C. Casserley*

Introduced 1908
Designed by Charles T. Hurry Riches
Built by Robert Stephenson
Number built 3 (one became 'P1')
Number inherited by BR 2
Last example withdrawn May 1955

Rhymney Railway 'P1' Class 0-6-2T

Nos 76, 77

As mentioned above, in 1915 Hurry Riches took RR No 5 and replaced its round-topped boiler with one with a Belpaire firebox, being redesignated as Class 'P1'. This square-topped firebox was invented by Belgian engineer Alfred Belpaire, and had a greater surface area at the top of the firebox and a less cluttered arrangement of stays, promoting greater steam production. However, its shape made attaching it to a circular

No 77 was the second 'P1' 0-6-2T, built new by Hudswell Clarke in 1917. It is seen here in pouring rain at Cardiff on an unseasonable 8 July 1947. Its predecessor, No 76, was withdrawn and scrapped at the end of 1950, while No 77 lasted until the end of 1953. *H. C. Casserley*

boiler more difficult. The Belpaire firebox was widely adopted by the GWR and LMS.

No 5 became GWR No 76, and was joined by another example, RR No 31, in 1917, built by Hudswell Clarke. As GWR Nos 76 and 77, they were rebuilt with GWR boilers and thus became identical to the similarly rebuilt original 'P' Class locos.

Introduced 1915
Designed by Charles T. Hurry Riches
Built by Robert Stephenson
Number built 2 (one rebuilt from 'P' Class)
Number inherited by BR 2
Last example withdrawn November 1953

Rhymney Railway 'A' Class 0-6-2T

Nos 52-75

In all, Hurry Riches introduced 53 0-6-2T locomotives on the Rhymney Railway, primarily as goods locos – the company's stock of engines at the Grouping amounted to 123, so the 0-6-2 tanks were clearly an important constituent. But then, goods traffic was the company's lifeblood, and was what allowed it to pay up to a 10% dividend to shareholders. In 1908 the total tonnage of goods over the RR's lines totalled some 9 million tons, the bulk being coal for shipment from the Bute Docks at Cardiff, as well as from Penarth and Barry.

Between the 'R' and 'R1' Classes came the 'A' Class of 0-6-2Ts, built between 1910 and 1918, with slightly smaller driving wheels. Again intended for freight traffic, they were also used on passenger duties. They fell into several batches. The first ten locos were built by Stephenson in 1910 and numbered 10-14 and 115-119 on the RR. In 1911 six more followed from Hudswell Clarke (Nos 15 and 18-22). These engines had round-topped boilers. In 1914 three more came from Hudswell, two more in 1916, then finally three more from Stephenson in 1918. These last eight (numbered 23 to 30) were Class 'A1', and had Belpaire fireboxes.

All passed to the GWR at the Grouping, and were renumbered in a single sequence from 52 to 75; they were also much rebuilt with GWR boilers from 1929 onwards. Once in BR stock, the first withdrawal came in April 1948, but the last four did not succumb until July 1955.

In shabby 'British Railways' livery, No 63 was photographed t Cardiff East Dock on 5 May 1951, having just been transferred from Radyr. It was withdrawn and scrapped in September 1952. Note the GWR taper boiler. *H. C. Casserley*

Introduced 1910
Designed by Charles T. Hurry Riches
Built by Robert Stephenson (13), Hudswell Clarke (11)
Number built 24
Number inherited by BR 24
Last example withdrawn July 1955

Rhymney Railway 'R1' Class 0-6-2T

Nos 35-44

Under the Railways Act of 1921 the Rhymney Railway was one of the many independent companies merged to become part of the new larger Great Western Railway, one of the 'Big Four' from 1923. Thus these engines were only a few months old when taken into GWR stock, which perhaps explains their relative longevity.

The former Rhymney Railway Class 'R1' 0-6-2Ts were nearly all allocated to Radyr and Cardiff East Dock sheds. No 36, wearing East Dock's 88B shedplate, is seen there on 8 July 1956. It was one of the last two survivors of the ten, being withdrawn and scrapped in October 1957. No 35 avoided being scrapped until 1958, having been used as a stationary boiler at Worcester shed for a couple of years. *T. B. Owen, Colour-Rail*

Nos 39-42 (RR numbering) were built in the second half of 1921 by Hudswell Clarke, the Leeds company famous for its industrial tank engines; the remaining six (Nos 43-47 and 62) followed at the end of the year from Beyer Peacock, of Gorton, Manchester. They were a development of the earlier 'R' Class (qv above), with some internal differences.

They were renumbered 35 to 44 in GWR ownership, and three were rebuilt with taper boilers, looking similar to the standard '5600' Class. All passed to BR at nationalisation, most shedded at Cardiff East Dock.. Nos 36 and 38 were the last of

Introduced 1921
Designed by Charles T. Hurry Riches
Built by Hudswell Clarke (4), Beyer Peacock (6)
Number built 10
Number inherited by BR 10
Last example withdrawn October 1957

the South Wales railways' 0-6-2Ts when withdrawn in October 1957, outliving the last TVR 'A' Class engines by two months

Rhymney Railway 'AP' Class 0-6-2T

Nos 78-81

These four 0-6-2Ts were built by Hudswell Clarke in 1921 just before the Rhymney Railway was absorbed by the GWR. Designed, like the 'Ps', for passenger work, they had superheaters and larger cylinders and were classified 'AP'. With larger tanks and bunkers, they were heavier than the 'Ps' and had a slightly higher tractive effort.

RR Nos 35 and 36 emerged from Hudswell Clarke's works in August 1921, and Nos 37 and 38 in November. The first two became GWR Nos 78 and 79, the latter two Nos 80 and 81, and all were withdrawn in 1954-55 and scrapped.

Introduced 1921
Designed by Hudswell Clarke
Built by Hudswell Clarke
Number built 4
Number inherited by BR 4
Last example withdrawn August 1955

All four 'APs' spent some or all of their BR careers allocated to Rhymney shed. No 79 is seen at Rhymney on 13 September 1951. *R. M. Casserley*

Rhymney Railway 'S' Class 0-6-0T

All four 'S' Class 0-6-0Ts spent their BR lives allocated to Cardiff East Dock shed, and No 96 is seen there, still in steam, on the evening of 13 April 1954. It was withdrawn during that month.
David Holmes

Nos 93-96

Introduced 1908
Designed by Charles T. Hurry Riches
Built by Hudswell Clarke
Number built 4
Number inherited by BR 4
Last example withdrawn May 1954

As mentioned earlier, 123 Rhymney Railway locomotives passed into GWR hands at the Grouping, in some 15 classes, 10 of which were 0-6-2Ts. By contrast, the Class 'S' and 'S1' locomotives were 0-6-0 tanks. These four were built by Hudswell Clarke in the summer of 1908. As with the other classes detailed above, they were all rebuilt with GWR taper boilers from 1930 onwards. Originally numbered 608 to 611 by the GWR, the first two were renumbered 93 and 94 in GWR days, while Nos 610 and 611 followed suit (to 95 and 96) under BR auspices in 1948-49. All were withdrawn between September 1953 and May 1954.

Rhymney Railway 'S1' Class 0-6-0T

Nos 90-92

Three further slightly heavier but otherwise similar 0-6-0T locomotives were added to stock in 1920. They were built with Belpaire fireboxes, so were not rebuilt with GWR boilers later in their lives. Numbered 604-606 by the RR, the first and third were renumbered 90 and 92 by the GWR, and No 605 became BR No 91 in April 1948, after nationalisation. All were disposed of during 1954.

Introduced 1920
Designed by Charles T. Hurry Riches
Built by Hudswell Clarke
Number built 3
Number inherited by BR 3
Last example withdrawn June 1954

Still with 'GWR' on its tanks, 'S1' Class No 92 was also photographed at Cardiff East Dock, on 5 May 1951. Again, all three had been allocated there since nationalisation. *H. C. Casserley*

Cardiff Railway 0-6-2T

No 155

The Cardiff Railway was an important concern, even though it was only 11 miles in length, as it allowed access to the city's docks to both the Taff Vale Railway and the Rhymney Railway, among others. The Bute Docks Company became the Cardiff Railway Company on 6 August 1897, and the line opened between 1909 and 1911. However, difficulties in its relations with both the TVR and Barry Railway, on which it needed to rely for access to the valleys, stunted the company's growth and potential. The CR subsequently suggested a merger with the TVR and the Rhymney Railway, but this was thwarted by claims of unfair competition from other South Wales railways, aware that the Taff Vale and Barry concerns were already extremely profitable. Thus the Cardiff Railway never achieved great success in its own right, but remained independent until it became a constituent part of the GWR at the Grouping.

The Cardiff Railway bequeathed 36 steam locomotives to the GWR, 13 of which were of the popular 0-6-2T wheel arrangement, built for the company by Kitson & Co and numbered 151-163 by the GWR. Only six Cardiff Railway locomotives, from three different classes, passed to BR on nationalisation. No 155 was the sole survivor of a batch of three 0-6-2Ts built in 1908, and withdrawn by BR in September 1953. The other locomotives were four 0-6-0PTs (see below), and one 0-4-0ST, No 1338 of 1898, which was preserved and at the time of writing is on static display at Didcot Railway Centre.

Introduced 1908
Designed by Ree
Built by Kitson
Number built 13
Number inherited by BR 1
Last example withdrawn September 1953

No 155 was fitted with a GWR taper boiler in 1928, and is seen at Cardiff East Dock, also on 5 May 1951. The loco was withdrawn and scrapped at the end of 1953. *H. C. Casserley*

Port Talbot Railway 0-6-2T

No 184

Robert Stephenson 0-6-2T No 184 was rebuilt with a GWR boiler in 1925 but, as the sole survivor of its class, did not last long under BR ownership, being withdrawn just 10 months after nationalisation, and scrapped in January 1949. It was photographed at Port Talbot. *R. M. Casserley collection*

Introduced 1898
Designed by Robert Stephenson
Built by Robert Stephenson
Number built 11
Number inherited by BR 1
Last example withdrawn October 1948

The Port Talbot Railway & Docks Co, to give it its full name, was incorporated in 1894 and promoted by mine-owners to bring coal down from the valleys via Maesteg. As well as enlarging the docks at Port Talbot, by the time the line was completed, in 1897-98, the company served more than 50 collieries. In 1898 an arrangement was made with the GWR whereby the larger company would work this prosperous 48-mile system, but the PTR remained independent until absorbed by the Great Western at the Grouping.

Only two Port Talbot locomotives became BR property at nationalisation, and 0-6-2T No 184 was one of them (see No 1358 below). It was the last survivor of a class of 11 built by Robert Stephenson & Co. Known as 'Stephensons', they were built six years earlier than, but were somewhat similar to, the larger Rhymney Railway 'M' Class (see above). Despite being successful engines, four of them were soon sold to other South Wales railways; two went to the Rhondda & Swansea Bay Railway in 1901, and the others to the Neath & Brecon in 1903. The remaining seven passed to the GWR in 1922.

In 1925 the GWR rebuilt two of the class with the then new No 10 standard boiler and high domed cab, whereby they resembled a smaller version of the later GWR '5600' Class of 1924. These new standard boilers were designed to be fitted to engines from absorbed companies that were worth retaining; for example, the No 9 was used on Barry Railway engines, and the No 11 for locos from the Cardiff and Taff Vale companies. The No 10 was also fitted to Rhymney Railway rebuilds. As we have seen, not all locos of a certain type were rebuilt, resulting in variations of appearance within classes.

Alexandra Docks 0-6-2ST

No 190

The Alexandra (Newport) Dock Company came into being in 1865, and combined with the Newport Dock Company to become the grandly named Alexandra (Newport & South Wales) Docks & Railway Company (ANDR) in 1882. The new company also took over the Old Town Docks in 1884. The main intention was to handle as much as possible of the vast output of the rich coalfields of the Cynon and Rhondda valleys, and to do this a railway was also promoted, the Pontypridd, Caerphilly & Newport Railway, which used its own tracks as well as running powers over the lines of five other companies. Incorporated in 1878, it was not completed for many years. Although only 23 miles long, the numerous sidings and connections meant that by 1922 the PC&NR consisted of more than 100 miles of track. By 1904 the North and South Docks at Newport were equipped with 17 hydraulic coal hoists and 31 cranes of various types; in 1914 the storage sidings covered 50 acres, and by 1932 they were capable of holding some 12,000 wagons. To move this traffic around the port the docks acquired an assortment of powerful locomotives.

In 1922 the ANDR was amalgamated into the Great Western Railway Docks Department, and 39 engines became GWR property. A varied selection of six eventually came onto BR's books, and 0-6-2

No 190, with its outside cylinders and sizeable saddle tank, had a long, low, chunky profile. It is seen here in GWR days at Newport on 12 August 1934. *Great Western Trust*

Introduced 1908
Designed by Andrew Barclay
Built by Andrew Barclay
Number built 3
Number inherited by BR 1
Last example withdrawn April 1948

saddle tank No 190 was one of them. One of three, originally numbered 29-31 and acquired from Andrew Barclay Sons & Co in 1908, it was designed for heavy shunting. It was rebuilt by the GWR in 1923 with shorter tanks and a GWR smokebox, but was disposed of within four months of nationalisation.

Taff Vale Railway 'H' Class 0-6-0T

Nos 193-195

Introduced 1884
Designed by Tom Hurry Riches
Built by Kitson
Number built 3
Number inherited by BR 3
Last example withdrawn November 1953

A branch line was constructed in 1863 by the Cwmclydach Colliery Company to link the pit in the Rhondda Valley with the Taff Vale Railway at Tonypandy. The line was just over 2 miles long and included the three-quarter-mile Pwllyrhebog Incline at 1 in 13. Locomotives were assisted by a cable running round two drums at the head of the incline, driven by a stationary engine and geared in such a way that ascending empty trains were counterbalanced by descending full ones. Although privately built, the line was acquired by the TVR in 1896.

Three 0-6-0 Kitson tank locomotives were built in 1884 to work the incline, and they were distinguished by markedly tapered boilers containing a tapered inner firebox to allow water to cover the firebox crown even when the engines were working on the incline. The large dome was also mounted above the firebox. The driving wheels were of a relatively large diameter for such a small loco, at 5ft 3in, in order to clear the cable sheaves. These engines, of Class 'H', were numbered 141-143 by the TVR, and when they passed into GWR hands they became Nos 792-794. Finally, in 1948-49 they became BR Nos 193-195.

The incline ceased operation in 1951, and the trio were withdrawn between then and late 1953. Two of them, Nos 193 and 195, were sold to the National Coal Board and worked on until scrapped in 1960 and 1957 respectively.

Although built by Kitson, the engines were designed by the TVR's Locomotive Superintendent Tom Hurry Riches (1846-1911), father of the Rhymney Railway's Charles. Tom began an apprenticeship with the TVR at the age of 17, then spent some years at sea before becoming General Manager of the Bute Ironworks, where he designed and built iron roofs and bridges, as well as assisting with the company's engines, machinery, steamers and dredgers. He returned to the TVR in 1872, and

The three former Taff Vale Railway 0-6-0Ts Nos 195, 194 and 193 were photographed together at Treherbert on 11 September 1951. *R. M. Casserley*

No 195 was withdrawn a couple of months later and sold to the NCB at Treorchy. Still carrying its GWR cabside number plate, but up on blocks for all wheels to be dropped, it approaches the end of its life in 1957. It was scrapped in April of that year. *J. Harrison, Colour-Rail*

the following year became Locomotive Superintendent, at that time the youngest in Britain. He stayed in the post until his death in 1911 at the age of 64. He was President of the Institution of Mechanical Engineers in 1907.

Barry Railway 'B' Class 0-6-2T

Nos 198, 212, 213, 231

The Barry Railway grew out of the discontent of mine-owners with the near monopoly of coal traffic enjoyed by the Taff Vale Railway and Cardiff Docks; the latter had been established by Lord Bute and were sufficient to serve his coal-exporting needs, but had no additional capacity. As a result a secondary route was proposed, terminating at Barry, where more easily accessible docks could be developed. The 1883 Barry Dock & Railway Bill was defeated by expected opposition, but when introduced again the

Introduced 1888
Designed by J. H. Hosgood
Built by Sharp Stewart
Number built 25
Number inherited by BR 4
Last example withdrawn November 1949

following year it was passed, the company becoming the Barry Railway in 1891. The company had the advantage of owning both dock and railway, while other railway companies used docks over which they had no control. It was a very successful line, paying high dividends, but at the expense of maintenance; reports in 1906 and 1909 showed that up two-thirds of locomotives were out of service at any one time, awaiting repair.

Eventually the Barry Railway operated 68 route miles of track, including branches, from the docks to the Rhondda Valley, together with connections to other companies' lines. It also had 140 miles of sidings, 100 in and around the docks alone. By 1910 Barry had overtaken Cardiff as the largest exporter of South Wales coal.

In 1888 the first 15 Class 'B' 0-6-2Ts were ordered from Sharp Stewart & Co Ltd of Glasgow, being a large version of the earlier Class 'A'. They were numbered 6 to 20 by the Barry Railway. A further ten followed in 1889-90, numbered 23-32. The first 15 became GWR Nos 198-201, 203, 204 and 206-214, and the other ten were Nos 223-232. Only four survived into British Railways ownership; No 198 was withdrawn immediately, and the other three had all gone by the end of 1949.

Ironically, Barry Docks was later to become the famous Woodham Brothers' scrapyard, the intended graveyard of

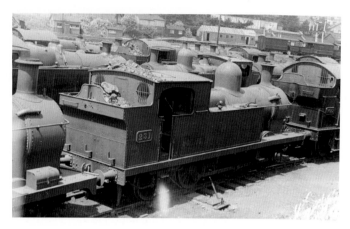

The last survivor of the four former Barry Railway 'B' Class 0-6-2Ts, No 231, is seen at its home shed at Barry on the eve of nationalisation, 6 July 1947. *H. C. Casserley*

hundreds of redundant British Railways locomotives, but from where many were rescued and restored, providing an early foundation for today's railway preservation industry.

Taff Vale Railway 'O3' Class 0-6-2T

Nos 410, 411

One of the oldest of South Wales's railways, the Taff Vale was authorised in 1836, and ran from Merthyr Tydfil to Cardiff Docks. It carried prodigious amounts of coal, and in the 1870s and 1880s the company's dividend reached 17½%! A measure of the amount of traffic handled is that, with a total of 124 miles of track, the TVR possessed 271 locomotives. A large number of these were 0-6-2 tanks, a design very popular throughout South Wales for hauling coal trains.

After using 4-4-0 and 4-4-2 types for passenger work, the TVR's long-serving Locomotive Engineer Tom Hurry Riches turned to the 0-6-2 wheel arrangement as an all-purpose design for new tank locomotives in 1891. In 1894 and 1897 he introduced his 14 'O1' Class 0-6-2Ts. One of these, No 28 (GWR No 450) survives in preservation, having been sold first to the Longmoor Military Railway, then the NCB at Hetton Colliery. In 1899 the Class 'O2' followed, nine 0-6-2Ts built by Neilson, Reid & Co of Glasgow. Again, an example has been preserved, No 85 (GWR No 426), thanks once more to having been bought by the NCB for use at Philadelphia Colliery in County Durham.

The 'O3' Class, a development of the 'O2', was introduced between 1902 and 1905, comprising 15 more 0-6-2 tanks. Of this class, none were preserved, and only two found their way

Introduced 1902
Designed by Tom Hurry Riches
Built by Kitson
Number built 15
Number inherited by BR 2
Last example withdrawn March 1948

No 410 was rebuilt with a GWR boiler in 1930, together with GWR side tanks, bunker and a high domed cab roof. In that condition it was photographed at its home shed of Cardiff Canton on 9 May 1937. *Great Western Trust*

onto BR's books at nationalisation, the first of the 15 having been withdrawn by the GWR as early as 1928. BR disposed of the pair within three months, and both were scrapped before the end of 1948

Taff Vale Railway 'O4' Class 0-6-2T

Nos 200-11, 215-220, 236, 278-299

As O. S. Nock remarked, 'It was on the local railways of South Wales that the 0-6-2 tank type came to reign supreme. It was ideal for the mineral hauls and for the local passenger work

alike, and it was only in the rather special operating conditions of the Barry Railway that the 0-6-2 did not become an all-purpose standard.' In the 'O4' Class we see the fourth development of the TVR 0-6-2T, introduced by Riches in 1907. The previous 'O' series tanks had progressively higher boiler

Introduced 1907
Designed by Tom Hurry Riches
Built by Manning Wardle (7), Beyer Peacock (24),
Vulcan Foundry (10)
Number built 41
Number inherited by BR 41
Last example withdrawn July 1955

pressures, but with the 'O4', while the cylinder dimensions were the same, the boiler was much larger, as was the grate area.

The first seven locomotives emerged from Manning Wardle in 1907; 14 more were built by Beyer Peacock the following year, and ten more in 1910. That same year another 10 were built by the Vulcan Foundry. All were renumbered by the GWR from a hotchpotch of TVR numbers, then renumbered again in 1946 into the non-consecutive range 200-11, 215-220, 236 and 278-99 – in fact, some did not receive these new numbers until after nationalisation, and three did not receive them at all prior to being withdrawn. The last four engines to be dispensed with were Nos 204, 208, 215 and 290, in July 1955, all residents of Cardiff East Dock shed.

TVR 'O4' Class No 204 was one of the Vulcan Foundry batch, dating from September 1910. It is seen here still in GWR livery and with a GWR boiler at Aberdare on 17 June 1951. Then a Cardiff Canton engine, it moved to Aberdare shed in March 1952, and was one of the last quartet to be withdrawn, in July 1955. *T. B. Owen, Colour-Rail*

Barry Railway 'B1' Class 0-6-2T

Nos 238, 240, 246, 248, 258, 259, 261-263, 265, 267-272, 274-277

The 'B1' was a larger version of the 'B' Class 0-6-2T (qv), with increased water and coal capacity to enable the engines to haul trains of empty wagons (or occasionally trains of pit-props from Barry Docks) from Cadoxton Yard, east of Barry, to Trehafod Junction, where the line met the Taff Vale Railway north-west of Pontypridd, without the need to take on extra water. They would also take loaded coal trains from Trehafod Junction back to Cadoxton. The 'B1s' also took miners' trains between Barry and Porth, as well as excursion trains to the popular resort of Barry Island. They could also be seen at the head of the 'Ports to Ports Express', the unofficial name for a Newcastle-Banbury-Cheltenham-Cardiff-Barry service operated by the GCR and GWR, introduced in 1906, over the Barry Railway section of the route.

The first batch of nine was built by Sharp Stewart in 1890, then two years later the Vulcan Foundry built another ten. Eighteen more were ordered from Sharp Stewart in 1894 and 1900, then interestingly the final five were built in 1900 by Société Franco-Belge. This company, founded in Brussels in 1859, built many types of railway vehicles for home use and for export. A new factory was established at Raismes, in northern France, in 1882, assembling machines using Belgian-produced components. The company survived to be acquired by Alstom in 1982, and the present factory in Valenciennes operates as an Alstom subsidiary, specialising in metro vehicles, trams and double-deck trains.

Just under half of the 'B1s' passed into BR ownership, and nearly all were shedded at Barry; the last three were withdrawn in April 1951. Some gained an extra lease of life as works shunters at Swindon, the last being scrapped at the beginning of 1953.

Introduced 1890
Designed by J. H. Hosgood
Built by Sharp Stewart (27), Vulcan Foundry (10), Société Franco-Belge (5)
Number built 42
Number inherited by BR 20
Last example withdrawn April 1951

Although having been withdrawn from regular service in November 1949, No 258 is seen at Swindon on 30 April 1950, presumably one of those kept on as works shunters. It was the last example of the class to be scrapped, in January 1953. Built in 1894, it carried its original Barry Railway boiler to the end. *H. C. Casserley*

Taff Vale Railway 'A' Class 0-6-2T

Nos 303-309, 312, 316, 322, 335, 337, 343-349, 351, 352, 356, 357, 360-362, 364-368, 370-391, 393, 394, 397-399

The first of the class numerically, but among the last to be built in February 1921, No 303 is seen at Barry in June 1955, with a GWR boiler. It was withdrawn from Barry in May 1956.
T. B. Owen, Colour-Rail

When Tom Hurry Riches died 'in harness' in 1911, he was succeeded by John Cameron, a Scotsman who had been apprenticed to William Stroudley on the London, Brighton & South Coast Railway, then moved to the LSWR. In 1885 he joined the TVR as Works Manager, then became Locomotive Superintendent until his retirement in 1922.

Introduced 1914
Designed by John Cameron
Built by Hawthorn Leslie (27), Nasmyth, Wilson (12), Vulcan Foundry (13), North British (6)
Number built 58
Number inherited by BR 58
Last example withdrawn August 1957

The first of his new 'A' Class 0-6-2Ts appeared in 1914, and were of a similar design to Hurry Riches's 'O4' Class (qv), but had larger wheels and were intended for passenger work. There were two different cylinder sizes and boiler pressures within the class. They were built in seven batches, and neither their TVR numbers nor their GWR/BR numbers were consecutive. The first 13 were constructed in 1914, six by Hawthorn Leslie and seven by the Vulcan Foundry. The North British Locomotive Co added six more in 1915, then a further half-dozen were built by Vulcan the following year. Nasmyth, Wilson & Co built 12 in 1919, and finally Hawthorn Leslie added 21 in 1920-21.

All 58 passed to the GWR at the Grouping, and all were rebuilt with GWR boilers between 1924 and 1931. The class was still intact at nationalisation, the first example not being withdrawn until November 1952 (No 344). The last seven survivors (Nos 370, 373, 381, 383, 390, 398 and 402) were withdrawn together in August 1957 from Abercynon shed. Some examples were used as works shunters at Swindon before being cut up.

Llanelly & Mynydd Mawr Railway 0-6-0ST

No 359

This historic line was the earliest company promoted to work a railway and dock as a single undertaking. The Carmarthenshire Tramroad was a tramway authorised in 1802, and ran horse-drawn trains from 1803. It carried coal to Llanelly Docks, together with ironstone and limestone, which were used in the Stradey Iron Works, established in 1798. The tramroad closed in 1844, and it was more than 30 years before local pressure saw the reopening of the line, and its extension to Cross Hands.

The line reopened in 1883 and was operated by the newly formed Llanelly & Mynydd Mawr Railway Co. The LMM had it own fleet of steam locomotives, and most passed with the company into the hands of the Great Western Railway at the Grouping. The GWR worked the line using mostly pannier tanks, and it continued as the main route for coal from the Gwendraeth Valley until the closure of Welsh 'super pit' Cynheidre Colliery in 1989, which had opened in 1954. In 1965 the NCB bought ex-GWR 0-6-0PT No 1607 of Llanelly, and that worked at Cynheidre until 1969.

Only two former LMM locomotives survived to become part of British Railways' stock in 1948. This saddle tank, No 359 *Hilda*, was built by Hudswell Clarke of Leeds in June 1917. Sadly neither

Hudswell Clarke 0-6-0ST No 359 *Hilda* is seen at its home shed of Danygraig, Swansea, on the eve of nationalisation, 7 July 1947. It carries a replacement GWR boiler, at which time it was also fitted with a small warning bell. The locomotive was withdrawn and scrapped in 1954. *H. C. Casserley*

Introduced 1917
Designed by Hudswell Clarke
Built by Hudswell Clarke
Number built 1
Number inherited by BR 1
Last example withdrawn February 1954

locomotive survived in preservation to be used on a third incarnation of the line, the heritage Llanelly & Mynydd Mawr Railway, incorporated in 1999. The primary objective of this new company is to reinstate this historic line by using derelict land on the site of the former Cynheidre Colliery. The new LMM has already erected a loco shed and stock shed on the site, and a platform at a new Cynheidre station. The running line will initially be more than half a mile in length, and there will also be a visitor centre, gift shop and cafe, creating an eco-friendly tourist attraction and educational resource.

Brecon & Merthyr Railway '45' Class 0-6-2T

Nos 431-436

The Brecon & Merthyr Railway had two distinct classes of 0-6-2 tank engines. One was the '36' Class (qv), very similar to the Rhymney Railway 'R' Class (qv), and the other was this class of six engines, known as the '45' Class. These were designed more in the style of the Taff Vale and Rhymney types, especially the latter's 'P' 0-6-2Ts (qv), with a smaller grate area and larger-diameter wheels for working loaded coal trains down to Newport Docks.

Three of the engines, B&M Nos 45-47, emerged from Robert Stephenson's Newcastle works in August and September 1915. That company built very few locomotives in that year, and none at all in 1916, being engaged in munitions and Admiralty work – then between 1917 and 1920 the War Ministry ordered more than 80 Robinson-type 2-8-0s for use on the continent. This is perhaps why the second batch of three 0-6-2Ts, Nos 48-50, was not built until the beginning of 1921. Within a couple of years they were GWR engines, renumbered 1372-75, 1668 and 1670; under the 1946 renumbering programme they became Nos 431-436, although five of the six had to wait until 1948-50 to receive their new numbers. Between 1927 and 1936 they all received GWR superheated boilers except No 436, which was fitted with a former Rhymney Railway boiler. Nos 435 and 436 were the last pair to survive, being withdrawn in January and February 1954 respectively.

Introduced 1915
Designed by James Dunbar
Built by Robert Stephenson
Number built 6
Number inherited by BR 6
Last example withdrawn February 1954

Former Brecon & Merthyr 0-6-2T No 435 was withdrawn from Ebbw Junction shed in February 1954, but was still to be seen at Swindon Works on 31 October of that year, perhaps undertaking internal shunting duties? *N. L. Browne, Frank Hornby collection*

Alexandra Docks 0-6-0T

Nos 666, 667

Introduced 1917
Designed by Kerr Stuart
Built by Kerr Stuart
Number built 10 (two acquired by Alexandra Docks)
Number inherited by BR 2
Last example withdrawn April 1955

With GWR-style 'British Railways' on the tank side, and with nearly six years of active life still ahead of it, No 666 is seen at Newport Pill shed on 19 June 1949. *Colour-Rail*

During the First World War, in 1915-16, Kerr Stuart & Co of Stoke-on-Trent built 72 0-6-0Ts for the French Government Artillery Railways to 600mm gauge. Then in 1917 the company built ten 0-6-0 tank engines, known as the 'Victory' Class, for the Railway Operating Division (ROD), a division of the Royal Engineers; the ROD controlled and operated standard and narrow gauge railways behind the British fronts. Another wartime order was for 18 'Wren' Class locos for use by the War Ministry on various aerodromes.

After the war the patriotically named 'Victory' locomotives were disposed of to collieries, docks, etc, and in 1919 Alexandra Docks purchased two of them, ROD Nos 604 and 602, which were numbered 34 and 35 respectively. When they passed to the GWR they were renumbered 666 and 667, and received some alterations at Swindon.

Another 'Victory' Class loco came to the docks from the Brecon & Merthyr Railway, then was sold to the Ashington Coal Co, finishing its days as an NCB loco in 1951. Others went to Manchester Collieries, the East Kent Railway (qv No 30948),

the Tirpentwys Coal & Coke Co, Lambton & Joicey, and the United Steel Co. One operated by Aberaman Colliery was not scrapped until 1969.

The two locos spent their BR lives at the former Alexandra Docks shed at Newport Pill, from where No 667 was withdrawn in November 1954, and its sister the following April.

Alexandra Docks 0-6-0ST

No 680

Fox, Walker & Co, of the Atlas Works, St George, Bristol, started building steam locomotives in 1864, mostly four- and six-coupled saddle tanks for industrial use. The company was taken over by Thomas Peckett in 1880 and became Peckett & Sons, but the well-established output of industrial saddle tanks continued. Two such, of Peckett's 'B1' type, were built in 1886 and 1890 for Alexandra Docks, and the first of them, No 680, was briefly a BR engine, having been given a modest amount of 'Swindonisation' when the property of the GWR. The other engine was sold by the GWR to a colliery, where it outlived its sister by five years.

These were very small locomotives, only 23 feet long over the buffers, and No 680 spent most of its working life on the Tanat Valley line. Various railway schemes had been put forward in the Welshpool and Oswestry areas, but it was the passing of the Light Railways Act of 1896 that enabled the construction of this line from Porthywaen Junction to Blodwell Junction and Llangynog. It officially opened in 1904, but by the early 1920s was deeply in debt, and was acquired by the Cambrian Railways in 1921. In turn the Cambrian became part of the GWR group in 1923. No 680 was withdrawn from Oswestry shed in December 1948 and scrapped. The Tanat Valley line just outlived it, with services ending in January 1951 and most of the line abandoned in July 1952. Goods traffic survived until January 1964.

No 680, with its GWR number plate and Peckett builder's plate on the bunker side, was photographed at its home shed of Oswestry on 28 May 1932. *H. C. Casserley*

Introduced 1886
Designed by Peckett
Built by Peckett
Number built 2
Number inherited by BR 1
Last example withdrawn December 1948

Today a heritage railway project, also known as the Tanat Valley Light Railway, is based by the lime kilns in Nantmawr, and hopes to operate trains from Nantmawr to Llanddu by Blodwell Quarry. The first one-third of a mile of track saw its first trains in November 2009.

Cardiff Railway 0-6-0PT

Nos 681-684

Introduced 1920
Designed by Hope
Built by Hudswell Clarke
Number built 4
Number inherited by BR 4
Last example withdrawn February 1955

Former Cardiff Railway 0-6-0PT No 681 was built in 1920 as a saddle tank, and was rebuilt as a pannier by the GWR. It is seen out of use in Swindon shed yard on 24 April 1955. It had been withdrawn in February of that year, and was scrapped in June. *Brian Morrison*

Two classes of Cardiff Railway locomotives entered BR ownership without any surviving into preservation. The 0-6-2Ts of 1908 have already been mentioned (qv), and the other was a class of four 0-6-0s built as saddle tanks by Hudswell Clarke in 1920, and numbered 14, 16, 17 and 32. These were the last Cardiff Railway engines delivered to the company before it became part of the GWR at the Grouping. As GWR Nos 681-684 they were rebuilt as pannier tanks between 1926 and 1939. All four spent their entire BR careers

at Cardiff East Dock shed, and were withdrawn between October 1953 and February 1955.

Barry Railway 'E' Class 0-6-0T

Nos 783, 784

Introduced 1889
Designed by J. H. Hosgood
Built by Hudswell Clarke
Number built 5
Number inherited by BR 2
Last example withdrawn August 1949

The 'E' Class of five tank engines was designed for light shunting duties around Barry Docks, and the small size of the locomotives, only just over 33 tons and with a driving wheel diameter of only 3ft 6½in, made them ideal for working on the Barry Island breakwater. The Barry Railway extended its line to Barry Island in 1896 and to Barry Pier and breakwater in 1899. Access to the breakwater was via a 1 in 80 descent through a narrow 280-yard rough-hewn tunnel with sharp curves, which prevented larger locomotives from using the route.

Two locomotives (Barry Railway Nos 33 and 34) were built in 1889 and another two (Nos 50-51) the following year; one more (No 53) appeared in 1890. The first of the five locomotives was withdrawn in 1932 (No 782). Nos 781 and 785 were rebuilt as 0-4-2 tanks for auto-train working, and the remaining two 0-6-0s were early BR casualties, disappearing before the end of 1949.

Ex-Barry Railway 0-6-0T No 784 was withdrawn from Barry shed in August 1949, and is seen here, minus coupling rods, at Swindon on 1 September. It was scrapped the following month. *R. M. Casserley*

Llanelly & Mynydd Mawr Railway 0-6-0T

No 803

No 803 was one of the two former Llanelly & Mynydd Mawr Railway locomotives to pass into British Railways' stock at nationalisation. For details about this historic line, see the entry above for 0-6-0ST No 359 *Hilda*.

This side-tank locomotive was built by Hudswell Clarke in January 1911 and originally carried the name *Ravelston*. In 1927, having become part of the Great Western Railway fleet, it was rebuilt with a renovated boiler, Belpaire firebox, GWR smokebox and extended bunker, at which time the name was removed.

Like *Hilda*, No 803 was withdrawn from Danygraig shed, but three years earlier, in March 1951.

Introduced 1911
Designed by Hudswell Clarke
Built by Hudswell Clarke
Number built 1
Number inherited by BR 1
Last example withdrawn March 1951

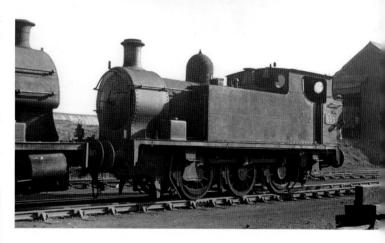

Unique Hudswell Clarke 0-6-0T No 803 was photographed at Danygraig shed on the same day as the LMM's other surviving engine, No 359 *Hilda* (qv), 7 July 1947. *H. C. Casserley*

Cambrian Railways '89'/'15' Class 0-6-0

Nos 844, 849, 855, 864, 873, 887, 892-896

Introduced 1903
Designed by Jones
Built by Robert Stephenson (5), Beyer Peacock (10)
Number built 15
Number inherited by BR 11
Last example withdrawn October 1954

The characterful Cambrian Railways was formed in 1864 by the amalgamation of a number of local railways and branch lines across mid-Wales around Oswestry (the company's headquarters), Newtown, Llanidloes, Machynlleth, Aberystwyth, Ellesmere and Whitchurch. It also included the Welshpool & Llanfair and Vale of Rheidol light railways, some 300 miles in all.

In 1911 the Cambrian had 91 locomotives on its books, and by the time of the Grouping in 1923 94 standard-gauge and five narrow-gauge engines had been transferred to the GWR. Among them were the Class '89' 0-6-0 tender engines (the first tender engines so far encountered in this survey). They became the GWR's '15' Class, and resembled that company's famous 'Dean Goods' 0-6-0s of 1883-99. The majority were built by Beyer Peacock, with five by Robert Stephenson.

Cambrian 0-6-0 No 895 arrives at Oswestry on 22 July 1954 with the 1.25pm local service from Gobowen. This was a Beyer Peacock product of 1903, and was withdrawn a few months after this picture was taken. *Brian Morrison*

The first member of the class was withdrawn by the GWR in May 1922, that company having absorbed the Cambrian on 1 January, just prior to the Grouping. Eleven engines became BR property, but all had gone by the end of 1954.

'1701' or '1854' Class 0-6-0PT

Nos 906, 907, 1705, 1706, 1709, 1713, 1715, 1720, 1726, 1730, 1731, 1752-1754, 1758, 1760, 1762, 1764, 1769, 1799, 1855, 1858, 1861-1863, 1867, 1870, 1878, 1884, 1888, 1889, 1891, 1894, 1896, 1897, 1900

The '1701' or '1854' class was one in a long evolutionary line of tank locomotives, built from 1890 and embodying parts from earlier engines. All were initially built as saddle tanks, but were converted to panniers from 1909 onwards; they were then also fitted with Belpaire fireboxes, the square top of which was not compatible with a saddle tank. Some had open cabs, and some enclosed.

Nos 1854-93 were built in 1890-91, and Nos 1701-20 in 1891. Nos 1721-40 appeared in 1892, and Nos 1751-70 in 1892-93. The final batch, Nos 905-07, 1791-1800 and 1894-1900, took to the rails in 1895.

Loco Nos 1710 and 1756 were sold to the Rhondda & Swansea Bay Railway, to become Nos 36 and 35 respectively, and Nos 1715 and 1882 to the Neath & Brecon Railway. At the Grouping these of course returned to GWR stock. No 1729 was scrapped in 1943 following damage in an air raid.

Most of the class worked in South Wales, but a few were allocated elsewhere, for example Didcot, Taunton and Oxley. The first examples were withdrawn in the late 1920s, but 36 passed in BR hands. All achieved at least one million miles in service. Only two made it into 1951, No 907, withdrawn in March, and the last, No 1861, in November.

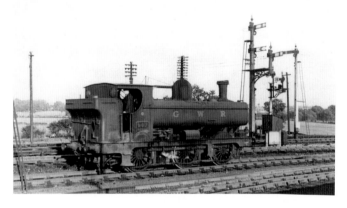

'1701 or '1854' Class 0-6-0PT No 907 of 1895 was one of 36 of a class of 120 to become BR engines. Still wearing GWR livery, the locomotive was allocated to Didcot from 1948 until March 1951, when it was withdrawn. It was photographed there on 12 October 1949. *H. C. Casserley*

Introduced 1890
Designed by William Dean
Built by GWR, Swindon
Number built 120
Number inherited by BR 36
Last example withdrawn November 1951

'850' and '1901' Class 0-6-0PT

Nos 992, 1903, 1907, 1909, 1912, 1917, 1919, 1925, 1930, 1935, 1941, 1943, 1945, 1949, 1957, 1964, 1965, 1967-1969, 1973, 1979, 1989-1991, 1993, 1196, 2000-2002, 2004, 2006-2014, 2016-2019

William Dean was Locomotive & Carriage Superintendent on the GWR from 1877 until 1902. He succeeded Joseph Armstrong, and Joseph's brother George was the Divisional Locomotive, Carriage & Wagon Superintendent at Wolverhampton from 1864 until 1897, responsible to Dean. It was at the Stafford Road Works in Wolverhampton, established in 1849 and enlarged in 1860 and 1881, that these '850'/'1901' Class engines were built. Locomotive building was transferred to Swindon in 1908, although Stafford Road remained busy with repair work.

The '850' Class of 0-6-0 saddle tanks were designed by George Armstrong, and has been described as the GWR equivalent of William Stroudley's 'Terrier' 0-6-0Ts on the LBSCR. They were versatile and good performers, earning them long service lives.

The locomotives were built in 14 batches from 1874, and those built from No 1216 to 2020 (1876-95) were considered as the '1901' Class. They were converted to pannier tanks from 1910, when the square-topped Belpaire boilers were fitted, and many received larger bunkers from 1924.

The engines worked widely throughout the GWR, from South Wales to Birkenhead, and from Devon to Oxford, Gloucester and Swindon. Some were sold to industrial concerns, and in the mid-1920s many were used on empty stock workings at Paddington. Once into BR days, withdrawals started in earnest in 1950/51. Nos 1935, 1991, 1996, 2010 and 2012 were still operational in 1953, and the last example, No 2012,

One of the last survivors of a class originally numbering 170, the last George Armstrong-designed engines in service, '1901' Class No 2008 was withdrawn from Birkenhead in March 1958, and is seen looking forlorn at Swindon on the 15th of that month. *T. B. Owen, Colour-Rail*

outlived its sisters by quite a margin, being withdrawn from Birkenhead as late as June 1958 at the age of 66, the last Armstrong-designed engine in service.

Introduced 1874
Designed by George Armstrong and William Dean
Built by GWR, Wolverhampton
Number built 170
Number inherited by BR 44
Last example withdrawn June 1958

'County' Class 4-6-0

Nos 1000-1029

Introduced 1945
Designed by Frederick Hawksworth
Built by GWR, Swindon
Number built 30
Number inherited by BR 30
Last example withdrawn November 1964

Seemingly rather 'out of numerical order', although initially allocated numbers in the '96xx' series, the 'Counties' were the final development of the GWR's celebrated two-cylinder 4-6-0 family, and were introduced as a heavy mixed-traffic engine. They were also the last GWR passenger design before nationalisation.

The 'Counties' resulted from Hawksworth's project for a new GWR 'Pacific' express locomotive design, and incorporated some features destined for this proposed 4-6-2; it is said that one departure from traditional GWR practice was to be the use of outside Walschaerts valve gear. In the event, the 'Pacific' project was stillborn in the new nationalised era, and the

The last surviving 'County' 4-6-0, No 1011 *County of Chester,* stands at Ruabon with a Festiniog Railway Preservation Society special train on 26 September 1964. It was withdrawn later that year and scrapped in March 1965.
Colin Whitfield/www.railphotoprints.co.uk

running gear of the 'Counties' was very similar to that of Hawksworth's earlier developments with the 'Modified Hall' 4-6-0s.

A new Standard No 15 boiler was fitted with a higher pressure of 280psi, a high degree of superheat, and smaller wheels at 6ft 3in diameter (the 'Castles' and 'Kings' were 6ft 8½in and 6ft 6in respectively). The boiler was developed from that of the LMS Stanier Class 8F; 80 of these 2-8-0 locomotives had been built at Swindon as part of the war effort, so Hawksworth had been able to study the design closely.

These and other new features made the 'Counties' more powerful than the 'Castles', on paper at least, and according to W. A. Tuplin this was done to match the tractive effort of the Southern Railway 'Pacifics'; however, when the latter had their boiler pressure reduced to 250psi, the GWR followed suit from 1956 onwards.

The first 'County' had an experimental double chimney, but this was replaced by a more slender example on all 30 of the class. The locomotives were coupled to a new design of flat-sided, all-welded 4,000-gallon tender. In appearance the 'Counties' were distinguished by their continuous splashers and straight nameplates, arguably less attractive than the more curvaceous lines of earlier 4-6-0s.

The last of the 'Counties' emerged from Swindon Works in April 1947, only months before nationalisation. In the BR era all 30 performed useful work throughout the Western Region, working alongside the 'Castles' on main-line expresses as well as hauling less glamorous freight and parcels trains.

Although the locomotives' introduction immediately after the war saw a return to the pre-war lined-green passenger livery, and they were free-steaming engines, albeit with a tendency to rough-riding, the 'Counties' were received only coolly by enginemen and enthusiasts alike. There also seems to have been no obvious role or need for them. More were planned, but no more were built – yet further examples of the 'Modified Halls' and 'Castles' were built by BR, and the 'grandfathers' of the 4-6-0 family, the 'Saints', were still running until 1953.

Possibly this coolness of attitude was responsible for none of the 30 locomotives being preserved. Withdrawals began in 1962, and by the end of the following year there were only eight left in service. The last, No 1011 *County of Chester*, was taken out of service at Swindon shed in November 1964 and scrapped the following spring.

However, that situation is currently being remedied by a new-build 'County' currently under construction at the Didcot Railway Centre under the auspices of the Great Western Society. The replica No 1014 *County of Glamorgan* is named in honour of the location of Woodhams' scrapyard in Barry, which yielded so many withdrawn steam locomotives for preservation, and the fact that Vale of Glamorgan County Council has made a significant contribution. The frames are from 'Modified Hall' No 7927 *Willington Hall* and the boiler from LMS 8F No 48518. It will also incorporate a number of original parts from other scrapped 'Counties', including the chimney from No 1006 *County of Cornwall*.

'1101' Class 0-4-0T

Nos 1101-1106

In 1905 work began on the King's Dock at Swansea (named in honour of King Edward VII, who cut the first sod), intended to cater for increasing tinplate exports; it was finished by 1909. At the same time a breakwater was built south of the new dock, enclosing about 150 acres of water to form the Queen's Dock, opened in 1920 and named for Queen Mary, who, with King George V, opened the new facility, which handled the import and export of oil.

To replace older Swansea Harbour Trust and Powlesland & Mason 0-4-0 tanks, which had been absorbed by the GWR at the Grouping in 1923, these six new short-wheelbase dock locomotives were ordered from the Avonside Engine Co in 1926 to a design by the GWR's Chief Mechanical Engineer, C. B. Collett. They had domed Belpaire boilers (which they retained throughout, not being reboilered by the GWR), and were unusual in having outside cylinders and Walschaerts valve gear, a reversal of usual GWR practice.

The six engines worked principally around the King's and Queen's Docks; all were taken over by British Railways, and all were shedded at Danygraig shed, east of Swansea Docks, for the whole of their BR careers.

No 1101 was withdrawn at the end of 1959, and the other five taken out of service en bloc in January 1960.

Collett-designed Swansea Docks shunter No 1101 looks in poor condition at Danygraig shed on 25 October 1959. The loco was withdrawn the following month, the first of the six to go. *Colour-Rail*

Introduced 1926
Designed by Charles Collett
Built by Avonside
Number built 6
Number inherited by BR 6
Last example withdrawn January 1960

Swansea Harbour Trust 0-4-0ST (Barclay)

No 1140

Swansea's development as an important South Wales port on the River Tawe began in the early 18th century, with the rapid growth of coal-mining and iron-making, as well as copper-smelting and the manufacture of tinplate. In 1791 the Swansea Harbour Trust was established to oversee the development of permanent harbour facilities, and to 'repair, enlarge and preserve the Harbour of Swansea'. Breakwaters were constructed to protected the river entrance and form a small tidal harbour.

In 1798 the 18-mile Swansea Canal joined Ystradgynlais and Swansea, and the area became globally important for metallurgical processing and manufacture. This led to further development of the docks; the North Dock was completed in 1852, and the South Dock in 1859.

By the 1870s the port was handling more than 1½ million tons a year, and it was said that 'there is no other harbour in the Kingdom where such an amount of work is done on a given space as at Swansea'. The new Prince of Wales Dock was completed in 1881, and extended in 1898. By the turn of the century 2 million tons of coal was being exported each year, and tinplate was also a major traffic. As already mentioned, the King's Dock was added in 1909, and the Queen's Dock in 1920.

The North Quay frontage was let to the Great Western Railway, the Neath & Brecon Railway and the Rhondda & Swansea Bay Railway. To handle traffic within the docks, the Harbour Trust operated its own fleet of locomotives, alongside those provided by Powlesland & Mason after 1903. The first locomotives were acquired in 1905, three 0-4-0STs from Andrew Barclay Sons & Co of Kilmarnock. They had the characteristic Barclay 'square' saddle tanks, and had GWR safety valve casings and warning bells in front of the cab.

The SHT controlled the port of Swansea until it and other South Wales ports were transferred to the GWR at the Grouping, when 14 locomotives were inherited, then they

More than 50 years old, diminutive 0-4-0 dock tank No 1140 stands at Swansea East Dock shed in September 1956. Apart from a short spell at Swansea Victoria, this was its home throughout the BR years. It is said that these locos were unpopular with crews due to the cramped cab and small boiler. *J. Harrison, Colour-Rail*

Introduced 1905
Designed by Andrew Barclay
Built by Andrew Barclay
Number built 3
Number inherited by BR 1
Last example withdrawn May 1958

became part of the Docks & Inland Waterways Executive of the British Transport Commission at nationalisation in 1948. One of the Barclay trio was still active; originally SHT No 5, it became GWR No 701, then was renumbered in June 1948 as 1140. It was withdrawn and scrapped in 1958; several examples from industrial users survive in preservation, one of which has been spotted numbered and liveried in the guise of No 1140.

Swansea Harbour Trust 0-4-0ST (Peckett)

Nos 1141, 1143, 1145

Introduced 1906
Designed by Peckett
Built by Peckett
Number built 3
Number inherited by BR 3
Last example withdrawn November 1960

These three SHT Pecketts were virtually identical to Powlesland & Mason's trio of 0-4-0STs, which became BR Nos 1150-52 (qv below). They were Peckett Class 'E' locos, and their 3ft 7in driving wheels and short wheelbase made them particularly suitable for use in locations such as docks, with their tight curves. All six – these three and the three P&M locos – passed into BR hands. Originally SHT Nos 11, 12 and 18, they became

Peckett 0-4-0ST No 1145 spent all its BR life allocated to Danygraig shed. Withdrawn from there in July 1959, it was photographed out of use on 25 October. It was scrapped in January 1960. *Colour-Rail*

GWR Nos 929, 968 and 1098 respectively, before gaining their 1946 GWR renumbering scheme numbers, which were applied by BR between 1948 and 1950.

By 1946 most of the locomotives inherited by the Great Western at the 1923 Grouping had been withdrawn, as had most of the older GWR engines numbered below 2000. In order to take account of the resultant gaps and make the numbering more consistent throughout, the pre-Grouping engines were given new numbers. Nos 30-96 were given to former Rhymney Railway engines, Nos 193-399 to Taff Vale and Barry locos, and Nos 421-436 to those from the Brecon & Merthyr. Powlesland & Mason engines were renumbered 1150-53, and SHT examples 1140-47.

Swansea Harbour Trust 0-4-0ST (Hudswell Clarke)

No 1142

This Hudswell Clarke 0-4-0ST was the most powerful locomotive of that type owned by the SHT. Built in the summer of 1911, like its sisters it worked around Swansea Docks, allocated to Danygraig shed, until June 1957, when it was transferred to Clee Hill shed, a sub-shed of Shrewsbury (84G), to work the former Ludlow & Clee Hill quarry railway at Titterstone Clee Hill, near Ludlow in Shropshire. It replaced 'Y3' Sentinel (qv) No 68164, which had arrived from Wrexham in November 1956 and was withdrawn in September of the following year.

The 6-mile Clee Hill quarry line was opened in 1864, and included a 3-foot-gauge 1¼-mile rope-worked incline. In 1867 the quarry owners made working arrangements with both the GWR and LNWR, and in 1893 those two companies absorbed the line as part of the jointly owned Shrewsbury & Hereford Railway. At its peak the quarry sent out about 6,000 tons of roadstone per week, and once employed more than 2,000 people.

No 1142 was withdrawn in November 1959 and scrapped in April the following year. The standard-gauge quarry railway remained intact until abandoned in the early 1960s; however, quarrying resumed in the late 1980s.

Introduced 1911
Designed by Hudswell Clarke
Built by Hudswell Clarke
Number built 1
Number inherited by BR 1
Last example withdrawn November 1959

No 1142 was a Danygraig engine until it was transferred to Clee Hill in 1957. It is seen here at its home shed, complete with characteristic warning bell, on 17 April 1955. *T. B. Owen, Colour-Rail*

Swansea Harbour Trust 0-4-0ST (Hawthorn Leslie)

No 1144

No 1144, GWR No 974 until renumbered in September 1948, is seen at Swansea East Dock on 8 September 1951. Note the warning bell in front of the cab. *H. C. Casserley*

Introduced 1909
Designed by Hawthorn Leslie
Built by Hawthorn Leslie
Number built for SHT 1
Number inherited by BR 1
Last example withdrawn January 1960

Only one Hawthorn Leslie-built loco was inherited by BR from the former SHT fleet. R. & W. Hawthorn Leslie & Co Ltd had a long history in locomotive manufacturing, as well as shipbuilding, and was founded in Newcastle-upon-Tyne in 1886 by the merger of shipbuilder A. Leslie & Co and loco-builder R. & W. Hawthorn Ltd (founded in 1817 as marine engineers). The Hawthorn brothers had been at the Rainhill Trials, and moved into loco-building with six engines for the Stockton & Darlington Railway. As a shipbuilder, one of their best known vessels was HMS *Kelly* of 1938. In 1968 the company's shipbuilding arm became part of Swan Hunter & Tyne Shipbuilders, later British Shipbuilders.

Meanwhile, in 1902 the famous engineering firm of Robert Stephenson & Co moved from Newcastle to Darlington, and Hawthorns acquired land adjoining the former's Forth Banks works for extensions. In 1937 the locomotive-building interests were disposed of to Robert Stephenson, to become Robert Stephenson & Hawthorns Ltd. Locomotive manufacturing continued, supplying engines to main-line and industrial railways, including many for export.

Burry Port & Gwendraeth Valley Railway 0-6-0ST

No 2176

Introduced 1907
Designed by Avonside
Built by Avonside
Number built 1
Number inherited by BR 1
Last example withdrawn March 1955

Avonside 0-6-0ST No 2176 was photographed inside its home shed at Llanelly on 9 September 1951. *H. C. Casserley*

The locomotive-building firm of Stothert, Slaughter & Co established its Avonside works in Bristol in the early 1840s as a partnership between Henry Stothert and Edward Slaughter. The company built engines to Daniel Gooch's design for the young Great Western Railway (one of the broad-gauge 'Hawthorn' Class 2-4-0s of 1865-66 was named *Slaughter*, but was soon renamed *Avonside* to allay possible passenger misgivings!). In 1866 the firm was renamed the Avonside Engine Company, and from 1889 built standard designs of four-coupled and six-coupled industrial saddle tanks. In 1907 this saddle tank was built for the BP&GVR as No 7, later becoming GWR No 2176, and rebuilt with GWR fittings. A resident of Llanelly shed throughout its BR career, it was withdrawn from there in March 1955.

Until 1927 the engine was named *Pembrey*, after the village on the Carmarthenshire coast between Burry Port and Kidwelly. Most of the village was created during the century-long coal-mining boom, when it was a port. However, the harbour was prone to silting and was abandoned in favour of Pembrey New Harbour, a mile further upstream on the Burry Estuary, soon renamed Burry Port Harbour. Traffic between the BP&GVR and the GWR was exchanged at the latter's Pembrey & Burry Port station, alongside a separate station belonging to the smaller company.

'2181' Class 0-6-0PT

Nos 2181-90

In 1939-40 '2021' Class (qv) engines Nos 2133, 2125, 2074 (the oldest, from 1899), 2145, 2149, 2118, 2143, 2087, 2105 and 2157 (the youngest, from 1905) were given enhanced braking gear with larger brake cylinders to enable them to work steeper gradients and trains of up to four carriages. Two of them, renumbered 2181 and 2182, were allocated to St Blazey to work the Goonbarrow branch; the others spent most of their BR days at Croes Newydd and Stourbridge.

Introduced 1897 (original locos); rebuilt 1939-40
Designed by William Dean
Built by GWR, Wolverhampton
Number built 10
Number inherited by BR 10
Last example withdrawn August 1955

Stourbridge-based '2181' 0-6-0PT No 2189 shunts at Stourbridge Junction on 10 September 1949. This was the class's first casualty, being withdrawn in October the following year. *H. C. Casserley*

Burry Port & Gwendraeth Valley Railway 0-6-0ST

Nos 2192, 2193

Black Hawthorn & Co built industrial tank locomotives in Gateshead, and became one of the area's leading manufacturers up to 1896, when it ceased trading, having built some 1,100 engines. The company was bought by Chapman & Furneux,

Introduced 1900
Designed by R. A. Carr
Built by Chapman & Furneux
Number built 2
Number inherited by BR 2
Last example withdrawn February 1952

Chapman & Furneux 0-6-0ST No 2193 *Burry Port* of 1901 is tucked away inside Llanelly shed on 15 June 1951.
T. B. Owen, Colour-Rail

which built a further 70 locomotives for northern collieries and other industrial concerns. The last example emerged in 1902, when the goodwill, drawings, patterns and templates were acquired by R. & W. Hawthorn Leslie & Co of Newcastle.

In 1900 and 1901 the Burry Port & Gwendraeth Valley Railway ordered two 0-6-0 saddle tanks, which became the company's Nos 1 and 3; the latter was a slightly smaller engine.

When the engines were absorbed into the GWR at the Grouping they became Nos 2192 and 2193, but still carried their original names, *Ashburnham* and *Burry Port*. As already mentioned, coal was initially moved down the Gwendraeth Valley by a canal, opened in 1768. A second canal was cut by the 3rd Earl of Ashburnham in 1798, which eventually became the BP&GVR. The country seat of the Earls of Ashburnham was Ashburnham in Sussex, and their wealth was substantially drawn from the village of Pembrey and its port, which was later superseded by Burry Port; as late as 1873 the family owned more than 7,500 acres in the principality, and the 3rd Earl was also Viscount St Asaph. The titles became extinct in 1924, not long after the BP&GVR itself ceased to exist.

No 2192 was withdrawn and scrapped in 1951, having spent its BR years at Neath. No 2193 was a Llanelly engine, and survived for nearly a year longer.

Burry Port & Gwendraeth Valley Railway 0-6-0ST

Nos 2194, 2195

Introduced 1903
Designed by Eager
Built by Avonside
Number built 2
Number inherited by BR 2
Last example withdrawn February 1953

These two saddle tanks were built by Avonside for the BP&GVR in 1903. Numbered 4 and 5, they were built in 1903 and 1905 respectively, and were named *Kidwelly* (after another small port served by the BP&GVR on the Gwendraeth Estuary) and *Cwm Mawr*. The latter was the northern terminus of the line, reached in 1913; there had been plans to extend the railway up

the valley beyond there to join the Carmarthen-Llandilo line at Llanarthney, but these never came to fruition.

As GWR engines following the Grouping they were renumbered 2194 and 2195 and the names were retained; No 2194 was 'Swindonised' and gained the standard bunker and fittings.. Later in the 1920s the locos went to Weymouth to work the quay tramway. This 1-mile line had opened in 1865, worked by horses, then by locomotives from the 1880s. The tramway's restricted clearances and sharp curves necessitated the use of small engines, and the former BP&GVR pair were ideal. They worked there, taking trains to and from the steamer quay, until replaced by pannier tanks in 1939/40. At that point No 2195 was withdrawn and lost its nameplates, but a few months later was reinstated, minus its name, and returned to Weymouth during 1945 and 1946; it was later allocated to Swindon. No 2194, still *Kidwelly*, moved to Cardiff, then spent its BR career mostly at Taunton. Both locomotives were withdrawn in the early part of 1953.

No 2194 *Kidwelly* was shedded at Bridgwater in July 1948, but otherwise was a Taunton engine. Once familiar on the Weymouth Quay tramway, the quaint saddle tank is seen here shunting at Bridgwater on 5 September 1952. Note the shunters' truck or 'runner' behind the loco. These wagons, which were largely a GWR feature, had full-length footboards and handrails for shunters, so they could ride on them during movements around sidings and depots. They also had a toolbox placed assymetrically, on which was usually painted the depot name, as here in Bridgwater. Jacks, chocks and other tools could also be carried by these trucks. *H. C. Casserley*

Awaiting the cutter's torch, former Burry Port & Gwendraeth Valley Railway 0-6-0ST No 2195 stands on the Swindon Works 'dump' line on 30 August 1953, having been withdrawn in January. *Brian Morrison*

Burry Port & Gwendraeth Valley Railway 0-6-0ST

No 2196

Introduced 1906
Designed by Avonside
Built by Avonside
Number built 1
Number inherited by BR 1
Last example withdrawn January 1956

Four Avonside-built BP&GVR locomotives passed to the GWR. This one, delivered in 1906 as the company's No 6, was very similar to No 7/2176, built the following year, in terms of weight, power and wheel diameter, but had a much taller-looking, chunkier profile. In GWR days it underwent the usual modifications – done by Kitson of Leeds – and was renumbered 2196, keeping its *Gwendraeth* name. At nationalisation in 1948 No 2196 was shedded at Burry Port, a sub-shed at Llanelly, then spend the remainder of its working life at Llanelly. It was taken out of use in January 1956.

No 2196 was photographed in Llanelly shed on the same day as sister Avonside 0-6-0ST No 2176 (*see page 37*), 9 September 1951. *H. C. Casserley*

Burry Port & Gwendraeth Valley Railway 0-6-0T

No 2197

Introduced 1909
Designed by Hudswell Clarke
Built by Hudswell Clarke
Number built 1
Number inherited by BR 1
Last example withdrawn October 1952

Of the 15 BP&GVR locos absorbed by the GWR in 1922, nine were products of Hudswell Clarke of Leeds. This was the BP&GVR's No 8, delivered in March 1909 and named *Pioneer*. This suitably upbeat name was popular during the 19th century; according to Jim Pike's *Locomotive Names: An Illustrated Dictionary*, No 8 was the 13th and last to use the name, which stretched back to 1841, and an 0-4-2 of the Manchester & Leeds Railway – a pioneer indeed!

The loco became No 2197 under the GWR, and spent its BR days at Llanelly shed, being withdrawn from there in October 1952. It was cut up at Caerphilly Works that month. It may have

No 2197 *Pioneer* nears the end of its days in what is probably Llanelly shed on 15 June 1951. *T. B. Owen, Colour-Rail*

been sent there for repair, but was found to be beyond help, a situation that was usually the result of cracked frames. It was reported shunting in Crwys Road sidings en route to the works, but within a few days had been cut up.

Burry Port & Gwendraeth Valley Railway 0-6-0T

No 2198

This was numerically the last of the 15 BP&GVR engines taken over by the GWR, 13 of which made it into BR ownership, and was the last survivor, not being withdrawn until March 1959. No 2198 was a slightly larger version of the previous year's No 2197, with a marginally higher tractive effort. Joining the BP&GVR as No 10, it was subsequently rebuilt by the GWR, and was dispensed with by BR at Llanelly shed in March 1959, where it had been allocated since nationalisation. It was never named.

Introduced 1910
Designed by Hudswell Clarke
Built by Hudswell Clarke
Number built 1
Number inherited by BR 1
Last example withdrawn March 1959

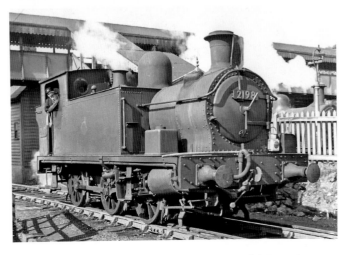

No 2198 is at work in the sidings east of Pontardulais station on 26 May 1956. Note the shovel in front of the chimney!
John Stretton collection

'2600' 'Aberdare' Class 2-6-0

Nos 2612, 2620, 2623, 2643, 2651, 2655, 2656, 2662, 2665, 2667, 2669, 2680

In 1899 the first of the so-called 'Kruger' Class of 2-6-0s appeared, described by W. A. Tuplin as 'perhaps the most nightmarish locomotive ever conceived in Britain up to that time.' The prototype was actually built as a 4-6-0, but was rebuilt as a 2-6-0, and the remaining nine were also 'Moguls'. By this time Dean was nearing the end of his long tenure as Locomotive & Carriage Superintendent at Swindon and, while still nominally in charge, it was his assistant, George Jackson Churchward, who was gradually assuming responsibility for the job to which he was formally appointed in 1902. Thus it was Churchward, perhaps feeling able to experiment in Dean's name, who put his theories of boiler design into practice with the 'Krugers', parts of which (they had all been withdrawn by about 1906) were incorporated into the first of the better-looking 'Aberdare' 2-6-0s that followed from 1900.

Introduced 1900
Designed by William Dean
Built by GWR, Swindon
Number built 81
Number inherited by BR 12
Last example withdrawn October 1949

The 'Aberdares' were essentially a freight version of Dean's 'Bulldog' and 'Atbara' 4-4-0s, and mainly worked heavy coal trains between Aberdare and Swindon, hence the class nickname. The prototype, numbered 33, appeared in August 1900, and was renumbered 2600 in December 1912.

Nos 2621-80 were built in three batches in 1901-02; the next ten, in 1903, took the earlier numbers 2611-20, then Nos 2601-10 (taking the numbers vacated by the withdrawn 'Krugers') emerged in 1906-07. All but the first of the third production batch (No 2661 onwards) received tapered boilers, becoming a milestone in British locomotive history as the first six-coupled engine to carry this type of boiler, which was to become the standard used by the nationalised British Railways half a century later. In fact, it was only the second engine to carry a Churchward tapered boiler, the first having been fitted to an 'Atbara' 4-4-0 in September 1902. The Belpaire firebox curved inwards towards the top, and also sloped gently towards the front of the cab.

They were distinctive locomotives with their double-framed driving wheels but single-frames for the leading truck. From 1929 many were attached to larger ex-ROD tenders of GCR design, and they continued to handle coal traffic until replaced

'Aberdare' 2-6-0 No 2655, with its distinctive double-framed driving wheels, is seen at Bristol on 4 July 1947. It became a BR engine the following year, and was one of the last four in service when withdrawn in June 1949. *H. C. Casserley*

by heavier 2-8-0 and 2-8-2T types. Some members of the class were withdrawn during the 1930s, and some were reprieved as war reserve engines in 1939, being reinstated in 1940. Eighteen of those that served through the war notched up more than a million miles each. Withdrawals began again towards the end of the war, but a dozen examples passed into BR hands, albeit only briefly, as all had gone within two years of nationalisation.

The 'Aberdares' were an evolutionary step towards the prototype for all Churchward's subsequent standard classes, 4-6-0 No 100 *William Dean*, built in 1902.

'2721' Class 0-6-0PT

Nos 2721, 2722, 2624, 2727, 2730, 2734, 2738, 2739, 2743-46, 2748, 2749, 2751, 2752, 2754-57, 2760, 2761, 2764, 2767, 2769, 2771, 2772, 2774, 2776, 2780, 2781, 2785-87, 2789-95, 2797-99

These pannier tanks were virtually identical to the earlier '655' Class (qv) apart from small detail differences. They were part of an evolutionary process via the '1501', '1813' '1854' classes, and the design would go on to influence the '5700' Class, which first appeared in 1929 and eventually numbered no fewer than 863 locomotives (including the '6700' and '9700' variants). Pannier tanks of GWR design continued to be built well into BR days, with the '9400' class of 1947-56. In fact, between 1860 and 1956 almost 2,400 GWR-designed tank locomotives were built, and after 1898 the company always had at least 1,000 examples on its books. The biggest visual change over the years was the fitting of the square-topped Belpaire firebox from about 1910, which required that the original curved saddle tank arrangement be changed to pannier tanks on each side of the boiler.

While Churchward was famous for his innovations and forward thinking in locomotive design, including his well-known predilection for standardisation, this did not apply to tank engines, and the GWR only introduced one entirely new design between 1897 and 1928. Apart from the replacement of saddle tanks by panniers, fully enclosed cabs were another gradual improvement, superheating was introduced in 1929, and boiler pressures increased.

The '2721' tanks, intended for branch-line passenger and mixed-goods traffic throughout the GWR, were numbered 2721-2800, although No 2800 became No 2700 in 1912 so that the pioneer 2-8-0 No 97 could become No 2800. They were the last 19th-century Swindon engines; the first batch, of 58 locomotives, appeared between 1897 and 1900, and a further

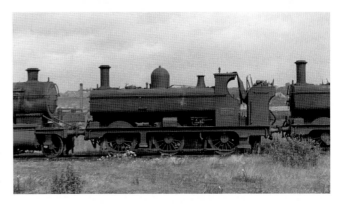

No 2738 was a '2721' Class pannier tank that retained its open cab, and is seen at Newport Pill, its home shed, on 6 July 1947. It was withdrawn from there at the end of 1949, and scrapped the following year. *H. C. Casserley*

Introduced 1897
Designed by William Dean
Built by GWR Swindon
Number built 80
Number inherited by BR 44
Last example withdrawn November 1950

22, the '2779' sub-class, followed in 1900-01. Forty-one engines received fully enclosed cabs, and most were fitted with larger bunkers; all had been converted to pannier tanks by the 1920s.

No 2756 was sold to the Rhondda & Swansea Bay Railway in 1921 as that company's No 33, but returned to the GWR the following year. Gradually the older engines were replaced by the newer '5700' Class tanks after 1929, and withdrawals began in 1945; by 1950, when all the '5700s' were in service (the '96xx' series), the last '2721s' could be consigned to scrap.

'Saint' ('2900') Class 4-6-0

Nos 2902, 2903, 2905, 2906, 2908, 2912, 2913, 2915, 2916, 2920, 2924, 2926-55, 2979-81, 2987-89

The fact that the 'Saints' were one of the most influential locomotive designs developed by the Great Western Railway – and indeed revolutionised British locomotive design – makes it all the more surprising that none survived into preservation.

The prototype locomotive was Britain's first express passenger 4-6-0, No 100 *William Dean* (in tribute to Churchward's predecessor at Swindon) of March 1902. It was very different in appearance and very modern-looking, and

caused quite a stir. It had a domeless parallel boiler (later replaced by a tapered 'half cone' example) and outside cylinders (a first for a GWR engine) whose valves were actuated by valve gear between the frames (Churchward had a strong dislike of outside motion). This was followed by No 98, the second prototype, built with a tapered boiler and redesigned valve gear and cylinders.

Churchward had studied American boiler design, and was also influenced by developments on the continent; with regard to the latter, he purchased a French De Glehn 4-4-2 'Atlantic' compound locomotive for comparative trials on the GWR. A third prototype,

Introduced 1902
Designed by G. J. Churchward
Built by GWR, Swindon
Number built 77
Number inherited by BR 47
Last example withdrawn October 1953

'Saint' Class 4-6-0 No 2920 *Saint David* (in lined black livery with red-backed nameplates) is seen at Banbury on 15 June 1952 during an SLS 'Saints' farewell tour. No 2920 took the train from Birmingham Snow Hill to Stourbridge Junction, Kidderminster, Worcester, Cheltenham, Gloucester, Stroud, Swindon, Banbury, Leamington Spa and back to Snow Hill. During the tour, one of many organised by W. A. 'Cam' Camwell in the 1950s and '60s, visits were also made to Gloucester and Banbury sheds and Swindon Works. *K. Cooper, Colour-Rail*

No 171, was built as a 4-6-0, with the boiler pressed to 225psi. It ran in this form until 1904, and was then converted to an 'Atlantic' in 1907 for comparison with the French engine. Meanwhile 19 engines were ordered from Swindon.

The adhesion advantage of the third coupled axle was soon apparent, and the earlier 'Atlantics' were rebuilt as 4-6-0s, the form in which the production batches would emerge. The 19 engines Nos 172-190, built as 'Atlantics', were converted to 4-6-0s in 1912-13 to match the rest of the class. They were rather austere in appearance, with straight frames running through below the cab, and a vertical step in front of the cylinders; they were subsequently renumbered 2971-90.

The five production batches, of 55 locomotives, numbered Nos 2901-2955, emerged from Swindon between 1906 and 1913, and were named after Ladies, Saints and Courts, while the former 'Atlantics', No 2971 onwards, carried names from the novels of Sir Walter Scott – despite this variety, the class

was known as the 'Saints'. The production engines had the familiar GWR curved frames at either end.

Another significant change was that the massive reversing lever of the earlier engines was replaced by an easier-to-handle screw reverser. Different boilers were fitted over the years, and by 1912 all were superheated (the first superheater fitted to a GWR engine was the Schmidt type on No 2901 *Lady Superior*). In their youth these revolutionary engines worked the GWR's principal expresses, but were eventually superseded by the newer four-cylinder 'Stars' and 'Castles'.

In 1924 one of the class, No 2925 *Saint Martin*, was rebuilt as the prototype 'Hall' Class 4-6-0, and renumbered 4900. No 2935 had Caprotti valve gear, the only GWR locomotive fitted with poppet valves.

When No 2920 *Saint David* was withdrawn from service in October 1953, the class became extinct. However, the lack of one of these seminal locomotives in preservation is being rectified by the Great Western Society's 'Saint Project', which is a 'back conversion' of a 'Hall' Class to create a brand-new 'Saint', to be known as No 2999 *Lady of Legend*. It has taken many years for this ambition to come to fruition; it was back in 1974 that the GWS purchased 'Hall' No 4942 *Maindy Hall* from Barry scrapyard with the specific intention of using it as the basis for a new 'Saint'. It will be one of the early 'Scott' 'Atlantic' conversions with an inside-steam-pipe cylinder block and straight frames, to distinguish it from the many GWR engines with curved frames already in preservation. It will also feature the original lever reversing gear and a top-feed boiler, as applied progressively to the class from 1911. It will eventually be outshopped in pre-Great War fully lined Edwardian livery with 'garter' coat of arms and full brass embellishments. It will also have the capability to run in 'Atlantic' form as a 4-4-2, when it will be numbered 191 and named, appropriately, *Churchward*. Intended to steam for the first time at the end of 2015, at last an infamous gap in steam locomotive preservation will have been filled!

'ROD' Class 2-8-0

Nos 3002, 3004-06, 3008-44, 3046-49

In 1915 the Royal Engineers formed the Railway Operating Division (ROD), which began operating in Europe in February 1916. It was largely recruited from the staff of Britain's railways, and was responsible for the control and operation of railways and their rolling stock. It was originally intended that French and Belgian locomotives would be used, but the operators kept them away from the front lines, and the war was evidently going to be more prolonged that initially expected, so a variety of British

engines were brought into use, at first on loan. A need for standardisation resulted in the ROD choosing the Great Central Railway's '8K' Class 2-8-0 design. In 1917 325 were ordered (311 of which went to France for war service), followed by a further 196 in 1918, 521 in all. The 126 built for the GCR itself, and 19 larger-boilered versions of Class '8M', brought the total built to 666. The 521 'RODs' were built by North British (369), Robert Stephenson (82), Nasmyth Wilson (32), Kitson (32) and the GCR at Gorton (6).

Several ROD 2-8-0s were borrowed by the GWR during the war, but they were returned to the Government at the end of

Introduced 1917 (based on a GCR 1911 design)
Designed by John G. Robinson
GWR examples built by North British (369), Robert Stephenson
(82), Nasmyth Wilson (32), Kitson (32), GCR, Gorton (6)
Number built 521
Number bought by GWR 100
Number inherited by BR 45
Last example withdrawn October 1958

hostilities. Then in 1919 the GWR bought 20 newly built examples, and numbered them 3000-19. A further 84 were hired in July 1919 and numbered 3020-99 and 6000-03, but these again were returned in October 1922. Finally, in 1925 the GWR bought 80 of the engines (including some of those that had been hired) and numbered the whole batch 3020-99.

In 1926/27 the original 20 2-8-0s and Nos 3020-49 were deemed worthy of a complete overhaul and were 'Swindonised' with top feed and brass safety valve, although they retained their parallel boilers with domes. The rest became Nos 3050-99 and were given a light overhaul, 'run into the ground' and then withdrawn, starting as early as 1927; locomotives in relatively good condition had their numbers changed so that they had lower ones.

In 1940, during the Second World War, the GWR once again borrowed some 2-8-0s, this time 30 examples from the LNER (by now Class 'O4'), returning them between 1941 and 1943.

One of the better examples of the 'RODs', No 3015 was a North British engine bought almost new in 1919. It is seen here in 1951 on the kind of train for which is was designed, and became one of the last two survivors of the GWR 'RODs', withdrawn in October 1958. *Huw Daniel, Colour-Rail*

None of the poorer batch of 'RODs' lasted long enough to be taken into BR ownership, although their tenders were reused. However, 45 did become BR engines, and some soldiered on until 1958.

'3100' Class 2-6-2T

Nos 3100-04

Introduced 1906; rebuilt 1938-39
Designed by G. J. Churchward
Built by GWR, Swindon
Number built 5
Number inherited by BR 5
Last example withdrawn January 1960

The 2-6-2T 'Prairie' tank is a design very much associated with the Great Western Railway, and was developed from the first prototype, No 99 of 1903 (see '5101' Class below).

The nickname 'Prairie' arose from the North American origin of the 2-6-2 wheel arrangement. (Indeed, the notation of wheel arrangements in this manner also originated in America, with Frederick Methvan Whyte (1865-1941), a mechanical engineer on the New York Central Railroad, who introduced the format of 'leading wheels-coupled driving wheels-trailing wheels' in 1900.) In 1885 six locomotives with a 2-6-2 wheel arrangement were built by Baldwin for New Zealand Railways, and in 1898 a further example was built for the McCloud River Railroad. In 1900 Brooks built several of the type for the Chicago, Burlington & Quincy Railroad, intended for use on the mid-western prairies. These were mostly tender locomotives, but in Britain, where the 'Prairie' nickname was also adopted, they were generally tank engines.

On the GWR the 'Prairie' tank family had a complex pedigree. The Churchward '3100', '3150' and '5101' classes and

'Large Prairie' 2-6-2T No 3102 of Stafford Road shed, Wolverhampton (84A), leaves the yards north of Wolverhampton on 20 July 1954 with a pick-up freight. *Brian Morrison*

Collett's later '3100', '6100' and '8100' classes were known as 'Large Prairies', while the '4400', '4500' and '4575' classes were the 'Small Prairies'.

These five '3100' Class engines arose from a rebuilding project by C. B. Collett in 1938, when five of Churchward's '3150' Class (Nos 3173, 3156, 3181, 3155 and 3179) were given a higher boiler pressure and smaller wheels for banking purposes, increasing their nominal tractive effort to 31,170lbf. They were renumbered 3100 to 3104 respectively, and one of them, No 3103, shedded at Ebbw Junction throughout, was not withdrawn until January 1960.

'3150' Class 2-6-2T

Nos 3150, 3151, 3153, 3154, 3157-61, 3163-65, 3167-72, 3174-78, 3180, 3182-90

Introduced 1906
Designed by G. J. Churchward
Built by GWR, Swindon
Number built 41
Number inherited by BR 33
Last example withdrawn September 1959

In this early nationalisation shot, No 3186 looks smart in black livery with the early BR 'cycling lion' logo at its home shed of Laira in June 1949. *W. H. G. Boot, Colour-Rail*

The parent class from which the five locomotives above were rebuilt was the '3150' Class, itself a development of the original '3100' (later '5100') Class. These engines, built between 1906 and 1908, used the larger and heavier Standard No 4 boiler, so had greater boiler capacity, but were consequently heavier and more route-restricted. They were used mainly as heavy suburban passenger traffic engines, but during their BR careers most were shedded at Severn Tunnel Junction, where they would no doubt have undertaken banking duties through the Severn Tunnel, and possibly headed the car trains that used the tunnel up until 1966, when the first Severn Bridge opened. When the shed opened in 1908 it had an allocation of some 90 engines, one-third of which were 2-6-2Ts.

The line though the tunnel fell at 1 in 90 from the Welsh side, then rose at 1 in 100 to the eastern portal. 'Banking' (or perhaps more accurately 'pilot') engines were attached to the front of freight trains (and occasionally passenger trains) at Severn Tunnel Junction – rear-end banking was not permitted. After assisting the train through the tunnel to Pilning, the 'Prairie' tanks would be moved to the rear (remaining uncoupled) to bank the train on to Patchway, then a path would have to be found in the heavy Anglo-Welsh traffic to return the banker(s) to Severn Tunnel Junction.

Most of the '3150s' made it into BR days, more than 20 being allocated to Severn Tunnel Junction (86E), where in the early years of nationalisation there were still about 100 freight trains (predominately coal) passing through each way every day except Sundays, more than half of which used the tunnel.

Withdrawals of the '3150s' began in 1947 and continued progressively through to 1959.

'Bulldog' ('3300') Class 4-4-0

Nos 3335, 3341, 3363, 3364, 3366, 3376, 3377, 3379, 3382, 3383, 3386, 3391, 3393, 3395, 3396, 3400, 3401, 3406-08, 3417-19, 3421, 3426, 3430-32, 3438, 3440-55

Introduced 1899
Designed by William Dean
Built by GWR, Swindon
Number built 156
Number inherited by BR 45
Last example withdrawn November 1951

William Dean introduced his 'Duke of Cornwall' '3252' Class 4-4-0s (qv) in 1895; initially working West of England expresses, their relatively low weight later made them useful engines throughout the GWR system. In 1898 one of the engines was rebuilt with a larger domed boiler, which became the prototype for the Standard No 2. This locomotive, with outside frames curved over the driving wheels, became No 3312 *Bulldog* and, although still looking like a 'Duke', it was the first of a new class, to be named after the first example. In all 121 'Bulldogs' were built, and more were added when 20 'Dukes' were rebuilt; finally, the last batch of 15, the 'Bird' sub-class, emerged in 1909-10. This made the 'Bulldogs' one of the GWR's larger classes.

In 1899 No 3352 *Camel* was built with the final form of the parallel No 2 boiler and a Belpaire firebox but no dome. A further

One of the early 'Bulldogs', No 3341 *Blasius* (the name of several saints), is on pilot duties at the south end of Exeter St David's station on 31 August 1949. It was withdrawn the following November. *Lens of Sutton Collection (PMA 2154)*

40, Nos 3332-51 and 3353-72, appeared in two batches in 1899-1900, and were initially known as the 'Camel' Class, the later ones having straight frames. Tapered boilers (of the 'half-cone' type, the taper being on the rear half of the barrel only) appeared with No 3443 *Birkenhead* of 1903, and 29 more engines were built in this style in 1903-04; a 'three-quarter-coned' boiler was fitted to some from 1906, and when *Bulldog* was so equipped the class assumed the 'Bulldog' name.

The 'Bird' sub-class, Nos 3441-55, was a development of the 'Bulldog' with deeper outside frames and a new type of bogie. These engines emerged in two batches between 1909 and 1910. In 1912 the whole class was gathered together in a new numbering sequence from 3300 to 3355.

Between 1927 and 1930 some of the 'Bulldogs' lost their names, apparently so that names such as *Penzance*, *Cardiff* and *Paddington* wouldn't confuse passengers into thinking they were the train's destinations.

When 'Bulldog' No 3365 *Charles Grey Mott* was withdrawn in January 1930, its frames were used with the boiler of 'Duke' No 3265 to create the first of the 'Earl' Class, becoming No 3265 *Tre Pol and Pen*. Twenty-nine more followed in 1936-39, and gained the popular portmanteau nickname of 'Dukedogs'. Apparently the Earls whose names graced the hybrid locomotives objected to being associated with such relatively antiquated machines, so the names were transferred to some of the new 'Castle' 4-6-0s! All the 'Dukedogs' became BR locos, and one, No 9017 *Earl of Berkeley*, is preserved, so they are outside the scope of this book – although the loco has the frames of 'Bulldog' No 3425!

One of the 'Bird' sub-class was No 3454 *Skylark*, seen here during an SLS rail tour from Birmingham Snow Hill to Swindon and return on 17 June 1951. Visits were made to Oxford and Didcot sheds, and Swindon Works and shed. *Skylark* and sister engine No 3453 *Seagull* were the last two surviving 'Bulldogs', being withdrawn in November of that year. *Colour-Rail*

Withdrawals of 'Bulldogs' and 'Dukedogs' began in the early 1930s, but 30 'Bulldogs' and all 15 'Birds' became BR engines. They saw out their days on secondary duties on former Cambrian lines and the old Midland & South Western Junction Railway. No 3377 (formerly *Penzance*) was the only 'Bulldog' to carry BR livery – the rest remained in GWR colours. However, they did little work in their final days, often being stored out of use, and all had gone by the end of 1951.

'3500' ('455') 'Metropolitan' Class 2-4-0T

Nos 3561, 3562 , 3582, 3585, 3586, 3588, 3589, 3592, 3597, 3599

These locomotives were built in ten lots over a 30-year period, and were described by O. S. Nock as 'very fast and "handy" little engines'. Their original use was on London suburban services, including the underground section of the Metropolitan Railway from Paddington to Moorgate Street and later Aldgate, which gave the class its nickname. They also operated on other routes, including the Hammersmith & City, Richmond and West London lines.

The early batches were numbered 455-70, 3-6 (briefly numbered 1096-99 when new), 613-32, 967-86, 1401-20, 1445-64 and 1491-1500. The 10 locomotives that passed to BR at nationalisation were from the 3561-70 series of 1894, and the last two batches built in 1899.

The different batches had detail differences: early examples had inside frames for all axles, and there were other variations in wheelbase, water tank and coal bunker size, leading to descriptions of 'small', 'medium' and 'large' types. The first locomotives had no cabs (to keep the crews alert, according to Armstrong), but later half cabs and fully enclosed cabs were fitted. In their later years, from the end of the 1920s, about 40 engines gained 'auto-train' gear for push-pull working.

The last of the 'large' 2-4-0 'Metro' tanks, No 3588 of 1899, stands forlornly at Swindon on 30 April 1950. Withdrawn at the end of the previous year, it was cut up in June. *H. C. Casserley*

Introduced 1869 (surviving locos 1894)
Designed by Joseph Armstrong/William Dean
Built by GWR, Swindon
Number built 140
Number inherited by BR 10
Last example withdrawn December 1949

Before the electrification of the Metropolitan in 1903 about 50 'Metro' tanks carried condensing apparatus, which diverted exhaust steam to the upper parts of the water tanks to reduce emissions; those so fitted were normally cabless, and were consequently sometimes dubbed the 'Get Wets'. After electrification only about a dozen condensing locomotives were required, mainly to take goods trains to Smithfield Market.

The 'Metros' continued to work on outer suburban services from Paddington until replaced by the '6100' 'Prairie' tanks and '9700' 0-6-0PTs in the early 1930s. They were also to be seen around Swindon, Oxford and Gloucester, in South Wales and the West of England, even efficiently heading cross-country trains such as Gloucester-Cardiff services.

Early withdrawals took place following electrification of the Metropolitan lines, and a good number of others went during the 1930s. About 25 survived the Second World War, and the ten Dean-built BR survivors were 'large' 'Metros' from the last two lots.

'3571' Class 0-4-2T

Nos 3574, 3575, 3577

These attractive 0-4-2 tanks had their origin in George Armstrong's '517' Class. Designed for local passenger work, those earlier tank locos were built in 13 lots at Wolverhampton Works between 1868 and 1885, with various detail variations over the years. The earlier examples were built as saddle tanks, then converted, while later ones had side tanks from new. At first they were mainly found on the Northern Division handling Birmingham and Wolverhampton suburban traffic. Later about half of the class members were fitted for auto-train working, and were distributed around the network as required; the remainder were relegated to shunting duties. Long-lived engines, most ran between a million and a million and a half miles, and the final example was not scrapped until just before nationalisation.

'517' Class No 1477 was partially rebuilt in 1895, and nine further engines followed to become the '3571' Class, Nos 3571-80. They had large boilers with longer fireboxes (Belpaire fireboxes from 1912), as well as wider outside frames. Large bunkers were also fitted, but only one received an enclosed cab, and none were auto-fitted. Withdrawals began in the late 1920s, but these three survived into BR days, although by then they were little used, and all had disappeared by the end of 1949. They had spent most of their lives in the Chester and Birkenhead areas, but the last example, No 3574, saw out its days at Worcester shed.

'3571' Class 0-4-2T No 3574 waits forlornly in the yard at Swindon on 16 February 1950. It had been withdrawn from Worcester the previous December, and was cut up in March. In front of it appears to be 'Saint' Class No 2929 *Saint Stephen*, also withdrawn in December 1949 and scrapped in March 1950. *T. B. Owen, Colour-Rail*

Introduced 1895
Designed by William Dean/George Armstrong
Built by GWR, Wolverhampton
Number built 10
Number inherited by BR 3
Last example withdrawn December 1949

'4400' Class 2-6-2T

Nos 4400-10

The '4400' Class was the first of the GWR's 'Small Prairie' tanks (see '3100' Class entry above). The prototype was built in 1904 and numbered 115, and was a small version of the '3100'/'5100' 'Prairie', designed for light branch work. No 115 was later renumbered 4400, and such was the success of these smaller-wheeled locos (4ft 1½in against 5ft 3in) that ten more were

Wellington-shedded 'Small Prairie' No 4409 approaches Much Wenlock with the 7.50am Craven Arms-Wellington train on 10 September 1949. The loco was withdrawn in February 1951 from Laira, Plymouth. *H. C. Casserley*

Introduced 1904
Designed by G. J. Churchward
Built by GWR, Swindon (No 4400) and Wolverhampton
Number built 11
Number inherited by BR 11
Last example withdrawn September 1955

built at Wolverhampton between 1904 and 1906 (originally numbered 3101-10, they became 4401-10). The locos' high power-to-weight ratio made them the ideal branch-line locomotive, and went on to inspire future LMS and British Railways Standard 2-6-2Ts.

The 'Small Prairies' were popular due to their lively acceleration, although their small wheels limited their speed. This would have made them ideal for suburban work, with many stops and starts, but they were put to work on some of the GWR's more hilly routes, operating the Princetown branch on Dartmoor and the Much Wenlock branch in Shropshire.

The '4400s' ultimately led to the '4500' (1906-27) and '4575' (1927-29) Classes, with slightly larger driving wheels (4ft 7½in), to complete the 'Small Prairie' family. The larger wheels gave these later engines extra speed – up to 60mph – and 75 '4500s' were subsequently built. The first batch were the last locos to be built at Wolverhampton, and No 4507 became the last Wolverhampton-built loco to remain in service with BR, surviving until 1963. Three are preserved.

The '4575' Class was a further development, with even larger side tanks (with sloping tops to improve visibility for the driver) and a greater water capacity. One hundred of these

After nearly 50 years in service, Churchward '4400' Class 2-6-2T No 4406 of 1906 has probably its last photograph taken inside Swindon Works Cutting-up Shop on 5 November 1955. This was one of the last three survivors of the class, all having been withdrawn that September (No 4406 from Newton Abbot, 83A). *Brian Morrison*

were built, the last in 1929 under C. B. Collett, and 11 are preserved.

The entire '4400' Class remained intact in 1948 and the last example was not withdrawn until September 1955. Given their usefulness on branch lines, it is a pity that none lasted long enough to be taken into preservation.

'4700' Class 2-8-0

Nos 4700-08

The class prototype, No 4700, was built in 1919, designed as a powerful freight engine, but the following class of eight entered traffic as mixed-traffic machines in 1922-23. These were the last locomotives designed by Churchward, who retired as Chief Mechanical Engineer at the end of 1921.

These were Britain's only mixed-traffic 2-8-0s – the only others of that wheel arrangement that regularly hauled passenger trains were the Somerset & Dorset 7Fs – and were the only British eight-coupled class to have driving wheels as large as 5ft 8in. They were similar in appearance to Churchward's earlier '2800' Class 2-8-0s of 1903-19, but had larger driving wheels than the earlier class, which had been designed specifically as a freight engine, and the drive was on the second coupled axle rather than the third. They were also the first Swindon design to have the steam pipe outside the smokebox. They were primarily intended for fast overnight freight work, earning them the nickname 'Night Owls'.

Introduced 1919, 1922
Designed by G. J. Churchward
Built by GWR, Swindon
Number built 9
Number inherited by BR 9
Last example withdrawn May 1964

A portrait of power: in fully lined green BR passenger livery No 4704 poses at Old Oak Common on 27 October 1957. This was one of the last three of the class to be withdrawn, all taken out of service in May 1964. *Rail Photoprints*

Although their axle loading restricted their route availability, their mixed-traffic potential was only really recognised after nationalisation, when their ability to haul holiday expresses during busy summer Saturdays was much appreciated, and they were turned out in fully lined BR passenger green livery.

When new, No 4700 carried Churchward's Standard No 1 boiler, but within two years it was decided that it needed a larger one, so received the Standard No 7 in 1921 when it became available; the rest of the class were built with the larger boiler. The prototype had the distinction of attending the Stockton & Darlington Railway Centenary event held at Darlington in 1925.

Although the class remained intact until as late as 1962, all nine locomotives had been scrapped by 1964 and none was preserved. To remedy this the Great Western Society is in the process of constructing what would have been the next member of the class, No 4709. This will use a mixture of new parts and others sourced from former Barry scrapyard

locomotives. Thus six of the eight 5ft 8in driving wheels will be donated by '5101' Class 2-6-2T No 4115, the cylinder block and some brake components are from '2800' Class No 2861, and various other components from '5205' Class 2-8-0T No 5227. (No 2861 was one of the 'Barry Ten', the last locos to remain at the famous South Wales scrapyard, and remained stored there until 2010, when it was bought for use in the new locomotive. In 2013 it was the last engine to leave Barry and was moved to the Llangollen Railway, where it was cut up to release the donor components.) The plates for the new frames were cut and machined in 2012, and the loco is being built alongside other 'new-builds' Nos 6880 *Betton Grange* and 'Patriot' 45551 *The Unknown Warrior*.

As well as now having sourced all the donor parts, the three groups have jointly funded an apprentice at Llangollen to work on all three projects as well as attending college, of great benefit to the groups and helping to ensure a supply of young engineers for the future.

'5400' Class 0-6-0PT

Nos 5400-24

In 1930 one of the ageing auto-fitted Dean '2021' 0-6-0 pannier tank locomotives (qv) was rebuilt to produce the prototype of this new class, which was intended to replace earlier life-expired engines that had been fitted with push-pull equipment. It had much larger wheels (more than a foot larger in diameter), a larger boiler and a larger bunker, to produce a more powerful, faster engine. Subsequently 25 engines were built to this design, the new ones having a round-edged cab, a style that was to be utilised on all future pannier tanks. The prototype only lasted two years before being scrapped and replaced by a completely new engine with the same number.

A further variation of the design, with smaller wheels, was introduced in 1932-37, to work the more steeply graded South Wales lines; these were the 40 '6400' Class panniers (Nos 6400-39), three of which have been preserved. Three of the '5400' engines made it to Barry scrapyard, but had been cut up by 1965 before they could be saved.

Introduced 1931	
Designed by C. B. Collett	
Built by GWR, Swindon	
Number built 25	
Number inherited by BR 25	
Last example withdrawn October 1963	

ABOVE Three withdrawn engines languish at Oswestry on 25 April 1964. '5400' Class No 5421, on the left, had been withdrawn there in September 1962. Next to it are two other Oswestry residents, '1400' Class 0-4-2T No 1438 and '7400' Class pannier tank No 7428, both also withdrawn in the autumn of 1962. Despite apparently standing there unused for some 18 months, none was saved before succumbing to the cutter's torch in the summer of 1964. *T. B. Owen, Colour-Rail*

LEFT '5400' Class No 5410, a resident of Yeovil Town shed, stands in Yeovil Town station on 24 August 1963. It was withdrawn in October and cut up a year later. *Colour-Rail*

'5800' Class 0-4-2T

Nos 5800-19

Introduced 1932	
Designed by C. B. Collett	
Built by GWR, Swindon	
Number built 20	
Number inherited by BR 20	
Last example withdrawn April 1961	

ABOVE '5800' Class 0-4-2T No 5813, still with 'GWR' showing clearly on its tank, heads a Leamington-Stratford local at Bearley on a lovely sunny evening in 1955. A Bristol engine for most of its BR life, it ended its days at Leamington shed in November 1957. *J. Eggleshaw, Colour-Rail*

The '5800' Class 0-4-2Ts were identical to the earlier '1400' ('4800') Class engines, which themselves were a development and an updating of George Armstrong's aged '517' Class via the '3571' Class (qv) of the 1890s. Collett kept the best features of the originals, but added modern refinements. The '1400s', initially known as the '4800' Class when introduced in 1932, were designed for branch-line passenger work. Seventy-five engines were eventually built up to 1936, and they were designed to work with auto-coaches, allowing 'push-pull' working and obviating the need for the engine to run round the stock at journey's end.

As branch lines closed following nationalisation the attractive little '1400s' became increasingly redundant; the last four were withdrawn in November 1964, although happily four examples, Nos 1420, 1442, 1450 and 1466, have been preserved, so do not appear in this book.

While the '1400s' were still in production, in 1932 the 20 '5800s' were built, distinguished from the others by not being fitted with auto-train equipment; they also lacked the characteristic Swindon top feed and GWR Automatic Train Control (ATC) equipment (although some were fitted with it later). This lack of 'auto' gear was the death knell of the class, and all had been scrapped before the '1400s' disappeared.

RIGHT Still with plenty of coal – but also plenty of rust – the last example of the '5800s', No 5815, awaits its fate at Swindon on an unknown date. *T. B. Owen, Colour-Rail*

'6700' Class 0-6-0PT

Nos 6700-79

With some dozen examples preserved, the GWR's ubiquitous '5700' Class pannier tanks, of which a total of 853 were built (including later derivatives), do not merit an entry in this book. Built between 1929 and 1950, it was the most prolific GWR class and one of the largest on Britain's railways as a whole. Although described as 'light goods and shunting engines', they were also used on branch-line, suburban and shorter main-line journeys. In the 1950s and 1960s 13 redundant engines were sold to London Transport, extending their lives to the early 1970s, and seven others found further industrial use, most of which are among the preserved examples.

Most of the first batch of 300 '5700s' had vacuum brakes and steam heating, and some were also fitted with the GWR's

Introduced 1930	
Designed by C. B. Collett	
Built by Bagnall (25), Yorkshire Engine (25), GWR, Swindon (30)	
Number built 80	
Number inherited by BR 80	
Last example withdrawn May 1964	

Automatic Train Control (ATC) equipment. However, the first 50 locomotives of the '6700' Class had only steam brakes, no ATC and plain three-link couplings, limiting them to shunting and light freight duties. They could also negotiate smaller-radius curves.

The first 25 of the '6700' Class (Nos 6700-24) were built by W. G. Bagnall Ltd, and the second 25 (Nos 6725-49) by the Yorkshire Engine Co. This was unusual for the GWR, but there

'6700' Class Nos 6765 and 6777 were the last two survivors of a class of 80, and had been built as recently as 1949 and 1950. Both were withdrawn in May 1964, but No 6765, seen here, had already suffered two periods in store at Barry shed, in 1958-59 and 1962. With a cloth covering its chimney, it was photographed at Barry on 12 July 1959, during the first of those periods of inactivity. *R. M. Casserley*

was a precedent in that in 1928 the building of 50 '5600' Class 0-6-2Ts had been put out to Armstrong Whitworth. This contracting of loco construction was partly funded by interest-free Government loans intended to relieve unemployment during the Depression years. Also, in accountancy terms new locomotives could be seen to be more economical than the repair or refurbishment of older ones.

Nos 6700-49 were initially stored for a couple of years before being allocated, as there was already of surfeit of '5700s' available. Thereafter they spent most of their lives allocated to South Wales sheds. Following nationalisation a further 30 engines were built at Swindon under British Railways auspices, the last emerging at the end of 1950. Some of these had very short working lives of less than 10 years but, despite the fact that all but four of the BR-built locos survived into the early 1960s, none was rescued from the scrapyard. The last two to go, in May 1964, were Nos 6765 and 6777, from Swansea East Dock and Upper Bank (Swansea) respectively.

'Grange' Class 4-6-0

Nos 6800-79

Introduced 1936
Designed by C. B. Collett
Built by GWR, Swindon
Number built 80
Number inherited by BR 80
Last example withdrawn December 1965

A glaring omission from the catalogue of preserved locomotives is the GWR's 'Grange' Class. A 4-6-0 with 5ft 8in driving wheels had been part of Churchward's standardisation plans as early as 1901 (producing locomotives suitable for a wide range of duties yet sharing a small number of standard components), but it was not until 1936 that Collett brought the proposal to fruition with the 'Granges', introduced to replace the '4300' 2-6-0s (qv) dating back to 1911. More than 300 of these were widely used throughout the GWR system, but were showing their age, so it was proposed to replace them with two classes of 4-6-0 carrying

different boilers, the 'Manors' and the 'Granges' (their names neatly continuing the theme begun with the 'Castles' and 'Halls').

The 'Granges' would reuse many parts of the '4300' 'Moguls', such as the driving wheels, motion and cab steps; the cylinders were the same size, but the design was different, so they could not be recycled. The locomotives were very similar to the 'Halls', with a slightly smaller driving wheel diameter, but, being smaller, can be distinguished by the running plate being raised over the cylinders. Eventually it was intended to replace all the '4300s', but the Second World War intervened and only 80 'Granges' were constructed. They were mixed-traffic machines, and saw use on all the GWR main lines, being shedded as far apart as Paddington, Penzance, Fishguard and Birkenhead. Their power and mixed-traffic status meant that they could be found on most types of traffic, often being used to haul perishable goods, such as fruit and broccoli, and excursion trains.

All the 'Granges' passed into BR ownership. The first to be withdrawn was No 6801 *Aylburton Grange* in 1960, but there were still 71 in service by the end of 1963, and 45 by the close of the following year. However, all had gone within the next 12 months in the great cull of GWR steam.

Happily, 33 years after the demise of the last 'Grange', the 6880 Society was formed in 1998 to recreate what it describes as 'the 81st Grange', No 6880 *Betton Grange* – this was the next member of the class scheduled to come off the assembly line at Swindon Works. The main frames and cab for No 6880 have had to be constructed from new, the work commencing in September 2004. In 2005 the society acquired the boiler from 'Modified Hall' No 7927 *Willington Hall* (its frames and wheels will

A 'Grange' in a classic role and a classic GWR setting, at Doublebois, west of Liskeard, on 13 September 1958. No 6808 *Beenham Grange* is coupled ahead of an unidentified 'Castle'. A Penzance-based engine, it was withdrawn from Oxley in August 1964. *T. B. Owen, Colour-Rail*

contribute to the new-build 'County' Class 4-6-0 (qv)), and also has the spare tender frame from No 4936 *Kinlet Hall*. The wheels are from '5101' Class 'Prairie' tank No 5199, and the front bogie borrowed from No 5952 *Cogan Hall*. It is therefore appropriate that an example of a locomotive built from the parts of others should likewise be assembled from a 'kit of parts'!

In poor condition just a month before withdrawal from Worcester shed, 'Grange' 4-6-0 No 6819 *Highnam Grange* is seen at Worcester on 17 October 1965. *T. B. Owen, Colour-Rail*

'7400' Class 0-6-0PT

Nos 7400-49

Introduced 1936
Designed by C. B. Collett
Built by GWR, Swindon
Number built 50
Number inherited by BR 50
Last example withdrawn April 1965

Just as the '5800' Class 0-4-2Ts were a version of the '1400' Class without auto-train equipment, so the '7400' 0-6-0 pannier tanks were a non-fitted variant of the 1932-37 '6400' Class; while the former were classified '2P', the latter were '2F'. The '6400s', three of which are preserved, were introduced in 1932, and all 40 examples were 'auto-fitted' to operate branch trains in 'push-pull' mode. Both classes were descendents of a long pedigree of tank locomotives stretching back to Armstrong's '850' Class of 1874 and Dean's '2021' Class of 1891 (both qv), a basic design that was therefore almost 60 years old. Distinguishing features were larger driving wheels and a more up-to-date appearance, together with a higher boiler pressure of 180psi, giving a useful increase in power. Another smaller difference was that the '6400' cab and bunker had an arc where they joined, whereas on the '7400s' the join was straight. The smaller '7400s' could be used on routes where the otherwise very common '5700' Class engines were prohibited, but this distinction was eliminated

A fine study of '7400' 0-6-0PT No 7440 shunting at Llangollen on 25 August 1959. Built in January 1950, it was a Croes Newydd engine for 10 years, but was withdrawn from Carmarthen shed in October 1962, aged just 12½. How useful would such a little-used engine be on today's heritage Llangollen Railway! *Russell Leitch, Colour-Rail*

when route availabilities were reassessed in 1950. They were widely distributed and could be found working branch-line passenger, freight and milk trains, as well as undertaking station pilot and shunting duties.

The first batch of 30 emerged from Swindon Works between July 1936 and June 1937, then BR built a further 20 of the same design (Nos 7430-49) in two batches in 1948 and 1950. This meant that when the latter were withdrawn, some were as young as nine years old, and the oldest only 15, a considerable waste of resources. None were preserved.

Shedded at both Oxford and Fairford throughout its BR days, No 7412 was a stalwart of services on the Fairford branch, and is seen at the branch terminus on a chilly looking 11 February 1961. This picturesque branch closed in June 1962, and No 7412 went into store at Oxford the following month, being withdrawn a year later and scrapped. *R. Denison, Colour-Rail*

'8100' Class 2-6-2T

Nos 8100-09

Introduced	1906; rebuilt 1938-39
Designed by	G. J. Churchward; rebuilt by C. B. Collett
Built by	GWR, Swindon
Number built	10 (rebuilds)
Number inherited by BR	10
Last example withdrawn	June 1965

The elegant and powerful-looking '8100' Class 'Prairies' were widely dispersed. No 8102 spent the first 12 years of its BR life in South Wales, before moving to Bristol, Westbury and Worcester after 1963, being withdrawn from the latter in May 1964. It is seen here at Newport High Street in March 1961. *A. Sainty collection, Colour-Rail*

The '5100' Class of 'Prairie' tanks of 1906 were conversions from the earlier '3100' Class, and renumbered in the 51xx series. These were modified to become the '5101' Class of 1935, but Nos 5100, 5123, 5118, 5145, 5124, 5126, 5120, 5116, 5133 and 5115 were rebuilt in 1938-39 with higher-pressure boilers and slightly smaller wheels, and given the numbers 8100 to 8109 respectively. They were the last of the so-called 'Large Prairies' built by the GWR, and appropriately No 8100 incorporated the frames of the original prototype 'Prairie' tank, No 99, built in 1903. It had been intended to similarly convert all the old '3100s', and 50 '8100s' were on order when the Second World War curtailed production.

The '8100' Class were fast and powerful locomotives, and were designed to supplement the '6100' Class 2-6-2Ts on London suburban duties, their smaller driving wheels providing better acceleration. However, as it turned out they were widely distributed throughout the system, from the Midlands to South Wales and the Bristol area; they were also to be seen at the head of the 'Pembroke Coast Express' for part of its journey.

Dating originally from 1906, these 1930s rebuilds were all withdrawn between 1957 and 1965.

'8300' Class 2-6-0

No 8393

Following a visit to America, H. Holcroft, a member of Churchward's staff, reported on 2-6-0 locomotives being used there on branch lines for both passenger and goods traffic. This was something that Churchward wanted, so a design for a 'Mogul' was drawn up using standard parts. Thus was born the '4300' Class, whose members were, according to Tuplin, 'economical all-round engines, able to make a fair shot at every haulage job from pick-up goods to top-rank express

Introduced	1928 (variation of '4300' Class of 1911-32)
Designed by	Churchward; converted by Collett
Built by	GWR, Swindon
Number built	65 (converted)
Number inherited by BR	1 (unconverted)
Last example withdrawn	October 1959

passenger work.' This was Britain's first modern 2-6-0 design, and between 1911 and 1932 342 were built, numbered in the 4300-99, 5300-99, 6300-99 and 7300-41 series. During the First World War 11 examples from the 5300 series went to France for service with the Railway Operating Division, and one of these has been preserved. Later, when members of the class were withdrawn in the 1930s, the wheels and motion of 80 of them (including 12 of the '8300' conversions) were used in the construction of the 'Grange' Class (qv), until the Second World War brought a halt to the conversions.

During the 1920s it was found that these 'maids of all work' were suffering excessive flange wear on the leading coupled wheels, so to relieve this Nos 4351, 4385, 4386 and 4395 had a

No 8393 was the last of the '8300' Class, 1928 conversions of '4300' Class 2-6-0s. It is seen at Par on 26 May 1947, and when the ballast weights were removed in September of the following year it reverted to its original number, 5393. *Great Western Trust*

heavy 30cwt casting added on the front buffer beam to redistribute some the engine's weight to the pony truck; the four were renumbered 8300, 8334, 8335 and 8344. The experiment proved successful, so between January and March 1928 65 engines (Nos 5300-02, 5304-05, 5307-09, 5313-15, 5318, 5320, 5322, 5325-29, 5331-35, 5337-38, 5340-44, 5350-54, 5357-66, 5368-69, 5372-74, 5376, 5378-79, 5381-84, 5386-91 and 5393) were similarly converted. These were renumbered to

the 83xx series, but retained the last two digits of their original number, so for example No 5326 became 8326. When the weights were removed in the 1940s the engines reverted to their original numbers.

Only one engine, No 8493, remained to be reconverted when the engines passed into BR ownership in 1948. Its ballast weights were removed in September 1948 and it became No 5393 again until withdrawal a decade later in October 1959.

'3252' 'Duke of Cornwall' Class 4-4-0

Nos 9054, 9064, 9065, 9072, 9073, 9076, 9083, 9084, 9087, 9089, 9091

Introduced 1895
Designed by William Dean
Built by GWR, Swindon
Number built 60
Number inherited by BR 11
Last example withdrawn July 1951

These 60 locomotives (initially referred to as the 'Pendennis Castle' or 'Devon' Class) were designed by Dean with the possible collaboration of his assistant Churchward. They were built in five batches between 1895 and 1899, with outside frames curved over the driving wheels and parallel boilers with a large dome and distinctively long smokebox; their original tenders, however, had a shorter than normal wheelbase to allow them to fit on the smaller turntables in use west of Newton Abbot. They were originally numbered 3252-91 and 3312-31. No 3252 was named *Duke of Cornwall*, giving its name to the class, and they were intended for use on the hilly routes of the West of England, where Dean's single-wheelers were unsuitable. Between 1902 and 1909 20 of the class were rebuilt with larger, tapered boilers and renumbered 3300-19 to become the 'Bulldog' Class (qv). By then the remaining locomotives were becoming uneconomical to maintain, and as an experiment 'Duke' No 3265 *Tre Pol and Pen* was rebuilt with straight frames from scrapped 'Bulldog' No 3365 *Charles Grey Mott*, becoming the prototype for the hybrid 'Dukedog' Class (officially the 'Earl' Class) of 1936-39. These were numbered 3200-28, later 9000-28, and one of them, No 9017 (3217), named *Earl of Berkeley*, survives in preservation. The conversion resulted in a lower axle weight, giving the engines a wider availability. It had been intended to convert more, but the Second World War intervened.

'Duke of Cornwall' Class No 9087 *Mercury* was a mid-Wales engine throughout its BR career, and is seen here at Aberystwyth in June 1949, a month before withdrawal. *T. B. Owen, Colour-Rail*

Having thus spawned two 'spin-off' classes, the remaining 'Dukes' worked on. Their numbers were gathered together into the sequence 3252-91, formerly carried by the first batch of 'Dukes'. In 1946 the last 11 were renumbered in the 9000 series, retaining the two last digits of their '3200'-series numbers; thus No 3254 *Cornubia* became No 9054.

Having worked the important services between Exeter and Penzance until 1900, they were gradually replaced in the West Country by the 'Bulldogs' and the new '4300' Class 2-6-0s. By the early 1920s they had been reallocated to such places as Reading, Didcot, Bristol and Shrewsbury, working local and branch passenger services and some goods trains. Later they became associated with the former Midland & South Western Junction and Cambrian Railways routes. When the 'Manor' 4-6-0s arrived, the 'Dukes' finally bowed out. The last example, No 9089 (named *St Austell* until 1930), was withdrawn from Oswestry shed in 1951, but most of the 'Dukedogs' served until 1957, the last few until 1960.

'9700' Class 0-6-0PT

Nos 9700-10
The '9700' Class pannier tanks were a development of the GWR's standard '5700' 0-6-0PTs, designed by Collett but essentially an updated version of much earlier classes. These were numerically the largest GWR class, with a total of more than 850 built from 1929, including the derivatives.

The first member of the '9700s', No 9700 itself, was rebuilt by Beyer Peacock from '5700' Class No 8700 in 1931. The purpose of the new version was the fitting of condensing apparatus to allow it to work on the underground lines from Paddington to Smithfield meat market in London; the apparatus fed the exhaust steam back into the water tanks,

Introduced 1933
Designed by C. B. Collett
Built by Beyer Peacock (1), GWR, Swindon (10)
Number built 11
Number inherited by BR 11
Last example withdrawn November 1964

'9700' Class 0-6-0PT No 9707 was photographed at Westbourne Park on 7 July 1962. The condensing apparatus and Weir feed pump can clearly be seen, as well as the unconventional deeper 'pannier' tanks. This engine, an Old Oak Common resident in 1962, was one of the last three, withdrawn from Taunton shed in September 1964. *Frank Hornby*

which were shorter than usual to accommodate the pipework, but deeper, to retain a suitable water capacity. As the condensing process naturally heated the water in the tanks, a special type of feed-water pump, the Weir pump, was fitted to the right-hand side of the boiler to feed water into it, as conventional injectors would not work with hot water. Another refinement, to allow the engines to work over the electrified underground lines, was a special type of ATC equipment that could be raised above the centre power rail; tripcock valves, such as those used on underground stock, were used instead.

Once the new design had proved itself, 10 further locomotives, Nos 9701-10, with modifications such as the tank

arrangement mentioned above, were built at Swindon. No 8700 was renumbered 9700, and a new No 8700 was built to replace it in the '5700' Class.

The 'new' Smithfield meat market had been rebuilt in 1868, incorporating 'cut and cover' railway tunnels and a triangular junction beneath it, on the line between King's Cross and Blackfriars via Snow Hill Tunnel. Extensive underground sidings were laid out, allowing the transfer of animal carcases to the cold store building or direct to the meat market via lifts – animals had previously arrived by road 'on the hoof'. The sidings closed in the 1960s, and the former railway tunnels are now used for storage, parking and as basements, with most meat arriving by road

The *Morning Post* stated that 'beneath the floor of this large building there is a world of railways, and sidings, and cranes, and lifts, designed to facilitate the supply of the market with its thousands of tons of meat and poultry. The Metropolitan Railway will provide access to this market for the meat-laden trains of the Great Western, Midland, Great Northern, South Western, and Chatham & Dover Lines; and by this system of underground communication will relieve to a great extent the street traffic... Of the area below the market one half ... belongs to the Metropolitan Railway Company, and the southern half to the Great Western, which has the right of passing over the rails of the Metropolitan.'

When this traffic ceased in the early 1960s the locomotives became redundant, and all 11 disappeared between 1959 and 1964.

2

Locomotives of the former Southern Railway and its constituents

LSWR 'A12' 'Jubilee' Class 0-4-2

Nos 612 (DS3191), 618, 627, 629, 636

Introduced 1887
Designed by William Adams
Built by LSWR, Nine Elms (50), Neilson (40)
Number built 90
Number inherited by BR 4
Last example withdrawn November 1951

No 629 would have been BR No 30629 if it had lived long enough, but, like the four surviving members of the class in regular service, it was withdrawn within the first year of nationalisation. It is seen here at its home shed of Eastleigh on 11 September 1948, three months before it succumbed. *H. C. Casserley*

William Adams was born on 15 October 1823 in Limehouse, east London, the son of the resident engineer of the nearby East & West India Docks Company. He went on to serve as the Locomotive Superintendent of the North London Railway (1858-73) and the Great Eastern Railway (1873-78), before joining the London & South Western Railway. There he designed more than 500 locomotives, until he retired in 1895 at the age of 72, dying nine years later in Putney.

Adams's 'A12' 0-4-2s were built in six batches between 1887 and 1895, all but 40 at the LSWR's Nine Elms works (predecessor to Eastleigh Works). Prior to 1887 LSWR locomotives had been built by outside contractors, and the 'A12s' were the first to be built when 'in-house' construction resumed at Nine Elms. They were unusual for their time in that the 0-4-2 wheel arrangement was already being phased out by the other companies that used it (the Great Northern and Glasgow & South Western, for example). The other well-known examples were the LBSCR's 'Gladstone' Class, but despite their success the 'A12s' were the LSWR's only 0-4-2s. Because the first batch appeared in the year of Queen Victoria's Golden Jubilee they gained the nickname 'Jubilees'.

They were mostly used on heavy excursion and troop trains, as well as fast goods services to the west, in north Devon, and around Weymouth and Southampton. They were the first LSWR locomotives to carry cast brass number plates, with polished numbers on a red background.

The majority of the first 30 engines were coupled to second-hand tenders from Beyer Peacock goods engines purchased by Adams's predecessors, later replaced by Adams tenders from scrapped locomotives. The fifth batch, of 40 engines, was built

by Neilson & Co of Glasgow, with detail differences. The splashers were adorned with brass beading, later removed by Drummond as unnecessary adornment!

Built with Adams-type stovepipe chimneys, these were later replaced by the Drummond type, and some engines gained Drummond-type boilers, while a few were fitted with both Westinghouse air brakes and vacuum brakes.

Appropriately, No 555 had the honour of hauling Queen Victoria's funeral train from Gosport to Fareham on 2 February 1901.

All the engines passed to the Southern Railway at the 1923 Grouping, and the first examples were withdrawn in 1928. Just four of the Neilson-built batch survived in BR service, but were withdrawn from Guildford and Eastleigh sheds in 1948 without ever carrying the 'plus-30000' BR numbers allocated to them. No 629 had previously been withdrawn in January 1939, but was reinstated as part of the war effort. A fifth locomotive, No 612, withdrawn in 1946, was used to supply steam to loco boilers at Eastleigh being tested after welding repairs, and in this role it outlasted its classmates by three years.

LSWR 'C14' Class 0-4-0T

Nos 30588, 30589, 77S

Introduced 1906; rebuilt 1913-23
Designed by Dugald Drummond; rebuilt by Urie
Built by LSWR, Nine Elms
Number built 10
Number inherited by BR 2
Last example withdrawn April 1959

Almost as tall as it is long, 'Engineers Dept' No 77S worked at the Redbridge sleeper depot until withdrawal and scrapping in 1959. It was photographed there on 22 May 1957. *H. C. Casserley*

These tiny engines started life as a class of 10 2-2-0 tanks, built at Nine Elms for £875 each, to work push-pull trains on lightly used routes, where there was increasing competition from road transport, and where Drummond's earlier 'railmotors' had proved unsuccessful. However, the engines proved to be underpowered themselves whenever traffic rose above a certain level, they had a propensity for slipping, and their small coal capacity precluded all but the shortest runs. They soon gained the nicknames 'Potato Cans' or 'Rockets'. They were based on 'railmotor' power units, and could be coupled to one or more carriages as demand dictated. At first their outside cylinders were located between the driving wheels.

In 1910 two 0-4-0 versions of the design were built, classified as 'S14', with the cylinders now forward of the driving wheels, but the design was not perpetuated.

In 1912 Robert Urie took over from Drummond, and ordered four of the 'C14s' to be rebuilt as 0-4-0 tanks; in the event, only two, Nos 743 and 745, had been so treated when the First World War broke out. The remaining 2-2-0Ts continued to see sporadic service during the war, but only Nos 741 and 743 ran as complete units with their railmotor carriages on a wartime service between Bournemouth West and the cordite factory at Holton Heath. Six other examples and one of the rebuilds were bought by the War Office to work in munitions facilities and dockyards; the two 'S14s' were also sold, and all were scrapped after the war.

Nos 741 and 744, having been leased by the Admiralty in 1917 for dockyard shunting, were subsequently returned to the LSWR and in 1922 and 1923 were rebuilt as 0-4-0Ts, joining the surviving 1913 rebuild No 745, and went on to put in many

One of the other two survivors, No 30589 of 1907, is seen from the other side in 1953. *B. J. Swain, Colour Rail*

more years of useful work. No 745 became departmental loco No 77S and spent the remainder of its life, until April 1959, at the Southern Railway's Redbridge sleeper depot. The other two worked at Southampton Town Quay, where they were well suited to the tight curves and limited clearances. No 741 became E0741 in 1925, then 3741 in 1931, and finally BR No 30588 in 1950, while No E744/3744 assumed its BR number 30589 in 1948. They were both withdrawn in 1957. Because of their unique design, the locomotives had to carry their original boilers for the whole of their lives.

On 14 June 1952 No 30589 became the only 'C14' to handle a passenger train other than a railmotor when it hauled a two-coach RCTS rail tour along the Bishops Waltham branch.

LSWR 'D15' Class 4-4-0

Nos 463, 30464-72

The LSWR opened a carriage and wagon works at Eastleigh in 1891, then in 1903 a large locomotive shed was built there to replace the existing maintenance and repair shops at Northam, near Southampton. In January 1910 locomotive building was transferred from Nine Elms to the new Eastleigh workshops.

It was from Eastleigh that Drummond's last LSWR design emerged in 1912. He had already built several classes of 4-6-0s that had proved to be less than successful, and his reversion to the 4-4-0 wheel arrangement was considered surprising. His new design, built in two batches of five (Nos 463-67 and 468-72), had a typical, some might say 'clumsy', Drummond appearance, with a short smokebox and a boiler with a large grate, pitched high to enable it to clear the trailing axle. Originally the engines were coupled to large eight-wheel tenders, their water capacity reflecting the lack of water troughs on the LSWR, but later six-wheeled examples were used. Drummond's successor, Urie, fitted the engines with small Eastleigh superheaters, which were again replaced by Maunsell after the Grouping, and these successive revisions improved the locomotives' appearance somewhat.

Unlike his previous 4-6-0 designs, Drummond's 'D15s' were very good performers, and on Bournemouth and pre-

Introduced 1912
Designed by Dugald Drummond
Built by LSWR, Eastleigh
Number built 10
Number inherited by BR 10
Last example withdrawn January 1956

No 30465 is captured at speed near Eastleigh in July 1953. This was the last of the class, withdrawn in January 1956. *S. C. Townroe, Colour-Rail*

electrification Portsmouth services were considered very superior to the earlier 'T14' 4-6-0s, with economical fuel consumption and ease of maintenance. They also used Walschaerts valve gear rather than the Stephenson variety. Until Bulleid's 'light Pacifics' took over, they were also often to be found at the head of Brighton-Plymouth trains.

On 7 November 1912, while the last three 'D15s' were still being completed, Drummond suffered a severe scald while on the footplate, and his leg had to be amputated. Although still in good health at the age of 72, the shock was severe enough to kill him the following day. Urie, while acknowledging the

merits of the 4-4-0s, built no more, preferring the 4-6-0 layout. Drummond had certainly shaken up the Locomotive Department at Eastleigh, being described by C. Hamilton Ellis as 'as rough a block of Scottish granite as ever rolled down the banks of the Clyde, knocking chips and scraping moss from other rocks.'

No 463 was converted to oil-burning during the post-war coal shortage, but was one of the first two engines to be withdrawn in 1951, without receiving its BR number. No 30465 was the last to be taken out of service, at Eastleigh, in January 1956.

East Kent Railway 0-6-0T

No 4

The East Kent Light Railway was part of the famous Colonel Stephens 'empire' of economically constructed rural light railways in England that took advantage of the Light Railways Act of 1896. Holman Fred Stephens was the line's engineer, and later became director and manager. The line opened for goods traffic in 1912 and for passengers four years later, and ran from Shepherdswell to Wingham (Canterbury Road) station, with a branch from Eastry to Richborough Port. The line's original intention was to link the collieries in the newly developed Kent coalfield with the new port at Richborough. In the event, however, the EKR only served one productive mine, at Tilmanstone, linking it the few miles to the SECR main line at Shepherdswell.

Never a 'Southern Railway' line as such, the company remained independent until nationalisation, but at that point, after a long period of decline, BR withdrew the passenger service of two trains each way on weekdays on 30 October 1948, and closed the line in stages between 1949 and 1951. The colliery link survived, but was effectively killed off by the miners' strike of 1984.

The EKR had a total of ten locomotives, and five passed into BR hands. No 5 was a Neilson-built ex-LSWR 4-4-2T, which became BR No 30583 and is now preserved, while Nos 6, 100 and 1371 were ex-SECR 0-6-0s sold to the EKR and reacquired upon nationalisation, becoming BR Nos 31371, 31372 and 31383 respectively, all scrapped in 1949-51. The fifth was this Kerr Stuart 0-6-0T, one of that company's 'Victory' Class locomotives of the same design as the Alexandra Docks 0-6-0Ts Nos 666 and 667 (qv).

EKR No 4 at Shepherdswell on 18 July 1936. It would have become BR No 30948, but was scrapped after closure of the light railway a year or so after nationalisation. *H. C. Casserley*

Introduced 1917
Designed by Kerr Stuart
Built by Kerr Stuart
Number built 10 (1 to EKR)
Number inherited by BR 1
Last example withdrawn February 1949

Originally built for the Inland Waterways Docks Department of the Royal Engineers as No 11, then ROD No 610, it was bought by the EKR as No 4 in 1919. Passing to BR in 1948, it was withdrawn and scrapped in 1949 without receiving its allocated BR number, 30948.

LSWR 'G6' Class 0-6-0T

Nos 30160, 30162, 237, 30238 (DS682), 239, 240, 257, 30258, 259, 30260, 261-5, 30266, 267-9, 30270, 271, 272 (DS3152), 273, 30274, 275, 30276, 30277, 278, 279, 348, 30349, 351, 353, 354

In 1893 Adams was asked by the LSWR to design a new class of compact and versatile shunting locomotive to cope with increasing traffic and to replace an assortment of ageing examples. The resultant engine was intended as an 0-6-0 version of Adams's 'O2' Class passenger locomotive, and was his only 0-6-0 design. The engines were built at Nine Elms in six batches, ten locos in 1894, four in 1896 (as more powerful replacements for the 'B4' 0-4-0Ts at Southampton Docks), five

Introduced 1894
Designed by William Adams
Built by LSWR, Nine Elms
Number built 34
Number inherited by BR 34
Last example withdrawn November 1961

in both 1897 and 1898, and two batches of five in 1900. The boiler was the same as that used for the 'O2s', for standardisation purposes. The 'G6s' were Adams's last LSWR locomotives, as he retired in 1895 and was succeeded by Drummond, who, impressed with their performance, ordered the remainder, which differed from the original ten in utilising the boilers of Beattie 'well tanks' and other withdrawn locomotives.

The 'G6s' worked exclusively in goods yards on the LSWR system, even in Southern Railway days, with the exception of two examples that were sent to the GWR's Reading freight yard to assist with a shortage of motive power during the Second World War. The engines were highly successful in undertaking the tasks for which they had been designed, and were respected by crews. They rarely undertook passenger work, though some worked as bankers on the incline between the GWR and SR stations at Exeter until the early 1930s.

All 34 engines became BR property, but BR's numbering was not strictly in order of building, and in fact only 11 of the locomotives carried numbers in the 'plus-30000' form.

Very little rebuilding took place, apart from boiler changes and the replacement of Adams's stovepipe chimneys with lipped examples, and all were eventually fitted with vacuum brakes.

In June 1950 No 272 was transferred to departmental service at Meldon Quarry in Devon, as No DS3152. It was replaced by DS682 (the former 30238) in 1960, and is seen here at Eastleigh on 21 August of that year, destined to be scrapped. *Colour-Rail collection*

Two engines entered departmental service at Meldon Quarry in Devon, first No 272 in June 1950 as DS3152, replaced by DS682 (the former 30238) in the summer of 1960. Meanwhile, No 30237, withdrawn in February 1949, enjoyed a second career in industrial use as No 39 at the Redbourn Ironworks in Scunthorpe until September 1960.

The first casualty was No 348 in August 1948, and 22 had disappeared by the end of 1951. The last to be withdrawn was No 30277 at Guildford, towards the end of 1961, marking the demise of this very useful locomotive class.

LSWR 'G16' Class 4-8-0T

Nos 30492-95

Introduced 1921
Designed by Robert Urie
Built by LSWR, Eastleigh
Number built 4
Number inherited by BR 4
Last example withdrawn December 1962

By 1910 the LSWR's internal and exchange goods traffic in London was beginning to overwhelm the existing facilities at Nine Elms, so the following year, and again in 1915, land was acquired at Feltham, a location that offered excellent access to both the LSWR's own main lines and those of other companies via the North London line. Work commenced in 1916, assisted by about 200 German prisoners of war, and the yard opened in stages between 1917 and 1921. It featured two automated gravity shunting humps, electrically operated points, and 32 miles of track, able to deal with 2,500 wagons a day, making it possibly the busiest marshalling yard in the country at that time. With the reduction in wagonload freight traffic obviating the need to marshal trains, by the 1960s Feltham yard became redundant and closed in 1969.

All 95 tons of 'G16' 4-8-0T No 30495 makes an impressive sight at Feltham shed on 21 August 1960. It remained in service until the end of 1962. *Colour-Rail collection*

To handle shunting over the humps at Feltham, in 1921 Urie designed these four huge 4-8-0T shunting engines, based on his 'S15' Class 4-6-0 freight engines; at 95 tons, they were the LSWR's most powerful locomotives and were the widest standard-gauge steam locomotives ever to run in Britain.

The same engine is seen out on the road at the head of a long goods train at Acton on 7 July 1956. *S. M. Watkins, Colour-Rail*

A series of trials during the Maunsell years found that the 'G16s' were capable of hauling loaded trains of up to 850 tons on the main line, although they took more than half a mile to stop from 20mph!

The boilers were identical to those used on Urie's 'H16' 4-6-2 tanks (qv), while the cylinders and motion were interchangeable with the 'H16' and 'N15' 4-6-0s. They had larger side tanks than the 'H16s', and the tanks had sloping tops towards the front to aid the driver's visibility.

Although they were tried out on other duties, most of the quartet's life was spent allocated to Feltham shed, and they provided sterling service, even in run-down condition, during the war. It was only when diesel shunters were introduced in the 1950s that the 'G16s' became redundant; they were transferred to other duties, but the spread of electrification meant that there were plenty of surplus steam locomotives, and the four giants were disposed of in 1959 (Nos 30492 and 30493) and 1962 (the remaining pair).

LSWR 'H15' Class 4-6-0

Nos 30330-35, 30473-78, 30482-91, 30521-24

Introduced 1914
Designed by Robert Urie/Richard Maunsell
Built by LSWR, Nine Elms (6), Eastleigh (20)
Number built 26
Number inherited by BR 26
Last example withdrawn December 1961

Robert Wallace Urie was appointed Chief Mechanical Engineer of the LSWR in 1912 following Drummond's sudden and tragic death (see 'D15' entry above). Like Drummond he was a Scot, and after an apprenticeship in Glasgow he had joined the Caledonian Railway as a draughtsman under Drummond, then moved with his boss to the LSWR in 1897, where Drummond became Locomotive Superintendent and Urie was Works Manager at Nine Elms. Urie transferred to a new works at Eastleigh in 1909, and remained there until his retirement in

1922. Unlike the forbidding and autocratic Drummond, Urie was more approachable and a less formidable physical presence!

Urie's first design was the 'H15' 4-6-0, responding to a serious lack of suitable large engines on the LSWR, especially for heavy freight. The new engines had two outside cylinders with Walschaerts valve gear for easy maintenance. The first ten (Nos 482-91) appeared in 1914, and were the subject of experiments with different superheaters. In the event, Urie designed and patented his own, known as the Eastleigh superheater, which he fitted to all future 'H15s'.

In 1914 one of Drummond's 1905 'E14' Class was rebuilt as the 11th 'H15', No 335, the first loco to have the Eastleigh superheater. The early engines had a lower running plate that was raised above the cylinders, with a single straight splasher above the driving wheels; later examples had a higher straight running plate. In all, 26 locomotives were built in six batches, including the 'one-off' No 335, the last appearing in 1924.

The class was an amalgam of four different groups of engine that really had little in common beyond cylinder and driving wheel size. The first-built were what became BR Nos 30330-34, which were Drummond 'F13' 4-6-0s of 1905 rebuilt by Maunsell in 1924-25 (they had distinctively tall cabs with some loftily positioned controls, which led to the nickname of 'Cathedrals'; in general, the class seems to have spawned the strange nickname 'Chonkers'). No 30335 was the 1907 'E14' rebuild, converted to an 'H15' in 1915. Nos 30842-91 followed, Urie's own design of 1914. The ten locos Nos 30473-78 and 30521-24 were Maunsell's version of the 'H15', built in 1924. Modifications made by Maunsell included the fitting of smoke deflectors. The engines were coupled to Drummond 'watercart'

'H15' No 30335 leaves Andover with a short freight in September 1958, less than a year before its demise. This engine had been rebuilt from a 1907 'E14' 4-6-0, becoming an 'H15' in 1915. *T. B. Owen, Colour-Rail*

eight-wheeled tenders, enabling them to travel further over a system that had no water troughs.

With their 6-foot driving wheels and free-steaming boilers, the 'H15's were excellent workhorses, and were used to haul fast, heavy freights, especially stone trains in the Okehampton area. The class remained intact until the mid-1950s, but all had been withdrawn by 1961, like so many others as a result of the 1955 BR Modernisation Plan.

The same engine is dismantled for scrap at Eastleigh on 29 August 1959, having been withdrawn from Salisbury shed that June. *J. Sutton, Colour-Rail*

LSWR 'H16' Class 4-6-2T

Nos 30516-20

As part of the development of the new yard at Feltham (see 'G16' entry above), and in addition to the four 'G16' 4-8-0T tanks, Urie also designed these five 4-6-2 tanks. The 'G16s' were dubbed the 'Black Tanks' (liveried in that colour) for shunting the new yard, while the 'H16s', the 'Green Tanks', were turned out in passenger green to work transfer freights between Feltham and other companies' yards. They were originally numbered 516-20, then when they passed to the Southern Railway in 1923 the numbers were prefixed by 'E' until the early 1930s.

As mentioned in the 'G16' entry, the 'H16s' shared many components and design features with their counterpart 'Black Tanks'; they had an identical boiler, motion and bogies, and similar cylinders. The driving wheels were of a greater diameter, and the larger bunker was carried by the trailing truck, with extra water capacity (and no slope at the front of the tanks). This made them heavier than the 'G16s', at more than 96 tons.

Their main work was on transfer goods trains between Feltham and Brent Sidings on the Midland main line and Willesden on the LNWR's West Coast Main Line. They were also occasionally used on passenger specials, such as during Ascot Race Week, but their limited water supply and rough riding when running bunker-first made them less than ideal for that role. All five passed into BR's hands, and during the 1950s they were regularly used to move empty stock between Clapham Junction and Waterloo, then later on oil trains to and from the Fawley branch, near Southampton. The advent of diesels rendered them redundant, and all five were withdrawn from Feltham shed at the end of 1962. One of them, No 30517, was twice used to haul rail tours in the South London area during its final weeks.

Introduced 1921
Designed by Robert Urie
Built by LSWR, Eastleigh
Number built 5
Number inherited by BR 5
Last example withdrawn November 1962

ABOVE 'H16' No 30520 doubled-heads with a new BR Standard 2-6-0 at Eastleigh in 1961. *Colour-Rail collection*

BELOW The same engine, minus its motion, awaits the attention of the scrapman at Eastleigh on 10 November 1963, a year after withdrawal. *Colour-Rail collection*

LSWR 'K10' Class 4-4-0

Nos 135, 137, 139-46, 150-53, 329, 340, 341, 343, 345, 380, 30382, 383-86, 389-94

To fulfil a serious need for mixed-traffic locomotives on the LSWR, Drummond designed a small-wheeled 4-4-0 of a type he had previously used when he was Locomotive Superintendent of the Caledonian Railway. The driving wheels of the 'K10' were the same diameter as his earlier 'M7' 0-4-4Ts and its boiler was also interchangeable with the 'M7', as well as the '700' Class 0-6-0 (qv) and the extinct 'C8' Class, Drummond's first 4-4-0 for the LSWR, of which they were a development. The locomotives were built at Nine Elms in eight batches of five through 1901 and 1902, and were generally coupled to a six-wheel tender, which was thought to be big enough for the needs of the local stopping passenger trains and medium-range goods trains that the engines were designed to handle; however, some examples were seen with larger 'watercart' eight-wheelers. No 137, built in September 1902, was the 650th engine to emerge from Nine Elms.

These neat and attractive engines were nippy in performance (reaching speeds into the 70s on occasions) and saw wide service in the LSWR's Western Section, being nicknamed 'Grasshoppers'. When the larger 'L11s' (qv) appeared a year or so later, the 'K10s' became the 'Little Hoppers', and the new 4-4-0s the 'Large Hoppers'.

Unfortunately the 'K10s' had the same steaming problems as the earlier 'C8s', and could not sustain power over long distances, but they performed usefully on secondary routes. They were never superheated, which might have improved the situation. Despite their 'mixed-traffic' label, the LSWR was mainly a passenger railway, so goods duties were less common.

'K10' 4-4-0 No 391 was photographed at Clapham Junction on 13 August 1949; this was one of the engines coupled to a larger eight-wheel tender. Under the LSWR the livery was sage green with yellow lettering on the tender, and black and white lining. This was perpetuated under Bulleid on the SR, although the 'Southern' lettering on the tender was changed to the 'Sunshine Yellow' style, as seen here. No 391 was taken out of service at its birthplace in October and scrapped. *H. C. Casserley*

Introduced 1901
Designed by Dugald Drummond
Built by LSWR, Nine Elms
Number built 40
Number inherited by BR 31
Last example withdrawn July 1951

During the Second World War one 'K10' was lent to the War Department, returning in 1942, while five others were lent to the LMS for use on the Somerset & Dorset line, as well as stints at Gloucester, Bristol and Nottingham. Withdrawals started in January 1947, but 31 engines passed into BR ownership, though only one, No 30382, received its allocated BR number.

KESR 0-8-0T

No 949

In 1904 the Rother Valley Railway became known as the Kent & East Sussex Railway, managed by the 'light railway king' Col H. F. Stephens. The name change had been adopted ready for a projected extension to Maidstone, which was never built, but the line opened from Tenterden to Headcorn in 1905.

The reasons for the KESR's acquisition of this large 0-8-0T are not clear; it may have been intended for the failed Maidstone line, or for through working to Tonbridge. What is clear is that its size, wheel arrangement, rigidity and inflexibility made it unusual and most unsuitable for a light railway with steep gradients, where an 0-6-0 might have been more at home. The website of the Colonel Stephens Railway Museum at Tenterden gives a fascinating account of this locomotive's career. Not only was *Hecate* too big, but its coal capacity was

Introduced 1904
Designed by Hawthorn Leslie
Built by Hawthorn Leslie
Number built 1 (for KESR)
Number inherited by BR 1
Last example withdrawn March 1950

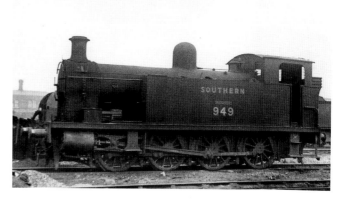

A pre-nationalisation portrait of No 949 *Hecate* at Nine Elms on 15 June 1946. The locomotive never became BR No 30949, but retained its name throughout its life. *H. C. Casserley*

insufficient for the length of run; what is more, having flangeless intermediate wheels on lightly maintained tracks was asking for trouble.

Hecate arrived on the KESR in May 1905 and was given the number 4, ready for the opening of the Headcorn extension, but was soon found to be unsuitable, although at busy times her haulage capacity outweighed her other disadvantages. In 1915 *Hecate* was loaned to the East Kent Railway, were it worked coal trains to Shepherdswell. Returning to the KESR in 1921, the engine was thoroughly overhauled and put into working order, but was given little to do.

After Col Stephens's death in 1931, the KESR faced bankruptcy and a shortage of motive power. As a result a deal was struck with the Southern Railway, and *Hecate* was swapped for two carriages, a Beattie saddle tank (see LSWR '0330' Class below) and a spare boiler. After further repairs at Ashford, *Hecate* became SR No 949 in 1933. Eventually the locomotive was found work at Nine Elms and Clapham Junction goods yards, where it became known affectionately as 'Old Hiccups' because of its faltering exhaust. Passing to BR on nationalisation in 1948, *Hecate* was allocated the number 30949, but never carried it, although its nameplate was retained to the end. The engine remained in this role until it suffered a collision with a 'King Arthur' Class 4-6-0, which damaged the leading main frame. As a result 'Old Hiccups' coughed its last, and was taken out of use and scrapped in March 1950.

LSWR 'L11' Class 4-4-0

Nos 30134, 148, 154, 155, 30156, 157, 158, 30159, 161, 30163, 30164, 167-70, 30171, 172, 30173-75, 30405-07, 408, 30409, 410-14, 435-37, 30438, 439-41, 30442

Introduced 1903
Designed by Dugald Drummond
Built by LSWR, Nine Elms
Number built 40
Number inherited by BR 40
Last example withdrawn April 1952

As mentioned in the 'K10' entry above, these 4-4-0s were a slightly larger version of the earlier engines, and became known as the 'Large Hoppers'. These 'excellent engines' (O. S. Nock) were built in eight batches of five between 1903 and 1907.

Again, the 'L11s' incorporated a large number of standard parts, improving interchangeability with other classes. For example, the boiler was the same type as fitted earlier to the 'T9' 4-4-0s; it had water tubes fitted across the firebox to increase the heating surface, but this caused maintenance problems, and they were subsequently removed by Drummond's successor, Urie. Like the 'K10s', the 'L11s' were never superheated. They had six-wheeled tenders as standard, but at the end of their lives a few had eight-wheel Drummond 'watercarts'.

Eight locomotives were converted to oil-firing as part of a Government trial during the post-war coal crisis in 1947-48, and were not reconverted prior to scrapping.

'L11' No 154 was one of eight members of the class converted to oil-burning in 1947-48, and it is seen here out of use with what appear to be several more in the yard at Eastleigh on 9 July 1949, although it seems it was not officially withdrawn until March 1951. Ahead of it is Adams 'X6' 4-4-0 No 657 of 1885, which had been withdrawn in 1940 and had been used as a stationary boiler at Exmouth Junction shed between 1941 and 1944. It was eventually scrapped in November 1949. *H. C. Casserley*

LSWR 'L12' Class 4-4-0

Nos 30415-429, 430, 30431-34

Drummond's 'T9' 4-4-0s of 1899-1901, wrote O. S. Nock, 'could well have been judged as Dugald Drummond's finest-ever locomotives, with a magnificent steaming boiler, ample firegrate, and a beautifully designed layout of Stephenson link motion which gave an astonishingly free-running engine.' As one example, No 30120, has been preserved, the 'T9s' are not included here, but Drummond's 'L12s' of 1904-05 were yet another development, with a large boiler; however, as with the 'S11s' (qv), they failed to achieve the fame of the 'T9s'. Indeed, the 'L12' Class gained notoriety in 1906 where one of its members, No 421, was involved in the infamous Salisbury crash, when reportedly travelling at twice the permitted speed through the station; although not considered a factor in the smash, it brought to an end any competition

In fine condition, the last survivor of the 'L12' Class 4-4-0s,
No 30434, is rostered for the Railway Enthusiasts Club's 'Hants
& Surrey' rail tour (reportedly the club's first) on 26 September
1953, two years after the majority of its classmates had been
scrapped. The special visited the Longmoor Military Railway,
and the loco is seen here at Tongham, near Farnham.
T. B. Owen, Colour-Rail

for speed between the LSWR and GWR for West of England
boat-train traffic.

The 'L12s' were very much express passenger locomotives,
and 'as originally turned out were the most handsome engines
Drummond ever built' (Nock). They took advantage of various
technological advances that had taken place in the five years
since the introduction of the 'T9s'. They were the last
development of Drummond's 4-4-0s, stretching back to his

Introduced 1904
Designed by Dugald Drummond
Built by LSWR, Nine Elms
Number built 20
Number inherited by BR 20
Last example withdrawn February 1955

unsuccessful 'C8' Class of 1898. They once more used the same
frames as the 'T9', but returned to the use of large driving
wheels of 6ft 7in diameter for fast running. They had 'T9'-type
boilers with the cross water tubes in the firebox, and had a
noticeably higher centre of gravity, which made them
unbalanced at speed on curves, as was demonstrated at
Salisbury. The smokebox was extended when Urie later fitted
superheaters, which helped to improve their somewhat
'stubby' appearance. All were coupled to large Drummond
'watercart' eight-wheel tenders, as there were no water
troughs on the LSWR.

In 1926 three class members, Nos 421, 423 and 424, were
experimentally converted to oil-burning.

The 'L12s' were initially allocated to Nine Elms, Bournemouth
and Salisbury for express passenger rosters. They later also
appeared at Exmouth Junction, where they shared with the
'S11' Class haulage of the ocean liner specials to and from
Plymouth. Although generally well-liked by footplate crews, the
'L12s' showed no real improvement over the 'T9s', but all passed
to BR at nationalisation. Withdrawals soon began, however, and
the last examples were relegated to local rural freight duties. All
but two disappeared during 1951; No 30415 survived to be
taken out of use at Fratton shed in January 1953, and the last,
No 30434, ended its days at Guildford two years later. Its boiler
was subsequently used as a stationary boiler at Eastleigh Works
Erecting Shop between 1956 and 1959.

LSWR 'S11' Class 4-4-0

Nos 395, 30396-400, 401, 30402-04

The 'S11' represented another stage in the development of
Drummond's successful 'T9' 4-4-0s. One problem facing the LSWR
in the design of its express passenger engines was speed versus the
ability to deal with steep gradients, especially west of Salisbury (the
1 in 75 of Honiton bank, for example) and into the West Country.
When Drummond tried his new 'T9' 4-4-0s over the LSWR's
undulating route to the West it was clear that their reputation for
fast running – they were, after all, nicknamed 'Greyhounds' – was
not matched by their hill-climbing ability. Their driving wheels
were too large. The 'S11s' were therefore designed with a larger
boiler (the largest yet built at Nine Elms, although at the same
pressure as that of the 'T9') and slightly smaller 6-foot-diameter

In July 1951 'S11' No 30403 passes Branksome shed with a
Salisbury train. On shed is a 'Black 5', and 'Britannia' No 70009
Alfred the Great is also present. The following September
No 30403 was withdrawn from Bournemouth shed.
S. C. Townroe, Colour-Rail

Introduced 1903
Designed by Dugald Drummond
Built by LSWR, Nine Elms
Number built 10
Number inherited by BR 10
Last example withdrawn October 1954

drivers with patented balanced crank axles to reduce 'hammer blow' on the track (and obviating the need for balance weights built into the driving wheels). Once again they used the same frames as the 'T9', and all ten locomotives were fitted with the Drummond eight-wheel 'watercart' tender; they were later superheated by Urie in 1920-22.

In the event, however, the larger boiler and smaller wheels did not have the desired result in the West Country, and the engines were proving slower and more cumbersome than expected. The 'T9s' were still preferred for their higher speeds downhill and on the level, even if they were slower when climbing; the large boiler was also thirsty, a problem on a system without water troughs, and being high-mounted led to instability on curves.

In 1941 all ten 'S11s' were lent to the LMS to be used on the Somerset & Dorset line, whose joint lessees were the Southern and the LMS; they were also found occasionally working around Saltley, Burton-upon-Trent and Peterborough. They were eventually returned to the SR between 1944 and 1945.

Although not entirely successful in their intended role, the 'S11s' were generally useful locomotives until displaced by such newer engines as Urie's 'N15' 4-6-0s of 1918-27.

LSWR 'T1' Class 0-4-4T

Nos 1-3, 5, 7-10, 13, 20, 361, 363, 366, 367

Introduced 1888
Designed by William Adams
Built by LSWR, Nine Elms
Number built 50
Number inherited by BR 14
Last example withdrawn June 1951

William Adams claimed that he felt safer riding a bogie engine, and that a four-coupled design with large driving wheels would remain stable at relatively high speeds. Stroudley, his counterpart on the LBSCR, was keen to discontinue the use of the 0-4-4 wheel arrangement, considering that the springs of the rear bogie had too strong an influence over the front driving wheels. Adams disagreed, and introduced his Class '415' 4-4-2 'Radial' tank in 1882, the 'A12' Class 0-4-2 in 1887, and the 'T1s' in 1888. The original 'T1' Class consisted of 20 0-4-4Ts built in two batches of ten in 1888 and 1889, and were numbered 61-80. They have been described as a tank engine version of his 'A12' 'Jubilee' Class of 1887 (qv), with smaller driving wheels. The prototype, No 61, was built at Nine Elms in June 1888, and quantity production began in December. They were used on fast suburban duties alongside the 4-4-2 tanks, and quickly proved popular and handy engines.

In 1890 the smaller 'O2' 0-4-4Ts appeared, which were equally popular, and went on to famously serve on the Isle of Wight.

Construction of the 'T1s' continued, with Nos 1-20 appearing in two batches in 1894 and 1895, then came the final ten, Nos 358-67, in 1896. (In typical LSWR style, they reused the numbers of retired or duplicated engines). These 30 engines were

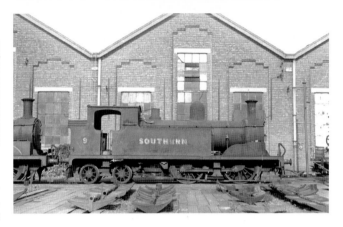

'T1' (former 'F6') 0-4-4T No 9 poses in the works yard at Eastleigh on 11 September 1948, having been taken out of service in July. It was cut up in October. *H. C. Casserley*

officially classed as 'F6', and all the original 'T1s' had been withdrawn by 1936; the survivors were eventually reclassified as 'T1'. As well as hauling London suburban services, they were to be found all over the LSWR network, although not common in the West of England. However, two new engines were sent to work the Sidmouth branch, while others were shedded at Plymouth, Fratton, Andover, Bournemouth and Salisbury.

It was not until 1933 that the first example was scrapped, and the class was scheduled to be withdrawn by 1940. However, wartime requirements extended their lives, and Nos 1-6 were lent to the LMS to work on the SDJR in 1941, returning in 1945. Nos 1 and 2 had been shedded at Highbridge, the others being allocated to Templecombe.

Fourteen examples from the 1894-96 batches made it into BR ownership, but by the summer of 1951 all had been withdrawn. However, the boiler and smokebox from one of them was subsequently discovered in a factory in Essex, and was bought as the possible basis of a 'new-build' 'T1'; it is currently in store at the Avon Valley Railway, at Bitton near Bristol. It has also been suggested that the boiler might be used to recreate an Adams 'Jubilee', which might prove a popular choice.

'T1' No 366, one of the 1896 batch, was photographed in 'buffed-up' condition at Eastleigh on 11 September 1948, but was to be withdrawn the following month. *H. C. Casserley*

LSWR 'T14' Class 4-6-0

Nos 443-45, 30446, 30447, 459, 460, 30461, 462

Introduced 1911
Designed by Dugald Drummond
Built by LSWR, Eastleigh
Number built 10
Number inherited by BR 9
Last example withdrawn June 1951

The last 'Paddlebox', No 30461, stands at Nine Elms on 27 August 1949, with less than two years ahead of it. The elaborate Drummond one-piece splasher has been replaced by the Maunsell raised running plate, but the front 'double-breasted' casting is still distinctive. Note also the stubby stovepipe chimney. *H. C. Casserley*

Drummond's success with his 4-4-0 designs, especially the 'T9', had led to an acceleration of passenger services on the LSWR, which in turn had generated traffic requiring longer trains and therefore more powerful locomotives. The 4-6-0 wheel arrangement seemed to be the answer; Drummond had already produced his first 4-6-0s, the 'F13' Class, in 1905, which were all rebuilt by Maunsell as 'H15s' (qv) in 1924-25. In 1908 the five 'G14' Class locomotives appeared, but all had been scrapped by 1925. His track record with this design was therefore not encouraging, and his last attempt at a 4-6-0 was the 'T14' Class, which incorporated many features seen on his earlier designs, including large splashers over the driving wheels (the design of which in this case, with a central circular inspection 'porthole', led to the nickname of 'Paddleboxes' or 'Paddleboats'). The driving wheels were of 6ft 7in diameter. The 'T14s' had four cylinders, all in line beneath the smokebox, those inside driving the front axle and the outside ones the second axle. This big front-end casting, curving to join the smokebox to the outside cylinders, gave rise to another nickname, 'Double Breasters'. Walschaerts valve gear was used, with the inside-cylinder valves operated by rockers. The engines were coupled to large eight-wheel tenders (the heaviest fitted to any ex-SR locomotive).

Although the most successful of Drummond's 4-6-0s, the 'Paddleboxes' did not match the success of his 4-4-0s, being heavy on coal and water, and with axleboxes that were prone to overheating. They were allocated to Nine Elms and used exclusively on expresses to Bournemouth and Salisbury, although timekeeping was often a problem, despite a good turn of speed on the level. After less than ten years they were replaced by Maunsell's 'N15s', but Maunsell took the opportunity to make modifications to the older engines for use on secondary services, including superheating and the removal of the 'paddlebox' splashers to improve access for maintenance, replaced by a simple raised running plate. Mechanical lubricators helped reduce hot axleboxes. Boiler pressure was reduced, but coal and water consumption remained high. One improvement came about by accident; when No 447 needed a new chimney in 1940, no Drummond spares were available, so a short 'stovepipe' chimney was fitted, which led to a significant improvement in steaming due to better draughting. All but one of the class were subsequently fitted with this type of chimney.

No 458 was destroyed in an air raid on Nine Elms shed in 1940, but the remaining nine engines all passed to BR in 1948. Only three carried their allocated BR numbers, and within three years of nationalisation all the members of this distinctive class had been scrapped. No 30461 was the last to be taken out of service, in June 1951, having covered just over a million miles.

SR 'Z' Class 0-8-0T

Nos 30950-57

To handle shunting over the humps at Feltham yard, Urie designed his large 'G16' 4-8-0Ts (qv), based on his 'S15' Class 4-6-0 freight engines. When the LSWR became part of the Southern Railway in 1923, its new Chief Mechanical Engineer, Maunsell, thought about building more of these huge engines, but felt that their firebox was too large for a shunter, and the superheater was likewise an unnecessary luxury, so decided to design his 'Z' Class 0-8-0Ts instead. These were three-cylinder tank locomotives intended for heavy shunting duties; the

Introduced 1929
Designed by Richard Maunsell
Built by SR, Brighton
Number built 8
Number inherited by BR 8
Last example withdrawn December 1962

three cylinders provided more even driving power, improving acceleration between frequent stops, and also produced a softer exhaust beat. More would have been built at Eastleigh but for the onset of the Depression years; in any event, the subsequent advent of diesel shunters would soon make such engines redundant.

The eight coupled wheels provided good traction while still able to negotiate the tight curves in goods yards; there was sufficient side-play to allow 4½-chain-radius curves to be taken. A further need was the ability to have power available even after periods of standing idle, as often happened in marshalling yards, and the boiler had a large steam chest able to deliver short, sharp bursts of power with the minimum of blowing off at the safety valves. The engines were fitted with 1,500-gallon water tanks to reduce the need for regular refilling, and they had sloping tops to aid driver visibility. They were popular with crews, being easy to control and not prone to slipping; at Eastleigh, for example, trains were marshalled against a 1 in 250 gradient without difficulty. They could be kept continuously in steam for a week, but could apparently be uncomfortable to ride on and were heavy on coal.

Although largely designed at the former SECR's Ashford Works, the locomotives were built at the former LBSCR works at Brighton, so they used an existing Brighton design of boiler. They had outside Walschaerts valve gear driven from the third axle, and a specially built inside gear driven from the second axle. They had both steam and vacuum brakes, and steam heating so that they could shunt passenger stock if necessary. They had a very distinctive front overhang of some 11 feet, albeit shorter than originally envisaged, terminating in a deep buffer beam, which could be a disadvantage on tight curves in some yards.

The 'Zs' worked at the marshalling yards at Hither Green, Norwood Junction, Exmouth Junction and Eastleigh. During the Second World War three were lent to the War Department to work at No 2 Military Port at Cairnryan, near Stranraer, Scotland, returning to the SR in 1943.

'Z' Class No 30951 shunts in Exmouth Junction yards in July 1962. It was withdrawn the following December. *A. Sainty collection, Colour-Rail*

As more diesel-electric shunters were delivered in the 1950s, the 'Zs' moved to less demanding shunting work, then eventually they all moved west to Exmouth Junction shed to be used as banking engines on the steep incline between Exeter St David's and Central stations. When this area came under the control of BR's Western Region in 1962, they were replaced by ex-GWR pannier tanks, and all the 'Zs' were withdrawn. A private attempt was made to preserve No 30952 for use on the Bluebell Railway; it was stored in working order at Exmouth Junction and Fratton sheds for a couple of years until the enterprise fell through, and it was eventually cut up at Cashmore's yard, Newport, early in 1965.

LSWR '0395'/'0496' Class 0-6-0

Nos 30564-81

Introduced 1881
Designed by William Adams
Built by Neilson
Number built 70
Number inherited by BR 18
Last example withdrawn October 1959

These six-coupled engines were the first main-line goods locomotives produced by Adams for the LSWR. All 70 were built by Neilson & Co in eight batches between 1881 and 1886, with a complicated number sequence that bore no resemblance to the order of building. The last 36 engines of 1885-86 were slightly longer and heavier, and were classified as '0496', 496 being the LSWR's number of the first of them. All had six-wheel tenders. At that time they were the only inside-cylinder engines that Adams had built.

Between 1916 and 1918 50 of the class were sold to the Railway Operating Division, and none were returned – four were lost in the Mediterranean when the ship carrying them

The final surviving example of Adams's '0395' Class, No 30567 of 1883, poses at Victoria on 25 January 1959. This was one of two members of the class to be fitted with a Drummond-type boiler. Only two engines were still in use at this date: No 30566 went in February 1959, and No 30567 in October. *Colour-Rail collection*

was torpedoed and sunk. The ROD put 36 of them on its Palestine Military Railway, while nine took part in the campaign in Mesopotamia, joined by seven from Palestine in 1918. Sixteen locos were transferred to the new Mesopotamian Railways in 1919, then in 1920 Palestine Railways was established, operating 29 of the '0395s' that remained in the country; 22 were scrapped in 1928, and the rest worked until 1936, not being scrapped until the end of the Second World War. Apparently some of the engines were taken over by the

War Department in Egypt during the war, where their tenders were used as water carriers in the Western Desert.

Meanwhile, the 20 examples that remained in the UK passed to the Southern Railway, which withdrew two of them; the final 18 entered BR stock and were renumbered in a continuous series from 30564 to 30581. Withdrawals started again in 1953, with the last example, No 30567 (previously 154, then 3154), surviving until October 1959, reaching the grand age of 76.

Southampton Dock Co '0458' Class 0-4-0ST

No 30458

In 1892 the Southampton Dock Company and its fleet of eight locomotives, mostly 0-4-0 saddle tanks, were absorbed into the LSWR. Three engines were sold off in 1896, but the remainder were joined by three others that had been acquired by the LSWR from the Docks Company, used for working Southampton Town Quay and Pier.

Two of the locomotives were 0-4-0STs built by Hawthorn Leslie in 1890, Nos 457 *Clausentum* (named after a Roman settlement thought to have been in modern-day Bitterne, a suburb of Southampton) and 458 *Ironside* (named after Edmund Ironside, the King of England who defeated the Danes in Wessex in 1016). They acquired these numbers when transferred to the LSWR's Running Department in March 1901 and were sent to work the Town Quay and Pier, being replaced in the docks by two Adams 'B4' 0-4-0Ts of 1891. No 457 later became No 734 and remained in service until September 1945, when it was withdrawn, while No 458 became No 3458 and survived into British Railways ownership. With the number 30458 it spent its BR years allocated to Guildford shed, where it was shed pilot until withdrawn in June 1954 (as the last surviving Docks Company engine), and cut up at Eastleigh Works that August. It was replaced by 'B4' Class 30086 *Havre* until it too succumbed in 1959.

In October 2014 one of *Ironside*'s nameplates and a brass cabside '458' number plate were sold at auction for £6,600 and £750 respectively. At the same sale *Clausentum*'s whistle also went under the hammer for £80.

Following withdrawal from Guildford shed in June 1954, 64-year-old No 30458 is seen at Eastleigh in August of that year; behind it is one of the preserved LBSCR 'Terrier' 0-6-0Ts. By contrast, on the right is diesel-electric shunter No 13010, new in January 1953; renumbered D3010 in 1958 and 08006 in 1974, it was withdrawn and scrapped in 1980, aged only 27! *Colour-Rail collection*

Introduced 1890
Designed by Hawthorn Leslie
Built by Hawthorn Leslie
Number built 2 (for SDC)
Number inherited by BR 1
Last example withdrawn June 1954

LSWR '700' Class 0-6-0

Nos 30306, 30308, 30309, 30315-17, 30325-27, 30339, 30346, 30350, 30352, 30355, 30368, 30687-701

In his previous roles as Locomotive Superintendent of first the North British Railway (1875-82), then the Caledonian Railway (1882-90), Drummond had built 133 0-6-0s for the former and 244 for the latter. In 1895 the LSWR had a need for a new class of modern goods locomotives, but William Adams was ill, and permission was sought to approach outside contractors to undertake the work. Adams subsequently retired on health

Introduced 1897
Designed by Dugald Drummond
Built by Dübs
Number built 30
Number inherited by BR 30
Last example withdrawn December 1962

grounds in that year, and was replaced by Drummond, who gave the LSWR his '700' Class 0-6-0s, which were almost identical to the earlier engines, and built in a single batch by Dübs & Co and its Queen's Park Works at Polmadie, Glasgow.

Henry Dübs had been a managing partner at Neilson & Co until 1863, when he left to set up his own company. It was Dübs that built a large batch of Drummond's 'T9' 4-4-0s in 1899, exhibiting one of them at the Glasgow Exhibition in 1901. In 1903 Dübs became one of the constituent companies merged to form the North British Locomotive Co.

Originally numbered 687-716, Nos 702-16 were soon renumbered in a 3xx series using numbers previously carried by withdrawn locomotives to free up numbers for the new 'T9s'. Logically the 0-6-0s should perhaps have been known as the '687' Class, as No 700 was actually the 14th loco constructed.

The '700s' took over haulage of heavy goods trains from Adams's '0395' and 'Jubilee' classes, and also appeared occasionally on passenger trains, gaining the nickname 'Black Motors'. They proved to be well designed, requiring few modifications during their long careers. They had many standard parts common with the 'C8' and 'K10' classes, and a boiler identical to that used on the 'M7'. In the 1920s Urie rebuilt them with superheaters, which required a longer smokebox, frame extensions and a higher-pitched boiler.

A further, more logical renumbering was proposed by the Southern Railway following the Grouping, but was not proceeded with.

In due course the newer Urie 'S15' 4-6-0s, Maunsell 'Q' 0-6-0s and Bulleid 'Q1' 0-6-0s made inroads into '700' Class duties, but they continued to give reliable service. Apart from

'Black Motor' No 30368 of 1897 is at work at Basingstoke on 30 March 1957 – note the distinctive diamond-shaped Dübs worksplate on the splasher. The addition of superheaters involved lengthening the smokebox and frames, giving the engines a somewhat front-heavy appearance. This was one of the last engines to be withdrawn, at the end of 1962.
T. B. Owen, Colour-Rail

No 30688, which was involved in a head-on collision with an EMU at Staines in 1957, all survived until the early 1960s, the final seven being taken out of service in December 1962.

Plymouth, Devonport & South Western Junction Railway '756' Class 0-6-0T

No 756

Introduced 1907
Designed by Hawthorn Leslie
Built by Hawthorn Leslie
Number built 1
Number inherited by BR 1
Last example withdrawn October 1951

The Plymouth, Devonport & South Western Junction Railway (PD&SWJR) was established in 1883 to build a line from Lydford to Devonport via Tavistock, Bere Alston and St Budeaux. Work started in March 1887 and the double-track line, just over 22 miles long, opened to traffic in 1890. Its importance was that it gave the LSWR an independent access to Plymouth, avoiding the GWR's Tavistock branch line.

In 1908 a branch was opened from Bere Alston to Callington, using older mineral lines that were regauged to standard gauge. This branch was engineered under the supervision of Col H. F. Stephens, and although leased, like the main line, to the LSWR, it was operated independently. To work the new extension the PD&SWJR ordered three locomotives from Hawthorn Leslie & Co. Two were 0-6-2Ts (see the next entry) and one was an 0-6-0T, given the number 3 and the name *A. S. Harris* after one of the company's directors.

No 3 was delivered to Bere Alston station on 31 October 1907 with the painted name *H. S. Harris* – the mistake was

quickly spotted and replacement brass nameplates with the correct name were fitted.

In 1922, just before the Grouping, the PD&SWJR was absorbed by the LSWR, and No 3 was renumbered 756. It gained Southern Railway livery in 1926-27, and its number was prefixed by 'E', denoting Eastleigh Works, which now maintained the former PD&SWJR locomotives; the 'E' was dropped in 1931.

Former PD&SWJR 0-6-0T No 756 *A. S. Harris* was shed pilot at Stewarts Lane (73A) during its brief BR career, and was photographed there on coal duties on 7 April 1951, six months before withdrawal – note the large smiley face chalked on the front of the dome! *B. W. L. Brooksbank, Initial Photographics*

In June 1929 the SR replaced No 756 on the branch with an 'O2' Class 0-4-4T, and the 0-6-0 tank was moved to the Wenford Bridge branch. It subsequently found employment at Winchester, Fratton, Bournemouth, Brighton, Tonbridge, Folkestone and Dover, and worked as shed pilot at Eastleigh until 1931. It was then moved to perform the same function at Nine Elms until 1939. In 1948 it was used briefly as a stationary boiler to supply steam at Dover.

Passing into BR ownership, it was transferred to Stewarts Lane shed and allocated the number 30756, but it was never applied. The engine was withdrawn on 27 October 1951 after problems with the firebox had been discovered, and was scrapped at Eastleigh.

Plymouth, Devonport & South Western Junction Railway '757' Class 0-6-2T

Nos 30757, 30758

Introduced	1907
Designed by	Hawthorn Leslie
Built by	Hawthorn Leslie
Number built	2
Number inherited by BR	2
Last example withdrawn	December 1957

Former PD&SWJR 0-6-2T No 30758 *Lord St Levan* moved from Plymouth Friary shed to Eastleigh in the spring of 1956, and is seen there, with rust encroaching, on a unknown date, presumably during that year, at the end of which it was withdrawn. Originally classed as '1MT', in 1953 it became '1P2F', as seen here. *K. Cooper, Colour-Rail*

As mentioned in the previous entry, the Plymouth, Devonport & South Western Junction Railway (PD&SWJR) opened its branch from Bere Alston to Callington in 1908, and three locomotives were purchased from Hawthorn Leslie to work it. Two were 0-6-2T goods engines; numbered 4 and 5, they were given the names *Earl of Mount Edgcumbe* and *Lord St Levan* respectively, after directors of the company. They were dispatched from the manufacturer on Boxing Day 1907, and were in appearance larger versions of No 3, and very powerful.

At the Grouping they became SR Nos 757 and 758, and continued to work on the Callington branch into BR days

except for a brief period in August 1926 when No 5 took part in trials on the newly opened North Devon & Cornwall Junction Light Railway of 1925, linking Torrington with Halwill Junction.

After nationalisation the pair became Nos 30757 and 30758, but 'O2s' and Ivatt 2-6-2Ts had assumed their duties on the branch by the early 1950s. Both engines could be seen at Plymouth in 1955, then two years later both went to Eastleigh. *Lord St Levan* was withdrawn in December 1956 and scrapped in early 1957, but *Earl of Mount Edgcumbe* survived for a short period as shed pilot before being cut up in December 1957.

SER/SECR 'B'/'B1' Class 4-4-0

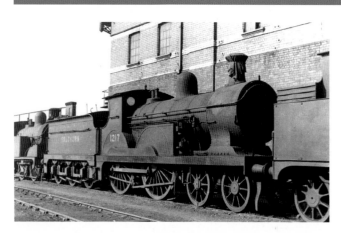

'B1' 4-4-0 No 1217, built at Ashford Works in 1898, stands out of use, yet still sporting its handsome lines, at its home shed of Reading South on 25 September 1948. It was officially withdrawn in June 1950. *H. C. Casserley*

Introduced	1898
Designed by	James Stirling/Harry Wainwright
Built by	SECR, Ashford (9), Neilson Reid (20)
Number built	27 (as rebuilt by Wainwright from 1910)
Number inherited by BR	16
Last example withdrawn	February 1951

Nos 1013, 1217, 1440, 1443, 1445, 31446, 1448-55, 1457, 1459

James Stirling succeeded his older brother Patrick as Locomotive Superintendent of the Glasgow & South Western Railway before moving to the South Eastern Railway in 1878. He remained there until 1898, on the eve of the working union between the SER and the London, Chatham & Dover Railway that resulted in the formation of the South Eastern & Chatham

Railway (SECR) in 1899. His last design before retirement from the SER, and his most successful, was his handsome 'B' Class 4-4-0. These were an enlarged version of his earlier 'F' Class 4-4-0s (qv), and, having followed the family tradition of using cutaway cabs and domeless boilers, these were a new departure, having a larger boiler with a brass casting over the safety valves and a squarer, better-protected cab, which gave rise to the nickname 'Square Cabs'; they were also known as 'Flying Bedsteads'! They also had much more modern tenders, with springs under the footplate, and a greater water capacity.

Twenty 'B' Class engines were built in 1898 by Neilson Reid (the company that had been Neilson & Co until that year, when James Reid became sole proprietor after the departure of Walter Neilson to start his own company). They were numbered 440-459. A further nine were then built at the SER's Ashford Works in 1898-99, and given an assortment of numbers between 13 and 217, numbers that they retained under the SECR. In 1901 Nos 454 and 459 were fitted with Holden's oil-burning system, but it was felt to be too expensive to be adopted generally and was removed in 1904.

After the Grouping the letter 'A' was added to the numbers, then 1000 was added. Stirling's successor, Harry Wainwright, made improvements to the already successful engines by fitting most of them with new domed, higher-pressure boilers and a slightly longer firebox; just two retained their domeless Stirling boilers until withdrawal. They now became known as the 'B1' Class, and were virtually identical to Wainwright's modified 'F1' Class (qv). When Maunsell took over, he increased the size of the smokeboxes and reduced the cylinder size.

During the Second World War several of the class were turned into makeshift air raid shelters by positioning them over pits, immobilising them and surrounded them with sandbags.

Sixteen of the class passed into BR ownership, but only one carried its allocated BR number, 31446, from July 1948. All but three had been withdrawn by the end of 1949, the remainder succumbing in 1950-51.

SECR 'D1' Class 4-4-0

Nos 31145, 31246, 31247, 31470, 31487, 31489, 31492, 31494, 31502, 31505, 31509, 31545, 31727, 31725, 31736, 31739, 31741, 31743, 31745, 31749

Introduced 1901; rebuilt 1921-27
Designed by Harry Wainwright; rebuilt by Maunsell
Built by As Class 'D': Dübs (5), SECR, Ashford (9), Sharp Stewart (2), Robert Stephenson (3), Vulcan Foundry (1)
Number built 21 ('D1' rebuilds)
Number inherited by BR 20
Last example withdrawn November 1961

Class 'D1' No 31470 was built at Ashford in 1906, and rebuilt there by Maunsell 20 years later. With a red-livered 'birdcage' set, it climbs Somer Hill bank past a fine bracket signal in June 1957; behind is a panoramic view over Tonbridge. *N. Sprinks, Colour-Rail*

Harry Wainwright's first express passenger engines for the SECR were the 'D1' Class 4-4-0s of 1901, two years after the South Eastern Railway and the London, Chatham & Dover Railway had formed a joint managing committee to create a working union (in fact, no such company as the South Eastern & Chatham Railway actually existed as such). Fifty-one 'Ds' were produced by Ashford Works and Sharp Stewart of Glasgow between 1901 and 1907. The SER's Wainwright was responsible for the overall design, with detail work by his chief draughtsman at Ashford, Robert Surtees, formerly of the LCDR, and between them they produced very fine-looking locomotives with elegant curves (their brass dome covers earning them the nickname 'Coppertops'). They responded well to hard work and helped to build a better reputation for the SECR than its constituents had enjoyed during the years of rivalry. At first they worked trains to the Kent coast and Hastings, but by the 1930s had been relegated to secondary duties. In 1948 28 passed to BR, and one, No 31737, has been preserved as part of the National Collection.

In 1919-21 Wainwright's successor from 1913, Richard Maunsell, rebuilt 11 of Wainwright's 'E' Class 4-4-0s with Belpaire fireboxes and new cylinders with piston valves, and so successful was the resultant 'E1' Class that in 1921-27 he similarly rebuilt 21 'Ds', the resultant locomotives being classified 'D1'. Larger and more powerful, but still usefully light in weight, they were needed to cope with increasing loads on the Chatham line, and were to all intents and purposes identical to the 'E1s', albeit perhaps less elegant than the original design. Because Ashford was short of capacity, only 11 could be dealt with there; the first 10, together with the plans and drawings, were sent to Beyer Peacock in Manchester. They were fitted with superheated boilers and long-travel valves, giving higher power with better fuel consumption. As O. S. Nock remarked, the rebuilding 'provided a stud of efficient modern engines which could be used at will anywhere on the old SECR system, and which put up some very fine running with the seaside expresses from Victoria to Margate and Ramsgate.'

Like the 'E1s', the 'D1s' could be found throughout the South Eastern Division, especially on Kent Coast services. When

these routes were electrified in the late 1950s, steam withdrawals inevitably followed; some of the class moved west and were reallocated to Eastleigh. One engine had been withdrawn in 1944, three more were lost in 1950/51, then between 1959 and 1961 the remainder disappeared. One of the class's last duties in Kent was acting as pilot engine for the 'Night Ferry' service.

No 31739 of Bricklayers Arms shed (73B), one of the last three survivors of the class, was on duty on 28 October 1961, the last day of the Westerham branch. It and Nos 31489 and 31749 were withdrawn the following month. *Colour-Rail collection*

SECR 'E' Class 4-4-0

Nos 31036, 1157, 31159, 31166, 1175, 31176, 31273, 31275, 31315, 1491, 31512, 31515, 31516, 1547, 31587

Introduced 1905
Designed by Harry Wainwright
Built by SECR, Ashford
Number built 26
Number inherited by BR 15
Last example withdrawn May 1955

Wainwright's 'E' Class 4-4-0s were a development of his 'D' Class (see previous entry). The success of the 'Ds' encouraged Wainwright to build five similar locomotives with a Belpaire firebox in order to produce additional power, as well as an extended smokebox and fluted coupling rods (one of the main distinguishing features between the 'Es' and the 'D'/'D1' engines, together with smooth-sided splashers; they also had slightly smaller driving wheels, leading to a higher tractive effort). They entered traffic in 1906, and the success of the design prompted the building of further examples until the class numbered 26 locomotives by 1909. In 1911-12 two engines, Nos (10)36 and (1)265, were superheated, which improved their fuel efficiency, but unfortunately the additional weight prevented them from working over the former LCDR routes, so no others were converted. In the late 1940s O. S. Nock rode on the footplate of No 1275 'and found her as smooth and free-running a 4-4-0 as I have ever ridden upon.'

The 'Es' were gracefully styled engines, like their 'D' Class predecessors, and were shedded at Battersea to work boat

trains from London to Dover and Folkestone, as well as other Kent coast expresses on the South Eastern Section. The boat trains were very heavy during this period, and at the height of the tourist season is was often necessary to run two trains to carry the passengers of a single, well-loaded steamer. They continued on these duties until the Wainwright/Maunsell Class 'L' 4-4-0s (see below) appeared after 1914. They were then relegated to secondary fast passenger services.

In 1919 Richard Maunsell decided to rebuild one of the 'E' 4-4-0s, No 179, changing its appearance and improving its performance. Ten more followed, becoming known as the 'E1' Class, described in the following entry.

The 15 unrebuilt 'E' Class engines passed to BR at nationalisation, and all but four went on to carry BR '3xxxx' numbers, but a dozen of them were taken out of service during 1951. The other three were withdrawn in 1953, 1954, and 1955.

The RCTS 'Invicta' special (the headboard being the Kent coat of arms and motto) ran on 12 September 1954 from Liverpool Street to Sheerness, Minster Junction, Ashford, Oxted and eventually London Blackfriars. Six locos were used, and 'E' Class No 31166 and 'D' No 31737 (later preserved) handled the last leg from Ashford to Blackfriars. The pair are seen here at Ashford; No 31166 is in plain black livery with 'Sunshine' figures, and has a borrowed lined-out tender with sans-serif lettering.
T. B. Owen, Colour-Rail

SECR 'E1' Class 4-4-0

Nos 31019, 31067, 31160, 1163, 31165, 31179, 31497, 31504, 31506, 31507, 31511

Introduced 1919
Designed by Harry Wainwright
Built by Beyer Peacock (10), SECR, Ashford (1) (as rebuilt by Maunsell)
Number built 11 (as rebuilt)
Number inherited by BR 11
Last example withdrawn November 1961

'E1' No 31507, built as an 'E' Class at Ashford in 1908 and rebuilt by Beyer Peacock in 1920, stands at its home shed, Bricklayers Arms, in April 1961, a few months before withdrawal in July. *Colour-Rail collection*

In 1917 the SECR Board decided that when the boat trains to Dover and Folkestone were reinstated after the war, they would be centred on Victoria station in London and use the former LCDR routes. As early as 1907 designs for 4-6-0 engines had been prepared at Ashford, which would have looked like elongated 'E' Class engines, but these were rejected by the Civil Engineer on the grounds of excessive axleloads. A solution to the problem of providing adequate motive power within an acceptable axleload was found in rebuilding 'E' Class locomotives with a superheated Belpaire firebox and new cylinders with piston valves (the same process was followed in converting the 'D' 4-4-0s into 'D1s' – see above). No 1179 of 1908 was the prototype for the rebuilding, and emerged from Ashford in 1919. It proved a successful experiment, so ten more were similarly rebuilt by Beyer Peacock in Manchester in 1920-21. Ten more were to be converted in 1921, but these were built as Class 'D' 4-4-0s instead.

The 'E1s' were duly charged with handling the heaviest boat trains until superseded in the mid-1920s, in Southern Railway days, by former LSWR 'N15' 4-6-0s. During the General Strike of 1926 four 'E1s' were converted to oil-burning, but were soon reconverted to coal.

Once ousted from the boat trains, the 'E1s' were transferred to express duties to Ramsgate, then in the 1930s several moved to the former LBSCR lines in Sussex to work Brighton-line expresses. During the Second World War the 'E1s' also worked the Redhill-Reading line.

Four 'E1s' were relatively early BR casualties, but three survived as late as the early 1960s, the last, No 31067, built in 1908 and rebuilt by Beyer in 1920, being withdrawn from Stewarts Lane in November 1961.

SECR 'F1' Class 4-4-0

Nos 1002, 1028, 1031, 1042, 1078, 1105, 31151, 1215, 1231

Introduced 1883; rebuilt 1903-19
Designed by James Stirling; rebuilt by Harry Wainwright
Built by SECR, Ashford
Number built 76 (as rebuilt)
Number inherited by BR 9
Last example withdrawn March 1949

'F1' Class No 31151 was the last survivor of the class, and was photographed at Reading on 25 September 1948. It was the only member of the class to receive its BR number, and was withdrawn in March of the following year. Note the distinctive 'Southern' tender, with outside frames and leaf springs above the valance. *H. C. Casserley*

James Stirling was Locomotive Superintendent of the South Eastern Railway from 1878 to 1898 and, like his better-known brother Patrick, built engines with domeless boilers. The 'F1' Class 4-4-0s are another example of an older class being rebuilt by its designer's successor, but in this case none of the original 'F' Class survived to be taken into British Railways stock. In all, 88 'Fs' were built between 1883 and 1898 and, known as Stirling's 'Mails' from the valuable and hotly contested traffic they would handle, they were graceful engines with 7-foot-diameter driving wheels, which might seem strange given the hilly nature of the routes they were to work.

Between 1903 and 1919 76 of them were rebuilt by Wainwright with domed boilers and new cabs (providing

better protection for the crew), becoming Class 'F1', and ensuring that a number of them would work on into early BR days. (A similar rebuilding was done by Wainwright on Stirling's 'B' Class 4-4-0s, to create the 'B1s' – qv – which were almost identical. One way to tell them apart was that their tenders were different: those of the 'F1s' had outside frames with outside leaf springs, while the 'B1' examples were more conventional, with inside frames.)

In due course the 'F1s' became SECR engines, and despite their large coupled wheels they performed well until superseded by, for example, Wainwright's 'D1' and 'E1' rebuilds. They worked on the main lines, but increasingly on secondary routes around Kent and across to Guildford and Reading. All but one

of them passed to the Southern Railway in 1923, with random numbers between 2 and 250. During the Second World War nine of the class were lent to the LMS, between 1941 and 1944.

By the time the railways were nationalised in 1948 only nine locomotives survived, and only one of these, No 31151, received its allocated BR number. The first locomotive was dispensed with as early as February 1948, and all had gone by just over a year later.

SECR 'J' Class 0-6-4T

Nos 31595-99

Introduced	1913
Designed by	Harry Wainwright
Built by	SECR, Ashford
Number built	5
Number inherited by BR	5
Last example withdrawn	September 1951

This small class of 0-6-4 passenger tanks was Wainwright's last design for the SECR. They fulfilled a need for a versatile mixed-traffic locomotive with good acceleration to keep suburban traffic moving smartly on the heavily used lines around south London; another requirement was an axleload light enough to fall within the restrictions on some of the lines. They were also designed to work on other companies' lines beyond the SECR. The five locomotives were built at Ashford during 1913, a year when the SECR was experiencing an acute shortage of motive power, made worse by a backlog due to the closure of Longhedge Works before Ashford had sufficient capacity to cope. These and other alleged shortcomings led to Wainwright being asked to resign 'on grounds of ill-health' in that year.

The class had two side tanks holding 350 gallons each, and a rear tank with a capacity of 1,300 gallons. Originally they had non-sequential numbers between 126 and 614, re-used from withdrawn locomotives. The Southern Railway renumbered them as A595-A599 (the 'A' signifying Ashford), and they duly became BR Nos 31595-99.

All five 'J' Class 0-6-4Ts spent their brief BR careers shedded at Ashford, and No 31597 is seen there on 4 May 1949. It was withdrawn in October the following year. *John Stretton collection*

The 'Js' were originally used on the London-Redhill section and the Addiscombe Road line, but were later sent to the Ashford area when electrification overtook them.

They proved quite successful handling a variety of secondary passenger and freight services, and all had exceeded a million miles by the time they were finally withdrawn between 1949 and 1951, when they were superseded by Fairburn 2-6-4Ts. No 31596 (SECR No 129) was the last 0-6-4T to remain in service on British Railways.

No more than the original five were built, possibly due to wartime conditions, and the fact they did not fit in with the ideas of Wainwright's successor, Maunsell.

SECR 'L' Class 4-4-0

Nos 31760-81

The working union between the SER and LCDR in the form of the SECR presented problems for Wainwright in that the latter company's main line was more lightly engineered with more weight restrictions, which made developing standard steam locomotives suitable for both companies' routes difficult. Initially Wainwright's 'D' and 'E' Class 4-4-0s were equal to the task, but by 1912 it became obvious that more powerful engines would be needed as loads increased. The SECR Board therefore asked Wainwright to design a locomotive suitable for the SER lines, but his original concept using non-superheated steam and slide valves was criticised as old-fashioned. As already mentioned,

Introduced	1914
Designed by	Harry Wainwright/Richard Maunsell
Built by	Beyer Peacock (12), Borsig (Berlin) (10)
Number built	22
Number inherited by BR	22
Last example withdrawn	December 1961

this and other problems faced by the company's motive power department led to Wainwright's premature retirement in 1913, before the new engines could be ordered. Wainwright was more an artist than an engineer, and was not a strong administrator; by contrast, Maunsell, his successor, was less an engine designer than a workshop manager, and felt unqualified to pronounce on the unfinished designs, so took the unusual step of taking advice from his former chief draughtsman on the Great Southern & Western Railway at Inchicore, Dublin. As a result some alterations were made.

The new 'L' Class was a handsome and powerful design, and following Wainwright's departure his assistant, Robert Surtees, incorporated superheating and piston valves, and ordered 12 engines to be built by Beyer Peacock in Manchester. When Richard Maunsell took up office in January 1914 he ordered a further batch of ten from A. Borsig of Berlin, as no British manufacturer could meet the required date. Fortunately, given the international situation, delivery of all ten was completed just weeks before the outbreak of the First World War in August. They arrived in kit form and were assembled by Borsig engineers at Ashford Works, and the Borsig men also travelled on the footplate during the trial runs. They were the only British express steam locomotives to be built in Germany, and acquired the nickname 'Germans'. The Beyer Peacock examples were delayed and actually arrived slightly later.

The 'L' 4-4-0s were used on the South Eastern main lines in Kent and Sussex until the 1920s, when they were superseded by the more powerful 'L1s' (see next entry), then in the 1930s the newer 'King Arthur' and 'Schools' Classes arrived. By then the LCDR lines had been improved, so the 'Ls' could now be used there, but overall there was less and less for them to do. All 22 locomotives passed to British Railways, but became increasingly redundant when the Bulleid 'light Pacifics' took over their services in the early 1950s. Some were transferred to Eastleigh and Brighton for use on cross-country services, but withdrawals began in 1956.

No 31760, the first member of the 'L' Class, built in August 1914, has its smokebox cleaned at Tonbridge in May 1956. This was one of the eight examples to stay in service until 1961, moving from Tonbridge to Nine Elms in May 1959. *S. C. Townroe, Colour-Rail*

August Borsig's company was established in 1837 as an iron foundry, and built its first steam locomotive in 1841. It subsequently grew to become the second largest locomotive manufacturer in the world. Shells, gun barrels and torpedo tubes were manufactured during the Great War, then locomotives as reparations after it. The locomotive business ended in 1931, but after several changes of ownership the company survives today, the present Borsig Group having been created in 2006, now Malaysian-owned and an international market leader in the field of pressure vessels and heat exchangers.

SR 'L1' Class 4-4-0

Nos 31753-59, 31782-89

Introduced 1926
Designed by Richard Maunsell
Built by North British
Number built 15
Number inherited by BR 15
Last example withdrawn February 1962

Maunsell's 'L1' 4-4-0s were a development of the earlier 'L' Class (see above), with a higher boiler pressure and smaller cylinders. They also had long-travel piston valves, Maunsell superheaters, side-window cabs and other detail alterations. So successful were these refinements that members of the 'L' Class were similarly modified as they visited the works.

Although Maunsell's more modern and powerful 'N15' 'King Arthur' and 'Lord Nelson' 4-6-0s were already in production, there was an outstanding order for 15 express engines on the books from the Grouping in 1923, so the 'L1s' filled a serious motive power gap on London-Folkestone services. Maunsell did not rebuild Wainwright's 'L' Class, which were still comparatively young, as he did with the 'Ds' and 'Es', but instead amended Wainwright's drawings to produce his

The last surviving 'L1', No 31786, outlived its classmates by a couple of months, and was used on several enthusiasts' rail tours prior to withdrawal in February 1962. A Gillingham (73D) engine, it is seen here at Ramsgate shed on 14 June 1959, having apparently worked in with a special. *Colour-Rail collection*

own 'L1' Class. They looked very similar to the rebuilt 'Ds' and 'Es', but a lack of works capacity meant that all 15 were built by the North British Locomotive Co. Also, like the other 4-4-0 rebuilds, they proved to be robust and reliable and enjoyed a useful three-decade career.

SECR/SR 'N1' Class 2-6-0

Nos 31822, 31876-80

Introduced 1923
Designed by Richard Maunsell
Built by SR, Ashford
Number built 6
Number inherited by BR 6
Last example withdrawn November 1962

Work-worn 'N1' 'Mogul' No 31878 passes through Ashford at the head of a freight on an unknown date. Note the distinctive vertical metal cover above the buffer beam to protect the inside cylinder. *Colour-Rail collection*

Maunsell's first new design for the SECR after Wainwright's departure was the two-cylinder 'N' Class 2-6-0 of 1917, which proved a considerable improvement over his predecessor's 0-6-0 and 4-4-0 designs. Fifteen were ordered in 1919 following the relaxation of wartime Government restrictions on locomotive production, but lack of capacity at Ashford delayed production until 1920-23. Further examples brought the class total to 80 by 1934. Although successful, Maunsell anticipated a requirement for an even more powerful locomotive, but axleloads were still restricted on parts of the SECR system. He therefore tried a three-cylinder version of the 'N', using a conjugated valve-gear operated from the outside Walschaerts gear, developed by his assistant, Harold Holcroft, who had joined him from Swindon. Holcroft had previously worked on the GWR's '4300' Class, and was a supporter of Churchward's standardisation policy – thus the 'N1s' used components common with the 'Ns'. Detail design was the responsibility of another of Maunsell's team, James Clayton, whose background was the Midland Railway at Derby. Thus the engines incorporated several 'foreign' design features.

Because production capacity at Ashford was so stretched, Maunsell built his prototype 'N1' using parts already constructed for the 'Ns' then being built – specifically, No 822. The 'N' Class boiler was higher pitched to accommodate the inside cylinder, and a distinctive vertical cover above the buffer

beam protected it. The prototype appeared in 1923, just as the SECR became part of the Southern Railway, of which Maunsell was appointed Chief Mechanical Engineer. Comparative trials with other absorbed locomotives were inconclusive, and it was not until 1929 that the Southern ordered five more 'N1s', with some new refinements and larger tenders; improvements in the permanent way and the lifting of weight restrictions meant that a third set of Walschaerts valve gear could now be used. The new engines appeared during 1930, but no further examples followed, as the mechanically similar and contemporary 'U1' Class engines were found more versatile.

The 'N1s' initially worked on the Central Section, in particular over the Tonbridge to Hastings route, on which they were allowed by virtue of their smaller outside cylinders (the two-cylinder 'Ns' were too wide); they also hauled through expresses to the GWR and LMS. During the war their capacity to haul heavy trains at moderate speeds was put to great use. The last of Maunsell's modifications was the addition of smoke deflectors from 1934. His successor, Bulleid, made no significant alterations to the class, and all six were well used into BR days over both the Central and Eastern Sections of the Southern Region. With the encroachment of electrification, all the 'N1s' moved to Tonbridge where they worked through to Redhill and onto the Brighton line and other parts of the Central Section. The entire class was withdrawn from Stewarts Lane shed in November 1962 and scrapped in 1963/64.

LCDR 'R' Class 0-4-4T

Nos 31658-63, 31665-67, 31670, 31671, 1672, 1673, 31674, 31675

William Kirtley was the nephew of Matthew Kirtley of Midland Railway fame, and trained under his uncle at Derby. He became Locomotive Superintendent of the London, Chatham & Dover Railway from 1874 until the merger with the South Eastern Railway to form the SECR in 1899.

Ex-LCDR 'R' Class 0-4-4T No 31666 was the last of a class of 18 built in 1891-92. Withdrawn from Tonbridge shed (74D) in December 1955, it is seen here four months earlier at Tunbridge Wells West. *D. A. Kelso, Colour-Rail*

The LCDR was a regular user of locos with the 0-4-4 wheel arrangement for suburban and local passenger trains, and Kirtley's 'R' Class was built by Sharp Stewart in 1891-92 as a development of his earlier 'A2' Class. When the two companies came together to form the SECR, there were both SER *and* LCDR 'R' Class engines on its books, the former 0-6-0 and the latter 0-4-4, an enduring source of confusion!

All the engines were fitted with condensing apparatus for working the 'Widened Lines' of the Metropolitan Railway, whose loading gauge allowed access to the City for trains from the LCDR as well as the GNR and MR. Suburban electrification eventually forced them out to more rural duties. As with many pre-Grouping classes inherited by the Southern Railway, the numbering of the 'R' Class was complex; originally Nos 199-216, they became SECR Nos 658-675 from 1899. In 1923 the

Introduced 1891
Designed by William Kirtley
Built by Sharp Stewart
Number built 18
Number inherited by BR 15
Last example withdrawn December 1955

Southern renumbered them A658-A675, and again in 1931 as 1658-75, then finally their BR numbers were 31658-75, although these were not carried by Nos 1672 and 1673.

Three of the class were scrapped for spares in 1940, but the remaining 15 passed into national ownership. The longest-lived was No 31666, which had the distinction of being the last LCDR locomotive to be withdrawn from service.

SER/SECR 'R1' Class 0-6-0T

Nos 31010, 31047, 31069, 31107, 1127, 31128, 31147, 31154, 31174, 31335, 31337, 31339, 31340

Introduced 1888; rebuilt from 1910
Designed by James Stirling; rebuilt by Harry Wainwright
Built by SER, Ashford
Number built 13 (as 'R1' rebuilds)
Number inherited by BR 13
Last example withdrawn April 1960

RIGHT Ex-SER 'R1' Class 0-6-0T No 31010 was one of the four with cut-down fittings that had enabled them to work through Tyler Tunnel on the Whitstable branch prior to the line's closure in 1952. Its rather squat appearance is seen here at Folkestone Junction shed in May 1959. In that month No 31010 moved from Dover Marine shed to Nine Elms, where it was withdrawn in August. *A. E. Doyle, Colour-Rail*

BELOW Ex-SER 'R1' No 31047 assists at the rear of a boat train ascending the 1 in 30 gradient from Folkestone Harbour, with Nos 31010 and 31107 working hard at the head, on 12 July 1958. No 31047 was the last of the class to be scrapped, in April 1960, the other two having gone eight months earlier. *T. B. Owen, Colour-Rail*

The South Eastern Railway classified its locomotives by simply using the next letter of the alphabet for each successive new class. The SECR and the Southern Railway under Maunsell did the same, and if a class was significantly modified or rebuilt, a number was added. So when Wainwright rebuilt Stirling's 'R' Class, they became the 'R1' Class. Confusingly, as mentioned above, Wainwright also rebuilt W. Kirtley's 'R' Class, and they also became SECR 'R1' Class!

Stirling's 'R' Class numbered 25 locomotives, built in six batches between 1888 and 1898; designed for shunting, they had characteristic Stirling domeless boilers and rounded cab roofs. Interestingly, the SER had been the only large British company not to employ 0-6-0 tanks. There were rarely seen in London, being generally used for shunting in Kent, and for occasionally hauling passenger trains on the Whitstable branch and the Elham Valley line.

In 1910, now as SECR engines, Wainwright rebuilt No 69 with a domed, higher-pressure 'H' Class boiler, and a dozen more (randomly numbered) were similarly modified, between one and four each year, until 1922 – these were the 'R1s'. The unrebuilt 'R' Class examples had all been withdrawn by 1943, but the 'R1s' passed into British Railways ownership. They had Wainwright's design of 'pagoda' cab, and some had sandboxes for the leading wheels as an aid to adhesion when working the steeply graded

Folkestone Harbour branch, where as many as four or five locomotives might be needed to assist a heavy boat train up the 1 in 30 incline to the main line. The 'R1s' were eventually replaced there in 1959 by ex-GWR '57xx' pannier tanks.

Four of the class (Nos 31010/069/147/339) were modified by Bulleid, retaining their Stirling round cab roofs and having truncated chimneys and domes to enable them to work through the undersized 1,012-yard Tyler Tunnel on the Whitstable branch; one, No 31069, was subsequently reconverted.

Although none of these locomotives was preserved, one lived on in model form when Hornby Dublo launched its two-rail electric model railway system in 1959. The plastic model carried BR livery, and was coloured either black (as No 31337) or green (No 31340). It remained available until 1964, by which time the class had been extinct for four years.

SECR 'R1' Class 0-4-4T

Nos 31696-98, 1699, 31700, 31703-06, 1717-09, 31710

Introduced 1900
Designed by William Kirtley, modified by Harry Wainwright
Built by Sharp Stewart
Number built 15
Number inherited by BR 13
Last example withdrawn April 1956

Both the LCDR and SER employed 0-4-4T locomotives for local passenger services: a recent class on the former was William Kirtley's 'R' Class, while the SER had James Stirling's 'Q' Class. When more were needed soon after the SECR came into being in 1899, it would have been possible to build more of either, but a standardised design for use across the combined network was favoured. However, this would take time, so meanwhile a modification of the LCDR 'R' Class was decided upon.

These 15 locomotives were built to Kirtley's original 'R' Class design (qv), but with Wainwright modifications that included a larger cylinder diameter, larger coal bunkers and larger bogie

Push-pull-fitted SECR 'R1' Class 0-4-4T No 31703, a Tonbridge engine throughout its BR days, is seen at Ashford on 15 July 1950. Comparison with the earlier picture of ex-LCDR 'R' Class No 31666 will show how similar the locomotives were. *H. C. Casserley*

wheels. Later all the 'Rs' were rebuilt with the larger cylinders and Wainwright's 'H' Class boiler, so there was little to distinguish between the two classes.

Like the original 'Rs', the 'R1s' were intended for suburban passenger work, later taking more rural duties when electrification spread. Seven of the 'R1s' were later fitted with push-pull apparatus for working branch-line services. Ten were intended for use on former LCDR routes, and the remainder on SER lines. They were originally included in the 'R' Class, but were reclassified as 'R1s' in 1901. No more were built as Wainwright's 'H' Class was soon ready.

Two of the class were scrapped in 1929, but the remaining 13 entered BR stock, and all were dispensed with between 1949 and 1956, when the last, No 31704, was withdrawn.

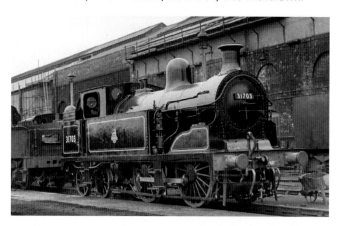

SECR 'S' Class 0-6-0ST

No 1685

The SECR's 'C' Class 0-6-0 tender goods engines were produced as a standard design for use across both constituent systems by Harry Wainwright, and 109 were produced between 1900 and 1908. One, No 1592/31592, has been preserved, having spent its last years in departmental use as No DS239; based on the Bluebell Railway, in 1999 it starred as the 'Green Dragon' in the TV film of *The Railway Children*.

During the First World War a secret 'Q' port was built on the River Stour at Richborough in Kent, and was used to ferry men and munitions across the Channel to France and Belgium. A great deal of military materiel, including locomotives, was dispatched using sea-going barges.

Introduced 1900; rebuilt 1917
Designed by Harry Wainwright; rebuilt by Richard Maunsell
Built by Neilson Reid
Number built 1, as rebuilt
Number inherited by BR 1
Last example withdrawn September 1951

A branch linking the port to the main line was constructed, and a heavy shunting engine was required to operate it. To provide such an engine, in 1917 Maunsell converted Wainwright 'C' Class No 685 into a saddle tank. The frames were extended at the back so that a bunker and a fully enclosed cab could be fitted, and a 1,200-gallon saddle tank was placed atop the boiler, all serving to increase the locomotive's available adhesion weight. This became the sole member of the 'S' Class, and after use at Richborough it was sent to Bricklayers Arms to be employed as a shunter as SR No 1685. Reportedly the last saddle tank on the Southern Railway at the time of nationalisation, it was withdrawn in September 1951.

The unique 'S' Class 0-6-0ST No 1685 is seen at Bricklayers Arms on 4 May 1946. Note the wartime graffiti on the bunker, with the 'Kilroy' figure and the words 'Wot no steam', while written on the cabside is the affectionate name 'Old Fanny'. *H. C. Casserley*

LCDR/SECR 'T' Class 0-6-0T

Nos 1602, 31604, 500S

The 'T' Class 0-6-0 tanks were introduced by Kirtley for shunting and local goods work, and all were built at the LCDR's Longhedge Works. The first two emerged in 1879, and the class had grown to ten by 1893, the eight later locos having longer frames to accommodate a larger bunker and a Westinghouse pump for the brakes. They worked at Herne Hill and Victoria sidings, although one was to be found at Dover Docks.

When the SECR was formed in 1899 they were renumbered, then during the First World War they served with the ROD, often being seen across the Channel at Boulogne; to avoid confusion with other ROD engines their numbers were prefixed by '5'.

Only three of the class passed to British Railways in 1948. The first had been withdrawn in 1932, with two others sold into industrial use in 1936. No 1607 was also to have been withdrawn, but instead was overhauled in 1938 and sent to work at Meldon Quarry to replace a Manning Wardle 0-4-0ST of 1881, which had worked there since 1927 as No 225S. Renumbered 500S, it worked at Meldon until 1948, being replaced by former LSWR 'G6' (qv) 0-6-0T No 72, renumbered as DS3152.

No 1604 was placed in store during January 1939 as part of a reserve of locomotives that could be used in the event of hostilities, but instead worked on the East Kent Railway until 1945, then returning to Herne Hill with fellow survivor No 1602.

When inherited by BR in 1948 the only other ex-LCDR engines still at work were members of the 'R' and 'R1' Classes. No 1602 and 31604 (which carried its BR number from May 1950) were sent from Stewarts Lane to storage at Reading, from where they were withdrawn in July 1951 and November 1950 respectively. That left only one other 'T' Class loco in Britain, No 1600, one of the pair sold to Frazer & Co of Hebburn-on-Tyne in December 1936, which ended its days working at Haydock Colliery in 1957, still in SR unlined black livery.

Former LCDR 'T' Class 0-6-0T No 1602 was shedded at Stewarts Lane before moving to Reading South in 1950. This pre-nationalisation picture is dated 18 June 1946. *H. C. Casserley*

Introduced 1879
Designed by William Kirtley
Built by LCDR, Longhedge
Number built 10
Number inherited by BR 3
Last example withdrawn July 1951

SR 'U1' Class 2-6-0

Nos 31890-910

Maunsell's first 2-6-0 tender loco design was the 'N' Class of 1917, and he simultaneously built a corresponding 2-6-4 tank engine, the prototype of the 'K' Class, which finally numbered 20 machines. Known as the 'River' Class, from their names, in 1927 No 800 *River Cray* was involved in a serious accident near Sevenoaks that threw doubt on the safety of the design and led to the withdrawal of the whole class. As a result they were subsequently rebuilt as 2-6-0 tender engines and dubbed the 'U' Class of 1928. They were very similar to the 'N' 'Moguls', but had larger-diameter wheels.

In the same way that a three-cylinder version of the 'N' became the 'N1' Class (qv), in 1925 Maunsell took the 'River' Class 2-6-4T *River Frome* and rebuilt it with three cylinders. When the 'Rivers' were rebuilt, so too was the three-cylinder 'K1', to become the prototype of the 'U1' Class of three-cylinder 2-6-0s, No 1890, in 1928. Again, the rebuild was very similar to the 'N1', but used three sets of Walschaerts valve gear from the outset, and again there was a notable Midland Railway style about the aesthetics, from the work of Maunsell assistant James Clayton, a former Midland Railway engineer. This was the final development of the Maunsell 2-6-0 family, and represented a continuation of Churchward's standardisation policies on the GWR, sharing certain characteristics with his '4300' Class 'Moguls', whereby parts were interchangeable between different classes. As with the 'N1s', the smaller cylinders increased the route availability of the 'U1s' compared with the 'Us'. A slab front above the front buffer beam, similar to that of the 'N1s', protected the inside cylinder and its associated valve gear between the frames, and the cabside cutaway extended into the roof.

By 1931 the class numbered 21 engines, being built in preference to more 'N1s'. The production batch had higher running plates, dispensing with the driving wheel splashers of No 1890, and smoke deflectors were fitted to the whole class from 1933, in common with most Maunsell locomotives; because of the high running plate they were of reduced height.

Introduced 1928
Designed by Richard Maunsell
Built by SR, Ashford (1), Eastleigh (20)
Number built 21
Number inherited by BR 21
Last example withdrawn July 1963

'U1' 'Mogul' No 31898 gets away from Southampton in September 1957. *B. J. Swain, Colour-Rail*

The 'U1s' gave valuable service and were popular with crews. They were capable of speeds in excess of 70mph, and possessed excellent traction and acceleration qualities. Their greater route availability led them to become regulars on the restricted Tonbridge to Hastings route, together with the 'N1s', and they could also be used on Central Section services; however, trials on the Somerset & Dorset line found that they were less suited to stiff gradients, and west of Exeter crews preferred the hill-climbing abilities of the smaller-wheeled 'Ns'.

The useful 'Moguls' only becoming redundant when the Kent Coast electrification scheme was completed in the early 1960s, and Bulleid's 'light Pacifics' began to usurp their duties. The entire class was withdrawn in 1962-63, and sadly none made it into preservation.

SR 'W' Class 2-6-4T

Nos 31911-25

Introduced 1931
Designed by Richard Maunsell
Built by SR, Eastleigh (5), Ashford (10)
Number built 15
Number inherited by BR 15
Last example withdrawn August 1964

As mentioned in the previous entry, following the Sevenoaks crash of 1927 the SR 'K' ('River') Class 2-6-4 tanks were withdrawn and rebuilt as 'U' 2-6-0 tender engines. The new 'W' Class of three-cylinder 2-6-4Ts was introduced in 1931-32 specifically for freight duties, especially short-distance, inter-company and inter-regional goods traffic around London's many marshalling yards. Under Maunsell's standardisation policies, they incorporated parts common to the 'N', 'N1', 'U' and 'U1' classes.

The Southern Railway had three principal yards in London, at Feltham, Norwood and Hither Green, and exchanged traffic with other yards, such as Old Oak Common, Willesden, Cricklewood and Ferme Park, via the West London Line. Traffic to, from and between these yards had to fit in amongst an intensive service of suburban electric services, so any goods trains had to be able to move smartly, with good adhesion and acceleration, especially over the relatively steep gradients of

'W' 2-6-4T No 31924 moved from Feltham to Exmouth Junction in November 1962, and was used for banking trains between Exeter St David's and Central stations. Here it is seen awaiting its next duty on 21 August 1963. Note the substantial steps to the rear of the outer cylinders, giving access to the tank fillers. *Colour-Rail collection*

the many flyover junctions in the south London network. Because short journeys would be the norm, a tank locomotive was the favoured option.

More of the 'Z' Class 0-8-0s of 1929 (qv) were considered at first, but the solution decided upon was a smaller-wheeled, three-cylinder version of the ill-fated 'K1' Class, using surplus bogies, leading wheels and tanks. Robust braking equipment, both steam and vacuum, was installed to cope with both fitted and unfitted goods trains; unusually the engines had additional brakes on the trailing bogies. The boilers were to be the same as those used on the 'N', 'N1' and 'U1'.

Ten engines were to be built at Eastleigh using frames made at Ashford, and Brighton boilers, but the Depression led to the frames being put in store, and the boilers used elsewhere. However, in 1931 construction resumed and just five 'Ws' were completed early the following year. The remaining five, together with five more, were eventually constructed and delivered by 1935-36, but were built at Ashford as Eastleigh

was busy with the 'Schools' Class. The first engines were right-hand drive, but the last ten had left-hand controls.

Although dedicated freight engines, during exchange trials after nationalisation 'Ws' were used on the non-electrified lines between Victoria and Tunbridge Wells and Ashford and Tonbridge, but like their forebears they were found unstable at speed.

The engines were generally shedded at Hither Green, Stewarts Lane and Norwood Junction, but in 1962 a number moved west to Exeter, to bank Southern Region trains from St David's up to Central station. All were withdrawn in 1963-64.

SECR '1302' Class 0-4-0 Crane Engine

No 1302

This Neilson crane tank was one of two similar machines built for the South Eastern Railway at a cost of £1,335 each, and delivered in April 1881. They differed from all other crane tanks built for British railways in that the crane was attached to the front end, constructed around the chimney. It became SER No 302 (the other was No 409) and worked initially at Folkestone Harbour until 1905, when it moved to Ashford Works until 1914. It then went to Dover and Richborough,

Introduced	1881
Designed by	James Stirling
Built by	Neilson
Number built	1
Number inherited by BR	1
Last example withdrawn	July 1949

BELOW Former SECR Crane Tank No 1302 of 1881, coupling rods removed, stands in Ashford Works yard on 2 July 1949. It was scrapped during that month. Note how the crane is constructed at the front end around the chimney. *H. C. Casserley*

ABOVE Another view of Crane Tank No 1302 at Battersea shed on 22 May 1948. The twin-cylinder mechanism, allowing the crane to lift 2½ tons, can clearly be seen. *P. E. Saxby, Frank Hornby collection*

returning to Ashford the following year. It was back at Richborough in 1918, then returned to Ashford.

Under the Southern Railway it was renumbered A234S, but by 1927 was out of use at Ashford. In 1929, overhauled, it went to Lancing Carriage Works until 1938. In that year it was overhauled again and gained an enclosed cab; originally it had only a small canopy supported by pillars, to afford the driver the best view when operating the crane. Renumbered once more to 1302, its final duty was shunting the CWS milk dock at

Stewarts Lane, which included a sharp curve – it is not known whether the crane was ever used during this period. It was a BR engine for just 19 months, and never carried its allocated number of 31302; out of use by the autumn of 1948, it was withdrawn in July 1949 and scrapped at Ashford.

The crane had twin cylinders and could lift 2½ tons within a radius of 7ft 2in. When withdrawn it had accumulated a total mileage of just 118,163.

LBSCR 'B4' Class 4-4-0

Nos 2044, 2051, 2054, 2062, 2063, 2068, 2074

Locomotives with BR numbers in the 32xxx series were former London, Brighton & South Coast classes. The 'B4' 4-4-0s were Billinton's last passenger tender locomotives for the LBSCR. Born in Yorkshire in 1845, Robert J. Billinton was Locomotive Superintendent of the Brighton company from 1890 until his death in November 1904. He succeeded William Stroudley, having previously been his head draughtsman; after a spell with the Midland Railway, he returned to Brighton after Stroudley's death, and was himself succeeded by Douglas Earle Marsh.

Billinton's earlier 'B2' Class 4-4-0s had proved disappointing, and had failed to improve on and replace Stroudley's 'B1' 0-4-2s on the principal London-Brighton expresses. It was hoped, therefore, that his new 'B4s' would do better, and when the first two, Nos 52 and 53, emerged from Brighton Works between December 1899 and January 1900, their design and performance proved to be sound. Because of a backlog of work at Brighton, a third example (No 54) could not be completed until May 1900, so the LBSCR ordered 25 from Sharp Stewart at £3,990 each, which were all delivered in the second half of 1901; soon nicknamed 'Scotchmen', they were also referred to as 'Canadas', from the name of the first-built, No 47. Finally, five further examples were built at Brighton in 1902, using Sharp Stewart boilers.

Being the largest and most powerful express locomotives to be seen on the LBSCR, they were used to handle the heaviest South Coast services, their bold proportions gaining them the

Introduced 1899
Designed by Robert Billinton
Built by LBSCR, Brighton (8), Sharp Stewart (25)
Number built 33
Number inherited by BR 7
Last example withdrawn May 1951

nickname 'Busters' (they were also known as 'Sirdars', after the second of the class). They continued in that role until replaced in about 1912 by the larger 'H1', 'H2', 'J1' and 'J2' classes, when they were relegated to lighter duties. In that year No 59 *Baden Powell* was fitted with a large Phoenix superheater, requiring a very much extended smokebox, to the detriment of the engine's aesthetics; the experiment was not a success.

Interestingly, in 1935 the Southern Railway withdrew and dismantled Nos 2059 and 2068, but a shortage of motive power led to the components being combined to create a new No 2068. No 2074 was withdrawn in 1937, but reinstated on the outbreak of war in 1939, and lasted into BR days.

Some members of the class carried names relating to the Royal Family (and were used on Royal Trains) or the recent Boer War – names like *Princess Royal*, *Sandringham* and *Windsor*, or *Cecil Rhodes*, *Ladysmith* and *Mafeking*. *Empress* and *Sirdar* (the latter as pilot engine, running ahead of the train) worked Queen Victoria's funeral train from the LSWR at Fareham to London Victoria. From a late start, the train made good time and arrived in London 2 minutes early; apparently the German Kaiser sent an equerry to the driver to convey his congratulations! Some examples managed to retain their names when the Southern Railway inherited all but two of the class, which had been converted to 'B4X' form (qv).

Seven 'B4s' passed to BR, but they never carried their allocated BR numbers and all had been cut up by the spring of 1951.

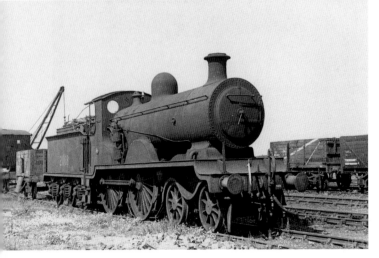

The elegant lines of R. Billinton's 'B4' Class are well illustrated by this portrait of No 2068 at its home shed of Eastbourne on 9 August 1947. It was one of the last four survivors, all disposed of in May 1951. Note the wartime allocation of 'York' on the buffer beam. *H. C. Casserley*

LBSCR 'B4X' Class 4-4-0

Nos 32043, 2045, 2050, 2052, 2055, 2056, 2060, 2067, 2070, 32071, 32072, 2073

Introduced 1922
Designed by Robert Billinton; rebuilt by Lawson Billinton
Built by LBSCR Brighton (3), Sharp Stewart (9)
Number built 12, as rebuilt
Number inherited by BR 12
Last example withdrawn December 1951

Lawson B. Billinton (1888-1954) was the son of Robert Billinton, and succeeded his father as Locomotive Superintendent of the LBSCR when Marsh's tenure of office ended in 1912, retaining the post until the Grouping. He had worked his way up through the LBSCR, starting under his father.

In 1918, Billinton junior rebuilt one of his father's Sharp Stewart-built 'B4' 4-4-0s with a new superheated boiler. After thorough trials, a further 11 were rebuilt between 1922 and the beginning of 1924, well into Southern Railway days, and these became the 'B4X' Class. The first three were built at Brighton, and were among the most powerful engines in the country at the time. However, the new boiler would not fit on the 'B4' frames, so by the time the design and construction had been modified these were virtually new engines, containing little of the originals other than wheel centres and bogies, though classed as 'rebuilds'. The wheelbase was lengthened and the larger boiler pitched higher. Unfortunately, the original valve gear was retained, which was not a good fit, and served to negate the steaming power of the excellent 'K' Class boiler, affecting both acceleration and top speed compared with other contemporary locomotives.

With the Grouping imminent, the first two engines, Nos 55 and 60, were turned out in grey rather than the LBSCR umber

'B4X' 4-4-0 No 32071 stands on the turntable at Reading on 25 September 1948. It was built by Sharp Stewart in 1901 as 'B4' No 71 *Goodwood*, becoming 'B4X' No B71 in 1923. Its last shed was Eastbourne, and it was one of only three of the class to carry a BR number, applied in July 1948; it was withdrawn in October 1951. *H. C. Casserley*

livery, and remained so until painted green by the Southern Railway; this gave rise to the nickname 'Greybacks'. They were the last engines designed and built by the LBSCR, the last ten appearing after the Grouping.

Maunsell decided against building more; their performance was unsatisfactory, and it was found that they cost more to maintain than, for example, the former SECR 'D1' and 'E1' rebuilds. However, they had to soldier on until the late 1920s, latterly on secondary duties. Withdrawals of the 'B4s' and 'B4Xs' took place between 1934 and 1939, but the war reprieved others, meaning that 12 'B4Xs' passed into BR's hands. However, all were taken out of service between August and December 1951.

LBSCR 'C2' Class 0-6-0

Nos 2435, 2436, 2533

Introduced 1893
Designed by Robert Billinton
Built by Vulcan Foundry
Number built 55
Number inherited by BR 3
Last example withdrawn February 1950

The 'C2' was Billinton's first main-line 0-6-0 goods locomotive for the Brighton company, and 55 were built by the Vulcan Foundry at Newton-le-Willows near Warrington. This company had been founded in 1830 by Charles Tayleur, a Director of the Liverpool & Manchester Railway, who entered into partnership with Robert Stephenson in 1832; the Vulcan Foundry name was adopted in 1864. Because of their builder, the class gained the nickname 'Vulcans'.

The locomotives were intended to supplement Stroudley's earlier 'C1' Class of 1882-87. Brighton Works had insufficient

'C2' 0-6-0 No 2436, one of only three remaining unrebuilt members of the class that would pass into BR ownership in 1948, stands at Norwood Junction on 28 July 1945. It is flanked by two other Billinton LBSCR engines: on the right is 'E4' 0-6-4T No 2498, and just visible on the left is 'E3' 0-6-2T No 2456. *H. C. Casserley*

capacity to handle the construction, so ten were ordered from Vulcan; further batches followed until by 1902 the class numbered 55 engines. They had the same cylinders and motion as Billinton's 'D3' 0-4-4T suburban tanks (qv), but larger fireboxes, and were fitted with Westinghouse air brakes so that they could work passenger trains if required. Their tenders had outside frames, bearings and springs.

Unfortunately the 'C2s' were not as powerful as the Stroudley engines, but were reliable and capable of a good turn of speed, so came to be used on secondary passenger trains and excursions. Freight traffic increased greatly in the early years of the 20th century, so in 1908 45 'C2s' were rebuilt, and improved, with a larger boiler, becoming the 'C2X' Class (see next entry). However, the post-war Depression led to a downturn in freight, and seven 'C2s' were taken out of service in 1937, so just three unrebuilt examples remained in service at nationalisation. None received their allocated BR number, and all had been cut up by the middle of 1950.

LBSCR 'C2X' Class 0-6-0

Nos 32434, 32437, 32438, 32440-51, 32521-29, 32532, 32534-41, 32543-54

Introduced 1893; rebuilt from 1908
Designed by Robert Billinton; rebuilt by Douglas Earle Marsh
Built by Vulcan Foundry (originals)
Number built 45
Number inherited by BR 45
Last example withdrawn February 1962

After Robert Billinton's death in office in 1904, his successor, Douglas Earle Marsh, rebuilt 45 of the 'C2' 0-6-0s (see previous entry) with a larger boiler, becoming the 'C2X' Class; the rebuilding continued as late as 1940. Marsh had worked under Dean at Swindon and Ivatt at Doncaster.

The need for a more powerful goods engine arose from a rapid growth in freight traffic in the early years of the 20th century. Marsh's first move was to introduce his 'C3' Class 0-6-0 (qv) in 1906, but these turned out to be poor performers. Then in 1908 he rebuilt a 'C2' with a larger-diameter C3 steel boiler and extended smokebox, pitched higher than the originals. This modification proved successful, and the so-called 'Large Vulcans' eventually numbered 45 by 1912. Although superseded by Lawson Billinton's more powerful 'K' Class 2-6-0s (qv) from 1913, the 'C2Xs' worked on through the Great War, and three more 'C2s' had been rebuilt by the end of 1922. The Southern Railway then rebuilt a further ten in 1924-25, two in 1939 and two in 1940. In SR days the 'C2s' and 'C2Xs' all had their domes

No 32541 was one of the engines that carried the double-domed boiler – the front dome originally carried top feed apparatus. It was photographed at its home shed, Norwood Junction, on 11 February 1960, and was withdrawn just under a year later. *Colour-Rail collection*

and chimneys shortened to fit within the new Group-wide loading gauge.

After the war Marsh's successor, Billinton junior, adopted a boiler with two domes, one containing the top feed apparatus, and various engines carried these at some time in their careers. Although this system of top feed was discontinued in 1930, the engines continued to carry the second dome.

The 'C2X' locomotives continued in their valuable role as secondary goods engines, and all passed to BR on nationalisation. A couple were withdrawn in 1957, but the last was not taken out of service until the beginning of 1962.

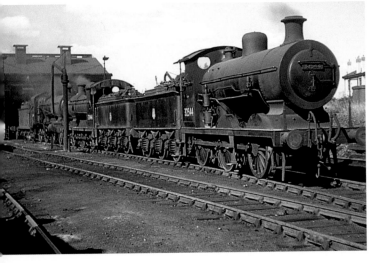

Two 'C2Xs', Nos 32544 and 32444 (with L. Billinton 'K' Class 2-6-0 No 32346 beyond), stand at Norwood Junction shed in July 1956. Built in 1901 as 'C2' No 544, No 32544 was converted to 'C2X' form in 1911 and withdrawn from Norwood Junction in November 1961. *P. Glenn, Colour-Rail*

LBSCR 'C3' Class 0-6-0

Nos 32300-03, 2306-09

Introduced 1906
Designed by Douglas Earle Marsh
Built by LBSCR, Brighton
Number built 10
Number inherited by BR 8
Last example withdrawn January 1952

The 'C3' was the only six-coupled goods engine built for the LBSCR by Marsh, and ten examples, intended to replace the older 'C2s' (qv) on heavy freight trains, were built at Brighton between March and September 1906. The first five had smaller cylinders than the second five, although all were later standardised on the smaller version. Their original tenders were replaced by smaller ones from 'B2' engines that had been rebuilt as 'B2Xs', and four of the class later carried Lawson Billinton's double-domed boiler from 1920.

The engines were indifferent performers with a high fuel consumption and a tendency to run hot at speed, and the 'C2X' rebuilds were much preferred by the Running Department; indeed, the 'C2Xs' outlived the 'C3s' by a decade. Most of the class were allocated to Horsham, and consequently gained the nickname 'Horsham Goods', as well as 'Marsh Goods'. The first

'C3' 0-6-0 No S2301 appears to have only recently gained its 'British Railways' title and number at Brighton in early 1948. It became No 32301 in August of that year, but was withdrawn from Fratton (71D) early in 1951 and cut up. *R. M. Casserley collection*

two of the class to be withdrawn went in 1936 and 1937, but the remaining eight became BR engines, although only half of them carried their BR numbers. All were withdrawn between the end of 1948 and early 1952.

LBSCR 'D1'/'D1/M' Class 0-4-2T

Nos 2215, 2234, 2235, 2239, 2252, 2253, 2259, 2269, 2274, 2283, 2286, 2289, 2299, 2358, 2359, 2361, 2605, 2699, 700S, 701S

Introduced 1873
Designed by William Stroudley
Built by LBSCR, Brighton (90), Neilson (35)
Number built 125
Number inherited by BR 20
Last example withdrawn December 1951

The powerful 'D1' 0-4-2 tanks, known originally as the 'D Tanks', were designed by Stroudley for suburban passenger duties, and were an extremely long-lived class, the last, in departmental service, being withdrawn in December 1951 at the age of more than 70 years! With 125 examples built between 1873 and 1887, the 'D1s' were also the LBSCR's most numerous class.

The 'D1s' were the designer's second tank engine class, intended to handle heavier trains than could be managed by his famous 'A1' Terrier' 0-6-0Ts of 1872. They continued in this role for two decades until superseded by R. Billinton's 'D3'

0-4-4Ts (qv), introduced from 1892. However, they remained in use on secondary passenger duties and occasionally freight trains across the Brighton system.

In 1910 Marsh experimented by rebuilding one example, No 79A *Carshalton*, with larger cylinders and boiler, and this became the solitary member of the 'D1X' Class; although more powerful, it proved unsteady at speed, so no further rebuilding was proceeded with, and the engine was scrapped in 1934. Marsh also reboilered the 'D1s', some for the second time.

The first locomotive was withdrawn in December 1903, but 84 survived to be absorbed by the Southern Railway at the Grouping of 1923. They remained popular with crews, often being preferred to newer engines, and found useful work

Seventy-four-year-old Stroudley 'D1' 0-4-2T No 2299, in faded, flaking Southern livery, looks out of use at Eastleigh in 1948, although it was not officially withdrawn until May of the following year. *S. C. Townroe, Colour-Rail*

during the war; six were loaned to the LMS for use in Scotland (at Ayr, Inverness and Wick), and nine were fitted with water pumps to fight any fires that might occur as a result of incendiary bomb attacks on depots; a powerful steam pump was installed over the rear buffer beam, able to supply four powerful water jets at the rate of a ton a minute.

No 627 was the first of many 'D1s' to be 'motor-fitted', enabling them to work push-pull trains; compressed air was used to operate the regulator remotely from the driving cab of the leading carriage. Converted to oil-firing and coupled to two trailer carriages, No 627 was put to work on the Epsom Downs branch.

Four of the class had their bunkers cut down and side tank capacity reduced in order to work the Lyme Regis branch, but not successfully.

Twenty survivors passed into national ownership in 1948, most being the 'motor-fitted' examples, classified as 'D1/M'. However, many had already been in storage for some time.

One example, No 2357, escaped BR ownership be being sold to the Whittingham Hospital Railway in Lancashire for £750, where it operated until it was found to be beyond economic repair in 1956.

The 'D1' was an important design, influencing future locomotives by Stroudley, such as his own 0-4-2 tender engine for longer-distance trains, and those by his assistants Robert Billinton (his 'D3' Class) and Dugald Drummond (who developed almost identical 0-4-2Ts for the North British and Caledonian companies, not to mention his later successful 'M7' 0-4-4Ts for the LSWR).

Two 'D1s' entered Departmental service in 1947, and were used as oil pumps to supply engines that had been converted to oil-firing. Nos 2244 and 2284 were renumbered 700S and 701S and, based at Eastleigh and Fratton, lasted until 1949 and 1951 respectively, the latter being the longest-lived of this long-lived class! Sadly, not one of these useful engines was preserved .

LBSCR 'D3' and 'D3X'* Class 0-4-4T

Nos 32364, 32365, 2366, 2367, 32368, 2370, 2371, 32372, 2373, 2734, 32376, 2377, 32378-80, 2383, 32384-86, 2387, 32388-91, 32393-95, 2397*, 32398

Having worked under Stroudley at Brighton, Billinton moved to the Midland Railway at Derby as Chief Draughtsman before returning south after Stroudley's death. He was therefore familiar with the 0-4-4 wheel arrangement, which Johnson had introduced to the MR in 1875-1900. Like the Johnson examples, the 'D Bogie', or 'D3' Class 0-4-4T design, Billinton's first for the LBSCR and the company's first 0-4-4, was built for working rural and semi-fast main-line passenger trains. It was intended to be an 'improved' version of, and replacement for, Stroudley's 'D1' tanks (see above). The design also had components shared with other of Billinton's designs.

The 'D3s' were first used in the Tunbridge Wells area and other London outer-suburban duties. One locomotive, No 363, an early casualty in 1933, was named after the Chairman of the LBSCR, Sir Julian Goldsmid, who was so fond of it that its outline was used as the LBSCR's loco crews' cap badge.

Introduced 1892
Designed by Robert Billinton; Douglas Earle Marsh*
Built by LBSCR, Brighton
Number built 36
Number inherited by BR 28
Last example withdrawn October 1955

The 'D3s' were, like other Billinton and Stroudley engines, reboilered over time, and after the First World War, with the spread of electrification, they tended to work more on rural lines in Kent and Sussex, and later, for example, on the Hastings-Ashford line, as well as on carriage shunting duties. The Southern Railway converted most for 'push-pull' duties, although they were considered rough riders compared with the earlier 'D1' tanks, and some spent time in store. However, early in the Second World War they were put back into service, and some spread to the far corners of the SR network, including Salisbury. One interesting wartime story involves SR No 2365, which was attacked by a Luftwaffe fighter. Gunfire either caused the boiler to burst, or the plane, flying very low, hit the dome, but the resultant escape of steam caused the enemy craft to crash nearby, killing the crew. The engine crew escaped unhurt, and No 2365 was repaired and reboilered and returned to service.

Harold Holcroft, in *Locomotive Adventure*, considered the 'D3s' as less than 'willing horses', giving the impression that they were 'tight chested'. Nonetheless, 28 of the class passed to BR following nationalisation and continued to work 'motor trains', although now in poor repair. Former SECR 'H' and LSWR 'M7' tanks were increasingly taking over their

'D3' 0-4-4T No 32390 (originally named *St Leonards*) outlived the rest of the class by two years. All the others had gone by the time this picture was taken at Horsham shed in August 1954, and No 32390 was withdrawn from Brighton in October the following year. *S. C. Townroe, Colour-Rail*

duties during the early 1950s, and most 'D3s' had been withdrawn by 1953, although No 32390 lasted another two years covering for failed 'M7s' around Tunbridge Wells, operating services to Horsham and heading rail tours, before being scrapped at Brighton Works.

In 1909 Nos 396 and 397 were rebuilt by Marsh with larger boilers, new cylinders and a circular smokebox mounted on a saddle; the boiler pressure was also increased. The pair were reclassified as 'D3X', but the experiment was deemed unsuccessful and no further engines were converted; indeed, one 'D3', No 2364, carried its original Billinton boiler until the mid-1930s. 'D3X' No 2396 was scrapped in 1937, and No 2397 survived in BR ownership for just seven months, being withdrawn in July 1948.

LBSCR 'E1' Class 0-6-0T

Nos 2097, 2112, 32113, 2122, 2127, 32128, 32129, 2133, 32138, 32139, 2141, 32142, 32145, 32147, 32151, 2153, 2156, 2160, 2162, 2164, 32606, 2609, 32689, 2690, 2691, 32694, W1-W4

Introduced 1874
Designed by William Stroudley
Built by LBSCR, Brighton
Number built 80
Number inherited by BR 30
Last example withdrawn July 1961

The 'E1' 0-6-0 tanks were designed by Stroudley to handle short-distance goods trains and piloting duties. Originally known as the 'E Tanks', they were reclassified 'E1' during the Marsh era. The first batch was built at Brighton in 1874-75, and so successful were they that by 1891 80 were in service throughout the LBSCR system, mainly on goods duties but occasionally secondary passenger trains. They carried names taken from places in Europe. The last six engines were built during Billinton's tenure, and were slightly different in design.

In the mid-1890s the 'E1s' began to be replaced by Billinton's 'E3' and 'E4' tanks (qv), and the first was withdrawn as early as 1908, broken up for spares. Further withdrawals took place until halted by increased locomotive requirements during the First World War.

In 1911 Marsh rebuilt one of the 'E1s', No 89 (later SR 2389, then BR 32389), with a larger boiler, being reclassified as 'E1X'. However, it was rebuilt as an 'E1' in 1930 when it needed a new boiler and an 'E1X' type was not available.

Under the Southern Railway further members of the class were withdrawn or sold into industrial use. One of these, No

'E1' 0-6-0T No 32694, built at Brighton in 1875, survived until July 1960 working at Southampton Docks. The engine is seen here on the 17th of that month. *Colour-Rail collection*

B110 (originally No 110 *Burgundy*) was sold in 1927 to the Cannock & Rugeley Colliery Co, where it worked until 1963. This example, never a BR engine and much modified while in NCB ownership, is now preserved and being restored by the Isle of Wight Steam Railway in the guise of No W2 *Yarmouth*.

Ten 'E1s' were rebuilt by Maunsell in 1927-29 as 0-6-2Ts, becoming Class 'E1R' (qv). In 1932-33 four 'E1s' moved to the Isle of Wight and were renumbered: No 2136 *Brindisi* became W1 *Medina*, No 2152 *Hungary* became W2 *Yarmouth*, No 2154 *Madrid* became W3 *Ryde*, and No 2131 *Gournay* became W4 *Wroxall*. On the island they were mostly used on goods trains, but were occasionally used on passenger services; found to be unsteady at speed, they were rebalanced at Ryde Works between 1933 and 1936.

Thirty 'E1s' entered BR stock in 1948, but they were increasingly replaced by the new diesel shunters. The last survivor was No 32694, allocated to Southampton Docks until taken out of service in 1961. On the Isle of Wight, No W4 was the last to go, in October 1960.

The last survivor of the class on the Isle of Wight was No (W)4 *Wroxall* (originally No 131 *Gournay* of 1878). Seen here at Ryde on 13 August 1960, it was withdrawn in November of that year. *Colour-Rail collection*

LBSCR 'E1R' Class 0-6-2T

Nos 32094-96, 32124, 32135, 32608, 32610, 32695-97

Introduced 1927 (from 1874-91 originals)
Designed by Richard Maunsell (from Stroudley originals)
Built by LBSCR, Brighton
Number built 10
Number inherited by BR 10
Last example withdrawn November 1959

Between 1927 and 1929 Maunsell rebuilt ten of Stroudley's 'E1' 0-6-0Ts with a radial trailing truck and an enlarged cab and bunker, to achieve an axle loading of less than 16 tons. In this form they were classified as 'E1R', and worked on Southern Railway branch lines in the West of England, including Calstock, Barnstaple and the former North Devon & Cornwall Junction Light Railway route between Torrington and Halwill Junction.

'E1R' 0-6-2T No 32124, formerly SR 'E1' 0-6-0T No 2124 and originally named *Bayonne*, poses at Exeter St David's on 17 March 1956. It was withdrawn from Exmouth Junction shed in January 1959. *T. B. Owen, Colour-Rail*

They were also used as bankers on the steeply graded connection between St David's and Queen Street stations in Exeter.

They retained their original 'E1' numbers and European place names (although No 96 *Salzberg* carried the incorrectly spelled name of Salzburg throughout!). Although all ten passed into BR hands, shedded at Plymouth Friary, Exmouth Junction and Barnstaple Junction, they had all been done away with by the end of 1959.

'E1R' 0-6-2T No 32094 is stripped ready for cutting in the Erecting Shop at Eastleigh Works in 1955. *S. C. Townroe, Colour-Rail*

LBSCR 'E2' Class 0-6-0T

Nos 32100-09

As mentioned earlier, in 1911 Douglas Earle Marsh rebuilt one of Stroudley's 1874 'E1s' (qv) with a larger boiler, classifying it 'E1X'. Only one was so converted before Marsh's unexpected retirement in July of that year, officially because of ill-health, but possibly as a result of alleged accounting irregularities! Lawson Billinton took over, and his plan was to introduce his own 'E2' 0-6-0Ts to replace the increasingly worn-out 'E1s'. The

Introduced 1913
Designed by Lawson Billinton
Built by LBSCR, Brighton
Number built 10
Number inherited by BR 10
Last example withdrawn April 1963

'E2s' were his first design for the Brighton company, and were intended for shunting and short-distance goods trains; they were also used for empty coaching stock duties at the LBSCR's London termini. Five examples were built in 1913-14, and their success led to an order for a further five, with a greater water capacity accommodated in larger side tanks extended over the front driving wheel; delayed by the war, these were delivered in 1915-16.

The last two 'E2' 0-6-0Ts were Nos 32104 and 32109, withdrawn from Southampton Docks in April 1963. No 32104 is seen shunting there on an unknown date. Note that this was one of the original five engines of 1913, without the extended side tanks. *Colour-Rail collection*

In 1914 a couple of 'E2s' were adapted for push-pull working between London Bridge and Crystal Palace, marshalled in the middle of a rake of six coaches, but their inadequate coal capacity and unsteadiness at speed counted against them, and the experiment was soon abandoned.

Electrification in the mid-1930s saw the locomotives relegated to marshalling yard and harbour duties, including use at Southampton Docks until replaced by diesel shunters in 1962. Another of their pre-war duties was to bring in the stock for the 'Night Ferry', then bank the train out of Victoria.

All ten of the 'E2s' became BR engines, and by the end of 1961 all were shedded at Southampton Docks, from where the last, No 32104, was withdrawn in April 1963.

Meanwhile, the class had found a quite unexpected fame as the model for artist Reginald Payne, and his successor C.

Reginald Dalby, in their depiction of 'Thomas the Tank Engine' in the well-known 'Railway Series' books by Rev W. Awdry – with several modifications due to 'artistic licence'! Thomas first appeared in 1946, and some sources claim the LNER 'J' tank classes as the inspiration, while Rev Awdry himself, after making a home-made wooden engine, apparently used a Tri-ang LMS 'Jinty' as his model while telling the stories to his son Christopher, later replaced by the Tri-ang 'E2'. It can be seen that 'Thomas' has the extended water tanks of the second batch of engines!

Hornby produced an OO model 'E2' between 1979 to 1985, which formed the basis for the company's subsequent 'Thomas' model. Bachmann has also produced several differently coloured 'E2'-based models in its 'Junior Range', but these are based on 'Thomas' as seen in the more recent popular TV series.

LBSCR 'E3' Class 0-6-2T

Nos 32165-70, 32453-56, 2457, 32458-62

Introduced 1894
Designed by Robert Billinton
Built by LBSCR, Brighton
Number built 16
Number inherited by BR 16
Last example withdrawn November 1959

The 'E3' Class 0-6-2Ts were one of four main variations on the radial tank theme designed by R. Billinton for the Brighton company. The 'E3s' and 'E6s' were goods engines, with coupled wheels of 4ft 6in, while the 'E4s' and 'E5s' (both qv) had 5-foot and 5ft 6in wheels respectively for passenger work.

The prototype for the class was actually a William Stroudley design, an 0-6-2T radial tank intended to replace his older 'E1' 0-6-0s and dubbed the 'E Class Special'. However, when Stroudley died in December 1889 only one was under construction, and his successor, Billinton, halted work and made some modifications to the design. The locomotive emerged in 1891 No 158 *West Brighton* (the name of Hove station until 1894), and was originally classified as 'F' before becoming 'E3'. It was allocated to Fratton, and worked goods trains along the coast line.

Billinton ordered a further 16 locomotives to a slightly modified design, which appeared in 1894-95 and were known

'E3' 0-6-2T No 32166 of 1894 poses at Brighton on 29 December 1956, in fine condition and fitted with a Westinghouse brake. It was withdrawn and cut up in the autumn of 1959. *T. B. Owen, Colour-Rail*

as 'Small Radials'. Numbered 165-170 and 453-462, they were intended for local goods trains and heavy shunting. The majority were named after Sussex villages, although No 453 *Broadbridge* was wrongly named *Charles C. Macrae* for a brief period in later years.

Although primarily goods engines, they were frequently found on passenger services (for which duties a Westinghouse air brake was fitted), but their small wheels were hardly suited to this role, and led Billinton to introduce his 'E4' Class, with larger 5-foot-diameter wheels; one of these, No 32473 *Birch Grove*, survives in preservation.

They all received new Marsh boilers, some with a higher pressure, and extended smokeboxes from 1918. In 1935 the Southern Railway withdrew the prototype, by then No 2158, but the remaining 16 engines went on to became part of BR's stock in 1948, and all but one received their allocated BR numbers. The last survivor, Norwood Junction's No 32165 (originally named *Blatchington*) was withdrawn in November 1959.

'E3' No 32459 was a Bricklayers Arms engine for its entire BR career until withdrawn from there in June 1956. Here it is being dismantled at Brighton on the 23rd of that month. *H. C. Casserley*

LBSCR 'E4X' Class 0-6-2T

Nos 32466, 32477, 32478, 32489

Billinton's 'E4' Class of 0-6-2 'Radial Tanks' do not warrant an entry in this book as one of their number, No 32473 *Birch Grove*, withdrawn in October 1962, was purchased by preservationists the following year and taken to the Bluebell Railway in East Sussex, where it has been based ever since, apart from occasional visits to other heritage lines. After a long period of restoration between 1971 and 1997, the engine was back in steam in time for its centenary in 1998. Overhauled again in 2008-10, *Birch Grove* is now the only Robert Billinton-designed locomotive in preservation.

Seventy-five 'E4s' were built between 1897 and 1903, and proved to be sturdy long-lived engines, handling local passenger, goods and branch-line trains for half a century. They continued to find work into BR days, as station pilots and hauling empty carriages around Waterloo and Clapham Junction.

Introduced	1909, as rebuilt
Designed by	Robert Billinton; rebuilt by Douglas Earle Marsh
Built by	LBSCR, Brighton
Number built	4
Number inherited by BR	4
Last example withdrawn	January 1959

The four 'E4X' rebuilds lasted almost ten years in BR ownership. The last of the quartet, No 32477, is seen at its home shed of Norwood Junction on 24 July 1954, with 3½ years of useful work still ahead of it. *H. C. Casserley*

Between 1909 and 1911 Marsh, Billinton's successor, rebuilt four of the class with much larger boilers and extended smokeboxes, and these were classified as 'E4X'. All four became BR engines, and all received their allocated BR numbers, working on for almost a further ten years.

LBSCR 'E5' Class 0-6-2T

Nos 32399, 32400, 32402, 32404-06, 2567, 32568, 32571, 2572, 32573-75, 32583-85, 32587, 32588, 2589, 32590-94

Introduced	1902
Designed by	Robert Billinton
Built by	LBSCR, Brighton
Number built	30
Number inherited by BR	24
Last example withdrawn	January 1956

In April 1903 Robert Billinton was the subject of an 'Illustrated Interview' in *The Railway Magazine*, and he took the opportunity to describe and illustrate his new 0-6-2 radial tank engine with 5ft 6in coupled wheels and an altogether modern look. As O. S. Nock points out, these 'were undoubtedly intended to be a twentieth century development of the Class "D" 0-4-2 , and to be multiplied accordingly.'

The 'E5s' were similar to, but a larger version of, the same designer's 'E4' Class, and were intended for semi-fast secondary passenger work. Having developed his 0-6-2 tanks through the 'E3s' and 'E4s', the 'E5s' had larger wheels and larger fireboxes. Thirty were built at Brighton; the first 10 emerged between

November 1902 and April 1903, and the remaining 20 in 1903-04. As well as being quicker, they had a greater coal and water capacity. At 60 tons, they were at the time the largest LBSCR tank locomotives. Sadly, just as the last of the 'E5s' was being completed, Billinton died on 7 November 1904. His successor did not believe in naming locomotives, so these were almost the last to be so honoured, again using village names from the South of England.

Before the First World War one of the class, No 591 *Tillington*, worked the 'Grand Vitesse' van trains from London Bridge to Newhaven, and was also the last engine to wear the Brighton company's yellow livery, until 1917.

Another of their regular duties was the so-called 'Managing Directors' Train', which arrived at London Bridge at 10.48am, as

'E5' 0-6-2T No 32406 was built in November 1904 as LBSCR No 406 *Colworth*, and is seen here a year or two before it was withdrawn in August 1951. The class's elegant chimneys were placed forward on the short smokeboxes, giving the engines a rather front-heavy look. *Lens of Sutton Collection (42188)*

well as a morning train from Chichester to Victoria via Midhurst and Pulborough, which, it is rumoured, was run as a favour to the aristocratic owners of Cowdray Park and Petworth House!

During 1906 some of the engines ran as 2-4-2Ts, a modification introduced by Marsh and involving the simple removal of the forward coupling rods. The experiment proved unnecessary, and they reverted to the 0-6-2 form three years later.

All the 'E5s' were absorbed by the Southern Railway at the Grouping, and the first to be disposed of was not until 1936,

with another being the victim of a collision in 1944. Four had been rebuilt by Marsh to become the 'E5X' Class (qv), and the remaining two dozen duly entered BR stock in 1948. However, the advent of larger 2-6-4 tanks in the early years of nationalisation allowed these older engines to be retired, and all had been withdrawn by 1956. The last three, Nos 32571, 32583 and 32593, were taken out of use at Norwood Junction, Basingstoke and Dover Marine respectively. No 32593 had been as a temporary stationary boiler at Dover during 1951.

LBSCR 'E5X' Class 0-6-2T

Nos 32401, 32570, 32576, 32586

> **Introduced** 1911, as rebuilt
> **Designed by** Robert Billinton; rebuilt by Douglas Earle Marsh
> **Built by** LBSCR, Brighton
> **Number built** 4
> **Number inherited by BR** 4
> **Last example withdrawn** January 1956

Just as Marsh rebuilt four of Billinton's 'E4s' with larger boilers, so four of the 'E5s' were similarly treated. The original engines had proved themselves successful, so in 1911 Nos 401 *Woldingham*, 570 *Armington*, 576 *Brenchley* and 586 *Maplehurst* were given the boiler used on March's 'C3' 0-6-0s and reclassified 'E5X'. As with the 'E4Xs', this did not produce a great improvement in performance, and the higher centre of gravity led to unsteady riding, so the experiment was not perpetuated.

No 32401 temporarily carried an ex-'C6X' boiler with a second dome, which had formerly carried the top feed apparatus.

Single-line staffs are exchanged with military precision at Cranleigh, on the Guildford-Christ's Hospital line, in August 1954. The engine is 'E5X' 0-6-2T No 32570, which was withdrawn from Brighton 18 months later, rendering this small class extinct.
S. C. Townroe, Colour-Rail

LBSCR 'E6' Class 0-6-2T

Nos 32408, 32409, 32410, 32412-18

> **Introduced** 1904
> **Designed by** Robert Billinton
> **Built by** LBSCR, Brighton
> **Number built** 12
> **Number inherited by BR** 10
> **Last example withdrawn** December 1962

As mentioned earlier, Billinton's 'E3' and 'E5' 0-6-2Ts were goods designs, with smaller coupled wheels. The 'E6s' were a development of the 'E5' (qv), slightly longer with driving wheels 12 inches smaller in diameter, larger cylinders, outside brake rods, higher water tanks and tapered chimneys. The first emerged from Brighton Works at the end of 1904. The 'E5s' and 'E6s' were the only Brighton-built engines to remain largely unaltered during their entire careers.

The 'E3' goods class was suitable for all but the heaviest freights, their smaller wheels enabling quicker acceleration on the congested inner London suburban lines, and the 'E6s' achieved the same result. A dozen locomotives were built by

'E6' 0-6-2T No 32417 was one of the last three of the class withdrawn in December 1962. Minus coupling rods and with 'R.I.P.' chalked on the cabside, the engine is seen on the dump at Hove on 7 June 1963; it was cut up the following October.
K. C. H. Fairey, Colour-Rail

Brighton Works between December 1904 and December 1905. It had been intended that the last two would be built as 0-8-0Ts for heavy shunting duties, but when Billinton died in November 1904, although some components had already been manufactured, the order was changed by Marsh so that all the class were built as 0-6-2Ts (although the last two had heavier, fluted coupling rods intended for the 0-8-0s). The engines mostly worked from sheds such as Norwood Junction, in the heart of the LBSCR's goods-marshalling area.

The first half-dozen carried names, but No 414 *Piccadilly* was the last Brighton engine to carry a name, with just a few exceptions. The last four 'E6s' were never named.

All ten 'E6s' passed to the Southern Railway, and all but two became BR stock in 1948. The last three were withdrawn at the end of 1962.

LBSCR 'E6X' Class 0-6-2T

Nos 32407, 32411

Introduced 1911, as rebuilt
Designed by Robert Billinton; rebuilt by Douglas Earle Marsh
Built by LBSCR, Brighton
Number built 2
Number inherited by BR 2
Last example withdrawn February 1959

The 'E6' 0-6-2Ts (see above) were successful goods locomotives, and in typical Marsh fashion two members of the class, Nos 407 and 411, were taken from stock and rebuilt with the larger 'C3' Class 0-6-0 boiler, mounted on a saddle, and an extended smokebox, being reclassified 'E6X'. They were certainly very powerful, but suffered higher fuel consumption than the originals, so the experiment was discontinued. No 32407 temporarily carried a double-domed boiler, which was later carried by 'E5X' No 32401.

The 'E3Xs' spent their long careers on shunting duties and hauling local goods trains, and both passed through both Southern Railway and BR hands.

'E6X' 0-6-2T No 32407 spent its BR career allocated to Norwood Junction, where it was photographed on 23 February 1957; it was withdrawn in November. This engine had carried a double-domed boiler, but at the end was fitted with a conventional single-dome example. Note the handrail on the dome. *Frank Hornby*

LBSCR 'H1' Class 4-4-2

Nos 32037-39

Robert Billinton died in 1904, and his successor was Douglas Earle Marsh. He had been a pupil of William Dean at Swindon. On the death of Patrick Stirling, Locomotive Superintendent of the Great Northern Railway, in 1895, Henry Ivatt took over at

Introduced 1905
Designed by Douglas Earle Marsh
Built by Kitson
Number built 5
Number inherited by BR 3
Last example withdrawn July 1951

Doncaster, and Marsh was appointed his assistant, and manager of the famous 'Plant'. From there he moved to Brighton, where he was very much a 'new broom', immediately making unpopular changes in locomotive liveries and discontinuing engine naming. It was also announced that his first design would be an express passenger locomotive, an 'Atlantic' that was almost identical to Ivatt's GNR '251' Class,

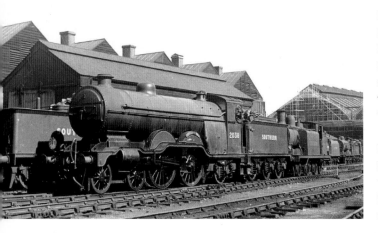

In the very early days of British Railways, and still in full Southern livery, No 2038 *Portland Bill* (named by the SR in May 1925) stands at Brighton on 24 July 1948. Renumbered 32038 in July 1949, it survived until July 1951. Note the attractive undulating running plate. *H. C. Casserley*

with, according to O. S. Nock, 'more regard for publicity than the traffic needs for such a great machine.' Indeed, Marsh took with him a complete set of 'Atlantic' drawings from Doncaster, and marked only detailed changes in red ink before passing them on to the contracted manufacturer, Kitson & Co of Leeds. One stylistic change was arching the running plate over the driving wheels and again over the cylinders, while the chimney and cab were standard Billinton items.

The boiler, larger than any thus far used on the LBSCR, was virtually identical to that of the GNR engine, except for a higher pressure, and the piston stroke was longer, but the 'Atlantics' were not hugely more powerful than Billinton's existing 'B4' 4-4-0s of 1899-1902, and few LBSCR crack expresses required more power. Lawson Billinton was refused permission to superheat the engines, which did not take place until Maunsell's tenure during Southern Railway days. By that time the new 'King Arthur' and 'River' Classes were taking the SR's express services, so the 'H1s' were put on to the boat trains connecting with the Newhaven-Dieppe ferries. At the same time they were at last named, carrying the names of notable landmarks in Southern England. Only one had carried a name in LBSCR days, despite Marsh's dictum, and that was No 39, named *La France* in 1913 when it worked a train from Portsmouth to London carrying the French President; the name was carried until 1926, when it became *Hartland Point*.

After the Second World War the 'Atlantics' found less and less work, and two of them, No 40 *St Catherine's Point* and No 41 *Peveril Point*, were withdrawn in 1944.

No 2039 *Hartland Point* (named *La France* by the LBSCR in 1913 and renamed by the SR in January 1926) was fitted with sleeve valves by Bulleid in 1947 as part of his experiments in preparation for his 'Leader' Class. The engine remained in that condition until it was broken up in March 1951; it is seen here circa 1949 near Lewes. *A. J. Pike, Frank Hornby collection*

In July 1947 Bulleid rebuilt No 39, by now SR No 2039, with sleeve valves as part of his trials in preparation for his revolutionary 'Leader' Class (qv); the loco never ran again in normal traffic, and was never rebuilt to its original form.

The three surviving 'Atlantics', Nos 32037 *Selsey Bill*, 32038 *Portland Bill* and 32039 *Hartland Point*, became BR engines briefly, all being withdrawn in 1951 and scrapped.

LBSCR 'H2' Class 4-4-2

Nos 32421, 32422, 2423, 32424-26

Early in 1911 it became known that Marsh's health was beginning to give concern, and he was in no condition to develop the additional express passenger engines that the LBSCR needed. Instead a superheated version of the 'H1' was ordered, with drawing office work undertaken by Marsh's Chief Draughtsman, B. K. Field. Marsh resigned at the end of the year, and was succeeded by Lawson Billinton, son of Robert. Meanwhile, the new 'Atlantics' emerged from Brighton between June 1911 and January 1912, and shared with the earlier 'H1s' the express services to Brighton, as well as the 'Brighton Limited' and 'Southern Belle' Pullman trains. They could be distinguished from their predecessors by larger cylinders and less undulating running plates.

As with the non-superheated 4-4-2s, they were eventually replaced on the principal services by the new 'King Arthur' and 'River' Classes, but they remained at work on such duties as the Newhaven-Dieppe ferry boat trains. Other workings on which they were found included heavy rush-hour trains from Victoria to East Grinstead, and Brighton-Plymouth services as far as Portsmouth. They were also to be seen on heavy inter-regional summer Saturday holiday trains, which they collected from the LMS at either Kensington Olympia or Mitre Bridge, near Willesden Junction. Following absorption by the Southern

Introduced 1911
Designed by Douglas Earle Marsh
Built by LBSCR, Brighton
Number built 6
Number inherited by BR 6
Last example withdrawn May 1958

'H2' 'Atlantic' No 32424 *Beachy Head* looks immaculate at Eastleigh shed in 1958, but is destined for scrapping. *S. C. Townroe, Colour-Rail*

Railway, like the 'H1s' they were at last given names in 1926, commemorating coastal landmarks of Southern England.

The ferries ceased during the Second World War, and after 1945 the 'Atlantics' found less work, and were either stored or transferred to other areas of the Southern Railway network. No 2423 *The Needles* was withdrawn in 1949 without carrying its BR number, three others lasted until the autumn of 1956, and the last, No 32424 *Beachy Head*, was withdrawn in May 1958.

However, that has proved not to be the end of the story, as in October 2000 the Bluebell Railway announced its intention to reconstruct an 'H2' 'Atlantic', which would take the name

Beachy Head. Its boiler will be that from a GNR 'Atlantic', which as already mentioned in the 'H1' entry above, was virtually identical to that carried by the Brighton engines. An LBSCR 'C2X' tender, latterly used as a water carrier at Guildford, was eventually acquired by the group via Woodham's scrapyard at Barry and the Madame Tussauds 'Royalty and Empire Exhibition' exhibition at Windsor station! The Brighton Atlantic Project continues to progress, and the locomotive is now in an advanced state of construction, so one of these graceful Marsh engines will eventually be seen once more on railway network of Southern England.

LBSCR 'I1X' Class 4-4-2T

Nos 2001-04, 32005, 2006-10, 2595, 2596, 2598, 2599, 2601-04

Marsh's lack of originality in loco design was demonstrated in his 'copy' of the GNR 'Atlantic' to produce his 'H1' Class, and even more so in his 'I1' 4-4-2 tanks of 1906-07, which were again closely copied from a GNR design, but one that was already ten years old and almost obsolete! His GNR counterpart, Ivatt, was building powerful 0-6-2Ts, and the Brighton company had recently built 30 of Billinton's capable 'E5' tanks to that wheel arrangement, so it is surprising that Marsh built what O. S. Nock describes as the 'feeble and outdated' 'I1s'. The first batch of ten carried the numbers 595 to 604, and used the wheels, coupling rods and other parts from retired Stroudley 'D1' and 'D2' locomotives. The remaining ten, oddly, carried lower numbers – in fact, Nos 1-10 – but had a longer coupled wheelbase.

The new tanks quickly developed a reputation as bad steamers and poor performers, which was a distinct disadvantage in their intended role on secondary passenger trains. Once they became Southern Railway property following the Grouping, Maunsell turned his attention to improving them, and between 1925 and 1932 he reboilered all of them with boilers left over from his rebuilding of the 'B4' and 'I3'

Introduced 1925-32 (rebuilt from 1906-07 originals)
Designed by Douglas Earle Marsh; rebuilt by Richard Maunsell
Built by LBSCR, Brighton
Number built 20
Number inherited by BR 18
Last example withdrawn July 1951

No 32005 was the only member of the originally 20-strong 'I1X' Class to carry its BR number, seen here together with the early SR-style 'British Railways' on the tank side. The last of the class to be withdrawn, in July 1951, it was already in store when photographed at Eastbourne shed on 17 April. *W. G. Boyden, Frank Hornby collection*

Classes. These became the 'B4Xs' and 'I3Xs' respectively, while the new 'I1s' duly became the 'I1X' Class, and their performance was greatly improved; perhaps it would have been further improved if piston valves had been fitted in place of the slide valves, but this was not done.

Two locomotives, Nos 2600 and 2597, were withdrawn by the SR in 1944 and 1946 respectively, but the remaining 18 engines passed to BR in 1948, albeit briefly, as all had been sent for scrap by the middle of 1951. BR added 30000 to the SR numbers, but only No 32005 actually carried a BR number.

LBSCR 'I3' Class 4-4-2T

Nos 32021-23, 2025, 32026-30, 32075-79, 2080, 32081-91

Marsh's 'I1' and 'I2' Class 4-4-2Ts had been far less successful than the locomotives they had been intended to replace, but it was perhaps 'third time lucky' with the 'I3s', which had a much larger firebox, and were a tank engine version of R. Billinton's 'B4' 4-4-0s of 1899-1902 (qv), with large 6ft 9in-diameter driving wheels.

The 'superheating' of steam was a subject much under discussion at this time: steam straight from the boiler is 'wet', but when heated by being fed back via superheater elements into the boiler firetubes it becomes much drier and greater in volume, leading to perhaps a 25% greater economy in coal consumption compared with unsuperheated steam. However, at this time the main railway companies were generally prosperous and coal was in plentiful supply, so there was no

Introduced 1907
Designed by Douglas Earle Marsh/Lawson Billinton
Built by LBSCR, Brighton
Number built 27
Number inherited by BR 26
Last example withdrawn May 1952

strong incentive to spend money to effect relatively small economies. Also, royalties had to be paid to the German patent-holder, Schmidt.

In 1907 Marsh ordered two locomotives for comparative purposes, one using a superheater boiler. No 21, built in the autumn of 1907, used conventional 'saturated' steam, while No 22, of March 1908, incorporated a Schmidt superheater in an extended smokebox, smaller wheels but larger cylinders. The 'I3' Class, as they became, were among the first locomotives in Britain fitted with superheaters – certainly the first express passenger engines – and were the largest and best of the LBSCR 4-4-2Ts. Even though the superheated engine performed better than the other, the LBSCR remained unconvinced, so in 1909-10 Marsh built four more superheated locomotives and six without superheating. Eventually the Directors were convinced, and five more locomotives appeared later in 1910. The 'I3s' proved capable of operating the heaviest LBSCR expresses on all routes without difficulty.

Meanwhile, on the London & North Western Railway C. J. Bowen Cooke was the new Chief Mechanical Engineer. He arranged comparative loco trials between the LNWR and other companies, and in 1909, anxious to introduce superheating himself, he proposed exchange working between the LNWR and the LBSCR on the 'Sunny South Express', whose running was already shared by the two companies. An 'I3' 4-4-2T was partnered with an LNWR 'Precursor' 4-4-0, the LBSCR engine running between Rugby and Brighton and return (Rugby to Willesden Junction being run non-stop) without refuelling. The 'I3' created a favourable impression on the LNWR, convincing the company of the value of superheating; the subsequent 'George the Fifths' were all fitted with Schmidt superheaters.

'I3' No 32091 was the last of the class to be withdrawn, from Brighton in May 1952. It is seen here at Three Bridges, its previous shed allocation, on 10 June 1950. In LBSCR days a heaped bunker like the one shown here enabled these superheated engines to run from Rugby to Brighton without replenishment. *H. C. Casserley*

More 'I3s' were built, yet the first three were constructed without superheaters, emphasising the continuing mood of uncertainty at Brighton. The final ten were actually built by L. Billinton, developed from Marsh's design; when the LBSCR became part of the Southern Railway, all the 'I3s' were converted by Maunsell between 1925 and 1927 using his own design of superheater.

As with other early SR steam classes, electrification pushed them towards semi-fast and other secondary services, in the Crowborough, East Grinstead and Tunbridge Wells areas, and more distant places including Salisbury and Dover. During the Second World War two 'I3s' were loaned to the GWR at Gloucester and Worcester. The first withdrawal came in 1944, but the remainder passed to BR, although they had been disposed of by the spring of 1952, all having recorded very high mileages. The last to go, No 32091, had the dubious distinction of being the first former LBSCR express passenger locomotive to be cut up at Ashford.

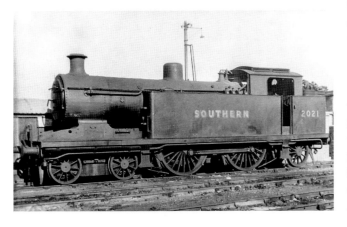

'I3' 'Atlantic' tank No 2021 was one of a pair built by Marsh in 1907-08 for comparative trials between 'saturated' and 'superheated' boilers. No 2021 was the conventional engine, but was fitted with a superheater and extended smokebox in 1919. From 1941 to 1943 it was one of two loaned to the GWR, and is seen here at Tunbridge Wells West in about 1947. *John Stretton collection*

LBSCR 'J1' Class 4-6-2T

No 32325

As the 'I3s' were being built at Brighton there came news of a large new express engine under construction with a 'Pacific' 4-6-2 wheel arrangement. An enlarged version of the 4-4-2T 'I3' with outside cylinders and a bigger boiler, it was clearly intended as the prototype of a new class.

No 325 was completed in December 1910, and could be considered Marsh's masterpiece. It was to have been numbered 36, then 100, then 325 was settled on, left vacant by the scrapping of the Stroudley 'Single' No 325 *Abergavenny*. Despite his rule about engine naming, Marsh was persuaded to allow the new engine to perpetuate the name of the older one. Another engine was to have been built with Walschaerts valve gear, for comparison, then a class of 20 was proposed – but Marsh's health was in decline, and 'H2' 'Atlantics' were built instead.

The 'J1' was the first 4-6-2 express tank engine to be built in Britain, and its intended role was to haul the heaviest London-Brighton expresses. It was fitted with a Schmidt superheater and Stephenson valve gear. The driving wheels were 6ft 7½in in diameter, the bunker held 3 tons of coal and the tanks 2,300 gallons of water; at 89 tons it was the LBSCR's largest express

> **Introduced** 1910
> **Designed by** Douglas Earle Marsh
> **Built by** LBSCR, Brighton
> **Number built** 1
> **Number inherited by BR** 1
> **Last example withdrawn** June 1951

A Southern Railway-era portrait of No 2325 *Abergavenny* (in LBSCR days the name was painted on the tank side) at Eastleigh in April 1938. *Colour-Rail collection*

passenger tank locomotive until the arrival of L. Billinton's 4-6-4 'Baltic' tank in 1914 (see 'N15X' entry below).

A second locomotive was ordered in May 1911, but Marsh had soon departed on extended sick leave and all work stopped.

As Southern Railway No 2325, it and its sister loco No 2326 *Bessborough* (see below) were displaced by the spread of electrification, and began to be used more on lighter express services. After the electrification of the Brighton main line in 1935 they were transferred to Eastbourne shed, working between there and London on the 'Sunny South Express' until the war, when they went into storage, then moved to Tunbridge Wells. In June 1951 both engines were replaced by new LMS-design Fairburn 2-6-4Ts and were withdrawn from Brighton shed.

LBSCR 'J2' Class 4-6-2T

No 32326

Marsh stepped down due to ill health in 1911, so his successor, Lawson Billinton, made detailed changes to the design and work on the second 4-6-2 tank resumed. Completed in March 1912, this time the engine had outside Walschaerts valve gear and slightly smaller water tanks, and was classified 'J2'. It was named *Bessborough* (although the original name was to have

> **Introduced** 1912
> **Designed by** Douglas Earle Marsh/Lawson Billinton
> **Built by** LBSCR, Brighton
> **Number built** 1
> **Number inherited by BR** 1
> **Last example withdrawn** June 1951

been *Grosvenor*). Like its sister, No 326 performed well, but was considered the quicker of the pair. With the 'H1' and 'H2' 'Atlantic' tender engines, both 'Pacific' tanks were used on the heaviest trains into Southern Railway days.

No 326's cab was altered in 1913, and after the Grouping the chimney and dome of both *Bessborough* and *Abergavenny* were cut down to fit the new SR loading gauge. The subsequent history of No 326/2326/32326 mirrors that of its sister No 32325 – see above – and they were both withdrawn in June 1951.

'J2' 4-6-2T No 2326, the former *Bessborough*, was photographed in full Southern livery at Tunbridge Wells West on the eve of nationalisation in September 1947. *J. M. Jarvis, Colour-Rail*

LBSCR 'K' Class 2-6-0

Nos 32337-53

Introduced 1913
Designed by Lawson Billinton
Built by LBSCR, Brighton
Number built 17
Number inherited by BR 17
Last example withdrawn December 1962

One of Lawson Billinton's businesslike 'K' Class 'Moguls', No 32343, is seen in October 1959. The whole class was withdrawn en bloc at the end of 1962. *Colour-Rail collection*

Being primarily a passenger railway, the LBSCR had relatively little need for heavy freight locomotives, but those that were used needed to have smart acceleration to avoid blocking intensively used passenger lines, especially when those lines were electrified. These 2-6-0 mixed-traffic engines, built to avoid the increasing practice of having to double-head Marsh's rebuilt 'C2X' 0-6-0s, were Billinton junior's most powerful design for the company, and probably the most successful overall. The first batch of five emerged from Brighton Works just before the outbreak of the First World War, and a further five followed in 1916, delayed by Government restrictions and difficulty in obtaining materials. During the conflict they did sterling work on supply, troop and munitions trains to South Coast ports; they could reportedly haul trains of up to 1,000 tons at 30-35mph. Ten more were to be built after the war; seven appeared in 1920-21, but after the Grouping in 1923 the Southern Railway decided not to proceed with the remainder.

Billinton's new 'K' Class incorporated several innovations: they were the first 2-6-0s operated by the LBSCR, and the first to carry Belpaire fireboxes. The boilers were superheated, Stephenson valve gear and piston valves were used, and surplus steam was redirected into the large tenders to preheat the feedwater. Although primarily goods engines, they had steam sanding apparatus and steam carriage heating equipment so they could be used on passenger trains.

After the first two engines were built in 1913, slight modifications were made as a result of thorough testing, and by 1916 there were ten at work. Following the war, Billinton considered a 2-6-2T version, but the Civil Engineer objected to the elongated wheelbase, and the lower water capacity would prove to be a problem. In the latter years of the LBSCR era Billinton used the 'Ks' as test beds for various experiments with specialised equipment.

In Southern Railway ownership the engines were used on the Central Section, which had a more generous loading gauge, but by the outbreak of the Second World War modifications to the chimney, dome and cab gave them a wider availability. In comparative trials with freight engines from other SR constituent companies, the 'Ks' were found to be more expensive to run than Maunsell's 'Ns' and Urie's 'S15s', so no more were built, although in the long run the 'Ks' proved to be more reliable and robust than the other classes. Once again, the 'Moguls' did invaluable work during the Second World War, especially in preparation for the D-Day landings in 1944.

All 17 of the 'K' Class passed to BR in 1948, still in good shape and doing useful work; even as freight declined, they found a new role on Newhaven boat trains following the withdrawal of Marsh's 'Atlantics' in the mid-1950s. It was accountancy considerations rather than physical condition that led to the entire class being withdrawn at the end of 1962. Most went into store at Hove before being broken up in 1963-64. Sussex's Bluebell Railway, a pioneer in preservation, originally hoped to obtain a variety of historically significant Southern locos, and a 'K' was on its 'wish list', but at the time the money was not available (being used to purchase the line's freehold), so sadly the opportunity was lost.

Lawson Billinton considered the 'K' class to be his finest design, and during his retirement he constructed a one-sixth-scale working model. This was sold in recent years for more than £40,000.

LBSCR Class 'N15X' 4-6-0

Introduced 1914-22 (as 4-6-4T); rebuilt as 4-6-0 1934-36
Designed by Lawson Billinton; rebuilt by Richard Maunsell
Built by LBSCR, Brighton
Number built 7
Number inherited by BR 7
Last example withdrawn July 1957

Nos 32327-33

Rather than further develop his new 4-6-2 tanks (qv 'J1' and 'J2' above), Billinton went one step further with his 4-6-4 'L' Class 'Baltic' tanks, the LBSCR's last entirely new locomotive design. As the LBSCR was a relatively short line, large tank locomotives with adequate water capacity were seen as ideal. Billinton therefore set about enlarging the design of the

The last of the 'N15X', or 'Remembrance', Class, No 32331 *Beattie*, makes a fine sight on a Ramblers Association special at Windsor & Eton Riverside on 23 June 1957, just a month before withdrawal. *T. B. Owen, Colour-Rail*

they were only half full, leading to derailments, so the water space was reduced within the tank. There was a suggestion that this problem could be solved by rebuilding them as tender engines, but this was discarded – although that very conversion was to take place 20 years later.

The second batch of seven had well tanks and shallower side tanks, although still within the same shell for the sake of class uniformity, and proved to be fast, stable and powerful locomotives. The Stephenson Locomotive Society, which had a close association with the Brighton company, suggested that one of the 'Ls' should be named *Stephenson*, becoming one of a dozen locomotives from a Manchester & Leeds 0-4-2 in 1839 to a BR electric 136 years later to be named in honour of the 'father of railways'; the naming took place in 1921. The last of the seven, No 333, was chosen to be the LBSCR's war memorial engine, to be named *Remembrance*; an additional plaque read: 'In grateful remembrance of the 532 men of the L.B.& S.C.Rly. who gave their lives for their country, 1914-19'.

In the early 1930s the engines were made redundant by electrification of the Brighton main line; they were too heavy for secondary duties, but still had plenty of life left in them, so the SR's CME, Maunsell, decided to rebuild them as 4-6-0 tender locos, extending their useful lives and putting them to work alongside his new 'N15' 'King Arthurs' on the Western Section. The 1934-36 rebuilds, similar in appearance to the 'Arthurs', and fitted with SR-style smoke deflectors, thus became reclassified as 'N15X' (the 'X' being the traditional LBSCR designation for a rebuilt/modified locomotive). They were coupled to large eight-wheel bogie tenders. At the same time the remaining five engines were named; *Charles C. Macrae* became *Trevithick*, and the others also commemorated locomotive engineers of the past, as suggested by Maunsell's assistant, Harry Holcroft – *Hackworth*, *Cudworth*, *Beattie* and *Stroudley*. The existing names *Stephenson* and *Remembrance* were transferred to the new engines.

Crews were disappointed to discover that the 'new' 'N15s' were no real improvement on the existing 'King Arthurs', and they gained a reputation for rough-riding and as relatively poor performers. They were thus put to work on secondary duties, cross-country and inter-regional trains around the Basingstoke area, rather than on the crack West of England expresses for which they had originally been intended. During the Second World War five of the class were loaned to the GWR to assist with freight traffic.

All seven 'Remembrances' passed to British Railways, but by then they were being usurped by the increasing numbers of Bulleid 'Pacifics', and they were all withdrawn from service between 1955 and 1957, No 32327 *Trevithick* as a result of collision damage at Woking on 23 December 1955.

The sad sight of 'N15X' No 32328 *Hackworth* being dismantled at Eastleigh in June 1955. It had been taken out of service in January of that year. *S. C. Townroe, Colour-Rail*

'Pacific' tank locomotives, with more capacity for both water and coal.

Reversing Marsh's earlier dislike of named engines, the first 'Baltic' tank, No 327, was named *Charles C. Macrae* (an LBSCR Director, and Chairman from 1920 to 1922) and was completed at Brighton in April 1914. It was, as described by O. S. Nock, 'a remarkably handsome machine though entirely in the style developed by the elder Billinton and continued by Marsh.' It was intended that the class would number seven machines, but only two were built at first; the remaining five did not appear until 1921-22. They were the most powerful engines in the South of England, and it was claimed that they had the capacity to run from London Victoria to Portsmouth non-stop, a distance of 87 miles.

The two outside cylinders with Walschaerts valve gear were the largest ever fitted to a Brighton locomotive. Initially there was a problem with water surging in the huge side tanks when

SR/BR 'Leader' Class 0-6-6-0T

Nos 36001-04

Introduced 1949
Designed by Oliver Bulleid
Built by SR/BR, Brighton
Number built 2, plus 2 not completed
Number inherited by BR 2, plus 2 not completed
Last example withdrawn November 1950

Novel, controversial, far-sighted, revolutionary – just some of the adjectives applied to Bulleid's remarkable new steam locomotive design. It arose as a result of a requirement by the post-war Southern Railway for a high-powered, high-availability, low-maintenance, mixed-traffic steam locomotive to replace ageing stock, such as the 'M7' tanks. Bulleid's design was basically two three-cylinder six-wheeled bogies (to spread the considerable weight) articulated beneath a single boiler, and the concept was to push the boundaries of steam locomotive design and by so doing incorporate some of the advantages of the emerging modern diesel and electric locomotives and obviate some of the operational disadvantages and labour-intensiveness of the conventional steam loco. There were cabs at both ends, diesel-like, and the firebox and fireman were located in the middle. Design work began in 1946, and development continued into BR days following railway nationalisation in 1948.

In July 1946 Bulleid wrote to the SR's General Manager, Sir Eustace Missenden, to announce that his new design would satisfy the requirements of the Traffic Manager and Civil Engineer, would have a top speed of 90mph, would be able to handle any train that a 'Q1' or 'light Pacific' could work, and would be able to run over almost all the SR network – claims that would ultimately not be fulfilled.

As with any machine of so innovative a design, there were many obstacles and disappointments – so many, that eventually the long-drawn-out and very costly developmental work was cancelled by British Railways. There were initially to be five locomotives in the 'Leader' Class, but just one, No 36001, was completed, steamed and operated out on the line. No 36002 was also completed, but never steamed, while Nos 36003 and 36004 were only partially built when the project was abandoned. By 1951 Bulleid had left BR to became CME of the railways of the Irish Republic (where he produced a peat-burning locomotive of similar design), and during that year what remained of the 'Leader' Class was quietly scrapped. An order for a further 31 had been placed in 1947, but impending nationalisation and general lack of progress rendered this stillborn. In 1953 a press report claimed that the modern equivalent of some £15 million had been absorbed by the 'Leader' project.

The 'Leader' employed oscillating sleeve valves, the moving parts lubricated by oil baths, echoing contemporary internal-combustion engine practice. Unfortunately, this arrangement proved overly complicated, as was the case with the cylinder blocks, which were difficult to machine accurately. The bogies were designed to be interchangeable, making the engines much easier to maintain and overhaul, and the boiler, perhaps

The only 'Leader' 0-6-6-0T to run out on the line, No 36001 is seen at Eastleigh receiving finishing touches in June 1949. One unpopular aspect of the design was that, although the locomotive was tall, at nearly 13 feet, the size of the bogie meant that the driving cab ceilings were uncomfortably low. Despite the diesel-like appearance of the 'Leader', the driving wheels were 5ft 1in in diameter, compared with, for example, the 3ft 9in of a Type 40 diesel-electric. *S. C. Townroe, Colour-Rail*

the design's most successful element, was a good steamer, incorporating the designer's 'thermic siphons' in the firebox as used in his SR 'Pacifics'.

The firebox was lined by firebricks, rather than using a water jacket as in a conventional boiler. The grate area was relatively small and the firing space was cramped and almost unbearably hot for the poor fireman – although oil-firing, as originally envisaged, would have alleviated this somewhat. (This discomfort led to the uncomplimentary and punning nickname of 'Bleeder', as well as 'Chinese Laundry'). The smokebox proved problematic, as its innovative design made maintaining a vacuum difficult, and the sharp exhaust blast ejected ash and embers into the air. The overall body casing allowed the engine to be washed in a carriage-cleaning plant, like a diesel locomotive.

No 36001 undertook a year of trials, but the results were far from encouraging, and did not endear the project to the rather reactionary members of the new nationalised Railway Executive. Fuel consumption was heavy; it was mechanically unreliable; the working conditions for both fireman and driver were unpleasant (the driver's cab at the smokebox ended suffered from excessive heat, so the engine was usually driven from the other end only, requiring frequent turning); the offsetting of the boiler, firebox and coal bunker (to accommodate a linking corridor between the cabs) affected the centre of gravity, which could only be rectifying by adding counterweights, increasing the already considerable weight; and the firebrick lining of the firebox collapsed into the fire (and several modifications failed to overcome the shortcomings of the lining). Because the firing compartment was so hot, the fireman's access door was kept open to provide ventilation. Since the fireman could only enter from one side, should the locomotive overturn on that side he would have no opportunity to escape, something that the ASLEF union was quick to point out.

Although a first-rate steamer, and when handled properly an effective runner, No 36001 was never used on a revenue-earning service because of the risk of adverse publicity for the new BR should it fail. On its final outing, on 2 November 1950, it reportedly hauled 15 coaches uphill at an average speed of 50mph, and running alone it reached 90mph near Winchester, apparently riding as smoothly as a passenger coach. But it was all too late. Since nothing survives of the engines, the 'Leader' project remains one of the great 'might-have-beens' of British locomotive development.

LSWR '0330' Class 0-6-0ST

No 4

This final locomotive in the list of former Southern Railway locomotive classes that passed to BR but of which none were preserved is included by the skin of its teeth!

William George Beattie was Locomotive Engineer of the LSWR between 1871 and 1878, following his father, Joseph Beattie; he had joined the LSWR as a draughtsman at Nine Elms Works in 1862. His '330' Class 0-6-0T saddle tanks, known as 'Saddlebacks', were ordered from Beyer Peacock in three batches in 1876, 1877 and 1882, and were put to work on shunting duties. Between 1894 and 1911, all 20 were placed on the duplicate list, and their numbers were prefixed by '0'. The first examples were withdrawn by the Southern Railway, and at the end of 1930 there were only five left. Of these, No 0335 was sent to the Kent & East Sussex Railway in 1932 with two carriages and spare boilers in return for 0-8-0T No 949 *Hecate* (qv). The last SR examples went in 1933, but No 0335, renumbered 4 by the KESR, remained in serviceable condition on that line long enough to pass into BR hands at nationalisation in 1948. It was not allocated a BR number, and its brief BR career ended in May, when it was withdrawn; it was scrapped in August.

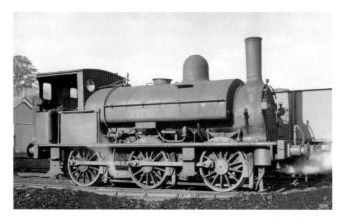

Former LSWR/SR 0-6-0ST No 0335, by now KESR No 4, poses on the Kent & East Sussex Railway at Rolvenden in 1947, just before it briefly became BR property. *J. M. Jarvis, R. M. Casserley collection*

Introduced 1876
Designed by William Beattie
Built by Beyer Peacock
Number built 20
Number inherited by BR 1, from KESR
Last example withdrawn May 1948

3

Locomotives of the former London Midland & Scottish Railway and its constituents

LMS Fowler 3MT 2-6-2T

Nos 40001-70

Henry Fowler, born in Evesham in 1870, began his railway career as an apprentice to Aspinall at the Horwich Works of the Lancashire & Yorkshire Railway in 1887. He then worked under George Hughes and became Gas Engineer to the company from 1895 to 1900. In the latter year he moved to the Midland Railway, where in 1909 he succeeded Deeley as Chief Mechanical Engineer. In 1919 he was knighted for his work for several Government departments during the First World War.

During the 1920s locomotive development at Derby was largely static, and with just a few exceptions remained firmly entrenched in the Midland's 'small engine policy' tradition, where double-heading was frequent for lack of suitably powerful locomotives. This policy gave rise to a rhyme:

'M is for Midland with engines galore
Two on each train and asking for more.'

Fowler was easygoing and tolerant of interference in loco matters from above. He also seems to have been a much-

Introduced	1930
Designed by	Sir Henry Fowler
Built by	LMS, Derby
Number built	70
Number inherited by BR	70
Last example withdrawn	December 1962

respected 'engineer's engineer', happy in the company of fellow members of the Institutions of Civil and Mechanical Engineers.

In 1923 he became CME of the young LMS, which in its early years suffered from conflicts between its constituent companies, each struggling to exercise its respective influence. He retired in 1930 to concentrate on research, and two years later was replaced by William Stanier from the GWR, the 'new broom' that LMS President Josiah felt the company needed. Sir Henry died in 1938.

Although BR's first class of ex-LMS locomotives numerically, having been LMS Nos 15500-69, then, from 1934, Nos 1 to 70, these were a late Fowler design, and not a successful one. Having introduced his 4MT 2-6-4T class in 1927 (qv), these 2-6-2 tanks followed in four lots between 1930 and 1932. They were designed for general suburban and branch-line duties, but their pre-Stanier parallel boilers were inadequate and they were poor performers.

Nos 40022-40 were fitted with condensing apparatus to enable them to work on the Metropolitan 'Widened Lines', to which the Midland main line was connected at St Pancras. Nine of the class were also fitted with push-pull equipment in order to work 'motor' trains. Whatever their shortcomings, the class remained intact until 1958, but more than half had been withdrawn by the end of the following year, the last survivors being dispensed with in 1962.

3P 2-6-2T No 40026, a Kentish Town engine until withdrawal at the end of 1962, stands at St Pancras on an unspecified date, in a scene that has changed beyond all recognition since the station's 'International' transformation. This was one of the class fitted with condensing apparatus to enable them to work on the Metropolitan 'Widened Lines'. *Colour-Rail collection*

LMS Stanier 3MT 2-6-2T

Nos 40071-209

Despite his locomotives being perhaps the defining image of LMS motive power from 1932 until nationalisation – and even beyond into BR 'Standard' days – William Arthur Stanier was born in the heart of Great Western country at Swindon in 1876. Not surprisingly, his father worked for the GWR, as William Dean's Chief Clerk, and William followed his father into the Works, where he was a draughtsman until becoming Inspector of Materials in 1900. In 1904 Churchward made him Assistant to the Divisional Locomotive Superintendent in London, then in 1912 he returned to Swindon as Assistant Works Manager, then Works Manager eight years later.

Introduced	1935
Designed by	William Stanier
Built by	LMS, Derby
Number built	139
Number inherited by BR	139
Last example withdrawn	December 1962

When Henry Fowler retired, Stanier was head-hunted by the LMS and, though reluctant to leave Swindon, where he would have loved to become Chief Mechanical Engineer, he left with the GWR's blessing, but took with him a distinct 'Great Westernness' influenced by his mentor, Churchward. He was knighted in 1943 and elected a Fellow of the Royal Society

3P 2-6-2T No 40087 stands out of use at its home shed of Nuneaton on 12 April 1963, having been withdrawn the previous November. It was scrapped in August. Note the juxtaposition of electrification gantries and semaphore signals in this transition period on the West Coast Main Line. *Colour-Rail collection*

Stanier reversed the company's 'small engine' policy, and revolutionised its locomotive affairs.

One of the GWR features that Stanier brought to the LMS was Churchward's celebrated taper boiler innovation, and these 2-6-2Ts were a taper-boiler version of Fowler's earlier class (see above), but otherwise of similar dimensions. Unfortunately, like the Fowler class they were considered poor performers, perhaps more so, and far from their designer's best work.

Designed as mixed-traffic engines, their roles included local, suburban and branch-line passenger services as well as empty stock trains and banking duties. The cab was well-designed, with the rear bunker sides angled inwards to give good visibility through the rear windows when running in reverse. Another distinguishing feature was that the tops of the side tanks had a pronounced slope towards the front.

The first two batches, LMS Nos 71-144, built in 1935, had domeless boilers, while the remainder (two batches totalling 39 in 1937, and two further batches totalling 26 in 1938) had a separate top-feed and steam dome. Between 1940 and 1956 six members of the class were fitted with larger boilers in an effort to improve their performance, but the exercise was found not to be cost-effective.

Just as with their Fowler predecessors, the class remained intact until 1958, half had been withdrawn by the end of 1961, and the last 16 were taken out of service in December 1962.

the following year, when he retired from the LMS; he was the only railway engineer other than George Stephenson to receive this honour. He was also President of the Institution of Mechanical Engineers. Appointed to the LMS on 1 January 1932, with the encouragement of LMS President Josiah Stamp

MR/SDJR Johnson/Fowler 2P Class 4-4-0

Nos 40322-26

Introduced 1914; rebuilt 1921	
Designed by Samuel Johnson; rebuilt by Sir Henry Fowler	
Built by MR, Derby	
Number built 5	
Number inherited by BR 5	
Last example withdrawn October 1956	

These five Johnson-designed engines, identical in design to the '40332' Class (see below), were built for the Somerset & Dorset Joint Railway, in which the Midland Railway was a partner with the London & South Western Railway, and which remained outside the Grouping arrangements of 1923. They were rebuilt by Fowler in 1921, as MR Nos 322-26, and worked on the SDJR until absorbed into LMS stock in 1930. They were withdrawn by BR between 1951 and 1956.

Former SDJR 2P No 40326 is back at its birthplace on 8 May 1955, working as station pilot. Shedded at Templecombe at nationalisation, it then travelled north to Skipton, Leeds and Hellifield until 1952, when it returned to Derby. It was withdrawn in May the following year. *John Stretton collection*

MR Johnson/Deeley/Fowler 2P Class 4-4-0

Nos 40332, 40337, 40351, 40353, 40356, 40359, 40362, 40364, 40370, 40377, 40383, 385, 391, 394, 40395-97, 400, 40401, 40402, 403, 40404, 40405, 406, 40407, 408, 40409-27, 40430, 40432-34, 40436, 437, 40438, 40439, 40443, 40444, 446, 40447, 40448, 40450, 40452-55, 456, 40458, 40459, 40461-64, 466, 468, 40470-72, 40477, 40478, 479, 40480, 40482, 483, 40484-89, 490, 40491, 492, 40493, 494, 40495, 496, 40497-505, 506, 40507-09, 510, 40511, 512, 40513-16, 517, 40518-29, 530, 40531-43, 544, 545, 40546-48, 549, 40550-53, 554, 555, 40556-60, 561, 40562

2P 4-4-0 No 40543 is signalled to take the Nuneaton and Birmingham line at Wigston North Junction, south of Leicester, in 1959. Built at Derby in 1901, the 2P was withdrawn from Leicester Midland shed in January 1961, having been allocated there throughout its BR days. *G. D. King, Colour-Rail*

Samuel Johnson was a very experienced locomotive engineer by the time he joined the Midland Railway in 1873, having worked for several locomotive manufacturers as well as the Great Northern, the Manchester, Sheffield & Lincolnshire, the Edinburgh & Glasgow, the North British and the Great Eastern companies. But it was at Derby that he appears to have found his niche, succeeding Matthew Kirtley as Locomotive Superintendent until 1903.

Most of the passenger engines he built for the Midland were of the 4-4-0 type rather than the 4-2-2 'singles' of the Kirtley era, although he designed those too. A series of 12 4-4-0 classes were produced between 1876 and 1901, and at first they were able to handle normal express passenger duties. However, as trains became heavier they were used double-headed, and eventually relegated to secondary work when more powerful engines were introduced. They were frequently rebuilt over their long lives, sometimes involving the replacement of almost all their original parts.

> **Introduced** 1882; rebuilt from 1904 and 1912
> **Designed by** Samuel Johnson; rebuilt by Richard Deeley and Sir Henry Fowler
> **Built by** MR, Derby
> **Number built** 235
> **Number inherited by BR** 160
> **Last example withdrawn** September 1962

Johnson's original 30 4-4-0s of 1876-77 were never rebuilt, but the remainder, built between 1882 and 1901, were rebuilt by Deeley from 1904 onwards, some with extended smokeboxes and Belpaire fireboxes. Between 1901 and 1912 Deeley rebuilt 15 of the class without superheaters, and three of these, Nos 383, 385 and 391, lasted into BR ownership

Most of the engines were rebuilt again between 1912 and 1923 by Fowler, with superheaters and new frames, thus becoming virtually new engines, and the subsequent standard LMS design of Class 2 passenger engine was based on the same design (see below). The reason for describing the exercise as 'rebuilds' may have been that the royalty paid to the Schmidt superheater company was less for a rebuild than for a new engine. BR took over 160 of this class of 2Ps, and they worked on all parts of the system, from the North West to the Midlands, and from Carlisle to North Wales and Gloucester, with a handful on the Somerset & Dorset line.

LMS Fowler 2P Class 4-4-0

Nos 40563-90, 40592-638, 40640-700

> **Introduced** 1928
> **Designed by** Sir Henry Fowler
> **Built by** LMS, Derby
> **Number built** 138
> **Number inherited by BR** 136
> **Last example withdrawn** December 1962

This class was designed by Sir Henry Fowler, and 138 locomotives were produced between 1928 and 1932 as the next generation of Class 2 4-4-0s, becoming the standard LMS Class 2 design; they naturally followed on from the earlier examples introduced by Johnson from 1882 and rebuilt by Deeley and Fowler in the 20th century (see above). They had slightly smaller driving wheels compared with their predecessors, higher-pressure boilers and reduced boiler mountings to enable them to work over all areas of the LMS. Like the earlier engines, they were often used double-headed, perpetuating

the Midland Railway's 'small engine' policy that pertained until the Stanier era.

All but two of the class passed to BR on nationalisation – Nos 591 and 639 had been scrapped following at accident on 6 September 1934 when two local trains collided head-on at Port

Fowler 2P 4-4-0 No 40564 emerged from Derby Works at the end of April 1928, and was allocated to Templecombe shed for the whole of its life with BR. It is seen here looking a little the worse for wear double-heading with SDJR 7F 2-8-0 No 53810 of 1925 at Radstock North station on a Bournemouth-Sheffield Saturdays-only service on 2 September 1961. No 40564 lasted until February 1962, and the 7F until December 1963; happily, two of the 2-8-0s survive in preservation. *Dave Cobbe collection, Rail Photoprints. co.uk*

Eglinton Junction, near Glasgow, due to missed signals.

Originally numbered 563-700, they all received 'plus 40000' BR numbers between 1948 and 1951. Being able to work throughout the former LMS system, the locomotives were found far and wide, being allocated to sheds in the former Glasgow & South Western Junction area of Scotland, such as Stranraer, Hurlford and Dumfries, the North West and the East and West Midlands, as well as North Wales. Many became especially associated with the former Somerset & Dorset line, being allocated to the sheds at Templecombe and Bath Green Park; indeed, three, Nos 633-35, had been built for the SDJR in 1928, and only entered LMS stock when the larger company absorbed the S&D stock in 1930.

The class remained virtually intact until 1959, when mass withdrawals began. By the end of 1961 only 15 remained in service, and the last, No 40670, one of the Scottish allocation, succumbed in December 1962.

It is a sobering thought that between 1948 and 1962, the era of BR's 'Modernisation' plans, from these three 2P classes *alone* some 300 locomotives were consigned to scrap.

MR Johnson/Fowler 3P Class 4-4-0

Nos 711, 715, 720, 40726, 727, 40728, 729, 731, 734-36, 739, 40740, 40741, 40743, 40745, 40747, 748, 756, 757, 40758, 762

Introduced 1900; rebuilt from 1913
Designed by Samuel Johnson; rebuilt by Sir Henry Fowler
Built by MR, Derby
Number built 80
Number inherited by BR 22
Last example withdrawn September 1952

Heavier and faster locomotives were required by the Midland for the new corridor trains running over the Settle & Carlisle route. The new Class 3 4-4-0s introduced in 1900 were a major departure from previous Johnson styling, and also brought with them significant changes in Midland locomotive matters. The most radical change was the use of the Belpaire firebox, which took Midland style firmly out of the Victorian age. In all, 80 of the 'Belpaires' were built, and in their original form they were coupled to huge eight-wheel bogie tenders.

The first 10 engines, with 170psi boilers, emerged from Derby in 1900-01; the next 60 had a larger, higher-pressure boiler and were built between 1902 and 1904, and the final 20 came out in 1904-05 with boilers pressed to 200psi. Seventy-three of the class were rebuilt by Fowler between 1913 and 1925 with superheated boilers and larger cylinders. All had 6ft 9in driving wheels with inside cylinders (the seven unsuperheated engines were withdrawn shortly after the Grouping).

In 1900 *The Railway Magazine*'s Charles Rous-Marten wrote: 'This new type has virtually come in with the new century, and is a complete departure from Midland tradition in several respects … its advent constitutes an epoch in Midland, if not also in British, locomotive practice.'

The first batch were sent to Leeds to work the Carlisle route, with first-class results, establishing themselves as very speedy engines. O. S. Nock recalls a report that one of them attained 96mph running downhill from Blea Moor towards Settle, but this was at a time when excessive train speeds were causing public

Former MR 'Belpaire' 3P 4-4-0 No 40758 stands at Leeds Holbeck shed on 29 April 1949, clearly showing its flat-topped firebox. This engine was one of only ten of the original class of 80 still in use at the end of that year, and one of only eight to carry its BR number, applied the previous August. It was taken out of service in March 1951, by which time it was allocated to Bedford. *H. C. Casserley*

disquiet, so this feat, whatever the undisclosed circumstances, was not publicised. It was not until the introduction of the 'Compounds' (see below) that such advances were made again.

In many ways the Class 3s were superior to the Johnson/Fowler 2Ps of 1882-1901 (rebuilt 1912-23), although they were heavy on coal, so the standard LMS 4-4-0 was developed from the Fowler 2Ps of 1928-32 (all qv).

One of the 'Belpaires', No 714, was destroyed in the collision at Charfield, between Gloucester and Yate, on 13 October 1928

when hauling a southbound mail train. The driver overran signals and hit a goods train that was reversing into a refuge siding to clear a path for the express. Rebounding from the collision, the mail hit an up goods train that happened to passing through Charfield station in the opposite direction at the same time. Fifteen lives were lost in the ensuing conflagration.

Withdrawals of the remaining engines began in 1935, and although 22 3Ps passed to British Railways, all had been withdrawn within five years.

LMS Fowler 4P 'Compound' Class 4-4-0

Nos 40900-39, 41045-199

Normally steam produced by a locomotive is used just once in a cylinder, then exhausted to the atmosphere. 'Compounding' involves the expansion of steam through two cylinders; after use in a high-pressure cylinder, it is passed to a larger-diameter low-pressure cylinder before being exhausted. This provides a 10-15% increase in power output. Compounding had been used on the continent and in Britain since the 1870s, but in 1898 W. M. Smith, chief draughtsman at the North Eastern Railway's Gateshead Works, invented a system for compound expansion utilising one inside high-pressure cylinder coupled to two outside low-pressure cylinders, which was used experimentally on three NER locomotives.

This system was used in 1902 by Samuel Johnson in his '1000' Class 2P 4-4-0s, one of which, No 1000 itself, is preserved as part of the National Collection. His design was modified by Deeley for a further batch of engines in 1905-06; overall, they are generally considered to have been the only really successful compound engines to run in Britain. The final version acted as the basis for the 195 locomotives built by Fowler for the LMS from 1924, becoming that company's standard compound design, and the only class of LMS 4-4-0s with outside cylinders. Between 1924 and 1927 190 engines were built, initially by Derby Works, then Horwich Works in conjunction with outside contractors. They had 6ft 9in driving wheels, 3 inches smaller than the earlier classes. Five final examples, Nos 935-39, were built by Derby in 1932, and more were on order, but when

Introduced 1924
Designed by Sir Henry Fowler
Built by Vulcan Foundry (75), LMS, Derby (75), LMS, Horwich (20), North British (25)
Number built 195
Number inherited by BR 195
Last example withdrawn July 1961

Stanier took over in that year these were cancelled, as he had different ideas for the development of LMS motive power.

The first batches took the numbers 1045 to 1199, then confusingly later engines were numbered 900 to 939. Some had shorter chimneys to suit the Scottish loading gauge, while others incorporated various modifications. They were put to work in many parts of the new LMS system, not only on former Midland lines but also on the Caledonian and Glasgow & South Western routes, and on the West Coast Main Line, heading the Birmingham '2 hour' expresses (although treated with some distrust there, due to memories of Webb's earlier unsuccessful compounding experiments). Those used in Scotland were well liked, being more economical in operation than former LNWR and Caledonian 4-6-0s, as proved during a series of comparison tests at the end of 1924 over the fiercely graded Leeds-Carlisle route. The LNWR engine, a 'Claughton', was free-running, but steamed poorly and was heavy on fuel. The Caledonian engine steamed better, but performed relatively poorly, while the 'Compound' showed the best and most economic performance, and was therefore chosen as the LMS standard. However, tests on the Somerset & Dorset line at the same time compared a 'Compound' with a 'simple' ex-MR 2P 4-4-0, where the former did not markedly outperform the latter due to its inability to develop sufficient tractive effort at low speeds.

Strangely, within three months of the Charfield collision (see previous entry), on 8 January 1929 the driver of 4P 'Compound' No 1060, on an up express from Bristol to Leeds, overran signals in fog approaching Ashchurch and collided with a goods train that, as at Charfield, was being shunted out of its way. Four people were killed, including the driver of the

4P 'Compound' 4-4-0 No 41071 emerged from the darkness at Leeds on 23 October 1958. A Holbeck engine (having been previously allocated to Kettering, Kentish Town, Bedford and Millhouses), this was its last year of service. *W. P. de Beer, Colour-Rail*

'Compound'. Both accidents stressed the need for the adoption of Automatic Train Control to prevent overrunning of signals.

The relatively complex mechanism of the 'Compounds' suffered from poor maintenance during and after the Second World War, and they were put on secondary services to which they were not suited, gaining a poor reputation as a result. The class remained fairly intact until 1954-55, but only two remained in service by the end of 1960, vanishing the following year.

MR Johnson 0F Class 0-4-0ST

Nos 1509, 41516, 41518, 41523

Introduced 1883
Designed by Samuel Johnson
Built by MR, Derby
Number built 30
Number inherited by BR 4
Last example withdrawn February 1958

In 1883 the first 0-4-0, and the first saddle tank, built by the Midland Railway emerged from Derby Works. Classified by the MR as '1322', '116A' and '1134A', the first batch of five engines, the '1322' Class, was designed for shunting in the Works yard, replacing and improving on four old Manning Wardle engines. One source claims that they were nicknamed 'Jinties' from their 'J' class boilers, a name that was later wrongly applied to the Class 3 0-6-0 tank engines. They were numbered 1322-26, and were not fitted with a cab, merely a 'protection plate at the front' and guard-rails at the back. The chimney and dome, the latter fitted with twin Salter safety valves, passed through the saddle tank. The engines were renumbered 1500-04 in the MR's 1907 renumbered scheme, and were withdrawn between 1921 and 1934 except for No 1323, which was rebuilt in 1921 with new frames and emerged as No 1533.

A further batch of five was built during 1889 and 1890, becoming Nos 1505-07 in 1907, and five more in 1893 and 1897-1903. Of the latter, No 1523 was fitted with an all-over cab, the top of which extended beyond the rear buffer beam and had two round windows, for working in the Swansea area. Normally such engines sported outside cylinders, but the Midland, in line with most of its engines, preferred inside cylinders.

These tanks spent their working lives in docks, works and brewery sidings where curves were tight – in particular, they became a familiar sight around the breweries of Burton-on-Trent.

The first withdrawals took place as long ago as 1905, and most had disappeared by 1930. Four passed to BR in 1948. The oldest, No 1509 of 1890, entered departmental stock as a works shunter at Derby Works until it was scrapped in 1949, without carrying its allocated BR number; it carried a bell on the front of the saddle tank above the smokebox. No 41516, like No 41523 a Burton engine, retained its original open cab throughout.

ABOVE 0F 0-4-0ST No 41523 was shedded at Burton to work on the town's brewery lines from 1948 until withdrawal in March 1955. It is seen here, complete with its all-over cab, at Derby in that month awaiting its fate. *J. Davenport, Colour-Rail*

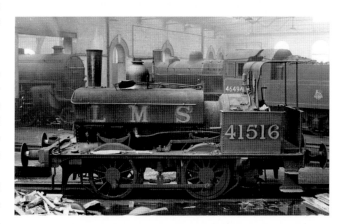

ABOVE No 41516 was another Burton engine throughout its BR career, but retained its original open cab, as seen here in Burton shed on 15 May 1953, 2½ years before withdrawal. *H. C. Casserley*

MR Deeley 0F Class 0-4-0T

Nos 41528-37

Richard Mountford Deeley (1855-1944) was the son of an accountant with the Midland Railway at Derby, and was educated in Chester. In 1873 he started work with a hydraulic engineering firm in Chester, and two years later became a pupil of Samuel Johnson at Derby, undertaking much experimental work. He had worked his way up to Works Manager by 1902, and the following year became Assistant Locomotive Superintendent, finally succeeding Johnson in 1904.

His most notable contribution to MR locomotive development was in the field of compounding (see above), but the company's board refused to sanction the building of larger, more powerful locomotives, and increasing friction on this matter with the new board under Sir Guy Granet from 1906 led him to resign in 1909, following which he continued to research and take out patents on a number of engineering matters.

Deeley's period of office was thus quite short, and resulted in only a handful of new designs, one of which was these 0-4-0 tank locos, built, like their Johnson predecessors (see above), for shunting docks and yards with sharp curves. These were successful engines, 50% larger than the saddle tanks, with

Introduced 1907	
Designed by Richard Deeley	
Built by MR, Derby	
Number built 10	
Number inherited by BR 10	
Last example withdrawn December 1966	

0F 0-4-0T No 41537 was allocated to the former MR Barnwood shed at Gloucester, to work at the city's docks, from 1948 until it was withdrawn in September 1963. It is seen here at Gloucester Docks in June of the previous year. Its Walschaerts valve gear is unusual, as are the overhead wiring warning plates, in an area a long way from electrified lines! *J. M. Wiltshire, Colour-Rail*

larger cylinders and, very unusually for the Midland, outside Walschaerts valve gear (a feature shared only with No 58100, the 0-10-0 Lickey banker).

The first five, Nos 1528-33, were built in 1907, followed by five more, Nos 1534-37, in 1921-22, with minor detail differences. All ten became LMS, then BR, engines, and the class remained intact until 1957, when two were withdrawn. The last two, Nos 41528 of 1907 and 41533 of 1921, were not dispensed with until the end of 1966.

LMS Stanier 2P Class 0-4-4T

Nos 41900-09

Introduced 1932	
Designed by William Stanier	
Built by LMS, Derby	
Number built 10	
Number inherited by BR 10	
Last example withdrawn March 1962	

These 0-4-4Ts were nominally Stanier's first design when he joined the LMS in 1932, and they were a modernised version of Johnson's 1P 0-4-4Ts (qv), 30 of which were built in 1875-76. In fact, the design had already been drawn up by Ernest Lemon and the Midland Railway's School of Engineering and the engines ordered before the new CME's arrival. Lemon had served his apprenticeship with the North British Locomotive Co, then worked for the Highland Railway and the Midland Railway; he became Manager of the latter's Carriage Works, and in 1923 was appointed Divisional Carriage & Wagon Superintendent at Derby. In 1931, on Fowler's retirement, he briefly became CME until Stanier was brought in from the GWR. These engines therefore feature none of the Stanier design characteristics he

2P 0-4-4T No 41900 calls at Upton-on-Severn, between Ashchurch and Malvern, with a single-coach service on 21 February 1959. All the class were withdrawn en bloc and placed in storage in November of that year. No 41900 was stored at Barnwood (Gloucester), but then moved to Leamington Spa for a few more months of service before a final 18 months of storage at Wellington, culminating in withdrawal in March 1962. *G. H. Hunt, Colour-Rail*

brought with him from Swindon. Indeed, they originally carried stovepipe chimneys, apparently due to an oversight by Stanier, as the new LMS design had not then been finalised; they were all later fitted with Stanier chimneys.

They were originally numbered 6400-09 but, in order that these numbers could be given to the Ivatt 2-6-0s of 1946, they were renumbered 1900-09.

In 1937 the last two class members were fitted with 'push-pull' equipment for working 'motor' trains, and the others were similarly equipped by BR in 1950-51 (No 41906 in 1957). These useful engines could be found all over the former LMS system, from the North West to Gloucester, the Midlands and the Home Counties. However, all but No 41900 were withdrawn en bloc in November 1959, while the class leader soldiered on until March 1962.

LTSR Whitelegg 2P '51' Class 4-4-2T

Nos 2092-103, 41922, 41923, 2107, 41925, 2109

Introduced 1900
Designed by Thomas Whitelegg
Built by Sharp Stewart (12), North British (6)
Number built 18
Number inherited by BR 17
Last example withdrawn March 1953

The London, Tilbury & Southend Railway was jointly promoted by the Eastern Counties Railway and the London & Blackwall Railway, and was initially leased to the contractors, Peto, Brassey and Betts. The first section opened in 1854, from Fenchurch Street and Bishopsgate, and was extended in 1856 and 1858, eventually reaching Southend.

Jointly with the Midland Railway, the LTSR constructed the Tottenham & Forest Gate Railway, allowing trains to run through from St Pancras to Tilbury Docks. In 1884 the line reached Shoeburyness, and in 1892-93 a branch to Grays was opened. The MR purchased the LTSR in 1912 and, although Midland 'branding' was applied, LTSR locos continued to work the line until replaced by Stanier 2-6-4Ts in the 1930s.

Thomas Whitelegg (1836 or 1837-1911) was the Locomotive, Carriage & Wagon and Marine Superintendent for the LTSR, at its Plaistow Works, from 1880. In fact, he was the company's first Locomotive Superintendent, because the railway had been leased to the contractors from 1854 to 1875, and between then and 1880 rolling stock had been hired from the Great Eastern Railway. He had previously worked for Sharp Stewart, Neilson, Ruston Proctor, and the GER..

The LTSR favoured the 4-4-2 tank locomotive arrangement for its heavy outer-suburban services. The first were introduced in 1880, designed by the GER's William Adams, and his classic 4-4-2T '1' Class engines became known as the 'Tilbury Universal Machines'. Whitelegg perpetuated the design with a second, enlarged series constructed between 1900 and 1903, the '51'

Class. The first 12 were built by Whitelegg's former employer Sharp Stewart of Manchester, and the North British Locomotive Co supplied a further six in 1903. They were numbered 51-68 and named after places in London and Essex, until the names were removed by the MR, which also renumbered the class 2158-75, then the LMS gave them the numbers 2092-109 in 1930. No 2109 ran for a while with a top feed injector housed in a second dome, and its appearance occasioned the nickname 'The Camel'.

No 2105 was withdrawn in 1947, but the remainder passed to BR in 1948, renumbered once more as 41910-926, although only three served long enough to carry their allocated BR numbers. From their original Thames-side stamping ground they migrated to the Midlands, many being allocated to Nottingham; they were used on the Uppingham branch in Rutland, and apparently one was even tried on the Somerset & Dorset line.

Between 1905 and 1911 a dozen of the original '1' Class were rebuilt with larger boilers, forming the basis of the third series of 4-4-2Ts, the '37' Class, and construction continued into LMS days, when 35 further engines were built between 1923 and 1930. One of the 12 rebuilt engines, from 1909, has been preserved; in 1956 No 41966 was restored to LTSR livery as No 80, named *Thundersley*, and is part of the National Collection.

The last two of the '51' Class, Nos 2093 (which would have become 41911) and 41922, were withdrawn from Toton and Nottingham respectively. The very last of the Tilbury 4-4-2Ts was LMS-built No 41947, withdrawn in December 1960.

The former LTSR '51' Class 4-4-2Ts were elegantly proportioned locomotives, and with the other two classes of similar engines were the mainstay of LTSR passenger services for many years. No 41922 (originally LTSR No 63 *Mansion House*, then MR No 2170 and LMS No 2104) eventually migrated north to Wellingborough and Nottingham, being withdrawn from the latter shed in March 1953. It is seen here, still looking in good shape, at Derby Works on 17 April, awaiting the cutter's torch. *John Stretton collection*

LTSR Whitelegg 3F '69' Class 0-6-2T

Nos 41980-93

Introduced 1903
Designed by Thomas Whitelegg
Built by North British (10), Beyer Peacock (4)
Number built 14
Number inherited by BR 14
Last example withdrawn June 1962

LTSR '69' Class 0-6-2T No 75 *Canvey Island* of 1908 went through several number changes until becoming BR No 41986 in 1948, and is seen here in September 1957 at Plaistow shed. All but one of the 14 class members were withdrawn in 1958-59; No 41986 succumbed in February 1959, and was described by the photographer as 'a rare bird'. *W. Potter, Colour-Rail*

At the time of the Midland's acquisition of the LTSR in 1912, all but two of the smaller company's 82 locomotives were tanks, and 70 of those were of the 4-4-2T wheel arrangement. The remaining ten were these 0-6-2T goods engines, known as the '69' or 'Corringham' Class (after the name of No 69).

The locomotives were ordered in three batches; six came from the North British Locomotive Co in 1903 (they had actually been ordered from Dübs & Co, which became part of NBL in that year), and four more in 1908. The final four were also ordered from NBL, but lack of capacity at the Queen's Park works meant that the order went to Beyer Peacock; delivered at the end of 1912, they went straight into Midland Railway stock. All but the last four again carried local place names until they were removed by the MR.

The class carried a series of numbers; the original ten were LTSR Nos 69-78, the Midland renumbered the class of 14 2180-93, then they became LMS Nos 2220-13, then 2180-93 again;

after the war they became Nos 1980-93, finally having 40000 added to their numbers by BR.

Unlike the 4-4-2 tanks, all the 0-6-2Ts stayed on the LTSR system. All but one were withdrawn in 1958-59, while No 41981 managed another four years, being taken out of service from Tilbury shed in June 1962.

LMS Fowler 4P/4MT Class 2-6-4T

Nos 42300-424

The infamous Sevenoaks accident of August 1927 involved a Maunsell 'River' Class 2-6-4 tank, which cast doubt on the safety of the design, and all were withdrawn and subsequently rebuilt as SR 'U' Class 2-6-0 tender engines (qv). That same year Sir Henry Fowler was contemplating the construction of his own class of 2-6-4 tanks, and checked with the accident's Inspecting Officer before allowing building at Derby to go ahead. In the event his locomotives proved very successful, and

Introduced 1927
Designed by Sir Henry Fowler
Built by LMS, Derby
Number built 125
Number inherited by BR 125
Last example withdrawn September 1966

were the first of a family of five classes with this wheel arrangement, including the LMS-inspired BR Standard engines of the 80000 series introduced in 1951. In all, 800 2-6-4Ts were produced over the 29 years from 1927 to 1956 by four different mechanical engineers: 125 by Fowler, 243 by Stanier, 277 to Fairburn's design, and 155 Riddles BR Standards.

These 125 Fowler parallel-boiler locomotives were turned out by Derby between 1927 and January 1934; the last 30, Nos 2395-424, had side-window cabs. Classified 4P by the LMS, BR reclassified them as 4MT.

Fowler 4MT 2-6-4T No 42410 is in ex-works condition at Crewe in about 1961. This was one of the last 30, built with side-window cabs, and plenty of protection for the crew when running bunker-first. This was the last survivor of a class of 125 engines, not being withdrawn until September 1966, but this was not enough to save it from the cutter's torch. *The late Alan H. Bryant ARPS, Rail Photoprints*

Most of the class were used on longer-distance commuter trains around such centres as London and Manchester. Their length and wheel arrangement gave them a relatively light axle loading that provided a wide route availability. Their outstanding feature was the use of long-lap, long-travel valves, which made them extremely free-running engines. O. S. Nock recalls the impact they had when introduced to outer-suburban services into London Euston in 1934, where previously life-expired LNWR 'Precursor' tanks, 'very tired old ladies', had been used. With the new engines 'we travelled up to Euston on the wings of the wind!' Always travelling bunker-first, speeds of 77-78mph were recorded, with a completely silent exhaust after the first half-mile or so.

Some of the class were allocated to Tebay shed and were used to bank heavy passenger and goods trains up to Shap. Others handled long-distance services from Shrewsbury to Swansea.

Sadly, even though there were still 14 of the class in service by the end of 1964, and two examples lasted into 1966, none were preserved, but recently there has been a proposal in the railway press to create a 'new build' Fowler 2-6-4T, using what few drawings are still available, together with reference to the very similar Irish 'WT' Class No 4 of the NCC, owned by the Railway Preservation Society of Ireland and awaiting restoration. Meanwhile, a model of one of the class, No 2308, in LMS lined crimson lake livery, has been produced by Hornby.

LMS Stanier (two-cylinder) 4P/4MT Class 2-6-4T

Nos 42425-94, 42537-672

Introduced 1935
Designed by William Stanier
Built by LMS, Derby (133), North British (73)
Number built 206
Number inherited by BR 206
Last example withdrawn September 1967

The second class of 2-6-4T was the 37 three-cylinder examples built by Stanier in 1934 for the former London, Tilbury & Southend route (Nos 42500-36). These were the new CME's version of Fowler's original, but fitted with three independent sets of Walschaerts valve gear, the characteristic Stanier domeless taper boiler, sloping tops to the tanks, and smaller cylinders. These successful and hard-working engines spent their whole lives on the LTSR section until replaced by electric multiple units. The class leader, restored as LMS No 2500, is preserved as part of the National Collection.

These were followed by the third incarnation of the design, Stanier's two-cylinder version of 1935-43, which proved to be equally as capable as the three-cylinder engines. They were all built at Derby except for 73 engines contracted out to the North British Locomotive Co in 1936-37. The first nine, Nos 2537-44, were built in 1935, followed by 70 in 1936-37, simultaneously with the NBL examples. Six further lots appeared between 1938 and 1943. Classified 4P by the LMS, BR reclassified them as 4MT.

As an aside, one of the class, No 2429, appeared in the classic 1945 David Lean film *Brief Encounter*, partly filmed at Carnforth station ('Milford Junction'). It was the engine that pulled Celia Johnson's branch-line train to 'Ketchworth' each evening, and appears three times in the film.

The class was allocated to sheds right across the LMS network, primarily on the Western and Central Divisions (the former LNWR and LYR lines), but did not get as far as Scotland. Withdrawals commenced in 1960, and 15 survived into 1967, almost at the end of steam on BR.

When Stanier became an advisor to the Ministry of Production in 1942 as part of the war effort, construction of

further 2-6-4 tanks was left to his deputy since 1938, Charles Fairburn, who became acting CME. When Stanier retired in 1944 Fairburn took over the post, by which time the production of his modified two-cylinder 2-6-4T was under way. Fairburn's design had a shorter wheelbase, and could be distinguished from the Stanier engines by the gap in the running plate ahead of the cylinders. Fairburn died unexpectedly in 1945 of a heart attack at the age of only 58, but construction continued right through to 1950, under the aegis of BR, when Brighton Works took over from Derby. In all, 277 Fairburn 2-6-4Ts were produced, providing the model for the BR Standard equivalent. A couple of the Fairburns have been preserved, as well as 15 of the 'Standards'.

One of the longest-lived of the Stanier two-cylinder 2-6-4 tanks was No 42644, built in November 1938 and withdrawn from Trafford Park in March 1967. It is seen here on the previous 3 December at Bury while working the LCGB's 'Rossendale Forester Railtour'. *The late Colin Whitfield, Rail Photoprints*

MR Johnson/Fowler 3F Class 0-6-0

Nos 43174, 43178, 43180, 43181, 43183, 43185-89, 3137/43750

For its goods traffic the Midland Railway remained committed to the 0-6-0 tender and tank engines, which evolved over a long period from the 1850s to the First World War, the main change being the gradual introduction of superheating and flat-topped Belpaire fireboxes. The many classes provide a complex evolutionary history. Between 1875 and 1908, under Johnson and his successor Deeley, the MR built 935 0-6-0 goods tender engines, at its own works and those of outside contractors. Although there were small variations between different batches, both as delivered and as rebuilt, they can be regarded as a single series, one of the largest classes of engine in British railway history.

These 11 engines, inherited by BR in 1948, were a series of Derby-built engines of the MR '1698' Class of 1885-88, rebuilt by Fowler with larger boilers from 1916 onwards. After 1920 they gained Belpaire fireboxes and Deeley-style cabs; instead of the earlier square cab side-sheet, the splasher of the rear coupled wheel merged with the front of the cab.

At first the engines retained their original numbers, but BR renumbered the unrebuilt engines in the 58114 series (qv), and these 11 became 3137 and 43174 to 43189. In 1952 No 3137 was renumbered 43750 to free up 43137 for one the Ivatt 'Moguls' then being built, which were numbered up to 43161.

Introduced 1875 (rebuilt examples from 1885-88)
Designed by Samuel Johnson; rebuilt by Sir Henry Fowler
Built by MR, Derby
Rebuilt engines inherited by BR 11
Last example withdrawn December 1960

3F No 43174 heads south on the up goods line at Wellingborough North signal box. The date is unknown, but it is some time before February 1958, while this engine was a Bedford (15D) resident. It then went to Sheffield Grimesthorpe, and was withdrawn from there in February 1960. *Colour-Rail collection*

MR/SDJR Johnson/Deeley 3F Class 0-6-0

Nos 43191-94, 43200, 43201, 43203-05, 43207, 43208, 43210-14, 43216, 43218, 43219, 43222-26, 43228, 43231-35, 43237, 43239, 43240-54, 43256-59, 3260, 43261, 43263, 3265, 43266-68, 43269, 43271, 43263-75, 43277, 43278, 43281-84, 43286, 43287, 43290, 43292-301, 43305-10, 43312-15, 43317-19, 43321, 43323-27, 43329-37, 3338, 43339-42, 43344, 43351, 43355-57, 43359, 43361, 43364, 43367-71, 43373, 43374, 43378, 43379, 43381, 43386-89, 43392, 43394-96, 43398-402, 43405, 43406, 3408, 43410, 43411, 43419, 43427-29, 43431, 43435, 43436, 3439, 43440, 43441, 43443, 43444, 43446, 43448, 43449, 43453, 43454, 43456, 43457, 3458, 43459, 43462-64, 43468, 43469, 43474, 43476, 43482, 43484, 43490, 43491, 43494, 43496, 43497, 43499, 43502, 43506, 43507, 43509, 43510, 43514, 43515, 43520-24, 43529, 43531, 43538, 43540, 43544, 43546, 43548, 43550, 43553, 43558, 43562, 43565, 43568, 43570, 43572, 3573, 43574, 43575, 43578-87, 43593-96, 43598-600, 43604, 43605, 43607, 43608, 43612, 43615, 43618-24, 43627, 43629-31, 43633, 43634, 43636-39, 43644, 43645, 43650-53, 43656-58, 43660, 43361, 3662, 43664, 43665, 43667-69, 43673-76, 43678-84, 43686, 43687, 43690, 43693, 43698, 43705, 43709-12, 43714, 43715, 43717, 43721, 43723, 43724, 43727-29, 43731, 43734, 43735, 43737, 43742, 43745, 3747, 43748, 43749, 43751, 43753-57, 43759, 43760,

3F 0-6-0 No 43754 had been allocated to Barnwood shed, Gloucester, since nationalisation, and is seen here standing in the Tewkesbury line platform at Ashchurch station on 1 August 1961. In June the following year it went into store, and was finally withdrawn in the November. *T. J. Edgington, Colour-Rail*

Introduced 1875 (rebuilt examples from 1888-1902)
Designed by Samuel Johnson; rebuilt by Richard Deeley and
  Sir Henry Fowler
Built by MR, Derby (20), Neilson (170), Kitson (90), Dübs (50),
  Sharp Stewart (85), Vulcan Foundry (20)
Number built 435
Number inherited by BR 324
Last example withdrawn February 1964

43761, 43763

This large class of 0-6-0s comprised several original Midland Railway classes: '1798' (1888), 'Neilson Goods' (1890-91), 'J' (1890-92) and 'M' (1892-1902). They were a version of the Johnson/Fowler 3F 0-6-0s (see previous entry), but with larger wheels of 5ft 3in diameter (as opposed to 4ft 11in), and were also rebuilt from locomotives of the earlier classes, initially by Deeley from 1903 onwards, then by Fowler after 1916, with Belpaire fireboxes and Deeley cabs. Again at first the engines retained their original numbers, but when BR renumbered the unrebuilt engines in the 58000 series, those remaining of the rebuilds had 40000 added to their numbers, becoming Nos 43191-763, thus forming a separate number sequence, which included No 43750, the renumbered No 3137 (see previous entry).

Ten of the class were bought by the Somerset & Dorset Joint Railway (in which the Midland had a stake) in 1896 and 1902, and were numbered 62-66 and 72-76. All were subsequently taken back into LMS stock in 1930, and were given the numbers of previously withdrawn locomotives.

3F 0-6-0 No 43216 was one of the 10 engines acquired by the Somerset & Dorset Joint Railway in 1902, and returned to LMS stock in 1930. It spent all its BR days in former SDJR territory, latterly at Templecombe, including a period in store there. It is seen here, looking rather shabby, at the shed on 24 September 1961; it was withdrawn the following August. *Colour-Rail collection*

3F 0-6-0 No 43680, a Kitson-built engine from 1901, spent all its BR life allocated to Saltley shed in Birmingham. Succumbing to rust, it is seen there on 15 June 1962, prior to withdrawal in August. *G. Parry collection, Colour-Rail*

MR Deeley 3F Class 0-6-0

Nos 43765-67, 3769, 43770, 43771, 3772, 43773, 43775-79, 43781, 43782, 3783, 43784-87, 43789-93, 43795, 3796, 43797-801, 3802, 43803, 43804, 3805, 43806-12, 3813, 43814, 43815, 43817-19, 3820, 43821-26, 3827, 43828, 43829, 3830, 3831, 43832, 43833

Built new by Deeley and introduced in 1903, the year he took over from Johnson, these 0-6-0s followed his predecessor's design (see previous entry). By that year the Midland had 450 Johnson engines, and no fewer than 500 older Kirtley double-framed 0-6-0s, so there was no shortage of motive power. There was still no call for larger engines, so the same time-honoured design was perpetuated, and

Deeley 3F No 43808 was one of the last six engines of the class still operating in 1962, and is seen here on 5 May of that year looking rather work-stained at the head of a very short goods train at Hitchin, on the East Coast Main Line. It has perhaps worked there along the old Midland Railway Bedford-Hitchin line, which once provided the MR with access to London via the GNR before its own St Pancras extension was built. The line closed to passengers in January 1962, and to goods in 1964. *Colour-Rail collection*

Introduced 1903
Designed by Richard Deeley
Built by MR, Derby
Number built 70
Number inherited by BR 63
Last example withdrawn September 1962

older engines were rebuilt by Deeley with new boilers. Twenty of the new engines appeared during 1903, then 20 more were completed between February and September 1904. Another six were turned out in January and February 1906, and four more in December 1906 and January 1907. The final order for 20 emerged between January and May 1908, with a different boiler.

As with all the 3F classes, they underwent considerable rebuilding, and from 1916 onwards they were fitted with Belpaire boilers and larger cabs by Fowler. They were used almost exclusively on goods trains, and sometimes heavier trains were double-headed in MR days.

In 1923 482 0-6-0s passed into LMS ownership, including this class, and they became the forerunners of the larger superheated 4F Class, two prototypes of which were built by Fowler in 1911. These 4Fs were the final development of the Midland 0-6-0 family, and full production followed from 1917 until 1921. The LMS subsequently adopted the design as its standard freight engine, and 580 more were built between 1924 and 1941, bringing the total of both classes to an astonishing 772. Several examples of these later classes have been preserved.

The 3Fs lost much of their work in the early 1960s with the closure of many branch lines and collieries and the introduction of diesels. Just six remained at the beginning of 1962, shedded around the former LMS network at Bedford, Leicester, Rowsley, Buxton and Gorton – the last went in September of that year.

LMS 'Patriot' Class 4-6-0

Nos 45500-45551

We now skip numerically through three LMS classes, two of Fowler's 4F 0-6-0s and Stasier's 'Black Fives' – together numbering a staggering 1,500 locomotives inherited by BR, with almost 20 still working on heritage railways – before arriving at a notorious gap in the preservation lists: the 'Patriots'.

Although they had done good work in their early years, towards the end of their lives the London & North Western Railway four-cylinder 'Claughton' 4-6-0s were inconsistent performers with a high coal consumption. Some were tried with larger boilers or Caprotti valve gear, showing that improvement was possible. In 1930 Fowler decided to completely rebuild two of the class with three cylinders, three sets of Walschaerts valve gear and long-travel valves. When Nos 5971 *Croxteth* and 5902 *Sir Frank Ree* emerged from Derby, only their driving wheels and a few other items were original components.

These new locomotives were successful and an order was placed for 50 more, with a longer wheelbase and other detail differences. They were soon nicknamed 'Baby Scots' – as they had an outline similar to but smaller than the 'Royal Scot' Class – but had become officially 'Patriots' by about 1936. Forty of

Introduced 1930
Designed by Sir Henry Fowler
Built by LMS, Derby (12), LMS, Crewe (40)
Number built 52
Number inherited by BR 52
Last example withdrawn December 1965

the new engines were nominally rebuilds of 'Claughtons', even though they were effectively new engines; rebuilds could be charged to the revenue account, rather than to capital. The last ten were classified as new builds. Nonetheless they retained some 'Claughton' items, including the whistle! 'Claughton' whistles were also re-employed on 'Royal Scots', and although for listeners this helped the perpetuate memories of the old North Western, a 1957 *Railway Magazine* correspondent considered that the sound 'is somehow out of keeping with these sleek and handsome machines. Those whistles belong to a sterner and wilder past.'

In 1934 the original pair were renumbered 5500-01, and the 40 'rebuilds', which had taken the numbers of the 'Claughtons' they replaced, were renumbered Nos 5502-41. The ten new engines were to have been numbered 6030-39, but appeared as 5542-51. A further five engines were ordered as Nos 6040-44, but they were actually built as the first of Stanier's new 'Jubilee' Class, and their numbers carried on from the 'Patriot' sequence, becoming Nos 5552-56.

Some of the 'Patriots' retained their old 'Claughton' names, while the two original conversions were renamed *Patriot* and *St Dunstan's*. Some continued a tradition of military names, while others bore the names of holiday resorts served by the LMS. Seven remained unnamed, although they had been allocated names in 1943.

As a result of the successful rebuilding of two 'Jubilees' in 1942, between 1946 and 1948 Ivatt rebuilt 18 'Patriots' with a

A splendid portrait of an unrebuilt 'Patriot'. The locomotive is Preston-allocated No 45518 *Bradshaw* of 1933, at the head of the up 'Mancunian' on Castlethorpe troughs, north of Wolverton on the West Coast Main Line, in August 1958. *Bradshaw* lasted until October 1962 T. B. Owen, Colour-Rail

Stanier boiler, cab and tender, a double chimney and new cylinders; as a result they were reclassified from 6P5F to 7P. 'Royal Scots' were similarly treated, and the new 'Patriots' were now considered the equal of the rebuilt 'Scots'. From 1948 they were fitted with smoke deflectors of the same pattern as the 'Scots'. The two original class members and the first ten 'rebuilds' remained unrebuilt, because of their non-standard parts.

The 'Patriots' took on very much a mixed-traffic role, light enough to be just as at home on suburban trains as express and local passenger services, as well as parcels, fish or fitted freight trains. However, one commentator has said that a 'Patriot' needed to be handled 'understandingly' and 'humoured' – 'hammer it you could not'. The smokebox was prone to leaking, and the injectors could be temperamental. Nonetheless, the three-cylinder layout was more reliable than four. When an unrebuilt 'Patriot' was tested against a 'Jubilee' between Wolverhampton and Euston in 1934, the 'Patriot' showed a slightly higher coal consumption, while against a superheated and a non-superheated 'Jubilee' both the 'Patriot' and superheated 'Jubilee' were superior to the untreated 'Jubilee'.

The fact that an example of the class was not saved for preservation is to be rectified by the LMS-Patriot Project, launched in April 2008 at the Llangollen Railway's Spring Gala. The Project is aiming to build a new £1.5 million 'Patriot', to be known as No 45551 *The Unknown Warrior* (a name chosen through a competition in the railway press, and most fitting for what is intended to be a new 'National Memorial Engine', as *Patriot* was for the LMS). The Project is endorsed by the

The rebuilt 'Patriots', with their taper boiler, double chimney and smoke deflectors, had very much the 'Stanier' look. No 45526 *Morecambe and Heysham* is far from 'home' on 22 August 1964 at Shrewsbury shed. Allocated to Carlisle Upperby at the time, it appears to have come in on a special. No 45526 was one of only three 'Patriots' in service in 1964, being withdrawn in December. *Colour-Rail collection*

Royal British Legion, and No 45551 will carry a Legion crest above its nameplate.

New main frame plates have been cut, and other new parts are being manufactured. Six brand new wheel sets were assembled in 2013, and Project members are working closely with the Vehicle Acceptance Body (VAB) to allow the new locomotive to be main-line certified.

LNWR Bowen Cooke rebuilt 'Claughton' Class 4-6-0

No 6004

Introduced 1913; rebuilt by Beames 1928	
Designed by Charles Bowen Cooke	
Built by LNWR, Crewe	
Number built 130	
Number inherited by BR 1	
Last example withdrawn April 1949	

This class of four-cylinder 4-6-0s took its name from Sir Gilbert Claughton, Chairman of the LNWR at the time of its introduction, and 130 locomotives were built between 1913 and 1921. They proved not to be a success; restrictions on the loco's weight by the Civil Engineer and other limitations meant that they were underboilered, inconsistent performers, expensive to maintain and run, and suffered from numerous other mechanical shortcomings. Although a flat-topped Belpaire firebox was used for the first time on the LNWR, the inner firebox was shaped to fit a round-topped boiler, so its

full potential was unrealised. However, the four cylinders were well-designed and, despite some outstanding running in their early days, Bowen Cooke was aware of his engines' overall shortcomings, and proposed to deal with them after the war. He made a number of trips to France in connection with the working of military railways, and this work, together with dealing with the aftermath of the war effort at Crewe, took a toll on his health, and he died in 1920 aged only 61.

The LNWR numbered the class haphazardly, using numbers and names from withdrawn locomotives, with the exception of

Rebuilt 'Claughton' No 6004 heads away from Berkhampsted with a down goods train on 18 March 1947. Shedded at Edge Hill, Liverpool, this was the kind of work allotted to this LNWR 'dinosaur' in its later years. *H. C. Casserley*

the war memorial engine, the original *Patriot*, which was deliberately given the number 1914. Under the LMS the class was renumbered 5900-6029, No 1914 becoming 5964.

In an attempt to improve their performance, 20 'Claughtons' were rebuilt by the LMS under Bowen Cooke's successor, H. P. M. Beames, with larger boilers, and ten were fitted with Caprotti valve gear. Others formed the basis of the 'Patriot' Class (see previous entry).

The 'Royal Scot' 4-6-0s appeared in 1927, usurping much of the work of the 'Claughtons', and within ten years all but four had been scrapped. Three of them were found to be not worth further repairs, and were taken out of service in 1940-41, leaving as the sole survivor No 6004, which carried the name *Princess Louise* until 1935. This engine was regularly used on fitted freight trains between London and Edge Hill, Liverpool, and duly became BR property in 1948. Although allocated the number 46004, it never carried it and was withdrawn and scrapped in 1949.

The once elegant No 6004, built at Crewe in 1920, was withdrawn in April 1949, and is seen here awaiting its fate, minus its tender, in Crewe Works yard on 7 May. It was cut up in August.
H. C. Casserley

LNWR Webb 1P Class 2-4-2T

Nos 46001, 46003, 46004, 6605, 46616, 46620, 6628, 6632, 46635, 46637, 6639, 46643, 46654, 46656, 46658, 6661, 6663, 46666, 6669, 6673, 6676, 6679, 46680, 6681, 6682, 46683, 6686, 46687, 6688, 6691, 6692, 46701, 6710, 6711, 46712, 6718, 46727, 6738, 6740, 6742, 6747, 46749, 46757

Introduced 1890
Designed by Francis Webb
Built by LNWR, Crewe
Number built 160
Number inherited by BR 43
Last example withdrawn September 1955

F. W. Webb's involvement with the LNWR began early, when he became a pupil of Francis Trevithick in 1851, while still a teenager. John Ramsbottom succeeded Trevithick, and Webb became his Works Manager at Crewe in 1861, as well as his Chief Assistant. Although working away from the LNWR for a period, Webb succeeded Ramsbottom in 1871, and remained in control at Crewe for 30 years.

In 1874 he introduced his 'Precursor' Class of 2-4-0 simple-expansion passenger engines, which were in turn based on Ramsbottom's 'Newton' Class, and were to be used between Crewe and Carlisle. In 1890 this class of 2-4-2 tanks was introduced, a tank engine version of the 'Precursor' type, with driving wheels

of 5ft 6in, the same as the tender engine; 160 were built between 1890 and 1897. There was also a smaller-wheeled version, 180 of which were built, but all had gone by 1948.

Although the first example was withdrawn in 1921, 157 engines passed to the LMS, and 43 engines survived to enter BR stock. They remained virtually unaltered throughout their lives, although a number were fitted with 'push-pull' equipment in order to work 'motor' trains. In BR days they were to be found all over the former LNWR system, in North and South Wales, the North West and the Midlands (at Northampton, Warwick and Bletchley, for example) – and even a few in southern Scotland.

Only four of the 'Precursor tanks' (not to be confused with George Whale's 4-4-2Ts of 1906-09, which had the same nickname, but had disappeared before nationalisation) were still in service by the end of 1953, and the last two, Nos 46604 and 46616, lasted until the autumn of 1955. The latter had been in store at Swansea since April 1953, but the former was at Warwick, no doubt working the push-pull service between Leamington and Rugby.

The longest-lived of Webb's 1P 2-4-2Ts, motor-fitted No 46616 of 1891, is in store at Abergavenny Junction in September 1953. Out of use since April, it was not officially withdrawn until September 1955, and had been scrapped by the end of that year.
T. B. Owen, Colour-Rail

LYR/Wirral Railway Aspinall 2P Class 2-4-2T

No 46762

Introduced 1889
Designed by John Aspinall
Built by LYR, Horwich
Number built 330 (of LYR Class '5')
This ex-Wirral Railway withdrawn February 1952

This lost 'class' should perhaps not be included, as the sole surviving locomotive was initially a member of the Lancashire & Yorkshire Class '5' until sold to the Wirral Railway in 1921. The following year the LYR and LNWR merged, prior to both becoming part of the LMS in 1923. The Wirral Railway was also an LMS constituent, so this engine passed into LMS ownership with the rest of the Class '5' – and one of them, No 50681, is preserved as part of the National Collection. However, the LMS numbered its absorbed Wirral engines in the same sequence as LNWR engines, otherwise it would have joined other LYR engines as No 50638. It worked on the Western Division of the LMS as No 6762, following on from the numbers of LNWR 2-4-2Ts. At nationalisation it still had that number, so became 46762, completely different from the numbers of its erstwhile classmates.

The LYR was an enthusiastic user of 2-4-2 'Radial' tank locomotives, beginning with Aspinall's design in 1889; by 1911 330 had been built, with various modifications over time.

The Wirral Railway was formed in 1891, and grew to link places like Hoylake, West Kirby, New Brighton, Seacombe and

Former LYR 2-4-2T No 46762, briefly a Wirral Railway engine, ended its days as station pilot at Preston. It is seen here working hard bunker-first as it banks a freight train out of the station on 21 April 1951. *H. C. Casserley*

Birkenhead. It obtained powers to electrify its lines in 1900, but this did not take place until LMS days, in 1938. Meanwhile the company purchased Class '5' 2-4-2T No 1041 from the LYR in 1921, and it became Wirral No 6. Just a couple of years later it was an LMS engine, and remained alone numerically for more than four years, in BR days allocated to Preston shed and working as station pilot at the city's station until being withdrawn and scrapped in 1952.

It was the only former Wirral Railway engine to enter BR stock, and retained its original round-topped boiler throughout.

LNWR Webb 2P Class 0-6-2T

Nos 6876, 6878, 6881, 6883, 6899, 46900, 6906, 6909, 46912, 6917, 6920, 6922, 6924, 6926, 6931

Introduced 1898
Designed by Francis Webb
Built by LNWR, Crewe
Number built 80
Number inherited by BR 15
Last example withdrawn February 1953

For Manchester suburban traffic, the LYR CME, W. Barton Wright, experimented with a lengthened redundant 0-6-0 and fitted a rear bunker above a pair of trailing wheels. Webb saw the advantages of such an arrangement, and introduced his celebrated 0-6-2T 'Coal Tanks', the side-tank version of his standard 17-inch 'Coal Engine' 0-6-0, in 1881. Three hundred

Former LNWR Webb 0-6-2T 'Watford Tank' No 6917 stands at Leighton Buzzard with a train for the Dunstable branch in the early months of BR, on 2 October 1948. It was shedded at Bletchley at this time, and was withdrawn six months later and scrapped at Crewe without ever carrying its allocated BR number.
John Stretton collection

had been built by 1897, all but eight were inherited by the LMS, and 64 survived to enter British Railways ownership. One, BR No 58926, originally LNWR No 1054, was preserved, and has been seen in action on several heritage railways over the years.

A passenger version, the so-called 'Watford Tanks' or '18-inch Passenger Tanks', was introduced by Webb in 1898, and they were the LNWR's largest tank locos until George Whale's 4-4-2T 'Precursor tanks' appeared in 1906. The cylinders, motion, boiler and coupled wheels were identical to the 18-inch 'Cauliflower' 0-6-0 goods engines, and they incorporated

the latest Webb modifications – fluted coupling rods, steel buffer beams and metal brake blocks – as well as train heating equipment. Only 80 were built, fewer than might have been expected, as some were altered during construction to a useful tender version to supplement hard-pressed main-line power.

The tanks were intended for the Euston-Watford outer-suburban services (hence their nickname), as well as similar services around Birmingham and Walsall, and Manchester to Buxton. Previously, long-in-the-tooth retired main-line locomotives hauling trains of elderly stock tended to be the norm. They were immediately successful and showed that Webb could produce exactly what was required very quickly; it is said that they pulled well and ran fast, and many ended with high mileages. The London area examples were not displaced from the Watford services until 1932. Some were fitted with 'push-pull' apparatus.

As described by author Rodney Weaver, 'the last survivors of these hard-working and most useful locomotives were withdrawn in early BR days, their grimy condition making it hard to imagine the gleaming black machines they once had been.' Only two of the 15 survivors carried their allocated BR numbers, and one of these, No 46900, a resident of Monument Lane shed in Birmingham, was the longest-lived, lasting until February 1953. Indeed, Monument Lane became a final home for 10 of the last 15 examples, and as late as the winter of 1951 the 'Western Lines' north-end pilot at New Street was No 46900. This was significant: they were passenger engines, so should an ailing locomotive arrive from Euston en route to Wolverhampton, the pilot could provide assistance. In fact, a few years earlier Monument Lane's 'Watford Tanks' had occasionally assumed main-line duties, assisting 'Scots' and 'Jubilees' through to the Black Country.

LMS/BR Stanier 0F Class 0-4-0ST

Nos 47000-09

William Stanier designed these short-wheelbase saddle tanks, but the first five were built by Kitson & Co of Leeds at the end of 1932. They must have been among the last Kitson locos, as the company built fewer than 100 engines between 1925 and 1938, and in the latter year the patterns, drawings and goodwill of the company were acquired by Robert Stephenson & Hawthorns, a receiver having been appointed in 1934.

The engines, originally numbered 1500-04, were designed for light shunting in yards where tight track curvature would present problems for locos with longer wheelbases. In 1935-36 they were renumbered 7000-04. In 1953 British Railways built a further five at Horwich Works, with the BR numbers 47005-09; these differed from the originals by having shorter saddle tanks and larger coal bunkers.

The class was allocated to a variety of locations, including sheds at Derby, Burton, Bank Hall, Hasland, Birkenhead, Chester and Preston. Nos 47002 and 47008 were shedded at Lostock Hall, and when Preston shed closed the saddle tanks undertook daily journeys between the sheds to assist with light engine movements. They were also the only engines capable

Introduced 1932
Designed by William Stanier
Built by Kitson (5), BR, Horwich (5)
Number built 10
Number inherited by BR 10
Last example withdrawn December 1966

of shunting the very sharply curved coalyard at Greenbank Sidings, north of Preston station, accessed via the main line; however, their very short wheelbases did not always activate the main-line track circuits, so they were subsequently hauled in each direction by one of Preston's station pilots, usually a 'Jinty' 0-6-0T. Both were withdrawn in September 1964, No 47002 allegedly as a result of a blowback accident that badly burned a fireman.

They are perhaps best remembered for their work during the last years of the Cromford & High Peak Railway in Derbyshire. Nos 47006 and 47007 were allocated to Sheep Pasture shed in 1963 and 1958 respectively, while Derby's No 47000 was also used there. Sheep Pasture shed was one-loco affair, at the top of the incline of the same name. One steam loco at a time worked trains along the level section from Sheep Pasture to the bottom of the Middleton Incline, where rope-haulage took over again. Apparently No 47007 was dubbed 'James Bond' by local children, for obvious reasons! It was the first of the class to be withdrawn, in late 1963, while Nos 47000 and 47006 lasted until the second half of 1966. The last survivor was No 47005, latterly shedded at Barrow Hill, Staveley and Langwith Junction, and scrapped by Arnott & Young the following year.

In June 1963 BR 0F 0-4-0ST No 47005, built at Horwich Works 10 years earlier, was allocated to Barrow Hill shed, Staveley, to work within Staveley Chemical Works, where it was photographed, looking very smart, in 1964. It was the last surviving member of the class, being withdrawn in December 1966, aged only 13.
Rail Photoprints collection

LMS Fowler 2F Dock Tank Class 0-6-0T

Nos 47160-69

Introduced 1928
Designed by Sir Henry Fowler
Built by LMS, Derby
Number built 10
Number inherited by BR 10
Last example withdrawn September 1964

The LMS acquired numerous docks, harbours and piers from its constituent companies, ranging from large facilities such as those at Barrow-in-Furness and Grangemouth to ferry harbours such as Holyhead, Heysham, Stranraer and Fleetwood. To service these facilities Fowler designed this class of ten short-wheelbase shunting engines.

Naturally, the railways in and around the docks contained sharp curves, so a short-wheelbase locomotive was essential. These were usually of the 0-4-0 wheel arrangement, but with the growth in freight traffic a more powerful engine was required. Fowler's design had six coupled wheels, but the wheelbase was only 9ft 6in, allowing the engines to negotiate curves as tight as 2½ chains radius, aided by the use of Cartazzi self-centring axleboxes. Invented by F. I. Cartazzi, an engineer on the Great Northern Railway, and Loco Superintendent of the Great Indian Peninsula Railway, these radial axleboxes were supported on inclined planes, so that the weight of the locomotive provided a centring force for the axle assembly.

Although designed at Horwich, the engines were built at Derby, so several Derby features such as cab, bunker and boiler fittings, as well as the Derby boiler, gave the locomotives a somewhat Fowler 'Jinty'-like appearance.

Because of the Cartazzi axlebox arrangement, unusually the engines had cylinders and Walschaerts valve gear outside the

Fowler 2F dock tank No 47165 is at work at Fleetwood Docks on 27 September 1961. At this time the docks were in serious decline, the Isle of Man ferry having ceased in that year. The following month No 47165 moved inland to Agecroft and Bolton, and finally Horwich Works in 1963. It and No 47164 were the last two survivors of the class, both withdrawn from Horwich in September 1964. *Colour-Rail collection*

frames; these were usually situated between the frames for dock engines, being considered safer when people were working in close proximity to them. Otherwise they were of typical dock tank design, with oval buffers.

They became the standard LMS dock tank. Originally numbered 11270-79, in 1933 they became Nos 7100-09, then in 1939 Nos 7160-69. In BR days five were allocated to Scottish docks and branch lines, shedded at St Margarets and Dalry Road (Edinburgh) and Greenock, and five to England, principally Birkenhead, Bidston and Fleetwood. Some were also used for a while as BR departmental locomotives.

LMS Sentinel 0-4-0T two-speed shunter

Nos 47180-83

Introduced 1930
Designed by Sentinel
Built by Sentinel
Number bought by LMS 4
Number inherited by BR 4
Last example withdrawn November 1956

The Scottish engineering firm of Alley & MacLellan began operating at the Sentinel Works in Glasgow in 1875; one of its best-known products was the steam lorry, and that part of the business became the Sentinel Waggon Works, based in Shrewsbury. The company also built a number of geared steam locomotives, which could be controlled by a single engineman and used as little as 15lb of coal per mile while shunting, but were too slow to be used on normal passenger and goods trains.

Sentinel No 47182 spent the whole of its BR career allocated to Ayr shed, where it was photographed on 18 August 1955. It was taken out of service the following February. *W. G. Boyden, Frank Hornby collection*

Between 1923 and 1957 some 850 steam locomotives were built by Sentinel for railways at home and abroad, and BR inherited seven examples from the LMS. These four were small vertical-boilered, two-speed chain-driven 100hp shunting locomotives, and were purchased by the LMS in 1930. Originally numbered 7160-63, in 1939 they became Nos 7180-83. They were Sentinel's 'CE' ('Central Engine') design, and in their box-like appearance were very similar to the LNER's 'Y1' (one of which is preserved) and 'Y3' (qv) Sentinel classes. All four were delivered new to the LMS shed at Shrewsbury in July 1930.

Like other standard Sentinel shunters, they had four wheels and a vertical water tube boiler, which was fired from the top down the centre flue. They were superheated and worked at a pressure of 275psi. The cylinders were 6¾ by 9 inches, originally horizontal, but after 1925 often vertical. The crankshaft was driven at 500rpm, and transmission to the wheels was by means of chains, engaging with sprockets on the crankshaft and wheel. The chain could be tensioned by a radius bar that moved the axles in either direction.

In BR days No 47182 spent all its time allocated to Ayr, but the others were more widely travelled, all being allocated to Sutton Oak, near St Helens, and Shrewsbury at one time. No 7183, for example, was first allocated to Accrington and later Lower Darwen. During the Second World War it was allocated to various sheds in the Manchester area and loaned for a while to one of the local Royal Ordnance factories. At Sutton Oak by January 1948, No 47183 moved to Shrewsbury in January 1949 for use at Clee Hill. Following a brief spell at Crewe South, it returned to Shrewsbury for further use at Clee Hill, being withdrawn from there on 29 September 1963. It was noted in the scrap shed at Crewe Works on 23 October 1955, awaiting is fate. The locomotive's worksplate was recently sold at auction for £1,050.

LMS Sentinel 0-4-0T single-speed shunter

No 47184

This additional Sentinel shunting locomotive was bought by the LMS in 1932. It looked quite different from the two-speed vertical-boiler Sentinels (see previous entry) and the LNER 'Y1' Class (qv). It was the smallest of the four Sentinel classes used by the LMS.

Although widely used in industry, LMS No 7164 was the company's only example of the Sentinel 'BE' ('Balanced Engine') design, where the boiler and engine were placed at opposite ends of the frames, separated by the water tank. It was renumbered 7184 in 1939, thus becoming No 47184 in BR ownership.

One duty undertaken by this locomotive was shunting at the Mitchells & Butlers Brewery at Cape Hill, Birmingham,

Introduced 1932	
Designed by Sentinel	
Built by Sentinel	
Number bought by LMS 1	
Number inherited by BR 1	
Last example withdrawn December 1955	

connected by rail to the Harborne branch at Rotton Park Road station. When the brewery's own loco was under repair the company hired one from BR and, as well as the Sentinel, LYR 'Pugs' Nos 11221 and 51218 were also seen. The loco would be based at the brewery all week, then return to Monument Lane shed on Saturday afternoon for servicing and maintenance.

Having been shedded at Sutton Oak (three times), Preston and Wrexham Rhosddu, No 47184 spent its last four years at Crewe South, from where it was withdrawn in December 1955 and scrapped early the following year. However, a similar industrial Sentinel, No 7232 *Ann*, has been preserved in the guise of LMS No 7164 at the Embsay & Bolton Abbey Steam Railway, to give a flavour of what the LMS engine looked like.

LMS Sentinel 0-4-0T No 7184 was photographed at Crewe Works on 27 May 1949. It received its BR number, 47184, that November, then was allocated to various sheds before finally returning to Crewe South in 1951 for subsequent withdrawal and scrapping.
Frank Hornby collection

SDJR Sentinel 0-4-0T shunter

Nos 47190, 47191

The Somerset & Dorset Joint Railway bought these two vertical-boilered, chain-driven Sentinels to shunt coal wagons on the colliery lines around Radstock, where they were both shedded. They were built to a reduced height as they had to pass under a low arch on the branch to Tyning pit. They were given the

SDJR numbers 101 and 102, and replaced three older saddle tanks. They were the last new locomotives acquired by the SDJR, because from the beginning of 1930 the joint company's assets were divided between the two operating partners, the LMS and the Southern Railway. The LMS acquired the Sentinels and renumbered them 7190-91, and they subsequently became BR Nos 47190-91. It has been suggested that this was an

Introduced 1929
Designed by Sentinel
Built by Sentinel
Number bought by SDJR 2
Number inherited by BR 2
Last example withdrawn March 1961

unusual purchase, given that the LMS was disposing of many of its old LYR 0-4-0Ts at the time, many of which were sold into industrial use. Perhaps they were bought for longer-term evaluation purposes; in LMS days No 7191 was at Kettering shunting the goods yard between 1932 and 1935, and at Highbridge in 1942-44.

Neither of the Radstock Sentinels was preserved, but a similar locomotive, No 37 *Joyce*, is under restoration by the Somerset & Dorset Railway Heritage Trust at Midsomer Norton station. It formerly worked at Croydon Gasworks, and is an historic engine in its own right.

Former SDJR Sentinel 0-4-0T No 47191 shunts a rake of coal wagons at Radstock in July 1953. It remained there until the autumn of 1959, when it was withdrawn *S. C. Townroe, Colour-Rail*

MR Johnson '2441' Class 3F 0-6-0T

Nos 47200-59

Samuel Johnson's first design after joining the Midland Railway in 1873 was his 1F 0-6-0T, 40 of which appeared between 1874 and 1876, built by Neilson & Co and the Vulcan Foundry. Between 1878 and 1899 240 further examples were built both at Derby and by outside contractors, and in 1907 they were renumbered 1620-1899. They became the standard Midland Railway shunting engines; some had full cabs, other half-cabs, and they were a familiar sight across the MR and later LMS systems for many decades. Ninety-five of them passed into BR ownership, and seven were still at work in 1964; half-cab No 41708, built in 1880, was the oldest locomotive then working on BR, and happily has been preserved.

A further 60 slightly larger engines were built by the Vulcan Foundry between 1899 and 1902, and initially numbered 2441-60 and 2741-80, thus becoming known as the '2441' Class; they were later renumbered 1900-59. Thirty-eight were fitted with condensing apparatus for working over the Metropolitan 'Widened Lines' via St Pancras, and thus many were shedded in the London area, principally Kentish Town and Cricklewood. In 1914 no fewer than 42 were allocated to Kentish Town, and there were still 12 in 1920, while Cricklewood had 29; the latter retained the largest allocation until scrapping began in the late 1950s.

By 1902 the Midland presumably had enough locomotives of this kind, but between 1924 and 1931, under Fowler, the newly formed LMS built a further 415 0-6-0Ts, the celebrated 'Jinties', and some ten of these very useful engines have been preserved. The original '2441' Class engines could be distinguished from the

Introduced 1899
Designed by Samuel Johnson
Built by Vulcan Foundry
Number built 60
Number inherited by BR 60
Last example withdrawn December 1966

Johnson MR 3F No 47202 of 1899 was the last survivor of 60 0-6-0Ts built between that year and 1902. It is seen here shunting a rake of empty mineral wagons at Agecroft, then its home shed, on 13 December 1965, just a year before withdrawal. Note the condensing apparatus (the pipe between smokebox and tank), a relic of its many years shedded at Kentish Town and working over the Metropolitan 'Widened Lines'. *Colour-Rail collection*

LMS-built examples by their shorter smokeboxes and rectangular bunkers, and the water tanks were higher and narrower.

During the 1930s the '2441' Class engines were renumbered 7200-59. As built, they all had enclosed cabs and the distinctive Johnson round-topped boilers with Salter safety valves in the dome, but between 1919 and 1942 Fowler rebuilt them all with Belpaire boilers, reclassifying them 3F.

Interestingly, although now widely known as 'Jinties', for most MR locomen that term belonged to a completely different type, a four-coupled saddle tank built at Derby in 1883, which was fitted with the company's Type J boiler, from which the nickname was derived.

Despite their age, the whole class remained intact upon nationalisation, and three were still in service in 1966. The last two, Nos 47201 and 47202, both built in 1899, were withdrawn from Patricroft and Newton Heath respectively at the end of that year.

LNWR Webb 'Bissel Truck' 1F Class 0-4-2PT

Nos 47862, 47865

These 20 short-wheelbase London & North Western Railway engines were variously known as 'Dock Tanks' or 'Bissel Tanks'. They were built at Crewe between 1896 and 1901, and the wheelbase was only 7ft 3in, thus making them suitable for docks and sidings with sharp curves. They were made larger, and thus more powerful (they had 80% of the tractive effort of a 'Jinty' 0-6-0T), by the addition of the 'Bissel truck' under the cab.

The 'Bissel truck' (more correctly 'Bissell') was invented in 1857 by American engineer Levi Bissell. When separate carrying wheels have their pivot within the truck, it is known as a bogie, but the Bissel truck has its pivot nearer the centre of the locomotive. Thus it is able to turn about its vertical axis as well as swing radially from side to side. Where the engine's frame rests on the truck there are a pair of inclined planes, lower at the centre, with corresponding planes on the truck frame; thus as the truck moves from side to side it lifts the outside of the locomotive, slightly canting it into the curve. The advantage of this more flexible arrangement is that the truck does not force the driving axles into an unnatural alignment on curved track.

Although described as pannier tanks, they were not strictly so as the tank was a single structure that sat atop the boiler; the locomotives were more accurately square saddle tanks. The

Having gained a few dents and scratches, 1901-built No 47862 stands in the yard at Crewe Works on 17 October 1954. The square-section saddle tank (not strictly pannier tanks) can clearly be seen, as well as the Bissel truck. *R. Butterfield, Initial Photographics*

tanks were not particularly attractive, and the solid wheels and frame of the Bissel truck were likewise rather cumbersome in appearance. The cab was enclosed, and wooden buffers were originally fitted as more suitable for the engines' shunting role. A large toolbox was fitted on the right-hand running plate.

All 20 locomotives passed to the LMS, which allocated them the numbers 6400-19, but only five had been renumbered before the numbers were changed again to 7850-69 in 1927. The first example was withdrawn in 1929, and two, Nos 7862 and 7865, survived to enter BR service in 1948, earning their keep as shunters at Crewe Works. No 47865 was withdrawn in November 1953, followed by No 47862 in November 1956.

Introduced 1896
Designed by Francis Webb
Built by LNWR, Crewe
Number built 20
Number inherited by BR 2
Last example withdrawn November 1956

LNWR Bowen Cooke 6F '1185' Class 0-8-2T

Nos 7875, 47877, 47881, 47884, 7885, 7887, 7888, 7892, 47896

The LNWR eight-coupled goods engine family traces its ancestry back to Webb's 'A' Class locomotives of the early 1890s. Various further classes of new engines and rebuilds followed until George Whale and Charles Bowen Cooke introduced the 'G' Class in 1910-12, becoming the principal workhorse for freight traffic towards the end of the LNWR era. The LMS rebuilt the 'Gs' to 'G1'/'G2A' form (qv).

These 30 '1185' Class 0-8-2Ts were designed under the supervision of C. J. Bowen Cooke as a tank version of the 'G' 0-8-0s, and emerged from Crewe between 1911 and 1917. A

Introduced 1911
Designed by Charles Bowen Cooke
Built by LNWR, Crewe
Number built 30
Number inherited by BR 9
Last example withdrawn February 1953

pony truck was added at the rear to support the weight of the rear tank and the coal bunker. The engines were intended for heavy shunting duties in large yards, especially those that had previously required two locomotives. They carried unsuperheated 'Precursor' Class boilers, and the driving wheels were coupled by three overlapping connecting rods (the centre rod fitting outside those on either side), to assist when travelling round sharp curves; the third pair of wheels were flangeless. They were fitted with steam brakes, but vacuum brakes were also provided should the engines be called upon to handle fitted or passenger stock in an emergency. They were also the first LNWR locomotives to be fitted with a lever-operated reverser, which was quicker in operation that the earlier Ramsbottom-style screw reverser, especially with the many changes of direction required when shunting. Initially small 13-inch-diameter buffers to Bowen Cooke's design were fitted, but these tended to lock due to the locomotive's long overhang on sharp curves, so buffers with a larger 18-inch diameter were soon substituted. Their initial livery was black with the insignia 'L N W R' on the side tanks in 12-inch letters.

During the Depression many of the class spent time in store for want of work, and many were scrapped from 1934 onwards. However, nine survived into the BR era all shedded in the North West. Only four of them received their allocated BR numbers, and they were soon withdrawn from February 1948 onwards. The final example, No 47877, outlived its fellows by some two years, finishing work at Wigan Springs Branch shed in February 1953. Despite being essentially shunting engines, No 47884 achieved the highest calculated service mileage of a creditable 732,425 miles, and three others managed around 700,000.

6F 0-8-2T No 47877 was the last survivor of a class of 30 locomotives built between 1911 and 1917. As a BR engine it was shedded at Speke Junction until August 1950, and is seen at work there on 21 April. It had received its BR number in May 1948, but two years later is still lettered 'LMS' on the tank side. *H. C. Casserley*

LNWR Beames 7F '380' Class 0-8-4T

Nos 7930, 47931, 7932, 7933, 7936, 47937, 7938, 7939, 7948, 7951, 7953, 7956, 7958, 7959

Introduced 1923
Designed by Capt Hewitt Beames
Built by LNWR, Crewe
Number built 30
Number inherited by BR 14
Last example withdrawn December 1951

When C. J. Bowen Cooke died in 1920, Capt H. P. M. Beames was appointed to succeed him. However, the LNWR and Lancashire & Yorkshire Railway merged in 1922, and after only two years in the Chief Mechanical Engineer's office Beames was ousted by the LYR's more elderly George Hughes. Hughes retired from the LMS in 1925 and Beames was overlooked when Sir Henry Fowler was appointed CME. When Fowler retired in 1930, Ernest Lemon took over the post, although on a somewhat temporary basis until Stanier was headhunted from the GWR in 1932. Beames thus missed the top job once more, but was always magnanimous in the face of disappointment; he wrote to Stanier to say that, though disappointed, there was no one under whom he would rather serve. Beames retired from the LMS in 1934, and died in 1948.

His only new locomotive for the LNWR was his '380' Class 0-8-4T, 30 of which were built in 1923-24, primarily for use in

South Wales, where the LNWR's lines were characterised by severe gradients. For example, the climb to the Heads of the Valleys line from Abergavenny was 1 in 38, with sharp curves.

The '380s' were basically an extended version of Bowen Cooke's '1185' Class 0-8-2T (see previous entry), with a longer bunker. They were intended for hauling heavy goods trains over short distances, and the larger bunker carried some 30% more coal than the 0-8-2Ts, while the tanks carried 70% more water, capacities that compared favourably with some tender engines. As with the 0-8-2Ts, Webb 18-inch-diameter buffers were fitted, and most of the class carried LNWR black livery, although six appeared in LMS red livery from the start.

As they appeared during the early months of the LMS, before the new group's numbering scheme had been finalised, the first 13 carried LNWR numbers; the remaining 17 carried LMS numbers 7943-59, and the first batch were renumbered 7930-42 between 1926 and 1928. The first was withdrawn in 1944, but 14 survived to become BR engines. Allocated the numbers 47930 and 47959, only two locomotives actually carried their BR number; six had been withdrawn before the end of 1948, and only one lasted into 1951.

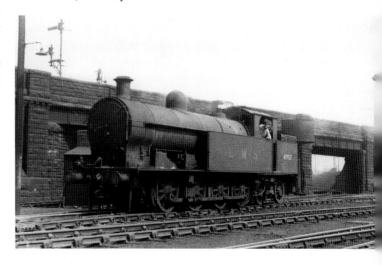

This is Beames 7F 0-8-4T No 47937. Although built for the steep LNWR lines of the South Wales valleys, most were allocated to Edge Hill shed, Liverpool, during their short BR careers; No 47937 is seen there on 18 April 1950, six months before withdrawal. Note the characteristic cast-iron wheels with their 'H'-section spokes, and the two sandboxes above the two front driving wheels. Also just visible are the steps on the smokebox front to allow footplatemen to reach the top lamp-iron on these huge engines! *H. C. Casserley*

LMS Fowler/Beyer Peacock 'Garratt' Class 2-6-0+0-6-2T

Nos 47967-99

Introduced 1927
Designed by Sir Henry Fowler and Beyer Peacock
Built by Beyer Peacock
Number built 33
Number inherited by BR 33
Last example withdrawn March 1958

The 'Garratt' articulated locomotive design – with a single boiler mounted on a central frame between a pair of two-cylinder engines – was developed by Herbert Garratt, a British locomotive engineer who worked on various colonial railways. He first applied for a patent in 1907, and approached locomotive builder Kitson & Co, which was not interested. Eventually he managed to interest Beyer Peacock & Co, which went on to built 'Garratts' of various wheel arrangements and gauges for railways around the world.

In LMS days a particularly heavy and lucrative traffic was coal trains from Toton yard, between Nottingham and Derby, and Brent Sidings, Cricklewood, in north-west London. The Midland's erstwhile 'small engine' policy meant that these trains were usually worked by double-headed 0-6-0s. This was considered increasingly uneconomical, so three Garratt locomotives were ordered from Beyer Peacock, and constructed in 1927. Their tractive effort of 45,620lb was roughly twice that of a single superheated 4F 0-6-0 – depending, of course, on the ability of a fireman to feed the large firebox effectively. The three engines were thoroughly tested and found effective; LMS President Sir Josiah Stamp stated that 'in addition to saving one set of enginemen per train, they will displace 68 old freight tender engines.'

A further 30 Garratts were therefore ordered, emerging between August to November 1930. All had conventional bunkers, but from 1931 all except the first two of the 1927 trio were fitted with Beyer Peacock's self-trimming revolving coal bunker, whose axis sloped towards the footplate; the top of the container had double doors to allow coaling. The floor was sufficiently steep to work coal forward when the bunker was revolved or oscillated, relieving the fireman of the tedious and strenuous task of doing the job manually. It also reduced the amount of coal dust on the footplate. Three or four revolutions of about 30 seconds each were normally sufficient to bring enough coal forward.

However, it seems that footplate crews were not trained in how to handle these huge engines. Although twin water cranes were in existence for watering double-headed trains, the distance between the Garratt water fillers did not conform.

The length and bulk of the LMS 'Garratts' can be readily gauged by this ground-level shot of No 47987, seen from the water tank end at its home shed of Toton on 23 June 1956. The top of the rotary bunker can be glimpsed at the far end. This engine met its end in May of the following year *T. B. Owen, Colour-Rail*

Working a loose-coupled freight train of something like 1,300 tons with a Garratt presented particular problems. The trains were so long that they sometimes spanned lengths of track with different gradients, so starting a train, to pick up the couplings one by one, had to be done with the utmost care.

The original 1927 locos were numbered 4997-99, and the remainder 4967-96. They were later renumbered 7967-7999, to free up numbers required for the new 'Black Five' 4-6-0s. The Garratts were all shedded at Toton, Hasland (near Chesterfield) and Wellingborough (the convenient halfway point between London and the East Midlands). Toton shed's roundhouses had to have longer roads provided for them.

Unfortunately design shortcomings limited the locos' effectiveness. The bearings were of inadequate size for such a large locomotive (the axle loadings were 'absurdly high', according to one author, leading to heavy flange wear) and short-travel valves were used, which meant that the class did not achieve high mileages between overhauls. Beyer had built a 2-8-0+0-8-2T for overseas, which would have spread the weight better, but the company did not have an entirely free hand in the design of the LMS engines. There were also failures of the rotary bunkers and exhaust steam injectors, filling the water tanks en route was time-consuming, and maintenance was hampered by a shortage of spares.

Always heavy on coal and maintenance costs, withdrawals of these leviathans began in 1955, and by early 1958 all had gone. Preservation would have been expensive and difficult – and which heritage railway of the early days could have accommodated such a monster?

LNWR Whale 4F 19-inch Goods Class 4-6-0

Nos 8801, 8824, 8834

George Whale (1842-1910) began work for the LNWR in 1858, at Wolverton Works under James McConnell. In 1862 the company transferred locomotive construction and repair at Crewe, under John Ramsbottom, and Whale moved north. By 1898 he was responsible for all LNWR locomotive running, and in 1903 he took over the Locomotive Superintendent's job on Webb's retirement.

Whale began by converting some of his predecessor's unsuccessful compound engines to simple form. In 1904 he introduced his new 'Precursor' 4-4-0s, followed by the 4-6-0 'Experiment' Class in 1905, which together formed the basis for subsequent LNWR classes, one of which was the '19-inch Express Goods' or 'Experiment Goods' of 1906. This was essentially an 'Experiment' passenger engine with smaller 5ft 2½in driving wheels, a long continuous splasher without coupling-rod splashers, and larger cab windows; the lower axles also allowed a slightly deeper firebox. They were very successful engines, designed to be a mixed-traffic 4-6-0 replacement for the old Webb 0-6-0 'Cauliflowers', mainly intended for goods trains but also able to handle special passenger traffic if required. One idiosyncrasy of the new engines was that the sandboxes were almost impossible to fill, being inside the frames just forward of the first two driving wheels; this problem was solved by relocating them, one behind the forward footstep and the other in the driving splasher.

Crewe built 170 engines between 1906 and 1909, and they were numbered haphazardly, reusing numbers from withdrawn locomotives. All 170 passed to the LMS in 1923, which gave

Introduced 1906
Designed by George Whale
Built by LNWR, Crewe
Number built 170
Number inherited by BR 3
Last example withdrawn February 1950

This undated LMS-era portrait shows Whale '19-inch Express Goods' 4-6-0 No 8834.

R. M. Casserley collection

them the power classification 4F and renumbered them into a single sequence from 8700 to 8869. Withdrawals began in 1931, and by the time of nationalisation in 1948 only three remained in service. They did not last long in BR ownership; Nos 8801 and 8834 were withdrawn from Patricroft and Wigan Springs branch respectively before the end of 1948, while No 8824 followed in February 1950, also from Springs Branch; none of the three ever carried its allocated BR number. No 8824 was the last LNWR 4-6-0 in service, only just outliving the last of the 'Prince of Wales' 4-6-0s, which had gone in October 1949.

LNWR 'G1' and 'G2A' Class 0-8-0

Nos 48892-99, 48901-15, 48917, 48918, 48920-22, 48924-27, 48929-36, 48939-45, 48948, 48950-54, 48962, 48964, 48966, 49002-181, 49183-205, 49207-14, 49216-335, 49337-73, 49375-79, 49381-94

(For simplicity, this list assumes that every locomotive carried its BR number, although many did not)

Introduced 1893; 'G1' rebuilds 1912, 'G2A' rebuilds 1936
Designed by Francis Webb (originals), George Whale and Charles Bowen Cooke ('G' Class), Bowen Cooke ('G1' rebuilds), Hewitt Beames ('G2')
Built by LNWR, Crewe
Number built 512
Number inherited by BR 442
Last example withdrawn September 1955 ('G1'), December 1964 ('G2A')

The genealogy of the LNWR 0-8-0 goods engine family is very complex. It began with a prototype engine in 1892 and subsequent 'A' Class built by Webb in 1893-1900. His 'B' Class four-cylinder compounds followed in 1901-04, some of which were converted to 2-8-0s ('E' and 'F' Classes). The 'G' Class two-cylinder simples were introduced by Whale and Bowen Cooke between 1910 and 1912, with large 160psi non-superheated boilers. In 1912 one was rebuilt with a superheated 160psi boiler, followed by 170 more between 1912 and 1918, becoming the superheated 'G1' Class. In addition, 278 older locomotives – the majority of classes 'A', 'B', 'C', 'D', 'E', 'F' and 'G' – were rebuilt to 'G1' specification between 1917 and 1934. The 'G2' Class was a Beames version from 1921-22, with a

superheated 175psi boiler. Subsequently, from 1936 onwards many 'G1s' were rebuilt with this higher-pressure boiler, to become the 'G2A' Class, which also incorporated improvements to the brakes and valve gear. To confuse matters further, when being overhauled some 'G2As' were rebuilt with lower-pressure boilers, thus reverting to 'G1' form!

As with other LNWR classes, numbering was haphazard, using the lowest available numbers. The LMS renumbered them in a more logical series, though by no means corresponding to order of construction, the 'G1s' and 'G2As' being combined within that sequence. The 449 'G1s' were

Ex-LNWR 'G2A' 7F 0-8-0 No 49142 is in its element at the head of a mineral train near Chapel-en-le-Frith in 1953. Allocated to Bescot in 1948, this engine wandered between Stockport Edgeley, Nuneaton, Edge Hill and Wigan before returned to Bescot in 1962, being withdrawn there at the end of that year. These 0-8-0s had been the LNWR's principal heavy freight engine, and it was only in the late 1950s that 'G2A' withdrawals began in earnest. *Colour-Rail collection*

never in service at the same time, as some were being converted to 'G2As' while some 'Gs' were still being converted to 'G1s'! With the 60 'G2s', the number of superheated 0-8-0s of LNWR origin eventually totalled well over 500. The rebuilding policy continued well into LMS days and some of the class were still in service until as late as 1964.

Originally the 'G1s' were unfitted with steam brakes for the engine only, but from 1914 they had vacuum brakes and screw couplings so they could work passenger trains if necessary; over time earlier engines were similarly equipped. Some time after the First World War steam heating was added, not so much for passenger trains but for the banana specials from Garston Docks.

All the ex-LNWR engines inherited by BR had the same general appearance. They were impressive-looking machines, with their extended smokeboxes (to accommodate the superheater header) and Belpaire boilers, and in the Manchester area they were known as 'Fat Nancies'. The 'G1s' were known as 'D Superheated' by the LNWR Traffic Department, and together with the 'G2s' eventually became known as 'Super Ds', a nickname now applied generally to the 0-8-0 engines. The prototype 'G2', No 49395, has been preserved, but the huge number of BR 'G1s' and 'G2As' have all passed into history.

LNWR Fowler 7F Class 0-8-0

Nos 49500-674

(For simplicity, this list assumes that every locomotive carried its BR number, although many did not)

Introduced 1929	
Designed by Sir Henry Fowler	
Built by LMS, Crewe	
Number built 175	
Number inherited by BR 173	
Last example withdrawn January 1962	

These LMS 0-8-0s were a 'Midlandised' development of the LNWR Beames 'G2' 0-8-0 (see previous entry), and were sometimes referred to by what would have been their LNWR class, 'G3'. The Joy valve gear of the 'G2' was replaced by Walschaerts, and long-travel valves were used. They were fitted with Belpaire boilers and had a higher boiler pressure than the earlier locomotives, but had the same power rating of 7F. The 'Midlandising' gave them very much a 'Midland' rather than an 'LNWR' appearance, but incorporated a number of characteristic Midland shortcomings, including axle and motion bearings that were not up to the job given the long wheelbase (the Midland having built nothing larger than an 0-6-0 for general freight working) and broke up rapidly, causing frequent overheating. Other minor defects included leaking injector steam and delivery pipes, and consequently they suffered from high maintenance costs.

Nevertheless, they had good steaming qualities and were economical when in service, and 175 were built in eight lots between 1929 and 1932. They gained the enginemen's nickname of 'Baby Austins' or 'Austin Sevens', after the popular motor car of the period. In 1932 Nos 9672-74 were fitted with

They were not the most successful or long-lived members of the MR/LMS 0-8-0 family, but Fowler's 7Fs clearly betrayed their Derby design origins. In this undated picture, No 49667, of Bury shed from 1948 until 1953, then Newton Heath, is seen near Sowerby Bridge in scruffy external condition. The shedplate might possibly read '26A', the code for Newton Heath, so it is probably a post-1953 picture. No 49667 was withdrawn in May 1959. *J. M. Bairstow, Colour-Rail*

ACFI feedwater heaters; this was a French design (the acronym standing for 'Accessoires pour les Chemins de Fer et l'Industrie'), whereby steam-driven pumps drew water from the tender and heated it with exhaust steam. The apparatus consisting of a feed pump and two heat-exchanging drums on top of the boiler behind the chimney, and these 'backpacks' gave rise to the additional nickname of 'Hikers' (also applied to similarly equipped 'B12' 4-6-0s on the LNER). The heaters were removed during the Second World War, and after the war in 1947 five

0-8-0s (Nos 9511, 9533, 9613, 9642 and 9670) were converted to oil-burning; No 49511 was reconverted to coal in 1949, but the others were scrapped in that year.

Indeed, some 60 class members were withdrawn during 1949, and fewer that 10 remained a decade later. The last example, No 49508, was withdrawn from Agecroft shed in the early weeks of 1962. Ironically, more than two dozen of the LNWR 'G2s' – almost half the class, and ten years older – outlived the Fowler engines that had been designed to replace them.

LYR Hughes 5P '8' Class 4-6-0

Nos 10412, 10423, 10429, 10432, 10442, 10448, 50455

'Dreadnought' was a nickname applied to several large, invincible-looking steam locomotives around the turn of the 20th century, referring to what was then the principal design of British battleship. The original, the Royal Navy's HMS *Dreadnought* of 1906, gave its name to a new kind of fighting ship, with 'all big gun' weaponry and steam turbine propulsion. 'Dreadnoughts' became an important symbol of national power, but the term gradually fell out of use after the First World War.

In 1908 the LYR was concerned to meet ever-increasing passenger loads, and Hughes designed his first 4-6-0 for the company, the Class '8' 'Lanky Dreadnoughts'. The engines had four cylinders and 6ft 3in driving wheels, a Belpaire firebox and Joy valve gear, and the first 20 were built in 1908-09. However, severe teething troubles beset the class; they were sluggish, poor performers and heavy on coal. This was partly due to having been designed to cope with the trans-Pennine routes rather than for fast running on less demanding routes. The wheelbase was kept as short as possible and allowance was made in the driving wheels and coupling rods to enable negotiation of fairly sharp curves. The engines were designed for good acceleration after frequent stops, rather than sustained running, and ease of maintenance also needed to be borne in mind. It is said that the lubricating system was inadequate for long runs, causing hot axleboxes, and that the smokeboxes leaked, allowing char to reaching the cylinders, causing problems with the piston valves.

To remedy the locomotives' shortcomings it was decided to rebuild them with superheaters, Walschaerts valve gear, and other modifications. The war postponed this plan until 1921, when the LYR also merged with the LNWR, and 15 of the 'Dreadnoughts' were rebuilt. They now emerged as the engines they had originally intended to be; 14 more were built before the Grouping, and were the most powerful engines in

On 1 July 1951 BR approached the Manchester Railway Society and Stephenson Locomotive Society to support a 'special excursion' (train C820) from Blackpool to York and return, using the last surviving LYR Class '8' 4-6-0 No 50455 (one of the 1923-25 LMS-built batch). In BR lined black, with 'British Railways' on the tender, the veteran is seen at York before its final run back to Blackpool, where it was shedded. *E. Oldham, Colour-Rail*

Britain until Gresley's 'Pacifics' appeared in 1922. So improved were they that the LMS built a further 41 during 1923-25 (some of which had already been ordered by the LYR, and 20 of which came from an order for 30 4-6-4Ts, changed to 4-6-0s during construction).

In 1925 Hughes's 'Dreadnoughts' participated in tests against LNWR 'Prince of Wales', 'Claughton' and compound LNWR classes, but these were hardly like-for-like comparisons. Dabeg feedwater heaters were fitted to some locomotives used on the Blackpool Club trains, leading to considerable savings in coal.

LMS No 10456 was converted to a four-cylinder compound in July 1926 by Fowler as part of his work to develop a compound 'Pacific' design.

The five unmodified locomotives of the original batch were withdrawn in the 1920s, and most of the others went in the 1930s – arising from the fact that at the Grouping the LMS inherited 393 different locomotive classes, and LMS President Sir Josiah Stamp thought it desirable to reduce this to just ten!

Ultimately just seven of the 4-6-0s entered BR stock, and only one of them, No 50455, received its allocated BR number, being the last to be withdrawn in October 1951; all the others had gone by August 1950.

Introduced 1908; rebuilt 1921-25
Designed by George Hughes
Built by LYR, Horwich
Number built 75
Number inherited by BR 7
Last example withdrawn October 1951

LYR Aspinall/Hughes 3P '6' Class 2-4-2T

Nos 10835, 50891, 50893, 10901, 10903, 50909, 50925, 10934, 10943, 10945, 10950, 10951, 10952, 50953

Introduced 1898; rebuilt 1912
Designed by John Aspinall; rebuilt by George Hughes
Built by LYR, Horwich
Number built 64 (20 new, 44 rebuilds)
Number inherited by BR 14
Last example withdrawn August 1952

John Audley Frederick Aspinall (1851-1937) was described by Denis Griffiths in *Locomotive Engineers of the LMS* as 'not only a brilliant engineer, in the complete sense, but … also an equally exceptional manager.' After an early apprenticeship at Crewe under Ramsbottom and a spell as Locomotive Engineer for the Great Southern & Western Railway in Ireland, he became CME of the Lancashire & Yorkshire Railway in 1886. He later became the company's General Manager from 1899 until his retirement in 1919.

In 1889 Aspinall introduced his very successful 2-4-2T 'Radial tank' design, a wheel arrangement much used by the LYR; in all, 330 were built up to 1911. The first of them (No 1008/10621/50621) was the first locomotive to be built at Horwich, emerging from the Erecting Shop on 20 February 1889; it is now preserved as part of the National Collection.

There was much debate at the time concerning the relative advantages of the 0-4-4 and 2-4-2 wheel arrangements for short-distance passenger traffic. The 0-4-4 was emerging as the winner, with Aspinall having had experience of them in Ireland, and Barton Wright having built many for the LYR. However, Aspinall disliked the concept of unguided driving wheels. He consulted the LNWR's Webb, who was a supporter of the 2-4-2 arrangement, as was Holden on the GER, so a 2-4-2T it was to be. Aspinall's design had a larger boiler and firebox, working at a higher pressure; they were simple, straightforward engines with no innovative components, yet they encountered no teething troubles and were met with general acclaim by the traffic department.

When Aspinall became the LYR's General Manager he was succeeded as CME by Henry Hoy, then by George Hughes in 1904. In 1911 Hughes built 20 new 2-4-2Ts, developed from Aspinall's earlier design, with superheated Belpaire boilers, extended smokeboxes and longer bunkers. From 1912 44 engines of the earlier class were rebuilt to the new form, becoming LYR Class '6'.

By nationalisation in 1948 there were still 14 in use, but withdrawals began almost immediately. By the end of 1951 only one remained, No 50925, but that had been dispensed with by August of the following year.

No 10925 was the last of the Aspinall/Hughes 2-4-2T 'Radial tanks'. Built in 1910 and later rebuilt with a longer bunker (seen here well filled!), it was one of 14 of the class inherited by BR. Still carrying its LMS livery and number at Wakefield on 11 March 1948, it became BR No 50925 in September of that year, and lasted until August 1952, when it was withdrawn from its home shed of Sowerby Bridge (25E). *H. C. Casserley*

LYR Aspinall rebuilt 2F '23' Class 0-6-0ST

Nos 51307, 51313, 51316, 11318, 51319, 11320, 51321, 51323, 11342, 51343, 51345, 51348, 51353, 51358, 51361, 51371, 51375, 51376, 51379, 51381, 51390, 51396, 51397, 11400, 51404, 11405, 51408, 51410, 51412, 51413, 51415, 51419, 51423-25, 11427, 51429, 51432, 51436, 11438, 51439, 51441, 11443, 51444-47, 51453, 51457, 51458, 51460, 51462, 51464, 11467-69, 51470-72, 51474, 11475, 51477, 51479, 51481, 11482, 51484, 51486, 11487, 51488-91, 11492, 11495, 51496-500, 51500, 51503, 51504, 51506, 51510-14, 51516, 51519, 51521, 51524, 51526, 51530, 11304, 11305, 11324, 11368, 11394

Introduced 1891 (rebuilt from 0-6-0s of 1876-87)
Designed by John Aspinall (rebuilt from Barton Wright originals)
Built by LYR, Miles Platting, plus Kitson, Sharp Stewart, Beyer Peacock, Vulcan Foundry; rebuilt LYR, Horwich
Number rebuilt 230
Number inherited by BR 101 (including 5 in departmental stock)
Last example withdrawn September 1964

William Barton Wright (1828-1915) was appointed Chief Locomotive Superintendent of the LYR in 1875, having started his career as an apprentice under Gooch on the GWR, followed by a spell with the Madras Railway in India. Wright's first job on the LYR was to rectify a run-down locomotive situation, and in 1877 the company's carriage works was moved from Miles

Platting to Newton Heath, providing more space at Miles Platting for locomotive building. Meanwhile, in 1876 Wright's new standard 0-6-0 goods engine was introduced; the first was built by Kitson & Co, and others followed from Miles Platting as well as other outside contractors until by 1887 the class numbered 280.

Wright's successor John Aspinall produced his own class of 0-6-0 in 1889, which remained in production until 1918, eventually totalling 468 machines, 245 of which lasted to become BR engines, and one of which, No 52322 of 1895, is preserved. They were intended to replace the ageing Barton Wright 0-6-0s, but the LYR also had a severe shortage of shunting engines, so Aspinall took the opportunity to rebuild some of the redundant older 0-6-0s as saddle tanks. In all, 230 were rebuilt at Horwich Works between 1891 and 1900, leaving just 50 as tender engines. The spare tenders were used economically for new Aspinall engines.

All the tanks and remaining tender engines passed to the LMS in 1923; 25 of the unrebuilt 0-6-0s became BR engines, and one of them, No 52044, is happily preserved.

Ninety-six of the saddle tanks also became BR property, together with five that worked at Horwich Works, retaining their LMS numbers 11304, 11305, 11324, 11368 and 11394. No 11305 was not taken out of service until 1964, being then the oldest engine working for BR. Four others, carrying BR numbers, worked at Horwich and Crewe. What had originally been produced as an urgent replacement for worn-out stock became a long-lived and useful engine serving the LYR, LMS and BR for the best part of eight decades.

Although none of the BR engines were saved for preservation, the LMS had withdrawn 1881 Beyer Peacock-built engine No 11456 (LYR No 752) in 1937 and sold it to a

2F 0-6-0ST No 51371 had originally been built as a tender engine by Kitson in 1878. Rebuilt as a saddle tank in the 1890s, it was still hard at work when photographed at its home shed of Newton Heath in 1960. Four examples survived to the end of that year, No 51371 being withdrawn in March 1961.
Colour-Rail collection

colliery near Wigan. In 1947 it became National Coal Board property, and was withdrawn in the late 1950s. After nine years out of use, it was preserved, in poor condition, in 1967, by what was to become the Lancashire & Yorkshire Railway Trust. Moved to the Keighley & Worth Valley Railway in 1971, it was returned to steam in May 1977 and took part in the celebration of 150 years of the Liverpool & Manchester Railway at Rainhill in 1979. It is currently disassembled at Haworth, requiring a good deal of work to return it to service.

LYR Aspinall 1F Dock Tank '24' Class 0-6-0T

Nos 51535-37, 51544, 51546

Introduced 1897	
Designed by John Aspinall	
Built by LYR, Horwich	
Number built 20	
Number inherited by BR 5	
Last example withdrawn September 1961	

Like 'Dreadnought', 'Klondyke' was a nickname applied to various different classes of locomotive, and arose from the famous Canadian 'gold rush' of 1897-98. One such class was the LYR Class '24' Dock Tanks, 20 of which were built by Horwich in 1897. They were compact engines with a short wheelbase for shunting dock sidings. They were built with flat-topped Belpaire fireboxes (among the first British locomotives to be so fitted), but, unlike many other types, from 1917 these were replaced by round-topped boilers. They originally had steam reversing gear and crosshead-driven vacuum pumps, but screw reversers were fitted later, and the original single-bar slidebars were replaced by double bars on some engines.

1F 0-6-0T Dock Tank No 51536 was allocated to Bank Hall shed, near Liverpool's docks, throughout its BR career. On 18 May 1950 an assortment of LMS and BR numbers and liveries are seen on three of the shed's resident engines; on the left is what appears to be 0F 0-4-0ST No 7002, while beyond No 51536 is LYR Aspinall 0-4-0ST 'Pug' No 51229. All three survived into the 1960s.
R. M. Casserley

The first locomotive to be withdrawn was in 1917, and six had gone by 1922. The LMS dispensed with nine more, but five survived to enter BR stock. They were all shedded at Bank Hall or Aintree for working in Liverpool's docks. No 51535 was fitted with wooden buffers, but the others had ordinary spring buffers, and, for dock work, they carried simple spark arresters.

No 11537 was the last ex-LMS engine to receive its BR number when it became No 51537 as late as September 1954. It was also the last survivor of the class, being withdrawn from Aintree in September 1961.

Furness Railway Pettigrew 3F 'D5' Class 0-6-0

Nos 52494, 52499, 52501, 52508-10

This is the only appearance of the Furness Railway in these pages. The company was incorporated in 1844, intended primarily for the conveyance of mineral traffic (slate and iron ore) from mines to the sea at Barrow, it was subsequently extended to Whitehaven and Carnforth, Ulverston, Coniston and Lakeside. The mineral wealth of the area made the Furness a prosperous concern, and when that business declined it turned successfully to tourist traffic.

Glasgow-born William Frank Pettigrew (1858-1941) was the Furness's Locomotive Superintendent between 1896 and 1918, having previously been assistant to William Adams on the London & South Western Railway. His first locomotives for the Furness were 0-6-0s, to handle the mineral traffic that was the company's lifeblood. O. S. Nock comments on Pettigrew's 'addiction to the simplest and most straightforward design practice', and it is a measure of the success of his 'D5' 0-6-0s of 1913-20 that the six examples that entered BR stock were the only Furness engines to be nationalised.

The 'D5s' were the final development of FR six-coupled goods engines, and were the largest and most powerful. Four were built initially by the North British Locomotive Co, with

Introduced 1913	
Designed by William Pettigrew	
Built by North British (15), Kitson (4)	
Number built 19	
Number inherited by BR 6	
Last example withdrawn August 1957	

large superheated boilers (the superheaters were not successful and were later removed). During and after the First World War 15 more followed, with boilers 6 inches longer. Although intended for freight traffic, they were fitted with vacuum brakes and steam heating so they could be used for excursion trains. In spite of their small 4ft 7½in wheels, they were capable of a good turn of speed when required.

Their tenders were the largest yet used by the FR, and were standard with the large 4-4-0 'K4' Class passenger engines built at about the same time.

The LMS renumbered the class 12494-512, and rebuilt most of them with LYR Belpaire boilers. Interestingly, when No 12509 (BR 52509) was withdrawn at Horwich Works in 1956, all the liveries it had ever carried could be discerned through the fading paint if observed at the right angle in the right light: the British Railways 'lion and wheel' emblem, on top of the letters 'LMS', then the large LMS numbers '12509', and underneath it all, very faintly, the letters 'FR'.

Four of the class were scrapped as early as 1930, at only 12 years old, but six passed to BR, all but one surviving until 1956/57. The last ex-Furness engine in BR service was No 52510 (FR No 33).

On 5 September 1954 the SLS and Manchester Locomotive Society ran the 'West Cumberland Rail Tour' along former Furness lines around Sellafield, Workington and Whitehaven. Two of the FR 'D5' 0-6-0s were used, Nos 52494 and 52501, which were subsequently withdrawn in April 1956 and June 1957 respectively. The train of five ex-LMS corridor coaches is seen here at Workington Central behind No 52501. *Chris Banks collection, Colour-Rail*

LYR Hughes 3F '28' Class 0-6-0

Nos 12528, 52541, 52542, 52545, 52549, 52551, 51554, 51557-59, 52561, 12688, 52569, 52572, 12574, 52575, 52576, , 12578, 52579-83, 12586, 52587, 52588, 12590, 52592, 52598, 12602, 12607, 52608, 52609, 52615, 51616, 12618, 52619

Aspinall introduced his Class '27' 0-6-0 goods engine for the Lancashire & Yorkshire Railway in 1889, and they continued to be built right through to 1918, during the Hoy and Hughes regimes, with some modifications. Eventually there were 468 in service, with two cylinders, a non-superheated round-topped boiler and Joy valve gear.

Introduced 1889 (rebuilt from 1912) and 1912 (new)
Designed by John Aspinall (rebuilt by Hughes), George Hughes
Built by LYR, Horwich
Number built 83
Number inherited by BR 37
Last example withdrawn March 1957

George Hughes used one of the Class '27s' for experiments in superheating, and after extensive trials the LYR authorised the building of a batch of superheated engines in 1909, with round-topped boilers. At the time of the Grouping in 1923 300 of these robust, practical engines passed to the LMS, and in due course 245 of them passed to the nationalised British Railways, the last 16 lasting into 1962. One of them, 1895-built No 52322 (LYR No 1300), was preserved.

Meanwhile, in 1912 Hughes introduced a version of the Class '27' that was superheated from the outset, with Belpaire fireboxes. Twenty were built new, and 63 were rebuilds of the Aspinall Class '27', undertaken between 1913 and 1922, with extended footplate, front sandboxes and larger cylinders; six of the new engines and 31 of the rebuilds survived to become BR property.

Although none was preserved, one has been immortalised as 'James the Red Engine' in 'The Railway series' by Rev W. Awdry. 'James' is in fact a 2-6-0 rather than an 0-6-0, but Awdry

Most of the Aspinall/Hughes 3F 0-6-0s remained in their home counties of Lancashire and Yorkshire, but curiously Nos 52608 and 52619 spent their last days on LNWR metals, allocated to Rhyl shed (6K). No 52608 is seen at Rhyl on 27 August 1954; it was taken out of use the following February. *R. M. Casserley*

himself described the engine as an 'experimental rebuild' with 5ft 6in driving wheels – the addition of the pony truck was suggested by the real loco's large front overhang. The sandboxes are also omitted.

By the end of 1955 only two engines survived, Nos 52551 and 52576, withdrawn in March and February 1957 respectively.

LYR Aspinall 6F '30' Class 0-8-0

Nos 52727, 52782, 12806, 52821, 52822, 52825, 12827, 12828, 52831, 12834, 12837, 52839

The LYR employed 0-8-0s to move its heavy coal traffic across the Pennines, the large-boiler varieties being nicknamed 'Lanky Bombers'. Eventually these were replaced by Fowler 'Austin Seven' 0-8-0s, then subsequently by the 'WD' 2-8-0s. Between 1900 and 1908 130 LYR 0-8-0 coal engines, designed by Aspinall (although they appeared after he ceased to be CME), were constructed at Horwich Works. They had 20-inch-diameter inside cylinders, the largest carried by an LYR locomotive at that time, but were initially fitted with small boilers. The boilers incorporated a novel corrugated firebox of Hoy's design, the corrugation making it stronger and obviating the need for potentially troublesome firebox stays. However, this type of firebox was not entirely successful, being prone to distortion and leakage. Between 1910 and 1918 Hughes fitted 70 of the engines with larger boilers, some superheated (30 were original engines rebuilt, and 40 were new engines – see next entry). Withdrawals of the remaining 60 began in 1926, and only one example, No 52727 of 1903, survived to pass into BR stock. The Hughes rebuilds were withdrawn from 1927 onwards, but 11 (one rebuild and 10 new examples) lasted into early BR days.

Aspinall 6F 0-8-0 No 52727 was the only original small-boilered example to pass into BR stock. Built in 1903, it is seen here at Wigan on 13 September 1950. It was withdrawn from Wigan shed (27D) the following month *H. C. Casserley*

Introduced 1900/1910
Designed by John Aspinall/George Hughes
Built by LYR, Horwich
Number built 130/40
Number inherited by BR 1/11
Last example withdrawn February 1951

One of the original small-boilered engines, No 1452, was rebuilt as a four-cylinder compound, with 15½in by 26in high-pressure cylinders and 22in by 26in low-pressure cylinders; tests showed a 25% saving in coal compared with the simple version. As a result ten more compounds were built between 1906 and 1907. They were considered to be very successful engines, but no more were subsequently built. In 1907 the 1,000th locomotive to be built at Horwich Works was No 1471, one of these compounds. They were all withdrawn in 1926-27.

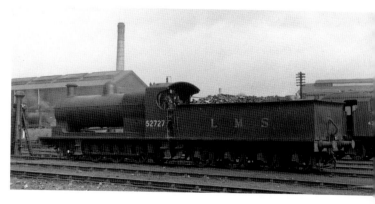

LYR Hughes 7F '31' Class 0-8-0

Nos 12841, 52856, 52857, 52870, 12873, 12877, 52886, 52906, 52910, 12913, 52916, 12935, 52945, 12952, 12956, 52962, 12971

Introduced 1912
Designed by George Hughes
Built by LYR, Horwich
Number built 155
Number inherited by BR 17
Last example withdrawn December 1951

Only three of the Hughes LYR Class '31' superheated 0-8-0s lasted into 1951 – Nos 52897, 52870 and 52945. All the class had been allocated to either Rose Grove or Aintree at nationalisation, but a number migrated to Wigan (23D/27D). The last example, No 52857, was the only one to be allocated to Low Moor, where it was withdrawn at the end of 1951. It is seen here at Lostock Hall shed on 26 May 1950 – note the side-window cab.

Frank Hornby collection

Between 1912 and 1918 Hughes built a superheated, Belpaire-boiler version of his large-boilered 0-8-0s (see previous entry) – 115 were new-builds, and 40 rebuilt Class '30s'. Of the rebuilt engines, only LMS No 12971 of 1900 became a BR locomotive until it was withdrawn and scrapped in 1949 (it was also one of only three BR examples with a side-window cab). The others were new-built engines.

CR unsuperheated '140' 'Dunalastair IV' Class 4-4-0

No 14363

Introduced 1904
Designed by John McIntosh
Built by CR, St Rollox
Number built 19
Number inherited by BR 1
Last example withdrawn October 1948

We now turn to Scotland, where John Farquharson McIntosh (1846-1918) began his railway career as an apprentice with the Scottish North Eastern Railway at Arbroath aged just 14; the SNER was later taken over by the Caledonian Railway. He lost a hand in an accident in the mid-1870s, but continued to rise through the CR ranks until he became deputy to the Chief Mechanical Engineer John Lambie at the company's works at St Rollox in Springburn, Glasgow. Lambie died suddenly in 1895 and McIntosh replaced him.

McIntosh had only been in office for six months where the competitive London-Scotland 'Races to the North' commenced, and he responded by introducing probably his most famous and important design, and his first class for the CR, the 'Dunalastair' series of 4-4-0s, which at the time were among the largest engines in the country. They took their name from that of the prototype, which emerged from St Rollox in January 1896; 'Dunalastair' was the Perthshire estate of the Caledonian's

then Deputy Chairman, J. C. Bunten. As noted by author Thomas Middlemass, the first 15 engines 'were an immediate and unqualified success; their speed and haulage capacity set completely new standards in British locomotive performance.'

The design was a development of a similar one by Lambie in 1894, which had in turn evolved from Dugald Drummond locos of 1884, but boasted much larger boilers that steamed well. The successively larger and more powerful versions (a 'locomotive dynasty', as dubbed by O. S. Nock) began with the '721' Class ('Dunalastair I') of 1896. The following year came the '766' Class ('Dunalastair II', some of which were rebuilt with superheaters in 1914). In 1899-1900 came the '900' Class ('Dunalastair III' – qv), again some of which received superheaters in 1914-18. Finally came the '140' Class, or 'Dunalastair IV', of 1904-10. The last engine of the 1910 batch was fitted with a superheater, becoming the first engine in Scotland to be so equipped, and one of the first in Great Britain; others were subsequently rebuilt with superheaters in 1915-17 – see below.

Still in full LMS livery, the sole BR saturated 'Dunalastair IV' 4-4-0, No 14363, was photographed at Aviemore on 9 June 1948. Sadly, a year later it was cut up, having been withdrawn in October 1948. *W. G. Boyden, Frank Hornby collection*

The tenders also increased in size with each successive version, until those of the 'Dunalastair IVs' weighed almost as much as the engine!

The 'Dunalastair IVs' were numbered 140-150, 923-27, 137, 138 and 136 by the Caledonian, and 17 passed to the LMS, becoming Nos 14349-65. Two engines, built in 1907 and 1908, had been superheated in 1917 and 1915 respectively, becoming

the first of the superheated 'Dunalastair IVs' – see later entry. The last survivor of the saturated engines was LMS No 14363, which as nationalisation dawned was allocated to Aviemore shed (32B). It lasted less than a year as a BR engine, being withdrawn from there in October 1948. It was scrapped at Kilmarnock Works in June the following year.

HR 'Loch' Class 4-4-0

Nos 14379, 14385

Introduced 1896
Designed by David Jones
Built by Dübs (15), North British (3)
Number built 18
Number inherited by BR 2
Last example withdrawn April 1950

Jones 'Loch' 4-4-0 No 14379 *Loch Insh* of 1896 poses at Aviemore in LMS days on 9 April 1946. It was a BR engine for three months in 1948, and was followed to the scrapyard by sister engine *Loch Tay* in April 1950. *H. C. Casserley*

The Highland Railway was the result of an amalgamation of smaller companies in 1865, together with those building the line from Inverness to the Far North. Eventually the system extended to just over 500 miles, most of it single line and, not surprisingly from the terrain through which it ran, often difficult to work. Traffic was not heavy, and at the Grouping in 1923 the locomotive stock only amounted to 173.

Manchester-born David Jones (1834-1906) was apprenticed to Ramsbottom on the LNWR, and joined what would become the HR in 1855, working under William Stroudley and Dugald Drummond. In 1870 he became Locomotive Superintendent and, as well as rebuilding older engines to extend their lives, he introduced new designs, like Britain's first 4-6-0 in 1894 and his final design for the HR, the 'Loch' Class main-line passenger 4-4-0s of 1896-1917. These had a very high power-to-weight ratio and carried Jones's special chimney with a louvred front; the supposed purpose of this was to provide a draught when the engine was running with its steam cut off, as often happened for long descents on the steeply graded Highland network. Jones retired in 1896, after being severely scalded during a locomotive test. Author Thomas Middlemass remarks that Jones had been offered the position to succeed Stroudley on the LBSCR, and considers this possibility an interesting 'might-have-been'.

The first 15 'Lochs' were introduced in 1896 and built by Dübs & Co of Glasgow. So successful were they that three more were hurriedly built in 1917 in response to urgent wartime

requirements, rather than building more locos by Jones's successor, Peter Drummond. The final trio were built by Dübs's successor, the North British Locomotive Co. The appearance of the 'Lochs' was typical Jones, with outside cylinders and a domed cab roof. All were named after Scottish lochs (including some misspellings!), and were generally used north of Inverness, replacing some of Jones's earlier 4-4-0s on the main line between there and Perth, as well as on the Kyle of Lochalsh line, being the heaviest engines permitted to work that route.

The 'Lochs' all passed to the LMS at the Grouping, and were classified 2P; nine were rebuilt with Caledonian-type boilers, but this was not entirely successful and the engines became heavy on coal. Withdrawals began in 1930, and only two examples, Nos 14379 (HR 119) *Loch Insh* and 14385 (HR 125) *Loch Tay* (both original 1896 examples) were left when BR was formed in 1948. *Loch Insh* was withdrawn from Aviemore almost immediately, in March, while *Loch Tay* remained at work from Forres shed until April 1950.

HR Drummond 'Small Ben' Class 4-4-0

Introduced 1898
Designed by Peter Drummond
Built by HR, Lochgorm (9), Dübs (8), North British (3)
Number built 20
Number inherited by BR 10
Last example withdrawn February 1953

Nos 14397, 54398, 54399, 14401, 14403, 54404, 14409, 14410, 14415, 14416

When David Jones retired in 1896 he was succeeded at Lochgorm Works by Peter Drummond (1850-1918), younger brother of the better-known locomotive engineer Dugald, of

'The one that got away.' The final remaining 'Small Ben' 4-4-0, No 54398 *Ben Alder*, languishes at Dawsholm shed in this undated view. After some 13 years in store it was eventually cut up in 1966. Luckier were the Jones 4-6-0 No 103, behind it, and beyond that GNSR 4-4-0 No 49 *Gordon Highlander*, both still very much with us today. *Colour-Rail collection*

London & South Western Railway fame (and a former employee of the HR's Locomotive Department). Peter remained with the Highland until 1911, and the following year joined the Glasgow & South Western Railway until his death.

Drummond's first design was the 'Ben' 4-4-0, generally divided into the 'Small Bens' and 'Large Bens' – or, locally, 'Wee Bens' and 'Big Bens'. All were named after Scottish mountains, 'ben' being a Gaelic word for a mountain peak. There was in fact little difference between the two types, the 'Large Bens' simply having a larger boiler with a larger tube heating surface. The cylinder dimensions and wheel diameter (6 feet) were identical. The 'Bens' had a typical Drummond family 'look', and were not unlike Dugald's contemporary 'T9' 4-4-0s for the LSWR.

Unusually for an HR engine, the 'Bens' had inside cylinders. The first eight were 'Small Bens' built by Dübs & Co of Glasgow. On emerging from the works No 1 originally carried the name *Ben Nevis*, but this was not a popular choice as Britain's highest mountain was actually in North British Railway territory! The

engine was therefore renamed *Ben-y-Gloe* before entering service.

A further nine 'Bens' were built at the HR's own works at Lochgorm, Inverness, in 1899-1901, then a third batch of three were North British Locomotive Co products of 1906.

The 'Bens' ranked among the most powerful British locomotives of the day, and were superb performers. C. Hamilton Ellis remembers a Highland driver remarking, 'Ye'll never find an easier an' more straightforward engine than our "Sma' Ben". I tell ye, man! Your mither could drive her an' get sixty out of her too.'

The six 'Large Bens' followed in 1908-09, built by North British, but they were all withdrawn by the LMS between 1932 and 1937. Withdrawal of the 'Small Bens' began in 1931, but half the class survived to enter BR ownership. All had been rebuilt by the LMS with Caledonian-type boilers.

Sadly, the last survivor was the subject of a failed preservation plan. No 54398 *Ben Alder*, withdrawn from Wick shed in February 1953, was placed in storage with the intention of preserving it to original Highland Railway condition; however, after languishing at Boat of Garten, Forfar and Dawsholm sheds pending a decision, it was eventually cut up by Motherwell Machinery & Scrap at Wishaw as late as 1966, becoming dubbed 'the one that got away' – although the Scottish Railway Preservation Society has raised the suggestion of a 'new-build' example.

CR superheated 'Dunalastair III' Class 4-4-0

No 14434

As already mentioned in the entry for the 'Dunalastair IV' 4-4-0s (see above), this was a family of 4-4-0s spanning the years 1896-1910. The 'Dunalastair IIIs', or '900' Class, appeared in 1899-1900, and were an enlarged version of the 'Dunalastair II'. The firebox was 6 inches longer and 3 inches deeper, the coupled wheelbase 6 inches longer and the boiler set 3 inches higher, necessitating a shorter chimney in order to remain within the loading gauge. They were similar in most respects to the 'IVs' that followed except being some 5 tons lighter. The CR numbered them 900-02 and 887-99, and four of the class were rebuilt with superheaters in 1914-18, elevating them to a 3P classification rather than 2P. Twelve were inherited by the LMS, numbered 14337-48.

The 'IIIs' were built with eight-wheel bogie tenders carrying 4,125 gallons of water and 4½ tons of coal. In LMS days newer and more powerful locomotives took over the longer-distance traffic from the 'Dunalastairs', and they were demoted to lesser duties, gaining lighter and simpler six-wheel tenders from other scrapped CR locomotives, with the same coal

Introduced 1899	
Designed by John McIntosh	
Built by CR, St Rollox	
Number built 16	
Number inherited by BR 1	
Last example withdrawn April 1948	

capacity but only 3,570 gallons of water.

The 'Dunalastair IIIs' entered service without fanfare, originally allocated to Polmadie, Carlisle, Perth and Edinburgh. The Polmadie engines were used on the 'Corridor' and on some of the Glasgow-London night services, regularly taking loads of around 300 tons up Beattock bank without assistance. They handled some of the heaviest jobs, including several runs at an average start-to-stop speed of more than 55mph, quite an achievement at that time, and one that no English railway could match on a regular basis. Eventually the 'Dunalastair IVs' began to assume some of these duties, followed in due course by the Stanier 'Black Fives' towards the end of the 1930s.

The first 'Dunalastair' to be withdrawn from service, other

than as a result of accident damage, was 'III' No 14343 in 1933 – no reason is known, and the next withdrawal did not take place until 1937. By 1944 only five 'IIIs' remained, working in the Highlands, their withdrawal possibly postponed by wartime requirements. Just one, No 14434, shedded at Aviemore, became a BR engine, but only for four months, being disposed of in April 1948.

This LMS-era portrait of the last of the superheated 'Dunalastair III' 4-4-0s, No 14434, shows it at the head of the 5.15pm train to Aviemore at Inverness on 9 April 1946. It was a BR engine for just four months, being withdrawn from Aviemore shed in April 1948. *H. C. Casserley*

CR superheated 'Dunalastair IV' Class 4-4-0

Nos 54438-41, 54443-60

Introduced 1904 and 1910 (originals), 1915-17 (rebuilds)
Designed by John McIntosh
Built by CR, St Rollox
Number built 24
Number inherited by BR 22
Last example withdrawn August 1958

The unsuperheated 'Dunalastair IVs' are described in an earlier entry. Two of them were superheated in 1917 and 1915, becoming LMS Nos 14438 and 14439 respectively and gaining a higher 3P classification. Twenty-two further superheated engines were built new between 1910 and 1914; the first 11 (1910-12) were officially Class '139', and the other 11 (1913-14) Class '39', but all are generally referred to as 'Dunalastair IVs'. All but one became LMS engines (CR No 121 had been destroyed in the infamous Quintinshill collision of May 1915). The LMS numbered them 14440-60; No 14442 was withdrawn in 1946, but the remaining 20, together with the original two rebuilds, passed to British Railways upon nationalisation. Withdrawals commenced in early 1948, but it was ten years before the last disappeared.

Superheated 'Dunalastair IV' 4-4-0 No 54444, built in 1911, is seen demoted to humbler duties as station pilot at Carlisle in about 1952. It was at that time allocated to Dumfries shed (62B), from where it was withdrawn in October 1953. *John Stretton collection*

CR Pickersgill 3P (Classes '113' and '72') 4-4-0

Nos 54461-508

In 1914 William Pickersgill (1861-1928) succeeded McIntosh as the Caledonian's Locomotive, Carriage & Wagon Superintendent. Cheshire-born, he started work with the Great Eastern Railway in 1876, where he was a Whitworth Exhibitioner. In 1894 he succeeded James Johnson as the Locomotive Superintendent of the Great North of Scotland Railway, and continued the development of that company's 4-4-0 locomotives. When he joined the CR he further developed the McIntosh 4-4-0 type with his '113' Class of 1916, of which 16 were built; six (CR Nos 113-16, 121 and 124) emerged from the CR's St Rollox Works, and ten (CR Nos 928-37) were

Introduced 1916
Designed by William Pickersgill
Built by CR, St Rollox (16), North British (22), Armstrong Whitworth (10)
Number built 48
Number inherited by BR 48
Last example withdrawn December 1962

constructed by the North British Locomotive Co. They were an enlarged version of the 'Dunalastair IV' and visually very similar – they could almost have been dubbed 'Dunalastair V'.

They were followed in 1920-22 by 32 4-4-0s of the '72' Class (CR Nos 66-97), built in three batches by St Rollox (10),

Former Caledonian Railway Class '113' 4-4-0 No 54467 was built by North British in 1916, and is seen here at Forfar in about 1959, the year that it was taken out of service from Perth shed (63A). Note the snowplough, and that someone has written 'CR' flanking the BR 'lion and wheel' emblem on the grimy tender! *Dave Cobbe collection, Rail Photoprints.co.uk*

The first engine was not withdrawn until 1953, when No 54481 was damaged in a collision at Gollanfield, east of Inverness. The situation remained unchanged until 1959, when further withdrawals took place, but by the end of 1961 there were still eight engines at work. On 13 March 1961 the *Glasgow Herald* published a letter from a correspondent who had written to the General Manager of the Scottish Region to suggest that a Scottish express passenger engine and appropriate historic carriages should be preserved, recommending the Pickersgill 4-4-0. 'Should one of these locomotives be preserved,' he wrote, 'Scotland would have the only example of an express train of the period immediately before the Grouping of 1923... The proposals which I have submitted to British Railways are being considered, and it is to be hoped that the Pickersgill 4-4-0 and the Caledonian Railway corridor coach will be scheduled for preservation by the Scottish Region.' Alas, this was not to be; the final engine, No 54463, was withdrawn from Polmadie shed at the end of 1962, and scrapped two years later with no reprieve.

Armstrong Whitworth (10) and North British (12). These were the CR's last express passenger locomotives, and the two classes were almost identical apart from minor detail differences and the slightly larger cylinder size of the '72s'. All 48 locomotives were taken over by the LMS in 1923, and by BR in 1948. Meanwhile, Pickersgill was appointed Mechanical Engineer of the Northern Division of the LMS, not retiring until 1925.

CR/LMS Pickersgill 4P '60' Class 4-6-0

Nos 54630, 14631, 54634-36, 14637, 54638-40, 14641, 54642, 14643-46, 54647-51, 14652, 14653, 54654

At the turn of the 20th century the Caledonian Railway's largest passenger engines were 4-4-0s, and the heaviest trains on the Carlisle-Glasgow route needed to be double-headed, with banking assistance at Beattock. Therefore in 1903 McIntosh designed a large 4-6-0 based on his 'Dunalastair' 4-4-0 design, the '49' Class. However, the new engines did not prove successful, and in 1906 McIntosh designed an improved version, the '903' Class, or 'Cardeans' (named after the first of the class). Despite being given a good deal of publicity by the CR, performance was

Introduced 1916
Designed by William Pickersgill
Built by CR, St Rollox
Number built 26
Number inherited by BR 23
Last example withdrawn December 1953

again unremarkable. All seven locomotives were superheated during 1911, which produced a modest improvement in coal consumption, but McIntosh built no more passenger 4-6-0s.

Pickersgill also tried different 4-6-0 designs, and his outside-cylinder Class '60' was his third attempt. Unfortunately these were no more successful, and were sluggish performers, so the CR had little choice but to continue to rely on 4-4-0 locomotives for its express passenger traffic.

Although extensively revised by the LMS in 1924, the two Class '49s' were withdrawn in 1933, and the four surviving 'Cardeans' had gone by 1930, eclipsed by new LMS designs such as the compound 4-4-0s and 'Royal Scot' 4-6-0s.

The first six of the '60' Class were built at St Rollox Works in 1916-17, and a further 20, slightly modified with larger cylinders, were built by George Hughes during LMS days in 1925-26, and outshopped in the pre-1928-style red livery; the

Solid-looking but lethargic, LMS-built Pickersgill Class '60' 4-6-0 No 54640 is seen at its home of Motherwell on 21 June 1949. It was withdrawn from that shed, where it had been allocated throughout its BR career, in October 1952. *H. C. Casserley*

earlier CR examples are believed to have been treated likewise. Although rugged and free-steaming, sadly the performance of the '60s' did not match their large size, and although intended for passenger traffic they ended their days as goods engines, gaining the nickname 'Greybacks', which perhaps referred to their long, grimy boilers (although 'greyback' is also Scottish vernacular for a louse!). Despite the engines' shortcomings, withdrawals only began in 1944, and 23 of the original 26 became BR engines in 1948. However, withdrawals began

again in that year, and there were only three survivors by the end of 1952. The last example, LMS-built No 54639 of 1926, was withdrawn from Hamilton shed at the end of 1953.

Pickersgill tried again with his three-cylinder '956' Class of four 4-6-0s in the early 1920s, the largest design of locomotive operated by a Scottish railway. Again visually impressive, they were no more successful than their predecessors, and were soon relegated to freight traffic. No further work was done on them, and all four were withdrawn between 1931 and 1935.

HR Cumming 'Clan' Class 4-6-0

Nos 14764, 54767

Frederick Smith (1872-1956) joined the Highland Railway in 1904 from the North Eastern Railway, and was appointed CME in 1912. His only locomotive design for the HR was his 4-6-0 'River' Class, the company's largest and most powerful locomotive. Unfortunately, the HR Civil Engineer was only concerned with the engines' deadweight driving axle loading, which was too high for the railway. However, Smith had taken this into account, and claimed that his engines had been designed to deliver a much reduced 'hammer blow' effect on the track, despite their dead weight. When the first two locomotives were delivered from Hawthorn Leslie to Perth in 1915 an argument ensued between the two men, who already had a difficult working relationship; the result was that the engines were rejected by the Engineer as being too heavy for a number of bridges and out of gauge, and the Board obliged Smith to resign. All six 'Rivers' were subsequently sold to the Caledonian Railway.

Smith's successor on the HR was Christopher Cumming, who remained in post until the Grouping. In 1917 he introduced his eight 4-6-0 'Clan Goods' engines, then in 1919, as a replacement for the ill-fated 'Rivers', a passenger version, described by O. S. Nock as 'grand engines'. Four were built in 1919, and four more in 1921. Like the goods engines, they had outside Walschaerts valve gear, but 6-foot driving wheels (9 inches larger than the goods class). They all bore the names of Scottish clans, and in 1921 No 53 *Clan Stewart* was used for experiments with oil-firing; it was later converted back to coal without any of the rest of the class being so treated.

An interesting story concerns the sudden ill-health of Cumming in 1922, when David Urie (son of Robert) was brought in from the Midland Great Western Railway in Ireland and was surprised to find all four of the 1919 batch of 'Clans'

Looking a little battered and the worse for wear, 'Clan' 4-6-0 No 54767 *Clan Mackinnon* stands in front of the famous portico at Inverness shed on 14 June 1949. By January of the following year this final member of the class was no more. *H. C. Casserley*

deliberately concealed in the dark recesses of Aviemore carriage shed, stored out of service with burnt fireboxes; they were quickly repaired at Lochgorm and put back into traffic. Urie found much evidence of slack post-war discipline in the Highland's Locomotive Department, and made himself unpopular by shaking things up a little!

In 1923 the whole class passed to the LMS, classified 4P. The first was taken out of service in 1944, and by 1948 only two remained to be taken into BR stock. No 14764 *Clan Munro* was withdrawn within a couple of months without being given its allocated BR number, while No 54767 *Clan Mackinnon* lasted until January 1950. Some of the clan names were later reapplied to the BR Standard 'Clan' Class 'Pacifics'.

Nock remarked on their performances during their later heyday on the Oban line in the 1930s, where they 'made a welcome relief from the puny nonsuperheated Pickersgill 4-6-0s [see previous entry], which in my experience were among the most useless engines ever to be put on British rails!... The Oban men pounded them without mercy on the fearsome gradients west of Callander...'

Introduced 1919
Designed by Christopher Cumming
Built by Hawthorn Leslie
Number built 8
Number inherited by BR 2
Last example withdrawn January 1950

HR P. Drummond 0P 'W' Class 0-4-4T

Nos 55051, 55053

The four Highland Railway 'W' Class 0-4-4Ts were built in 1905-06 at the company's Lochgorm Works at Inverness; indeed, they were the last of the 41 new engines to be built there. Thereafter outside contractors were used, and the works only handled rebuilding and repair until they closed under BR ownership in 1959.

The tank engines were intended for branch-line services. Nos 25 *Strathpeffer*, 40 *Gordon Lennox* and 45 were built in 1905, followed by No 46 in early 1906; the named locomotives had their names removed in 1920. All four passed to the LMS, becoming Nos 15051-54. No 15052 was withdrawn in 1930, and No 15054 in 1945, but the other two survived to become BR Nos 55051 and 55053.

They became well known in their later years when they worked the Dornoch branch, opened from The Mound in 1902. They were shedded at Helmsdale, further north up the main line towards Wick and Thurso, although there was a small shed at Dornoch for overnight stabling. The Dornoch branch

Introduced 1905	
Designed by Peter Drummond	
Built by HR, Lochgorm	
Number built 4	
Number inherited by BR 2	
Last example withdrawn January 1957	

required locomotives with very light axle loadings, and the first to be used was HR 0-6-0T No 56 of 1869, which worked there until at least 1919. Nos 55051 and 55053 later worked the branch until their withdrawal in June 1956 and January 1957 respectively, the latter being the last Highland Railway locomotive to remain in ordinary service, and still in almost original condition.

In 1957 BR Standard Class 2 No 78052 was used, joined later that year by ex-GWR pannier tank No 1646, and in 1958 by another 0-6-0PT, No 1649. The branch closed in the summer of 1960, and the GWR engines were withdrawn in December 1962.

Although both of the HR engines were cut up, they were almost identical to the Duke of Sutherland's private 0-4-4T locomotive *Dunrobin*, built in 1895 by Sharp Stewart. The 3rd Duke had a private station on the Golspie-Helmsdale stretch of the Far North line, and had running rights for his engine and two private carriages between Dunrobin Castle and Inverness. Happily, *Dunrobin* and the carriages were saved for preservation when the Duke sold them in 1949 following nationalisation of the railways. *Dunrobin* became a much-travelled engine, but in 2011 it was acquired by Beamish Museum, which hopes to be able to restore it to working order.

This splendid portrait shows what became the last Highland Railway locomotive to remain in ordinary service, 0P 0-4-4T No 55053 of 1905, gleaming in the sunshine at Dornoch with a mixed train for The Mound in July 1955. It was withdrawn in January 1957 and cut up the following year; the branch itself closed in the summer of 1960. *T. J. Edgington, Colour-Rail*

CR McIntosh 2P '19' and '92' Class 0-4-4T

Nos 15115, 15117, 55119, 55121-26, 15127, 55129, 15130, 55132, 15133, 55134-36, 55138-46

John McIntosh took over from John Lambie at St Rollox in 1895, and his Class '19' 0-4-4 tank engines introduced that year were similar to Lambie's 4-4-0Ts. The ten engines, numbered 19-28, were fitted with condensing apparatus for working the low-level lines of the Glasgow Central Railway. The original Glasgow Central station opened in 1879 on the north bank of the Clyde, and was enlarged in 1890. The low-level platforms were originally a separate station, serving the underground Glasgow Central Railway, authorised in 1888 and opened in 1896; the company was taken over by the Caledonian Railway in 1890. The condensing apparatus was later removed from most of the class.

Introduced 1895/1897	
Designed by John McIntosh	
Built by CR, St Rollox	
Number built 32	
Number inherited by BR 26	
Last example withdrawn October 1961	

The 22 members of the '92' Class followed in 1897-1900. They were very similar to the '19' Class, also carrying condensing apparatus, but had larger tanks and high-sided coal bunkers; Nos 92-103 were fitted with Westinghouse hot water feed pumps.

E. S. Cox, in his *Chronicles of Steam* (Ian Allan, 1967), described the low-level lines: '...how can I forget the descent from the lofty and in those days immaculate spaces of the main-line station into the murky depths of this steam-operated underground. A permanent woolly pall of steam clung under the low roof on the platforms whence drops of dirty moisture descended upon the waiting passengers; 0-4-4 condensing tank engines rather sensibly painted black operated the service, and freight trains of which there were plenty passing from east to west under the city also sported 0-6-0 tender engines on which a long and rather battered-looking copper pipe was supposed to convey the exhaust steam into the tender tank during the transit of the tunnels Whatever may have been the practice in earlier times, by the period of World War I condensing was undertaken as much in the breach as the observance, and so heavy became the through mineral workings that non-condensing engines had to be freely used. Conditions underground were really rather frightful, but how fascinating it all was…'

Most of the 32 engines entered BR service, although withdrawals commenced in 1948. The last pair, Nos 55124 (a '19' Class engine of 1895) and 55126 (a '92' built in 1897), lasted until the second half of 1961; the former was withdrawn from Dalry Road, but the latter had become an Oban engine in 1958.

2P 0-4-4T No 55124 was allocated to Dumfries shed between April 1950 and December 1960, before moving to Perth, then Oban. In June 1960 it was captured leaving Oban with the 4.55pm train to Ballachulish. The last of its class, it was withdrawn from Dalry Road shed in October 1961. *Michael Mensing, Colour-Rail*

CR Pickersgill 2P '431' Class 0-4-4T

Nos 55237-40

Introduced 1922
Designed by William Pickersgill
Built by CR, St Rollox
Number built 4
Number inherited by BR 4
Last example withdrawn November 1961

In 1900 McIntosh introduced a development of his earlier '19' and '92' Class 0-4-4Ts (see previous entry), the '439' or 'Standard Passenger' Class. Seventy-eight were built between 1900 and 1922, the last ten being built by Pickersgill in 1915 and 1922 with detail differences. None of them were built with condensing apparatus. They were LMS Nos 15159-236, and all but two passed to BR. One of them, CR No 419 (BR No 55189) of 1907, has been preserved and is the flagship of the Scottish Railway Preservation Society. It ended its days on pilot duties at its home shed of Carstairs, until withdrawn from there in a major cull of 200 steam engines in Scotland in December 1962. It appears on the society's letter heading and has represented the SRPS at numerous events on both sides of the border. It is currently out of service and undergoing a major overhaul.

The next development of the Caledonian's 0-4-4T family was Pickersgill's Class 431, built in 1922. There were just four engines, CR Nos 431-4, LMS Nos 15237-40. They had larger cylinders, a higher tractive effort and a cast-iron front buffer-beam to make them more suitable for use as banking engines by moving the centre of gravity forwards over the driving

Pickersgill 2P No 55238 was a Stirling engine when photographed at Oban on 5 May 1961. It was withdrawn four months later. *David Holmes*

wheels. They were used on the infamous Beattock incline on the West Coast Main Line between Carlisle and Carstairs, the highest point on the route north of the border; in the northbound direction the gradient varies between 1 in 69 and 1 in 88 to the summit. There was an engine shed at Beattock where the banking locomotives were kept on standby 24 hours a day. Two of the locos were still shedded there in 1948, but by the 1950s the quartet were widely distributed around Scotland. All four were withdrawn in the second half of 1961.

LMS (CR) McIntosh 2P '439' Class 0-4-4T

Nos 55260-69

These nine engines were a post-Grouping LMS build of McIntosh's '439' Class 0-4-4Ts. They were built by Nasmyth Wilson & Co of Patricroft, a firm better know for its exports of locomotives for overseas railways, especially in India; however,

in the 1920s the LMS ordered five 4-4-2Ts for the Tilbury line, and these ex-Caledonian tanks. The 0-4-4Ts departed only slightly from the originals, and from Pickersgill's Class '431s' (see above), being slightly heavier and a little more powerful. One, No 55260, was shedded at Beattock for eight years, but the others were to be found at Hurlford, Oban, Perth, Carstairs, Ayr, Ardrossan, Corkerhill and Greenock, with one residing as far north as Forres and Inverness. In 1926 LMS No 15264 was sent south to be evaluated on St Pancras suburban services.

The last of the LMS-built McIntosh-designed 0-4-4Ts, No 55260 of 1925, is seen at Carstairs in this undated view. However, it is carrying a 63A (Perth) shedplate, and it was allocated to that shed from December 1960 until February 1961, and from July 1962 until withdrawal in December of that year, being the last remaining member of the class. *Colour-Rail collection*

Introduced 1925
Designed by John McIntosh
Built by Nasmyth Wilson
Number built 9
Number inherited by BR 9
Last example withdrawn December 1962

CR Pickersgill 'Wemyss Bay Tank' '944' Class 4-6-2T

Nos 55350, 15351, 55352-54, 15355, 55356, 55359-61

These dozen engines were the only large passenger tank engines built for the Caledonian Railway, and were intended to haul the tightly timed expresses and boat trains from Glasgow and Greenock to the Ayrshire coast, hence they were often referred to as 'Wemyss Bay Tanks' (they were also nicknamed 'Wemyss Bay Pugs' or 'Big Pugs'). To handle this traffic they had a water capacity of 1,800 gallons and carried 3 tons of coal, and they weighed almost 92 tons. They were basically a tank version of Pickersgill's Class '60' 4-6-0 tender engines (qv), although they had slightly smaller dimensions. The only 'Pacific' tanks in Scotland, numbered 944-955 by the

Introduced 1917
Designed by William Pickersgill
Built by North British
Number built 12
Number inherited by BR 10
Last example withdrawn October 1953

CR, they were popular with Caley enginemen; with a 1 in 60 gradient between Port Glasgow and Upper Greenock, and 1 in 69 from Wemyss Bay to Inverkip, they had their work cut out. They also ran on the Edinburgh and Gourock lines.

By the Second World War they had been displaced by newer engines, and subsequently appeared on suburban trains in the Glasgow area; just before nationalisation they made a brief appearance on the Central low-level line. Two, LMS Nos 15357 and 15358, were scrapped in 1946, and the remainder were transferred by BR to Beattock for banking duties.

They were also occasionally to be seen shunting at Carlisle, and on local trains at Glasgow and Ayr while running in after attention at Kilmarnock Works. The last survivor, No 55359, ended its career at Beattock on banking duties, together with Caledonian 0-4-4Ts, LMS Fairbairn 2-6-4Ts and BR Standard 2-6-2Ts.

At nationalisation Pickersgill's Caledonian 4-6-2Ts, the former 'Wemyss Bay Tanks', were all shedded at Beattock for banking duties. On 1 June 1951 No 55361 is doing just that at the rear of a freight. It was taken out of service exactly a year later. *H. C. Casserley*

CR D. Drummond/McIntosh '264' and '611' Class 0-4-0ST

Nos 16010, 56011, 56020, 56025, 16026, 56027-32, 56035, 56038, 56039

Introduced 1885
Designed by Dugald Drummond, John McIntosh
Built by CR, St Rollox
Number built 34
Number inherited by BR 14
Last example withdrawn December 1962

'Caley Pug' 0-4-0ST No 56039 was a resident of Yoker shed throughout the 1950s, but is seen here at St Rollox in 1958. In February 1961 it transferred to Dawsholm, and was withdrawn from there in October 1962, the last but one of the class to remain in use. *Colour-Rail collection*

These 'Caley Pugs' were developed from a Neilson & Co design of 1878. The first eight (Class '264') were designed by Dugald Drummond, the CR's CME from 1882 to 1890, were built at St Rollox in 1885, and were numbered 264-271. Later examples were built during the tenure of John McIntosh in 1889 (six), 1890 (six), 1895 (four), 1900 (six), 1902 (two), and 1908 (two). The four 1895-1908 batches were designated Class '611'.

The 'Pug' nickname is familiar from the Lancashire & Yorkshire 0-4-0ST dock shunters, but in Scotland *all* shunters, whether saddle or side tank and regardless of duties, were known as 'Pugs'. These CR examples were designed for docks, harbours and other small yards with sharply curved trackwork, particularly those associated with the then booming fishing industry. They had open-backed cabs with no coal bunkers, so often ran with home-made wooden tenders to improve their limited coal capacity. They had outside cylinders and inside Stephenson slide valves. Some were later sold into private industry (including several gasworks and Harland & Wolff at Govan), and following nationalisation Nos 56027 and 56032 worked as pilots south of the border at Crewe Works, while No 56025 was the St Rollox Works shunter. Two class members, Nos 56020 and 56027, were shedded at Burton/Bromsgrove and Shrewsbury/Preston respectively in BR days.

These engines should not be confused with the earlier 1882-built North British Railway 'G' Class (LNER 'Y9'), one of which, No 68095, is now preserved. Dugald Drummond worked for the NBR before moving to the Caledonian in 1882. Before

moving he authorised the purchase of two Neilson-built 0-4-0STs, although his successor, Matthew Holmes, is credited with introducing the class on the North British. The '264' Class engines can be distinguished from the 'Y9s' by full-width spectacle plates and Drummond fittings (especially the smokebox door dart). Also the 'Y9s' usually had their safety valves located forward of the cab, rather than on the dome.

Although none of the 'Caley Pugs' escaped the cutter's torch, one lives on in model form. 'Smokey Joe' is a popular 'starter-level' Hornby Railways model based on No 56025, the St Rollox shunter, and has been in the range since 1981, initially in Caledonian Railway blue. In 1983 it adopted the 'Smokey Joe' guise and was billed as a 'character' locomotive inspired by a Glaswegian engine that carried that nickname.

The first engine was withdrawn in 1920, but 14 came into BR stock in 1948. The last, No 56029, a much-travelled engine, was withdrawn from Kipps (65E) at the end of 1962.

CR McIntosh 'Caledonian Dock Tank' '498' Class 0-6-0T

Nos 56151-73

The first two 'Caledonian Dock Tanks' of Class '498' (CR Nos 498 and 499) were introduced by John McIntosh in 1911. Under his successor Pickersgill, a further 21, with larger bunkers, were built between 1915 and 1921. As their familiar name suggests, they were intended to operate on sharply curved lines within dock complexes, and to aid this they had a very short wheelbase of only 10 feet. Compact and powerful engines, they were McIntosh's only design with outside cylinders.

Although 0-4-0 saddle tanks such as the 'Caley Pug' could negotiate sharp curves, their power was restricted, and the overhang of their 'tenders' restricted their turning capabilities. Six coupled wheels increased the pulling power considerably,

and in an interesting article about the class by J. Sinclair, one Greenock driver is quoted as saying that the engines could easily pull 40 standard goods wagons on level track.

The first of the class, No 498, was kept at St Rollox and allocated to that shed. It was often found shunting at nearby Braby's Eclipse Works, and the nickname 'Braby Pug' was applied to that engine and the class as a whole. No 499 went

Introduced 1911
Designed by John McIntosh
Built by CR, St Rollox
Number built 23
Number inherited by BR 23
Last example withdrawn April 1962

Short and compact, McIntosh 0-6-0T 'Caledonian Dock Tank' No 56152 poses at St Rollox in this undated view. This was one of the original pair built in 1911, shedded for many years at Grangemouth to work on the docks there. It was withdrawn in March 1959. Note the spark arrester fitting on the chimney *Colour-Rail collection*

to Grangemouth for harbour duties. The later engines were designated as dock tanks as a result of being allocated to sheds that featured dockyard duties on their work rosters.

Another nickname applied to the class was 'Wee Cuddies' (a 'cuddy' being a Scottish dialect word for donkey). Enthusiasts

sometimes referred to them as 'Beetlecrushers', and elsewhere the '498s' were dubbed 'Bulldogs' and 'Hercules'.

Later-built engines carried a larger bunker to increase their working times between servicing. In LMS days some engines were fitted with a most unattractive stovepipe chimney, while Nos 16151, 16152 and 16154 temporarily sported small spark arresters.

At least one member of the class found its way south when LMS No 16156 went to Burton-on-Trent to be evaluated for possible use on the brewery railways there, but it was found to be too heavy.

The 14 engines inherited by BR lasted for almost a decade before withdrawals commenced. The original two survived for just short of half a century, and No 56158 of 1915 was the last of the class to be serviced, in 1958. By April 1962 all had disappeared.

CR Lambie/McIntosh 3F '29' and '782' Class 0-6-0T

Nos 56230-69, 16270, 56271-350, 16351, 56352-76

John Lambie (1833-95) became Locomotive Superintendent of the Caledonian in 1890 following the departure of Dugald Drummond, and held the post until his death in February 1895. He designed his '29' Class 0-6-0T goods engine just before his death, and the nine engines were built, with some modifications, under the supervision of his successor, John McIntosh. Their leading dimensions were similar to Lambie's 0-6-0 saddle tanks, but with side tanks. They were initially fitted with condensing apparatus for working the Glasgow Central Railway low-level line, but this was removed in 1920-22. They were numbered 29 and 203-210.

The remaining 138 locomotives, the '782' Class – making this the Caledonian's most numerous goods tank engine class –

Introduced 1895	
Designed by John Lambie	
Built by CR, St Rollox	
Number built 147	
Number inherited by BR 147	
Last example withdrawn December 1962	

were built during the McIntosh and Pickersgill eras between 1898 and 1922. Twenty-eight engines were fitted with Westinghouse brakes. Remarkably the class remained intact throughout the LMS years (numbered 16230-376) and all passed to BR in 1948. Only two failed to carry their allocated BR numbers following nationalisation, and only seven engines had been lost by the end of 1954. Thereafter withdrawals became more numerous, but eight engines were still at work as 1962 dawned. Having been spread across Scotland from Carlisle to Inverness, and Ayr to Aberdeen, the last three, Nos 56302, 56325 and 56336, were part of the cull of Scottish steam during 1962, being withdrawn in December of that year from Dumfries (No 56302) and Motherwell.

Former Caledonian 3F 0-6-0T No 56347 was a Perth engine for the whole of its BR career, and is seen here at Forfar shed on 9 August 1962. It is recorded as having been withdrawn the previous month, but seems to be still in steam in this view. Note that it was one of the 28 engines fitted with the Westinghouse brake. *G. Parry collection, Colour-Rail*

GSWR P. Drummond/R. Whitelegg 3F '45'/'1' Class 0-6-2T

No 16905

The Glasgow & South Western Railway served a triangular area of south-west Scotland encompassing Glasgow, Stranraer and Carlisle. It mainly carried mineral traffic, especially from the Ayrshire coalfield. The GSWR later formed an alliance with the Midland Railway for the running of Anglo-Scottish expresses in competition with the Caledonian Railway. At the Grouping of 1923 the GSWR joined the MR and CR as constituents of the LMS, but Midland and Caledonian influences held sway. GSWR locomotives were now 'non-standard', and many were rapidly scrapped.

Peter Drummond, younger brother of Dugald, was CME of the GSWR from 1912, and among his designs was this 0-6-2 tank, based a class of 0-6-4Ts he had built for the Highland Railway; tank locomotives had hitherto generally been avoided by the GSWR. Eighteen were built initially, between 1915 and 1917, to handle Ayrshire coal traffic on the steeply graded lines in the area, as well as general short-distance goods trains. Originally known as the '45' Class, following the GSWR's renumbering in 1919 they became the '1' Class, together with a further ten built in that year by Drummond's successor, Robert Harben Whitelegg (son of the London, Tilbury & Southend's Thomas, both men having served that company).

The LMS originally numbered the class 16400-27, but later changed this to 16900-27. Only one of the class passed to briefly to BR, Whitelegg No 16905 of 1919, the last surviving GSWR locomotive. It was withdrawn from Carlisle Kingmoor shed on 17 April 1948, too soon to have received its BR number. Two other members of the class were sold to Ashington Colliery and lasted beyond 1948: No 16904 was scrapped in 1953, and No 16908 in 1956.

3F 0-6-2T No 16905 was the only member of the class to became BR stock, but was scrapped early in 1948. Two other engines, sold to Ashington Colliery, outlived the last surviving ex-GSWR BR loco, and one of them, No 16908, is seen as NCB No 2 at Ashington on 29 April 1952. *H. C. Casserley*

Introduced 1915
Designed by Peter Drummond/Robert Whitelegg
Built by North British
Number built 28
Number inherited by BR 1
Last example withdrawn April 1948

Peter Drummond also designed a class of three dock shunters for the company. One of them was sold to a colliery, and was subsequently saved from scrapping, to become the only GSWR locomotive to be preserved; it is now in the Glasgow Museum of Transport.

CR D. Drummond 2F '294' and '711' 'Jumbo' Class 0-6-0

Nos 57230-47, 57249-80, 57282-92, 57294-96, 57298-375, 57377-427, 57429-73

(For simplicity, this list assumes every locomotive carried its BR number, although a minority did not)

'Jumbo' is perhaps the most common locomotive nickname of all, deriving from the name of a mid-19th-century circus elephant. As Thomas Middlemass pointed out in *Steam Locomotive Nicknames*, 'the word … was usually employed to denote good-natured, if rather lumbering, strength' – ideal, therefore, for workaday goods engines.

Dugald Drummond's 'Jumbos' for the Caledonian were initially a class of 122 powerful 0-6-0s known as the '294' Class, or 'Standard Goods' (later BR Nos 57230-392), built between 1883 and 1892. They were based on an earlier class of 133 0-6-0s that Drummond had designed for the North British Railway. It has been said that the design betrayed a certain Stroudley influence (the tender in particular), Drummond having worked under Stroudley on the Highland Railway. They

were also the forerunner of his '700' Class, designed for the London & South Western Railway in 1897.

The first batch of 15 was supplied by Neilson & Co, and numbered 294-308. Nos 349-54 were constructed at St Rollox, then Neilson supplied a further 20 in 1884, numbered 517-26 and 680-89.

After Drummond's retirement in 1890, construction continued at St Rollox under John Lambie and John McIntosh (the '711' Class), until by 1897 the class numbered 244 engines in total, by far the most numerous on the Caledonian. Indeed, these unsung workhorses formed the largest class of locomotives in Scotland, and were held in great affection by footplate crews, mastering all types of traffic. Many were

Introduced 1883
Designed by Dugald Drummond
Built by CR, St Rollox (209), plus Neilson (35)
Number built 244
Number inherited by BR 238
Last example withdrawn November 1963

Caledonian 'Jumbo' 0-6-0 No 57276, which emerged from St Rollox Works in December 1885, is seen in this undated mid-1950s view, when it was allocated to Oban shed (63D). It is crossing the Connel Ferry road/railway bridge at the head of a Ballachulish-Oban pick-up goods. The engine was scrapped at the end of 1959. *J. M. Bairstow, Colour-Rail*

fitted with the Westinghouse brake, while some also carried vacuum brakes, so they could also be used on passenger trains. Some carried condensing apparatus for use on the Glasgow

Central low-level lines, and many had their original chimneys replaced by a less attractive stovepipe design.

Twenty-five machines saw service with the Railway Operating Division during the First World War.

The entire class was taken over by the LMS, and the first withdrawal was not made until 1946. All but half a dozen soldiered on into the BR era, the last six being dispensed with in November 1963, representing a lifespan of some eight decades. It is therefore perhaps surprising that not a single example was saved for preservation.

CR McIntosh 3F '652' Class 0-6-0

Nos 17629, 57630-35, 17636, 57637, 57638, 17639, 57640, 17641, 57642-45

In 1899-1900 McIntosh built an enlarged version of the 'Jumbo', the Class '812', and one of these, CR No 828/BR 57566, was lucky enough to be preserved, currently to be found on the Strathspey Railway. These engines carried the same boiler type as the '721' 'Dunalastair I' Class (qv), and 17 of them were fitted with the Westinghouse brake. In 'The Railway Series' books by Rev W. Awdry, the engines 'Donald' and 'Douglas', the 'the Scottish twins', are based on the '812' Class, and

Introduced 1908
Designed by John McIntosh
Built by CR, St Rollox
Number built 17
Number inherited by BR 17
Last example withdrawn November 1963

carried the fictional numbers 57646 and 57647 before arriving at Sodor.

In 1908-09 McIntosh brought out another class based on the 'Jumbo', the '652' Class; the engines were almost identical to the '812s' except that they had 'Dunalastair III'-type cabs with a different shape of cut-out. The 17 engines were built at St Rollox in four batches and, like their predecessors, were allocated to almost every part of the Caledonian system. In LMS days they even infiltrated former Highland and GSWR territory, and later could also be found on North British and Great North of Scotland sheds.

3F 0-6-0 No 57634 is a long way from its Caledonian home as it enters Aberlour station, on the Great North of Scotland Craigellachie-Boat of Garten line, in August 1954. Having started its BR career at Aviemore on the former Highland Railway, it was shedded at Keith when this picture was taken, ending its days at Dalry Road, Edinburgh, in August 1963. *Colour-Rail collection*

CR Pickersgill 3F '300' ('294'/'670') Class 0-6-0

Nos 57650-55, 57658, 57659, 57661, 57663, 57665-74, 57679, 57681, 57682, 57684, 57686, 57688-91

In 1912 McIntosh built four 0-6-0s known as the '30' Class, which were a superheated version of his '812' Class (see above); all had been scrapped by 1946. In 1918 his successor, Pickersgill, built 43 0-6-0s that were a composite of the '30' and '812'

Introduced 1918
Designed by William Pickersgill
Built by CR, St Rollox
Number built 43
Number inherited by BR 29
Last example withdrawn November 1963

Pickersgill 3F '300' Class No 57652 was one of the last three survivors of the class, all withdrawn in November 1963. It was a resident of Dawsholm shed (at Maryhill, Glasgow) from 1948 until it moved to Grangemouth, then Polmadie, in 1963. It is seen here at Dawsholm being watered on 11 June 1962. The overhead electrification warning plaques on the cab and boiler side look quite incongruous on this 1919 veteran! *Colour-Rail collection*

engines, and were known as the '300' Class (or '294' Class, not to be confused with Drummond's 'Jumbo' Class). They were built and numbered in three batches, 294-324, 280-81 and 670-79; the last six engines, built in 1919-20, were known as the '670' Class, and could be distinguished by having a higher-set boiler than the '812s' and 'teardrop'-shaped cab windows.

They all passed to the LMS in 1923, classified 3F, renumbered 17650-92, and most of them superheated. The first was withdrawn in 1934, but 29 survived in BR stock until the early 1960s. As with the 'Jumbos', the last three were withdrawn in November 1963.

HR P. Drummond 3F 'K' Class 'Barney' 0-6-0

Nos 17693, 17694, 57695, 57697, 57698, 17699, 17702

The 'K' Class were the only 0-6-0 tender locomotives built for the Highland Railway, and gained the nickname 'Barneys' for no clearly discernable reason. They had a characteristic Drummond family appearance. The first six (HR 134-139) were built by Dübs & Co in 1900, coupled to inside-bearing double-bogie tenders, not unlike the 'watercart' design used by Peter's brother Dugald on the LSWR; these were later transferred to other engines. Four more engines followed from Dübs in 1902; they did not have the bogie tenders, but incorporated another Drummond family characteristic, cross water tubes in the firebox. No 21 is recorded as retaining this boiler in unmodified form until 1934. The final two appeared in 1907, constructed by the North British Locomotive Co, of which Dübs had become a constituent part in 1903.

Although built as goods engines, all were fitted with vacuum brakes in order to be able to work passenger trains.

All 12 passed to the LMS, and the first was withdrawn in 1936. The LMS rebuilt some with Caledonian boilers, removing the firebox water tubes, although four were later refitted with Highland boilers. They were used in the Glasgow area in 1938 in connection with the Empire Exhibition, and also spent some time working trains in the Lanarkshire coalfields.

Seven became BR engines, and Nos 57695 and 57699 retained their Highland boilers throughout. No 57697 was fitted with a stovepipe chimney.

Introduced 1900
Designed by Peter Drummond
Built by Dübs
Number built 12
Number inherited by BR 7
Last example withdrawn January 1952

Only three of the seven Peter Drummond 0-6-0 'Barneys' carried their allocated BR numbers, and No 57695 was one of them. Built by Dübs & Co in 1900, and still carrying its original Highland Railway boiler, it is seen at its home shed of Corkerhill on 20 June 1949. It was withdrawn from Hurlford shed in January 1952, rendering this small class extinct. On the extreme left is LMS Fairburn 2-6-4T No 2194, another Corkerhill resident, not yet a year old and yet to receive its BR number. *H. C. Casserley*

HR Cumming 4F 'Clan Goods' Class 4-6-0

Nos 57950, 57951, 17953, 57954-56

The first four 'Clan Goods' 4-6-0s (or more properly the 'Superheated Goods', which actually preceded the passenger 'Clan' Class – qv) were nominally designed by Cumming and built by Hawthorn Leslie of Newcastle-upon-Tyne (the firm that had also built Smith's ill-fated 4-6-0 'River' Class). They were delivered in 1917, numbered 75-78, and four more followed in 1919 (Nos 79-82). Some claim that Cumming's 4-4-0 and 4-6-0 designs were more accurately the work of Hawthorn Leslie, particularly one of

Introduced 1917
Designed by Christopher Cumming
Built by Hawthorn Leslie
Number built 8
Number inherited by BR 6
Last example withdrawn October 1952

The Cumming 'Clan Goods' 4-6-0s had two outside cylinders with Walschaerts valve gear, driving 5ft 3in-diameter wheels. Although intended as goods engines, during their later careers they were all shedded at Inverness and worked passenger trains on the Kyle of Lochalsh line. No 57956 is seen at Kyle on 22 April 1952, a month before withdrawal. *H. C. Casserley*

the company's draughtsmen, J. E. Armstrong, and his team, and that Cumming himself was something of a 'shadowy figure'.

The 'Goods' engines had smaller driving wheels and were slightly more powerful than the subsequent passenger version. Although intended for heavy freight work between Perth and Inverness, their driving wheels were the same diameter as the celebrated Jones 'Big Goods', so passenger work had doubtless been envisaged, if only in a piloting role. In later years they were used for passenger work on the Kyle of Lochalsh line,

where their power was welcomed following the introduction of LMS corridor stock and the occasional dining car train.

All eight entered service with the LMS at the Grouping, where they were classified 5F. Initially numbered 14762-69, they later became Nos 17950-57. Two were withdrawn prior to nationalisation, so six became BR engines, and all but one lasted long enough to carry BR numbers. One succumbed in 1948, another in 1950 and a third in 1951. The last three had been withdrawn before the end of 1952.

LNWR Bowen Cooke 'Prince of Wales' Class 4-6-0

Nos 25648, 25673, 25722, 25752, 25787, 25827

As we enter the '58xxx' series of BR allocated numbers, we find ourselves in the realm of fascinating London & North Western Railway and Midland Railway oddments and relics, with 'duplicate list' numbers.

Bowen Cooke introduced his 'Prince of Wales' 4-6-0s in 1911, and they were basically a superheated version of his 'Experiment' 4-6-0s. They appeared without ceremony, and eventually became the most numerous and most generally successful LNWR passenger engine, well-liked by enginemen. Between 1911 and 1922 135 engines of the class were built at Crewe, as well as by outside contractors (unusually for the LNWR), as Crewe was unable to cope with the required output to handle increased traffic. Twenty were built by the North British Locomotive Co in 1915 and 90 by William Beardmore & Co of Glasgow in 1921-22. The latter company was initially well

known for the building of ships, armament, aircraft and motor cars – locomotive building only began in 1920, and just over half of the output between then and 1931 was for home railways, including the GER, LNWR, LMS and LNER. In 1924 Beardmore built an additional locomotive for display at that year's British Empire Exhibition at Wembley, specially named *Prince of Wales* for the occasion; this was subsequently purchased by the LMS as No 5845.

The first member of the class took the name *Prince of Wales* as it was built in 1911, the year of the future King Edward VIII's investiture at Caernarfon Castle. As was common LNWR practice, the remaining members of the class reused names and numbers from withdrawn locomotives, so both were completely haphazard. The Beardmore engines remained unnamed. When the entire class became LMS property, that company renumbered them more logically in the 5600-5844 series. In the mid-1930s most of the class were renumbered

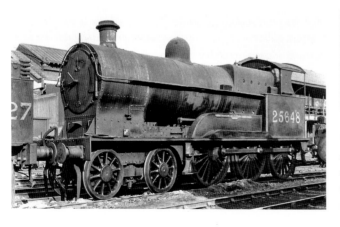

Introduced 1911
Designed by Charles Bowen Cooke
Built by LNWR, Crewe (135), North British (20), Beardmore (91)
Number built 246
Number inherited by BR 6
Last example withdrawn May 1949

How are the mighty fallen... 1915-built LNWR 'Prince of Wales' 4-6-0 No 25648 *Queen of the Belgians* stands minus tender at Crewe Works on 10 October 1948. It was cut up the following month. It still carried its nameplates – one wonders what happened to them. *John Stretton collection*

again in the duplicate list by the addition of 20000, becoming part of the 25600-844 series; this was to free up numbers for the new 'Jubilees'.

At the same time withdrawals began, the first engine going in 1933. Only 22 were left at the outbreak of the Second World War, when withdrawals were suspended, and just six survivors passed to BR in 1948; two of them were almost immediately taken out of service without a BR number being allocated. The remaining four lasted just over a year, and none carried its allocated BR numbers in the 58xxx series. (If the usual 40000 had been added to their LMS 25xxx numbers, it would have intruded on the new 6xxxx numbers allocated for former LNER locomotives).

The new engines looked heavy and crude in comparison with, for example, the near contemporary 'Saint' 4-6-0s of the GWR. All were built with round-topped boilers, but many were subsequently given Belpaire fireboxes. All remained inside-cylinder engines with Joy valve gear (which had an inherent weakness resulting from a necessary hole in the connecting rod, which in one instance caused a serious accident), except four that were fitted with outside Walschaerts gear in 1923-24, together with the Beardmore exhibition engine. These engines were nicknamed 'Tishies', after a racehorse of that name that frustrated owners and punters alike by crossing its forelegs when running, then falling over! The crossed rods of the Walschaerts valve reminded enginemen of that peculiarity.

LNWR Whale 'Precursor' Class 4-4-0

No 25297

The LNWR had two classes of locomotives known as 'Precursor'. The first was a 2-4-0 introduced by Francis Webb in 1874, and this second class was designed by George Whale in 1904, the year after he took over from Webb at Crewe.

Between 1904 and 1907 130 'Precursors' were built at Crewe, replacing the unreliable compound engines so favoured by Whales's predecessor (some took the numbers and names of withdrawn compounds). They were basically a larger version of Webb's 'Improved Precedent' Class, and were built with saturated boilers, although most were subsequently rebuilt with Belpaire fireboxes and superheaters between 1913 and the Grouping, effectively becoming two sub-classes. When built they were the heaviest 4-4-0 types in Britain.

Because the LNWR often reused numbers and names from withdrawn locomotives, the numbering of the 'Precursors' was haphazard. The first was No 513 *Precursor*, which gave its name to the class. It has been pointed out that these engines weren't a 'precursor' to anything, but, like 'Experiment', the name suggested something new and pioneering. This approach seems to have become less popular, and more patriotic or imperial-sounding class names were adopted, such as 'Prince of Wales' or 'George the Fifth'.

When the LMS absorbed the locomotives it gave them the power classification 3P, and the saturated engines were given numbers in the 5187-266 series, though not all survived long enough to receive them. The superheated engines became LMS Nos 5270-319 (5267-69 were not used). The LMS continued to superheat the engines until 1926, and the unsuperheated examples were withdrawn between 1927 and 1935. Superheated engines began to disappear from 1935, and survivors joined the duplicate list with 20000 added to their numbers, to free up numbers for the new Stanier Class 5 4-6-0s. The gradual modifications included various features introduced with the Bowen Cooke 'George the Fifth' Class of 1910 onwards (see below), including the wheels, larger cylinders, superheating and Belpaire boilers.

On the West Coast Main Line the 'Precursors' were gradually displaced by the newer 'Claughtons', 'Patriots' and 'Royal

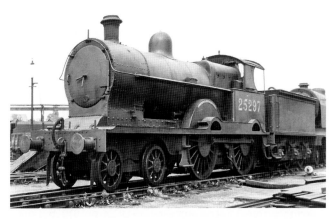

The elegant lines of LNWR 'Precursor' 4-4-0 No 25297 *Sirocco* are still evident as it languishes at Crewe Works, newly withdrawn, on 19 June 1949. It was scrapped in October. (The name had previously been carried by an 1874 Webb 'Precursor', No 1153.) *John Stretton collection*

Introduced 1904
Designed by George Whale
Built by LNWR, Crewe
Number built 130
Number inherited by BR 1
Last example withdrawn June 1949

Scots', and eventually the Stanier 'Pacifics', and were relegated to secondary duties, such as fast trains from Euston to Watford, Berkhamsted, Tring and Bletchley.

By the outbreak of the Second World War only seven survived, and just one joined the nationalised British Railways, No 25297 *Sirocco*. Shedded at Chester, it would have become No 58010, but was withdrawn in June 1949 before that number could be applied.

In an article in *Heritage Railway*, author Bruce Nixon remembered the 'Precursors': 'Part of the reason why few lasted beyond the 1930s was that they could be flogged so hard, they wore out. Also, LNWR locomotives were not favoured under the regime of Midland Railway traditions that dominated the first years of the LMS. By 1949 ... only one 4-4-0 survived. Funnily enough, it was one of the original "Precursors", built in 1905, modernised several times in its life and now relegated to the Denbigh to Chester branch line... I was fascinated by their unique appearance, with their beautiful curvaceous splashers for driving wheels and coupling rods, lovely engraved brass nameplates, circular wheel bosses, distinctive cabs with rectangular rear splashers incorporated into their sides, neat coal tenders, round smokebox door handles and three-part chimney castings. They looked altogether too elegant for such humble duties...'

LNWR Bowen Cooke 'George the Fifth' Class 4-4-0

Nos 25321, 25350, 25373

Bowen Cooke's 'George the Fifth' Class was a development of his predecessor Whales's 'Precursor' 4-4-0, with a modified front end and superheating. It is claimed that the locomotives were perhaps the most successful 4-4-0s of their day, very powerful for their size and more economical to build that, say, Churchward's contemporary designs on the GWR. O. S. Nock considered that the class represented the zenith of the inside-cylinder 4-4-0 type; he wrote that they had 'a special place in the eventful history of express train operation over Shap. In relation to the total engine weight, there have never been more competent locomotives on the line... There were times, indeed, when the virtually impossible was attempted.'

Two identical inside-cylinder 4-4-0s were built at Crewe in July 1910. One was the superheated No 2663 *George the Fifth*, the other the saturated No 2664 *Queen Mary*. This comparative experiment followed the successful running of a superheated Marsh 'I3' 4-4-2T (qv) between Brighton and Rugby in 1909. *George the Fifth* was considered the experimental engine, so nine more 'Queen Marys' appeared in October 1910, but once the advantages of superheating became evident it was more 'Georges' that were built in 1913-14, and the 'Queen Marys' were converted to superheating. All the engines were now absorbed into what became known as the 'George the Fifth' Class. As an acknowledgement to his predecessors, Bowen Cooke named the second 'Queen Mary', No 238, *F. W. Webb*, and the third, No 896, *George Whale*.

A total of 90 engines were built at Crewe between 1910 and 1915, including ten that had originally been 'Queen Marys', and these compact and elegant 4-4-0s continued to haul West Coast Main Line passenger trains into the late 1920s.

Introduced 1910	
Designed by Charles Bowen Cooke	
Built by LNWR, Crewe	
Number built 90	
Number inherited by BR 3	
Last example withdrawn May 1948	

The LMS revised the haphazard LNWR numbering into a more logical series of 5320-409, and any survivors in 1936/37 were renumbered in the duplicate list and had 20000 added to their numbers, to free up more numbers for the new 'Black Fives'. Some of the names were also removed so that they could be applied to the new 'Jubilees'.

LNWR practice subsequently fell out of favour on the LMS, and withdrawals commenced in 1935. By 1939 only nine engines remained, and BR inherited just three in 1948. In that year 'Precursor' *Sirocco*, the last 'Prince of Wales' 4-6-0 and the last 'Claughton', No 6004 (both qv) were lined up to be photographed at Crewe Works, in the hope that they would be saved. Sadly, all were subsequently cut up, and the final trio of 'Georges' had also gone by mid-year. It is interesting to speculate how different posterity's attitude might have been a decade later.

Indeed, more than six decades later the LNWR George the Fifth Steam Locomotive Trust is building a new member of the class with the aim of 'making good this gap in our steam locomotive heritage... An engine of this size and power is ideal for the permanent way and the requirements of most heritage lines yet powerful enough for main-line excursions, and as the sole representative of a 20th-century LNWR express locomotive [it] would present a fascinating and potentially popular drawcard and represent a slice of rail travel at its zenith.' The new-build engine is to be named, appropriately, *Prince George* in honour of the Duke and Duchess of Cambridge's young son.

The sad sight of one of the last surviving pair of 'George the Fifth' 4-4-0s, No 25373 *Ptarmigan*, in Crewe Works yard on 31 May 1947. It is probably already out of use, although it was not officially withdrawn until May of the following year, without ever carrying its BR number, 58012. *H. C. Casserley*

MR Johnson 6ft 3in 1P '1070' Class 2-4-0

No 20155

When Johnson succeeded Kirtley at Derby in 1873 his predecessor's 1070-1089 series of '890' Class 2-4-0s (MR Nos 127-146, built from 1874) was too far advanced at Sharp Stewart's works for him to place his stamp upon them, except his own design of chimney. The need for more engines was pressing – with the Settle & Carlisle line about to open – so immediately Johnson built ten more 2-4-0s (Nos 1, 9, 10, 13, 70, 71, 73, 74, 96 and 146) to his own modified design with inside rather than outside frames. He seemed undecided about whether to incorporate a four-wheel leading bogie, but in the event continued to built 2-4-0s until 1881, thereafter favouring the 4-4-0 arrangement. (He also rebuilt Kirtley's later engines to conform to his own design, and the classes eventually became almost indistinguishable.)

The new engines performed well on the Derby-Manchester route, but were not as popular as Kirtley's engines north of Leeds; after a few years on the Carlisle road, they moved to second-rate work in the Midlands, based at Nottingham (with one sent to Kentish Town). This was an inauspicious start to Johnson's career, but he went on to design far more successful 2-4-0, and later 4-4-0, locomotives. In 1907 all 30 engines (of Kirtley and Johnson origin) were renumbered in a single sequence from 127 to 156 in order of building.

All had their cylinders enlarged between 1887 and 1902, and during the LMS era some were rebuilt with Belpaire boilers between 1924 and 1927.

It was LNWR practice to allocate an old engine, often a 2-4-0, to principal depots to undertake departmental duties, such as hauling officers' saloons or for permanent way work. Between 1933 and 1936 Derby-built Johnson 2-4-0 No 155 (the former No 96, renumbered in 1907) was sent to Abergavenny for such a

After some years in LMS departmental use at Abergavenny, Johnson 2-4-0 No 20155 was transferred to Nottingham upon nationalisation, and is seen there, probably out of use, on 3 June 1950. This historic survivor, the last ex-Midland 2-4-0 in service, was broken up the following October *H. C. Casserley*

Introduced 1876
Designed by Samuel Johnson
Built by MR, Derby
Number built 10
Number inherited by BR 1
Last example withdrawn October 1950

purpose, carrying plates reading *Engineer South Wales*. Later renumbered 20155, it remained at Abergavenny until 1946, when it was transferred to Nottingham. It became the last Midland 2-4-0 engine in service, not being withdrawn until 28 October 1950, having clocked up a total of 1,425,151 miles.

MR Johnson 6ft 6in 1P '1282' Class 2-4-0

No 20185

Introduced 1876
Designed by Samuel Johnson
Built by Dübs
Number built 40
Number inherited by BR 1
Last example withdrawn August 1948

There were four varieties of Johnson 2-4-0s, and the '1282' Class was the second, with larger 6ft 6½in-diameter driving wheels. Dübs & Co, of which the Midland was a good customer, supplied two orders for 30 engines in 1876, MR Nos 1282-1301 and 1302-11. The first batch was fitted with Smith's simple vacuum brake for working London-Manchester services, while Nos 1302-11 had Westinghouse brakes for working Anglo-Scottish expresses. Ten more had been built by 1880, and they were all later renumbered 157-91 and 217-21.

When nationalisation dawned the last surviving 6ft 6in Johnson 2-4-0, No 20185 of 1876, finished its days at Barrow, where it was photographed a few months earlier on 12 June 1947. *H. C. Casserley*

O. S. Nock considered this and the 6ft 9in and 7-foot variations collectively 'the most beautiful passenger engines that have ever run on the railways of this country.' He considered Johnson an 'artist in metal', and went on to say, 'The drivers may have had their preferences between units of different batches, but taken as a whole, wherever they were used, they were generally very popular.'

The first to be withdrawn was in 1922, and some were rebuilt with Belpaire boilers from 1926. In 1934, in common with the other classes, they joined the duplicate list with 20000 added to their numbers.

A single example was left at nationalisation, No 20185, of 1876 vintage. Allocated to Barrow shed (11B), it was withdrawn from there in August 1948 without carrying its BR number, 58021.

MR Johnson 6ft 9in 1P '1400' Class 2-4-0

No 20216

The 6ft 9in series of 2-4-0s, the '1400' Class, was built between 1879 and 1881 and was the largest group of Midland 2-4-0s. Thirty were produced at Derby (Nos 1400-09 and 1472-91), while a further 30 were manufactured by Neilson & Co (Nos 1502-31). In 1907 they were renumbered 192-96, 207-16 and 222-271, before having 20000 added to their numbers when they were transferred to the duplicate list in 1934. Across the surviving classes this only involved about 20 engines, including three of the earlier Kirtleys, all the rest having been scrapped.

A number of the '1400s' were rebuilt by Deeley (who succeeded Johnson in 1903) with Belpaire boilers and his own design of smokebox door, chimney and dome. Ross pop safety valves were fitted, but these changes did nothing to improve the appearance of these attractive locomotives. In general the Belpaire engines lasted longer than the originals; eight were still serving the LMS in 1934, and most had the flat-topped firebox.

Again, only one example survived to fall into BR's hands, No 20216 (which would have become BR No 58022), built at Derby in 1879. At nationalisation it was allocated to Kettering shed (15C). The story goes that it was always kept well topped up with coal, although it had been withdrawn from service; apparently it was to be sent to Derby for scrapping as soon as the tender was empty, but it seems it was a favourite of the shed foreman, who consequently made sure the tender was always kept full!

Whatever the truth of that, in March 1949 it moved to Gloucester Barnwood (22B), and worked as station pilot at Cheltenham Lansdown. It was withdrawn in November 1949 and scrapped.

In 1877 the fourth variation of the 2-4-0 theme appeared, with ten further engines built with 7-foot-diameter driving

One of the last duties of the last Johnson 6ft 9in 2-4-0, No 20216, was as station pilot at Cheltenham Lansdown; it was photographed in the bay platform there on 30 July 1949, but it had been scrapped by the end of the year. *B. W. L. Brooksbank, Initial Photographics*

Introduced 1879
Designed by Samuel Johnson
Built by MR, Derby (30), Neilson (30)
Number built 60
Number inherited by BR 1
Last example withdrawn November 1949

wheels. They were Nos 1347-56, built at Derby, for use on the fastest main-line passenger trains, and allocated to Skipton and Saltley sheds. The cost of each locomotive is recorded as having been £1,572. They were renumbered 1347A-56A, and again to 101-10 in 1879, becoming Nos 197-206 in 1907. Ten more were subsequently built, Nos 272-81, but all had disappeared before the railways were nationalised.

MR Johnson 5ft 7in '1252' Class 0-4-4T

Nos 1239, 1246, 1247, 58033, 1251, 1252, 58036, 1260, 58038

For more than half a century the principal suburban and branch-line passenger engines used by the Midland had the 0-4-4T wheel arrangement. Between 1875 and 1900 the Midland Railway gained 205 of these tanks in three batches designed by Johnson for suburban passenger duties in the London area, and based on his '134' Class 0-4-4 tanks for the

Great Eastern Railway. The first batch was the '1252' Class, 30 engines built by Neilson & Co in 1875-76, being a development of the ten engines of the earlier '6' Class. Originally numbered 1262-81 and 1252-61, under the 1907 renumbering scheme they became Nos 1236-65.

The engines had 5ft 7in-diameter driving wheels, the largest on this type produced by the Midland and larger than subsequent batches (see next entry). Otherwise all the locomotives were built to the same basic design, with minor differences and gradually

Introduced 1875
Designed by Samuel Johnson
Built by Neilson
Number built 30
Number inherited by BR 9
Last example withdrawn May 1954

increasing dimensions, and remained active in their designated role until the mid-1920s. Some were temporarily fitted with push-pull equipment with vacuum-controlled regulators, and many of the 0-4-4Ts carried condensing apparatus to enable them to work on the 'Widened Lines'.

Many of the engines were fitted with Belpaire-firebox boilers, and nine of the class of 30 entered BR stock in 1948, but only three of them lived long enough to carry their BR numbers in the 5803x series. All bar one had been withdrawn by the autumn of 1950; the sole survivor, No 58038 (LMS No 1261), managed to work on until May 1954 from Plaistow shed, where it had been allocated since nationalisation (being the only member of the class to spend its BR days in the South East).

The last survivor of the first batch of Johnson 0-4-4Ts from 1875-76 was No 58038, which spent its BR days allocated to Plaistow shed (33A). It is seen here at Romford on 13 August 1949, with nearly five years of service still ahead of it. *H. C. Casserley*

MR Johnson 5ft 4in '1532' and '2228' Class 0-4-4T

Nos 1272, 58040-42, 1290, 58045-47, 1315, 1322, 1324, 58051-54, 1342, 58056, 1348, 58058-62, 1361, 1365, 1366, 58065, 58066, 1370, 58068-73, 1385, 1389, 58075-77, 1402, 1406, 58080, 1413, 58082-91

The second and third batches of 0-4-4Ts were known as the '1532' and '2228' batches, and were built between 1881 and 1900 by Derby Works, Dübs & Co and Neilson & Co. The main distinction between these and the earlier '1252' Class (see previous entry) was that they had smaller 5ft 4in driving wheels. In the 1907 MR renumbering, these engines fell into the number series 1266-1430. Most later received their allocated BR numbers, except for three that were withdrawn immediately after nationalisation in the early months of 1948.

Some of the first 15 built worked the service between Manchester London Road and Central via Stockport. Five of the Neilson engines, delivered in the summer of 1893, were fitted with condensing equipment for working the 'Widened

Lines'. Enclosed cabs were fitted, with two round windows in the front and back plates, except on the condensing locomotives, which had only a front weatherboard.

A fairly healthy total of 56 engines survived long enough to be taken into BR stock, and most lasted into the early 1950s; thereafter their numbers dwindled, although one, No 58086 (LMS 1423, a 1900 Dübs engine), lasted until August 1960. This was a much-travelled engine, having started its BR career at Kentish Town, then moving north to various sheds in Derbyshire and Yorkshire before transferring to Bath Green Park in March 1950, remaining on the Somerset & Dorset line until its final demise.

Introduced 1881
Designed by Samuel Johnson
Built by MR, Derby (105), Dübs (50), Neilson (10)
Number built 165
Number inherited by BR 56
Last example withdrawn August 1960

Shabby Johnson 1P 0-4-4T No 58062, an 1892 Dübs product, looks as if it has had a hard, long life as it gets away from Ockendon with a Tilbury line local service in about 1955. This was one of eight of the BR survivors to be shedded at Plaistow, in this case for his entire BR career, being withdrawn from there in February 1956. *Dave Cobbe collection, Rail Photoprints.co.uk*

LNWR Webb 'Chopper Tank' Class 2-4-0T

No 58092

Thomas Middlemass, in *Steam Locomotive Nicknames*, reckons that it was the sharp exhaust of these 'tough little tanks', together with the inflexible motion of their coupling rods at speed, that earned them the nickname 'Choppers'. Fifty were built between 1876 and 1885, intended mainly for local passenger work; No 2000 was the 2,000th locomotive built at Crewe, and was completed on Queen Victoria's birthday, 24 May 1876. It was one of the examples fitted with condensing gear for the Outer Circle Broad Street to Mansion House services; others were not so fitted, and were used on suburban services in the Manchester and Birmingham areas. Other than the 4-4-0T Metropolitan type ordered from Beyer Peacock in 1871, these were the first LNWR suburban tank engines.

In 1879 Crewe Works produced the first in a long line of 2-4-2 tanks, which were an enlarged version of the 2-4-0T; construction went on until 1898, and while 93 of them passed to the LMS in 1923, all had gone by 1932. The 2-4-2Ts, also dubbed 'Choppers', or 'Mansion House Tanks', were a natural development from the earlier class. Indeed, the final order for 2-4-0Ts had included a single 2-4-2T, built with an additional trailing radial axle supporting a larger-capacity bunker; it also had a tender-locomotive-type cab, but subsequent examples were fitted with cabs suitable for travel in both directions.

In the late 1890s 40 of the 50 'Chopper Tanks' were 'renewed' by being given an extended bunker with a trailing radial axle, and were absorbed into the 2-4-2T class. Conversely, in 1908 five locomotives built as 2-4-2Ts were converted to 2-4-0Ts to work push-pull services, beginning with the Red Wharf Bay branch on Anglesey.

Introduced	1876
Designed by	Francis Webb
Built by	LNWR, Crewe
Number built	50
Number inherited by BR	1
Last example withdrawn	March 1952

Veteran Webb 'Chopper' tank' No 58092, built at Crewe in October 1877, shunts at Sheep Pasture on the Cromford & High Peak line on 16 July 1951. It was withdrawn and scrapped early the following year. *R. J. Buckley, R. M. Casserley collection*

The remaining ten non-converted 2-4-0Ts were retained for working the Cromford & High Peak line, but all bar one had been withdrawn by 1936. The last survivor of the class was No 58092 (formerly LMS No 6428, then No 26428 on the duplicate list from March 1948), which was withdrawn from Buxton shed on 14 March 1952, at the ripe old age of 74½! How sad that such a historic and useful little engine was not saved.

MR Fowler 'Lickey Banker' 0-10-0

No 58100

The Lickey Incline, on the Bristol & Gloucester line between Bromsgrove and Blackwell, is the steepest sustained main-line railway incline in Britain, and presents northbound trains with 2 miles rising at 1 in 37¾; included for reasons of economy, it kept the Birmingham & Gloucester Railway in debt for all of its independent existence.

Additional locomotives were used to assist trains up the incline from the earliest days, including an 1845 McConnell 0-6-0ST, No 38 *Great Britain*, which handled the job for 56 years until 1901, establishing the concept of a specialised banking engine.

Then in 1919 Derby Works built what was then by far the largest locomotive on the Midland Railway, which had otherwise stuck to its 'small engine' policy. It was nominally designed by Fowler, but it was more likely the work of James Anderson, who was acting Chief Mechanical Engineer between 1915 and 1919 when Fowler was away on war work.

Introduced	1919
Designed by	Sir Henry Fowler
Built by	MR, Derby
Number built	1
Number inherited by BR	1
Last example withdrawn	May 1956

Constructed by the end of the latter year, the engine was first steamed at the beginning of January 1920 at Derby, arriving at Bromsgrove on the 20th of that month.

No 2290 was a four-cylinder 0-10-0 engine built specifically for banking duties on the Lickey (it was only the second ten-coupled locomotive built in Britain, the other being the GER's 'Decapod' of 1902). It soon gained the nickname 'Big Bertha', a wartime name applied to a huge German gun (in turn derived from Frau Berta Krupp, granddaughter of munitions magnate Alfred Krupp); it was also known as 'Big Emma', from 'M' for Midland.

From 1922 a duplicate superheated boiler was kept at Derby so that it could be periodically exchanged without the engine having to be out of service for too long. The engine had Walschaerts valve gear operating the huge and steeply inclined outside cylinders, but because there was not enough space under the smokebox to fit piston valves for the inside cylinders, the large outer piston valves also supplied the inside cylinders through crossover steam ports. This was a practical, uncomplicated arrangement, but the steam flow was poor; however, this was not crucial in an engine that would generally only be running at slow speed. The cylinders all drove the middle pair of wheels, which allowed adequately long connecting rods for all sets of motion.

A tender cab was incorporated, which would be necessary as the engine would spend half of its life travelling in reverse when returning to Bromsgrove. Altogether, this mighty engine and tender weighed 105 tons, and had a tractive effort of 43,315lb; because it was only to be used for banking, it was not given a power classification by either the LMS or BR. The tender could hold more than 2,000 gallons of water and 4 tons of coal; each ascent was reckoned to use about 7cwt. The engine had no need of a larger capacity, as both coal and water could be replenished easily and frequently between duties.

Brakes acted on all wheels, and a handbrake was also applied to the driving wheels, not just the tender wheels as was customary, as the 0-10-0's tender was relatively light compared to the bulk of the engine.

To make it easier to draw up to the rear of a train in darkness, a powerful electric headlight was fitted in 1921, run from a steam generator on the footplate. When BR Standard 9F 2-10-0 No 92079 took over the banking duties, it inherited the headlamp.

In 1924 'Big Bertha' made a few trials on mineral trains between Toton and Cricklewood, but otherwise was found only working from Bromsgrove. The LMS renumbered it 22290 (in order to be able to use 2290 for one of the new 2-6-4 tanks), and in 1949 BR gave it the number 58100 (as adding 40000 to its LMS number would have encroached on the ex-LNER 6xxxx locomotive number series).

In 1955, during servicing in Derby, ex-LNER Garratt No 69999 arrived to take over, together with BR 9F 2-10-0 No 92008 for trials as an assistant banker. The Garratt was very unpopular with local crews, and had gone back north by the end of the year. However, the 0-10-0's days were clearly

'Big Bertha', 0-10-0 No 58100, works hard assisting a freight up the Lickey Incline, approaching Blackwell some time in 1954. *Colour-Rail collection*

numbered, and it was finally taken out of service in May 1956 (not long after the Garratt), being scrapped just under a year later. During the last six or seven years of banking operations, duties were shared with ex-LMS 'Jinty' 0-6-0s. Steam banking continued for another eight years, but utilising much more modern locomotives, and even ex-GWR tanks.

By the time of her withdrawal, 'Big Bertha' had amassed an amazing 838,856 miles plodding up and down the incline.

MR Kirtley double-framed '700' Class round-topped firebox 0-6-0

No 58110

Matthew Kirtley had a preference for six-wheeled locomotives – 2-4-0s and 0-6-0s – and the many hundreds of 0-6-0 good locomotives built by him for the Midland Railway and rebuilt by his successors Johnson and Deeley were remarkably sturdy and long-lived, and amenable to adaptation with later larger boilers and other modifications over the years.

The '700' Class was developed from Kirtley's '480' Class double-framed goods engines, and even after subsequent modifications they could still be distinguished by the graceful

curve of the frame over each outside coupling rod crank.

Six '700' Class engines were withdrawn between 1903 and 1905, and in the Midland's 1907 renumbering scheme the remainder became Nos 2592-671, 2674-711 and 2713-867. In 1906 50 were sold to the Italian State Railway. During the First World War 78 of the class served with the Railway Operating Division, and three were loaned to the LSWR between December 1917 and February 1920. The ROD locomotives were returned to the MR in 1919-20, and all but one returned to service.

In the mid-1930s, to free up numbers for new classes, the LMS added 20000 to the numbers of the 20 or so surviving

Introduced 1863
Designed by Matthew Kirtley
Built by Dübs
Number built 470 (originally round-topped, some rebuilt with Belpaire fireboxes)
Number inherited by BR 1 (round-topped firebox)
Last example withdrawn November 1951

The last surviving Kirtley double-framed 0-6-0 still with a Johnson round-topped firebox was No 58110. Formerly shedded at Bourneville to work the Halesowen branch, it moved to Derby in April 1948, and was photographed shunting there on 12 June 1949. This wonderful antique was scrapped at Derby at the end of 1951. *H. C. Casserley*

0-6-0s, and some were famously retained at Bourneville shed long after the rest of the class had been scrapped. There they worked the Halesowen branch, being light enough to cross the severely weight-restricted Dowery Dell Viaduct (GWR pannier tanks were later used). Thus Bourneville was regularly visited by enthusiasts in the late 1940s to see what even then were seen as veterans from a distant era.

Just four of these archaic early Midland locos survived beyond the LMS, and one of them, LMS No 22630, built in 1870, retained its round-topped Johnson boiler with Salter safety-valves, and even had its BR number, 58110, applied (for the other three, see below). Initially classified as 2F, it was later downgraded to 1F. From Bourneville it moved to Derby in April 1948, and was considered useful for shunting, having a greater coal and water capacity than a tank loco, while the open cab helped visibility.

Of the earlier straight-framed 0-6-0s, No 2393, a Kitson engine of 1856, was the last of its kind to remain in service when it was withdrawn in 1927. Another, No 2320, withdrawn the previous year, was set aside for preservation, but ultimately it was decided to scrap it in 1932. Attempts were also made to preserve No 58110, but it was not to be, and following withdrawal in November 1951 it was broken up at Derby Works the following month at the age of 81.

MR Kirtley double-framed ('700' Class) Belpaire firebox 0-6-0

Introduced 1863
Designed by Matthew Kirtley
Built by Dübs
Number built 470 (originally round-topped, some rebuilt with Belpaire fireboxes)
Number inherited by BR 3 (Belpaire firebox)
Last example withdrawn March 1950

Nos 22846, 22853, 22863

Many of the '700' Class 0-6-0s were rebuilt by Johnson and Deeley with several variations of boiler, smokebox and cab, and three of the modified engines passed into BR's hands in 1948. On the LMS duplicate list they had been Nos 22846, 22853 and 22863, and would have become BR Nos 58111-13, had they live long enough to be renumbered.

Two of the three, Nos 22846 and 22863, built in 1873 and 1874 respectively, were Bourneville engines, and were withdrawn from there in 1949. No 22853, an 1873 Dübs product, was shedded at Saltley, where it managed to last until March 1950.

No 22853 is seen on shed at Saltley on 3 July 1948. Its Belpaire firebox can be seen, and a full cab, as distinct from No 58110's more open variety. The smokebox numberplate and shedplate have already been lost. *H. C. Casserley*

MR Johnson 4ft 11in '1142' and '1698' Class 0-6-0

Nos 58114-33, 22940, 58135-40, 22953, 58142-46, 22965, 58148, 58149, 22969, 22970, 58152-54, 22876, 58156-87, 58229-38, 3157, 58240-42, 3168, 58244, 3173, 58246, 58247, 3177

Johnson followed Kirtley's example and built vast numbers of 0-6-0 engines, the biggest difference being that they were single-framed, rather than Kirtley's later style of double-framed construction. In 1875-67 120 engines were ordered from outside contractors: Kitson & Co built 30 at £2,920 each, Dübs & Co contributed 30 at £2,635 each, then in 1876 Beyer Peacock built 30 at £2,650, and finally Neilson & Co added a further 30 at £2,635 each.

All the engines had 4ft 11in driving wheels, except the Neilson engines, which had wheels of 4ft 10in diameter; they had the standard Midland wheelbase of 8ft + 8ft 6in. Their working weight was 34 tons 3cwt for the engine and 28 tons 19cwt for a full tender.

In 1885 yet more 0-6-0s emerged, still with round-topped fireboxes, but this time from the Midland's own Derby Works, with slightly larger 18-inch-diameter cylinders. Sixty were built in five batches between 1885 and 1888. Like the outside-built engines, they had a working pressure of 140psi, but from 1903 onwards they were reboilered to 175psi. Many of this class, and later ones, were again rebuilt from 1926 with larger boilers with flat-topped Belpaire fireboxes and pressed to 140 or 160psi.

All the engines initially carried small Johnson cabs, but from 1917 onwards larger, more enclosed Deeley cabs appeared. Thus the class members had a very mixed appearance.

The first of the class was withdrawn in 1925, and in the 1930s some were renumbered in the duplicate list (having 20000 added to their numbers) when their original number sequences were required for new-build engines.

About half the class was still at work when British Railways was formed, and nearly half of those remained in service towards the end of the 1950s. Withdrawals began in earnest in the early 1960s, until only one remained, No 58182. 1961 had found it at Rugby, then it had moved to Barrow and finally Coalville in January 1963, where it had joined half-a-dozen other members of the class. They had been concentrated there

Because the veteran Johnson 2F 0-6-0s were small enough to negotiate Glenfield Tunnel on the Leicester West Bridge branch, they were retained at Coalville to handle the two daily freight trains. One of the half-dozen or so kept for this duty was No 58148 of 1876, seen here in what is clearly Midland territory at Desford on 14 November 1963, the month before it was withdrawn. Sister loco No 58182, withdrawn the following January, was then the oldest locomotive running on BR. *Colour-Rail collection*

Introduced 1875
Designed by Samuel Johnson
Built by MR, Derby (60), Kitson (30), Dübs (30), Beyer Peacock (30), Neilson (30)
Number built 180
Number inherited by BR 94
Last example withdrawn January 1964

to work the former Leicester & Swannington Railway route to Leicester West Bridge. This single line included the narrow Glenfield Tunnel, and these Johnson 2F veterans were small enough to squeeze through with the two daily freight trains.

When No 58182 was finally withdrawn in January 1964 it had the distinction of being the oldest locomotive running on BR, at the age of 88.

MR Johnson 5ft 3in '1357', '1798', 'J' and 'M' Class 0-6-0

Nos 58188-201, 3050, 58201, 3052, 58203, 58204, 3061, 58206, 58207, 3066, 58209, 3073, 58211-22, 3109, 58224-26, 3123, 58228, 58249, 3195, 3196, 58251, 58252, 3264, 58254, 3311, 3360, 58257-62, 3437, 58264, 58265, 3466, 3473, 3477, 58268, 58269, 3489, 58271-74, 3511, 58276-81, 3533, 58283, 3537, 58285-91, 3566, 58293, 3592, 3602, 58295, 3617, 3632, 58298-300, 3689, 58302-06, 3726, 58308-10

In total some 1,763 0-6-0s were built by or for the Midland Railway, including 56 built for the Somerset & Dorset and Midland & Great Northern routes. Although there were detail differences between the locomotives, they can be considered the largest single basic design of engine ever built by a British railway company.

These later engines carried what became the Midland's standard driving wheel diameter for an 0-6-0, 5ft 3in, and were the direct ancestors of all subsequent MR 0-6-0s.

Twenty were delivered by Dübs & Co in 1878, then in 1880

On 30 May 1959 three Johnson 0-6-0s (4ft 11in No 58167 and 5ft 3in Nos 58271 and 58283) were used for the Stephenson Locomotive Society's 'Birmingham Area Rail Tour', which traversed a selection of Black Country backwaters, including many lines now long since closed. Suitably spruced up, No 58271 attracts youthful attention at Birmingham New Street. A Monument Lane engine at the time, No 58271 was withdrawn just two years later. *J. Adams, Colour-Rail*

Introduced 1878
Designed by Samuel Johnson
Built by MR, Derby (30), Dübs (120), Robert Stephenson (30), Beyer Peacock (50), Neilson (175), Kitson (120), Sharp Stewart (85), Neilson Reid (85), Vulcan Foundry (20)
Number built 715
Number inherited by BR 108
Last example withdrawn July 1962

Derby Works turned out its first Johnson goods tender locomotive of this type. The Dübs locomotives cost £2,274 each and those built by Derby £1,990 9s 6d, so there was quite a saving to be made by building 'in-house'. Further batches followed from a wide variety of manufacturers, including Robert Stephenson, which built 30 in 1880-81, and a further 50 from Beyer Peacock in 1882-84, costing £2,234 and £2,460 each respectively.

Many of the engines were subsequently rebuilt with larger Belpaire boilers, becoming the Johnson/Deeley 3F Class 0-6-0s of 1888-1902 (qv), numbered 43191-763 by BR. Remarkably, not one of these hundreds of useful engines was preserved, despite the fact that the last of the rebuilt locomotives was not withdrawn until February 1964. The last of these unrebuilt engines survived until July 1962; No 58218, a Beyer Peacock product of 1883, was a Northampton engine until February 1953, moving then to Rugby for eight years before being withdrawn from Bescot in July 1962 at almost 80 years old.

LNWR Webb '17-inch Coal Engine' Class 0-6-0

Nos 28088, 58321, 58322, 28095, 28097, 58323, 28104, 28105, 58326, 28107, 8108, 58328, 28116, 28128, 28133, 58332, 28152, 28153, 28158, 28166, 58336, 8182, 28191, 28199, 28202, 28205, 28216, 28221, 58343, 28230, 28233, 28234, 8236, 28239, 58347, 28246, 28247, 28251, 58351, 58352, 28262, 58354, 38271, 28295, 28296, 28308, 28309, 28312, 28313

Webb succeeded Ramsbottom as Chief Mechanical Engineer at Crewe in September 1871, and inherited a very sound position as regards locomotive provision for Britain's 'Premier Line'. The first new locomotive design for the LNWR for which he was entirely responsible was the so-called '17-inch Goods Engine'

Introduced 1873
Designed by Francis Webb
Built by LNWR, Crewe
Number built 500
Number inherited by BR 49
Last example withdrawn October 1953

('17-inch' referring to the cylinder diameter), an 0-6-0 that was a development of Ramsbottom's 'DX' and 'Special Tank' designs. This was a straightforward, sturdy and reliable design, specifically for goods haulage, and E. L. Ahrons considered it to have been among the simplest and cheapest locomotives ever made in Britain. Economy was paramount, as the LNWR had a 'low cost' policy, which had driven down running costs from 10¾d per engine mile in 1857 to 7¾d by 1871.

Between 1873 and 1892 500 'Coal Engines' were built. In February 1878 what would now be called a 'publicity stunt' resulted in one of the class, No 1140, being built from scratch in 25½ hours. The last of the 500 emerged from Crewe in October 1892, after which no more 0-6-0s were built purely for freight

With what looks as though it may be a mis-match LMS tender behind them, the crew of Webb 'Coal Engine' No 58332, one of the class to survive as Crewe Works shunters, take a break at the north end of Crewe station on 13 September 1950. This and sister loco No 58343 were the last two survivors of a once 500-strong class. *H. C. Casserley*

work. They incorporated many features from earlier eras, including Ramsbottom's design of safety valve, a horizontally hinged smokebox door, wooden buffer beam and brake blocks, absence of brakes on the engine, and a tender design with grease axleboxes. However, they had Webb chimneys, cabs, coupling rods and cast-iron wheels. By the time of the final batch they had gained circular smokebox doors, steam brakes (albeit with wooden brake shoes) and 1,800-gallon as opposed to the original 1,500-gallon tenders. They were never fitted with vacuum brakes in LNWR days, so after the final disappearance of Webb's chain brake ('which very often did,' as one railway humorist put it) in 1892, they were used on goods trains only.

During the First World War many 'Coal Engines' were used by the Railway Operating Division, including some by the British Expeditionary Force and 42 by the Palestine Military Railway.

At the Grouping of 1923 227 members of the class passed into LMS stock, and 49 examples, between 56 and 75 years old, became BR engines upon nationalisation. However, some were already marked for withdrawal and were never allocated a BR number, and of those that were, only a dozen ran long enough to have them applied.

The 'Coal Engines' were the model for Webb's celebrated 1881 'Coal Tanks', an 0-6-2T version that gave greater operational flexibility over shorter journeys. In all, 300 were built until 1896, and one of them (BR No 58926), thanks to the efforts of Bangor shedmaster J. M. Dunn, was preserved as LNWR No 1054 and has been a popular performer on various heritage lines for many years.

Interestingly, three of the BR engines that retained their pre-duplicate-list LMS numbers, Nos 8108, 8182 and 8236, had been sold to the Shropshire & Montgomeryshire Railway in the 1930s. That line had been requisitioned by the War Department during the Second World War, and when it came into BR hands at nationalisation its entire stock was withdrawn, and the three engines were cut up at Swindon in 1950.

By the end of 1952 only ten 'Coal Engines' remained in service. Nos 58321/23/26/28/32/36/43/47 were retained for internal shunting duties at Crewe Works (although not officially regarded as 'service' locomotives), while LMS No 28128 (which would have become BR No 58330) and No 58354 were shedded at Barrow. The last pair, Nos 58332 and 58343, ceased work at their birthplace in October 1953.

LNWR Webb '18-inch Goods' or 'Cauliflower' Class 0-6-0

Nos 58362-65, 28338, 28339, 28345, 28350, 28370, 28372, 28385, 28392, 26403, 28404, 58275-78, 28441-43, 58381-83, 28458, 28460, 28464, 28484, 28487, 58389, 28494, 28499, 58392-94, 28511, 58396, 28513, 58398, 28521, 58400, 28526, 28527, 28529, 28531, 28532, 28542-44, 28547, 58409, 28549, 28551, 58412, 58413, 28556, 58415, 28561, 28575, 28580, 28583, 28585, 28586, 28589, 28592, 28594, 28597, 28598, 28608, 58426, 58427, 28618, 58429, 58430

Webb's celebrated 'Cauliflower' 0-6-0 express goods engines gained their nickname from the LNWR coat-of-arms carried on the central splasher, whose shape and intricacy of design rather resembled that vegetable. They were the only 0-6-0 class to be thus adorned, and were also known as the 'Crested Goods'.

These versatile and hardy engines had larger-diameter wheels than the 'Coal Engine' 0-6-0s (see previous entry), at 5ft 2½in; they were thus designed for faster running, replacing the earlier 'DX' class of 1858. The LNWR was developing long non-stop freight journeys between traffic centres, hence the need for the new engines. They were also often used on passenger trains (for example, in January 1937 No 8369 managed 74mph with a 280-ton train on the main line between Penrith and Carlisle).

A total of 310 engines were built at Crewe between June 1880 and 1902, and they were also the first LNWR engines to use David Joy's radial valve gear, enthusiastically adopted by Webb. The gear was tried out on No 2365, which had the older Crewe features of a horizontally hinged smokebox door, no brakes on the engine and cast-iron H-section driving wheels; after trials, nine more of the class were built in 1882 (No 2365

A 'Cauliflower' past its best: it is hard to imagine the elaborate LNWR coat-of-arms on the splasher of this elegant goods engine when it was built back in July 1901. Withdrawn from Widnes shed in December 1955, No 58427 makes a sad sight at Crewe the following June, awaiting the cutter's torch. *T. B. Owen, Colour-Rail*

Introduced 1880
Designed by Francis Webb
Built by LNWR, Crewe
Number built 310
Number inherited by BR 75
Last example withdrawn December 1955

was later exhibited at an Institution of Mechanical Engineers meeting at Barrow). The 'Cauliflowers' could be distinguished by the humps in the running plate to clear the connecting rod cranks, and the first ten had the H-section wheels, while later examples had more elegant spokes. Originally the engines had wooden brake blocks and wooden buffer beams, but the brakes were changed to the double-hanger all-metal type during LMS days. The engines were coupled to tenders with capacities of 1,800, 2,000 or 2,500 gallons.

A further batch followed from early 1887, with conventional driving wheels of cast steel and circular smokebox doors, which became standard on subsequent batches. Some years later Webb's 'Watford Tanks' represented a tank engine version of the class.

Webb equipped the 'Cauliflowers' the same boiler as his 'Precedent' Class, then in 1924 the LMS started to fit the engines with Belpaire fireboxes, and at least 140 were so modified. The new boiler featured pop safety valves, and the flat-topped firebox necessitated alteration to the spectacle plate, with different windows.

The LMS initially numbered the class 8315-8624, and between 1940 and 1944 20000 was added to the numbers to free up the originals to be applied to new 8F 2-8-0s.

When eventually displaced by larger engines, the 'Cauliflowers' were moved to lighter duties. For example, from 1932 they reigned supreme on the Cockermouth, Keswick & Penrith line for some 18 years. O. S. Nock travelled on one of them, which 'ran freely up to 57mph, and without any suggestion of rough or wild riding.'

The first 'Cauliflower' was withdrawn in 1922, and six were withdrawn immediately upon nationalisation without being allocated BR numbers. Only 26 BR engines actually carried their BR number. By 1950 the class had been reduced by more than half, and at the end of 1954 only seven remained; four had gravitated to Widnes shed (8D), with three others at Bangor, Penrith and Carlisle Upperby. It was the Penrith engine, No 58412, and Widnes's No 58427 that rendered the class extinct when they were withdrawn at the end of 1955. It is a particular disappointment that not one of these iconic 0-6-0 goods engines should have been preserved for posterity, complete with a 'cauliflower' on the splasher!

North London Railway 0-4-2ST Crane Tank

No 27217

The distinction of being the oldest locomotive inherited by the newly formed British Railways in 1948 goes to this charming little crane tank.

It was originally built in 1858 by Sharp Stewart & Co of Glasgow as a conventional 0-4-0 saddle tank to work the Hammersmith-Acton branch of the North & South Western Junction Railway. This company had been authorised in 1851 to link the LNWR and LSWR systems at Willesden and Old Kew Junction respectively, and the line opened in 1853. The North London Railway worked the passenger service at first, with the line being leased to the LNWR and LSWR until 1871, when the partners became the LNWR, NLR and MR. The company remained nominally independent until vested in the LMS in 1923.

The saddle tank was purchased by the NLR in 1859, and in 1872 John C. Park, the company's new Locomotive Superintendent, rebuilt it at Bow Works as an 0-4-2ST crane tank, the crane being constructed over the newly added trailing truck. The jib was marked 'Not to lift more than 3 tons'.

Introduced 1858; rebuilt 1872
Designed by Sharp Stewart
Built by Sharp Stewart
Number built 1
Number inherited by BR 1
Last example withdrawn February 1951

The crane tank was withdrawn in 1951, a few years short of its centenary, and sent to Derby Works to be broken up. It is seen there, derelict, on 3 April 1952; it lasted until October. *H. C. Casserley*

A fine portrait of former North London Railway 0-4-2ST crane tank No 58865, originally built in 1858 and converted to a crane in 1872. Having worked at Bow Works for almost 80 years, it is seen here at Devons Road shed on 24 August 1949, having gained its new BR number the previous March. *R. M. Casserley*

At first it had no cab, but was later fitted with one; the LMS added rectangular sheeting to enclose the crane and match the flat-topped saddle tank. It also later gained wheels with H-section spokes and Ramsbottom safety valves.

The NLR gave what it labelled simply 'Crane Tank' the numbers 37, 29 and 29A successively; when it passed to the LNWR on the takeover of the NLR in 1909, it became No 2896, then the LMS numbered it 7217, later placing it on the duplicate list as 27217. Its BR number was 58865. Throughout

this time it remained practically unaltered for almost 80 years, spending its life as works shunter at Bow.

It was hoped that the loco might reach its centenary, something that had not been achieved by a working British engine without drastic rebuilding. Unfortunately, although it attained the distinction of being the oldest surviving standard-gauge engine in service with BR, it was taken out of service at Devons Road shed (1D) in February 1951 and sent to Derby, where it was eventually broken up at the works there in October 1952.

LNWR Webb 'Saddle Tank' Class 0-6-0T

No 27480

> **Introduced** 1905; rebuilt from 1873-92 0-6-0s
> **Designed by** Francis Webb; rebuilt by George Whale
> **Built by** LNWR, Crewe
> **Number built** 45
> **Number inherited by BR** 1
> **Last example withdrawn** December 1948

Between 1905 and 1907 Webb's successor, George Whale, rebuilt 45 of the former's '17-inch Coal Engine' 0-6-0 tender engines (qv) as 0-6-0 saddle tanks. By so doing he extended the lives of these older locos, some of which were already more than 30 years old, so they could eke out their days as shunters.

Because the saddle tank was of a rather unattractive square profile, the engines were sometimes known as 'Box Tanks' (not to be confused with the 'Bissel Truck' 1F Class 0-4-2PT – qv). They were a development of the earlier 'Special Tanks' (see below), although visually more like the 'Bissel' 0-4-2Ts.

The class passed intact to the LMS, as Nos 7458-7502, and the first was withdrawn in 1924. In 1934 the surviving engines were transferred to the duplicate list, and had 20000 added to their numbers.

Just one of the rebuilds became a BR engine in 1948. LMS No 27480, built in February 1891 and rebuilt as a saddle tank in

This pre-nationalisation picture of the last surviving Webb/Whale 0-6-0ST 'Box Tank', No 27480, was taken at Wolverton Carriage Works in about 1946. The loco was subsequently scrapped at Crewe Works in 1949. Note the unusual side extension to the cab. *H. F. Wheeller collection via Roger Carpenter*

October 1906, was used at Crewe Works until it was taken out of service in December 1948, without ever carrying its allocated BR number, 58870.

LNWR Webb 'Special Tank' Class 0-6-0T (Service Locomotives)

Nos CD3, CD6, CD7, CD8, 3323

Ramsbottom's 'Special Tank' was his last design before he retired from the LNWR, and building continued under Webb. The design was a saddle tank version of Ramsbottom's 'DX' express goods 0-6-0 tender engines, 857 of which had been built between 1858 and 1874; the 'Specials' had the same cylinders and wheelbase, but slightly smaller driving wheels and boiler. Fifty were ordered initially, but only 20 had been delivered before Ramsbottom retired; their subsequent evolution took place during Webb's tenure, and incorporated such Webb features as his design of chimney, cast number plate and safety valve casing. In all 258 (260 or 278 according to some sources) were built between 1870 and 1880. Most retained the sloping Ramsbottom smokebox front until LMS days and, although

> **Introduced** 1870
> **Designed by** John Ramsbottom
> **Built by** LNWR, Crewe
> **Number built** 258
> **Number inherited by BR** 5
> **Last example withdrawn** November 1959

originally built with only weatherboards, some had received cabs by the 1890s, and many more by the First World War.

The term 'Special' on the LNWR, also applied to other engines besides these, may have indicated that they were fitted with vacuum brakes, and were thus able to work passenger trains. In the case of these tank engines, the name may have arisen because they were built for the special job of working the Abergavenny to Merthyr line.

The 'Special Tanks' were used for shunting but also frequently for station pilot and empty carriage stock workings. Their fuel capacity was more limited than the 0-6-2 'Coal Tanks', resulting in a smaller range.

Two of the engines were fitted with condensing apparatus and rectangular saddle tanks for use in Wapping Tunnel, Liverpool. From 1895 they were used on the American Special boat trains through Waterloo and Victoria Tunnels between Edge Hill and Riverside, and carried a fully lined livery and the names *Euston* and *Liverpool*.

The first example was scrapped in 1920, and those that entered LMS stock at the Grouping were numbered 7220-7457, together with eight in Departmental stock that were numbered separately. The last of those in public service was withdrawn in 1941, but five of the Departmental engines survived to be inherited by BR: four – Nos CD3 (formerly No 317), CD6, CD7 (No 2329) and CD8 *Earlestown* (No 2359) – worked as Carriage Department shunters at Wolverton Works, while LNWR No 3323 (formerly No 2322 of 1878, and briefly renumbered 43323

Three of the Ramsbottom/Webb 'Special Tanks' are lined up at Wolverton Works on 29 July 1956. No CD8 *Earlestown* is nearest the camera; the others carry plates that read 'CARR^E DEP^T WOL^N'. *T. B. Owen, Colour-Rail*

in error) was retained as a shunter at Crewe Works. The others were Nos CD2 and CD5, which were 0-4-2ST crane tanks at Wolverton, No CD4 at Crewe, and CD8 at Earlestown Wagon Works, near Newton-le-Willows, all of which were scrapped prior to 1948. No 3323 was scrapped in 1950, *Earlestown* went in 1957, and the other Wolverton engines succumbed in 1959.

*

One other locomotive inherited by BR from the LMS was a narrow-gauge 0-4-0ST of 1924, purchased from Bagnall in 1945. Named *Batley*, it worked at Beeston Creosote Works until scrapped at the end of 1955.

4

Locomotives of the former London & North Eastern Railway and its constituents

LNER 'A1' Class 4-6-2

Nos 60113-62

Introduced	1948
Designed by	Arthur Peppercorn
Built by	LNER, Doncaster and Darlington
Number built	50
Number inherited by BR	50
Last example withdrawn	June 1966

One of the last pair of Peppercorn 'A1' 'Pacifics' to remain in service in 1966, No 60124 (formerly named *Kenilworth*) is reduced to standby duty at Stockton on 19 September 1965. It is still only 16 years old. *Chris Davies, railphotoprints collection*

Sir Nigel Gresley's successor as Chief Mechanical Engineer of the London & North Eastern Railway from 1941 was Edward Thompson, and he caused controversy in 1945 when he rebuilt Gresley's prototype 'Pacific' of 1922, No 4470 *Great Northern*, as the prototype for his new class of 4-6-2s, and by doing so eradicated almost all of his predecessor's distinctive features. The rebuild had three cylinders each with a set of Walschaerts valve gear, and the wheelbase was lengthened as a result of the outside cylinders being positioned well behind the front bogie. The new engine was considered strikingly ugly at the front end, and it showed no improvement in performance over other existing 'Pacifics'. Thompson's motives in rebuilding *Great Northern* seem to have been standardisation of parts and ease of maintenance, but his action was seen as a deliberate slight towards Gresley. Most of Gresley's original 'A1' 'Pacifics' had already been rebuilt as 'A3s', any that remained unrebuilt being redesignated by Thompson as Class 'A10'.

In 1946 Arthur Peppercorn succeeded Thompson at Doncaster when the latter retired, and he continued the slow development work on the new 'Pacifics' based on Thompson's prototype. These were identical in layout to Peppercorn's own 'A2/3' Class, but with larger 6ft 8in wheels, double chimneys and double Kylchap blastpipes; later chimneys were lipped, which improved their appearance over the 'double stovepipe' originals. The cylinders were moved forward to the more conventional position beside the leading bogie. They were altogether excellent locomotives, and required less maintenance that any contemporary express engine. They were, however, unpopular with crews on account of their rough riding. On the Thompson 'Pacifics' this had been attributed to the wide spacing between the front bogie and front driving wheels, but the 'yawing' motion of the 'A1s' was much worse, especially when running fast south of the border. Free-steaming and economical they may have been, but O. S. Nock recalled that No 60159 *Bonnie Dundee* 'gave me the roughest ride I had ever experienced on a steam locomotive; indeed, there were times when we were lurching so much … that I was really scared.'

When the LNER became part of BR, Peppercorn remained as CME of the Eastern and North Eastern Regions. The 'A1s' had been ordered by the LNER, but were delivered after nationalisation. Peppercorn redesignated the rebuilt *Great Northern* as Class 'A1/1', and 49 further examples of his 'A1s' were rapidly built in four batches during 1948-49; the first, No 60114 *W. P. Allen*, entered traffic in August 1948. East Coast Main Line trains of the period weighed up to 550 tons, and the 'A1s' could handle them at a consistent 60-70mph on level track. Five of the class (Nos 60153-57) were fitted with Timken roller bearings throughout in an attempt to increase the period between heavy repairs; this was achieved, but no other class members were so fitted.

The names chosen for the new engines were a mixture of racehorses, the names of people associated with the history of the LNER, pre-Grouping LNER constituent companies, birds, names associated with Sir Walter Scott and his novels, and other place-related names.

The first engine to be withdrawn was No 60123 *H. A. Ivatt* in October 1962 after an accident, and by the end of 1965 only two were left, Nos 60124 *Kenilworth* and 60145 *Saint Mungo*; the latter was the last to go, in June 1966.

Though not perhaps as well-loved or iconic as the Gresley 'A3s' and 'A4s' (both of which classes have famous examples preserved), it was considered a pity than no 'A1' had been preserved, especially as they had given less than 18 years of service when scrapped. Efforts had been made to preserve *Saint Mungo*, but the necessary funds could not be raised. This omission was rectified when No 60163 *Tornado*, the '50th Peppercorn A1', was built between 1994 and 2008 by the A1 Steam Locomotive Trust based at Darlington; full main-line certification followed in January 2009. The new engine, costing in the region of £3 million, was considered not as a replica or restoration project, but as an evolutionary step incorporating improvements that may well have been made had steam continued.

The name *Tornado* was chosen in honour of the RAF aircraft and crew flying at the time in the Gulf War, and its number, 60163, would have been the next in the 'A1' sequence. As a new steam locomotive running on the 21st-century railway, *Tornado* has the TOPS number 98863 – '98' designates a steam locomotive, '8' is the power classification, and '63' is the last part of its number.

LNER 'W1' Class 4-6-4

No 60700

Introduced 1929
Designed by Nigel Gresley
Built by LNER, Darlington
Number built 1
Number inherited by BR 1
Last example withdrawn June 1959

Having been withdrawn from service, the unique 'W1' Class 4-6-4 No 60700, rebuilt in 'A4' style from the Gresley 'Hush Hush' experimental engine No 10000 in 1936-37, awaits its fate in Doncaster Works yard on 23 May 1959. *Brian Morrison*

One of the most interesting 'one-offs' inherited by BR in 1948 was the streamlined 4-6-4 No 60700. This engine's remarkable career had begun as an experiment by Gresley in the use of high-pressure boilers (not unlike Fowler's contemporary 4-6-0 No 6399 *Fury*). Developed in 1929 under circumstances of great secrecy (immediately earning it the nickname 'Hush Hush'), the locomotive emerged from Darlington as a four-cylinder compound; it was the first British locomotive to incorporate streamlining in its design (five years before the 'A4s'), and the first experimental engine to be used on regular public services. Some dubbed this massive engine the 'Grey Ghost', others, less politely, the 'Flying Sausage' or 'Galloping Sausage'. Its unusual but not unattractive front-end design was the result of wind tunnel experiments, and the chimney was almost invisible, a factor that apparently caused more public comment that any other feature of the new design.

At its heart was a high-pressure marine-type water tube boiler, developed over three years specially for the locomotive by shipbuilders Yarrow & Co of Glasgow. The resulting boiler was patented by Gresley and Harold Yarrow, and was quite unlike any used for stationary or marine applications. It was triangular in shape, with a large central steam drum placed above four water drums, linked by rows of slightly curved tubes through which water circulated. The firebox area was wide and spanned the frames, placing the water drums at the limits of the loading gauge, while the boiler area was narrower, the water drums there being placed between the frames. The space outside the tubes formed a pair of exhaust flues leading forwards. Longitudinal superheater tubes were placed between the steam generating tubes. The third area forwards contained the superheater headers, the regulators and smokebox. The boiler casing remained at a similar width throughout, giving an overall curved triangular appearance. The working pressure was a mighty 450psi, compared to the more conventional 180psi (220psi superheated) of an 'A3'.

The motion was based on Gresley's 'Pacifics', with the additional pair of wheels at the rear to carry the extra length. (The two trailing axles were independent, rather than forming a four-wheel bogie as at the front, thus being partially articulated – it has therefore been suggested that the wheel arrangement was strictly 4-6-2-2.) No 10000 was the only standard-gauge 4-6-4 tender locomotive to run on a British railway.

Steam was supplied to the inside high-pressure cylinders, and was then fed to the two larger low-pressure outside cylinders before being exhausted. Two sets of outside Walschaerts valve gear also controlled the inside cylinders via an ingenious system allowing for independent cut-off controls for each set of cylinders.

Initially it had been intended to name No 10000 *British Enterprise*, while a later 1951 plan was to give it the name *Pegasus*, but neither was implemented.

The locomotive was supplied with a corridor tender to allow it to run non-stop between King's Cross and Edinburgh. Various modifications were found necessary during testing and its runs in service, but unfortunately steaming remained relatively poor, and performance never reached the standards of an equivalent firetube boiler. By 1935 Gresley had decided that nothing more could be done to improve matters, and the water tube boiler made its last journey in October 1936. No 10000 was consequently rebuilt with a conventional boiler and 'A4'-style streamlining, together with a three-cylinder non-compound arrangement, re-entering service in 1937. Out of its 1,888 days of existence, 1,105 had been spent in Darlington Works. The water tube boiler was used for pressure testing and space heating, and was not finally scrapped until 1965, thus outliving the locomotive by some six years.

BR renumbered the rebuilt 4-6-4 No 60700, and replaced the corridor tender with a conventional one. In 1955 the front bogie frame broke, happily at slow speed, and was repaired. However, by 1959 this one-off was proving uneconomical and was withdrawn from Doncaster shed on 1 June 1959 and broken up.

GCR Robinson '1A'/'B8' Class 'Glenalmond' 4-6-0

Nos 1353-55, 1337, 1358

Introduced 1913
Designed by John Robinson
Built by GCR, Gorton
Number built 11
Number inherited by BR 5
Last example withdrawn April 1949

At the end of 1912, the Great Central Railway's Gorton Works turned out No 423 *Sir Sam Fay*, the first of a new series of express passenger locomotives of Class '1' (LNER 'B2'). The first was named after the company's energetic and enterprising General Manager from 1902 to 1922. The engines were designed by the GCR's CME, John G. Robinson, who according to O. S. Nock designed 'one of the most handsome ranges of steam locomotives ever run in Great Britain.' The inside-cylinder 'Sir Sam Fay' 4-6-0s were no exception, with their long splashers above a running plate that was raised above the driving wheels, and straight brass nameplates.

Before the last of the Class '1' engines had been completed, another 4-6-0 variation was being built at Gorton. The first engine was numbered 4, the fourth engine to carry this number, and was named *Glenalmond*, after the Scottish seat of the company's Chairman, Sir Alexander Henderson. This was the Class '1A', a smaller-wheeled (5ft 7in) version of the 'Sir Sam Fay', with a straight running plate, and between 1913 and 1915 ten further engines were constructed. They were numbered 279, 280 and 439-446, and four were named; apart from No 4 *Glenalmond*, they were Nos 279 *Earl Kitchener of Khartoum*, 439 *Sutton Nelthorpe* (a GCR Director) and 446 *Earl Roberts of Kandahar*. They were mainly used on goods trains, as well as on some slow passenger services and excursions.

The '1As' were the first locomotive type to be fitted with Robinson's boiler top-feed, which was carried by all but No 4, but which was subsequently removed during early LNER days.

LNER 'B8' No 1358 *Earl Kitchener of Khartoum* stands at Gorton on 27 July 1947. Built in December 1914, it became LNER No 5279, then 1358 in 1946. It did not last long enough to carry its BR number of 61358, being scrapped before the end of 1948. *John Stretton collection*

The LNER reclassified the engines 'B8' and added 5000 to the numbers; the first of the class, No 5004 *Glenalmond*, was referred to as Class 'B8/2', the others being Class 'B8/1'.

Under the LNER renumbering scheme of 1946 they became Nos 1349-59. When displaced by more modern LNER engines, the 'B8s' went to March to help with the GE Section's shortage of mixed-traffic locomotives. However, they were severely route-restricted and were returned to the GC Section by 1926.

Despite the fact that the 'Glenalmonds' shared the same shortcomings as the 'Sir Sam Fays', most survived until 1947, when rapid withdrawals of all GCR 4-6-0 types began. Five were briefly BR engines, but did not last long enough to receive their allocated numbers of 61353-58 (subsequently carried by LNER 'B1' 4-6-0s). All were shedded at Sheffield Darnall at nationalisation, and all had gone within 16 months, scrapped at either Gorton Works or Dukinfield Carriage Works.

GCR Robinson '9Q'/'B7' Class 4-6-0

Nos 1360-90, 61391, 1392-95, 61396, 1397 (61702-13)

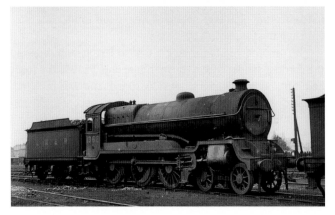

Robinson's ninth and last 4-6-0 design for the Great Central (and probably his most successful of that wheel arrangement) was a mixed-traffic version of his 'Lord Faringdon' (GCR '9P', LNER 'B3' – qv) express passenger locomotive, with the same size of boiler and cylinders, but smaller 5ft 8in driving wheels. The first three were built at the GCR's Gorton Works in 1921, then two more followed while the Vulcan Foundry produced a further ten. In the first half of 1922 Gorton turned out eight more, and the final batch of five was produced by the

This 'B7' 4-6-0 was built as GCR No 78 by the Vulcan Foundry in September 1921. It later became LNER No 5978, then 1363, but never carried its allocated BR number, 61363. It is seen here at Selby on 3 October 1949, having been withdrawn in the middle of the previous year. *H. C. Casserley*

Introduced 1921
Designed by John Robinson
Built by GCR, Gorton (23), Vulcan Foundry (10), Beyer Peacock (5)
Number built 38
Number inherited by BR 38
Last example withdrawn July 1950

neighbouring works of Beyer Peacock, and were apparently £1,500 cheaper than the Vulcan examples!

Although the smaller wheels enabled a shorter wheelbase, the relative positioning of the leading bogie, cylinders and middle driving axle (driven by the outside cylinders) was the same as for the 'Lord Faringdons'. The inside cylinders drove the front driving wheels. The rear driving wheels were 7 inches further forward than on the earlier engines; this allowed for a deeper ashpan, which was a considerable improvement on other GCR 4-6-0s.

When the 13 GCR-built engines passed to the LNER in 1923 they were classified 'B7/1', and the LNER ordered a final batch of ten, which were built at Gorton in 1923 and early 1924. These last examples, the 'B7/2s', had lower boiler mountings and cab and smaller chimneys to fit the new LNER Composite Loading Gauge.

The GCR engines initially worked from Gorton, Neasden, Woodford, Immingham, Leicester and Sheffield, while the LNER batch was divided between Gorton and Neasden. By 1943 all were allocated to Gorton.

The 'B7s' did much good work throughout the system, hauling fast heavy goods trains as well as some relief passenger and excursion traffic. However, their short-travel valve gear resulted in heavy coal consumption (though not more so than other contemporary LNER engines), which led to the locomen's nicknames of 'Black Pigs' and 'Collier's Friends'. They were also less disparagingly known as 'Faringdon Goods'. But, as O. S. Nock remembers Oliver Bulleid pointing out, 'when any large locomotive was stigmatised for burning a lot of coal … it merely meant that it was doing a lot of work'!

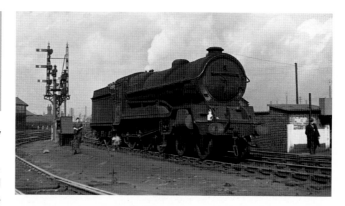

LNER-built 'B7/2' No 61711 of October 1923 was renumbered from 61391 in April 1949 to make its original number available for new 'B1' 4-6-0s. It was photographed at its home shed of Gorton on 28 May, and was the last survivor of its class, not being withdrawn until July 1950. *T. B. Owen, Colour-Rail*

As part of his move towards standardisation, Edward Thompson planned to rebuild the 'B7s' with just two 'B1'-type cylinders, making them slightly less powerful and a little lighter. However, it was Thompson's 'B1' 4-6-0s, built between 1942 and 1952 (together with 'K3s' and 'V2s'), that rendered the 'B7s' redundant, and the plan was never carried out.

When the 'B7s' entered BR stock, they were to have had 60000 added to their LNER numbers, but only two engines, Nos 61391 and 61396, actually carried their BR numbers. Most of the others had been withdrawn by the middle of 1949, when the last dozen survivors were renumbered 61702-13 to free up their former numbers for new 'B1s'. These 12 only lasted a further year or so, the last example, No 61711 (LNER No 1391, formerly BR No 61391), being withdrawn in July 1950.

As a postscript, in 1922 Robinson, then aged 66, was offered the post of CME of the new LNER. However, he felt that a younger man was needed, and the post went to his friend, the CME of the GNR, Nigel Gresley, who was 20 years his junior. The rest, as they say…

NER Raven 'S3'/'B16' Class 4-6-0

Nos 61400-02, 1403, 61404-07, 1408, 1409, 61410-78

NER Class 'S' (LNER 'B13' – qv) 4-6-0 No 1699 was the sole survivor of a class of 40, and survived as a Departmental loco until 1951. These engines had caused a stir on their introduction in 1899 as the first passenger 4-6-0s in the British Isles, and were the first stage in the development of NER engines of that wheel arrangement. The 'S2s' (LNER 'B15') followed in 1911, then the 'S3s' (LNER 'B16'), designed by Raven, in 1919. Originally classified as 'fast goods' locomotives, this was later changed to the more appropriate 'mixed traffic'.

The first ten of these three-cylinder machines were ordered in November 1918, with a further 25 ordered before the first batch was delivered. By 1924 70 had been built, in six batches

'B16/3' 4-6-0 No 61453 awaits the final call to Draper's scrapyard in June or July 1963. From 1948 until December 1962 this had been a York engine. *Railphotoprints.co.uk*

Introduced 1919; rebuilds from 1937 and 1942
Designed by Vincent Raven; rebuilt by Gresley and Thompson
Built by NER, Darlington
Number built 70
Number inherited by BR 69
Last example withdrawn July 1964

**In happier days, Leeds-based 'B16/1' No 61447 appears
to be shunting stock at Scarborough station in June 1959.
It was withdrawn from Mirfield (56D) in September 1961.**
K. C. H. Fairey, Colour-Rail

altogether. They were another very successful NER design, with tried and tested NER characteristics: Stephenson link motion, three sets of valve gear and outside admission. The boilers were superheated, and had a higher pressure than earlier engines. The 'B16/2s' were seven engines rebuilt by Gresley in 1937, with outside Walschaerts valve gear and the designer's conjugated gear operating the central cylinder. In 1944 further rebuilds were undertaken by Thompson, with three separate sets of Walschaerts valve gear; these were the 17 'B16/3s'.

In the 1930s the 'B16s' were employed on excursion trains to Yorkshire resorts, as well as football specials, some of which

were very heavy. It is said that on several summer Saturdays more than 30 of the class arrived at Scarborough.

From the 1930s the 'B16s' were allocated principally to Darlington, York, Hull Dairycoates, Leeds Neville Hill, Scarborough, Tyne Dock and Blaydon sheds, as well as occasionally migrating south.

All but one of the class passed into BR ownership in 1948, and most were shedded at York, Neville Hill and Dairycoates. The missing locomotive had the distinction of having been destroyed in the air raid on York shed in late April 1942 when 'A4' *Sir Ralph Wedgwood* was also lost.

Most of the 'B16/1s' lasted until 1959, but all had gone by the end of 1961. The last of the 'B16' family to remain in service was 'B16/2' No 61435, withdrawn from Hull Dairycoates in July 1964.

GCR Robinson '8G'/'B9' Class 4-6-0

Nos 61469, 1470, 61475, 1476

Robinson based his class of ten two-cylinder '8G' 4-6-0s on his 'Immingham' (LNER 'B4') 4-6-0s (see next entry) of the same year, but the driving wheels were considerably smaller, at 5ft 4in. The engines were built by Beyer Peacock as soon as that works had completed the 'B4s'. They were intended for fast freight duties and heavy perishables, and all were subsequently superheated by the LNER during the 1920s (becoming Class 'B9/2', the saturated examples being 'B9/1'; although the latter had all gone by 1929, it was not until 1937 that the remainder became simply Class 'B9').

Introduced 1906
Designed by John Robinson
Built by Beyer Peacock
Number built 10
Number inherited by BR 4
Last example withdrawn May 1949

The 'B9s' remained goods engines for their entire careers, although they were sometimes used on stopping passenger services and race specials. The Great Central allocated the class principally to Gorton and Lincoln; the former handled the main goods duties from Manchester to Marylebone, Hull and Grimsby, while the Lincoln engines hauled fast goods services to Manchester. After the Second World War they were concentrated in the Liverpool and Manchester areas, still

**'B9' 4-6-0 No 1475 received its BR number in February 1949, but
by May it became the last of its class to be taken out of service,
from Heaton Mersey shed. Awaiting its fate at Dukinfield on
13 June, the removal of its tender gives us one last look at the
footplate of this elegant Robinson engine. Its BR number, 61475,
was transferred to 'B16' No 61406 in December 1949, so the
latter number could be used on a new 'B1' 4-6-0 the following
year. Ahead of it is GCR Pollitt 'F2' 2-4-2T (qv) No 7104 of 1898,
also withdrawn in May 1949 and awaiting the cutter's torch.**
H. C. Casserley

mainly used for freight, with occasional use on Liverpool-Manchester passenger turns.

Towards the end of their lives they were all working on the lines of the former Cheshire Lines Committee (a joint arrangement between the Great Northern, Midland and Great Central companies, instituted in 1865/66; most trains were hauled by GCR engines). The 'B9s' handled most traffic except express passenger services.

The first member of the class was withdrawn in 1939, No 6111, later renumbered 1475, but the war extended its life; it

was not until 1947 that withdrawals began in earnest, and only four examples survived the 1948 nationalisation of the railways. Two of them had gone before the end of that year, and the other two, given BR numbers 61469 and 61475 (ironically the one initially withdrawn in 1939), soldiered on for a further six months. Both engines donated their BR numbers to Raven 'B16' 4-6-0s (see previous entry) when ten of the latter were renumbered to make way for new 'B1s' being built in 1950.

GCR Robinson '8F'/'B4' 'Immingham' Class 4-6-0

Nos 1482, 1483, 1485, 1488

Introduced 1906
Designed by John Robinson
Built by Beyer Peacock
Number built 10
Number inherited by BR 4
Last example withdrawn November 1950

The first sod of the Great Central's new dock complex at Immingham (eventually opened by the King and Queen in 1912) was cut on 12 July 1906, and four special trains carried guests to witness the occasion, from Marylebone, Manchester, Chesterfield and Cleethorpes. One of them was hauled by a brand new 4-6-0, the third of ten of Robinson's new '8F' Class, designed for working express goods and fish trains to London. Numbered 1095-1104, No 1097 was named *Immingham* in honour of the event, and gave its name to the class as a whole.

The 'B4s' were the third of four very similar classes of 4-6-0s, and although perhaps not the most elegant of Robinson's generally very attractive locomotives, they did good work over many years. They were quickly put to work on fish trains between London, Manchester and Grimsby. None were superheated during GCR days, but by the end of 1928 the LNER had converted all ten. As with other GCR locomotives, they were reduced in height to comply with the new LNER Composite Loading Gauge.

The 'B4s' were very similar to the new LNER 'B1' 4-6-0s, so incorporated a similar range of modifications over the years; for example, in the 1920s and '30s they were fitted with a variety of different domes and chimneys.

With fish as their intended traffic, the class was initially allocated to Neasden, Gorton and Grimsby; Neasden also employed the engines on Marylebone-Leicester expresses. The LNER moved them all to Sheffield, to handle a variety of main-line services, until displaced by Ivatt 'Atlantics' and ex-GCR 'B7' 4-6-0s, so they moved again to the Great Northern and Great Eastern sections. By 1926 all were allocated to the Yorkshire

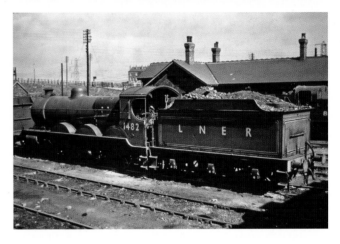

This fine portrait shows LNER 'B4' No 1482, the former Great Central '8F' No 1097 *Immingham*, at its home shed of Ardsley, the former GNR depot north of Wakefield, in April 1947.
D. Jenkinson, Colour-Rail

sheds of Ardsley and Copley Hill, to handle King's Cross services between Leeds and Doncaster, being light enough to cross the Calder Viaduct at Wakefield, for which 'Pacifics' were too heavy.

During the 1930s they were often seen on excursions, and operated more frequently in Eastern England; after the war they were increasingly displaced by the new 'B1' 4-6-0s. As with the 'B9s' (see above), the first was withdrawn on the outbreak of war, but quickly reinstated. However, the same engine, LNER No 6095, was 'written off' in 1944 following collision damage. The remaining nine were renumbered 1481-89, and five had been withdrawn by the time the railways were nationalised. The surviving quartet were all shedded at Ardsley, but Nos 1483, 1486 and 1488 had been taken out of use there by September 1949, leaving the sole survivor as *Immingham* itself, No 1482. It would have become BR No 61482, but was withdrawn at the end of 1950 without ever having the number applied. At that time it was the longest-surviving former GCR 4-6-0 locomotive, and in later more enlightened times would undoubtedly have been a candidate for preservation.

GCR Robinson '9P'/'B3' 'Lord Faringdon' Class 4-6-0

No 61497

The Henderson family had a remarkable association with the Great Central Railway, if only in the matter of locomotive names. Alexander Henderson (1850-1934) was a financier and MP. He was Chairman of the GCR for almost all of its independent life, from 1900 to 1922. He was created a baronet in 1902, and in that year the name *Sir Alexander* was given to '11B' Class (LNER 'D9') 4-4-0 No 1014. In 1907 a Class '8E' (LNER 'C5') engine was named *Lady Henderson*. In 1913 the GCR named its '11E' Class (LNER 'D10') after directors of the railway, and the first, No 429, was named *Sir Alexander Henderson* (No 1014's name being removed at the same time). In 1917 Henderson was elevated to the peerage, taking the name 1st Baron Faringdon; No 364 was renamed *Lady Faringdon*, No 429's name was removed, and newly built '9P' Class (LNER 'B3') 4-6-0 No 1169 was named *Lord Faringdon*. In 1948 the newly formed British Railways renamed ex-LNER 'A4' 'Pacific' No 60034 (formerly *Peregrine*) as *Lord Faringdon*. Thus the Henderson name was carried on steam locos for more than 60 years.

Incidentally, Henderson's youngest son Eric was similarly honoured in 1919 when '11F' 'Director' 4-4-0 No 506 was named *Butler-Henderson* (Eric having changed his surname to that form shortly after he married in 1910). And finally, having been mentioned earlier in these pages, the Hendersons' Scottish seat provided the name for another GCR locomotive, '1A'/'B8' Class No 4 *Glenalmond* of 1913 (qv). Both father and son served on the LNER Board after the Grouping.

The 'Lord Faringdons', as the '9Ps' became known, were Robinson's largest passenger locomotive design for the GCR, built to meet the demands of heavy wartime passenger traffic. The design is claimed to have inspired the London & North Western Railway's 'Claughton' Class (qv), the GCR's rival on the London-Manchester run, although it had little in common other than the four-cylinder arrangement. The outside cylinders were driven by the same set of valve gear as the adjacent inside cylinders by means of rocking shafts, then an arrangement very different from other railways' 4-6-0s; the inside cylinders drove the front pair of wheels while the outside cylinders drove the middle set. The 'B3s' had a similar general

Introduced	1917
Designed by	John Robinson
Built by	GCR, Gorton
Number built	6
Number inherited by BR	1
Last example withdrawn	April 1949

appearance to the 'B2' 'Sir Sam Fay' 4-6-0s, but the outside cylinders gave them a 'heavier' appearance. They were no more successful than the 'B2s' and, although fast and powerful, they were heavy on coal.

Six more engines followed the prototype in 1920, the last three with large NER-style double-side-window cabs. No 1165 was given the name *Valour*, thus serving as a mobile war memorial to the many GCR men who had died during the Great War. The engines were allocated to Gorton and Immingham (despite the latter having few passenger workings); the Gorton locomotives handled slower services to London, the frequent stopping and starting suiting the four cylinders and six coupled wheels.

All six became LNER engines in 1923, renumbered 6164-69. In 1929 Gresley rebuilt Nos 6166 and 6168 with Caprotti valve gear, and Nos 6164 and 6167 followed in 1938-39, resulting in a considerable saving in coal. The rebuilt engines were classified 'B3/2'.

After 1923 the 'B3s' moved to the Great Northern Section, operating the newly introduced King's Cross-Leeds Pullman service (just before the advent of the Gresley 'Pacifics'), which required an average speed of 54mph throughout. (It is said that at this time the name of No 1167 *Lloyd George* was removed because an ex-GNR director was a prominent Conservative MP!) They operated a variety of heavily laden services during the Second World War, but once peace returned it was decided to scrap the class. The new Gresley 'B17s', 'A1s' and 'V2s' were rapidly displacing the Robinson types from most principal expresses, exacerbated by the arrival of the Thompson 'B1s'.

In 1943 Edward Thompson rebuilt No 6166 to his 'B1' form, with Walschaerts valve gear, and it was reclassified 'B3/3', retaining relatively little of the original engine; the experiment was not repeated.

All but one of the class were withdrawn just before nationalisation, the sole survivor being the heavily rebuilt No 6166, the GCR's No 1166 *Earl Haig* and now renumbered 1497. It was renumbered 61497 in April 1948, and withdrawn from Immingham shed a year later.

Largely indistinguishable from a Thompson 'B1', the only ex-GCR 'Lord Faringdon' 4-6-0 to enter BR's books, No 1497 (formerly LNER No 1166), had been heavily rebuilt in 1943, with Walschaerts valve gear replacing the original Stephenson variety. It is seen here at Neasden shed just prior to nationalisation on 10 April 1947. In April 1948 it became No 61497 of Immingham shed, and was withdrawn from there exactly a year later.
H. C. Casserley

LNER Gresley 'B17'/ 'B2' Class 'Sandringham' 4-6-0

Nos 61600-72

In 1928 no new express passenger engines had been introduced on the former Great Eastern system in East Anglia since the Holden 4-6-0s of 1912 (LNER Class 'B12'), which were heavy on coal. Passenger traffic (and carriage weight) had become heavier, but there was a Civil Engineer's weight restriction on steam locos of no more than 44 tons on three axles, resulting from lightly constructed bridges; in addition, short turntables limited locomotive and tender length. The lack of suitable motive power came to a head following the General Strike of 1926, when poor coal led to dreadful locomotive performances.

Gresley was therefore ordered to come up with a 4-6-0 to replace the 'B12s', but many obstacles were put in his way, and time and again it was literally 'back to the drawing board'. Apparently he ended up by saying 'Don't waste more time on it: send the whole thing up to the North British Locomotive Company.' So, most unusually for the LNER, the design was put out to the Glasgow company in 1927, and most of the original Doncaster drawings were destroyed.

A three-cylinder design was produced, and although still slightly restricted in the routes that could be travelled, an order for ten engines was placed. The design borrowed some features from a batch of 'A1' 'Pacifics' that North British had produced in 1924, and the LNER requested some additional modifications. Delayed by ongoing difficulties, the first locomotive, No 2802 *Walsingham*, was not delivered until 30 November 1928, 13 weeks late.

Between 1930 and 1936 a further 52 engines were built in five batches by Darlington Works, and a final 11 were built by Robert Stephenson & Co in 1937; all the batches incorporated small modifications, dividing them into the sub-classes 'B17/1' to 'B17/4'. Despite these changes, all the 'B17s' gained a reputation as rough riders.

The NBL engines were named after historic and country houses in East Anglia, the next 20 having to cast the net wider to include properties in the East Midlands and North East England; the name of the first, No 2800 *Sandringham*, came to be applied to the whole class. By 1936 the engines were being coupled to larger and heavier tenders and, having more or less exhausted the stately home theme, the last 25 engines were named after well-known Football Association clubs in LNER territory, beginning with No 2848 *Arsenal*. Three of the first four were named after the FA Cup semi-finalists in 1936 – Arsenal, Sheffield United and Grimsby Town (the fourth, Fulham, not being an LNER destination!). Not surprisingly, these engines gained the nickname 'Footballers', and their distinctive nameplates were curved around an 8½-inch-high half-football, flanked by enamelled plates in the club colours.

While those engines that had replaced the 'B12s' in East Anglia handled the same traffic with no marked improvement, when the 'B17s' appeared on the Great Central Section, replacing older GCR 'Atlantics', they put in some remarkable performances. They also increasingly worked services such as the cross-country Ipswich-Manchester trains, and heavy boat trains. After the war they were once again restricted to the GE Section.

Introduced 1928 ('B2' 1945)
Designed by Nigel Gresley ('B2' Edward Thompson)
Built by North British (10), LNER, Darlington (52), Robert Stephenson (11)
Number built 73
Number inherited by BR 73
Last example withdrawn August 1960

ABOVE 'B17/4' 4-6-0 No 61649 *Sheffield United*, one of the 'Footballer' batch of ex-LNER 'Sandringhams', calls at Woodbridge, Suffolk, in September 1957. Built in 1936 and fitted with a large LNER 4,200-gallon tender, it was withdrawn from Ipswich shed in February 1959. *P. Glenn, Colour-Rail*

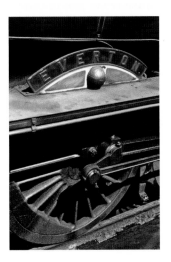

LEFT The distinctive nameplate style of the 'Footballers': this is No 61663 *Everton*, photographed on 5 July 1959. Note the incorporation of the club colours of blue and white. *T. B. Owen, Colour-Rail*

In September 1937 Nos 2859 and 2870 (later BR Nos 61659 and 61670) were fitted with 'A4'-type streamlining for working the new 'East Anglian' Liverpool Street-Norwich service; classified 'B17/5', they were named *East Anglian* and *City of London* respectively. The streamlining was, however, purely for publicity purposes, having no practical effect on at the speeds being run; it was removed in 1951, the 'East Anglian' having been withdrawn at the beginning of the war and not reintroduced until 1946, running until 1962.

Between 1943 and 1958 Thompson fitted 55 members of the class with the same boiler as his 'B1' 4-6-0s, and this variant became Class 'B17/6'.

Meanwhile, between 1945 and 1947 Thompson rebuilt nine engines with two cylinders, and these were reclassified 'B2'; they kept their original names. They showed an improvement in efficiency and power, but the 'B17/6s' still slightly outperformed them; only one further 'B2' conversion was carried out, in 1949, and the experiment was rendered redundant by the success of Thompson's 'B1' 4-6-0s.

In 1946 No 1671 *Manchester City*, based at Cambridge, was renamed *Royal Sovereign* in order to haul the Royal Train to and from Wolferton, the nearest station to Sandringham House. When what was then BR No 61671 was withdrawn in September 1958, the name and role was transferred to No 61632, formerly *Belvoir Castle*.

The first three 'B17s' to be withdrawn went between 1952 and 1953. The sub-class to last the longest was 'B17/6', which still had 16 members at the end of 1959. The last of them, 'Footballer' No 61668 *Bradford City*, was withdrawn from Stratford shed (30A) in August 1960. Many of the nameplates from the scrapped 'Footballers' were presented to their respective football clubs.

Recognising the fact that one of these important engines should have been preserved, in 2008 the B17 Steam Locomotive Trust was launched with the aim of building a new 'Sandringham' 4-6-0. After early difficulties in raising the necessary finance, the project was revived in 2011 with new management, a new structure and a clear strategy. Now a registered charity, the objective is the creation of a new 'B17' from scratch for operation on the main line and heritage railways. Incorporating modern materials and practices, the new engine will offer enhanced safety, reliability, strength, performance and ease of maintenance to meet the stringent requirements for railway operations in the 21st century. It is estimated that the new engine, No 61673 *Spirit of Sandringham*, will cost almost £3 million and take at least 11 years to complete.

In 2012 it was reported that another organisation, the North British Locomotive Preservation Group, is planning to build anew scrapped No 61662 *Manchester United*. Around two million supporters of the world-famous club are to be asked to contribute to the £1.8 million project, which it is hoped could be brought to fruition within five years. An original LNER tender from a similar locomotive has been located, and a replica 'B17' cab has been constructed to promote the project. So all is far from dead on the 'B17' front!

GCR Robinson '8'/'B5' 'Fish' Class 4-6-0

Nos 1680, 1681, 1685, 1686, 1688-90

This was the first of Robinson's nine 4-6-0 designs for the Great Central, and the first four followed a generally similar pattern, with two outside cylinders driving the centre pair of driving wheels, and separate splashers for each wheel. These Class '8' 4-6-0s were specifically designed to haul the express fish trains from Grimsby to London, hence their nickname of 'Fish Engines'. Fish by rail from that port had increased from some 74,000 tons in 1897 to more than 100,000 tons by 1900, and was still growing. A special 15-ton bogie fish van was also introduced in 1902, so important was the traffic. Gross income from railborne fish from Grimsby was almost £300,000 in 1911, two-thirds of which went to the GCR. Although primarily used for this purpose, the engines were also later used for passenger traffic.

The design was straightforward and 'handsomely proportioned' (O. S. Nock), with 6-foot driving wheels and two outside cylinders. The locomotives were finished in black, lined with red and white.

Introduced 1902	
Designed by John Robinson	
Built by Neilson Reid (6), Beyer Peacock (8)	
Number built 14	
Number inherited by BR 7	
Last example withdrawn July 1950	

(Wilson Wordell's 'S' Class 4-6-0s – see the next entry – were comparable machines, designed for similar duties.)

The engines were built in two batches. The first six were built in 1902 by Neilson, Reid & Co (successor to Neilson & Co in 1898), while the other eight emerged from the Beyer Peacock works in 1904. They were numbered 1067-72 and 180-87.

Initially the engines were coupled to relatively small tenders, long non-stop runs not being envisaged, although such runs became more possible when the GCR installed water troughs from 1903. However, between 1905 and 1906 larger tenders were substituted. The engines were rebuilt by the LNER with superheated boilers between 1926 and 1936.

The first Class '8s' were shedded at Grimsby and Neasden to handle the fish traffic, but later examples were allocated to Gorton and often used on London-Leicester express passenger trains. This variety of traffic is explained by the fact that at that time the '8s' were the largest GCR locomotive type.

The LNER distributed what it classified as 'B5' between Gorton, Immingham and Mexborough. The latter engines regularly

Seven Robinson 'Fish Engines' had brief careers with British Railways, all shedded at Mexborough. No 1681 is seen there on 11 April 1948, still in LNER livery; withdrawn just two months later, it never received its BR number. *W. G. Boyden, Frank Hornby collection*

hauled fish trains to the GWR via Banbury; later moving to Lincoln and Woodford, they continued to be used on fish trains, stopping passenger trains, and as station pilot at Lincoln Central.

During the Second World War the 'B5s' mainly worked Sheffield-Hull services, as well as banking trains between Wath and Dunford Bridge. As with other former GCR classes, it was

Thompson's 'B1s' that increasingly displaced them. One engine had been withdrawn in 1939, and others followed in 1947. The seven surviving examples were all shedded at Mexborough, and spent their last years banking trains on the Woodhead route at Dunford Bridge. No 1686, a Beyer Peacock engine of 1904, was the last to go, in July 1950.

NER W. Worsdell 'S'/'B13' Class 4-6-0

No 1699

Wilson Worsdell spent his early years as an apprentice on the Pennsylvania Railroad, USA, and the LNWR at Crewe before succeeding his brother Thomas as Locomotive Superintendent of the North Eastern Railway at Gateshead in 1890. He went on to build a series of very successful 4-4-0 classes. These included the 'M' Class of 1892, the heaviest express passenger class in Britain at the time, nicknamed 'Railcrushers'; it was one of these that ran between Newcastle and Edinburgh at an average speed of 66mph during the 1895 'Races to the North'. In 1899 the 'R' Class 4-4-0s followed, another outstandingly successful design.

But it was the 'S' Class 4-6-0s that really caused a stir. Also built in 1899, they were large, very handsome engines – 'impressive beyond measure,' according to O. S. Nock – and the first passenger 4-6-0s in the British Isles. The emphasis now was as much on comfort as speed, with longer trains of larger, more comfortable carriages. The first three locomotives had a short wheelbase to fit existing turntables, requiring small tenders and short single-side-window cabs, which were later replaced with more conventional ones.

The 'S' Class engines were intended to eliminate double-heading between Newcastle and Edinburgh. However, their general performance was coming up short of expectations, even though No 2006 gained a gold medal at the Paris Exhibition of 1900. They were outperformed by the smaller 'D20' 4-4-0s (qv), and were only used on principal express services for a few years before being eclipsed by newer designs; however, they did perfectly well on less demanding duties, and between 1905 and 1909 30 more were built to handle fast goods trains and excursions.

In early LNER days, as Class 'B13', they were used throughout the main-line network between Edinburgh and Doncaster, but the Depression years saw a decline in traffic and withdrawals started in 1928; all but one had gone before the outbreak of war. The survivor was No 761, which was withdrawn in September 1934 and entered Departmental stock. Its superheater was removed, and it was used as a counter pressure test locomotive for the road testing of other locomotives.

In *North Eastern Steam*, W. A. Tuplin describes the process as

The last example of the first 4-6-0 passenger locomotive design in Britain, former NER 'S' Class (LNER 'B13') No 761 was withdrawn from normal service in 1934, and used thereafter as a 'counter pressure test locomotive' based at Darlington. The elegant locomotive is seen here at York in 1937, clearly showing the addition of test equipment to the cylinders, and apparently coupled to a dynamometer car. *H. M. Lane, Colour-Rail*

Introduced 1899
Designed by Wilson Worsdell
Built by NER, Gateshead
Number built 40
Number inherited by BR 1
Last example withdrawn May 1951

follows: 'In this capacity No 761 was attached to the rear of a dynamometer car, itself attached to the locomotive under test. Setting No 761 in backward gear while running forward caused it to apply to the rear of the dynamometer car a resistance that was adjustable with the aim of maintaining a predetermined speed in spite of changes of gradient while the engine under test worked with a fixed regulator opening and fixed cut-off.'

No 761 was kept at Darlington North Road Works. In October 1946 it was renumbered 1699, then after 1948 BR moved it to the new Rugby Testing Station. It was eventually scrapped in May 1951 at Crewe Works, having outlived its classmates by some 13 years.

LNER Gresley 'V4' Class 2-6-2

Nos 61700, 61701

By the outbreak of the Second World War a sufficient number of various types of powerful modern locomotives were in service to cover practically all of the LNER's main-line requirements. However, there was still felt to be a need for a powerful utility design with a light axle loading. The 'V4' 2-6-2s were designed to fill this need, and turned out to be Gresley's last new design for the LNER before his untimely death from a heart attack in 1941 at the age of 64.

While 2-6-2 tanks were fairly common on Britain's railways, Gresley's 'V2' 2-6-2s of 1936 were hitherto the only major tender engine to use that wheel arrangement. Its advantage was that it allowed the fitting of a large firebox that did not interfere with the driving wheels, while the leading pony truck improved stability at high speeds.

Design work began in 1939, initially as a replacement for the ageing 'K2' 2-6-0s of 1912. The two 'V4s' were numbered 3401 and 3402, and incorporated the usual Gresley features, but on a smaller scale. They had three cylinders, and No 3402 had a 250psi boiler with thermic syphons, for comparison purposes with its partner, which had a conventional firebox; the former was altered to the conventional arrangement in 1945. By using modern construction techniques and light alloys, the weight was reduced from 74 tons to 70 tons 8cwt. With a maximum axleload of just 17 tons, the 'V4s' could be used over some 5,000 route miles, or more than 80% of the entire LNER network, almost twice that of the heavier 'V2' 2-6-2s. They had certain features in common with the 'V2s', including the monobloc casting for the cylinders and the same design of pony truck.

The lightweight characteristics of the new design, which favoured a high drawbar output for short periods rather than

Introduced 1941
Designed by Nigel Gresley
Built by LNER, Doncaster
Number built 2
Number inherited by BR 2
Last example withdrawn November 1957

sustained high power, ideal for Scottish lines, was emphasised by the name applied to No 3401, *Bantam Cock*. No 3402 was not officially named, but it is perhaps not surprising that Eastfield shed crews gave it the unofficial nickname of 'Bantam Hen'!

No 3401 went to the Great Eastern Section and No 3402 to Scotland. *Bantam Cock* was more powerful than the resident 'Sandringhams', and provided a much more comfortable ride. Later No 3401 joined its partner in Scotland, where they worked passenger services in and around Edinburgh before moving to the West Highland line in 1943. They performed well on the faster stretches of line, but their wheel arrangement made them less effective than the 'K4' 2-6-0s when climbing.

It might be assumed that the 'V4s' were intended to become the prototypes of a new standard class of lighter, general-purpose engine to replace the increasingly ageing types inherited from the LNER's constituent companies. However, after Gresley's death Thompson decided that no further 'V4s' would be built; wartime economies and difficult maintenance conditions led him to substitute a two-cylinder 4-6-0 mixed-traffic engine of his own design, which became the large and successful 'B1' Class 4-6-0s. These provided a similar tractive effort and were subsequently adopted as the LNER's standard mixed-traffic engine.

In the 1946 renumbering scheme the 'V4s' became Nos 1700 and 1701, then BR Nos 61700 and 61701. In 1949 they were replaced by 'B1s' and ex-LMS Stanier 'Black Fives'. Now resident at Eastfield shed in Glasgow, they hauled mainly goods trains and occasional passenger services. In 1954 they both moved to Aberdeen Ferryhill shed to replace wartime 'WD' 'Austerity' 2-8-0s, which were unsuitable for the required fast running. However, when their boilers needed replacement in 1957 it was decided to scrap both of these non-standard engines.

'V4' 2-6-2 No 61701, as partner to No 61700 *Bantam Cock*, soon gained the unofficial nickname 'Bantam Hen'. Both engines spent most of their BR career at Eastfield shed, Glasgow, until they moved to Aberdeen Ferryhill in May 1954. *Bantam Cock* succumbed in March 1957, and in May of that year, six months before withdrawal, its companion catches the evening light at Ferryhill, apparently being moved by a 'WD' 2-8-0. *J. G. Wallace, Colour-Rail*

GNR Gresley 'H2' and 'H3'/'K1' and 'K2' Class 2-6-0

Nos 61720-94

Introduced 1912
Designed by Nigel Gresley
Built by GNR, Doncaster (30), North British (20), Kitson (25)
Number built 75
Number inherited by BR 75
Last example withdrawn June 1962

The 2-6-0 'Mogul' wheel arrangement (the nickname is thought to derive from the name of the first to be built in Britain, for the GER in 1878-79) was rare in this country until the Midland Railway imported some from America (where the 2-6-0 was very common) at the turn of the 20th century. At first thought of as an American interloper, the 'Mogul' gained favour after 1912 with Churchward's '43xx' 2-6-0s (qv GWR '8300' Class), and others that quickly followed from the Brighton, Caledonian and Glasgow & South Western companies. The design's advantage was that the pony truck reduced wear on the leading driving wheels and provided a steadier ride at higher speeds.

For Gresley's new design for the Great Northern, which also first appeared in 1912, he chose the 2-6-0 arrangement, and initially ten were built (GNR Class 'H2'), numbered 1630-39. They were characteristically GNR engines except for the outside Walschaerts valve gear and the running plate raised over the driving wheels. They were the first design to use Gresley's own patent double-swing-link pony truck design, much used by him thereafter. They were intended primarily as goods engines, particularly the newly introduced braked goods trains, and needed to be able to work heavy trains at up to 40mph. They were soon working the fast night goods to Doncaster, as well as more mixed-traffic duties and passenger trains when necessary. Early in the First World War they also hauled ambulance trains.

The sound and motion of the Walschaerts gear, and the engines' lively running at speed, soon led to them gaining the nickname 'Ragtimers', after the lively syncopated US music style developed since the 1890s.

The design's weakness lay in the boiler, which was too small, so when further engines were built from 1914 (GNR Class 'H3') a larger boiler was fitted. They continued to be fully occupied with goods work – 'as fast freight engines they were second to

One of the Scottish 'K2/2s', No 61779, gets into its stride with a lightweight southbound passenger train at Aberdeen in April 1954. It was a Kittybrewster engine at this time, moving to Keith in June, from where it was withdrawn six years later.
J. B. McCann, Colour-Rail

none,' according to O. S. Nock – but were also used on other duties as conditions required.

A total of 65 'H3s' were built in five batches between 1914 and 1921, both at Doncaster and by the North British Locomotive Co (having been started by Beyer Peacock, which was unable to complete the batch due to wartime pressures) and Kitson & Co.

In LNER days the two varieties of boiler size led to the engines being classified as 'K1' (the first 10) and 'K2' (the rest). Between 1931 and 1937 the smaller-boilered engines were rebuilt to 'K2' standard, rendering the 'K1' Class extinct, although the two variations were referred to as 'K2/1' (the rebuilds) and 'K2/2' (the original K2s).

To suit the new LNER loading gauge, all GNR locomotives were fitted with shorter chimneys and lower dome covers, a lower cab roof, and smaller safety valves.

From 1924-25 the 'K2s' were regularly seen on both the West Highland line and in East Anglia, sharply contrasting railway environments! In Scotland the crews were not too enamoured of the GNR intruders, with their right-hand drive, GNR pull-out regulator and poorly sheltered cabs, and their perceived unsophisticated design earned them the local nickname of 'Tin Lizzies'. Eventually in 1934 the Scottish 'K2s' were fitted with side-window cabs, and at the same time 13 were given the names of Scottish lochs.

The entire class passed to BR, and served throughout the former LNER system until the first was withdrawn in 1955. Scrappings accelerated after 1958, and five were converted for use as stationary boilers at New England and King's Cross sheds into the early 1960s. The last of the surviving engines was No 61756, which spent its last year at Colwick, then King's Cross.

One of the named Scottish 'K2/2' 2-6-0s, No 61774 *Loch Garry*, stands in the shed yard at its home shed of Eastfield on 23 June 1957. It was withdrawn just under a year later. *Brian Morrison*

GNR Gresley 'H4'/'K3' and LNER Thompson 'K5' Class 2-6-0

Nos 61800-992

These new Gresley 'Mogul' express goods locomotives were a more powerful development of the designer's earlier 'H3' Class (see previous entry), and were classified 'H4' (LNER Class 'K3'). They were noteworthy in having 6-foot-diameter boilers, which at the time were the largest carried by any British locomotive, making them also the heaviest eight-wheeled engine in the country. Thus they can be considered to be first manifestation of Gresley's future 'big engine' policy. Almost 200 were built over 17 years, and the design was adopted as an LNER standard.

The first ten locomotives (GNR Nos 1000-09, LNER Nos 4000-09) emerged from Doncaster Works in 1920-21 right into the world of the General Strike, where coal trains were hard to find, but the 2-6-0s found work hauling prodigiously long passenger trains, sometimes up to 20 coaches. Six further batches followed, built by the GNR and LNER at Darlington and Doncaster, as well as by Armstrong Whitworth, Robert Stephenson & Co and the North British Locomotive Co. Each batch incorporated minor changes (such as a reduced height to comply with the LNER's Composite Loading Gauge), so they were classified accordingly from 'K3/1' through to 'K3/6'. The last was delivered in early 1937, construction only coming to an end with the advent of the 'V2s', which proved themselves worthy replacements.

Using three cylinders as against the two of the 'H2s', Gresley reduced their diameter but kept the same boiler pressure, thus increasing the tractive effort by 36 per cent. The 'H4s' proved themselves excellent mixed-traffic locomotives, the master of almost all main-line duties, especially fast fitted freights such as those to Manchester and Liverpool, although their bulk restricted their route availability.

Introduced 1920 ('K5' 1945)
Designed by Nigel Gresley ('K5' Edward Thompson)
Built by GNR, Doncaster (10), LNER, Darlington (93), LNER, Doncaster (20), Armstrong Whitworth (40), Robert Stephenson (10), North British (20)
Number built 193
Number inherited by BR 193
Last example withdrawn December 1962

Initially the austere cabs had no side windows, but in 1939-40 these were introduced, together with padded seats. The latter would have been welcome, as throughout their careers the 'K3s' were infamous for their rough riding, which shook loose cab bolts and caused damaged to the engine and tender dragbox. This quality and their syncopated exhaust beat earned them the nickname 'Jazzers', after the dance craze of the period. In his book *Bill Harvey's Sixty Years of Steam*, the author says that he 'found that rough-riding locomotives generally steamed well, possibly because the vibration shook the ash and cinders out of the fire and kept the air spaces clear'!

When Edward Thompson succeeded to the post at Doncaster, it was well known that he had an aversion to all things Gresley, especially the three-cylinder arrangement with conjugated valve gear for the middle cylinder, and in 1945 he rebuilt 'K3' No 206 (later No 1863) as a two-cylinder engine, classifying it as 'K5'. Very little of the original engine remained, and the resulting machine was lighter and slightly less powerful, but proved more fuel-efficient. It also rode better, and the absence of the central cylinder improved ease of maintenance. Ten more 'K3s' were to have been similarly rebuilt, but in the event the order was cancelled and no further engines were so treated. The sole 'K5' spent its last eight years at Stratford, East London, before being scrapped in the summer of 1960.

In Thompson's 1946 renumbering scheme the whole class became Nos 1800 to 1992, with 60000 added to form their BR numbers. The class remained largely intact at the dawn of the 1960s, but the last 22 engines were withdrawn en bloc in December 1962. Three were kept as stationary boilers, with the last being finally taken out of use from Colwick shed in 1965.

The large size of the boiler is evident in this view of LNER-built 'K3/2' No 61973 doing what it was built to do on the East Coast Main Line south of Retford in July 1960. A Staveley engine at this date, No 61973 was one of the last survivors of this once numerous class, being withdrawn from Doncaster shed in November 1962. *P. J. Hughes, Colour-Rail*

GNR Ivatt 'D3' Class 4-4-0

No 62000, 2116, 2122-26, 2128, 62131, 2132, 2133, 62135, 2137, 2139, 2140, 2143-45, 2148

Introduced 1896; rebuilt 1912-28
Designed by Henry Ivatt
Built by GNR, Doncaster
Number built 51
Number inherited by BR 19
Last example withdrawn October 1951

'D3' 4-4-0 No 62000 was originally LNER No 4075, built in 1897. In 1944 it was rebuilt with a new side-window cab and painted green for working officers' saloons. In this new guise it initially carried the number 1, but this was shortly changed to 2000. It was one of only two engines to carry the full LNER coat-of-arms (the other being No 4472 *Flying Scotsman* when on display at the British Empire Exhibition in 1924-25). At nationalisation it was shedded at Grantham, and is seen there on 4 June 1950, by which time it was one of only four 'D3s' still running. It was withdrawn in October the following year. *H. C. Casserley*

Henry Ivatt succeeded Patrick Stirling as Locomotive Superintendent of the Great Northern in 1896, and held the post until his retirement in 1911, when Gresley took over. By 1896 Stirling's engines were no longer powerful enough for the heavier expresses, and almost immediately Ivatt introduced the GNR's first 4-4-0 design, which was very similar in appearance to the GNR's final series of 2-4-0s.

The new engines were classified 'D2' by the GNR (or the '400' Class, after the number of the prototype – the classification of the 4-4-0s by the GNR and LNER is nothing if not confusing!), and altogether 51 were built in five batches between 1896 and 1899. The last ten were built with the running plate raised above the driving wheel centres to match the style of the new GNR 'C2' 'Atlantics' then being built.

As built the 'D2s' carried Ivatt's standard 4ft 5in-diameter boiler, then in 1898 Ivatt introduced a new boiler with a larger diameter and a longer firebox; this meant that it could not be easily fitted to the 'D2s', so only two had been modified to carry it by the time of the Grouping in 1923.

In 1912 Gresley introduced yet another new boiler, slightly larger again but with a shorter firebox, which made it suitable for fitting to the 'D2s'. This was gradually done between 1912 and 1928, and the rebuilt engines were classified 'D3' by both the GNR and the LNER. The new boilers were pitched higher, with shorter chimneys. By 1928 all but two of the 'D2s' had been rebuilt, resulting in a new class of 49 'D3s'.

The 'D2s' had been intended for secondary duties, and they could also be seen piloting Stirling single-wheelers on heavier

main-line trains. They were shedded at various points along the East Coast route and in Yorkshire, then in the 1920s their sphere of activity was broadened to include rural services in Nottinghamshire and Lincolnshire.

In 1935, when the first examples were withdrawn, these 4-4-0s were spread across the LNER system, from Hitchin to Immingham, and Penrith to Louth and Boston. Many were put into store, but were reprieved by the requirements of the Second World War. When BR inherited the 'D3s' there were just 19 left, and only three lived long enough to carry their allocated BR numbers. All but one had been taken out of service by the end of 1950, the last survivor being No 62000, the illustrated locomotive.

NBR Holmes 'M'/'D31' Class 4-4-0

Nos 62059, 62060, 2062, 2064-66, 2072 (62281-83)

Introduced 1884-99; rebuilt 1911-24
Designed by Matthew Holmes
Built by NBR, Cowlairs
Number built 48
Number inherited by BR 7
Last example withdrawn December 1952

The North British Railway had its origins in the first Anglo-Scottish railway, built between Berwick-upon-Tweed and Edinburgh in 1846, eventually expanding with the acquisition of 50 smaller subsidiaries (including the West Highland Railway in 1908) to become one of the most extensive of Scotland's

railway companies. Unfortunately it was not fortunate in its choice of locomotive superintendents; the first five (between 1846 and 1874) were sacked or forced to resign due to professional or financial incompetence! The sixth was Dugald Drummond, and he was succeeded in 1882 by Matthew Holmes (1844-1903).

The NBR employed the 4-4-0 as its standard passenger tender engine (it operated more than 200 between 1871 and 1921), and Holmes built three classes for the company. The first was the '574' Class of 1884, intended for light Edinburgh-Glasgow expresses. Between 1890 and 1895 the '633' Class appeared; designed for heavier duties resulting from the opening of the Forth Bridge, these engines also handled the Edinburgh to Aberdeen leg of the famous 'Races to the North'

In 1895. Then the '729' Class followed in 1898; they were larger still, to cope with the ever-growing traffic on the NBR.

Holmes was succeeded by William Reid (1854-1932) in 1903, and by Walter Chalmers from 1920 until the Grouping; because the NBR became part of the LNER in 1923, Chalmers was unable to develop new designs, but he went on to work briefly for the LNER. Both Reid and Chalmers rebuilt Holmes's 4-4-0s, the '574s' by Reid in 1911. Then, as the older classes' boilers fell due for renewal, they were replaced by Reid boilers between 1918 and 1922. The last 18 engines, the '729s', were rebuilt by Chalmers with a distinctive straight chimney and helical springs on all axles, unlike the earlier classes, which had used a mix of laminated and helical springs.

In 1949 former NBR Holmes 'M' Class No 62059 (LNER/BR 'D31') was renumbered 62281, as one of the last three survivors of the class. During its brief BR career it was shedded at Carlisle Canal shed, and is seen there in about 1950. This very elegant engine was the last of its class to be scrapped, at the end of 1952. *John Stretton collection*

As the Grouping approached the rebuilt engines were gathered together into a single class, the Class 'M', which became LNER Class 'D31'. At first the LNER classified the former '729s' as 'D31/2', but the distinction was soon discontinued.

All three former classes had unusual 'steam-jacketed cylinders', where the exhaust steam passed around the cylinder before exhausting through the chimney.

As larger locomotives were introduced, the 'D31s' were increasingly used on stopping trains as well as cross-country and branch-line services. Under the LNER, together with some ex-GNR Ivatt 'D1' 4-4-0s, they even infiltrated former Great North of Scotland Railway territory.

The first 'D31' casualties came in the early 1930s, leaving just 16 after the war. Withdrawals then accelerated, and only seven made it onto BR's books. By this time they were still occasionally working over the 'Waverley' route. The last three survivors were renumbered 62281-83 in 1949 to make way for newly constructed 'K1s', and the last of them, No 62281 (formerly 62059), succumbed at the end of 1952.

NER W. Worsdell 'Q'/'D17' Class 4-4-0

Nos 2111, 2112

Wilson Worsdell's 20-strong 'M1' Class 4-4-0s appeared in 1893, numbered 1620-39. They were fast, elegant machines, and Nos 1620 and 1621 both took part in the famous 'Races to the North' of 1895, between them making a record-breaking run from York to Edinburgh at an average speed of 66mph. No 1621 was subsequently preserved, and is now part of the National Collection repainted in its old NER colours. Expecting further rivalry between the East Coast and West Coast companies the following year, the North Eastern built two more engines in 1896, Nos 1869 and 1870, with large 7ft 7¼in driving wheels, the largest ever used in Britain – indeed, according to O. S. Nock, the largest in the world. Clearly built

Introduced	1896
Designed by	Wilson Worsdell
Built by	NER, Gateshead
Number built	30
Number inherited by BR	2
Last example withdrawn	February 1948

for racing, unfortunately that kind of speed was not required again, but this 'Q1' Class pair (LNER 'D18') were fast engines.

Also in 1896, Gateshead turned out the first ten of the 'Q' Class, Nos 1871-80, with smaller driving wheels of 7ft 1¼in diameter. These were followed by 20 more in two batches of ten, Nos 1901-10 and 1921-30. They were generally similar to the 'Q1s', apart from the wheel size, larger cylinders, and a cab fitted with a clerestory roof. 'For beauty of appearance,' says Nock, 'the "Q" and "Q1" engines must stand second to none among 19th-century designs.'

These 4-4-0s were built for use on East Coast express passenger services, so were fitted with a Westinghouse air brake (fitted in the centre of the generous splasher), as well as

The classic, late-Victorian lines of NER Class 'Q' (LNER 'D17/2') are well in evidence in this undated view of one of the last two survivors, No 2112 (the former No 1902). It was scrapped within two months of nationalisation before it was able to become BR No 62112. *R. M. Casserley collection*

a vacuum ejector. From 1913 the 'Qs' received with new cylinders and piston valves, together with superheaters.

The LNER decided to combine the NER 'M1' and 'Q' Classes into Class 'D17'; Class 'M1' was known as 'D17/1', and Class 'Q' as 'D17/2'. Most had Ramsbottom safety valves, and were not fitted with the standard LNER Ross pop valves; indeed, one of the last survivors, 'D17/2' No 2111, carried Ramsbottom valves in an NER-type brass column until the end.

To work York-Edinburgh trains the 4-4-0s were shedded at St Margarets, Newcastle and York, with engines changed at Newcastle. From 1899 the new Worsdell 'D20' 4-4-0s began to displace the 'Ms' and 'Qs', and in the new century the NER 'Atlantics' appeared, further eclipsing the older engines; by 1920 only half of the 4-4-0s were allocated to main-line sheds. Engines based at Hull handled ordinary passenger trains across Yorkshire, while those at Gateshead usually worked services to Berwick or Carlisle.

The first 'D17' withdrawal took place in 1928 following a collision. Normal withdrawals started in 1931, and by the outbreak of war only two 'D17/1s' and seven 'D17/2s' were still at work. The former were withdrawn in 1945 (No 1621 being preserved), and five of the 'D17/2s' were scrapped during 1943-45. The last two, Nos 1873 and 1902, by now renumbered Nos 2111 and 2112, just made it in to BR ownership, but had been scrapped within two months of nationalisation. They had ended their days doing pilot work, working local stopping services and hauling the inspection saloon.

GNR Ivatt 'D2' Class 4-4-0

Nos 2150-57, 2160, 2161, 2163, 2165, 2167, 2169, 62172, 2173, 2175, 2177, 2179-81, 2187-90, 2193-95, 2197-99

The 'D2' 4-4-0s were also known as the '1321' Class, from the GNR number of the first locomotive. They were an enlarged version of Ivatt's 'D4' 4-4-0 of 1898, which had all been rebuilt as 'D3s' (qv) by 1928. A total of 70 were built in seven batches of from five to 20 engines between 1898 and 1909. In 1923 Gresley rebuilt two 'D3s' as 'D2s', which brought the class total up to 72.

The engines had larger-diameter boilers than the 'D4s', so after the first five had been built the smokeboxes were also enlarged to suit; this involved moving the chimney and blastpipe forward so they remained in the centre of the smokebox. Ivatt, and Gresley after him, tried various different types of superheater on 23 'D2s', the last being fitted in 1937. The footplate was raised over the coupling rods, allowing better access to the oiling points.

The main work for the 'D2s' was secondary passenger trains throughout the GNR network, as well as some fast goods trains. They were also seen hauling occasional express passenger trains between Grantham and York, and assisting the Stirling 'Singles' out of King's Cross, and later, at the Grouping, the 'Atlantics', although this practice came to an end when the Gresley 'Pacifics' appeared.

As had been the case with the 'D3s', cracks were found in the frames in LNER days, and this seems to have been due to the amount of double-heading that the class had done. Some were patched, and some sent out for welding.

By the early 1930s the 'D2s' were mainly handling holiday excursions, while some were stored. It seems that they had a reputation as rough-riders. At nationalisation several members of the class were shedded at Yarmouth Beach and Melton Constable, on the former Midland & Great Northern Railway. Railwayman and author Dick Hardy recalled that the crews on that line 'thrashed work out of these old things that had not been coaxed out of them for many a year on their own territory.' Apparently the pioneer locomotive No 3400 was one of the 'wildest riders' he had travelled, and

'D2' 4-4-0 No 62172 was the only one of the former GNR 4-4-0s to carry a BR number, applied in March 1948. It is seen here getting away northwards from Nottingham Victoria station into the 1,200-yard Mansfield Road Tunnel on 4 June 1950. *H. C. Casserley*

Introduced 1898
Designed by Henry Ivatt
Built by GNR, Doncaster
Number built 70
Number inherited by BR 31
Last example withdrawn June 1951

at speed it was 'downright dangerous'. Author and former engine-driver Norman McKillop also noted that when running fast 'they had the most diabolical and varied repertoire of bangs, thuds, jerks and jumps of any locomotive I have ever stood on.'

The first was withdrawn in 1936, while the war led to a reprieve for others. In 1946 they were renumbered in the sequence 2150-2201, but between that year and 1948 21 were scrapped. However, a respectable total of 31 became BR engines. Scrappings started again immediately, and only one engine, No 62172, had its allocated BR number applied. This was also the longest-lived of the class, not being taken out of service at Colwick shed until mid-1951.

GNR Ivatt 'D1' Class 4-4-0

Nos 62203, 2205, 2207, 62208, 2209, 2214, 62215

Ivatt introduced three 4-4-0 classes during his time with the Great Northern Railway, and the 'D1s' were the final development, built in a single batch in 1911. They were similar to the 'D2'/'1321' Class (see above) except that they were the only 4-4-0s built with superheaters from new at Doncaster, and had piston valves; the cylinders were also slightly larger, which meant that the boiler was mounted slightly higher and the bogie moved forward. Confusingly the GNR classified them 'D1' together with '1321' 4-4-0s; later the LNER reclassified the '1321' locomotives as 'D2', leaving the 1911 engines as 'D1'.

Although they were not built for express passenger duties, at first the 'D1s' handled some of the GNR's heaviest main-line duties on the Grantham-York and Doncaster-Leeds routes. For a time they were also used on light Leeds-King's Cross dining car trains. However, after the First World War they began to be displaced by Gresley's newer 2-6-0s.

The LNER allocated a few of the class to Cambridge and New England, where they worked expresses to the university city and leave trains from RAF Cranwell. Most were based at Grantham and Leeds, but within a few years they were no longer needed on the East Coast Main Line, and were all moved to Scotland to replace various former North British Railway 4-4-0 types. This involved reducing their height to suit the NBR loading gauge, and Westinghouse pumps were fitted as well as vacuum brakes. Their duties were now local passenger services and serving as

Introduced 1911	
Designed by Henry Ivatt	
Built by GNR, Doncaster	
Number built 15	
Number inherited by BR 7	
Last example withdrawn November 1950	

By 1948 five of the seven remaining Ivatt 'D1' 4-4-0s were shedded in Scotland, the whole class having been moved north of the border in 1925. No 62208 was photographed at its home shed of Hawick on 20 June 1949. It was withdrawn from there the following July. Note the Wakefield mechanical lubricator for the cylinders and steam chests on the right-hand running plate. *W. G. Boyden, Frank Hornby collection*

pilot engines on main-line expresses, but the Scottish crews took an immediate dislike to these English cast-offs! They were considered rough-riders, gaining the local nickname 'Tambourines'. Because of their new lowly duties, they were also known as 'Ponies', their cabs were draughty, and they suffered various mechanical and steaming problems. Significantly, unlike most other Scottish types the 'D1s' never enjoyed regular rosters.

In 1930-32 seven of the class returned south of the border, being used on the Great Eastern and Midland & Great Northern Joint sections. As nationalisation dawned seven engines remained, five in Scotland, and two on the former M&GN. It was one of the Scottish engines, Stirling-based No 62209, that lasted longest, not going to the breakers until November 1950.

GNoSR Johnson/Pickersgill 'S' and 'T'/'D41' Class 4-4-0

Nos 62225, 62227-32, 62234, 2235, 62238, 62240-43, 62246-49, 62251, 62252, 62255, 62256

The Great North of Scotland Railway, a smaller concern that its name might suggest, was incorporated in 1846 and served the north-eastern corner of the country. Its routes radiated from Aberdeen to such coastal towns as Lossiemouth in the north and Peterhead in the east.

Apart from some 0-4-4 tanks used around Aberdeen, all the company's main-line locomotives were 4-4-0s. What became the standard form was introduced by James Manson, Locomotive Superintendent from 1883. He was succeeded by James Johnson in 1890, who continued the 4-4-0 tradition by ordering six new and more powerful engines from Neilson &

'D41' 4-4-0 No 62246, a Neilson Reid product of 1897 and shining in lined black British Railways livery, poses at its home shed of Keith (61C) in May 1950. Despite its seemingly fine condition, it was withdrawn in August the following year. *T. B. Owen, Colour-Rail*

Co. Numbered 78-83 and known as Class 'S', they were capable of rapid acceleration and high speed, and worked the principal main-line services with great success for several years. They were attractive locomotives and showed strong links with Midland Railway practice, which was hardly surprising as James was the son of Samuel Johnson, then Locomotive Superintendent at Derby.

When Pickersgill replaced Johnson in 1894, he ordered 26 further 4-4-0s with detail modifications between 1895 and 1898, also built by Neilsons (which became Neilson, Reid & Co in 1898) in two batches of 14 and 12. Sharp Stewart had tendered a lower price, but Neilson could offer the better delivery, so secured the contract. These were similar to Johnson's 'S' Class, and were known as Class 'T'; again they were fast machines. Ten more were ordered in 1899 – known as Class 'V' – but traffic was declining, and five of them were sold to the South Eastern & Chatham Railway.

Nine of the 'T' Class were reboilered between 1916 and 1923, making them indistinguishable from the 'S' Class, and the LNER completed the process, grouping both versions – the most numerous GNoSR locomotive classes – together as the 'D41' Class.

The GNoSR shedded the engines at Kittybrewster, Keith and Elgin, and as well as the usual passenger duties they also handled the relatively little freight carried by the company (it

Introduced 1893	
Designed by James Johnson/William Pickersgill	
Built by Neilson/Neilson Reid	
Number built 32	
Number inherited by BR 22	
Last example withdrawn February 1953	

never built any 0-6-0 goods engines, for instance, that were so prevalent on southern railways); the 4-4-0s even did some shunting. Eventually the later Pickersgill 'D40s' replaced the 'Ss' and 'Ts' from some of these duties (and one of them, BR No 62277 *Gordon Highlander*, is famously preserved).

During the Second World War the North British Section of the LNER was experiencing growth in traffic, while on the GNoS it was the opposite, so four of the latter's engines were transferred to the NB Section to help out, returning at the end of 1943.

After the war some 'D41s' were scrapped, but 22 passed to British Railways, all shedded at either Elgin or Kittybrewster. However, increasing use of 'B1' 4-6-0s hurried the 4-4-0s towards the breakers' yards, and only three were left at the end of 1952. The final duties for the class including working the Speyside line and Lossiemouth branch, and station pilot at Elgin. The final trio, Nos 62225, 62241 and 62242, were taken out of service in February 1953.

GCR Robinson '11B-D'/'D9' Class 4-4-0

Nos 62300-05, 2306, 62307-09, 62311-15, 62317-19, 62321, 2322, 62324, 62325, 2329, 62330, 2332, 62333

When Robinson took over at Gorton in 1900, his first two designs were his celebrated 'Pom Pom' 0-6-0 goods engine (LNER 'J11' – qv) and these typically elegant Class '11B' 4-4-0s (which by association were nicknamed 'Pom Pom Bogies' in some quarters). Both were built by contractors (Gorton being too busy to handle them), the 4-4-0s initially by Sharp Stewart & Co in Glasgow, and were based on older similar proven GCR designs. The boiler was larger and the pressure higher, providing more power. Forty were built between 1901 and 1904, in four batches, the last produced by the Vulcan Foundry.

In 1907 Robinson rebuilt two of the class with larger, saturated boilers and longer fireboxes, and these became Class '11C'. The experiment presumably led to no great improvement, and no further engines were similarly treated.

In 1909 there was another rebuilding, retaining the original boiler and firebox but adding a superheater (and hence a longer smokebox), and the slide valves were replaced by piston valves. The

Introduced 1901	
Designed by John Robinson	
Built by Sharp Stewart (30), Vulcan Foundry (10)	
Number built 40	
Number inherited by BR 26	
Last example withdrawn July 1950	

Former GCR 'D9' No 2321 of 1902 (shedded at Liverpool Brunswick) stands at Liverpool Central in the late 1940s (it was renumbered from 6037 in July 1946, and became BR No 62321 in March 1949). It was one of many members of the class scrapped in 1949. *John Stretton collection*

process began in 1913, and was completed by the LNER in 1927, these rebuilt engines being classified '11D'. The LNER brought all three variations together under the classification 'D9', with two sub-classes: 'D9/1' was applied to those engines that did not fit within the new LNER Composite Loading Gauge, and 'D9/2' to those that were cut down during the 1930s to fit. By 1939 all were thus altered, becoming a single 'D9' Class once again.

Four of the class were named. No 1014 (LNER 6014/2301) was named *Sir Alexander* until 1913 after the GCR's Chairman (see '1A'/'B8' Class entry above). LNER No 5104 was named *Queen*

Alexandra in 1907 when it was rebuilt to an '11C', 5110 *King George V* in 1911, and 6021 *Queen Mary* in 1913; the latter was named in the course of rebuilding as the pioneer '11D' locomotive. (Incidentally, in 1904 model-makers Bassett-Lowke produced a model of No 1014 *Sir Alexander*, together with coaches, as a marketing venture in association with the GCR.)

Replacing Harry Pollitt's earlier '11A' 4-4-0s on the GCR's newly opened London Extension, the engines were shedded at Gorton, Leicester and Neasden. Loads were generally light, but timings very tight, requiring an average speed of almost 60mph. As O. S. Nock writes, '…when attached to a six-car set of the new vestibule buffet car trains in their chocolate and cream livery, there was no doubt that the railway buffs in the southern shires of England began to waver in their former allegiances and incline towards the Great Central!'

It was only the advent of the 4-4-0 'Directors' and 4-4-2 'Atlantics' that ousted the 'D9s' from top-link work, and by the Grouping they were spread around the former GCR system, on a wide variety of duties. In the 1930s the new 4-6-0 designs sent the 'D9s' even further afield, to the Cheshire Lines routes and East Anglia, allocated to such places as King's Lynn, Cambridge and Bury St Edmunds; a prestigious roster at this time was the Peterborough-Liverpool Street mail train via Ely and Ipswich. They also worked on the former Midland & Great Northern system when the LNER took it over in 1936.

By the outbreak of war the engines were largely back in traditional GCR territory, and 26 entered BR stock, mostly concentrated in the Cheshire area. At nationalisation the former LNER Cheshire Lines became part of the London Midland Region, so ex-LMS engines were used in preference to LNER types, and the 'D9s' quickly became redundant. No 62305, a Trafford Park engine, was the final example, withdrawn in July 1950.

NER W. Worsdell 'R'/'D20' Class 4-4-0

Nos 62340-45, 62347-49, 62351-55, 62357-60, 2361, 62362, 62363, 62365, 62366, 2367, 62369, 2370, 62371-75, 2376, 2377, 62378-81, 2382, 62383, 62384, 62386-89, 2390, 62391, 62392, 62395-97

Introduced 1899
Designed by Wilson Worsdell
Built by NER, Gateshead
Number built 60
Number inherited by BR 50
Last example withdrawn November 1957

Worsdell's 'R' Class 4-4-0s were the most successful and economical of the succession of 4-4-0s built for the North Eastern Railway, and were developed from the earlier 'M' and 'Q' designs (qv). By the turn of the 20th century traffic growth on the East Coast Main Line saw the introduction of 'Atlantics' by the Great Northern and these enlarged 4-4-0s by the NER, which incorporated several new developments to improve their performance, including a larger boiler (the largest yet on the NER) with an increased pressure, and a longer firebox.

Ten engines appeared in 1899 and immediately proved successful and reliable. They were kept in tip-top condition by their regular crews, who took great pride in their appearance and working efficiency; this personal relationship between individual engines and the men who worked them ensured the best performances. Two further batches of ten emerged from Gateshead in 1900-01, the 30 engines being numbered 2011-30 and 2101-10. Five years later another 30 were built, bringing the class total to 60, even though by then the newer 'Atlantics' were available – it seems that the men preferred the 4-4-0s.

Eventually convinced of the benefits of superheating, the NER converted all but two of the 'Rs' between 1912 and the Grouping, the other two being dealt with by the LNER, which classified the engines 'D20'. All had both vacuum brakes and Westinghouse air brakes.

The first 'R' worked a double schedule with two crews working from Newcastle to Edinburgh and Leeds every day, six days a week, which was maintained almost unbroken for two years. In so doing No 2011 had amassed more than 284,000 miles by the time of its first general overhaul in March 1903!

By 1923 the Raven 'Atlantics' were handling the majority of the principal expresses, but there were still 54 'D20s' at work on the main line, including regular passenger rosters as well as excursion duties. In order to extend the lives of these ageing but very capable engines, in the mid-1930s the LNER modified the boilers and valves, then Thompson made further modifications when he took office in 1941. The rebuilt engines were classified 'D20/2', and the unrebuilt examples were

There were only seven 'D20' 4-4-0s left at the end of 1956, and one of them, D20/1' No 62378, is seen blowing off at York during that year. One of 16 locomotives that ended their days at Selby shed, it was taken out of service in November. *Dave Cobbe, railphotoprints collection*

'D20/1'. A few engines were altered in 1936, including raising the running plate clear of the coupled wheels, spoiling the overall handsome appearance; luckily, most retained the generous splashers that so characterised the class.

However, the Gresley 'Pacifics' and 'D49' 4-4-0s began to erode the duties of the 'D20s', and they were increasing demoted to secondary duties. By the mid-1930s they were spread across the former NER network, but still doing useful work, particularly under wartime conditions.

The first withdrawal took place in 1943, but only ten had gone by the time British Railways inherited the class. Still fairly widely spread, a good number were allocated to Selby (50C), working the newly popular post-war holiday trains to East Coast resorts. Another duty was hauling the Rowntrees workers' trains on York's Foss Islands branch.

The class numbers dwindled after 1950, and the last three, all shedded at Alnmouth (52D), went in November 1957.

NBR Reid 'J'/'D29' 'Scott' Class 4-4-0

Nos 2400-04, 62405, 2406, 2409, 62410-13

Glaswegian William Paton Reid (1854- 1932) was an apprentice at the North British's Cowlairs Works from 1879, and in due course became Locomotive Superintendent there in 1903.

His 'J' Class 4-4-0s were based on his 'K' or 'Intermediate' Class of mixed-traffic 4-4-0s (LNER 'D32' – see below), built in 1906, but with larger 6ft 6in driving wheels for express passenger work and a large tender to allow for non-stop running between Edinburgh and Carlisle over the 'Waverley' route. Reid reintroduced a policy of naming NBR locomotives, and appropriately the 'Js' were given names taken from Sir Walter Scott's 'Waverley' novels (although thought of as an archetypically Scottish word, the inspiration for the title of the first novel, *Waverley*, is thought to have been Waverley Abbey in Surrey). No 898/9898/2403/62403 carried the author's name prominently in capital letters, and the engines thus inevitably gained the nickname 'Scotts'. Some of the names were later reused on Peppercorn's 'A1' 'Pacifics'.

The first six were built by the North British Locomotive Co in 1909. Between April and June 1910 a 'Scott' and an 'Intermediate' (qv) took part in trials between Edinburgh and Perth, and the results were sufficiently encouraging to persuade the NBR to built six more 'Scotts'. However, the stipulated price was not more than £3,000 per engine, and NBL declined to built them for that, thus marking a parting of the ways between the railway and the manufacturer after a continuous four-year period. Consequently the next ten engines were built at the NBR's own works at Cowlairs in 1911. It had been intended to built 12, but the last two emerged as the NBR's first superheated engines; these were followed by 25 more, which the LNER classified as 'D30' (see overleaf).

The 'D29s' themselves were not superheated until the 1920s, and the process was continued by the LNER through to 1936, as the original boilers became life-expired. As with other classes already considered, the saturated engines were classified by the LNER as 'D29/1' and the superheated ones 'D29/2'.

The original NBR whistles of the 'Scotts' apparently had a particularly mellow note. The LNER fitted a spring-operated whistle lever, and when the spring eventually weakened the whistle would sound intermittently while the engine was running!

'D29' 4-4-0 No 62411 *Lady of Avenel* was the last survivor of Reid's 'Scott' Class, built in 1911. It is seen here in August 1952 at Thornton Junction, its home shed for the whole of its BR career. It was withdrawn in November. Mary Avenel is a character in Scott's *The Monastery* and its sequel *The Abbot*, both published in 1820 *D. A. Kelso, Colour-Rail*

Introduced 1909
Designed by William Reid
Built by North British (6), NBR, Cowlairs (10)
Number built 16
Number inherited by BR 12
Last example withdrawn November 1952

The 'Scotts' entered service on express trains between Edinburgh and Carlisle, as well as to Aberdeen, Perth and Glasgow, and were still handling such duties at the time of the Grouping in 1923, as well as stopping trains. The latter became increasingly common rosters as new engines took over the heavier principal services. The 'D29s' were also used for football specials and holiday excursions to the East Coast.

The new Thompson 'B1' 4-6-0s increasingly took over the duties of the older engines; one was withdrawn in 1946, and a further three in the second half of 1947. The remaining 12 became BR engines the following year, and the last, No 62411 *Lady of Avenal*, was not consigned to the scrapyard until November 1952, having been a Thornton Junction (62A) resident since the end of 1949.

NBR Reid 'J'/'D30' 'Scott' Class 4-4-0

Nos 62417-32, 62434-42

As mentioned in the previous entry, two of Reid's 'J' Class engines were built experimentally with superheaters in 1911. (There had been a single unsuccessful experiment with one of the earlier 'Scotts', No 897 *Redgauntlet*, in 1909.) They also had larger cylinders with piston valves, but lower-pressure boilers. Grouped with the earlier engines, they remained part of the 'J' 'Scott' Class, although the LNER classified them as 'D30'. They were also dubbed 'Superheated Scotts', as they once again carried names associated with the novels of Sir Walter Scott – including such gems as *Cuddie Headrigg*, *Jingling Geordie* and *Wandering Willie*!

The two prototypes, NBR Nos 400 *The Dougal Cratur* and 363 *Hal 'o the Wynd* (which became LNER Class '30/1'), were followed by 25 production machines ('D30/2') built in three batches, 15 between April and October 1914, five between June and August 1915, and a final five in 1920.

The engines were reboilered from 1921, but other than that only minor modifications were made. In 1939 the LNER at Doncaster considered a significant rebuilding programme for NBR 4-4-0s, but the war put paid to the plans.

The two prototype 'D30/1s' were initially allocated to St Margarets shed to work the non-stop expresses between Edinburgh and Carlisle, while the production locomotives worked fast trains throughout the NBR system, except on the West Highland line. During the First World War they were paired up on the famous 'Jellicoe' specials carrying naval

Introduced	1914
Designed by	William Reid
Built by	NBR, Cowlairs
Number built	27
Number inherited by BR	25
Last example withdrawn	June 1960

personnel on leave from the fleet moored in Scapa Flow.

In LNER days the 'Superheated Scotts' continued to work main-line trains, including Glasgow-Edinburgh expresses and main-line services connecting with the 'Flying Scotsman'; their ability to climb the 1 in 42 incline out of Glasgow Queen Street with trains of up to 400 tons, assisted by a banker, made them popular with footplate crews. As with other 4-4-0s, during the 1930s new types such as the ex-GCR 'Improved Directors' and 'D49' 'Shires' took over many of the 'D30' duties, and they began to move to more secondary passenger services, or as express train pilot engines.

One of the 'D30/1s', LNER No 9400 *The Dougal Cratur*, was withdrawn in 1945, and 'D30/2' No 2433 *Lady Rowena* on the eve of nationalisation. Replacement boilers were built as late as 1946, and the last 'D30' to receive a new one did so in 1951. The remaining 25 members of the class entered the BR era and remained largely intact until 1957, when withdrawals came thick and fast. Within three years all had gone, the final pair, Nos 62421 *Laird o' Monkbairns* and 62426 *Cuddie Headrigg*, being withdrawn from St Margarets and Stirling respectively in June 1960.

O. S. Nock has fond memories of being hauled by an NBR 'Atlantic' piloted by a 'Superheated Scott' out of Aberdeen: '... the combined roar of those two engines as they mounted the steep inclines out of Aberdeen, Stonehaven and Montrose was music to the ears of a locomotive enthusiast!'

Demoted to lowlier duties in their later years, the 'Superheated Scotts' increasingly handled secondary passenger services. This is 'D30/2' No 62423 *Dugald Dalgetty* at the head of a lightweight cross-country service at Humshaugh, on the ex-NBR Reedsmouth-Hexham line, in 1953. It was one of seven of the class allocated to Hawick since 1948, and was withdrawn from there in August 1957. Dugald Dalgetty features in Scott's *A Legend of Montrose* (1819). *Colour-Rail collection*

NBR Reid 'K'/'D32' 'Intermediate' Class 4-4-0

Nos 2443-46, 2448-50, 62451, 2453, 2454

Serving fishing ports on both the west and east coasts of Scotland, the North British Railway naturally handled large quantities of perishable traffic, and 0-6-0 tender engines were used until Reid introduced these mixed-traffic 'K' Class 4-4-0s specifically for that traffic, especially the light, fast fish trains. Essentially a mixed-traffic version of the 'Scotts', 12 engines were ordered in 1905 and built at Cowlairs Works in 1906-07. They were known as the 'Intermediate Passenger' or

Introduced	1906
Designed by	William Reid
Built by	NBR, Cowlairs
Number built	12
Number inherited by BR	10
Last example withdrawn	March 1951

'Intermediate Goods' Class, or simply 'Intermediates', and were classified 'D32' by the LNER. The series of 4-4-0s would continue through Classes 'D33' and 'D34' (both qv) right through to 1920.

NBR Reid 'Intermediate' 4-4-0 No 2445 runs light engine away from the south end of Edinburgh Waverley station, beneath the walls of the former Calton Gaol, on 24 April 1948. No 2445 was the penultimate member of the class to be withdrawn, from St Margarets at the end of 1949 – the last would be No 62451, 15 months later. *H. C. Casserley*

The 'D32s' had saturated boilers and 6-foot driving wheels, and in the mixed-traffic role they proved very successful and versatile, becoming the basis for future NBR 4-4-0 designs such as the 'D29'/'D30' 'Scotts' (qv) and 'Glens'. When the LNER inherited the class they were fitted with superheaters, the process completed in 1926 as boilers came due for renewal. As superheating progressed, the original engines became known as Class 'D32/1', and the superheated ones 'D32/2'.

The majority of the new engines were shedded at Eastfield, Glasgow, to handle long-distance express goods traffic. St Margarets also received a few, to work local services and longer-distance ones to Newcastle. They were also used for excursion traffic, and passenger services on the West Highland line. Following the First World War they were increasingly used on passenger rather than goods trains.

All 12 passed to the LNER, with half of them allocated to St Margarets for local services south to Berwick and Galashiels and north to Dundee.

As with so many of the former NBR 4-4-0s, it was the proliferation of Thompson 'B1s' that brought about their demise. By the end of the first year of British Railways their numbers had been reduced to just two, and these went in December 1949 (No 2445) and March 1951 (No 62451, the only example to carry its BR number), both from St Margarets shed.

NBR Reid 'K'/'D33' Class 4-4-0

Nos 62455, 62457, 2458, 62459-62, 2463, 62464, 62466

Introduced 1909	
Designed by William Reid	
Built by NBR, Cowlairs	
Number built 12	
Number inherited by BR 10	
Last example withdrawn September 1953	

In 1909-10 the success of the 'Intermediate' 4-4-0s (see previous entry) led to the building of a second series of 12 generally similar locomotives. They had the same tractive effort as the earlier 'Ks', but were coupled to tenders with a greater fuel capacity to allow non-stop working between Edinburgh and Carlisle. The NBR did not distinguish between the two series, but the LNER considered that they were sufficiently different to warrant two class designations, 'D32' and 'D33'.

This second series appeared while Cowlairs Works was at work on the 'Scott' 4-4-0s, but they had smaller driving wheels with a diameter of 6 feet as opposed to the 6ft 6in of the 'Scotts' and, as with the other mixed-traffic engines, they were not named.

When the class passed to the LNER in 1923 they were all fitted with superheaters as their original boilers were renewed, the process lasting until 1936. After superheating they resembled the subsequent 'D34' Class 'Glens'.

Like the 'D32s', they were used on perishable freights and passenger trains, but were more widely distributed, working from Aberdeen in the north to Carlisle in the south, as well as on the West Highland line. Again, as with the 'D32s' it was the spread of the new 'B1' 4-6-0s that ousted them from their regular duties. However, just two, Nos 2456 and 2465, were dispensed with by

the LNER, and two followed quickly after nationalisation without carrying their allocated BR numbers. The remaining eight had dwindled to three by 1952, and only one saw 1953, No 62464, a Dunfermline Upper (62C) resident since 1948.

No more 'D33s' were built; when further engines were required they took the form of the 32 superheated 'D34' 'Glens' (still classified as 'Ks' by the NBR), introduced by Reid in 1913 and constructed through to 1920. All but two became BR engines and the class was not taken out of service until 1961. One of them, No 62469 *Glen Douglas*, has been preserved by the Scottish Railway Preservation Society as NBR No 256, and can be seen on display in Glasgow's Riverside Museum.

At nationalisation 'D33' No 62466 was shedded at Perth South shed (63A), where it is seen on 18 June 1949. In 1950 it was moved to Dundee Tay Bridge, then Dunfermline Upper, from where it was withdrawn in October 1951. *H. C. Casserley*

GER J. Holden 'D56'/'D15' 'Claud Hamilton' and 'H88'/ 'D16' 'Super Claud' Class 4-4-0

Nos 62501-03, 2504, 62505-36, 62538-49, 62551-59, 2560, 62561, 62562, 2563, 62564-82, 2583, 62584-93, 2594, 62596-99, 2600, 62601, 2602, 62603-20

Introduced 1900
Designed by James Holden; rebuilt by Alfred Hill and Nigel Gresley
Built by GER, Stratford
Number built 121
Number inherited by BR 117
Last example withdrawn October 1960

After experience on the York, Newcastle & Berwick Railway (under his uncle Edward Fletcher) and the Great Western (where he became Chief Assistant to William Dean), James Holden (1837-1925) became Locomotive Superintendent of the Great Eastern Railway in 1885, succeeding Thomas Worsdell. However, his designs for that company depended a good deal on the work of draughtsman Frederick Russell, who became the Chief of Locomotive Design. This is true of the classic 'Claud Hamilton' 4-4-0s, nominally Holden's work but probably designed by Russell (as Holden, then in his 60s, was recuperating in Egypt at the time).

The initial batch of 41 engines was built in four batches from 1900 to 1903, and was classified 'S46' (LNER 'D14'), with round-topped boilers and the standard size of 7-foot driving wheels; they were the GER's largest and most powerful express locomotives. The first, prototype, engine shared its number with the year of its construction, 1900, and was exhibited in Paris that year, winning a gold medal. It carried the name of the long-serving Chairman of the GER, *Claud Hamilton*. Lord Claud John Hamilton MP (1843-1925) was as a director of the GER from 1872, Vice-Chairman from 1874, and Chairman from 1893 to 1922. As *The Oxford Companion to British Railway History* puts it, 'Hamilton devoted the main energies of his life to the company, not only at headquarters but also through constantly travelling over the system, observing its conduct and operation.' As a result of this naming, the class and all the variations that followed was referred to as the 'Claud Hamiltons', or just 'Clauds'.

The 'S46s' were followed by the 70-strong 'D56' Class, built in 1904-11 in seven batches with flat-topped Belpaire fireboxes,

later becoming LNER Class 'D15'. The 'S46s' had been numbered 1900-1909, and subsequent batches were unusually numbered in reverse order, i.e. Nos 1890-99, then 1880-89, and so on.

The 'Clauds' were singularly attractive engines, in GER royal blue livery lined in scarlet and with copper-capped chimneys, copious amounts of brass beading, elegant driving wheel splashers and perforated subsidiary coupling rod splashers, allowing access to the coupling rod pins when the rods were in the upper position. A further embellishment introduced by Holden was a polished steel ring around the smokebox door. They had spacious cabs with side windows (Holden was a Quaker and was very concerned about his enginemen's safety and comfort). The last four 'D56s' were built with superheaters, and from 1915 the earlier 'S46s' were so fitted, together with Belpaire fireboxes.

All 41 of the 'D14s' and the first ten 'D15s' were fitted with Holden's patented oil-burning apparatus, which not only improved the engines' performance but was a useful way of making use of the residue oil from the GER's gas plant, which produced gas for carriage lighting. This apparatus was discontinued in 1911, although some engines were occasionally refitted in times of coal shortage. The oil burning and allocation of engines to regular crews brought some excellent performances on the company's principal express services, seldom bettered in subsequent years.

In 1908 Holden's son Stephen succeeded him at Stratford, and he in turn was followed by Alfred J. Hill (1862-1927), who was Locomotive Superintendent until the Grouping of 1923. The year before, Hill designed a third variant, with a larger superheated boiler and Belpaire firebox, and ten were constructed in 1923, but still with the GER classification 'H88'. Nicknamed the 'Super Clauds', this variation became LNER Class 'D16'.

The LNER rebuilt the original 'D14s' to 'D15' Belpaire form through to 1931, at the same time rebuilding 29 'D15s' as 'D16' 'Super-Clauds', until there were 40 of the latter. Thus the 'D14s' became extinct, and the name *Claud Hamilton* was removed

Towards the end of their long and illustrious careers on the Great Eastern main lines, the remaining 'D16/3' 'Super Clauds' handled lowlier duties. This is No 62510 (formerly LNER No 8899, numerically the first of the 'D15' rebuilds) at Stoke, between Haverhill and Long Melford in Suffolk, with a Bury St Edmunds-Cambridge local on 24 September 1956. Then a Cambridge engine, it was withdrawn from King's Lynn in October 1957.
Dave Cobbe, railphotoprints collection

from LNER No 2500 and given to 'D16/3' No 2546 (BR No 62456).

The last major development took place in 1933, when a 'D15' was rebuilt by Gresley with a round-topped firebox, followed by further similar rebuilds of other 'D15s' and 'D16s'; these were classed as 'D16/3', and 104 were rebuild through to 1949.

Even as the 'Super Clauds' were being produced, the new 'B12' 4-6-0s were usurping some of their main-line duties. In LNER days the 'Clauds' were widely allocated across the system, from Stratford to Doncaster, and Norwich to Colchester. They were also occasionally seen on special services on the East Coast Main Line out of King's Cross, especially Royal Trains to Cambridge or King's Lynn, as well as regular services from King's Cross to Cambridge.

At nationalisation there were still 117 'Clauds' in service, including 14 'D15s', although all of those had been withdrawn by 1952. Withdrawal of the 'D16/3' 'Gresley rebuilds' began in 1945, but there were still 90 at work a decade later, and still

putting in useful work, for example on the Oxford-Cambridge line, which had been transferred from the London Midland to the Eastern Region. Some were even allocated to the former Cheshire Lines in 1949, where the crews preferred ex-LNER engines to incoming ex-LMS types.

It was reliability problems in the mid-1950s that hastened the withdrawal of these elderly locomotives, and No 62613 was the last 'D16/3' to be withdrawn, from March shed in October 1960.

The failure to preserve one of these classic 4-4-0s has long been seen as a notable omission, but the Claud Hamilton Locomotive Group is in the process of building a brand new 'Claud' for the 21st century. It will be a 'D16/2' 'Super Claud', and the project is estimated to take 10-20 years, dependent on funding. The new locomotive will be used primarily on heritage railways, but will carry modern equipment that will also provide the potential for main-line running. No 8783 *Phoenix* will be turned out in LNER apple green livery with a copper-capped chimney.

GCR Robinson '11E'/'D10' 'Director' Class 4-4-0

Nos 62650-59

'The "Directors" were beautifully proportioned locomotives,' wrote George Dow in his *Great Central* trilogy. 'They were ...as powerful as they looked and capable of high speeds.'

By the early 20th century Robinson's '11B' Class 4-4-0s were proving too small for the growing traffic on the GCR, with its newly opened London Extension, so he introduced his 'B1' 4-6-0 and 'C4' 'Atlantics', the latter being particularly successful. He then reverted to the 4-6-0 wheel arrangement for his 'Sir Sam Fays', but these were disappointing. So it was back to the 4-4-0 for his sturdy '11E' 'Directors', an arrangement that, with one fewer coupled axle, allowed a longer wheelbase and hence more space between the driving axles to accommodate the firebox, instead of it having to be positioned above one of the axles. Ten engines were built at Gorton in 1913, and so successful were they that ten more were ordered, but the First World War intervened, and it was not until 1920 that the so-called 'Large Directors' appeared.

A characteristic feature of the design was the long splasher over the driving wheels and connecting rods, but this was removed by the LNER to improve accessibility. All the engines were named after GCR directors (hence the class's familiar name). However, the name of the Chairman, *Sir Alexander Henderson*, was removed from the first engine, No 429 (later BR No 62650) in 1917 when Henderson became Lord Faringdon, and given to a Class '9P' (LNER 'B3') 4-6-0 (thus giving the class its popular name); it was replaced by *Sir Douglas Haig* until

Even in their declining years, the elegant lines of the Robinson 4-4-0 'Directors' are still evident in this rear view of No 62653 *Sir Edward Fraser* at Northwich in May 1953. This was one of the engines sent to work services on the former Cheshire Lines routes following nationalisation. Exactly 42 years old, No 62653 was withdrawn from Northwich in October 1955, rendering the class extinct. *J. B. McCann, Colour-Rail*

about 1920, when he became Earl Haig, then *Prince Henry* (the fourth child of King George V). No 437 (BR No 62658) was named *Charles Stuart Wortley* until about 1920, when he was elevated to the peerage, then became *Prince George* (another Royal son). There were actually 12 GCR board members, but two, Henderson and Viscount Cross, already had locomotives named after them. That left one board member without his 'own' engine, which was rectified when Class '1A' 4-6-0 No 439 was named *Sutton Nelthorpe* (see the GCR '9P'/'B3' 'Lord Faringdon' entry above).

The 'Directors' first went to Neasden to replace 'Atlantics', and by the outbreak of war they had proved themselves one of their designer's greatest triumphs, with 90mph being recorded

Introduced 1913
Designed by John Robinson
Built by GCR, Gorton
Number built 10
Number inherited by BR 10
Last example withdrawn October 1955

more than once. One of their more onerous duties was the 3.20pm Marylebone-Manchester Central train, with 212 miles being run by a single locomotive. The 2.15pm from Manchester was a similarly tough task, but the work put in by the 'Directors' on these schedules was remarkable.

After the war their position was usurped by the 'Improved Directors' of 1920-24, but they continued to work along the London Extension, allocated to Neasden and Gorton, and later further afield, especially during the Second World War. They even worked goods trains to Newcastle and Edinburgh.

On the eve of nationalisation all ten 'D10s' were allocated to Sheffield, but some subsequently moved to Brunswick, Trafford Park and Northwich for use on the former Cheshire Lines routes. Following nationalisation in 1948 the CLC lines were transferred to the London Midland Region (having been

an LNER/LMS partnership since the Grouping), and former LMS types took over. This rendered the original 'Directors' redundant, and they were all withdrawn between March 1953 and October 1955.

The 35 GCR '11F' Class 'Large' or 'Improved Directors' (LNER 'D11', BR Nos 62660-94) soldiered on, however, until the beginning of 1962, the last being placed in store at Sheffield Darnall shed after having been relegated to local services. From there they went to Doncaster for scrapping, except for No 62660 *Butler-Henderson*, which was restored to GCR condition at Gorton Works before being presented to the British Transport Commission's Curator of Historical Relics. After being on display at various places it was transferred to the Transport Museum at Clapham, and is now part of the National Collection at the NRM, York.

GCR Robinson '8B'/'C4' 'Atlantic' Class 4-4-2

Nos 2900-03, 2908-10, 2912, 2914-25

The 4-4-2 or 'Atlantic' type originated in the United States, where the Atlantic Railroad ordered the first in the 1880s. It was the Great Northern's Henry Ivatt that introduced the type to Britain, recognising the advantage of adding a trailing truck to the familiar 4-4-0 arrangement to support the firebox and improve the riding characteristics. His 'Small Boiler' 'C1' Class appeared in 1898, nicknamed 'Klondikes' from the recent gold rush. The pioneer engine, No 990, named *Henry Oakley* after the GNR's General Manager, was ultimately preserved.

Ivatt's second 'Atlantic' design was his larger-boilered 'C1' Class of 1902-10, and once again the first built, No 251 (LNER No 2800), was put aside for preservation, even before the class was finally taken out of service in 1950, and is likewise part of the National Collection.

By then the 4-4-2 wheel arrangement was finding favour on other railways. On the Great Central, with traffic anticipated to continue growing in the new century, Robinson ordered four experimental new locomotives from Beyer Peacock & Co in 1903 – two were to be 4-6-0s and two 4-4-2s, otherwise almost identical, so that the 'Atlantics' could be converted to

Introduced 1903	
Designed by John Robinson	
Built by Beyer Peacock (7), North British (12), GCR, Gorton (8)	
Number built 27	
Number inherited by BR 20	
Last example withdrawn December 1950	

4-6-0s later if necessary. In the event, the 4-4-2 type was chosen, being thought adequate for GCR traffic at that time. They had two outside cylinders, with inside Stephenson valve gear and slide valves.

Consequently a further 25 '8B' 'Atlantics' were built in three more batches between 1904 and 1906, by Beyer Peacock, the North British Locomotive Co and the GCR itself at its Gorton Works. They had deeper fireboxes, made possible by the lack of a third driving axle.

They were classic Robinson products of extreme elegance, painted in the Great Central's passenger livery of green with vermilion frames and wheel splashers carrying the GCR coat-of-arms. Their looks gained them the nickname 'Jersey Lilies', after the equally beautiful and alluring contemporary actress and socialite Lillie Langtry (1853-1929). (In *Steam Locomotive Nicknames*, Tom Middlemass describes how O. S. Nock refuted this theory, claiming that the engines' size and girth reminded Gorton men of a reputed 32-stone lady who ran a local Manchester pub!)

In 1908 one of the engines was rebuilt with three cylinders and, unusually for the GCR, Walschaerts valve gear, to be compared with the three-cylinder compound 'Atlantics' (LNER Class 'C5'). The engine was converted back to its original form in 1922.

This 'Jersey Lily' is now in her early 40s, and her looks have faded! However, something of her former beauty still shines through in this portrait of No 2921 at Gorton on 12 March 1948. At this time most of the 'Atlantics' were shedded at Boston and Lincoln, and this Boston engine has presumably been sent home to die, being officially withdrawn the following month.
H. C. Casserley

Between 1912 and 1936 all the class were superheated, and most of them had their slide valves replaced with piston valves, in conjunction with larger cylinders.

Between 1925 and 1936 they had their elegant Robinson chimneys replaced by the LNER 'flowerpot' type, cut down to fit the new Composite Loading Gauge. Variations in superheating, valves and reduction in height led to three sub-class designations.

When introduced the 'Jersey Lilies' graced the GCR's London Extension, being shedded at Gorton and Neasden to haul London-Manchester expresses. The GCR was connected to the GWR by lines from Culworth Junction to Banbury, and Grendon Underwood Junction to Ashendon Junction, north of Princes Risborough, so GCR 'C4s' sometimes took excursions to such far-flung places as Weymouth, Weston-super-Mare and Plymouth; indeed, an 'Atlantic'-hauled train from Manchester

to Plymouth set a long-standing British record for the longest through working of the day.

Leicester soon boasted the largest allocation of 'C4s', 16 by the Grouping, with the other 11 at Woodford. However, by LNER days the engines were beginning to struggle with heavier loadings, and by the early 1930s they were being displaced on express passenger trains by 'B17' 4-6-0s. Having been cut down to fit the LNER-wide loading gauge, the 'Atlantics' were able to work further afield at such diverse places as Cambridge, Lincoln and Ipswich.

In 1939 No 6090 was damaged in a collision at Banbury and scrapped, but wartime requirements kept the remainder in work. By 1945 the LNER's Standardisation Programme spelled the end for these elderly engines, although 20 managed to enter BR stock in 1948. However, all were done away with between January 1948 and the end of 1950, when the last half-dozen were dispensed with.

NER W. Worsdell 'V'/'C6' 'Atlantic' Class 4-4-2

Nos 2933, 2937

While Robinson was introducing the 'Atlantic' type to the GCR, on the North Eastern Railway Worsdell was doing likewise, with his two-cylinder 'V' Class engines, also designed to cope with heavier trains of heavier stock. Worsdell saw Great Northern 'C1' 'Atlantics' bringing trains into York, and had also been inspired by 4-4-2s he had seen at work in the USA during a visit in 1901.

The first engine, No 532, emerged from Gateshead Works at the end of 1903, just before Robinson's first '8B' rolled out of Gorton. It '...was one of those rare locomotives in which a huge boiler is poised so as to give an appearance of elegance rather than an effect of mere massive bulk.' (O. S. Nock) During the next year nine more were built, with higher cab roofs than the prototype and added windows, the first engine returning to the works to be similarly modified.

Worsdell's 'D21' 4-4-0s of 1908 had not been a great success so, rather than perpetuate that design, ten more 'V' 'Atlantics' were built in 1910. These incorporated minor differences, so the NER classified them as 'V/09'.

In 1911 Worsdell's successor, Vincent Raven, introduced his 'Z' Class 'Atlantics' (see next entry), and it seems that the footplate crews found these to be a more comfortable ride than the 'Vs'. However, the newer engines were more work for the firemen, being heavier on coal, but were acknowledged as more powerful by the drivers. All 20 'Vs' had saturated boilers, but between 1914 and 1920 new superheated boilers were substituted.

In early LNER days the 'Atlantics' continued to handle the principal East Coast Main Line expresses, being shedded at York, Gateshead, Heaton and Tweedmouth. When the Gresley 'Pacifics' began to arrive, some of the 'Atlantics' were relegated to standby duties at Darlington and Tweedmouth. They were also now used on fast freights, until eclipsed by the new 'K3' 2-6-0s.

The 'V' Class became 'C6' on the LNER, and the later 'Zs' were 'C7'. The former were several years older, so took on lighter duties, and were also increasingly seen on the

They were not as elegant as the contemporary Robinson 'Atlantics', but the long low running plate helped mitigate the effect of the massive boiler. This LNER-era portrait shows 'C6' No 696 (No 2939 after 1946) at York in 1938. This was one of the 18 engines scrapped between 1943 and 1948. *H. M. Lane, Colour-Rail*

Introduced 1903
Designed by Wilson Worsdell
Built by NER, Gateshead (10), NER, Darlington (10)
Number built 20
Number inherited by BR 2
Last example withdrawn March 1948

Newcastle-Carlisle line. By the end of the 1930s 'V2' 2-6-2s were making their presence felt, but wartime requirements kept the 'Atlantics' employed, although withdrawals began in 1943, when No 532 was scrapped. By the time British Railways was formed only two of the class remained, and both were taken out of service within three months of nationalisation, No 2933 from Hull Dairycoates and No 2937 from Gateshead; neither ever carried its BR number.

NER Raven 'Z'/'C7' 'Atlantic' Class 4-4-2

Nos 62954, 62970, 62972/3, 62975, 62978, 62981-3, 62988/9, 62992/3, 62995

Wilson Worsdell's successor on the NER was Vincent Raven (1859-1934). He had begun his career with the company in 1876 as an apprentice engineer with Fletcher at Gateshead, after which he rose through the ranks to became Chief Assistant Locomotive Superintendent at Darlington in 1893. He visited the USA on several occasions, and consulted the NBR about its 'Atlantic' locomotives. An innovator in both steam and electric traction, his war service earned him a knighthood in 1917. One of his daughters married Edward Thompson, who in 1941 became the LNER's CME.

As soon as took up his post at Darlington in 1910 he demonstrated his strong preference for three-cylinder engines by securing permission to build a dozen three-cylinder 'Atlantics', which were not unlike Worsdell's 'V/09' 4-4-2s, but with the additional cylinder. In 1911 Darlington was fully booked with work, so for the first time in many years the construction was put out to a contractor, and the order, increased to 20 locomotives, was awarded to the North British Locomotive Co at £4,485 each. For comparative purposes, ten had saturated boilers, and ten were superheated (Class 'Z/1'). The latter soon proved to be the better engines, so all were superheated between 1914 and 1915, reverting to simply Class 'Z'. Thirty further engines were built by Darlington between 1911 and 1918, bringing the total to 50.

The last-built engine was fitted with Stumpf 'Uniflow' cylinders, which were unusual in that steam flowed through them in one direction only. The cylinders had to be twice as long, so the front bogie had a longer wheelbase and smaller wheels. The arrangement was presumably good enough not to warrant rebuilding to original condition, but no further engines were modified.

In LNER days some members of the class were used by Gresley for experiments with different feed water heating systems, and rotary cam-operated valve gear. Whatever the results, none of the innovations were extended to the class as a whole. However, dynamometer car trials in the early 1920s proved the superiority of the three-cylinder 'Atlantics', and although all three sets of valve gear were located between the frames, the engines' mechanical simplicity and straightforwardness made them popular with maintenance staff.

Another experiment was the fitting of 'boosters' (small auxiliary steam engines) to the rear bogies of two engines; the bogies were extended to four axles and articulated between

Looking a little tired (but still in steam?) is Scarborough-based No 2992, photographed at York on 3 October 1948, a month before it was withdrawn from service and scrapped. The long, low unbroken running plate was a distinctive feature of the locomotives. *H. C. Casserley*

Introduced 1911
Designed by Vincent Raven
Built by North British (20), NER, Darlington (30)
Number built 50
Number inherited by BR 14
Last example withdrawn December 1948

the engine and tender, so the engines could be described as 4-4-4-4s.

Raven's 'Atlantics' handled the bulk of the NER's main-line traffic for some years, but when supplanted by his 'Pacifics' and relegated to secondary routes they proved less effective. Subsequently the arrival of Gresley's 'Pacifics' saw the old 'Atlantics' increasingly put out to grass on such routes as York-Scarborough and Newcastle-Carlisle, and they were sometimes used double-headed as replacements for failed 'Pacifics'. They were also seen on fast goods services.

It was the advent of the 'V2' 2-6-2s that finally saw off the 'Atlantics'. The war years extended their lives, but in 1943 withdrawals began. All but two of the class were allocated new LNER numbers in the 1946 renumbering, but only 24 lived long enough to receive them. Just 14 locomotives lasted into BR days – and then only very briefly, as all had been taken out of service by the end of 1948.

LNER Riddles 'O7' 'WD' 'Austerity' Class 2-8-0

Nos 63000-199

(For simplicity, this list assumes that every locomotive carried its 63xxx BR number, although many did not)

The 'Austerity' or 'WD' 2-8-0s appear twice in these pages. This entry describes those engines used by the LNER during and after the war and purchased by the company, and initially numbered 63000-199 by BR. The entry in the BR section describes their history when they became part of the 733-strong BR class renumbered 90000-732.

Robert Riddles (1893-1983) was apprenticed at Crewe under Bowen-Cooke, and was responsible for the major reorganisation of the works in LMS days, later doing the same at Derby. He was Stanier's principal assistant, then during the Second World War he was appointed Director of Transport Equipment at the Ministry of Supply, responsible for the supply of locomotives and rolling stock for military use overseas. As part of this task, from 1942 he developed 2-8-0 and 2-10-0 locomotives that were simpler, cheaper and more economical to build (given shortages of materials and manpower – his locomotives required 20% fewer man-hours) than the Stanier 2-8-0s that had initially been built for the war effort. In all 1,100 of these engines were built, and most returned to Britain after the war to find further domestic use.

A total of 935 2-8-0s had been built by May 1945 by the North British Locomotive Co (at both its Hyde Park and Queen's Park works) and the Vulcan Foundry. They were based on the Stanier 8F, with many interchangeable parts, a simpler parallel boiler with a round-topped firebox (of steel rather than copper). The boiler was not lagged, but incorporated a 2-inch airspace to provide insulation; the LNER later lagged the boilers in the conventional manner.

The firebox developed problems from being of too rigid a construction, and after the war cracks and failures of the stays were frequent. Walschaerts valve gear was used for the two cylinders, and at first both steam brakes and Westinghouse air brakes were fitted, although the latter was removed by the LNER.

Prior to the Normandy Landings the 'Austerities' were loaned to the 'Big Four' railway companies, the LNER taking 350, then in June 1944 all went to the continent. Meanwhile,

A number of the 'O7' 'Austerities' found themselves working freights on the northern section of the former GCR London Extension, shedded at Annesley and Woodford Halse. On 23 June 1948 No 63188 has found itself as far south as Neasden. Later in its life, as No 90509 after September 1950, it moved to Wigan in 1959, then Staveley, being withdrawn from the latter in August 1965, at just over 20 years old *H. C. Casserley*

No 7337 was extensively damaged at Soham (Cambridgeshire) by an explosion on an ammunition train; the Cambridgeshire town was saved by the quick thinking and heroism of the loco crew, who uncoupled the burning wagon and drew it clear; only the station was destroyed. Fireman Nightall and signalman Bridgers were both killed, and Driver Gimbert seriously injured; the footplatemen were awarded the George Cross.

After the war most of the engines returned home, and the LNER offered to buy 200 of them, including 190 of those that it already had on loan. They became LNER Class 'O7'. At the end of 1947 a further 270 2-8-0s were taken on loan. One was experimentally converted to burn oil in 1947-48.

Although acquired as heavy good engines, some wartime passenger workings were recorded. The Vulcan engines were run-in at Gorton, and were consequently used on the former GCR London Extension as far as Woodford.

The LNER's 200 'Austerities' were numbered 3000-3199; during 1948 these numbers were increased by 60000, and the majority of the class had these numbers applied. At the end of that year all the 'WD' locomotives, including the LNER examples, were purchased by BR, and the whole batch was then renumbered in the 9xxxx series, the LNER engines becoming Nos 90000-100 and 90422-520.

For their subsequent history see the entry in the BR section.

Introduced 1943
Designed by Robert Riddles
Built by North British (101), Vulcan Foundry (99)
Number built 200
Number inherited by BR 200
Last example withdrawn September 1967

GCR Robinson '8A'/'Q4' Class 0-8-0

Nos 63200-02, 3203, 63204, 3205, 3206, 63207, 3210, 3212-14, 63216, 63217, 3219, 63220, 3221, 63223, 3224, 63225, 3226, 63227, 3228, 3229, 3231, 63232-34, 3235, 63236, 3238, 63240, 3241, 63243

Introduced 1902
Designed by John Robinson
Built by Neilson Reid (3), Kitson (51), GCR, Gorton (35)
Number built 89
Number inherited by BR 34
Last example withdrawn October 1951

Former Great Central superheated 'Q4/2' No 63201, a Neilson Reid product of 1902, was photographed at its home shed of Barnsley on 7 April 1950. The picture clearly shows the unusual splasher arrangement of the 'Tinies'. This example was withdrawn the following January. *J. Howard Turner via Great Central Railway Society*

When Robinson got to grips with the modernisation of the Great Central loco fleet, his first design was the '9J' 0-6-0 of 1901, built initially by Neilson, Reid & Co. These goods engines were closely followed by the '11B' Class 4-4-0s (LNER 'D9' – qv). Then, at the end of 1902, another new type emerged, the massive Class '8A' outside-cylinder 0-8-0. A distinctive feature of the design was a combination of a double splasher over the centre pairs of wheels with single splashers over the outside sets; the double splasher contained the sandbox. The first three engines were shedded at Grimsby, where they distinguished themselves by hauling 55-wagon coal trains to the port from Hexthorpe, returning with 80 empties.

Although designed for the unglamorous world of heavy goods, the 0-8-0s had a hallmark Robinson handsomeness, with a long, low, straight running plate giving them a very businesslike appearance. The boiler and firebox were the same as the Class '8'/'B5' 'Fish' 4-6-0s (qv), and the wheels had a diameter of 4ft 7in, which, with the locomotive's adhesion weight of more than 60 tons, provided plenty of power at the rail for heavy haulage.

Their size, unlike anything thus far seen by GCR locomen, earned them the ironic nickname 'Tinies', and they were used mainly on the steeply graded Woodhead route, taking trains from Wath marshalling yard to Manchester, for which duties many were allocated to Mexborough shed.

Superheaters were fitted from 1914, and only a few remained saturated in pre-LNER days. The superheaters required a longer smokebox, and it was this that led to the adoption of a leading pony truck, transforming the design into the much-lauded Robinson '8K'/'O4' 2-8-0s from 1911 onwards.

In LNER days the class was split into four sub-classes depending on the various combinations of tender type and overall height, then later also distinguishing between saturated and superheated boilers.

Withdrawals began in 1934, and by 1938 it had been decided to do away with all the 'Q4s', but, as with so many other types, wartime shortages of heavy freight locomotives saw a good number remain in service. Of the 40 survivors, 13 were rebuilt by Thompson in 1942-45 to become 0-8-0 tank engines, known as Class 'Q1' (qv). All were eventually to have been rebuilt, but the programme was halted with the end of the war.

After the war, when large numbers of ex-ROD 'O4' and 'Austerity' 'O7' 2-8-0s were bought by the LNER, the 'Q4s' moved to the Great Northern Section and the West Riding, but were rapidly proving redundant. Withdrawals of the 34 that came into BR hands, all but one shedded at Ardsley, Barnsley and Grantham, began at once. Ten engines lasted as long as 1951, but all had gone by October.

NER W. Worsdell 'T'/'Q5' Class 0-8-0

Nos 3250-57, 3259-64, 3267, 3268, 3270-81, 63282, 3283-85, 63286, 3287, 3289, 63290, 3291-301, 3303, 3305-08, 3310-12, 63313, 3314-18, 63319, 3321, 63322, 3323, 3326, 3327, 63328, 3330-32, 63333, 3334-36, 63338, 3339

Wilson Worsdell's 'T' Class 0-8-0s were the first locomotives of that wheel arrangement on the North Eastern Railway (a company that also never owned a 2-8-0), and were designed specifically for heavy mineral traffic – coal and coke as well as

limestone and ironstone – which was increasing as the new century dawned. Most of it originated from the Durham area, but some also from the South Yorkshire collieries (for which an initial allocation was made to Hull).

The 'Q5s' were developed from Worsdell's earlier 'S'/'B13' (qv) and 'B14' 4-6-0 passenger classes, from which he took the basic outside-cylinder layout to produce a simple, robust 0-8-0 design with a relatively light axle loading for colliery track, and good brakes for descending steep inclines. As piston valves began to find favour over slide valves, Worsdell built 50 of the

Introduced 1901
Designed by Wilson Worsdell
Built by NER, Gateshead (70) and Darlington (20)
Number built 90
Number inherited by BR 77
Last example withdrawn October 1951

engines with slide valves (Class 'T1'), and 40 with piston valves (Class 'T'). In 1906 dynamometer car trials were carried out between West Auckland and Tebay to compare performance with the different valves, and the piston valves won the day.

The locomotives proved to be a successful design, so much so that Raven later developed it into his equally successful 'Q6' 0-8-0 of 1913-21, and ultimately the 'Q7' three-cylinder version in 1919-24 (examples of both of which have, happily, been preserved). The 'Q7s' were withdrawn en masse in 1962, but the 'Q6s' worked on until the second half of 1967, some by then almost 60 years old.

One of the earliest duties for the 'Ts' was working coal trains from the coal concentration point at Stella Gill, near Chester-le-Street, to Tyne Dock. A typical run might involve more than 1,300 tons, taking 52 minutes at a respectable average speed of 21mph. The engines would then return with 60 empties, lifting them up the initial 1 in 47 incline from Tyne Dock, then perhaps made up to 80 wagons for the onward journey to Stella Gill. They also worked over the Stainmore line until the NER's civil engineers decided that they were too heavy to risk over Belah Viaduct. However, until the 1930s a pair was based at Kirkby Stephen for goods trains to Tebay.

During the First World War all the 'T1' slide-valve locomotives served in France with the Royal Engineers' Railway Operating Department, and all came home safely.

A sad end for a robust workhorse: built at Gateshead in March 1902, 'Q5' 0-8-0 No 63260 stands withdrawn at Darlington on 24 June 1950, with 'Scrap' scrawled on the cabside and 'Boiler scrap' on the smokebox. None of the class escaped the cutter's torch. *H. C. Casserley*

Between 1932 and 1934 Gresley rebuilt 14 of what were by then Class 'Q5' with larger boilers from scrapped Hull & Barnsley Railway 'Q10s', and modified cabs.

As with the 'Q4s' it was the arrival of the wartime 'Austerity' 'O7' 2-8-0s that spelled the end for the ageing 'Q5s', and the first was withdrawn at the end of 1946. However, there were still 77 in service when the BR era dawned, although further withdrawals began at once. Only ten engines saw 1951, the last of which was taken out of use in October.

As the 'Q5s' were being scrapped, many of their tenders were transferred to 'Q6' 0-8-0s, and indeed the tender from scrapped No 3331 lives on coupled to preserved 'Q6' No 3395 (BR No 63395).

GNR Gresley 'O1'/'O3' Class 2-8-0

Nos 63475-86, 63488, 3489, 63491, 63493, 3494

When Gresley succeeded Ivatt in 1911, coal traffic between Peterborough and Ferme Park yard in London was growing and the existing locomotives were only just coping. Also, the company wanted to reduce the number of coal trains by lengthening them. To this end Gresley introduced his second design for the GNR, his 'O1' 2-8-0 (later reclassified by the LNER as 'O3'). The first five had emerged from Doncaster Works by early 1914, and gained the nickname 'Tangos' (a name that the class also shared with Gresley's later 'O2' 2-8-0s), after the South American dance that gained popularity on the dance floor after about 1907. Tom Middlemass claims that the name arose from the characteristic 'clank' of the engines' motion and their 'rather sinuous gait once they got going'.

The new engine's boiler was the largest Doncaster had produced at that time, the cylinders were also notably large, and the 4ft 8in driving wheels gave them a high tractive effort. They were also superheated from new. The boiler was based on that used by Ivatt on his 'Atlantics', but with the wide firebox replaced by a long narrow one.

When further locomotives were needed, the wartime situation made matters difficult, and some parts were ordered from America in 1917. In the end the order was given to the North British Locomotive Co, which produced a batch of ten 'O1s' in 1918, and five more in 1919.

The 'O1' incorporated several features from Gresley's first GNR design, the 'K1' 2-6-0 of 1912, including the outside cylinders with Walschaerts valve gear. The front pony truck provided support for the heavy and powerful front end, and also guidance for the locomotive during the many inevitable crossings to and from the slow lines during the journey to the capital.

The size of the boiler and cylinders led to the temporary experimental fitting of different feed water pumps, the initial fear being that conventional injectors would not be able to cope.

Introduced 1913
Designed by Nigel Gresley
Built by GNR, Doncaster (5), North British (15)
Number built 20
Number inherited by BR 17
Last example withdrawn December 1952

The huge boiler of the 'O3' 2-8-0 made the wheels look relatively small, but they had a 4ft 8in diameter. No 63484, a Doncaster engine since 1948 except for a spell at Retford in 1951, is seen here at Hexthorpe Bridge, Doncaster, on an unknown date. It was the last of the class to be withdrawn, in December 1952. *P. J. Hughes, Colour-Rail*

The intention was that the 2-8-0s would be able to take 80 wagons amounting to 1,300 tons, 20 more wagons than had previously been possible. The whole class was initially allocated to New England shed, Peterborough, but later there was also an allocation at Colwick to work daily coal trains from there to Peterborough. The New England engines also worked trains of empty wagons north to Doncaster.

As congestion on the main line worsened, a different approach was taken by employing a larger number of lighter trains worked by faster locomotives, such as the 'K3' 2-6-0s. This eventually led to the 'O1s' migrating north to Doncaster. Two went to Grantham in 1942 to work the steep iron-ore quarry branches from Highdyke to Stainby and Sproxton. They also hauled ore trains to Frodingham.

In 1944 the LNER reclassified the 'O1s' as 'O3s' to allow the 'O1' classification to be used for Thompson's rebuilds of Robinson's 'O4s'. By 1945 the whole class was at Doncaster, but the following year they moved to Frodingham to haul trains to and from the steelworks. At nationalisation all were allocated to either Doncaster or Retford, where they were used for lighter duties and from where they were successively withdrawn, the last four going in 1952.

LNER Thompson 'O1' Class 2-8-0

Nos 63571, 63578, 63579, 63589-92, 63594, 63596, 63610, 62619, 63630, 63646, 63650, 63652, 63663, 63670, 63676, 63678, 63687, 63689, 63711, 63712, 63725, 63740, 63746, 63752, 63755, 63760, 63768, 63773, 63777, 63780, 63784, 63786, 63789, 63792, 63795, 63796, 63803, 63806, 63808, 63817, 63838, 63854, 63856, 63863, 63865, 63867-69, 63872, 63874, 63879, 63886, 63887, 63890, 63901

Introduced 1944 (rebuilt from 1911-20 'O4' locomotives)
Designed by Edward Thompson (original locomotives designed by John Robinson)
Built by (original locomotives) North British (42), GCR, Gorton (4), Nasmyth Wilson (1), Kitson (5), Robert Stephenson (6)
Number built 58
Number inherited by BR 58
Last example withdrawn July 1965

The Robinson '8K' (LNER 'O4') 2-8-0s had a long and illustrious career on their native Great Central and beyond, as well as serving abroad during the First World War. Altogether 521 '8Ks' were built, and between their introduction in 1911 and the end of the Second World War they underwent several modifications requiring eight sub-classes. One of the original engines, 'O4/1' No 63601 of 1912, has been preserved.

When Thompson succeeded Gresley in 1941 he quickly initiated a programme of standardisation, and one of the engines envisaged was a heavy goods 2-8-0 to replace the many 0-8-0 and 0-6-0 types that had been acquired from constituent companies, as well as the older 2-8-0s. Because of wartime restrictions, it was decided that the most economical way to do this would be to rebuild ex-GCR 'O4s' with a 'B1'-type boiler and cylinders, Walschaerts valve gear, a leading pony truck as used on Thompson's contemporary 'L1' 2-6-4T, a side-window cab, and a standard LNER 4,200-gallon tender. In the event the original 'O4' pony truck was retained. The rebuilt engines became LNER Class 'O1'.

Work-worn 'O1' No 63784 was originally an 'O4' built by North British in 1918, subsequently rebuilt by Thompson. It is seen here in May 1953 rattling northbound through Charwelton on the GCR London Extension with a train of empties. Note the wagons in the down sidings, filled with iron ore from local quarries. The 'O1' was withdrawn from Staveley in August 1963, a few months after Charwelton station closed. *Colour-Rail collection*

The first rebuild was in 1944, No 6595 (later No (6)3795). (At the same time a total of 99 other 'O4s' were being rebuilt, also with 'B1' boilers but retaining their original cylinders, becoming sub-class 'O4/8' – the condition of the individual engines decided the type of rebuild.) The newly rebuilt engines underwent extensive trials, and by the end of 1946 40 were shedded at Gorton to work the Woodhead route, with others at March to haul Whitemoor-Temple Mills freights. The 'O1s' also took part in the 1948 Interchange Trials.

Fifty-eight engines were eventually rebuilt as 'O1s' through to 1949 (the last being No 63856 in October of that year), by which time Stanier 8F and 'Austerity' 2-8-0s, acquired by BR, were also helping to fill the post-war heavy freight locomotive gap. It had originally been intended to rebuild 160 'O1s'.

At the beginning of the BR era the various 'O4' sub-classes and the 'O1s' were numbered together in a single sequence. All but five 'O1s' were allocated to Annesley. The remaining five were at Tyne Dock, and were fitted with Westinghouse pumps to work the compressed-air hopper doors on the iron-ore block trains running from there to Consett. The first withdrawals started as late as 1962, and only eight 'O1s' were left at the beginning of 1965, all shedded at Staveley. Most then moved to Langwith Junction in June 1965, to be officially withdrawn en bloc the following month and scrapped at Drapers of Hull.

Interestingly, the 'O1s' were outlived by three of the classes they had been meant to replace, the 1913 Raven 'Q6' 0-8-0s, 1926 Gresley 'J38' 0-6-0s, and some of the original Robinson 'O4s' themselves.

GNR Gresley 'O2' Class 2-8-0

Nos 3921, 63922-87

Gresley's 'O2' Class 2-8-0s were a three-cylinder development of his earlier 'O1' (LNER 'O3' – qv) two-cylinder heavy freight loco. This was the first design to incorporate its designer's 'conjugated' valve gear, whereby the valves of the central cylinder were operated by shafts or levers from the outside cylinders, thus eliminating one set of motion. Gresley patented his design in 1916.

The first engine (No 461, later No 3461, then in 1946 No 3921) was built in May 1918, design work having commenced in 1916. This was a milestone locomotive, which convinced Gresley of the advantages of the three-cylinder arrangement, and he declared that he would employ it from then on. The boiler was the same as that used on his 'O1', as was the pony truck.

The three-cylinder arrangement was particularly useful when starting the heavy 1,300-ton block trains of coal, getting away in a clean and steady manner, and gaining speed uniformly without the jerking effect noticeable with two-cylinder engines. Starting and stopping was frequent on this heavily congested main line.

In 1919 a further batch of ten locomotives, classified 'O2/1', was ordered from the North British Locomotive Co, and they appeared in 1921, with a different cylinder and steam chest arrangement that used 2-to-1 motion levers rather than rocking shafts in the conjugated valve gear. The LNER later fitted these with lower cabs to suit its loading gauge; the cabs also had side windows.

In 1923 15 more engines were constructed at Doncaster, cut down to fit the LNER's new Composite Loading Gauge and classified 'O2/2'. The building of another 50 was considered in 1924, but was felt unnecessary in view of the number of war-surplus 'O4s' that were available.

However, in 1929 eight further 'O2s' were ordered, which did not actually enter service until 1932, due to the general trade depression of the time. Eight more followed in 1933, then finally 25 in 1942-43. These 41 locomotives and tenders were considered an LNER 'Group Standard', and were classified 'O2/3'. This brought the class total to 67.

Gresley 'O2' 2-8-0 No 63940 on home turf on the East Coast Main Line heading a train of iron ore from High Dyke in 1960. This was a Grantham engine throughout its BR career, until it moved to Doncaster for withdrawal with 29 others in September 1963. *Railphotoprints collection*

Introduced 1918/1921
Designed by Nigel Gresley
Built by GNR Doncaster (57), North British (10)
Number built 67
Number inherited by BR 67
Last example withdrawn November 1963

A final sub-class, designated 'O2/4' in 1945, consisted of five engines fitted with Thompson's 'B1'-type boiler in 1943-44, as part of his standardisation plans.

The 'O2s' initially worked from Peterborough's New England shed on coal trains to London. Later engines went to March to haul Whitemoor-Temple Mills coal trains, which eventually comprised 80 wagons. In the early 1930s railwayman and author Gerard Fiennes worked at Whitemoor and recalled that the 'O2s' were very powerful, working south to Temple Mills. However, there were difficulties in getting enough work out of them, although the speed was greatly increased when March Town were playing at home! The 'O2/4s' went first to Doncaster, then Colwick, to help with transport requirements in the build-up to D-Day. Later allocations included New England, Colwick, Grantham, Doncaster, March and Langwith, the latter to haul coal to various places from Mansfield.

The entire class became BR property in 1948, but the non-standard pioneer loco was quickly consigned to the scrapyard.

More than 20 of the remainder were gradually fitted with 'B1'-type boilers. After working throughout the former LNER system from Stratford through East Anglia to the East Midlands, mainly still employed on coal and iron ore trains, and having gravitated to Doncaster, Grantham and Retford sheds, the first 'O2s' were withdrawn in 1960. Thirty locomotives were withdrawn en masse in September 1963, and the final five succumbed in November, some having apparently been in storage for some time.

GNR Stirling/Ivatt 'J3' and 'J4' 0-6-0 Class

Nos 64105, 4106, 4107, 4109, 4110, 64112, 4114, 4115, 64116, 4117, 64118, 64119, 4120, 4121, 64122, 4123, 4124, 64125, 4127, 4128, 64129, 64131-33, 4135, 4136, 64137, 64140-42, 4145, 4148, 4150-52, 64153, 4158, 64160, 4162, 4163, 4167

Patrick Stirling's 'J7' Class 0-6-0s of 1867-73 became the basis for the Great Northern's 0-6-0 'Standard Goods', being later rebuilt to become GNR Class 'J8'. Another modification of 1873 produced the GNR's Class 'J6', 160 of which were built between then and 1896. Stirling died in office in 1895, and Henry Ivatt immediately built more of his predecessor's 0-6-0s, followed by his own final development of the design, with domed boilers (Stirling's had been characteristically domeless); 133 were built between 1896 and 1901, and were classified 'J5' by the GNR. Ivatt then started to rebuild the 'J6s' to 'J5' form with domed boilers, and eventually there were 125 of these rebuilds. Confusingly, the LNER called these engines Class 'J4', and there were 157 at the Grouping.

Introduced 1892; rebuilt 1912-28 as 'J3', and 1896 as 'J4'
Designed by Patrick Stirling and Henry Ivatt (original engines)
Built by GNR, Doncaster, plus Dübs and Kitson
Number built 153 ('J3'), 278 ('J4')
Number inherited by BR 41
Last example withdrawn December 1954

This broadside view shows one of the last eight 'J4s' on BR's books. No 64160 was one of the engines built for the Midland & Great Northern Railway by Dübs & Co in 1900, and was shedded at New England, where it was photographed on 26 August 1950. It was withdrawn at the end of the following year. *H. C. Casserley*

The final GNR 'J5s' were a batch of 25 built by Dübs & Co, and 12 of them were supplied to the Midland & Great Northern Joint Railway in 1900, in which the GNR was a partner. The M&GN rebuilt these engines between 1920 and 1927, and when the LNER took over sole working of the M&GN in 1936 they were included in Class 'J3' – however, eight were rebuilt to LNER 'J4' form, the only examples to be converted backwards!

Between 1912 and 1929 Gresley did his own rebuilding of the 'Standard Goods' design, with 153 engines rebuilt with larger domed boilers; they were classified by the GNR as 'J4', and subsequently became LNER Class 'J3'.

The GNR's 'Standard Goods' engines worked throughout the network on both main-line and local goods services, and a shortage of bigger engines meant that they were often double-headed with sister engines or other classes on Peterborough-London trains.

During the First World War 26 GNR 'J5s' (LNER 'J4s') were loaned to the ROD for operations in France. All carried Doncaster worksplates, even though some had been built by contractors. They all returned home in 1919/20.

At the Grouping of 1923 engines of both classes were allocated to such places as London, Peterborough, Grantham,

Class 'J3' 0-6-0 No 64140, a 1912 larger-boilered Gresley rebuild of a 1900 original, stands in the yard at its home shed of Retford (36E) on 19 September 1954. It was one of the last two survivors, both withdrawn in December. *Brian Morrison*

Retford and Doncaster, as well as Yorkshire, Lincolnshire and Nottinghamshire depots. The 'J3s' were mainly used for shunting, with occasional short excursion work.

At the outbreak of war in 1939 65 'J3s' and 'J4s' remained at work; some of the former migrated north to Tyneside and even Scotland. By 1948 there were still 41 of these veterans, by then undertaking only light duties. Only eight were 'J4s', and the last two (one of them a former M&GN engine) were withdrawn at the end of 1951. The last pair of 'J3s' lasted until the end of 1954, at Boston and Retford.

GNR Ivatt/Gresley 'J22'/'J6' Class 0-6-0

Nos 64170-279

Introduced 1911
Designed by Henry Ivatt, Nigel Gresley
Built by GNR, Doncaster
Number built 110
Number inherited by BR 110
Last example withdrawn June 1962

The versatile 'J6' 0-6-0s were as at home on heavy freight as local passenger services. This is No 64172, one of the original Ivatt-design examples of 1911, leaving Spalding with a local passenger train in February 1959. Just over a year later it was withdrawn from Boston shed (40F). *T. J. Edgington, Colour-Rail*

These 0-6-0s were the final flowering of the GNR 'Standard Goods' design, with a new standard superheated boiler. Ivatt retired in 1911, and the first 15, emerging from Doncaster Works at the end of that year, were entirely his design, and sported characteristic Great Northern lines. As well as being the first new class built with superheaters (of various designs) from new, they were the first GNR goods engines with piston valves. Classified 'J22' (or '521') by the GNR (the same class as earlier slide-valve engines that became LNER Class 'J5' – qv), the LNER recognised the distinction and put them in a separate class, 'J6'.

Gresley continued to built these engines until just before the Grouping as Class '536', but his machines had the boiler set slightly further back, necessitating a shorter cab and thus making the fireman's job easier. Gresley added 95 more 'J6s' in ten almost yearly batches; a further ten engines were planned, but these became 'N2' 0-6-2Ts instead, 107 of which were built between 1920 and 1929. A clear visual difference between the Ivatt and Gresley engines was that the former had the front sandboxes below the running plate, while on the latter they were above the running plate, incorporated in the front splashers.

The GNR experimentally fitted a number of feed water heaters to various members of the class, but all had been removed by the Grouping. The LNER likewise undertook short-lived experiments with the apparatus.

The 'J6s' were mainly used on GNR provincial services, working principally from New England, Colwick and Doncaster, as well as express goods until displaced by more modern 2-6-0s.

The crews nicknamed them 'Knick Knacks', from the odd noise they made when running with steam shut off.

The LNER allocated this versatile class widely; in Nottinghamshire, for example, they were just as happy on heavy trains of coal, or beer from Burton, or fast excursions to East Coast resorts. They were capable of a good turn of speed for what was essentially a goods engine, recorded at more than 65mph on occasions.

During the Second World War some of the class found themselves in unfamiliar surroundings, but otherwise their allocation remained much as before. The whole class duly passed to British Railways, demonstrating their usefulness by remaining virtually untouched until the end of 1957. However, more than half had gone within two years, and the last two saw out their last days at Ardsley and Copley Hill depots prior to withdrawal in June 1962. All but four were scrapped at Doncaster, the others at Stratford and Gorton.

GCR Robinson '9J'/'J11' 'Pom Pom' Class 0-6-0

Nos 64280-453

The 'Pom Pom' gun was designed by Hiram Maxim in the 1880s. Formally the 'QF [quick-firing] 1 pounder', the gun was used during the Second Boer War, able to fire a 1lb shell accurately over a distance of 3,000 yards. 'Pom Poms' were also used in the trenches and against aircraft during the First World War. The gun gained its popular name from the sound of its discharge, so it is not surprising that the sharp bark of the exhaust of these Robinson engines should be likened by enginemen to the weapon used so successfully in the recent Boer War.

The GCR's '9Js' were Robinson's first goods engine design for the company, and 'can be well described as the "prettiest"

Introduced	1901

Introduced 1901
Designed by John Robinson
Built by Neilson Reid (49), Beyer Peacock (25), GCR, Gorton (70), Vulcan Foundry (15), Yorkshire Engine (15)
Number built 174
Number inherited by BR 174
Last example withdrawn October 1962

'J11' 'Pom Pom' 0-6-0 No 64401 makes light work of a short freight train near Birch Vale on the former GC&Midland Joint branch from New Mills to Hayfield on 16 April 1957. In their last days such duties suited these veterans, and No 64401, a long-time Gorton resident, was withdrawn that October.
Colour-Rail collection

0-6-0s ever built,' according to O. S. Nock, while George Dow judged them 'sturdy, beautifully proportioned' engines in typical Robinson style. Based on the earlier 'J10', they had a larger, longer, higher-pressure boiler and firebox.

The first batch of 49 was built by Neilson, Reid & Co in 1901-02, then between 1903 and 1910 a further 11 batches appeared, built both by the GCR itself at Gorton, and by several outside manufacturers, an ample demonstration of how successful the new design had proved to be. The 'Pom Poms' had commodious Robinson cabs carrying an oval numberplate that became standard practice.

The whole class had slide valves and saturated boilers, apart from one experimental loco that became the first GCR locomotive to be superheated, employing the Schmidt equipment. Robinson quickly modified the superheater to develop his own design, which went on to became the LNER Group Standard. Engines built after 1913 were duly superheated as their original boilers came due for renewal, but the slide valves were retained.

During the First World War 18 'J11s' were used by the ROD in France. Serving on the continent between 1917 and 1919, all returned safely except a single tender, damaged in a collision!

The LNER was eager to include what it referred to as Class 'J11' within the new Composite Loading Gauge, so boiler and dome modifications were made to reduce the engine's height, a process that took until 1946 to complete.

Another compliment paid to the class was that Thompson chose a modified 'J11' as an LNER standard class. He subsequently rebuilt 31 of the class with long-travel piston valves, which required the boiler to be pitched higher; this in turn required a smaller chimney, so the elegant Robinson original was replaced by the somewhat disfiguring 'flowerpot' type. Variations in tender size, locomotive height, valve and boiler type led to four sub-classes.

The versatile 'Pom Poms' worked all kinds of traffic, from pick-up goods to express passenger, and were very popular with their crews. The LNER allocated them across the system, from Immingham to Neasden, and Leicester to Lincoln, and they were only eclipsed by the purchase of war-surplus 'O4' 2-8-0s. The 'Pom Poms' in turn displaced older 0-6-0s, and between 1927 and 1933 26 of them worked on the Great Eastern Section from Norwich, Lowestoft, Yarmouth and Cambridge before returning to their GCR homeland. They also worked briefly on the M&GN when the LNER took on responsibility for that system in 1936.

From GCR days the engines carried random numbers, but with the LNER renumbering scheme of 1946 they were numbered in a single sequence from 4280 to 4453. Becoming BR property in 1948, 60000 was added to the numbers and the class was still widely spread across the former LNER network, including former Cheshire Lines routes, where they worked until removed when the London Midland Region took over.

Although principally goods engines, in their later days they were increasingly used on local passenger trains – even the occasional express – until usurped by diesel units. They could be quick when required; the 'J11/3s' (the Thompson piston-valve rebuilds) were recorded at 60mph on more than one occasion.

There were still nearly 140 of these workhorses in service at the end of 1956, but then numbers dwindled until only 30 were still at work in 1962. The very last of the 174 'Pom Poms' was No 64354 of Retford (36E), taken out of service in October 1962.

NBR Reid 'B'/'J35' Class 0-6-0

Nos 64460-64, 64466, 64468, 64470-80, 64482-502, 64504-07, 64509-35

Reid's predecessor Holmes had provided the North British Railway with a useful and numerous class of 0-6-0s (LNER 'J36'), but in 1905 it was decided that more powerful locomotives were required. As well as a couple of classes of passenger engines (an 'Atlantic' and a 4-4-0), Reid introduced his 'B' Class of sizeable 0-6-0s in 1906.

The first 18 engines employed piston valves, the next six the more traditional slide valves. Unlike other designs, the slide valves proved to be better, and subsequent members of the

Introduced 1906
Designed by William Reid
Built by North British (40), NBR, Cowlairs (36)
Number built 76
Number inherited by BR 70
Last example withdrawn December 1962

class were built with them. Ten batches were constructed between 1906 and 1913, 40 in four batches by the North British Locomotive Co in 1906 and 1909-10, and the remainder by the railway itself at its own works at Cowlairs.

The first two Cowlairs engines, built in 1906, were different from the rest of the class, with detail modifications that led the LNER to classify them 'J35/2'. The remaining piston valve engines became Class 'J35/1', and the slide valve engines 'J35/3'.

These 0-6-0s were built for long-distance goods traffic, and were allocated at St Margarets, Eastfield, Carlisle and Dundee.

In 1914 Reid introduced his more powerful 'B' and 'S' 0-6-0s, and these overshadowed the older class, which were then used increasingly on coal trains and pick-up goods, although they also made appearances on summer holiday trains. Fifty-four of the class had Westinghouse brakes for passenger working.

All the 'J35s' were superheated by the LNER between 1923 and 1942, as the older saturated boilers fell due for replacement. In 1937 the superheated engines with piston valves became LNER Class 'J35/5', while those with slide valves were 'J35/4'. They were spread widely across the former NBR territory in Scotland, from Berwick to Dundee, and some were fitted with

One of the first batch of Reid 'J35' Class 0-6-0s built by the North British Locomotive Co for the railway of (almost) the same name, No 64463 was built in 1906 and is seen here at Carlisle (Canal) shed in August 1959. A Hawick engine at this time, it moved to St Margarets in November and was withdrawn from there in September 1960. *John Stretton collection*

rather ungainly tender cabs for protection when running tender-first in bad weather.

All but six (withdrawn between 1946 and 1948) became BR engines, and were employed on local goods and mineral trains. No further engines were lost until 1958, when withdrawals began in earnest. It fell to 'J35/4' No 64491, a former Bathgate slide-valve engine, withdrawn from Thornton Junction shed in December 1962, to render the class extinct.

NBR Reid 'B' and 'S'/'J37' Class 0-6-0

Nos 64536-639

Introduced 1914
Designed by William Reid
Built by NBR, Cowlairs (35), North British (69)
Number built 104
Number inherited by BR 104
Last example withdrawn April 1967

These powerful engines represented the final development of North British Railway 0-6-0 goods locomotive, and found much use on heavy wartime freights and mineral workings. They were a superheated version of the designer's 'B' Class (LNER 'J35' – see above) of 1906-13, with a larger boiler pitched high, piston valves and larger cylinders. Happily, unlike some of their contemporaries such as the GCR 'Pom Poms', they were not disfigured by having alien chimneys and domes fitted in LNER days.

The first three batches of five emerged from Cowlairs Works in 1914-15, then further examples followed after the end of hostilities, including an order for 34 placed with the North British Locomotive Co. Two further batches of 20 and 15 were built by North British, in 1919 and 1920 respectively, while Cowlairs produced another 20, bringing the class total to 104. Twenty engines from the later batches, built in 1919-20, had higher-pressure boilers, and were classified 'S'; in due

On 27 March 1964 the Branch Line Society organised a brake-van tour to and from Springburn, covering several north Glasgow branch lines. The locomotive used was 'J37' 0-6-0 No 64623, then shedded at Polmont; it was to survive until the end of 1966. *Railphotoprints collection*

course the NBR temporarily upgraded some 'Bs' to 'S' form, while the LNER converted them all to higher-pressure boilers, classifying them 'J37'. They were employed on long-distance goods trains, notably from Glasgow to Aberdeen and Carlisle to Dundee, as well as on the Mallaig extension of the West Highland line.

Between 1927 and 1938 the LNER altered the weight balance towards the rear axle, to improve running on long-distance express goods services; eventually most weight was concentrated on the middle axle. After the Grouping some members of the class found themselves south of the border, working from Berwick and Tweedmouth, and even Newcastle, while one was experimentally tried out in East Anglia in 1926. As well as goods rosters, the engines could also be found on summer excursion and relief trains.

The entire class survived to become part of BR stock in 1948, and some were reallocated to former LMS sheds, although for some reason these engines tended to suffer from overheated big-ends.

It was not until May 1959 that the first engine, class leader No 64536, was withdrawn, and only in the early 1960s did their numbers dwindle significantly. More than a dozen were still in service in June 1966, working short-distance goods and mineral trains in the Fife area, and four almost made it to the end of steam in 1968, being withdrawn in April 1967 from Dundee Tay Bridge shed. They were among the very last pre-Grouping designs still working on BR.

GER Hill 'E72' and 'T77'/'J18' and 'J19' Class 0-6-0

Nos 64640-74

Alfred J. Hill was apprenticed at the GER's Stratford Works in 1877 at the age of 15, and quickly rose through the ranks to become Assistant Works Manager in 1885, and Manager of the Locomotive Carriage & Wagon Works in 1899. In due course he succeeded Holden as Chief Mechanical Engineer in 1912. He retired at the Grouping of 1923, and died suddenly three years later while playing golf at Bexhill. Although his activities at Stratford were limited by wartime conditions, he made improvements at the works and is remembered as the man who introduced the Robinson superheater to the Great Eastern.

Holden's saturated 'G58' 0-6-0s were built between 1900 and 1910, and one, BR No 65567 of 1905, is preserved as part of the National Collection. Hill's Class 'E72' (LNER 'J18') of 1912 was a development of it – the goods equivalent of the 'Claud Hamilton' 4-4-0s – and the ten locomotives had superheaters, piston valves and larger cylinders. The frames had a front overhang to accommodate the long piston tail rods, which were shortened in 1916, reducing this unattractive feature of the locomotives. Thus altered, the engines were classified 'T77'

Introduced 1912/1916; rebuilt 1934-39
Designed by Alfred Hill
Built by GER, Stratford
Number built 35
Number inherited by BR 35
Last example withdrawn September 1962

(LNER 'J19'), and 25 were built in four batches (of ten and three fives) between 1916 and 1920.

Ten more were to be built, but this was reduced to five and they were modified to use the same boiler as Holden's 'B12' 4-6-0s, thus becoming GER Class 'D81' (LNER 'J20' – see below).

In 1934 Gresley began to rebuild the 'J19s' with large round-topped 'Claud Hamilton' superheated boilers (they had been built with Belpaire fireboxes), which also necessitated a larger cab, and they were classified 'J19/2'. Between 1935 and 1938 the ten 'J18s' were also rebuilt to this form.

The 'J18s', having no vacuum brakes, at first mostly worked goods trains on the Peterborough-March route. The 'J19s', meanwhile, had vacuum ejectors and could work fitted goods trains. Their allocation was therefore wider, across East Anglia from Stratford and Colchester to March and Lincoln. In LNER days engines based at Peterborough often worked on the former Midland & Great Northern Joint line, while in the 1950s a large number of 'J19s' shedded at Colchester worked frights to and from Whitemoor yard.

As BR engines the class remained intact until 1958, but they were then quickly disposed of, the last four examples disappearing during 1962 from March, Norwich and Stratford sheds.

'J19' 0-6-0 No 64655 was a long-time March resident, but ended up at Cambridge in early 1960. It is seen here on 7 May 1961 at Stratford, perhaps already withdrawn, as the official date for disposal was August of that year. *G. Parry collection, Colour-Rail*

GER Hill 'D81'/'J20' Class 0-6-0

Nos 64675-99

The 'D81' 0-6-0 was the final development of a long tradition of 0-6-0 Great Eastern goods engines. Although the company by this time had on loan 42 ex-ROD 2-8-0s, it was felt that post-war

traffic would increase still further, and the 'D81s' were built to fulfil this need. As was often the case with GER engines, the boiler and motion were borrowed from elsewhere, in this case being the same at those used on Holden's 'B12' 4-6-0s. The front end was similar to the 'T77', but the rear wheelbase was lengthened

Introduced 1920
Designed by Alfred Hill
Built by GER, Stratford
Number built 25
Number inherited by BR 25
Last example withdrawn September 1963

to accommodate the larger boiler. Because they were heavier than their predecessors they were able to use all the available boiler pressure, and the result was that the new engines became the most powerful 0-6-0s in Britain until Bulleid's 'Q1s' appeared in 1942. Twenty-five were built at Stratford in three batches (a five and two tens) between 1920 and 1922. Despite the longer wheelbase, spring-loaded side-control trailing axleboxes still enabled them to negotiate relatively sharp curves; only when plain axleboxes were substituted by the LNER did their availability become more limited.

In 1925 No 8280 was experimentally fitted with Lentz oscillating cam poppet valves, the first use of this equipment in Britain; this equipment was subsequently fitted to a number of LNER designs, starting with some 'B12' 4-6-0s in 1926, although the 'J20' reverted to conventional piston valves in 1937, the Lentz gear being expensive to maintain.

In 1941 a new round-topped boiler was designed to be used on unrebuilt 'B12s' and the 'J20s'; it was fitted to the latter between 1943 and 1956, and the engines became known as Class 'J20/1'.

Most members of the class were based at Cambridge and March, and were principally used on heavy coal trains between

From August 1954 until withdrawal in April 1962 'J20' 0-6-0 No 64696 was allocated to March shed (31B). It is seen here on light rural goods duties at Clare, between Haverhill and Long Melford, Suffolk, on 30 May 1960. *Colour-Rail collection*

Whitemoor and Temple Mills. In the early 1950s four were allocated to Hornsey for cross-London goods traffic. Although fitted with vacuum brakes, the engines were seldom used on passenger services before the 1930s, when seaside excursion trains were sometimes handled. The advent of further 2-8-0s after the Second World War began to displace the 0-6-0s to more rural duties but, like the 'J19s', the class remained intact until 1959. After that withdrawal was rapid, and by the autumn of 1963 all had gone to the scrapyard.

LNER Gresley 'J39' Class 0-6-0

Nos 64700-988

Introduced 1926
Designed by Nigel Gresley
Built by LNER, Darlington (261), Beyer Peacock (28)
Number built 289
Number inherited by BR 289
Last example withdrawn December 1962

In the early years of the LNER Gresley was faced with a stable of many and varied locomotive types from the constituent companies, so a 'Group Standard' system was developed, to centre development on certain key designs intended to replace the inherited assortment. The first Group Standard design was Gresley's 'J38' 0-6-0 (qv), 35 of which were put into service at the beginning of 1926. Later in the year the 'general service' equivalent appeared, the 'J39', like the 'J38' but with larger

wheels, necessitating splashers (absent on the 'J38s'). Both designs were worked out by the Darlington Drawing Office, and owed little to Doncaster practice.

Considered by some as the finest 0-6-0 type yet put into service, the design was characterised by straightforward machinery and an entirely new boiler, short and of large diameter, with a deep and well-proportioned firebox, ideal for free steaming. Eventually 289 were constructed through to 1941, making it the most numerous Gresley design. All were built at Darlington (many with boilers supplied by Armstrong Whitworth and Robert Stephenson) except for three batches totalling 28 engines, built by Beyer Peacock & Co in 1936-37.

Two 'J39s' survived withdrawal from Woodford Halse shed in November 1962 by becoming stationary boilers at the shed. This is one of them, the almost anonymous No 64747, photographed in that role on 20 August 1964. It was finally scrapped in December, six months before the shed closed.
Colour-Rail collection

The class was divided into three sections from the early 1930s to the early 1950s; the Class 'J39/1' engines (mostly the lower-numbered examples) had Group Standard 3,500-gallon tenders; 'J39/2' (mostly middle-range numbers) had 4,200-gallon tenders; and 'J39/3' (BR Nos 64842-45, 64855-59 and 64971-88) were the remainder, coupled to old NER and GCR tenders. There were also variations in the brakes fitted, depending on the area of deployment, and other much smaller variations – in lubricators, reversing gear, superheaters, etc – not surprising with such a large class built over 15 years.

The angular relationship between the driving wheel cranks and inside axle cranks on these powerful locomotives led to a twisting force on the axleboxes that resulted in heavy maintenance. Various axlebox modifications were tried without success.

Gresley's successor, Thompson, planned to use the existing 'J39s' as a replacement for all other 0-6-0 types with an axle loading of more than 18 tons, with his new 'B1' 4-6-0 intended to take on any future suitable duties.

The 'J38s' had all gone to Scotland, so the first 'J39s' also went there, and to the North Eastern Area, and it was not until after nationalisation that allocations broadened. They were powerful and versatile engines, so were put to work not only on general goods trains but also heavier traffics and, occasionally, passenger trains and summer excursions, where they could put in a good turn of speed.

All 289 engines survived to become BR property in 1948, but like others already considered their demise was swift. Withdrawals started in 1959; there were still nearly 90 in use by

'J39/1' 0-6-0 No 64813 was allocated to Tweedmouth shed (52D) for almost its entire BR career, and in this delightful view dating from June 1956 it is seen on what appears to be a mixed train at the terminus of the short Eyemouth branch. This was one of the last survivors of the class, withdrawn in December 1962.
J. G. Wallace, Colour-Rail

the beginning of October 1962, but all had gone by the end of the year, dogged by the ongoing problems with hot axleboxes. Two of them, Nos 64727 and 64747, were withdrawn from Woodford Halse shed, but survived until August 1963 and 1964 respectively as stationary boilers.

GNR Ivatt 'J21'/'J1' Class 0-6-0

Nos 65002-5, 5006, 65007-10, 65013, 65014

When Ivatt introduced his 'J21' fast goods 0-6-0s in 1908 – which soon developed into a mixed-traffic class – his standardisation policy ensured that they were based on his 'N1' 0-6-2 tanks (qv) of 1907, using the same boiler, motion and coupled wheels. This same boiler was also used on other classes, but on the 'J21s' it was never superheated.

Fifteen 'J21s' were built at Doncaster, and despite the standardisation ideals there were ultimately many detail variations between them; for example, their original full-

Introduced 1908	
Designed by Henry Ivatt	
Built by GNR, Doncaster	
Number built 15	
Number inherited by BR 11	
Last example withdrawn November 1954	

height chimneys and domes were cut down or replaced during the 1930s.

Nearly half the 'J21s' went first to New England shed, Peterborough, with smaller numbers at Ardsley, Colwick and King's Cross. Although mainly employed on fast goods trains, they were soon put onto passenger workings; in 1909 all three King's Cross engines worked August Bank Holiday excursions to Skegness.

As LNER Class 'J1', some were allocated to Bradford, where they worked local services as well as occasional summer seaside excursion trains to the Yorkshire coast. During the war the engines were dealing with wartime goods traffic, based at

Ivatt 'J1' 0-6-0 No 5007, a Leicester Central engine, calls at Melton Mowbray on 24 April 1948. It was renumbered 65007 in October 1949, and was withdrawn from Colwick in February 1952.
John Stretton collection

Gorton and Colwick. In 1945 they were briefly all based at Colwick, but four of the class were withdrawn in 1947, so only 11 became BR engines. No more were withdrawn until July 1951 (No 5006, scrapped before it could carry its BR number), then the remainder followed between February 1952 and November 1954; the last was No 65013 of Hitchin shed. While there it had been used to substitute for failed express engines on two occasions, one of which involved a 14-coach train from King's Cross whose 'Pacific' had to be taken off; No 65013 took the train forward unaided!

GNR Ivatt/Gresley 'J21'/'J2' Class 0-6-0

Nos 65015-20, 5021, 65022, 65023

When Gresley took over from Henry Ivatt the company's greatest need lay in goods locomotives. As traffic grew is was not unusual to find express passenger engines – 'Atlantics' and 4-4-0s among them – on fast fitted freights. Ivatt met this need by adapting his 'J22' (LNER 'J6') 0-6-0 of 1911 (qv) to produce the 'J21' Class. These used the same superheated boiler, cylinders and motion, but had larger-diameter wheels. They were also similar to the 'J21' 0-6-0s of 1908 (qv), but used piston valves and were superheated.

Ten 'J21s' were built at Doncaster in 1912, just after Ivatt's retirement. Once in charge, Gresley introduced his 'K1' ('H2', later 'K2') 2-6-0s (qv), and no more of these 0-6-0s were built.

Unlike many other pre-Grouping designs, the 'J21s' were never brought within the LNER's new Composite Loading Gauge, remaining as tall as the GNR's generous loading gauge permitted. They were allocated to King's Cross, New England and York shed to work the night fitted goods trains between London and York. The King's Cross engines were also used on daytime stopping passenger services to Cambridge, as well as occasional seaside excursions. However, their duties were soon

'J2' No 65016 poses at its home shed at Boston on 26 August 1950. It was withdrawn from there in October 1953. Note the famous 'Boston stump' on the right, the 272-foot tower of St Botolph's, the highest parish church tower in England. The building is also said to be England's largest parish church. *H. C. Casserley*

usurped by the new 'K1s', and by the Grouping the 'J21s' were based only at New England and Doncaster, where they continued to concentrate on goods duties, but were also found on local passenger services in Lincolnshire and around Nottingham, and on summer East Coast resort excursions.

The LNER classified the engines 'J2', and withdrew the first locomotive, No 3080, later 5024, in 1946, but the remaining nine became BR property at nationalisation. The next to go was No 5021 in 1950, without receiving its BR number, and the remaining eight, allocated to Colwick, Boston and Leicester Central, were withdrawn between March 1953 and July 1954.

Introduced 1912
Designed by Nigel Gresley
Built by GNR, Doncaster
Number built 10
Number inherited by BR 9
Last example withdrawn July 1954

MSLR/GCR Parker '9D', '9H' and '9M'/'J10' Class 0-6-0

Nos 65126-28, 65130-49, 65151, 65153-73, 65175-94, 5195, 65196-05, 65208, 65209

Thomas Parker (1829-1903) began as an apprentice on the Caledonian Railway, and moved to the Manchester, Sheffield & Lincolnshire Railway in 1858 as the company's Carriage & Wagon Superintendent. In 1886 he became Locomotive Superintendent, and introduced inside-framed designs to the

company, and Britain's first engines with Belpaire fireboxes (qv LNER 'N5'), both of which features characterised the company's engines after it became the Great Central Railway in 1897 and through to the Grouping of 1923. Parker also supervised the complete remodelling of the company's Gorton Works. He retired in 1893.

From around 1890 there was an increasing need for additional motive power, with more traffic and new lines being opened. Parker's Class '9D' 0-6-0s were a development of his earlier '9B' (LNER 'J9') engines, effectively a tender version of his 'N5' 0-6-2T, with Joy valve gear instead of Stephenson's. Initially 18 were built by Kitson & Co and Gorton Works in 1892-93 in two batches.

Parker was succeeded by Harry Pollitt (1864-1945), son of the MSLR's General Manager, Sir William Pollitt., and

Introduced 1892
Designed by Thomas Parker
Built by GCR, Gorton, and Kitson (58), Beyer Peacock (66)
Number built 124
Number inherited by BR 78
Last example withdrawn August 1961

perpetuated many of his predecessor's designs until he resigned the post in 1900. His Class '9H' 0-6-0s were similar to the '9Ds', with just detail differences, and 66 were built by Beyer Peacock in 1896-97.

More '9Hs' were built by Pollitt's successor, John G. Robinson, when a final batch appeared in 1901-02, with smaller tenders and further detail changes, at the same time as his own '9J' 0-6-0s (LNER Class 'J11' – qv) were already beginning to appear.

In 1908 one of the engines received a larger non-standard Belpaire firebox, which necessitated cab alterations and a higher cab roof. The GCR classified the conversion '9M'.

During the First World War seven of the class were loaned to the Caledonian Railway, with shorter GCR chimneys to fit within that railway's loading gauge.

At the Grouping the LNER placed the '9Ds' and '9Hs' together in its Class 'J10', by which time all the engines were standardised with 20-inch cylinders and the 'GC Standard No 1 Belpaire' boiler. The sole '9M' was initially included with the 'J11s', before being reclassified as a 'J10'.

The 'J10/4' sub-class had the 4,000-gallon tender, larger bearings, and had been reduced in height to fit within the LNER Composite Loading Gauge. No 65134 was built by Beyer Peacock for the Manchester, Sheffield & Lincolnshire Railway in 1897, as is seen here in July 1959 at Northwich shed, where it had been allocated for its entire BR career. It was withdrawn from there at the end of the year. *P. J. Hughes, Colour-Rail*

In 1927 the LNER divided the class into three sub-classes. The '9Ds' more than 13 feet tall became 'J10/1', while those reduced in height (with LNER 'flowerpot'-type chimneys) to fit within the LNER loading gauge were 'J10/2'. Likewise the '9Hs' with 4,000-gallon tenders became 'J10/3' and 'J10/4' on the same basis, and the '9Hs' with smaller 3,080-gallon tenders became 'J10/5' and 'J10/6'.

Though initially exclusively employed as goods engines, they later appeared on passenger excursions. The 66 examples built in 1896-97 were intended for use on the GCR's new London Extension, and Annesley had a large allocation. The Robinson engines served the Lancashire and Cheshire areas. The LNER distributed the class widely, including 13 to the Great Eastern Area between 1925 and 1933. By 1940 they were all based in Lancashire and Cheshire, mainly operating in North Wales, on the Cheshire Lines, and in the Wigan area.

The first engines were taken out of service in the 1930s, but there were still 78 active in 1948, and they were even more widely dispersed, some to the sheds of other constituent members of the 'Big Four'. Popular with ex-LMS crews, the last three to be withdrawn were allocated to the former LMS shed at Wigan Springs Branch. One of the last to be consigned to scrap, No 65157 of 1897, was by a narrow margin the very last MSLR locomotive in service.

GNR Ivatt 'J22'/'J5' Class 0-6-0

Nos 65480-99

Introduced 1909
Designed by Henry Ivatt
Built by GNR, Doncaster
Number built 20
Number inherited by BR 20
Last example withdrawn December 1955

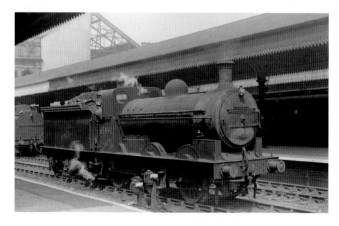

These 20 medium-powered goods 0-6-0s were built at Doncaster in two batches of ten, in 1909 and 1910. Classified by the GNR as 'J22', they had the same dimensions as Ivatt's 'J21' 0-6-0s (LNER 'J1' – qv) of 1908, except for wheels 6 inches smaller in diameter. In 1911 Ivatt introduced his heavier, superheated version of the 'J22' with piston rather than slide valves, which during Gresley's tenure became LNER Class 'J6' (qv), so no more of this particular 0-6-0 were built.

The engines originally had tall domes and chimneys, but the LNER cut these down by 3 inches. Superheaters were fitted to just two of the class, in 1923 and 1928.

The 'J22s' were initially employed on Peterborough-London coal trains, and during the First World War Colwick had some to handle through goods trains to Hornsey.

Increasing displaced by the 'J6s', the LNER, classifying the

During the BR era most of the Ivatt 'J5' 0-6-0s were shedded at Colwick, just east of Nottingham. No 65493 of 1909 was photographed at Nottingham Victoria station on 3 June 1950, when it still had more than four years of service left.
H. C. Casserley

engines 'J5', dispersed them along the East Coast Main Line and at Colwick. Eventually they all congregated at Retford, where they worked local coal trains, and some to New England. During the Second World War they were all in the Nottingham area, where they coped with heavy traffic from the Nottinghamshire and Derbyshire coalfields. As with many of the LNER's goods 0-6-0s, they were also occasionally seen on local passenger services, although mainly in summer as they were not fitted with steam heating apparatus.

All 20 entered BR stock in 1948, and none were dispensed with until March 1953. By now, all but one were stationed at Colwick, and withdrawals hastened. Only three saw 1955, the last two, Nos 65483 and 65498, being taken out of service in December of that year.

NER W. Worsdell 'P'/'J24' Class 0-6-0

Nos 5600, 65601, 5602-04, 5606-09, 5611, 5612, 5614, 65615, 65617, 65619, 5621-29, 5631-34, 5636, 5639, 65640, 5641, 65642, 5644

Thomas W. Worsdell introduced his Class 'C' 0-6-0 goods engines (LNER 'J21') to the North Eastern Railway in 1886, and between then and 1894 more than 200 were built, most of which were compounds with Joy valve gear. One of them, BR No 65033, passed into preservation. Thomas retired due to ill health in 1890 and his younger brother Wilson succeeded him, while the 'Cs' were still in production; Thomas remained a consultant for a further two years.

Wilson disliked both compounding and the Joy gear, and also felt that the 5ft 1¼in wheels were too large for a mineral engine; he therefore amended the final two batches of 'Cs' to use simple expansion, but the Joy valve gear and wheels had already been ordered. When Worsdell junior was finally able to design his own mineral engine, he planned to use Stephenson valve gear, simple expansion, and smaller driving wheels of 4ft 7¼in diameter, but this would have resulted in too powerful an engine for the company's needs, so instead he came up with a smaller engine using an existing boiler design. This became the Class 'P', and 70 were built between 1894 and 1898, five batches of ten emerging from Gateshead, and a final batch of 20 from Darlington in 1898.

When the need arose for more powerful engines, the design was adapted to take a larger boiler, becoming the 'P1' of 1898 (see below).

Wilson Worsdell retired in 1910, and between 1914 and 1920 his successor, Vincent Raven, modified the design by fitting piston valves and superheaters to 20 engines. However, the kind of work done by the 'Ps' did not benefit from superheating, and the process was discontinued. Those that retained their superheaters could be distinguished by their longer smokeboxes.

In 1918-20 three of the engines were fitted with tender cabs for working the exposed moorland branch to Rosedale.

When the LNER inherited the engines it classified them 'J24' and, since they were already within the new loading gauge, no alterations were necessary. With the 'J21s' hauling the faster freight services, the 'J24s' proved useful with slower traffic, their smaller wheels enabling them to start heavy trains more easily and keep them on the move. At first they were used to handle heavy coal trains between the Durham and Northumberland collieries and East Coast ports, and most were still doing so at the Grouping.

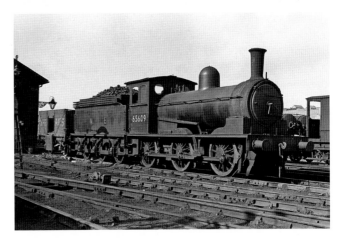

'J24' 0-6-0 No 65609 had a brief BR career. Allocated to Whitby shed, it is seen there on 8 July 1949. It lasted only until October. Note the spacious, covered-in cab characteristic of Worsdell locomotives, perhaps influenced by the brothers' experiences when visiting America; the fittings and high-quality workmanship were much appreciated by the crews! Note also the 1941 wartime 'NE' on the tender. *T. B. Owen, Colour-Rail*

Introduced 1894
Designed by Wilson Worsdell
Built by NER, Gateshead (50), NER, Darlington (20)
Number built 70
Number inherited by BR 34
Last example withdrawn December 1951

In 1924 ten of the class moved to Scotland to work on lightly laid branch lines, where their light weight was a bonus; five of them were still north of the border when the railways were nationalised in 1948.

During the Depression the 'J24s' found less and less work, and withdrawals commenced in the early 1930s; 14 had gone by 1936. Wartime needs reprieved others, but withdrawals began again in 1942, and only 34 became part of BR stock. Numbers quickly dwindled, and the last two, Nos 65601 and 65617 (two of only ten to carry their allocated BR numbers) were withdrawn from Newport (51B, between Middlesbrough and Thornaby) and St Margarets, Edinburgh, respectively.

One 'J24' was sold to the South Shields, Marsden & Whitburn Colliery Railway in 1939, and was scrapped in 1946. Another, No 5626, was bought by the National Coal Board in 1948 for use at Boldon Colliery, and was scrapped at Whitburn Colliery in July 1956, still carrying its LNER number.

NER W. Worsdell 'P1'/'J25' Class 0-6-0

Nos 65645-48, 5649, 65650, 5651, 65653-57, 5658, 65659-64, 5665, 65666, 65667, 5668, 65669-73, 5674, 65675-77, 65679-81, 65683-700, 65702, 5703, 5704, 65705, 65706, 5707, 65708, 65710, 65712-14, 5715, 65716-18, 65720, 5721, 65723, 65724, 5725, 65726-28

Introduced	1898
Designed by	Wilson Worsdell
Built by	NER, Gateshead (80), NER, Darlington (40)
Number built	120
Number inherited by BR	76
Last example withdrawn	June 1962

Even as the final 'P' 0-6-0s were emerging from Darlington Works, Wilson Worsdell was working on adapting the design to produce yet more power for mineral traffic. This was the 'P1', which used a boiler of the same size as his brother Thomas's Class 'C' (LNER 'J21') of 1886-94. The boiler was 4 inches longer than that of the 'J24', and the firebox 6 inches longer; the wheelbase was thus commensurately longer, but the design retained the smaller 4ft 7¼in wheels. Gateshead built two batches of 20 in 1898, Darlington produced two more batches of 20 the following year, then finally Gateshead built the last 40, again in two batches of 20, in 1900 and 1902. From 1902 all the engines were progressively fitted with larger cylinders, a process that lasted into LNER days.

Like the 'J24s', the engines carried saturated boilers, although eventually 28 received superheaters and piston valves from 1915 onwards – but as with the earlier engines the benefit was only marginal, and the number of superheated boilers dwindled into the 1930s.

The 'P1s' proved themselves useful freight workhorses, but the still larger 'T'/'Q5' 0-8-0s (qv) of 1901, 'P2'/'J26s' of 1904 (qv) and 'P3'/'J27s' of 1906 soon overtook them, and they were relegated to lesser but still vital trip and local goods workings, as well as shunting and banking (the latter particularly over Stainmore). Traffics included coal, stone and ironstone.

As with their predecessors withdrawals began in 1933, but engines that might otherwise have been disposed of were kept in store during the Second World War. Forty were loaned to the GWR in 1939-40 to work around Wolverhampton and Worcester, returning between 1943 and 1946. Seventy-six run-down examples were still at work in 1948, and almost half of those were still to be seen by the end of 1957. Thereafter withdrawals accelerated, but eight were still operating in 1962. Two of the last three were shedded at Tyne Dock for banking duties, while the third was a Gateshead resident. All three went in June 1962, rendering the class extinct.

One of the duties that fell to the last remaining 'J25' 0-6-0s was hauling ammunition trains on the former North British Railway's Rothbury branch to supply the nearby moorland firing ranges. In this undated view No 65687 is seen at the terminus with a mixed goods train. The locomotive was withdrawn in August 1959.
David Lawrence, Colour-Rail

NER W. Worsdell 'P2'/'J26' Class 0-6-0

Nos 65730-79

Introduced	1904
Designed by	Wilson Worsdell
Built by	NER, Darlington (30), NER, Gateshead (20)
Number built	50
Number inherited by BR	50
Last example withdrawn	June 1962

In 1901 George S. Gibb, NER General Manager, visited America accompanied by four senior officers, including Wilson Worsdell. The aim was to study US railway methods, and one outcome of the visit was the introduction of 'Atlantic' 4-4-2 locomotives to the NER. Another was a general increase in freight train loads, using new, larger 20-ton mineral wagons. Thus the average gross freight train load increased from 276 tons in 1903 to 402 tons 20 years later. To handle such loads the next member of the NER 0-6-0 family was the Class 'P2'; it had a large-diameter boiler with 50 per cent greater heating surface than the 'P1', and 4ft 7in-diameter wheels once again. 'They were "stocky" workmanlike engines,' wrote O. S. Nock. Although large, the boiler was pitched low, belying its huge

size. The firebox and frames were about a foot longer. Thirty of the 'P2s' were built at Darlington in 1904 and 1905, and 20 more at Gateshead in 1905.

For about ten years the 'P2s' handled long-distance goods and mineral trains, but were then ousted by the newer 'Q6' 0-8-0s of 1913, as well as 'B15' and 'B16' 4-6-0s.

A further version of the design appeared in 1906, the 'P3' (LNER 'J27'), with various modifications, including revised firebox dimensions. This new boiler was subsequently fitted also to the 'P2s' between 1910 and 1925.

Just before the First World War some engines had the cab spectacle shape changed from the original circular pattern, but 28 retained the original circular spectacles.

In 1923 the class became the LNER's 'J26', and the boiler was further modified in 1937, being fitted to engines right through to 1958. That was the year when the first locomotives were taken out of service by BR, and some engines had the new boilers swapped back for the older ones. None of the 'J26s' were superheated.

In pre-war LNER days the class was widely distributed throughout the North East of England and East Yorkshire, but during the war they were concentrated in the Tees area.

The whole class passed to BR in 1948, and remained intact for a decade. When Middlesbrough and Newport sheds closed in 1958, they were moved to the new Thornaby shed, but now withdrawals began and over the next four years the class was gradually scrapped, although some examples were temporarily reprieved for lack of suitable replacements. The widespread introduction of Type 2 diesels finally spelled the end, and the last ten 'J26s' were withdrawn en bloc in June 1962.

The final progression in this 0-6-0 series was the 'P3'/'J27', which had a deeper firebox and a higher boiler pressure. Between 1906 and 1923 115 were built at Darlington and by a

Work-worn 'J26' 0-6-0 No 65761 is at home at Middlesbrough on 30 March 1962. It had moved from Newport shed (51B) to Thornaby (51L) in May 1958, and only had three months left when this photograph was taken. *Colour-Rail collection*

variety of outside contractors, and they remained active in the North East until the end of steam there in 1967. The last-numbered, BR No 65894, has been preserved.

LNER Gresley 'J38' Class 0-6-0

Nos 65900-34

Introduced 1926	
Designed by Nigel Gresley	
Built by LNER, Darlington	
Number built 35	
Number inherited by BR 35	
Last example withdrawn April 1967	

Gresley designed two new classes of 0-6-0 for the LNER to replace the many ageing types inherited from the constituent companies. One was the 'J39' already covered (see above), the first of the 289 engines emerging from Darlington Works in September 1926. Meanwhile, between January and May 1926 the other class, the 'J38s', had appeared, the 35 examples also built at Darlington; however, no more were built as the 'J39' proved to be the more versatile machine. The 'J38s' and 'J39s' were the first LNER 'Group Standard' types.

In 1924 LNER plans for new goods engines mooted 103 new 0-6-0s, including 35 for Scotland. The other quantities were cancelled, in part due to the purchase of ex-ROD 2-8-0s, so just the Scottish engines were built as the 'J38s'.

'J38' No 65918 moved to Dunfermline Upper shed (62C) in January 1963, and was photographed at Alloa on 21 April 1965, when 23 of the original 35 locomotives were still at work. The last were withdrawn as late as April 1967. The 'J38' boiler was longer than that of the later 'J39', and the smokebox was correspondingly shorter. *T. B. Owen, Colour-Rail*

As with the 'J39s', these engines were very much a Darlington design, although the standard Doncaster goods engine wheel diameter of 4ft 8in was used. The wheelbase was longer than the 'J25'-'J27' series to accommodate a longer firebox with a greater heating surface.

The engines were duly dispatched to work main-line goods trains on former North British lines in Scotland, as well as heavy coal trains in the Fife and Lothian areas, but there were certain NER features with which the men were unfamiliar. One former railwayman, writing in 1982, considered that the engines' bearing surfaces were inadequate, and they were difficult to maintain. The tender brakes proved inadequate on the relatively steeply graded lines, but this was rectified, and eventually the Scottish crews grew accustomed to the 'J38s' and, although heavy on coal, they were powerful and free-steaming.

The 'J39s' carried a modified boiler, and from the end of 1932 spare examples were also often fitted to 'J38s', leading to the subclass 'J38/2', while unmodified engines were 'J38/1'.

When the 'K2' 2-6-0s and 'J39s' arrived on the scene, the 'J38s' concentrated on coal traffic between the Lothian coalfield and Edinburgh docks.

In BR days the 'J38s' had the distinction of being the last LNER class to remain completely intact. All 35 engines were still working at the end of 1962, then two were withdrawn in December of that year. There were still 21 active at the end of 1965, and three even survived into 1967. The last two, Nos 65901 and 65929, were withdrawn from Thornton Junction and Dunfermline Upper respectively on 22 April of that year, and had the further distinction of being the last Gresley-designed locomotives to serve with British Railways. They were cut up by Motherwell Machinery & Scrap, Wishaw, in September.

GER S. Holden 'Y65'/'F7' Class 2-4-2T

Nos 7093, 7094

Stephen Dewar Holden (1870-1918) was the son of the GER's James Holden, and followed his father into the post of Locomotive Superintendent from 1908 until his own retirement in 1912; he predeceased his father. Holden senior had been appointed in 1885, and the following year his son became a pupil at Stratford Works. He rose quickly through the ranks, but his time as Locomotive Superintendent was short, and he was mostly concerned with developing his father's designs.

These small 2-4-2 tanks were built in 1909-10 to replace his father's 'E22' (LNER 'J65') 0-6-0 tank engines of 1889-93, which were used for light passenger services. They proved not to be particularly successful or popular (the older 0-6-0Ts being preferred by enginemen), and only 12 were built (Nos 1300-11), two in 1909 and ten more, classified 'A67', in 1909-10. Their most distinctive feature, apart from their tall brass-rimmed, outward-tapering chimneys, was the size of the cab. As described by Cecil J. Allen, 'Overshadowing the whole machine was a cab of immense size, with high arched roof, windows in both sides, and huge windows fore and aft that extended from the roof down to the side tank and bunker level.' Not surprisingly, this feature soon gained them the nickname of 'Crystal Palace Tanks'.

All the engines had Westinghouse brakes, and four were fitted with compressed-air equipment for push-pull working, which required a second Westinghouse pump. A fifth had a mechanical system, as used on the former GCR lines. They were

GER 'Y65' No 1311 was built in January 1910. The LNER renumbered it 'F7' No 8311, in 1942 it was No 7598, and carrying that number it is seen here at St Margarets, Edinburgh (where it had been sent in the early 1930s) on 2 October 1946. That year it was renumbered 7094, but was withdrawn at the end of 1948 after a very brief career as a BR engine. *H. C. Casserley*

used for lightweight branch-line work in East Anglia – for example Saffron Walden, Mildenhall, Ramsey and Stoke Ferry – being allocated to sheds that handled such duties. In LNER days, as Class 'F7', they moved further afield, and in the early 1930s three were sent north to St Margarets shed, Edinburgh, where their copious glazing earned them a second nickname of 'Tomato Houses'! In Scotland the air brakes were replaced with a steam brake and vacuum ejector.

The LNER renumbered them 8300-11, and four members of the class were withdrawn in 1931; just six remained in 1942, when they were renumbered 7593-98 to free up numbers in the 83xx series for new 'B1' 4-6-0s. Surprisingly, two examples (having been renumbered 7093-94 in 1946) became BR engines in 1948, but did not last the year.

Introduced	1909
Designed by	Stephen Holden
Built by	GER, Stratford
Number built	12
Number inherited by BR	2
Last example withdrawn	November 1948

MSLR/GCR Parker '3'/'F1' Class 2-4-2T

Nos 7097, 7099, 7100

When Parker joined the Manchester, Sheffield & Lincolnshire Railway in 1886 there was a serious deficiency in tank engines for suburban and short-distance passenger services. For example, around Manchester local services were being handled by elderly 2-4-0 tender locomotives, particularly unsuitable when needing to run in reverse. This shortage was made good by the introduction of several classes, including these Class '3' 2-4-2Ts.

Between 1889 and 1891 24 were built, with round-topped boilers, radial axleboxes and Joy valve gear. Then in 1893 a further 15 were built; 12 were known as the 'Class 3 Altered', because their bunkers were 6 inches longer, while three were the same as the original engines. Between 1909 and 1929, by

Introduced 1889
Designed by Thomas Parker
Built by MSLR, Gorton, and Neilson
Number built 39
Number inherited by BR 3
Last example withdrawn January 1949

now Great Central engines, the entire class was fitted with the GC Standard No 2 Belpaire boiler. In 1915 three were temporarily fitted with superheaters.

Just before the Grouping three of the class had mechanical equipment fitted to allow them to operate push-pull trains, and the LNER added another. The system was not successful, and was removed later in the 1930s.

As LNER Class 'F1', the 2-4-2Ts continued to work Manchester-area services, although electrification in the early 1930s led to early withdrawals. However, five were still at work in 1945, and it is a measure of the success of the design that three lasted long enough to became BR property, although one was withdrawn almost immediately, from Gorton, and the others, shedded at Brunswick, Liverpool, had gone by the beginning of 1949.

Seen in early LNER days, former GCR Class '3' No 5589 stands looking smart at Neasden shed on 27 August 1927, apparently having work done on its safety valves, which have been removed and are resting on the tank top. Only four of the LNER Class 'F1' were left in 1946 when they were renumbered 7097, 7099, 7100 and 7101. Sadly No 5589 had already been scrapped by then. *H. C. Casserley*

GCR Pollitt '9G'/'F2' Class 2-4-2T

Nos 7104, 7105, 67106, 7107-09, 7111-13

Between 1893 and 1899 the MSLR's Gorton Works turned out 83 new locomotives, and the only contractor used by the company to supply it with engines was nearby Beyer Peacock, which built 153 locomotives during the same period and 'who from the outset had maintained a very friendly and profitable association with their next-door neighbours' (James Lowe). With the forthcoming London Extension, in 1895 it was arranged with Beyer Peacock that from January 1896 the firm would produce five engines per month (although some were partially constructed by the MSLR).

Harry Pollitt, who took over from Parker in 1893, based his Class '9G' 2-4-2T suburban tank design on his predecessor's Class '3' engines (see above), although the Joy valve gear gave way to Stephenson's, and they carried Belpaire boilers from new. As with the Class '3'/'F1s', the locomotives were fitted with the GCR No 2 Standard Belpaire boiler between 1909 and 1916.

Under LNER ownership the 'F2' 2-4-2Ts were progressively replaced by larger engines, and four were equipped with the company's vacuum mechanism to allow them to operate push-pull train services in East Anglia. Generally more widely dispersed than the 'F1s', the 'F2s' also operated services in the Manchester area, and sometimes deputised for Clayton and Sentinel railcars in Yorkshire and East Anglia.

Introduced 1898
Designed by Harry Pollitt
Built by Beyer Peacock
Number built 10
Number inherited by BR 9
Last example withdrawn December 1950

The first of the class was withdrawn in 1947, and the other nine enjoyed no more than 18 months in BR ownership. The last two, Nos 7108 and 7111, allocated to King's Cross shed, worked trains on the Alexandra Palace branch. Only one, No 67106, carried its allocated BR number, but for only four months, being withdrawn at the end of 1948.

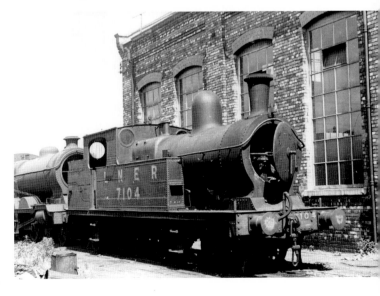

Ex-GCR 'F2' 2-4-2T No 7104 was withdrawn from Annesley shed in February 1949, and is seen here forlornly awaiting the scrapman at Dukinfield on 13 June. Beyond is ex-GCR 'B9' 4-6-0 No 61475, which had been withdrawn in May 1949. *H. C. Casserley*

GER J. Holden 'C32'/'F3' Class 2-4-2T

Nos 7114, 7115, 7117, 7119, 7124, 7126, 67127, 67128, 7134, 7139-41, 7143, 67149, 7150

Wilson Worsdell introduced the 2-4-2T type to the Great Eastern in 1884, and these were added to by James Holden in 1903-09 to form LNER Class 'F4'. Some of these were further modified by James's son Stephen from 1911, to form Class 'F5' (for both, see below). Meanwhile James had introduced his 'C32' Class in 1893, with 5ft 8in driving wheels as opposed to the 5ft 4in of the other two classes. Five batches of ten were built, two in 1893, one in 1894, another in 1895, and the final ten in 1902. The final batch were pressed to 160psi, rather than the 140psi of the earlier ones, although the latter were fitted with the higher-pressure boiler between 1903 and 1910. The front axle carried the greatest loading, so the coupled wheels had a tendency to slip.

Many of the 'C32s' were fitted with condensing gear in order to work services out of Liverpool Street and Southend, but as the engines moved away from the capital this was removed from the majority. Thereafter the class was mostly found on rural services in East Anglia.

> **Introduced** 1893
> **Designed by** James Holden
> **Built by** GER, Stratford
> **Number built** 50
> **Number inherited by BR** 15
> **Last example withdrawn** April 1953

'F3' 2-4-2T No 7137 languishes at Stratford on 7 February 1948, having been withdrawn the previous year, so narrowly avoiding becoming a working British Railways engine. *H. C. Casserley*

The LNER classified the engines 'F3', and withdrew the first in 1936, but after the war there were still 37 at work; 22 went on the eve of nationalisation in 1947, and the remaining 15 passed into BR ownership. Only three carried their allotted BR numbers and all but one had been dispensed with by the end of 1950. The sole survivor, No 67127, lasted until April 1953, having worked from Ipswich and Lowestoft sheds since 1949.

Interestingly, one lives on in the form of its boiler. The Midland & Great Northern Joint Railway Society bought Worsdell 'J15' 0-6-0 No 65462 (LNER No 7564) when the last of that class was withdrawn in 1962 and four were put aside for possible preservation. In 1966 the boiler was given two partial hydraulic tests to determine the condition of the tubes, and it was discovered that it dated from before 1893 and had once been carried by an 'F3' 2-4-2T.

GER J. Holden 'M15'/'F4' Class 2-4-2T

Nos 67151, 67152, 7153, 67154, 67155, 7158, 67157, 67158, 7159-61, 67162-67, 7168-70, 67171, 7172, 7173, 67174-78, 7179-81, 67182, 7183, 67184, 7185, 67186, 67187

> **Introduced** 1884/1903
> **Designed by** Thomas Worsdell/James Holden
> **Built by** GER, Stratford
> **Number built** 160
> **Number inherited by BR** 37
> **Last example withdrawn** June 1956

As mentioned above, after many years utilising the 0-4-4T type for light passenger work, the 2-4-2T type was introduced to the GER by Thomas Worsdell in 1884, drawing on his experience with his previous employer, the London & North Western Railway, and incorporating many design features that were to became characteristically 'Great Eastern'. Forty were built in three batches in 1884 and 1886 and, classified 'M15' by the GER, they worked branch-line and suburban passenger services. They used Joy's valve gear (Joy had been a friend and colleague of Worsdell at Crewe), which was less than ideal for the locomotives' role and was very difficult to 'set' correctly, resulting in a high coal consumption. They thus quickly gained the nickname 'Gobblers', and many had been taken out of service by the Grouping.

Worsdell left the GER in 1885 and moved to the North Eastern Railway, where he produced the NER's 'A' Class 2-4-2Ts, almost identical to the 'M15s'. His successor, James Holden, designed several classes of 0-6-0 and 0-4-4 tanks for similar duties, but in 1903, with the opening of the new line between

Woodford, Ilford and Seven Kings via Fairlop and Hainault, and with many of the early 0-4-4Ts nearing the end of their useful lives, he reverted to the 2-4-2T design and a further 120 'M15s' were built in ten batches, but this time with Stephenson valve gear and other detail modifications. This solved the coal consumption problem – but unfortunately the disparaging nickname stuck. By 1909 there were 160 engines of Worsdell and Holden origin, and between 1911 and 1920 30 were further rebuilt by Stephen Holden (see below).

Most of the 'M15s' were employed on London suburban services until supplanted by the Hill/Gresley 'L'/'N7' 0-6-2Ts from 1914 onwards. Eighty of them had condensing equipment in order to work the East London line, although it was removed before the Second World War, and all had Westinghouse brakes. They subsequently moved to East Anglia and, as LNER Class 'F4', three (BR Nos 67151, 67157 and 67164) were sent to Scotland in

'F4' 2-4-2T No 67157 was one of three of the class sent to Scotland by the LNER to work the Fraserburgh and St Combs branch, shedded at Kittybrewster. It was the last survivor of the class, being withdrawn in June 1956. It is seen here a couple of months later at Kilmarnock Works just prior to scrapping. Note the 'cowcatcher'. *K. C. H. Fairey, Colour-Rail*

the 1930s to work the former Great North of Scotland branch to Fraserburgh and St Combs, fitted with 'cowcatchers'. Two of them also had LNER vacuum-operated push-pull equipment from 1941. They were eventually replaced by BR Standard 2MTs.

During the Second World War 15 'F4s' (and a single 'F5') were loaned to the Army to haul armoured coastal defence units, being allocated to various locations between Kent and Scotland. They subsequently carried plaques to mark their war service.

The first of the original Worsdell 2-4-2Ts went as early as 1913, and 118 engines fell under LNER ownership in 1923. The rest of the unrebuilt engines were quickly disposed of, all having disappeared by 1929. Then the rebuilds were progressively withdrawn; there were 37 on the eve of nationalisation, but only 26 by the end of 1948. A handful survived until the mid-1950s, mostly in East Anglia, but one example, No 67157, managed to hold out until June 1956, shedded at Kittybrewster, Aberdeen.

GER S. Holden 'M15R'/'F5' Class 2-4-2T

Nos 67188-219

Between 1911 and 1920 James Holden's son Stephen followed his father by rebuilding 30 of the 'M15s' with higher-pressure boilers, to form Class 'M15R'; the LNER classified these 'F5'. Again Stephenson valve gear was used in preference to Joy's and, like the 'F4s', the engines initially worked London suburban services. Most had condensing equipment fitted, and some engines still carried it into LNER days. The last two numerically, BR Nos 67218 and 67219, were built with large side-window cabs along the lines of the 'F7' 'Crystal Palace Tanks' (see above) and the 'F6s' (see below), and were mistakenly classified 'F6' until BR rectified the mistake and included them in Class 'F5', bringing the class total to 32.

In 1929-30 the LNER fitted eight of the class with trip-cocks and shorter chimneys to enable them to be used over the electrified East London line; a further seven were similarly equipped later. The LNER had undertaken to work central London sub-surface lines should electricity supplies be interrupted during the war.

On becoming BR engines seven 'F5s' were fitted with vacuum-operated push-pull gear; five (Nos 67193, 67200, 67202, 67203 and 67213) were allocated to Epping to work the Epping-Ongar shuttle (fitted with trip-cock apparatus to work between Epping and Leyton), while Nos 67199 and 67218 went to Great Yarmouth; the latter engine subsequently joined the others at Epping, and in November 1957 hauled the last steam trains on the branch. Meanwhile the remaining 'F5s' continued

Stratford-based 'F5' 2-4-2T No 67213 was one of five engines used by the LNER to operate the Epping-Ongar shuttle, and is seen here at Epping on 11 October 1952. The fireman is dealing with coal in the bunker, watched by a smartly uniformed schoolboy. The intended new-build 'F5' would be ideal to return to this line, now the Epping Ongar Railway heritage line. *Colour-Rail collection*

to work smaller branches in the eastern counties. The class remained intact until 1955, when withdrawals began, and only five were still active by the end of 1957. The last three, Nos 67195, 67212 and 67214, were taken out of service together in May 1958; two had been Lowestoft/Great Yarmouth-based, while No 67212 had been a long-time Stratford resident.

No 'F4s' or 'F5s' were preserved, but a project has been launched by the Holden F5 Steam Locomotive Trust to build a new 'F5', one of the pair that carried the 'F6'-type cab. The main frames, smokebox and many other parts and components have been acquired or manufactured. The work is being undertaken by Tyseley Locomotive Works, and it is intended that the finished locomotive will be outshopped as No 789 in GER blue livery.

Introduced 1911	
Designed by Stephen Holden	
Built by GER, Stratford	
Number built 32	
Number inherited by BR 32	
Last example withdrawn May 1958	

GER S. Holden 'G69'/'F6' Class 2-4-2T

Nos 67220-39

As mentioned above, two of Stephen Holden's 'M15R' 2-4-2Ts, built in 1904, had cabs with side windows like their larger contemporaries, the Class 'G69' 2-4-2Ts, and the LNER classified them with the 'F6s'. British Railways only corrected this in December 1948, and the engines reverted to their correct 'F5' route availability after a period of some 35 years.

The 'G69' engines themselves were the last development of the GER 2-4-2T family, with increased water and coal capacity that raised their overall weight by some 3 tons. They were still very similar to Worsdell's originals and those rebuilt/built by Stephen's father James, apart from their distinctive large, high cabs. Two batches of ten each were built at Stratford between 1911 and 1912, and they were fitted with condensing gear (removed in 1936-38) and Westinghouse air brakes.

When the LNER inherited the class it reduced the cab height by about 7 inches to bring the engines within the company's new Composite Loading Gauge. The company also added vacuum ejectors to all but one locomotive in 1927. The locomotives spent virtually their entire lives working London suburban services (until displaced by the newer 'N7' 0-6-2Ts and, later, the Thompson 'L1' 2-6-4Ts), and on East Anglian rural services.

All 20 continued to work until the end of 1954, when dieselisation began to encroach on their rural duties. Half had gone within the next 12 months, and the last two examples, Nos 67227 and 67230, were dispensed with at Colchester and Stratford respectively in May 1958, together with their 'F5' cousins.

Introduced 1911	
Designed by Stephen Holden	
Built by GER, Stratford	
Number built 20	
Number inherited by BR 20	
Last example withdrawn May 1958	

'F6' 2-4-2T No 67221 is at home in the GER rural heartland in this undated view at Cressing, on the Bishops Stortford-Witham line. The tall, commodious cab was a distinctive feature of the class. Since 1948 No 67221 had been shedded variously at Cambridge, Bury St Edmunds and Kings Lynn, and was withdrawn from Stratford in October 1957. *G. W. Powell, Colour-Rail*

NER W. Worsdell 'O'/'G5' Class 0-4-4T

Nos 67240-84, 7285, 67286-305, 7306, 67307-49

As mentioned above, when Thomas W. Worsdell left the Great Eastern Railway to join the NER as its Locomotive Superintendent, he took with him the 2-4-2T design he had developed at Stratford and introduced it as the NER's Class 'A' (LNER 'F8'). When his younger brother Wilson succeeded him in 1890, he discarded the 2-4-2T arrangement and returned to an 0-4-4 tank engine design. This was his 'O' Class of 1894,

Introduced 1894	
Designed by Wilson Worsdell	
Built by NER, Darlington	
Number built 110	
Number inherited by BR 110	
Last example withdrawn December 1958	

which had smaller wheels than the 'F8' but more coal and water capacity; some of the bunkers incorporated hoppers.

Between 1894 and 1901 110 'Os' were built in seven batches of 10 or 20 engines. They were intended to replace Edward Fletcher's much earlier 'BTP' Class 0-4-4Ts (LNER 'G6'), which were converted to became 0-6-0Ts, classified by the LNER as 'J77' (qv). The 'Os' were never superheated.

The reliability of the design is demonstrated by the fact that no major changes were made to the locomotives until they

Although otherwise exclusively North East England engines, in BR days three 'G5' 0-4-4Ts found themselves in North East Scotland, and two more were shedded at Stratford, then Cambridge from July 1951. One of that pair, No 67279, is seen at Audley End with a train of ancient stock on 9 June 1956; it was withdrawn that November. *Colour-Rail collection*

were inherited by the LNER, which made some modifications to the boiler after 1930 and again in 1937. They were robust workhorses and enjoyed a long career throughout the North East of England, on both rural branch lines and suburban services, with a good turn of speed when necessary. Some moved south in the 1930s to work the former GER Seven Sisters-Palace Gates branch.

They became LNER Class 'G5', and in pre-war days many were replaced by steam railcars. As a branch-line economy measure, and to extend their useful lives, 21 were fitted with LNER vacuum-operated push-pull equipment from 1937.

The class entered BR ownership in 1948 intact, but No 7306 was withdrawn in June without carrying its BR number; all but one of the remainder subsequently carried BR numbers, and it was only in 1952 that the class total dropped below 100.

Thereafter withdrawals were regular. Twenty-two were still extant at the end of 1957, and in July of that year No 67338 was used for a series of tests in Yorkshire on the durability of concrete sleepers following derailments. The last 11 were withdrawn en bloc during the last month of the following year, having been replaced by incoming diesel railcars and multiple units.

Although no example of the class was saved from the scrapyard, a replica of original class member No 1759 is being constructed by the Class G5 Locomotive Company for use on heritage railways, particularly in the North East, such as the Weardale, Wensleydale and Aln Valley lines, as well as main-line use. It will make an economical locomotive for smaller preserved railways, yet with considerable pulling power. As the group points out, the 'G5' was designed specifically for branch-line use so will comfortably handle four or five bogie coaches.

GNR Ivatt 'C2'/'C12' Class 4-4-2T

Nos 67350, 7351, 67352-54, 7355, 67356, 67357, 7358, 7359, 67360-69, 7370, 67371-76, 7377, 7378, 67379-87, 7388, 67389-95, 67397, 67398, 7399

Introduced 1898	
Designed by Henry Ivatt	
Built by GNR, Doncaster	
Number built 60	
Number inherited by BR 49	
Last example withdrawn December 1958	

Ivatt took over the reins at Doncaster in 1896, and one of his first designs was the 'C2' 'Atlantic' tank, reversing the 0-4-4T trend set by Sturrock and Stirling. The first ten were ordered from 'The Plant' at the end of 1897, intended for suburban duties in West Yorkshire. They proved very successful, and a further 50 emerged in five batches of ten between 1899 and 1907, to undertake similar duties in the London suburban area, replacing older and less powerful Stirling 0-4-4Ts.

The GNR numbered them 1009A, 1010, 1013-20 and 1501-50. The first locomotive, No 1009, was fitted with a rigid type of trailing axle, but the more successful and flexible 'radial truck' design was fitted to subsequent engines. The boiler was an Ivatt standard, complete with dome.

The last 50 of the class, built for use in London, had shorter chimneys and domes than the others, and also carried condensing gear, allowing them to operate over the Metropolitan 'Widened Lines'. (The GNR had invested heavily in the 'Widened Lines', and initially provided what was possibly the largest number of classes that could work over that sub-surface system.) The earlier engines also had square-shaped water tanks and bunkers, while later ones were distinguished by their rounded tank ends and bunkers with flared tops (later fitted to the earlier members). As London suburban traffic increased, the 'C12s' were displaced from the heavier trains by

larger 0-8-2Ts (LNER Class 'R1') from 1903, which in turn were replaced by Ivatt's well-known 'N1' 0-6-2Ts from 1907 onwards and Gresley's 'N2s' of the same wheel arrangement from 1920.

Thereafter the class moved out to the country, with the condensing equipment removed. In LNER days, now as Class 'C12', the locomotives worked mainly in West Yorkshire and Lincolnshire, although Hitchin had some for London services, and others were allocated to Hull (Botanic Gardens) to replace 'G5' 0-4-4Ts. Two were employed as station pilots at Peterborough North. In 1937 two went to Yarmouth Beach shed to work over the former M&GNJR system. Engines working on former GER lines in the Cambridge area handled trains to Saffron Walden, Sudbury and Colchester, and branch services between Swaffham and Thetford, and from Bury St Edmunds to Long Melford.

Some 15 or so 'C12s' found themselves allocated to Peterborough's New England shed at some time, especially towards the end of their lives. One of them was No 67365, seen here at Stamford Town station on the former Midland Railway Peterborough-Melton Mowbray line on 11 April 1957. 'C12s' worked the former GNR branch from Essendine to Stamford East, but after the latter station closed in 1957 trains used the Town station. No 67365 was withdrawn in May 1958, and the GNR Stamford branch closed just over a year later. *Colour-Rail collection*

Ten 'C12s' had been withdrawn by the end of the war, and were therefore not included in the post-war LNER renumbering scheme. Thus the remaining 50 were given a sequential number series, 7350-99. During the war members of the class could be seen around Manchester working services to Wigan, Warrington and Chester, although they were not popular with ex-GCR men.

No more engines were lost until 1947, when No 7396 was withdrawn, so just 49 passed into BR's books. In 1948-49 five were fitted with push-pull gear to operate branch-line services from King's Cross to Alexandra Palace, from Bulwell Common to Annesley on the former GCR, and from King's Lynn to South Lynn. Nonetheless, withdrawals continued steadily until just 16 survived at the end of 1957, and all had gone in 12 months.

GCR Robinson '9K'/'C13' Class 4-4-2T

Nos 67400-67439

The '9K' 'Atlantic' tanks were Robinson's first suburban tank design for the Great Central, aimed to satisfy growing suburban traffic requirements; they were graced with the elegant lines so characteristic of Robinson's locomotives, and are also considered to have been one of his most successful and long-lived products, some remaining in service for nearly six decades. The design was based on Harry Pollitt's '9G' 2-4-2T of 1898 (LNER Class 'F2' – qv), with extended firebox and smokebox. It was also very similar to a smaller 4-4-2T that Robinson had designed during his previous employment on the Waterford, Limerick & Western Railway in Ireland.

Forty locomotives were built in four batches by the Vulcan Foundry in 1903 and the GCR itself at its Gorton Works in 1903-05. The tanks held 1,450 gallons of water, and the bunker 4 tons of coal, producing a considerable all-up weight of more than 66 tons. They were turned out in GCR passenger green. Only one was superheated by the GCR, although the LNER fitted superheaters to the remainder between 1926 and 1935, when these attractive engines, by then classified 'C13', were disfigured by having their graceful Robinson chimneys and domes shortened to suit the new LNER loading gauge. The different combinations of chimneys, domes and boilers gave rise to three sub-classes.

Their intended duties were suburban and branch-line passenger trains, and they began their careers working in and out of London Marylebone station until replaced by the larger '9N' (LNER 'A5') 4-6-2 tanks of 1911-23, better able to compete with the spread of electric trains in North West London. By

Introduced 1903
Designed by John Robinson
Built by Vulcan Foundry (12), GCR, Gorton (28)
Number built 40
Number inherited by BR 40
Last example withdrawn January 1960

1922 they were to be seen more in the North West of England, on the former Cheshire Lines system and former GCR lines around Manchester, and especially in the Wrexham area, where they coped easily on the steep Welsh inclines. These versatile locos also handled suburban traffic around Sheffield, Nottingham and Doncaster

As the GCR installed water troughs in the same year that construction of the class began, they were fitted with scoops, but the equipment was rarely being used by the early 1930s and had been removed by 1935. In 1933 the LNER fitted six C13s with the GCR mechanically operated push-pull system, replaced by the LNER's own vacuum-operated gear in 1941.

In the mid-1930s the 'C13s' replaced the 'F1' 2-4-2Ts on suburban Manchester services, continuing to handle them into BR days, and proving superior even to later LMS 2-6-4 tanks.

The class remained intact until 1952, but only ten were left at the close of 1957, displaced by the spread of diesel trains after 1955. One example, No 67417, soldiered on alone from Gorton shed until January 1960.

Although more widely dispersed in later years, three 'C13' 4-4-2 tanks were allocated to Neasden in BR days to handle London suburban traffic. One of them was No 67418, seen here at the former Metropolitan Railway terminus at Chesham in June 1956. These engines worked the branch until Ivatt 2-6-2Ts took over, then the branch was electrified in 1960. Note the ancient push-pull compartment stock. No 67418 was withdrawn in December 1958. *L. V. Reason, Colour-Rail*

GCR Robinson '9L'/'C14' Class 4-4-2T

Nos 67440-51

The '9Ks' (LNER 'C13' – see above) 'gave a good account of themselves' according to George Dow, so in 1907 a heavier version was ordered from Beyer Peacock & Co, weighing in at some 70 tons. Twelve '9Ls' were built, in most respects similar to the '9K' design but with increased water and coal capacity; the side tanks were deeper and wider (projecting outwards of the cab), the bunker bigger, and the coal rails followed the shape of the raised bunker end plate to maintain a good view when running in reverse. They went into service on residential trains on the GC&GW line, working into and out of London Marylebone. In common with the company's mixed-traffic engines, they were painted black with stylish outlining in red and white.

All were built with saturated boilers, although one was superheated in 1914; as with the 'C13s', no further engines were thus treated until after the Grouping, the process being completed by 1935. Again, water scoops were fitted from new, but removed in the early 1930s. Like the 'C13s', the tall GCR-profile chimneys were replaced with shorter ones and lower domes by the LNER. Different variations of chimney and dome height and superheating led to three sub-classes until 1937, by which time all members of the class were standardised.

The 'C14s' all operated from Neasden shed until the 'A5' Pacific 'tanks arrived; in 1912-13 they moved away to work stopping

The last of the 12 'C14' 4-4-2Ts, No 67450, stands out of use, a sack covering the chimney, at Gorton in September 1959; it was officially withdrawn the following January. The higher cab roof, large bunker and projecting side tank distinguish it from a 'C13'. On the right is Robinson 'A5' 4-6-2 tank No 69817, of a class that replaced the 'C14s' in the London area; this engine was withdrawn from Gorton in April 1960. *P. J. Hughes, Colour-Rail*

passenger services along the GCR main line. By 1922 all but one were based around Nottingham (the other being at Woodford).

In 1934 four engines went to Bury St Edmunds temporarily, and later eight were allocated to Ipswich. Wartime saw them even further afield, at King's Lynn, Cambridge, Norwich, West Yorkshire and Manchester, proving efficient and popular in their new homes.

'N1' 0-6-2Ts displaced the 'C14s' from Yorkshire, and they moved to Gorton, where they worked Manchester area services alongside the 'C13s'. However, like their close cousins they were increasingly replaced by new diesel units and, having remained intact right through to 1957, the class had all been consigned to the scrapyard by the beginning of 1960, the last survivor being withdrawn from Gorton in January.

Introduced 1907
Designed by John Robinson
Built by Beyer Peacock
Number built 12
Number inherited by BR 12
Last example withdrawn January 1960

NBR Reid 'M'/'C15' Class 4-4-2T

Nos 67452-60, 7461, 67462-64, 7465, 67466-69, 7470, 7471, 67472-81

A leading bogie returned to North British Railway locomotives when Reid introduced his Class 'M' 'Atlantic' tanks in 1911, although this was a wheel arrangement that generally seems to have found little favour for tank engines north of the border. Thirty engines were built by the Yorkshire Engine Co of Meadowhall Works, Sheffield, in three batches of 11, 9 and 10, one in each year of 1911 to 1913. This was an unusually high number for an NBR passenger engine. Reid used the same boiler as for his 0-4-4T 'G9'

Two of the 'C15' 'Atlantic' tanks, shedded at Eastfield, spent their last days working local services between Craigendoran and Arrochar for several years after the demise of the rest of the class. Here No 67460 makes a spirited departure from Arrochar heading for Craigendoran on 19 September 1959. The pair were replaced by diesel railcars in 1960, and were scrapped in May.
Dave Cobbe collection, Railphotoprints

Introduced 1911
Designed by William Reid
Built by Yorkshire Engine
Number built 30
Number inherited by BR 30
Last example withdrawn April 1960

design of 1909, but a trailing axle was added to allow an increase in water and coal capacity. Because of their origin, the locomotives were known by the men as 'Yorkshire Tanks', or simply 'Yorkies'.

Their first task was handling suburban and stopping services between Edinburgh and Glasgow, as well as trains along the Clyde Coast. A new standard boiler was fitted from 1921, but none were superheated. In LNER days the 'C15s' gave way to new 'N2' 0-6-2Ts and 'V1' 2-6-2Ts (see below), and moved away to other parts of the former North British system.

In 1940 No 9135 (later No 7460/67460) gained vacuum-operated push-pull equipment in order to work between Craigendoran and Arrochar. In 1950 No 67475 (the former No 9016/7475) was similarly equipped and, after being withdrawn in April 1954, No 67474 took over, gaining the equipment that September. This ensured that the pair would outlive their sister 'C15's, working until April 1960 when they were replaced by diesel railbuses.

Meanwhile, many of the other 'C15s' were stored by BR or used as stationary boilers at, for example, Bo'ness Creosote Works and the M&EE's depot at Burntisland. The first example was withdrawn at the end of 1952 and, apart from the two push-pull engines, all had been sent for scrap by April 1956.

NBR Reid 'L'/'C16' Class 4-4-2T

Nos 67482-502

Between 1915 and 1921 21 further 4-4-2 tanks were built, but these had larger cylinders with piston instead of slide valves, a slightly higher-pitched boiler (necessitating a shorter chimney and dome) with – at last – Robinson-pattern superheaters (although one had a saturated boiler temporarily fitted by the LNER between 1943 and 1947). They also had a greater coal and water capacity, making the engines some 4 tons heavier. The North British Locomotive Co's Atlas Works turned out the first 15 in 1915-16, and a further half-dozen in 1921.

The first ten replaced the 'C15s' on heavier trains in the Glasgow area, continuing to do likewise elsewhere on the system, being shedded at, for example, North Berwick, St Margarets and Dunbar. From 1917 they were also able to be fitted with snowploughs for working the Peebles line from Galashiels.

In 1951 two members of the class were fitted with spark arrestors for working near the Rosslyn Castle gunpowder works, south of Edinburgh.

In early BR days the 'C16s' were found further afield at such places as Dundee, Dunfermline and Aberdeen as the older

Formerly allocated to Eastfield, 'C16' 4-4-2T No 67500 moved to Parkhead in November 1951, where it was photographed on 2 June 1957. It was finally withdrawn in October 1959.
T. B. Owen, Colour-Rail

Introduced 1915
Designed by William Reid
Built by North British
Number built 21
Number inherited by BR 21
Last example withdrawn April 1961

'C15s' were withdrawn, but they were themselves gradually put out of work by the 'V1' 2-6-2Ts (see below). The first engine to be withdrawn was No 67498 in August 1955, and eight were withdrawn in March/April 1960, as their fellow 'C15s' became extinct. Just three saw 1961, and the last, No 67485, a long-time Eastfield resident, went in April of that year.

Towards the end of 1954 No 67488 found fame when it appeared in the British Lion film *Geordie*, released in 1955, working near Gartmore on the Aberfoyle branch. Another 'C16', No 67499, withdrawn in November 1955, was overturned to demonstrate a German hydraulic re-railing apparatus, which was subsequently purchased by BR's Scottish Region.

LNER Gresley 'V1'/'V3' Class 2-6-2T

Nos 67600-91

The 2-6-2 'Prairie' tank design will forever be associated with the Great Western Railway since its introduction on that company's lines in 1903, and was not seen on the LNER until 1930. Since 1928 there had been plans for such a design to work the Metropolitan 'Widened Lines', based on Gresley's 'K1' 2-6-0 but utilising three cylinders, the central one using the designer's patented conjugated valve gear.

However, the derailment of Southern Railway 'River' Class 2-6-4T No 800 *River Cray* near Sevenoaks in 1927 had cast doubt upon the stability of large tank engine designs at speed, and the whole SR class had been withdrawn and rebuilt as 2-6-0 tender engines. As a result Gresley carried out tests that proved the stability of his own design, and the 'V1s' were put into production.

By the end of 1928 the destination of the new class had been changed to Scotland, to replace Scottish-based 'N2' 0-6-2Ts and

Introduced 1930 ('V3' 1939)
Designed by Nigel Gresley
Built by LNER, Doncaster
Number built 92
Number inherited by BR 92
Last example withdrawn November 1964

NBR 'Atlantic' tanks. Eighty-two engines were ordered between early 1929 and the end of 1936, emerging between September 1930 and early 1939, some of the early batches being delayed by shortage of money. A further 25 examples were authorised in 1940-41, but the order was cancelled in 1943.

The boiler was superheated, and the leading truck was the same type as used on the 'K3' 2-6-0, while the trailing pony truck was the radial type as used on the 'N2' 0-6-2Ts.

In 1936 the LNER's North East Area considered increasing the boiler pressure from 180psi to 200psi, to provide greater power and higher acceleration, and ten further engines were built to that form in 1939, being classified 'V3'. The LNER also began to rebuild the 'V1s' with the higher boiler pressure, and four had been so treated by 1948. BR continued the process, until a total of 73 had been built as such or converted.

The first 28 'V1s', built in 1930-31, worked suburban trains around Edinburgh, Glasgow and Helensburgh, and eventually more than 40 were handling Scottish suburban services. In the mid-1930s 25 worked in the North Eastern Area, replacing former NER Class 'A8' 4-6-2 tanks of 1913-22 and working particularly on Newcastle-Middlesbrough services. After the Second World War some restrictions were eased on the challenging coast line through Whitby and Scarborough, allowing the 'V1s' to work it successfully.

A brace of Heaton-based ex-LNER 2-6-2Ts, Nos 67652 and 67647, stand at Newcastle in 1956. Both were built as 'V1s' in 1936 and 1935 respectively, and No 67652 was uprated to 'V3' form in October 1952. No 67647 would follow suit in December 1959. Both were taken out of service during 1963. *Dave Cobbe collection, Railphotoprints*

Other 'V1s' were allocated to Stratford, Norwich and King's Lynn until replaced in London by Thompson 'L1s' of 1945-50. The total of 92 engines, in varying proportions of 'V1s' and V3s', remained intact until 1960, by which time there were 20 'V1s' left – all had gone by the end of 1962. The 'V3s', meanwhile, lived on for a further two years, the last 11 being withdrawn in one fell swoop in November 1964, the advent of diesel railcars taking over their passengers duties. Some had been put on parcels and empty stock trains until replaced by new Type 2 diesel-electrics.

LNER Thompson 'L1' Class 2-6-4T

Nos 67701-800

The Great Central Railway inside-cylinder '1B' Class tanks designed by Robinson in 1914 were the first 2-6-4Ts in Britain, and were classified 'L1' by the LNER (qv). All 20 were still in service in 1945 when Thompson's prototype engine of the same wheel arrangement, but with outside cylinders, emerged from 'The Plant' in May 1945. It was numbered 9000 and was the only LNER tank engine ever painted in LNER apple green livery. That year the GCR 'L1s' were reclassified 'L3' to release the 'L1' classification for Thompson's new engines.

Thompson's standardisation plan of 1941 originally listed the 'V3' 2-6-2T (qv above) as the standard heavy passenger tank engine, replacing the older GCR 'A5' 'Pacific' tanks and some of the 'N2' and 'N5' 0-6-2Ts. However, by 1945 it was felt necessary to

Introduced 1945
Designed by Edward Thompson
Built by LNER, Doncaster (1), BR, Darlington (29), North British (35), Robert Stephenson & Hawthorns (35)
Number built 100
Number inherited by BR 100
Last example withdrawn December 1962

'L1' 2-6-4T No 67741 hurries two 'Quad-art' sets of articulated compartment coaches along the East Coast Main Line near Hadley Wood in 1951 when less than two years old. It was a Hitchin engine at the time, and was one of the last 21 of the class withdrawn en bloc in December 1962, in this case from Colwick. *E. Oldham, Colour-Rail*

replace the 'V3' with a new, more powerful two-cylinder variant 2-6-2T. Further 'V3' orders were cancelled in 1943, and the Running Department was asking for a modern 2-6-4T locomotive. The boiler was based on that of the 'V3' but with a larger firebox, and the water tanks were to be longer, but could not be wider without affecting the boiler diameter. The front pony truck was a Thompson spring design, and the rear bogie was similar to that of the contemporary 'A1/1'. 'Thirty of the new 2-6-4Ts were ordered in April 1944, and the first, No 9000, appeared a year later 1945. An order for the production locomotives – 110 were planned – was also placed in 1944, but the first 29 did not emerge until after the nationalisation of the railways in 1948, following thorough and extensive trials using the prototype on varied duties. These trials were deemed to be successful, apart from an inevitable lack of braking on heavy goods trains (there being no tender brakes). The order was subsequently reduced to 100, the remainder being supplied by outside contractors.

The first 16 were by now numbered 9000-15, but in April/May 1948 they were renumbered 67701-16, and new engines were subsequently numbered in that sequence, freeing the 69xxx numbers for other classes.

When the engines entered service the reaction was mixed. They were the most powerful 2-6-4Ts to run in Britain, but their relatively small 5ft 2in wheels were more suited to slow, heavy goods work than the suburban passenger services with frequent stops for which they were primarily designed. The axleboxes and moving parts were therefore prone to overheating, the cabs were found to be draughty until modifications were made, and the welded side tanks tended to leak. Various 'fixes' were tried to cure the problems with axlebox wear, but without success. The engines required very careful handling by the crews, and the loud clanking noise they produced earned them the nickname 'Cement Mixers'.

The first 30 were allocated to Stratford, Neasden and Hull (Botanic Gardens). By the time the last was delivered in the autumn of 1950 they were to be found at Stratford, Neasden and Ipswich, as well as King's Cross, Hornsey, Hitchin, Norwich, Lowestoft, Darlington and Hull, primarily handling suburban and stopping passenger services; there were also occasional express passenger and freight duties. Replacing many elderly tank locomotive classes, they were themselves quickly displaced by the spread of diesel multiple units and electrification. The oldest was barely 12 years old when withdrawals began in 1960, brought about by electrification of the lines out of Liverpool Street, and the 100 had been quickly reduced to 21 by the autumn of the following year. Those engines had mostly congregated at Colwick and Ardsley, and they were all dispensed with that December.

GER Neilson '209'/'Y5' Class 0-4-0ST

No 8081

These tiny saddle tanks were a standard Neilson & Co design, and four were built for the Great Eastern Railway in 1874-76. They had a short wheelbase, ideal for locations with tight curves. The GER itself built four more to a modified design with a covered cab, steam brakes and a higher boiler pressure, and these entered service in 1897 (two) and 1903 (two). They were used for shunting in the goods yards at Devonshire Street and Canning Town in East London, as well as at Colchester, Lowestoft Harbour and Stratford Carriage Works.

The engines had unusually shaped saddle tanks with flat tops, and the coal bunker was atop the boiler between the tank and the cab. Because this space was inadequate, coal was often also stored along the running plate, and even on the tank.

The two 1897 engines (GER Nos 209 and 210) were scrapped in 1911, and one of the Neilson originals followed in 1914; these

Introduced	1874
Designed by	Neilson & Co
Built by	Neilson (4), GER, Stratford (4)
Number built	8
Number inherited by BR	1
Last example withdrawn	April 1948

replaced by the more powerful 'Y4' 0-4-0Ts (qv) of 1913. No 229 of 1876 was sold to the Admiralty in 1918, and the four remaining engines entered LNER ownership. Three were withdrawn between 1926 and 1931, but No 230 of 1903 (later No 7230, then 8081) survived as a shunter at Stratford Carriage Works until the early months of 1948, nicknamed the 'Coffee Pot'.

The Admiralty engine has survived. Used at the National Shipyard in Chepstow at the end of the First World War, it remained there until sold in 1982. After cosmetic restoration it was put on display at the North Woolwich Old Station Museum in 1984. When that closed in 2008 it moved to a new location near Lydney in the Forest of Dean, where it is currently awaiting restoration to working order.

One 'Y5' 0-4-0ST survived as a shunter at Stratford Works until withdrawn in early 1948. Ten years earlier, on 12 March 1938, No 7230 (later No 8081) of 1903 is seen in the smart lined black livery that it carried to the end. Kept in sparkling condition, it was frequently displayed at LNER exhibitions throughout the 1930s. Note the coal stored on the running plate and on top of the tank as well as in the tiny 'bunker'! *H. C. Casserley*

GER T. Worsdell 'G15'/'Y6' Class 0-4-0T tram engine

Nos 68082, 68083

Introduced 1883
Designed by Thomas Worsdell
Built by GER, Stratford
Number built 10
Number inherited by BR 2
Last example withdrawn November 1952

The inner workings of 'Y6' 0-4-0T tram engine No 68082 are revealed in Stratford Works on 30 June 1948, presumably during an overhaul. Note the controls fitted at both ends. *H. C. Casserley*

The GER's Wisbech & Upwell Tramway was a roadside line built to transport agricultural produce out and bring coal in. It opened to Outwell Basin in 1883 and thrived until road transport undermined its role. A Beeching casualty, it was to have closed in 1962, but managed to survive until 23 May 1966.

To operate the line the GER built three 0-4-0T tram locomotives (Nos 130-32), classified 'G15'. There were six passenger trains a day in each direction, initially limited to 8mph (later 14mph). The engines had to comply with Board of Trade rules that required speed restrictions, controls at both ends (and on both sides in these engines), and the fitting of a warning bell, cowcatchers and steel side aprons over the wheels. The safety valves discharged into a receiver that muffled any noise, so as not to frighten horses! The two small inside cylinders drove wheels that were just 3ft 1in in diameter. The overall wooden body gave the engines something of the appearance of a brake van. Westinghouse brakes were fitted in 1891.

Two further engines were constructed in 1885 (Nos 128-29) to operate the Yarmouth Union street tramway (which linked the town's quays with the Beach station), then five more were built for the Wisbech line, three in 1891-92 and two in 1897 (with higher-pressure boilers). However, the weight of traffic was such that more powerful motive power was required, and the 'G53' Class tram engines (LNER 'J70' – qv) appeared in 1903. Four 'G15s' were duly retired between 1909 and 1913.

In LNER days '7' or '07' was added as a prefix to the GER numbers, and the engines were reclassified 'Y6'. Individual members could now also be found at Ipswich, and at Neasden, possibly assisting with work on the British Empire Exhibition at Wembley. One of them even took part in the 1925 Stockton & Darlington Centenary procession.

During the war two 'Y6s' were loaned out to help with the war effort, and by the time of the LNER's 1943 renumbering these were the only two still in service, now Nos 8081 and 8082. They were renumbered again as 8082 and 8083 in 1946, and became BR engines two years later, as Nos 68082 and 68083. The former was withdrawn from Wisbech shed in May 1951, and the latter from March in November 1952. No 68083 was put aside for preservation, and was stored in Stratford Paint Shop for about a year; sadly, it was eventually cut up.

Although passenger trains had ceased in 1927, freight traffic on the Wisbech line continued to flourish, and by 1949 eight trains left Upwell on weekdays, and three on Saturdays during the fruit season. Unfortunately, by the early 1960s

No 68082 is seen from the same angle at Wisbech on 25 August 1950, with its brake-van-like body refitted, but no side-skirts or cowcatchers (propped against the wall on the right?). It was withdrawn in May the following year. *H. C. Casserley*

there was only one daily service. Two Drewry shunters (BR Class 04) had taken over in 1952, making the branch Britain's first all-diesel-operated line!

The Nene Valley Railway heritage line had planned to build a replica of a 'Y6' to represent 'Toby the Tram Engine' from Rev W. Awdry's 'Railway Stories' (although the original 'Toby' was inspired by a 'J70' 0-6-0T – qv). It was to be based on a Belgian Cockerill 0-4-0 tram engine, discovered near Brussels in 1987. Much work was done, but the project subsequently stalled through lack of finance, and the deaths of the two members who had brought the Belgian engine to Wansford.

NER T. Worsdell 'K'/'Y8' Class 0-4-0T

Nos 8090, 8091 (55)

In 1888 T. W. Worsdell introduced his Class 'H' 0-4-0 tanks, 19 of which were built between then and 1923. They became LNER Class 'Y7', and two survived to enter BR stock as Nos 68088 and 68089. No 68088 became a Departmental engine at Stratford Works, and after withdrawal in December 1952 was preserved.

Two years later Worsdell designed an even smaller version for use as a dock tank. This was the NER Class 'K', and was Thomas's last design for the company prior to his retirement in 1890. They engines originally had 'marine'-type boilers (with the grate located within a cylindrical flue), but these were replaced with more conventional tubed boilers in 1902-04.

The five engines, numbered 559-63, were specifically designed for dock work at Hull, and there they stayed into LNER days (apart from temporary loans elsewhere on war work). They were the smallest steam engines ever to work on the LNER – with 3-foot-diameter wheels and a weight of just 15½ tons – and possessed no coal bunker as such; the small amount of coal required was stored in a bin at the back of the footplate.

The Depression years of the mid-1930s saw three of the 'Y8s' scrapped due to lack of work and the increased use of Sentinel shunters. The survivors, now Class 'Y8' Nos 559 and 560, were renumbered 8090 and 8091 at the 1946 renumbering, and both duly passed into BR ownership, but not long enough to carry

LNER 'Y8' 0-4-0T No 8091 was shed pilot at York (50A) for several years and is seen there on 3 October 1948. Note the improvised coal storage arrangements, there being no bunker! It never carried its BR number 68091, but in 1954 was renumbered 55, and its side tank carried the legend 'Departmental Locomotive No 55'. It lasted in that role until scrapped in November 1956. *H. C. Casserley*

their allotted BR numbers of 68090/91. No 8090 was withdrawn in November 1948, but its sister became a Departmental engine and, numbered 55, worked as shed pilot at York (50A) for several years until it, too, was dispensed with in 1956.

Interestingly, between 1942 and 1946 No 8091 acquired the chime whistle from Gresley 'A4' 'Pacific' No 4469 *Sir Ralph Wedgwood*, which was damaged beyond repair during an air raid on York in June 1942.

It is thought that the museum at Beamish might be considering building a replica 'Y8', whose small size and 'marine'-type boiler would be ideal for the museum's short demonstration line.

Introduced 1890	
Designed by Thomas Worsdell	
Built by NER, Gateshead	
Number built 5	
Number inherited by BR 2	
Last example withdrawn November 1956	

GER Hill 'B74'/'Y4' Class 0-4-0T

Introduced 1913	
Designed by Alfred Hill	
Built by GER, Stratford	
Number built 5	
Number inherited by BR 5	
Last example withdrawn December 1963	

Nos 68125-29

Just one of these chunky, square-set tanks was built in 1913, to replace the much smaller Class '209' (LNER 'Y5' – qv) saddle tanks for shunting at Canning Town, East London. No 227 was a very powerful engine for its size, possibly the most powerful British four-wheel locomotive. It was, for example, more than three times more powerful than the NER 'Y8' just considered, was more than twice as heavy, but had the same wheelbase of

The 'Y4' 0-4-0T was a big engine on small wheels, ideal for dock and yard shunting. No 68125 was the first of the five to be built, in 1913, and is seen here at Stratford on 14 November 1954. It originally had toolboxes on top of each tank, but subsequently, like the later-built examples, carried a single toolbox on the left-hand running plate. Note also the coal rails added to increase the carrying capacity atop the firebox! No 68125 was taken out of service in September 1956. *T. B. Owen, Colour-Rail*

just 6 feet! Four more 'B74s' were subsequently built, two in 1914 (Nos 226 and 228), and two in 1921 (Nos 229 and 210); the latter pair were lower in height for working in the Bethnal Green area, and the first two were similarly treated in 1931. Their lives were spent shunting in the Stratford area, including the yards at Canning Town, Devonshire Street, Blackwall Docks and Mile End, where substantial power was required but curves were tight.

The engines had Belpaire boilers and, unusually, outside Walschaerts valve gear. They had no coal bunker, but there was a small coal storage area at the rear of the left-hand tank, and coal was also often carried on top of the firebox. BR added some coal rails to increase the carrying capacity.

Apparently, when driven at speed the engines used to adopt a 'plunging' action, made worse by poor-quality track; this often damaged the low-hanging cylinder drain cocks, which frequently had to be replaced.

In LNER days, as Class 'Y4', they were renumbered 7226-29, with 7210 in Departmental stock. In 1946 they were renumbered again, becoming 8125-29 respectively. They all survived into BR days, becoming Nos 68125-29. No 68129, the Departmental engine No 7210/8129, became No 33 in September 1952, employed at Stratford Works. All were shedded at Stratford, and while the other four were withdrawn between September 1955 and October 1957, No 33 lived on until December 1963, being scrapped early the following year.

LNER Sentinel 'Y3' Class 0-4-0T

Nos 8154, 68155, 68156, 8157, 8158-60, 8161, 68162-66, 8167, 8168, 68169, 68171, 8172, 8173, 68174, 8175-78, 68179-85

Introduced 1927
Designed by Sentinel
Built by Sentinel
Number built 32
Number inherited by BR 31
Last example withdrawn May 1964

Between 1923 and 1957 the Sentinel Waggon Works built some 850 steam locomotives for railways at home and abroad. In 1930 the LMS bought four of the company's 'CE' ('Central Engine') design (qv Nos 47180-83), but the LNER was by far the largest user of the type. The design was based on the Sentinel steam lorry, with the same type of vertical boiler and chain-driven wheels (which had no harmful 'hammer-blow' effect on the rails, ideal for lightly laid track).

The first to be acquired, between 1925 and 1933, were 15 single-speed machines, classified 'Y1' by the LNER and intended for use at Lowestoft harbour. Several went on to become Departmental locomotives, and one, BR No 68153 (Departmental loco No 54 from 1954 until withdrawal in 1961), has been preserved.

Between 1927 and 1931 the LNER also purchased a total of 32 of Sentinel's 'CEDG' ('Centre Engine, Double-Geared') locomotives, which had two gear speeds. Classified 'Y3', they were numbered 18, 21, 23, 35, 42, 49, 55, 60-65, 78, 81, 86, 87, 90, 94, 96, 98, 117, 148, 154, 155, 172, 189, 192, 193, and 196-98. They had a complex design of water-tube vertical boiler (allowing quick steam-raising), with an inner firebox. The two vertical cylinders were connected by a common crankshaft to camshafts that allowed the steam 'cut-off' to be set. A superheater was fitted into the top of the firebox, and coal was fed in from the top. A chain connected sprockets on the crankshaft to sprockets on each of the two axles. A spur wheel

allowed the working sprocket set to be changed, but only while the engine was stationary. Low gear, providing a maximum speed of 13½mph, would be used for shunting, while high gear was used for working a short train or running light at up to 36½mph.

All but one of the 'Y3s' passed into BR ownership and were numbered 68154-69 and 68171-85 (although some never carried their BR number). Between 1952 and 1956 ten of the Sentinels (Nos 68160/62/65/66/68/73/77/78/81/83) passed into Departmental stock following withdrawal from normal duties, and were numbered 57, 21, 5, 7, 38, 40, 41, 42, 3 and 8 respectively. (Until 1952 service locomotives retained their original numbers, but thereafter they were numbered in a new sequence from 1 to 59, and included examples from more than ten different LNER classes.) Two other 'Y3s' were sold into industrial service, one of which survived until 1962. The last Departmental loco, No 68166 (No 7), survived until 1964.

The last of the two-speed Sentinel 'Y3' engines was No 68166 (originally No 49 of 1930). It had worked at Boston Sleeper Depot until March 1953, when it was renumbered 7 in Departmental stock, and is seen here at Doncaster. It was withdrawn in May 1964. *Historical Model Railway Society, Colour-Rail collection*

LNER 'Super Sentinel' 'Y10' Class 0-4-0T

Nos 8186, 8187

In November 1929 the LNER purchased two unusual Sentinel 'DEDG' ('Double-Engined, Double-Geared') 0-4-0 locomotives, which became Class 'Y10'. They were to be used on the Wisbech & Upwell Tramway, and like their simpler predecessors, the 'Y6' Sentinels (qv), they were fitted with cowcatchers and sideplates covering the motion. Once again they featured a chain drive and a two-speed gearbox, although the ratios could only be changed when the locomotive was stationary. They were delivered in June 1930, and numbered 8403 and 8404.

Although four-wheelers and quite short, they had a cab with a full set of controls at both ends, the rear cab partially housing two standard Sentinel two-cylinder engines, while the vertical boiler was in the front cab, with the water tank in the middle. Unlike previous LNER Sentinels, coal was fed into the firebox near the bottom of the boiler rather than at the top.

The two 'Y10s' worked on the Wisbech line in 1930-31, but were not powerful enough for peak-season fruit trains, and

Introduced 1930	
Designed by Sentinel	
Built by Sentinel	
Number built 2	
Number inherited by BR 2	
Last example withdrawn February 1952	

were heavy on coal. After this short trial they were therefore moved away in May 1931 to Yarmouth to work the old quayside line (without their cowcatchers), where they subsequently made their home.

In February 1934 No 8404 was transferred to Kittybrewster (Aberdeen) for more dock work, then moved to Edinburgh docks before returning to Yarmouth in May. For a period during 1940 the two engines were moved to the safety of Norwich, returning to the coast later in the year.

In 1935 Sentinel offered the LNER a yet more advanced design, but it was considered not efficient enough and was not proceeded with.

In 1946 the pair were renumbered 8186 and 8187, and both passed into BR hands in 1948, shedded at Yarmouth South Town. No 8187 was withdrawn before the year was out, while its sister lasted until February 1952.

The complex numbering history of one of the two 'Super Sentinel' 0-4-0Ts is clear to see here. It was delivered as No 8403 in 1930, then briefly carried the intermediate number 7775, before being renumbered 8186. It never officially carried its allocated BR number of 68186, yet it has been neatly chalked on by the photographer for this picture at Yarmouth Vauxhall on 31 August 1951, five months before withdrawal. *H. C. Casserley*

GNoSR Manning Wardle 'X'/'Z4' Class 0-4-2T

Nos 68190, 68191

Manning Wardle & Co of Leeds was established in 1858, and concentrated on building contractors' and industrial tank engines. By the end of 1880 760 locomotives had been constructed, the majority of which were 0-4-0 and 0-6-0 saddle tanks (311 and 298 respectively).

Initially the Aberdeen Harbour Commissioners would only allow horse haulage around the docks, but when the GNoSR took over working the dock traffic in 1915 it was allowed to purchase two steam locomotives from Manning Wardle. Classified 'Y' (LNER 'Z5' – see next entry), it was discovered that they were overweight by 2 tons, so two more were purchased, Nos 114 and 115 (43 and 44 from 1915). These were actually 6 tons lighter, with smaller cylinders and driving wheels and a shorter wheelbase, but were almost as powerful and were classified 'X'; the LNER originally included them in Class 'Z5', but in 1927 they were reclassified 'Z4'. After the Grouping the

Diminutive Manning Wardle 0-4-2T 'Z4' Class No 68191 shunts at Aberdeen Docks in May 1955. It was taken out of use at the end of March 1959 and scrapped. *Colour-Rail collection*

'Z4s' became Nos 6843 and 6844; in 1946 they were renumbered 8190 and 8191. They carried their GNoSR livery of black with red and yellow lining throughout, with just the letters 'LNER' added, apart from during the war years when they were in unlined black.

Both 'Z4s' spent most of their working lives on the 1¾-mile branch from Kittybrewster to Aberdeen's Waterloo Docks, occasionally straying further afield on local goods trains, and sometimes hired out to private owners. When they passed to BR they became Nos 68190 and 68191, and still carried their original boilers, as there were no spares.

| Introduced 1915 |
| Designed by Manning Wardle |
| Built by Manning Wardle |
| Number built 2 |
| Number inherited by BR 2 |
| Last example withdrawn April 1960 |

No 68191 was withdrawn in March 1959, having been stored in Kittybrewster shed derelict since July of the previous year. No 68190 lasted a little longer, until April 1960.

GNoSR Manning Wardle 'Y'/'Z5' Class 0-4-2T

Nos 68192, 68193

| Introduced 1915 |
| Designed by Manning Wardle |
| Built by Manning Wardle |
| Number built 2 |
| Number inherited by BR 2 |
| Last example withdrawn April 1960 |

Despite carrying higher numbers than the 'Z4s', these were the first two steam locomotives purchased by the GNoSR to work Aberdeen Docks from 1915. As mentioned above, they were found to be too heavy to work the dock lines, and two lighter 0-4-2Ts (LNER 'Z4' – see previous entry) were acquired, also in 1915.

These 'Y' Class engines were numbered 116 and 117 (30 and 32 in 1915), and to help reduce their weight they initially operated with their water tanks only partially filled. They were later permitted to work alongside the 'Xs' (what they did in the meantime is unclear), and spent all their lives at Aberdeen, retaining their original boilers throughout, and being similarly liveried. The LNER numbered them 6830 and 6832, then in 1946 they were renumbered 8192 and 8193, subsequently becoming BR Nos 68192 and 68193.

By June 1956, when this picture was taken, 0-4-2T No 68192 was the only 'Z5' working at Aberdeen Docks, its sister engine having been withdrawn in April. It is seen on the quayside, and had nearly four more years' work ahead of it. Note the different livery style as compared with 'Z4' No 68191. *K. Bannister, Colour-Rail*

The first of the four 0-4-2Ts to be withdrawn was 'Z5' No 68193 in April 1956, and No 68192 was taken out of service at the same time as 'Z4' No 68190, in April 1960.

MSLR/GCR Pollitt '5'/'J62' Class 0-6-0ST

Nos 68200, 8201, 8203

Harry Pollitt became Locomotive Superintendent of the GCR in 1894, and continued building engines designed by his predecessor, Parker. In 1897 locomotives to his own designs began to appear, and the Class '5' 0-6-0 saddle tanks were designed for working the company's docks at Grimsby and similar locations that included tight curves. Twelve were built at Gorton in 1897, numbered 882-93. No 891 was the last locomotive built by the Manchester, Sheffield & Lincolnshire Railway, appearing in July 1897; the following month the company adopted the new name of Great Central Railway, so Nos 892 and 893 were the first GCR-built engines.

The class's initial allocation was to Grimsby, Immingham and Birkenhead docks, and they carried a warning bell and a distinctive

| Introduced 1897 |
| Designed by Harry Pollitt |
| Built by MSLR, Gorton |
| Number built 12 |
| Number inherited by BR 3 |
| Last example withdrawn November 1951 |

hooter instead of a whistle; originally fitted on the roof of the cab, these were later repositioned on the tank in front of the cab; the LNER later mounted the bells beneath the boiler. Some engines were also fitted with spark arresters on their chimneys. They carried 1½ tons of coal and 600 gallons of water.

In 1903 No 889 was rebuilt by J. G. Robinson as an 0-6-2ST, with a 4-ton Vulcan Foundry crane added over the trailing wheels. It was used as a shunter at Gorton until damaged in a

The last survivor of the 12 ex-GCR 'J62' 0-6-0 saddle tanks was No 68200. It was shedded at Wrexham Rhosddu, and was photographed there on 27 July 1951, four months before withdrawal. It appears to have 'Herbie' chalked on the side of the bunker – a local nickname? *W. Potter, R. M. Casserley collection*

collision in 1918, after which it was reconverted to standard Class '5' form.

The LNER classified the engines 'J62', and they were allocated to Immingham and Wrexham, with one at Staveley Works. Thereafter they were also occasionally seen at Bidston, Ipswich Docks, Chester, Trafford Park and Ardsley.

The LNER withdrew the first 'J62' in 1935, and between 1936 and 1938 three were loaned to Sir Robert McAlpine during the construction of Ebbw Vale steelworks in South Wales; one was withdrawn after being damaged. By 1945 only four of the 12 remained in service, by now numbered 8200-03 and shedded at Wrexham, Sheffield and Immingham. No 8202 was lost in December 1947, and the three survivors passed into BR's hands. Only No 68200 carried its allocated BR number, the other two having been quickly disposed of at the beginning of 1949. The final example was withdrawn from Wrexham Rhosddu shed in November 1951, almost 55 years old.

GCR Robinson '5A'/'J63' Class 0-6-0T

Nos 68204-10

Six Class '5A' 0-6-0Ts were built by the GCR in 1906, and were side tank versions of Pollitt's Class '5' saddle tanks (see previous entry); they used the same frames and motion, and the cylinders and wheels shared the same dimensions. They also had the same size of bunker, but carried an extra 350 gallons of water, and the cab and running plate were wider. They were built for working in docks such as those at Grimsby and New Holland, and carried warning bells when on these duties. They were numbered randomly: 60, 61, 89, 157, 321 and 538. The first two carried condensing gear for working in the Liverpool area, being shedded at Brunswick and Walton, and they were heavier than other members of the class. A seventh example, No 277, was added in 1914.

The '5As' were built to replace the company's Class '4' Manning Wardle (LNER 'J61') dock shunters. Apart from the Liverpool pair, they were allocated to the Immingham area, and would spend most of the working lives there.

As LNER Class 'J63', the engines had 5000 added to their numbers, then in 1946 were renumbered more logically as 8204-10. Some now found themselves temporarily allocated to such sheds as St Margarets in Edinburgh, Bidston, Wrexham, Chester and Frodingham, while Nos 5061 and 5157 were loaned to the Mersey Docks & Harbour Board during the war.

The 'J63s', still intact, passed into BR ownership in 1948. The first casualty was No 68208, withdrawn from Immingham in 1953, then No 68209 was taken out of service at Wrexham in

Introduced 1906
Designed by John Robinson
Built by GCR, Gorton
Number built 7
Number inherited by BR 7
Last example withdrawn February 1957

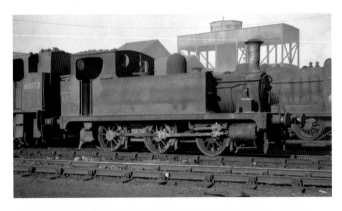

'J63' No 68210 was the last survivor of the seven-loco class; the other six had been built in 1906, and this one was added in 1914. It was a long-time Immingham shed resident, and was withdrawn in February 1957. Its number and BR emblem are barely visible in this undated view. *P. J. Hughes, Colour-Rail*

February 1955. The remaining five were all to be found at Immingham, but the advent of diesel shunters led to their withdrawal between March 1955 and February 1957.

GER Holden 'E22'/'J65'Class 0-6-0T

Nos 68211, 8213, 68214, 8215

When Holden took up post on the Great Eastern in 1885 he found to his surprise that there were just 15 0-6-0 shunting and

goods tank engines out of a total locomotive stock of more than 700. As a result, as E. L. Ahrons put it in 1918, 'The new shunting engines … began to pour out of Stratford Works for some time… The old days of painful and laborious movements

Introduced 1889
Designed by James Holden
Built by GER, Stratford
Number built 20
Number inherited by BR 4
Last example withdrawn October 1956

By 1956 only one of the former Great Eastern 'J65' 'Blackwall Tanks' remained, the 1893-built No 68214. It was withdrawn from Yarmouth Beach shed (32F) in October, and is seen awaiting the cutter at Stratford on 17 November. *Brian Morrison*

to and fro on the part of retired tender engines on half pay are now over as far as the Great Eastern is concerned.' By 1904 210 had been built, for the teeming London suburban services as well as rural, goods and shunting work.

Holden's first 0-6-0T design was the 'T18' of 1886 (LNER Class 'J66' – qv), intended for light passenger duties. These were followed in 1889 by the smallest of the GER 0-6-0T family, the 'E22' Class, with shorter frames, smaller cylinders, smaller side tanks and a shorter cab; the boiler was fully interchangeable with Class 'J66' and 'J67' locomotives, and these little engines weighed in at 36½ tons. They had a Westinghouse brake and screw reverse for passenger duties. The first ten (Nos 150-159) were built at Stratford in 1889, followed by a second batch (Nos 345-54) in 1893; the latter had slightly lower but wider tanks, with a slightly greater water capacity. Between 1899 and 1912 the whole class was reboilered.

Half of the class quickly became associated with the frequent-interval Fenchurch Street to Blackwall line, earning the engines the nickname of 'Blackwall Tanks'. They often ran with the front portion of the side rods disconnected, transforming them into 2-4-0 tanks. The others were to be found on small East Anglian branches – such as the Stoke Ferry, Eye and Mid-Suffolk lines – with allocations at such places as Ipswich, Cambridge and King's Lynn.

The LNER classified the engines 'J69', and added 7000 to their numbers. Several were now allocated to Parkeston to work on the quay, as well as handling local passenger trains to

Harwich. Others found their way to the Colne Valley & Halstead Railway. In 1926, during the General Strike, the Blackwall services were withdrawn, so more engines headed to the country. When some of the smaller East Anglian branches closed, or were upgraded, in the 1930s, withdrawal of the 'J69s' began; six were done away with in 1937 alone, by which time only five of the 20 remained, allocated to Ipswich and Parkeston and later renumbered 8211-15 in order of construction. Another was lost in 1947, and just four became BR engines the following year. In 1948 and 1949 two Yarmouth Beach-allocated engines were withdrawn, followed by No 68211 from Ipswich, where it had worked in the docks. The last to go was No 68214, withdrawn from Yarmouth in October 1956, where it had been a spare locomotive for the quay.

GER Holden 'C53'/'J70' Class 0-6-0T tram engine

Nos 68216, 68217, 8218, 68219-26

The roadside Wisbech & Upwell Tramway opened in 1883, and to operate it Thomas Worsdell designed three 0-4-0T tram locomotives, classified 'G15' (LNER Class 'Y6' – qv). By the turn of the 20th century these 0-4-0Ts were less able to cope with the peak-season harvest traffic, so Worsdell's successor, Holden, designed a more powerful six-wheeled version, with outside cylinders and, unusually, Walschaerts valve gear (the first GER engines to be so fitted). The boiler was the same size but operated at a higher pressure.

Despite having an extra pair of wheels, the wheelbase was only 2 inches longer than that of the 0-4-0T 'G15s', at 6ft 8in. Apart from the extra axle (invisible if the side plates were fitted), the wooden body was almost indistinguishable from that of the earlier engine, and it also had to comply with the same Board of Trade regulations, including the fitting of cowcatchers, warning bells, spark arrestors, governors set to 8mph, and protective side plates to cover the wheels and

The last four remaining ex-GER 'J70' tram engines were withdrawn during 1955. This is No 68225, one of the three built in 1921. It is seen at Stratford in March 1955, the month it was withdrawn from Ipswich. Note the modification to the Walschaerts valve gear! *T. B. Owen, Colour-Rail*

Introduced 1903
Designed by James Holden
Built by GER, Stratford
Number built 12
Number inherited by BR 11
Last example withdrawn August 1955

motion. As with the 'Y6', the safety valves discharged into the water tank, so reduce potential noise that might scare horses! The engines could be controlled from both ends, and Westinghouse brakes were fitted as standard.

Twelve 'C53s' were built in five batches: two in 1903 (Nos 135-36), three in 1908 (137-39), one in 1910 (130), then three each in both 1914 and 1921 (127, 128 and 131, and 125, 126 and 129 respectively). Nos 135 and 136 worked at Ipswich Docks, while the 1908 trio went to Yarmouth (two) and Vauxhall. The others were distributed between Wisbech, Yarmouth, Ipswich and Colchester.

The engines were serviced at Stratford, travelling under their own steam on the main line. With the governor disengaged, they had quite a turn of speed, looking for all the world like some kind of runaway brake van!

Under the LNER the tram engines were classified 'J70', and had 7000 added to their numbers. 'Y10' 'Super Sentinels' (qv) replaced those at Yarmouth in the early 1930s, but five continued to be based at Wisbech even after passenger services on the Upwell line were withdrawn, and right through into BR days; two were sufficient to operate the regular traffic, with the others helping out at harvest season. It is reported that No 7131 once struggled out of Upwell with 48 wagons containing about 400 tons of fruit!

The first 'J70' to be withdrawn was No 7138 in 1942, and the remaining 11 were subsequently renumbered 8216-26. In BR days two Drewry 0-6-0 diesel shunters began to work the Wisbech line from 1952, but No 68222 was kept as a back-up until March 1953. By the end of 1954 just four 'J70s' were still at work, at Colchester, Ipswich and Yarmouth. However, these too were replaced by diesel shunters, and the quartet (Nos 68222/23/25/26) were withdrawn in 1955.

Rev W. Awdry's 'Toby the Tram Engine' (first encountered in print in 1952 in one of famous 'Railway Stories') was inspired by a 'J70' that Wilbert and his son Christopher saw while on a holiday at Yarmouth. 'He is short and sturdy,' Awdry wrote in 'Toby and the Stout Gentleman'. 'He has cow-catchers and side-plates, and doesn't look like a steam engine at all.'

NER T. Worsdell 'E'/'J71' Class 0-6-0T

Nos 68230, 8231, 68232-36, 68238-40, 68242-46, 8247, 68248, 2849, 68250-56, 68258-60, 68262-73, 68275, 68276, 8277, 68278-84, 8285, 68286, 68287, 8288, 68289-309, 8310, 8311, 68312-14, 68316

In 1881-83 Edward Fetcher built his seven '44' Class 0-6-0 short-coupled saddle tanks, but this typical NER design found little favour with Thomas Worsdell when he joined the company in 1885; both he and his brother Wilson disliked saddle tanks, so a replacement standard shunting engine was introduced in 1886. This was the Class 'E' side-tank 0-6-0, with Stephenson rather than Joy valve gear, and simple expansion.

This very attractive design also proved to be a successful workhorse for light goods work and shunting, and altogether 120 were built at Darlington between 1886 and 1895. It was only when Wilson Worsdell succeeded his brother that

Introduced 1886
Designed by Thomas Worsdell
Built by NER, Darlington
Number built 120
Number inherited by BR 81
Last example withdrawn February 1961

production turned to Wilson's smaller-wheeled, larger-cylindered 'E1' Class (LNER 'J72') from 1898. (These continued to be built until 1925, then BR built 28 more in 1949-51, and one of the latter, No 69023, is preserved, with the name *Joem*.)

Over the course of production Class 'E' cylinder sizes varied, and they carried the same boiler as used on the later 'E1', so there was random swapping over the years. The 'Es' had steam brakes as standard, and some also had vacuum brakes for passenger work; a few were dual-fitted with Westinghouse brakes.

Many of the 'Es' worked at NER ports and docks, where their lightness and short wheelbase suited sharply curved tracks. They were also used for local trip workings between docks and goods depots.

The 'Es' were also much used as station pilots on the NER main line, duly fitted with vacuum ejectors. Two were specially

No E8310 was one of only eight of the 81 'J71' 0-6-0s to be withdrawn before carrying its BR number. It is seen at its home shed of York South (50A) on 3 October 1948; it was withdrawn at the end of 1950, more than ten years before the class became extinct. Behind it is No 8699, one of the 'J72s' that replaced many of the older 'J71s'. It became BR No 68699 in November 1948, and was withdrawn ten years later. Note the ex-LMS Garratt on the adjacent road. *H. C. Casserley*

maintained for these duties at York, serving there for more than six decades. They wore post-war LNER green livery, then BR green. Those undertaking pilot duties in the Newcastle and Gateshead areas had an ingenious mechanism employing a movable red spectacle glass whereby the driver could change the lamps at each end from clear to red, allowing frequent changes of direction without the laborious business of constantly changing the tail lamp from one end to the other. This system was still in use after nationalisation. Two other class members were used as shunters at Darlington Works and Shildon wagon shops.

As LNER Class 'J71', the engines were widely dispersed throughout the former NER system, although seldom north of Newcastle. During the 1930s they began to be replaced by the newer 'J72s', and the first withdrawal took place in 1933 during the Depression years. (Two were sold to collieries, and lasted with their new owners until 1954 and 1960.) Further engines were taken out of service as the years went on, although some were reprieved during the war, and a total of 81 engines survived into British Railways ownership. There were still more than 60 at work by the end of 1953, but diesel shunters rapidly began to take their jobs. Just 14 saw the dawn of the 1960s, and the last four were withdrawn together from West Hartlepool, Thornaby and Normanton shed in February 1961; the oldest was No 68233 of 1887, scrapped at the age of 74.

GNR Stirling 'J16'/'J55' Class 0-6-0ST

Nos 8317, 68319

Between 1874 and 1892 the Great Northern's first saddle-tank locomotives were introduced by Patrick Stirling. These were GNR Class 'J15', and a total of 95 were built by Doncaster Works (75), Robert Stephenson & Co (10), and Neilson & Co (10). Their domeless boilers, cylinders and wheel spacings were the same as the existing Class 'J6' 0-6-0s, but they had larger wheels. Meanwhile, in 1876/77 ten further, similar but shorter locomotives, also with domeless boilers, were built – these were classified 'J17'. The 'J15s' and 'J17's became LNER Classes 'J54' and 'J56' respectively.

In 1897 two of the 'J17's were rebuilt by Ivatt to the same specification as the 'J15s' but with a domed boiler, and these became the foundation of Class 'J16'. Subsequently many of the 'J15's were rebuilt by Gresley with domes – 28 had been so treated by the 1923, and a further 23 thereafter by the LNER, which classified the rebuilds 'J55'.

The 'J56s' had all been withdrawn by 1932, and the 'J54s' a year later. All had worked throughout the former GNR network until superseded by larger, heavier 0-6-0 side and saddle tanks, thereafter taking on lighter duties. By 1937 there were only

By 1937 there were only three LNER Class 'J55' saddle tanks still at work. No 3908 (8318 from 1946) was scrapped in 1947, but No 3859 (later No 8317) and 4990 (8319, and subsequently BR 68319) passed into BR hands. No 8317, carrying its earlier LNER number, was photographed at Copley Hill on 27 June 1937, with more than a decade's work still ahead of it. *H. C. Casserley*

three of the 'J55s' still at work; a further example was scrapped in 1947, leaving just two of the original 105 engines to pass into BR's hands the following year. No 8317 (built 1892 and rebuilt to 'J55' form in 1928) was done away with at Doncaster shed at the end of 1948, but 68319 (built 1891, rebuilt 1934) was given a BR number and worked as a Departmental loco at Doncaster Works for a further two years until withdrawn in December 1950 without having been given a Departmental number – indeed, it was cut up in August, before it had even been officially withdrawn!

> **Introduced** 1874; rebuilt from 1912
> **Designed by** Patrick Stirling; rebuilt by Nigel Gresley
> **Built by** GNR, Doncaster
> **Number built** 53 as rebuilt
> **Number inherited by BR** 2
> **Last example withdrawn** December 1950

NBR Reid 'F'/'J88' Class 0-6-0T

Nos 68320-54

With their short wheelbase of only 11 feet, these small NBR Class 'F' tank engines were designed by Reid to work in docks and industrial locations, where curves were sharp and headshunts short. They differed from the products of his predecessor Drummond by having outside cylinders, and being driven from the right-hand side. The 'Fs' became the NBR's standard light shunting engine.

Two batches of six each were built at Cowlairs in 1904 and 1905, with safety valves atop the dome and wooden block buffers (most of which were subsequently replaced by conventional examples by the NBR). Another half-dozen appeared in 1909, then ten in 1912 and a final seven in 1919; the last two batches saw the safety valves moved to the firebox.

The 1904/05 engines were rebuilt with new boilers by the LNER in 1925, by then classified 'J88'. Further new boilers were

Introduced 1904
Designed by William Reid
Built by NBR, Cowlairs
Number built 35
Number inherited by BR 35
Last example withdrawn December 1962

The first of the NBR 'F' Class, No 68320, built in December 1904 and latterly the LNER's No 9836/8320, was a St Margarets engine for the whole of its short BR career. It is seen here at Haymarket in August 1959, and was withdrawn the following June. Note the dumb buffers, to prevent buffer-locking on sharp curves.
Colour-Rail collection

fitted in 1929-33, and by BR in the early 1950s. The entire class survived to be nationalised, shedded at St Margarets, Thornton Junction, Polmont, Eastfield, Haymarket, Kipps, Stirling and Dunfermline, and rarely straying further afield. The class remained intact until No 68341 was withdrawn from Thornton Junction in November 1954 after falling into Kirkcaldy harbour following a loss of control. The advent of diesel shunters led to further losses through to 1958, and at the end of that year only 20 were still in service. That number was quickly reduced to just seven at the end of 1961, and all had gone within 12 months. The last survivor was No 68345, latterly a Kipps engine, going in December 1962.

NER W. Worsdell 'L'/'J73' Class 0-6-0T

Nos 68355-64

Wilson Worsdell succeeded his brother Thomas at Gateshead in 1890, and his first design for the North Eastern Railway was this Class 'L' 0-6-0. They were a larger and more powerful version of Thomas's 'J71' 0-6-0Ts (qv) of 1886-95, with larger boiler, cylinders and grate area.

Just ten were built in 1891-92, and instead of Stephenson valve gear they had Joy's, which Worsdell senior (and Darlington Works) preferred; since Thomas remained as a consultant with the NER for two years after his retirement, he probably influenced his brother's first design for the company. The engines were built specifically for use beside the Tyne on the 1,300-yard Quayside branch in Newcastle – which rose from the river at a ruling gradient of 1 in 25, mostly in tunnel – and the steep Redheugh incline from the famous Dunston Staiths up to Gateshead.

Only slight changes were made to the engines throughout their lives, principally in boiler construction and type of safety valves. When the Quayside branch was electrified by the NER

Introduced 1891
Designed by Wilson Worsdell
Built by NER, Gateshead
Number built 10
Number inherited by BR 10
Last example withdrawn November 1960

in 1905 the 'J73s' working there were reallocated. By 1923 most were to be found at Ferryhill (for working trains between there and Hartlepool) and Tyne Dock. In 1937 some also replaced the smaller 'J71s' in the Hull area, to work timber traffic on the docks. In 1948 all ten became BR engines, allocated to West Hartlepool, Selby (to work the marshalling yard at Gascoigne Wood) and Hull Alexandra Dock, with one briefly at Tweedmouth.

During the First World War NER Nos 544 and 545 were modified to haul large rail-mounted guns, and an extra Westinghouse pump was fitted for taking water from streams. In this guise they were apparently employed to guard the north and south banks at the mouth of the Tees.

When the first of the class was withdrawn in March 1955 it had given more than 62 years' service, and the others worked on until 1957, but between then and 1959 most were withdrawn, leaving just three to see the dawn of the 1960s. No 68361 was the last survivor, taken out of use at Hull Dairycoates in November 1960.

'J73' 0-6-0T No 68361 was the last survivor of the class of ten. As a BR engine it was shedded at Hull Alexandra Dock, Springhead and finally Dairycoats, from where it was withdrawn in November 1960. It is seen here at Springhead in June 1959, shunting a decrepit Carriage & Wagon Department brake van at the former Hull & Barnsley Railway Works. *K. C. H. Fairey, Colour-Rail*

H&BR M. Stirling 'G3'/'J75' Class 0-6-0T

No 8365

Scottish-born Matthew Stirling (1856-1931) was the son of Patrick of Great Northern Railway fame and nephew of James, who was Locomotive Superintendent on the Glasgow & South Western. He served his apprenticeship on the GNR, then became Chief Locomotive Superintendent of the newly formed Hull & Barnsley Railway in 1885. This line had been promoted to break the North Eastern Railway's stranglehold on Hull's railways, and ran the 53 miles to Cudworth on the Midland Railway, a couple of miles short of Barnsley. Stirling remained in that post until 1922, when the H&BR merged with the NER prior to both becoming part of the LNER the following year.

Matthew followed his father's design tenets, including domeless boilers and spartan cabs. The engines themselves were built by outside contractors, the first six by the Yorkshire Engine Co in 1901-02, and ten more from Kitson & Co in 1908. They originally had domeless boilers. The design was based on Stirling's earlier 'G2' 0-6-0T, but with smaller wheels. Nine 0-6-2Ts of the same basic design (LNER 'N12' – qv) also emerged from Kitson's at the same time, intended for transfer and short-trip workings.

When the H&BR joined the NER, the domeless boilers on 14 members of the class were replaced by a domed variety; two remained domeless until scrapped.

The first batch of six engines worked the Wath (H&BR) and Braithwell (GCR/H&BR/MR Joint) branches. The other ten worked as shunters at Cudworth, the western extremity of the H&BR, and Hull, principally the H&BR's Alexandra Dock. Once LNER property, as Class 'J75', they move further afield to various locations in Eastern England (even as far south as Peterborough). The Depression years led to all but one of the

During the late 1920s and '30s the ex-Hull & Barnsley 'J75' 0-6-0Ts moved away from their home turf, and No 2529 is seen here at Peterborough East on 29 May 1937. By 1939 this engine and all but one of the class had been withdrawn by the LNER; the sole BR engine, LNER No 2532 (No 8365 from 1946), worked at Liverpool until January 1949. *H. C. Casserley*

Introduced 1901
Designed by Matthew Stirling
Built by Yorkshire Engine (6), Kitson (10)
Number built 16
Number inherited by BR 1
Last example withdrawn January 1949

class being withdrawn before the outbreak of war in 1939. The sole survivor was placed in store, but later No 2532 (No 8365 from 1946) moved west to work at Huskisson Dock, Liverpool, shedded at Walton-on-the-Hill. It just lasted into British Railways ownership but was not renumbered, being withdrawn in January 1949.

LD&ECR 'J60' Class 0-6-0T

Nos 8366, 8368

Introduced 1897
Designed by Kitson
Built by Kitson
Number built 4
Number inherited by BR 4
Last example withdrawn August 1948

The Lancashire, Derbyshire & East Coast Railway was built to fulfil a need for a new east-west rail link, from Warrington to Sutton-on-Sea in Lincolnshire, with new docks at each end. It was largely financed by a group of coal owners and was the largest railway scheme, in terms of capital and mileage, ever approved by Parliament in a single session. It would be 170 miles long, including branches, but in the event the only section to become reality was the line between Chesterfield and Lincoln, via Langwith and Tuxford, which opened in 1897. The LD&ECR was purchased by the Great Central Railway as a going concern as from 1 January 1907.

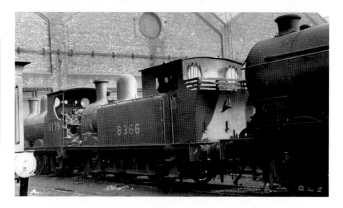

Only two former LD&ECR locomotives entered BR stock, the surviving 'J60' (GCR Class 'B') 0-6-0Ts Nos 8366 and 8368. Both were shedded at Wrexham Rhosddu, and No 8366 only survived until March 1948 before it was withdrawn and sent to Gorton to be scrapped; it is seen there on the 11th. Ahead is tenderless ex-GCR 'J10' No 5179 of 1901, which received its BR number in April 1948 and worked on until the end of 1952. *H. C. Casserley*

The LD&ECR was unusual in that its entire locomotive stud consisted of tank engines, and all were supplied by Kitson & Co – perhaps not surprisingly, as Sir James Kitson was a holder of LD&ECR Debenture Stock. These four locomotives, of typical Kitson design, were built in 1897, and numbered 9 to 12. When taken over by the GCR, they became that company's Class 'B', and were renumbered 1175-78. They were given Robinson-style chimneys, but these were later replaced by less attractive LNER 'flowerpots'.

The LD&ECR allocated three of the class to Langwith shed to be used for shunting the sidings at Warsop, while the other was often based at Tuxford and used as works pilot. The latter engine, by now classified by the LNER as 'J60', moved west to Wrexham, and was subsequently followed by the other three. There they mainly worked the Brymbo branch, where their modest size was ideal, although larger engines would have been preferred if they had been suitable; the 'J60s' had the disadvantage of small cabs. From 1937 No 6410 was usually allocated to Gorton for yard shunting duties. In 1956 what were now LNER Nos 6411, 6410, 6409 and 6408 became Nos 8366-69 respectively.

Nos 8367 and 8368 were withdrawn in 1947, and the other two were taken out of use at Wrexham Rhosddu shed within eight months of nationalisation without ever carrying their allocated BR numbers.

GER Holden 'T18'/'J66' Class 0-6-0T

Nos 68370-75, 8376, 8377, 68378, 68379, 8380, 8381, 68382, 68383, 8384, 68385, 8386, 8387, 68388

Introduced 1886
Designed by James Holden
Built by GER, Stratford
Number built 50
Number inherited by BR 20
Last example withdrawn September 1962

The 'T18' was Holden's first design for the Great Eastern, having taken up the post of Locomotive Superintendent in 1885. With the great growth in mineral traffic and the opening of the large marshalling yards at March and Temple Mills, these small and straightforward 0-6-0 tanks, incorporating the best of previous practice, were urgently required for shunting duties, a job previously done by superannuated main-line engines. The 50 locomotives were built in four batches – the first ten (GER Nos 275-84) emerged from Stratford in 1886, 20 more in 1887 (285-304), then two batches of ten each in 1888 (307-26).

The 'T18' was a very successful design, and provided the basis for all future GER 0-6-0Ts right through to the Grouping. Although essentially a shunter, one was experimentally fitted with a Westinghouse brake to work suburban services to Enfield, as a result of which the last batch of ten were similarly fitted, and had larger bunkers and other refinements enabling them to work passenger trains to Enfield and Chingford until replaced by 'J67s' in 1890. The whole class was reboilered between 1898 and 1908.

The class became 'J66' under the LNER, renumbered 7275-7304 and 7307-26. In 1946 the 19 surviving engines were renumbered again in a single sequence, 8370-88. They were spread widely, in London and throughout eastern England. In the 1930s and '40s they even found themselves allocated to non-GER sheds.

In 1926 four engines were sold to Sir Robert McAlpine & Co to help with the construction of Ebbw Vale steelworks, followed by another four on loan. In 1939 No 7297 was sold to the Mersey Railway (still an independent company); it became No 3 and was used to work ballast trains until it entered BR stock, together with the remaining 19 LNER engines, in 1948. In 1952 three of the class (Nos 68370/78/82) were transferred to Departmental stock at Stratford as Nos 32, 36 and 31 respectively, and the remainder had disappeared by 1955. It is probable that No 68370/32 had always worked at Stratford, and was notable as having been the first GER engine to be converted to oil-burning. It became the last surviving 'J66', being scrapped in September 1962 with the end of steam on the GE Section.

In 1952 three 'J66' 0-6-0Ts were transferred to Departmental stock at Stratford Works. One of them was Staveley resident No 68382 of 1888, which became Departmental No 31. It is seen here at Stratford a couple of years earlier on 19 August 1950. *H. C. Casserley*

NER W. Worsdell/Raven '290'/'J77' Class 0-6-0T

Nos 8390, 68391--93, 68395, 8396, 68397-99, 8400, 68401, 68402, 8404, 68405-10, 68412-14, 8415, 8416, 68417, 68420-32, 8433, 68434-38, 68440, 8441

Edward Fletcher's 'G6' Class 0-4-4 well tanks ('Bogie Tank Passenger', or 'BTP') for the NER were successful and sturdy locomotives. Twelve were built by Neilson & Co in 1874, followed by others from R. & W. Hawthorn & Co, until a total of 124 had been built, including 92 by the NER itself. However, in the late 1890s they were being replaced, and rather than do away with them altogether many were rebuilt as 0-6-0T shunters, becoming the NER's Class '290'. Forty were rebuilt at York Works in 1899-1904 (with round-cornered cab roofs), then when more redundant 0-4-4WTs became available the final 20 emerged from Darlington Works in two batches of ten, in 1907-08 and 1921, these later examples having square-cornered Worsdell cabs.

The rebuilding involved replacing the rear bogie with a third coupled axle. Larger cylinders were fitted, and the first rebuilds had new side tanks and smaller bunkers. The original wooden buffer beams gave way to steel, and standard buffers were fitted.

The 60 engines became LNER Class 'J77' in 1923, and withdrawn 'G6s' continued to donate boilers to the rebuilds. These hard-wearing and popular engines were found throughout the former NER system, working in sidings, marshalling yards and docksides, and from the 1920s also further afield, even beyond former NER territory. It was not until 1933 that withdrawals began, as a result of the Depression years. However, 46 survived long enough to become BR engines, and for six years only a few withdrawals occurred, increasing from 1956-57 as the new diesel shunters made their presence felt. Just seven saw the beginning of 1958, mainly shedded at North Blyth and South Blyth to work the coal staithes there, where their good power-to-weight ratio was an advantage. Five were still at work there in 1960, before making

'J77' No 68436 was built at Gateshead in 1880 as an 0-4-4 well tank, and was converted to an 0-6-0T at Darlington Works around the turn of the century. It then worked on for more than half a century, one of six that were shedded at Tweedmouth in BR days. Photographed there on 1 May 1956, it was withdrawn the following month. *Colour-Rail collection*

Introduced 1874; rebuilt from 1899
Designed by Edward Fletcher; rebuilt by Wilson Worsdell and Vincent Raven
Original builders of BR engines Neilson (4), Hawthorn (13), NER, Darlington (6), NER, Gateshead (21), NER, York (2)
Number built 60 (as rebuilt)
Number inherited by BR 46
Last example withdrawn February 1961

their final moves towards withdrawal. The last 'J77' to go was No 68408, a Hawthorn 0-4-4WT of 1875, later rebuilt at York, which remained in reserve at South Blyth until February 1961. Some of the class clocked up more than 80 years of service in their two guises.

Meanwhile, in 1950 two 'J77s' had been sold into the coal industry, one ending its days in South Wales in the early 1960s.

NBR Holmes 'D'/'J83' Class 0-6-0T

Nos 68442-61, 68463-81

As on the GER mentioned above (qv 'J66'), the North British tended to use obsolete tender engines to undertake short-distance goods and shunting duties. However, again like the GER, goods traffic was growing enormously, so in the 1890s Holmes rebuilt 20 0-6-0 tender engines as saddle tanks (from LNER Class 'J31' to 'J84'). Then in 1900-01 he introduced a new side-tank engine as his Class 'D' or '795', 20 of which were produced by both Neilson, Reid & Co and Sharp, Stewart & Co. Apparently, Neilson's were short of work and offered to built all 40 at advantageous rates and with a speedy delivery, but despite this the NBR decided to place the second 20 with Sharp Stewart. Built with steam brakes, ten were quickly converted

Introduced 1900
Designed by Matthew Holmes
Built by Neilson Reid (20), Sharp Stewart (20)
Number built 40
Number inherited by BR 39
Last example withdrawn December 1962

to Westinghouse brakes, then around 1916 they also received vacuum brakes.

Unaltered, all 40 passed to the LNER in 1923, reclassified 'J83', then in 1924-25 they were all rebuilt with new boilers and other slight modifications. Their main duties were transfer goods, yard shunting and mineral trains, as well as banking, across the whole of the former NBR system, until displaced by

Several 'J83' 0-6-0Ts were familiar as station pilots at major Scottish stations such as Glasgow Queen Street and Edinburgh Waverley. LNER No 9826 (later 8473, then BR 68473) did the honours at Waverley for many years until withdrawn in 1956, as did No 68481 until its own demise in February 1962. The Edinburgh pilots were kept in fine fettle and carried a bright green livery, as seen here in 1949. *J. Robertson, Colour-Rail*

the newer 'A' 0-6-2Ts (qv) of 1909. Those with suitable brakes were then used in carriage sidings and as station pilots.

One 'J83' was withdrawn in 1947, but the remainder became BR engines, and ten new boilers were built in 1951. Remarkably, the class remained otherwise intact until March 1956, after which the increasing number of diesel shunters meant that only 11 were still at work at the end of 1961, and the last half-dozen were withdrawn in the last months of the following year.

The 'J83s' were reliable, long-lived yet unsung workhorses, and enjoyed one of the lowest maintenance costs of any LNER class. They also clocked up higher mileages than any other LNER 0-6-0T; all but three recorded 1 million miles, and when No 9830 (later No 8477 and ultimately BR No 68477) was withdrawn from St Margarets shed on 29 December 1962, the last survivor, it could boast a total of some 2 million miles. Although its accumulation of miles then ceased, it spent another nine months as a stationary boiler at the shed before finally being sent to Motherwell Machinery & Scrap at Wishaw, where it was cut up in July 1964.

M&GNJR Marriott 'J93' Class 0-6-0T

Nos 8484, 8488, 8489

William Marriott (1857-1943) began his career as an apprentice with Ransomes & Rapier in Ipswich, then worked for a railway contractor building various lines in East Anglia. In 1883 he became Engineer with the new Eastern & Midlands Railway, then Locomotive Superintendent in 1885, retaining that post when the E&MR became part of the Midland & Great Northern Joint Railway in 1893. He retired in 1924, and the LNER took control of the M&GN in October 1936. (There is a William Marriott Museum at Holt station on the North Norfolk Railway.)

Most M&GN engines were the responsibility of the Midland Railway, although the company also acquired its own including these nine engines of the 'Shunting' Class, designed by Marriott and built at the company's works at Melton Constable between 1897 and 1905. Not surprisingly, the design incorporated a number of Midland design features. Although described by the company as new engines, six of them (Nos 93-98) were more possibly rebuilds of engines built by Sharp, Stewart for the Cornwall Minerals Railway in 1873-74, and acquired by one of the M&GN's constituent companies in 1880-81.

All the M&GN locomotives were taken over by the LNER in 1936, being officially added to LNER stock the following year. In 1942 these 0-6-0Ts were classified as 'J93', and were employed on shunting duties and station pilot work at Melton Constable, Norwich City, Yarmouth Beach and South Lynn; the

| Introduced 1897 |
| Designed by William Marriott |
| Built by M&GNJR, Melton Constable |
| Number built 9 |
| Number inherited by BR 3 |
| Last example withdrawn August 1949 |

latter engines were also used for working goods traffic (and later some passenger trains) to and from King's Lynn station and harbour.

No 97 (not yet having been renumbered by the LNER) was withdrawn in 1943, and five others (LNER Nos 8482/83/85/86/87) succumbed between 1945 and 1947, leaving just three to enter BR stock. Their career on the nationalised railway was only brief, however, as Nos 8484 and 8488 were withdrawn within six months, and the last, No 8489, was taken away for scrap in August 1949.

LNER 'J93' 0-6-0T No 8488 was built by the Midland & Great Northern Joint Railway at Melton Constable in 1904, and is seen here at its home shed of South Lynn on 15 April 1947. It became a BR engine on 1 January 1948, but was withdrawn almost immediately. Note the wartime 'NE' livery, and the 'hopper' bunker, fitted in the early 1930s to aid coaling at the M&GN's new coaling plants. *H. C. Casserley*

GER Hill 'C72'/'J68' 0-6-0T

Nos 68638-66

These tank locomotives were the final incarnation of the Great Eastern 0-6-0T family, what became LNER classes 'J65' (qv), 'J66' (qv), 'J67' and 'J69' (the last two classes, built between 1890 and 1904, being closely related, and one of which, 'J69/1' No 68633, has been preserved). As GER Class 'C72', they shared the same size of boiler, cylinders and driving wheel, and had the same wheelbase, as the 'E22'/'J65s' of 1902-04, but had modern, high-roofed cabs with side windows. They were built at Stratford in three batches of ten in 1912 (GER 41-50), 1913-14 (21-30), and 1923 (31-40, not appearing until after the Grouping) – the LNER later added 7000 to these numbers. The first ten were intended for passenger duties (and fitted with condensing gear until 1936-38), the other 20 as shunters.

The passenger engines were employed on the celebrated intensive 'Jazz' service from Liverpool Street to Enfield and Chingford, introduced in 1920. They were gradually replaced by the 'N7' 0-6-2Ts during the later 1920s, whereafter the 'J68s' were used as passenger pilot engines.

The LNER took over the 'C72s' in 1923, reclassified them 'J68', and made various modifications. The goods shunting engines were divided between Stratford and Peterborough East, while the 1923 batch were shedded at Stratford, before moving further afield to East Anglia and Lincolnshire.

In October 1939 No 7041 was loaned to the Government, which bought it in 1940 for use on the Longmoor Military Railway (with seven 'J69s'); it was renumbered WD85/70085. In May 1942 it moved to the Central Ordnance Depot at Bicester, then to Military Port No 1 at Faslane, until scrapped in 1946.

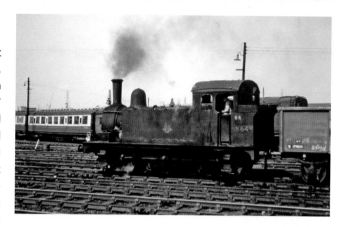

Showing its age at Stratford in 1955 is 'J68' No 68649 of 1913. This was one of the last three survivors of the class, withdrawn from Stratford in September 1961. Note the side-window cab. *Bruce Chapman collection, Colour-Rail*

Introduced 1912
Designed by Alfred Hill
Built by GER, Stratford
Number built 30
Number inherited by BR 29
Last example withdrawn September 1961

The remaining 29 engines were renumbered 8638-66 by the LNER in 1946, and all passed to BR in 1948, continuing to work for a further ten years until quickly superseded by new diesel shunters. Only three were left in 1961 (Nos 68642, 68646 and 68649), all being withdrawn from Stratford in September of that year.

GER Ruston & Proctor '204'/'J92' Class 0-6-0 Crane Tank

Nos 68667-69

The company of Proctor & Burton was established in Lincoln in 1840, and is best remembered as a manufacturer of narrow- and standard-gauge diesel locomotives and steam shovels. However, the company also built cars, internal combustion engines and steam locomotives. In 1857 the company became Ruston, Proctor & Co, when Joseph Ruston joined, and from 1866 built several four- and six-coupled steam tank engines, including five 0-6-0Ts for the Great Eastern Railway in 1868, to a design by the GER's then Locomotive Superintendent Samuel Johnson. Intended for shunting duties, they had no cabs.

In 1881, during the Adams years, the engines were rebuilt with half-cabs, then in 1891 James Holden rebuilt one of them

Introduced 1868; rebuilt as crane tanks 1891-94
Designed by Ruston Proctor
Built by Ruston Proctor
Number built (as crane tanks) 3
Number inherited by BR 3
Last example withdrawn September 1952

Former GER Stratford Works crane tank 'B', later LNER No 8667, was converted in 1891 from an 1866 Ruston Proctor 0-6-0T shunting engine. In March 1949 it became BR No 68667, and this photograph, taken on the 26th of that month, shows the newly applied number, in LNER-style shaded numbers. The engine was withdrawn in May 1952 and scrapped. *H. C. Casserley*

as a 3-ton crane for use at Stratford Works, with steam brakes, a larger-diameter boiler and lengthened frames. Two others were scrapped in 1889 and 1892, and in 1893 the remaining two were also converted to crane tanks. They were used on stripping work and moving components around the works, but by the 1930s the cranes had become redundant with the installation of a fixed overhead travelling crane. The trio became Stratford Works property in 1894 and were designated 'B', 'C' and 'D', remaining so until renumbered 8667, 8668 and 8669 respectively in 1946.

When they became part of LNER stock they were initially classified 'Z4', but in 1927 they became 'J92'. They all spent most of their working lives at Stratford Works, right through into BR ownership, becoming Nos 68667, 68668 and 68669 in 1949-50. The last survivor of the three, No 68668, was allocated the Departmental number 35 in September 1952, but was withdrawn during that month without ever carrying it. The crane tanks were replaced by three 'J66' tank locos, which were given Departmental numbers D31, D32 and D36.

GNR/LNER Gresley 'J23' and 'J51'/'J50' Class 0-6-0T

Nos 68890-991

The Great Northern had a long-standing tradition of using saddle tanks, but Gresley's new 'J23' 0-6-0T design of 1913 had large side tanks, which extended forward to the front of the smokebox, with a distinctive cut-out to allow access to the motion. The front of the tanks sloped downwards, to aid visibility from the cab while shunting. The main duties of the new class involved working the steeply graded lines in the West Riding as well as shunting, so a powerful tank engine with large cylinders seemed the ideal choice (the tanks adding useful adhesive weight). These long tanks gave rise to the nickname 'Submarines', but the engines are best known as the 'Ardsley Tanks', as most of the first batch were sent to work the large marshalling yards around Ardsley, south of Leeds. (They were apparently also dubbed 'Chinese Puzzles' by Scottish locomen, and 'Ally Slopers'.)

The first 30 were built between 1913 and 1919 in three batches of ten, using surplus boilers from Ivatt 'R1' 0-8-2Ts and classified 'J51'. They were found to have poor weight distribution, so the front of the tanks was blanked off, and additional tankage was provided under the bunker, which on the second and third batches was longer to maintain the coal capacity.

In 1922 and 1924 the LNER built 20 more of the locomotives, using further surplus boilers from withdrawn classes, which had a larger diameter. Although the GNR had classified them all as 'J23', these later batches became LNER Class 'J50', which was adopted as a Group Standard design; between 1926 and 1939 a total of 52 more were built, 29 in three batches in 1926,

Introduced 1913	
Designed by Nigel Gresley	
Built by GNR/LNER, Doncaster (88), LNER, Gorton (14)	
Number built 102	
Number inherited by BR 102	
Last example withdrawn May 1965	

three more engines in 1927, six in 1930, eight in 1938 and six in 1939 – these last two batches were built at Gorton Works. The Depression meant that none were built in the mid-1930s, even though the LNER was still short of medium-sized shunting engines; the shortfall was only really solved, despite the 14 Gorton engines, with the acquisition of 75 'Austerity' 'J94' 0-6-0Ts after the war.

In December 1939 the 'J50s' were divided into four sub-classes, depending on such details as fuel capacity, dimensions and the brakes fitted. Initially allocated to the West Riding, they later spread to Lincolnshire, East Anglia and the northern Home Counties. All passed to British Railways in 1948, most still in the West Riding, then in 1952 30 members of the class were allocated to Hornsey to work transfer freight trips to the Southern Region via the Metropolitan 'Widened Lines' (although not fitted with condensing apparatus), and occasionally empty carriage workings between Hornsey and King's Cross.

In 1949 a 'Jay-Gee' smoke eliminator was tested on No 8950, a device marketed by Utility Constructions Ltd of Wickford. Earlier a superheater had been tried on one engine, but the class remained unsuperheated.

It was not until 1958 that the first of the 102 locomotives was withdrawn, once more due to the arrival of diesel shunters. Over the next five years the numbers dwindled dramatically, until only a dozen were still working in 1963; the last ten were withdrawn en bloc in September. However, seven 'J50s' had been transferred to Departmental stock in 1961-62, numbered 10-16, and these lasted until May 1965.

The distinctive side tank arrangement of Gresley's 'J50' 'Ardsley Tanks' is clearly seen in this portrait of the former No 68976, built at Doncaster in 1930. In the early 1960s seven members of the class were transferred to Departmental stock and No 68976, now numbered 16, is seen at Doncaster on 4 April 1965. It was withdrawn the following month, and scrapped in September.
D. Wainman, Colour-Rail

GCR Robinson '1B'/'L1', later 'L3' Class 2-6-4T

Nos 69050-52, 9053, 69054, 69055, 9056-59, 69060-62, 69064, 69065, 9066-68, 69069

The *Manchester Guardian Review of Engineering* described J. G. Robinson's 2-6-4Ts of 1914 as 'one of the handsomest tank engines to have made their appearance anywhere in recent years', but the general consensus is that they were not one of their designer's best works; George Dow considered them somewhat ungainly and unsymmetrical. They were nonetheless notable as the first standard-gauge 2-6-4 ('Adriatic') tank engines to run in Britain (two had been built in Austria in 1908-11, and named from the sea that bordered Austria-Hungary until 1918). They were unusual in having inside cylinders, where subsequent versions on other railways favoured outside cylinders.

Robinson based his Class '1B' design on the Kitson Class 'D' 0-6-4Ts (later LNER Class 'M1') of 1904-06, which the GCR had inherited from the Lancashire, Derbyshire & East Coast Railway. These had been designed by Robert Thom, the LD&ECR's Locomotive Superintendent, for hauling coal trains to the East Coast at Grimsby. Thom became Assistant Works Manager at Gorton Works, and later Robinson's assistant. The tank capacity of the '1Bs' was the same, and the trailing bogie very similar. The superheated boiler was similar to that carried by the 'Director' 4-4-0s, which necessitated the leading pony truck. Inside cylinders and piston valves were fitted, the cylinders and motion being as far as possible interchangeable with those of the 'Sir Sam Fay' and 'Glenalmond' engines.

Twenty '1Bs' emerged from Gorton in goods black livery in four batches between 1914 and 1917, and enginemen were not impressed by the loco's aesthetic shortcomings, nicknaming them 'Crabs'. They were intended for heavy mineral traffic between Nottinghamshire and Derbyshire and Immingham Docks, but were fitted with water pick-up apparatus from

Although designed to haul heavy mineral trains to the East Coast docks, Robinson's '1B' 2-6-4Ts (LNER Class 'L3') were later relegated to lighter duties and occasional passenger turns. This is No 69052 at Northwich with a local goods train on 1 October 1953; a Northwich shed (9G) resident since 1948, it was withdrawn in August 1954. Although considered unattractive compared with their designer's usual standard, they were powerful-looking machines. *Bob Gellatly collection*

new, although the LNER removed this between 1931 and 1934. The engines were not as successful as Robinson might have wished; their braking proved inadequate for heavy duties, and the coal traffic was beginning to decline, so they were more often used on lighter goods trains, and occasionally passenger services between Rickmansworth and Aylesbury.

As LNER Class 'L1' they were allocated to sheds along the London Extension and Gorton, and six were used on the coal drops at Immingham Docks. In 1929 seven were employed to bank coal trains from Wath Yard up to Dunford Bridge.

Between 1945 and 1950 Thompson's outside-cylinder 'L1' Class 2-6-4s appeared, so the former GCR engines were reclassified 'L3'. One was withdrawn just before nationalisation, but the remaining 19 entered BR service. Withdrawals began quite quickly and by the end of 1950 there were only a dozen still working. Half of these had gone within the next two years, and the last example, No 69069, was dispensed with at Woodford Halse shed in July 1955.

Introduced	1914
Designed by	John Robinson
Built by	GCR, Gorton
Number built	20
Number inherited by BR	19
Last example withdrawn	July 1955

Metropolitan Railway 'K'/'L2' Class 2-6-4T

Nos 9070, 9071

These engines had a curious pedigree. The end of the First World War led to a decline in manufacturing at Woolwich Arsenal, and the Government was anxious to avoid unemployment, so in 1924-25 sponsored the construction of sufficient full sets of components to enable the building of 100 of Maunsell's South Eastern & Chatham Railway 'N' Class 2-6-0s, for that railway and others, with boilers sourced from outside contractors. Unfortunately no customers came forward, and in 1925 the Southern Railway, successor to the SECR, was able to

Introduced	1925
Designed by	George Hally
Built by	Armstrong Whitworth
Number built	6
Number inherited by BR	2
Last example withdrawn	October 1948

buy 50 of the sets at a knock-down price to construct at Ashford what became Nos 31826-75 (sardonically nicknamed 'Woolworths'). A further 26 sets went to the Great Southern Railway of Ireland, and the Metropolitan Railway purchased

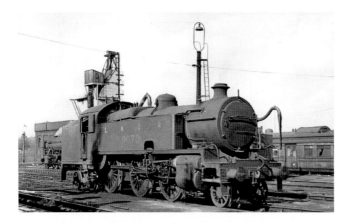

With its Maunsell ancestry apparent, 'L2' 2-6-4T No 9070 is seen at Neasden on 23 June 1948. One of six built in 1925 from an adapted set of parts built at Woolwich Arsenal and intended for SECR 'N' Class 2-6-0s, the two surviving examples were withdrawn in October 1948. *H. C. Casserley*

six, engaging Armstrong Whitworth & Co to use the parts to build 2-6-4 tank engines, numbered 111-116.

This adaptation of the 'N' Class components was overseen by the Met's new Locomotive Engineer, George Hally (who held that post from 1923 until 1933, when he was one of two Metropolitan officers to join the newly formed London Passenger Transport Board). He ensured that the new engines would require as little modification as possible of the Woolwich parts. Classified 'K', the engines inevitably had very much a 'Maunsell' appearance, and were the last new steam engines built for the Metropolitan.

Upon the formation of the LPTB in 1933, it was agreed that the LNER would operate the remaining steam services north of Rickmansworth. Four years later, in November 1937, the six 'K' Class 2-6-4Ts, together with other locomotives, were sold to the LNER and became Class 'L2' Nos 6158-63. They were used mainly on coal trains from Verney Junction, where the Met joined the LMS Bletchley-Oxford line, to the power station at Neasden, and occasionally passenger services. They were very slightly out-of-gauge, so were a tight fit at the Met's own platforms, and were prohibited from working through the tunnels south of Finchley Road.

As non-standard locomotives in the LNER stud, withdrawals started early, in 1943. Just two (LNER Nos 6158 and 6160, later 9070 and 9071) survived to become very briefly BR engines in 1948, both being withdrawn from Neasden in October of that year without carrying their allocated BR numbers.

Metropolitan Railway 'G'/'M2' Class 0-6-4T

Nos 9076, 9077

Charles Jones (b1870) joined the Metropolitan Railway in 1903 as an electrical engineer, then became Chief Resident Electrical & Mechanical Engineer in 1906, responsible for the company's new electrification schemes. He also designed two steam locomotive classes for the Met, one of which was the 'G' Class 0-6-4T, built by the Yorkshire Engine Co in 1915-16. (This Sheffield company was better known as this time for mining equipment and locomotive boilers, and only built 58 complete locomotives between 1913 and 1927.)

The four members of the 'G' Class, numbered 94-97, were the company's largest locomotive design to date, and incorporated some Great Central features, including the Robinson superheater and the general design of the motion, cab and bunker.

Introduced 1915	
Designed by Charles Jones	
Built by Yorkshire Engine	
Number built 4	
Number inherited by BR 2	
Last example withdrawn October 1948	

Together with the 'L2s' (see above), the 'G' 0-6-4Ts were taken over by the LNER from the London Passenger Transport Board in November 1937, becoming Class 'M2' and altered to fit within the LNER's Composite Loading Gauge (although they never worked beyond their Metropolitan home).

The engines were not particularly successful and because of their relatively long fixed wheelbase on the Met's tracks they suffered from cracked frames (to alleviate this a new class of eight 4-4-4Ts, the 'H2s', appeared in 1920-21). The 'M2s' were intended for mixed-traffic duties, although the 'H2s' eventually took over most of the passenger work. Both the LNER and BR classified the engines as being less powerful that the 'L2' 2-6-4Ts, which were generally preferred. Like the 'L2s', the 'M2s' were non-standard engines and therefore dispensed with fairly

Former Metropolitan Railway 0-6-4T No 9076 *Robert H. Selbie* receives attention at Neasden on 23 June 1948. Various numbers and fractions listed under 'L' and 'R' are chalked on the tank side, and a chock of wood appears to be holding the smokebox door shut. Note the nameplate in its unusual position on the front splasher. Whatever work was being undertaken, the locomotive and its fellow BR survivor, No 9077 *Charles Jones*, were withdrawn four months later. *H. C. Casserley*

quickly by the LNER, which under Thompson was increasingly keen on standardisation. No 6157 *Brill* (the former No 97) was withdrawn in 1943 (the engines were unusual in carrying names as well as numbers, and were the last Metropolitan steam locomotives to do so). No 6154 (94) *Lord Aberconway* followed in 1946, and the remaining two, LNER Nos 9076 and 9077 since 1946, briefly passed into BR ownership prior to withdrawal (with the 'L2s') in October 1948. No 9076 was named *Robert H. Selbie*, after the Met's General Manager from 1908 until his death in 1930, and No 9077 *Charles Jones*, after its designer.

H&BR M. Stirling 'F2'/'N12' Class 0-6-2T

No 9089

Introduced 1901	
Designed by Matthew Stirling	
Built by Kitson	
Number built 9	
Number inherited by BR 1	
Last example withdrawn August 1948	

After a shaky start, goods traffic on the Hull & Barnsley Railway was increasing at the turn of the 20th century, so the company bought five 'F1' (LNER 'N11') 0-6-2Ts from Kitson (a cancelled order from the Lancashire, Derbyshire & East Coast Railway, which was unable to pay for them), and Stirling designed his own 'F2' 0-6-2T. The class consisted of nine engines, and they were also built by Kitson, in 1901. The design once again incorporated features influenced by the designer's father Patrick, in the form of a domeless boiler and a round-topped cab.

In 1923 the engines became LNER Class 'N12', and four were rebuilt with new domeless boilers that had been started by the H&BR, while the others received domed boilers. Eventually all had domes.

The 'N12s' were used for hauling, marshalling and banking coal traffic from the West Riding end of the line, shedded at Cudworth, where the H&BR met the Midland Railway. Having vacuum brakes, they also occasionally saw service on passenger trains. Later the engines moved further afield, to Hull, Hartlepool and Ferryhill, and handled agricultural traffic on the Derwent Valley Light Railway at York.

Former Hull & Barnsley 'F2' (LNER 'N12') 0-6-2T No 9089 outlived its sisters by a decade, shunting at the carriage and wagon works at Tuxford until 1942. It then moved back to Hull's Springhead shed, where it and its crew pose for the photographer on 17 April 1947. It was withdrawn 16 months later. Note the Patrick Stirling-inspired round-topped cab. *H. C. Casserley*

The first of the class was withdrawn in 1936, and within two years all but one had been done away with. The survivor, No 2486, was allocated to Ardsley shed until 1938, then moved to Tuxford to work as a shunter at the former LD&ECR wagon repair works there (there had also been a loco works at Tuxford until 1927). In 1942 it moved back to Springhead shed in Hull, from where it was withdrawn in August 1948, having become No 9089 in 1946. It never carried its BR number.

NER W. Worsdell 'U'/'N10' Class 0-6-2T

Nos 69090-102, 9103, 69104-09

Quickly following on from his Class 'P' (LNER 'J24') 0-6-0s, Wilson Worsdell introduced a yet more powerful version for mineral traffic in the form of the 'P1' (LNER 'J25' – qv). By 1902 the NER needed what it described as a 'tank version of the J25 0-6-0 tender locomotive'. Darlington Works was therefore given an order for 20 engines of a new 0-6-2T 'U' Class, which emerged in 1901-02 and were similar to Thomas Worsdell's 'N8' 0-6-2Ts of 1886-90 (qv), but with larger tanks and bunker and smaller driving wheels, the same size as the 'P1s'.

The boilers were interchangeable with the 'J21s', 'J25s', 'N8s' and 'N9s' (qv), and boiler exchanges were therefore common, although the 'N10s' were never superheated.

The duties of the 'Us' were similar to the NER's other 0-6-2Ts,

Introduced 1902	
Designed by Wilson Worsdell	
Built by NER, Darlington	
Number built 20	
Number inherited by BR 20	
Last example withdrawn April 1962	

and they were allocated widely around North East England, most at Hull. During the war they handled some passenger and empty carriage duties, although it is suggested that these were unofficial turns, as the continuous brakes were being removed from the engines at about this time. (They had all been built with Westinghouse brakes, and the LNER fitted vacuum brakes. Later they became only steam-braked, although three had vacuum brakes refitted for pilot duties and carriage workings.) Having

carried fairly random numbers before 1946, as LNER Class 'N10' they became Nos 9090-109 in that year's renumbering programme.

The entire class entered BR service in 1948, although one, No 9103, was withdrawn from Gateshead shed as early as November of that year. Otherwise the class remained intact until 1955, but by the end of 1957 fewer than half remained. Just three engines (Nos 69097/101/109) saw in 1962, but were taken out of service from Bowes Bridge (one) and Gateshead (two) respectively on 9 April.

One of the last three 'N10' 0-6-2Ts, No 69097, was a long-time resident of Bowes Bridge, a sub-shed of Gateshead. Showing its 60 years of service, it was photographed there in April 1960, two years before withdrawal. *T. B. Owen, Colour-Rail*

H&BR M. Stirling 'F3'/'N13' Class 0-6-2T

Nos 9110, 69111-19

The nine 'F2' 0-6-2Ts (LNER 'N12' – qv) of 1901 continued to do good work at the western end of the Hull & Barnsley's line, then in 1914, at the Hull end, the new King George Dock opened as a joint venture between the H&BR and the North Eastern Railway. With the current locomotive stock fully stretched, there was clearly a need for fresh motive power, so more 0-6-2Ts were ordered, this time from the Newcastle firm of Hawthorn Leslie & Co, the name by which R. & W. Hawthorn Ltd became known after the 1884 amalgamation with A. Leslie & Co of Hebburn.

The ten new engines, built during 1913-14 and classified 'F3', were based on the tried and tested 'F2s', but with a greater water capacity, making them 2½ tons heavier. The first five were considered as replacements for older engines, whose numbers they assumed; the earlier locos had 'A' added to their numbers to distinguish them. The second five were numbered in a new sequence.

The LNER classified the engines 'N13', and they were fitted with new domed boilers between 1926 and 1934, of the type used on the older 'N12s', 'J75s' (qv) and 'J80s'; as these earlier engines were withdrawn, some donated their boilers to the younger 'N13s'.

The class were not vacuum-fitted, so were used exclusively as goods engines, shunting the yards at Springhead, Hull, and occasionally taking trip workings to Alexandra Dock or the yards at Dairycoates. Two were allocated at the western end of the H&BR at Cudworth, where they worked alongside the 'N12s'.

After the war the class was divided equally between Leeds Neville Hill and Springhead, while later one was allocated to Alexandra Dock, and that situation pertained throughout the

Former Hull & Barnsley 'F3' No 69119 (H&BR No 156, LNER 2537/9119) is seen at its home shed of Hull Springhead (53C) on 24 August 1952. It moved to Neville Hill, Leeds, in October 1953, and was withdrawn from there in July 1955. *R. M. Casserley*

Introduced 1913
Designed by Matthew Stirling
Built by Hawthorn Leslie
Number built 10
Number inherited by BR 10
Last example withdrawn October 1956

BR years. The first-numbered engine, No 9110, was withdrawn before 1948 was out, but the others were all renumbered 69111-19. No more were taken out of service until May 1953, four were still at work in 1955, and the last, No 69114, was dispensed with at Neville Hill in October 1956, gaining the distinction of being the very last Hull & Barnsley engine in service.

NBR Reid 'A'/'N14' Class 0-6-2T

Nos 69120, 69124, 69125

Glasgow Queen Street station opened on a cramped site in 1842, and was accessed through a tunnel just over a mile long falling at a gradient of 1 in 42 towards the station, built at the insistence of the owners of the Port Dundas Canal. After early experiments with banking engines, trains were rope-hauled up the incline

until 1909, when banking began once more. In that year Reid introduced his Class 'A' 0-6-2Ts, and eventually 105 were built, by both the NBR and LNER. The first batch of six, numbered 858-863, emerged from the works of the North British Locomotive Co in 1909 (which built its 3,000th engine in that year), and had a short cab. These were considered separate from the remainder of the class, and were classified 'N14' by the LNER, while all the others

The remaining three of a class of six former NBR 'N14' 0-6-2Ts survived to be taken into BR stock in 1948. Nos 69120 and 69125 were the last in service, and the latter (which, unlike the others used as Cowlairs bankers, had been a long-time Kittybrewster resident until a move to Aberdeen Ferryhill in 1950) is seen passing through Aberdeen with a rake of empty coaching stock on 29 July 1953. *Brian Morrison*

became Class 'N15' (see next entry). They had inside cylinders with piston valves and Stephenson valve gear.

The first three 'As' went to Eastfield shed, near Cowlairs station, where they were used for banking on the incline; they had a slip coupling operated by a rope and pulley arrangement from the cab, and spent their working lives banking trains on Cowlairs incline. Two others went to Burntisland to handle traffic from the Fife coalfield, and the last (No 863) was allocated to St Margarets, Edinburgh, to be available for emergency

Introduced 1909
Designed by William Reid
Built by North British
Number built 6
Number inherited by BR 3
Last example withdrawn March 1954

passenger work (it was fitted with continuous brakes). The two Burntisland locomotives joined the others at Eastfield in 1912, where they worked the incline for the remainder of their days. The LNER moved what was by then No 9863 from St Margarets to Haymarket, for the same emergency duties, until it went to Kittybrewster in 1927 as a shunter. There it stayed, as No (6)9125, until it moved to Aberdeen Ferryhill in 1950.

Reid had been a locomotive foreman on the NBR for many years, so realised the importance of simple, robust engines. His locomotives were highly standardised – the boiler used on the 'N14s' was common to more than 300 engines of several different classes – so very little modification was undertaken over the years, although during the 1921 coal strike two of the 'N14s' were briefly fitted with oil-burning apparatus.

These 0-6-2Ts were useful and long-lived engines, and the author of the online *LNER Encyclopaedia* notes that 'in a busy yard they appeared to be in perpetual motion – barely stopping to let a shunter hop on or off.'

In 1946 the six engines were renumbered 9120-25, and three (Nos 9121-23) were withdrawn the following year. The other three entered BR stock; Nos 69120 and 69124 remained Eastfield engines until the end, which came in March 1954 and November 1950 respectively. No 69125 was withdrawn from Aberdeen, also in March 1954.

NBR Reid 'A'/'N15' Class 0-6-2T

Nos 69126-224

After the first six 'A' Class 0-6-2Ts (later LNER Class 'N14' – see above) had been built, a further 99 were built over a period of 13 years, and these were classified 'N15' by the LNER. Eighteen were built by the North British Locomotive Co in 1910, followed by a further 20 in 1912 and nine in 1913; another dozen emerged from the same source in 1916, and a final ten in 1920. When the LNER took over in 1923 ten were already on order from Robert Stephenson & Hawthorns, and the last 20 were built at Cowlairs Works.

The first six of these 'As' were built with Westinghouse brakes and larger bunkers to work on the Cowlairs Incline. They differed

In a classic Glasgow Queen Street scene from May 1961, former NBR 'N15/1' 0-6-2T No 69163 banks the 'Queen of Scots' Pullman into the tunnel and up Cowlairs Incline, with 2nd Class Pullman Brake Car No 69 on the rear. The 'Queen of Scots' was introduced in 1928, and reintroduced after the war in 1948. During its career it left Queen Street at various times between 10 and 11 o'clock in the morning, and reached London between 7 and 8 in the evening; it was discontinued in 1963. No 69163 was withdrawn from Eastfield in February 1962. *Michael Mensing, Colour-Rail*

from the earlier members of the class in having the safety valves mounted on the firebox rather than atop the dome. These six were classified by the LNER as 'N15/2', and were shedded at Edinburgh St Margarets, Thornton and Glasgow Eastfield. Three of them had joined their earlier classmates on the Cowlairs Incline by 1923.

The remainder of the class were known as 'N15/1', and were intended for general freight duties, with smaller bunkers and longer cabs. Neither sub-class was subject to any great modification, although new boilers were fitted between 1921 and 1950. Interestingly, an original 'N14' boiler, with safety valves on the dome, survived into BR days, being fitted to No 69151 of 1912, and later carried by No 69222 of 1924.

The 'N15/1s' were spread widely around the NBR system, undertaking varied goods and shunting duties, but only on relatively short distances due to their limited water capacity. By 1935 the LNER allocated 21 to Eastfield, to work the Cowlairs Incline, and typically seven 'N14s' or 'N15s' would be engaged on this task each day.

All 99 'N15s' entered BR stock at nationalisation, and some were subsequently seen allocated to ex-LMS sheds. The class

Introduced 1910
Designed by William Reid
Built by North British (69), NBR, Cowlairs (20), Robert Stephenson (10)
Number built 99
Number inherited by BR 99
Last example withdrawn December 1962

remained intact until 1957, but the gradual introduction of diesels, including Type 2s on Cowlairs banking duties, led to a decline in numbers. By the end of the 1950s 54 were still at work, but 1962 saw the withdrawal of the final 21; eight went in October of that year, and the very last, in December, was No 69178, a Cowlairs-built example from 1923, taken out of service at Motherwell shed (66B).

MSLR Parker (GCR '9A')/'N4' Class 0-6-2T

Nos 69225, 9226, 69227-37, 69239, 69240, 9241, 69242, 9243, 68244-46, 9247

Between 1889 and 1894 there was a great influx of new locomotives on the Manchester Sheffield & Lincolnshire Railway to deal with increasing traffic and new lines being opened. There was a serious deficiency in tank engines for suburban passenger traffic and local goods, and Parker introduced the company's first 0-6-2T class in 1889, which the MSLR's successor after 1897, the Great Central Railway, classified '9A'. These had larger-diameter wheels than previous 0-6-0 classes and a greater coal and water capacity. They had Joy valve gear and round-topped fireboxes, and were built in four batches: Gorton built three engines in 1889 (Nos 161, 165 and 173, later 512-14), while the following year Neilson added 35. Then Gorton built a further three in 1891, followed again by 14 Neilson engines a year later. These engines were numbered 601-38 and 712-25. A further development followed from 1891, adding another 131 0-6-2Ts to GCR stock – these became LNER Class 'N5' (see next entry).

The last 14 '9As' were heavier thanks to a slightly longer bunker, and were referred to as Class '9A Altered'; at first the

Introduced 1889
Designed by Thomas Parker
Built by Neilson (49), GCR, Gorton (6)
Number built 55
Number inherited by BR 22
Last example withdrawn December 1954

LNER classified them 'N4/1' and 'N4/2', and added 5000 to their numbers (in 1946 the 24 surviving engines were renumbered 9225-47). Later they became 'N4/1' and 'N4/3', short- and long-bunkered respectively and outside the LNER Composite Loading Gauge, and 'N4/2' and N4/4', the same but altered with 'flowerpot' chimneys to bring them inside the new dimensions.

The 'N4s' were very similar to other MSLR/GCR engines, with the trailing axlebox design very similar to that used on the 'F1' 2-4-2Ts (qv). Additionally, as with many of the other classes, they were all rebuilt with boilers having Belpaire flat-topped fireboxes; all but three had been so converted by the time of the Grouping, and the process was completed in 1928.

Most of the class worked exclusively on coal and steel traffic around Sheffield and shunted the local marshalling yards. After 1923 they moved further afield, but rarely west of the Pennines, and never south of Leicester.

Eighteen 'N4s' were withdrawn by the LNER before the war, but the remainder continued to put in heavy work around Sheffield and Barnsley without complaint. There were still 22 at work at nationalisation in 1948, a few allocated to Mexborough but the majority at Sheffield Darnall. Only a further six had been lost by 1952, but the remainder were withdrawn between then and the end of 1954.

An 'N4' on home turf: this undated view shows an unidentified member of the class at the head of a local mixed goods at Sheffield Victoria. *Colour-Rail collection*

MSLR Parker (GCR '9C'/'9F')/'N5' Class 0-6-2T

Nos 69250-370

The '9A' (LNER 'N4') 0-6-2Ts (see previous entry) proved to be a success, so more were built between 1891 and 1901. Modifications included the replacement of Joy valve gear with Stephenson link motion, and the round-topped firebox of the 'N4s' with the flat-topped Belpaire firebox; indeed, prototype loco No 7, built at Gorton in 1891, was the first locomotive built for a British railway to use this design, and it became standard on GCR locos thereafter (and used elsewhere, but with less fervour). The company needed to be sure of this innovation, so it was nearly a year before the second engine appeared (No 47), then a third (No 171) a few months later. The trio were classified '9C'.

After adjustment to the valve gear layout, 39 engines were built by close neighbour Beyer, Peacock & Co (which had been using the Belpaire firebox for some years, on export locomotives), delivered in 1893-94. These were ordered by Parker's successor after 1893, Harry Pollitt, and more continued to built through to 1901, when Robinson was in charge at Gorton; these became GCR Class '9F'. In all, there had been 12 batches, with some variation in terms of boilers and superheating. The first to be superheated was No 771 (LNER No 9311) in 1915, which also had its side tanks extended to the front of the smokebox (with a cut-out between the leading and middle driving axles to allow access to the motion), and its bunker enlarged. It is thought that this was to enable it to haul passenger trains to and from Chester and Connah's Quay, which it did briefly, being the only member of Class '9O' (LNER 'N5/3').

These two classes of 0-6-2Ts were the Great Central's standard shunting and 'trip' locomotives for the rest of the company's existence. Some were sold on to other companies; Nos 754-55 went to the West Lancashire Railway (later part of the Lancashire & Yorkshire Railway) in 1894, and two went to the Wrexham, Mold & Connah's Quay Railway, returning to GCR stock when that company was taken over by the GCR in 1905.

All 129 engines passed to the LNER in 1923. Robinson had replaced the original stovepipe chimneys with his own elegant design, but these were in turn replaced by uglier 'flowerpot' examples to bring the engines within the LNER's Composite Loading Gauge; those with original chimneys were referred to as 'N5/1', the others as 'N5/2', until all had been modified by

'N5/2' 0-6-2T No 69262 is far from its original Great Central homeland as it passes through Essendine, on the East Coast Main Line north of Peterborough, with a lightweight goods train in 1959. This engine had begun its BR career at Northwich shed, then moved to Heaton Mersey in 1952. Its final home was New England from April 1958, and it ended its days there at the end of the following year. *D. M. C. Hepburne-Scott, Colour-Rail*

Introduced 1891
Designed by Thomas Parker
Built by Beyer Peacock (81), MSLR/GCR, Gorton (50)
Number built 131
Number inherited by BR 121
Last example withdrawn December 1960

1938. When the LNER acquired large numbers of war-surplus 'ROD' 2-8-0s, the 'N5s' were displaced from their Yorkshire home to more distant parts of the former GCR system. In the 1940s some moved to the Great Northern Section, at Copley Hill (for use as station pilots at Leeds Central), Retford and Newark.

Only ten 'N5s' had been withdrawn by nationalisation, so 121 passed to BR. As with so many other goods and shunting locomotives, they were increasingly replaced by new diesel shunters. From 1955 their numbers fell dramatically through to 1960, when the last 19 were dispensed with, many having spent some time in store; seven survived to November, and the last two, Nos 69296 and 69307, were taken out of service in December at Sheffield Darnall (which latterly had had the largest allocation) and Gorton respectively.

NER T. Worsdell 'B'/'N8' Class 0-6-2T

Nos 69371, 69372, 9373-76, 69377-79, 9380, 69381, 69382, 9383, 9384, 69385-87, 69389-95, 9396, 9397, 9398, 9399, 9400, 69401

Thomas W. Worsdell was appointed to the North Eastern Railway in 1885, having been Locomotive Superintendent of the Great Eastern since 1881. His first entirely new design for his new employer was the Class 'B' 0-6-2T, which was also a new wheel arrangement for the NER; the additional trailing axle

allowed an engine of greater power than preceding 0-6-0Ts. The first ten were simple-expansion locomotives with Joy valve gear, built at Darlington in 1886. Then, as an experiment, two further engines were built at Gateshead in 1888, one of which was a two-cylinder compound using the Worsdell-von Borries system, with a high-pressure cylinder of 18 by 24 inches, and a low-pressure one at 26 by 24 inches. The experiment was evidently a success, as 50 more compounds were built, while the simple-expansion engines were reclassified 'B1'.

Ex-NER T. W. Worsdell 'N8' Class 0-6-2T No 69381 of 1888 is on station pilot duty at Hull Paragon station on 30 August 1954. Shedded at Dairycoates throughout its BR career, it was withdrawn from there in June 1955. *Brian Morrison*

Introduced 1886
Designed by Thomas Worsdell
Built by NER, Darlington (54), NER, Gateshead (8)
Number built 62
Number inherited by BR 30
Last example withdrawn October 1956

Although compounding was generally not popular in Britain – especially before the introduction of superheating – Thomas Worsdell was very keen on the concept. He worked with influential German railway engineer August von Borries (1852-1906), who designed the first Prussian compound locomotive in 1880. He and Worsdell obtained several British patents together.

Starting a compound engine was often problematical, which proved a disadvantage when the 'N8s' were increasingly used on pick-up goods trains. Nonetheless, an 0-6-0 tender version, the Class 'C' compounds (LNER 'J21' – qv), followed.

The 'Bs' were used for medium-distance goods and mineral trains, and were soon a familiar sight on the Stainmore line, where their compounding was found economical, although less so when on short runs or shunting. For heavy loads of coke and coal they were used in pairs to run 'double loads' along that steeply graded line, although the distance involved taxed their water and coal capacity. In 1914 severe new weight

restrictions were placed on the Belah and Deepdale viaducts, and the 'Bs' were banned for several years as being overweight. They also took mineral trains from pit to port, notably Tyne Dock, Sunderland and Hull. At the turn of the century the 0-6-2Ts began to be displaced by large numbers of new 'J24', 'J25' and 'J26' 0-6-0s (all qv), and a large proportion of the class was allocated to Hull for local goods duties.

The 'Bs' were also found useful for passenger rosters (especially empty stock workings), and some were fitted with continuous brakes for this purpose from 1899. Later the LNER used them more widely in this role.

By the turn of the 20th century compounding was falling out of fashion, and Thomas's successor, his brother Wilson, converted the 'Bs' and 'Cs' to simple expansion. Between 1902 and 1912 all the 'Bs' were converted as new cylinders were required, then between 1915 and 1927 37 'N8s' were superheated.

In 1923 both the 'Bs' and 'B1s' were grouped together in LNER Class 'N8', and superheating was discontinued on cost grounds; some engines once more received unsuperheated boilers. The first withdrawal took place in 1929, then gathered pace, with nearly half having gone by 1938. There were still 30 at work when nationalisation dawned, most still at Hull Dairycoates, with others at Heaton, Tyne Dock, Consett and Sunderland. They were gradually dispensed with until just one was left in 1956, No 69390, which had in the preceding eight years seen service at all the above-mentioned sheds except Hull. It was withdrawn from Tyne Dock in October 1956.

NER W. Worsdell 'N'/'N9' Class 0-6-2T

Nos 9410, 9411, 9413-15, 69418, 9419-23, 69424, 9425, 69426, 69427, 9428, 69429

Ex-NER W. Worsdell NER 'N9' Class 0-6-2T No 69427 of 1893 awaits coal and water in the shed yard at Tyne Dock (54B) on 26 August 1954. It had received its BR number in early 1952, moved to Tyne Dock from Sunderland in March 1953, and was withdrawn in June 1955. *Brian Morrison*

Introduced 1893
Designed by Wilson Worsdell
Built by NER, Darlington
Number built 20
Number inherited by BR 17
Last example withdrawn July 1955

Wilson Worsdell took over the reins from his older brother Thomas in 1890, and more goods tank engines were required to supplement the 'B' 0-6-2Ts, so a new version of the same design was used. Twenty of what became NER Class 'N' were built at Darlington in 1893-94; they had Stephenson valve gear, slightly larger cylinders and were not compounded, but were otherwise very similar to the earlier class. To increase the water capacity, high side tanks were used, holding some 250 gallons more than the 'Bs', while a small 130-gallon well tank was added. They were never superheated. Between 1900 and 1923 ten of the class were fitted with air brakes to enable them to handle fish vans and other brake-piped vehicles.

At the Grouping the engines became LNER Class 'N9', and vacuum brakes were added to the air brakes between 1928 and 1931, although six eventually lost that equipment.

The 'N9s' spent most of their working lives on local goods trains around Hull and Hartlepool, especially on the docks, and in the Darlington area. At the outbreak of war the locomotives were concentrated at Darlington, Sunderland and Tyne Dock. The first engines were withdrawn in 1946, but 17 of them entered BR's books in 1948, most still shedded at Tyne Dock, Consett, Sunderland and Darlington, with odd ones at West Auckland and Northallerton. Just three survived into 1955 (of the five that lived long enough to receive their BR numbers); Nos 69424, 69427 and 69429 were withdrawn from Tyne Dock in June and July of that year.

GNR Ivatt Class 'N1' 0-6-2T

Nos 69430-37, 69439-79, 9480, 69481-85

No 190, Ivatt's first 0-6-2 tank engine design for the Great Northern, appeared at the beginning of 1907, and was intended for use on London suburban services. It was fitted with condensing gear, and its side tanks extended forward of the middle driving wheel splashers, creating weight distribution problems that unfortunately made it unsuitable for the Metropolitan 'Widened Lines'; it was consequently stripped of the condensing apparatus and dispatched to Yorkshire.

Towards the end of 1907 a further ten engines were built, slightly larger and heavier, with the radial wheels set further back. Revision of the coal bunker (with a water tank within it) and shorter side tanks resulted in more weight at the rear, rectifying the earlier problem while leaving the fuel capacity unchanged. A further 45 engines were ordered in four batches between the end of 1909 and autumn 1911, the last entering service in the summer of 1912. All but four (working in the West Riding) were fitted with condensing gear. The London engines had destination board brackets fitted to the smokebox door and the rear of the bunker. The boiler used was the same as that on the 'J1' and 'J5' 0-6-0s and 'D2' 4-4-0s (all qv).

In 1910 Ivatt experimented with a different design of condensing apparatus on one engine, using a 'nest' of smaller-diameter pipes to provide a greater radiating area to cool the steam as much as possible before it entered the tank. The engine soon reverted to its original arrangement.

During the First World War two 'N1s', Nos 1587 and 1590, were sold to the War Office for use on armoured trains in Norfolk and South East Scotland (known as HMT *Norna* and HMT *Alice*), which had been built at Crewe from parts supplied by the Great Western and Caledonian railways; they were bought back by the LNER for £1,000 in 1923.

Eleven members of the class were superheated, the first No 1598, in 1918. In 1922 Gresley compared the average coal consumption of the superheated engine with that of the others in the class, and it proved considerably lower. Eleven engines had been superheated by 1928.

Becoming LNER stock at the Grouping, the 'N1s' continued to work suburban trains in the capital as well as transfer goods to and from South London, proving very successful, although they suffered from excessive flange wear on the leading wheels. As with similar engines working in the Welsh valleys, they tended to work downhill with the radial wheels at the

On 6 September 1953 the Stephenson Locomotive Society's 'West Yorkshire Rail Tour' saw Ivatt's pioneer 'N1' 0-6-2T, No 69430 of 1907, at the former Midland terminus of Yeadon, north-west of Leeds. It was shedded at Copley Hill, and withdrawn from there at the end of 1956. *J. Davenport, Colour-Rail*

Introduced 1907
Designed by Henry Ivatt
Built by GNR, Doncaster
Number built 56
Number inherited by BR 55
Last example withdrawn April 1959

front. When the more powerful 'N2' 0-6-2Ts appeared in the early 1920s (one of which, No 69523 of 1921, has been preserved), they gradually took over the passengers duties of the 'N1s', and the latter were relegated to goods duties.

The LNER initially moved a total of 13 'N1s' to Yorkshire to work passenger trains and serve as station pilots in the Leeds, Bradford and Wakefield area, their condensing apparatus removed, followed by further locos during the 1920s.

The class, initially numbered 3190 and 4551-4605 by the LNER, was renumbered 9430-85 in 1946, and the first to be withdrawn was No 9438 in 1947. The remaining 55 entered BR stock the following year, and remained intact until 1951, when a further member (No 9580, which never gained its BR number) was taken out of service. Thereafter numbers increasingly dwindled until just seven remained at work at the end of 1958. Five went the following March, and the last two, Nos 69462 and 69477, ended their lives at Copley Hill shed, Leeds, in April.

In about 1923 the German firm of Bing Brothers produced an electric model of the 'N1' prototype, No 190, for Bassett Lowke.

NER Raven 'Y'/'A7' Class 4-6-2T

Nos 69770-88, 69789

Wilson Worsdell retired as Chief Mechanical Engineer of the NER in May 1910, and his assistant of 15 years, Vincent Raven, succeeded him. There were no immediate changes in policy, and Raven, an early proponent of electrification, was content to follow in his predecessor's footsteps as far as steam was concerned.

The design for these 4-6-2Ts was ready before Worsdell retired, but they did not appear until during Raven's tenure. Apparently they were authorised on 10 February 1910, but this order was cancelled, then re-authorised on 17 November; it is not known whether Raven introduced any changes in the meantime.

Worsdell had introduced his Class 'X' 4-8-0 tanks (see 'T1' Class below) for hump-shunting work (the last engines to be built new at Gateshead Works), and the 'Y' 'Pacific' tanks were the first such engines to built new by the NER (the 'A6s' and 'A8s' – see below – having been conversions). Unlike the 'Xs', these new heavy mineral 4-6-2Ts were going to be out on the road, so had a considerably larger boiler and smaller cylinders for higher speeds. Their work would be relatively short heavy hauls from pit to coal staithes, and a tank engine was chosen to avoid tender-first working. They had three cylinders and, with Stephenson piston valve gear, the drive of all three was on the leading coupled axle. They weighed 87½ tons, had 4ft 7¼in driving wheels, and carried 5 tons of coal and 2,300 gallons of water.

Introduced 1910	
Designed by Vincent Raven	
Built by NER, Darlington	
Number built 20	
Number inherited by BR 20	
Last example withdrawn December 1957	

One of the original requirements was that the engines should be able to haul 1,000 tons at 20mph on level track, and this they could do, although during a test near Shildon one engine slipped to a halt on a 1 in 185 gradient due to faulty sanding gear. Nonetheless, the same engine restarted the same load from rest on a 1 in 148 gradient, reaching 10mph in just over half a mile.

Just 20 engines were built in 1910-11, numbered 1113, 1114, 1126, 1129, 1136, 1170, 1174-76, 1179-83, 1185, 1190-93 and 1195; in 1946, as LNER Class 'A7', they were renumbered more logically as 9770-89. Seventeen of them were superheated between 1917 and 1932 (being classified 'A7/1'), requiring longer smokeboxes. In the mid-1930s the boilers were further modified to allow them to be interchangeable with a number of other LNER classes.

By the time the engines became LNER stock in 1923 they were mostly being used for shunting in the larger marshalling yards, and their power was of great value when propelling wagons over a hump. As heavy mineral traffic declined after the war, most of the 'A7s' were transferred to the Hull area, where they replaced life-expired Hull & Barnsley Railway types.

All 20 entered BR stock at nationalisation and survived until 1951, when No 9789 was withdrawn without having carried its allocated BR number. After 1954 withdrawals accelerated, and only three were still at work in 1957, having moved from Hull Dairycoates to Springhead just prior to their withdrawal on 16 December of that year.

The 'A7' 'Pacific' tanks were a businesslike long-and-low design, well exemplified by No 69784 photographed at Hull Springhead in May 1955. It had transferred from Dairycoates in August 1951, and was withdrawn in March 1956. *T. B. Owen, Colour-Rail*

NER W. Worsdell 'W'/'A6' 'Whitby Tank' Class 4-6-2T

Nos 66791, 9792, 69793-98, 9799

These 'Pacific' tanks did not begin life in that form. They were built by Worsdell in 1907-08 as two-cylinder Class 'W' 4-6-0 tanks, Nos 686-695, specifically to work the steeply graded Whitby-Scarborough line when the earlier Class 'O' 0-4-4Ts (LNER 'G5' – qv) of 1894-1901 proved not to be up to the task. The coastal Scarborough & Whitby Railway had opened in 1885, after a protracted development following the passing of the Act for its construction in 1872. It was a spectacular and scenic line, but included gradients as steep as 1 in 41 southbound and 1 in 39 northbound towards Ravenscar. The NER worked the line from 1898.

Introduced 1907; rebuilt 1914	
Designed by Wilson Worsdell, rebuilt by Vincent Raven	
Built by NER, Gateshead	
Number built 10	
Number inherited by BR 9	
Last example withdrawn March 1953	

The 'Ws' were the NER's first six-coupled passenger tank locomotives, and had a usefully increased adhesive weight over the 'O' 0-4-4Ts. At first the various tall iron viaducts along the coastal route were not strong enough for the new engines, and they worked in the Harrogate and Leeds areas; once the

After working the coast line between Whitby and Scarborough, former NER 'A6' 4-6-2T 'Whitby Tank' No 69791 spent most of its BR career shedded at Starbeck, Harrogate, where it was photographed in June 1950. It moved to Hull Botanic Gardens the following February, and was withdrawn from there six months later. *T. B. Owen, Colour-Rail*

weight restriction issues were solved, the 'Ws' worked the coast line effectively, especially in summer when holiday traffic was heavy. However, their one drawback was a limited capacity for coal and water (just 2 tons of coal and 1,500 gallons of water), and Raven rectified this by rebuilding the class between 1914 and 1917 with larger bunkers and water tanks; this made a trailing bogie necessary, turning the engines into the 4-6-2 'Whitby Tanks' (or 'Willies', or, after rebuilding, 'Woolley Willies'!).

They all passed to the LNER as Class 'A6', renumbered 9790-99 in 1946. Between 1937 and 1944 seven members of the class were fitted with superheaters

In 1934 the former NER Class 'A8' 'Pacific' tanks of 1913-22 (qv below) were put to work on the route, displacing the capable 'A6s', which then moved further afield, many to Hull. During the war they were also found elsewhere, such as Leeds,

Northallerton and Darlington; in 1945 nine of them worked from Harrogate on heavy wartime freight trains.

The first engine, No 9790, was withdrawn in 1947, but the remaining nine became BR property the following year. Another went at the end of 1948, and two in 1950. At the beginning of 1952 just one remained, No 68796, shedded at Hull Botanic Gardens, where it managed to survive shunting carriages at Paragon station until March 1953.

GCR/LNER Robinson/Gresley '9N'/'A5' Class 4-6-2T

Nos 69800-42

The '9N' Class 4-6-2 passenger tanks were one of the first of that arrangement to appear in Great Britain, and were Robinson's last such design for the Great Central. Generally, passenger traffic did not contribute greatly to the GCR coffers, so no new passenger engines appeared in 1910-11 until the '9Ns'. These were introduced to handle the suburban services on the GCR and GCR&GWR Joint lines out of Marylebone to the Chilterns, replacing the '9K' and '9L' 'Atlantic' tanks. (Originally it had been intended to run them as far as Leicester.) These trains comprised rakes of five carriages, setting new standards in commuter comfort ('most palatial' wrote O. S. Nock). This made them heavier than normal commuter trains (at more than 165 tons tare), so a powerful engine with good starting and stopping abilities on the steeply graded country lines was needed. The driving wheels were 5ft 7in in diameter, but the boiler was relatively small, since there would be little requirement for continuous steaming.

Ten were built at Gorton in 1911, another six in 1912, and a further five in 1917. A fourth batch of ten was ordered by the GCR, but did not appear until after the Grouping of 1923.

Resplendent in green passenger livery, free-running and always immaculately maintained, the '9Ns' were instantly popular with enthusiasts, and Bassett Lowke produced a scale model, the first GCR locomotive to be so honoured. The model, of class leader No 165, 'earned the enthusiastic commendation of Robinson himself' (Nock).

The '9Ns' were some of the first GCR engines to be superheated, and between 1915 and 1917 they were standardised on Robinson's own patent superheater design. Thereafter the engines remained virtually unaltered, although some (including all of the 1923

On home turf, former GCR Neasden-allocated 'A5' 4-6-2T No 69814 runs bunker-first with the 3.25pm Aylesbury to Marylebone local service between West Wycombe and High Wycombe on 6 June 1953. Over the following nine years the engine moved to Grantham, King's Cross, Lincoln and Colwick, and was one of the last three of the class to be withdrawn in November 1960. *Brian Morrison*

Introduced 1911
Designed by John Robinson
Built by GCR, Gorton (31), Hawthorn Leslie (13)
Number built 44
Number inherited by BR 43
Last example withdrawn November 1960

batch) were fitted with an experimental Automatic Train Control system known as 'Reliostop', which incorporated a lever below the running plate that contacted trackside equipment. Later, between 1947 and 1949, the Hudd and GWR ATC systems were tried on a number of the class.

Some of the class were temporarily converted to oil-burning as a result of coal strikes in 1921 (ten engines) and 1926-27 (six). All were also initially fitted with water pick-up gear, but this was removed in early BR days.

In 1921 one engine was fitted with a cab incorporating side windows (they had thus far not been so equipped), and thereafter all new '9Ns' had these cabs, and the earlier engines were similarly altered between 1924 and 1926. The LNER engines gradually received lower domes and Gresley chimneys to keep them within the new Composite Loading Gauge.

So sound was the '9N' design that Gresley decided to build 13 more, and they emerged from Hawthorn Leslie's works with detail differences in 1925-26, making 44 locomotives in total, now Class 'A5'. The LNER engines were not, however, intended for use on the Marylebone line, but to make good a serious shortage of passenger tank locomotives in the North Eastern area around Middlesbrough. Some others migrated north to the Bradford area, then by 1928 six of these had returned south to King's Cross to work trains to Hitchin and Baldock.

In 1937 the LNER took over the former Metropolitan Railway route (by now London Transport) between Rickmansworth and Aylesbury, replacing older 'H2' 4-4-4Ts with the 'A5s'.

One engine, No 5447, was withdrawn in 1942 with cracked frames, and in 1946 the remaining 43 were renumbered 9800-42. They passed to BR in 1948, but were gradually replaced by newer Thompson 'L1' 2-6-4Ts of 1945-50. The 'A5s' went to Lincolnshire, then some further north to Hull, and to work Darlington-Saltburn services. BR reclassified them as 'A5/1' (Nos 69800-29, the GCR originals, all allocated to Neasden in 1948) and 'A5/2' (69830-42), the Gresley-modified LNER batch.

The 43 engines remained in service until mid-1957, when two were withdrawn. Increasing dieselisation then took its toll, and by the end of 1958 there were only 18 survivors, reduced to just ten a year later. The last three, Nos 69808/14/20, which were all GCR originals (the last of the LNER batch was withdrawn in 1958), were taken out of service at Lincoln, Colwick and Immingham respectively.

NER Raven/Gresley 'A8' Class 4-6-2T

Nos 69850-94

Between 1913 and 1922 Raven introduced his three-cylinder 'D' Class 4-4-4 tank locomotives to work relatively short-distance fast passenger trains radiating from Darlington, along the coast between Saltburn and Scarborough, and fast residential services in the Leeds-Harrogate area. (The class lettering system had already reached 'Z', so these engines used what was by then the vacant 'D' classification.) The 4-4-4 wheel arrangement and cab design were chosen to provide good riding qualities in both the forward and reverse directions. Twenty of these handsome engines were built in 1913, but a second order the following year fell victim to the onset of war. Between 1920 and 1922 25 more engines were added, becoming the most numerous class of 4-4-4s in the country,

Introduced 1913; rebuilt 1931-36	
Designed by Vincent Raven; rebuilt by Nigel Gresley	
Built by NER, Darlington	
Number built 45	
Number inherited by BR 45	
Last example withdrawn June 1960	

and the only three-cylinder tank engines to that wheel arrangement. However, they did not prove particularly popular: although free-running locomotives, it was found that the double-bogie arrangement led to rolling at speed.

The engines became Class 'H1' under LNER ownership, and it seems that comparison with the ex-GCR 'A5' 4-6-2Ts (qv) and a series of trials throughout the North East area, revealing that their adhesion weight of 39 tons was insufficient, led to the decision to rebuild the 'H1s' as 'Pacific' tanks, undertaken during Gresley's tenure at Doncaster between 1931 and 1936. The new 'A8' 4-6-2Ts certainly demonstrated a better adhesive weight of 52 tons, with their additional coupled axle, and had better riding characteristics. O. S. Nock was of the opinion that 'these rebuilds were among the smoothest riding engines I have ever travelled on.' The first engine converted was 'H1' No 2162, and the subsequent rebuilding programme involved a modified superheated boiler, which from 1935 was adapted to become interchangeable with several other LNER classes.

Former NER 'A8' 4-6-2T No 69860 heads a lightweight passenger train at Whitby in November 1957. It was a Middlesbrough (51D) engine at this time, moving to Thornaby in May of the following year, from where it was withdrawn with the final nine others in June 1960. I. Davidson, Colour-Rail

As LNER Class 'A8', these new tanks were well equal to the task of working heavy suburban and long-distance coastal trains, replacing the earlier 'G5' 0-4-4Ts. Once again it was the spread of dieselisation that displaced the 'A8s' from these duties.

All 45 engines entered BR stock in 1948, and none was disposed of until two were withdrawn towards the end of 1957. Thereafter scrapping was rapid; less than half the class were still working in 1960, and they had all gone by the middle of the year, the last 13 being consigned to scrap in May and June.

GCR/LNER Robinson/Gresley '8H'/'S1' Class 0-8-4T

Nos 69900-5

The idea of a yard for the concentration of coal traffic arose following the visit of the GCR General Manager, Sam Fay, to the USA. There were some 45 collieries within a 10-mile radius of the GCR at Wath-on-Dearne, between Doncaster and Barnsley and right in the centre of the South Yorkshire coalfield, and their output had to be sorted wagon by wagon to numerous destinations, resulting in a very complex pattern of rail traffic. The gravitation yard at Wath was therefore planned at a cost of £191,000 and built by contractors Logan & Hemingway; it was fully opened in November 1907. More than a mile long, it employed two humps and two signal cabins, one at each end, controlling 15 reception roads. The humps fed 21 sorting sidings for each of the up and down directions – 36 miles of sidings in all, able to handle some 5,000 wagons per day. The coal wagons were 'tripped' to the yard from the collieries, then sorted into longer-distance trains for onward distribution. The 1984-85 miners' strike led to a steep decline in coal traffic, and the yard finally closed in 1988.

To propel the rakes of coal wagons over the humps, in 1907-08 Robinson designed four 'huge but not unwieldy' (George Dow) '8H' Class 0-8-4 tanks, which were inevitably nicknamed 'Humpies'. (They were also later known as 'Wath Daisies', and sometimes referred to by the ironic nickname 'Mickey Mouse'.) They were developed from Robinson's '8A' Class (LNER 'Q4' – qv) mineral engines, with a third cylinder that made them the most powerful engines in Great Britain at the time, as well as the first 0-8-4 engines in the country. The third cylinder also provided a more even power delivery than just two. Using the same boiler as the GCR 'Atlantics', they weighed in at all but 100 tons, with an adhesive weight of more than 75 tons. They demonstrated that they could handle a load of more than 1,000 tons against a gradient of 1 in 109, although even so they could slip in bad weather. The requirement was that they should be able to push a train of 80 loaded wagons (about 1,200 tons) over the hump, and were sometimes used in pairs to achieve this. They were fitted with powered reversing gear, to aid with the constant toing and froing in the busy yard.

Originally numbered 1170-3, in 1923 they became LNER Class 'S1' Nos 6170-03. To increase the power and improve adhesion, in 1930 Nigel Gresley fitted one of them, No 6171 (BR No 69901), with a reversible booster fitted to the outside-framed trailing bogie, which added power at slow speed or for starting heavy loads; this engine was classified 'S1/2'. Subsequently two new booster-fitted locomotives were built at Gorton in 1932, classified 'S1/3' (the original engines being

Former GCR 'S1' 0-8-4T No 69900 – all 99 tons 6cwt of it – is seen at its home shed of Mexborough on 11 May 1952. It moved to Doncaster in January 1954, and was withdrawn and cut up in early 1956. Whether any heritage line could have coped with such a monster had it been preserved is debatable!
K. C. H. Fairey, Colour-Rail

Introduced 1907
Designed by John Robinson
Built by Beyer Peacock (4), LNER, Gorton (2)
Number built 6
Number inherited by BR 6
Last example withdrawn January 1957

'S1/1'). It seems that the boosters did not work well in reverse, so were seldom used in that mode, and were eventually disabled in reverse; they were removed altogether in 1943. The 'S1/2' and 'S1/3s' were superheated, to increase the power to the boosters; the original 'S1/1s' were later similarly fitted. In 1946 the six engines were renumbered 9900-05.

The original 'S1s' worked in pairs on the two humps at Wath until replaced by the two 'S1/3s', after which they moved to the newly opened Whitemoor yard at March until replaced by diesel shunters in 1949; they then moved to Frodingham steelworks until returning to Wath in 1950. By 1953 diesel shunters were working successfully at Wath too, so the 'S1s' went to Doncaster, with one tried for a short period at Immingham Docks. All six engines were then placed in storage at Doncaster, and were scrapped between 1954 (No 69903) and 1956/57 (the remainder).

NER W. Worsdell 'X'/'T1' Class 4-8-0T

Nos 69910-22

In the year before he retired from the North Eastern Railway, Wilson Worsdell designed a three-cylinder 4-8-0 tank locomotive for heavy marshalling and shunting duties in the hump yards in the Thornaby and Middlesbrough area, as well as the yards at Gascoigne Wood, Hull and Tyne Dock. The effectiveness of such a three-cylinder design with a high tractive effort had recently been demonstrated by Robinson's 0-8-4Ts built for the Wath gravitation yard in 1907 (see above), although the NER engines were less powerful and lighter, and effectively had the GCR's trailing bogie at the front end. Worsdell employed 'divided drive', with the inside cylinder driving the leading axle, and the outside cylinders driving the second axle. An interesting feature of these 'X' Class tanks was that the three cylinders and valve chests were a single casting, foreshadowing the 'monobloc' construction adopted by Gresley many years later.

Six engines were built at Gateshead in 1909, followed by another four the following year, during Raven's tenure, numbered 1350-59. They are notable as the last engines to be built new at that historic works; there was no space between the main line and river to extend further, so all new construction was moved to Darlington.

Introduced	1909
Designed by	Wilson Worsdell
Built by	NER, Gateshead (10), LNER, Darlington (5)
Number built	15
Number inherited by BR	13
Last example withdrawn	June 1961

In 1923 the engines became LNER Class 'T1', and Gresley built five more in 1925, Nos 1656-60. They were to be found at work in the North East at Hull Dairycoates, Newport, Selby, Tyne Dock, Gateshead and Stockton. In 1929 No 1656 was used for a time further south at Whitemoor yard, near March, later replaced by Nos 1355 and 1358, although the 'S1's were ultimately preferred.

In 1935 a new boiler was designed to fit not only the 'T1's, but also the 'A6', 'A7', 'A8' and 'H1' classes, although only one 'T1' was superheated (the future BR No 69914, apparently due to a misunderstanding at Darlington Works); it reverted to a saturated boiler in 1951.

In 1937 the two former Whitemoor engines, Nos 1355 and 1358, were scrapped, but the remaining 13 continued to work coal trains at docks and marshalling yards throughout the North East. As coal traffic declined, so they moved to other sheds for further heavy shunting duties, and the 13 surviving engines, having been renumbered 9910-22 in 1946, duly became BR Nos 69910-22 in 1948. Withdrawals did not commence until 1955; there were only six working at the end of 1958, but one example, No 69921, managed to carry on until withdrawn from Tyne Dock in June 1961.

The last surviving 'T1' 4-8-0T was No 69921, built by the LNER in 1925. Having been allocated to Newport, Stockton, Hull, Goole and Selby since nationalisation, it was a Tyne Dock engine from September 1959, and was withdrawn from there in June 1961. This photograph at Tyne Dock is dated 7 September 1960.
T. B. Owen, Colour-Rail

LNER Thompson 'Q1' Class 0-8-0T

Nos 69925-37

'A new 0-8-0 tank locomotive: the L.N.E.R. saves steel to assist the War effort.' So ran a headline in *Railways* in 1942, announcing the conversion of 13 Robinson 'Q4' (GCR '8A') 0-8-0 tender engines into tank locomotives.

The large '8As' (qv) had emerged from Gorton Works and Kitson & Co between 1902 and 1911, and withdrawal had begun in 1934, but was delayed by a wartime shortage of goods locomotives. Of more use as tank locomotives for heavy shunting, it was decided to rebuild 25 'Q4s', but in the event only 13 were converted between 1942 and 1945, and they were classified 'Q1', a designation previously held by a class of Ivatt engines, extinct from 1934. The tanks retained the frames, cylinders and connecting rods of the 'Q4s', but the boiler was

Introduced	1902; rebuilt 1942-45
Designed by	John Robinson; rebuilt by Edward Thompson
Built by	Kitson (8), LNER, Gorton (5)
Number built	13
Number inherited by BR	13
Last example withdrawn	September 1959

shortened in order to accommodate a fully enclosed cab and the bunker. Some parts were used from a cancelled order for more 'J50' 0-6-0Ts, which the new 'Q1s' were intended to replace.

The first four rebuilds entered service in 1942-43 but were soon criticised for inadequate water capacity of 1,500 gallons, so the next nine engines, built in 1943-45, had a longer bunker that incorporated a water tank, but reduced the coal capacity. The first four (BR numbers 69925-28) were classified 'Q1/1', and the

While most of the 'Q1' rebuilds were allocated to Langwith Junction and Frodingham by British Railways, a couple went to Selby, and two to Eastfield, Glasgow. Class leader No 69925 is seen at the latter shed at on an unknown date in the early 1950s. This Kitson-built engine began life as a GCR 'Q4' 0-8-0 No 58 in 1903, and was converted to 0-8-0T form in June 1942 as No 5058. Renumbered 9925 in 1946, it was withdrawn on 31 August 1954 and cut up at Cowlairs in October. Note the LNER 'totem' on the bunker. *P. J. Hughes, Colour-Rail*

later engines (69929-37), now carrying 2,000 gallons, became 'Q1/2'. Any 'Q4s' that had been superheated lost their superheaters with the rebuilding, and steam brakes were fitted. In their new form the 'Q1s' were designated an LNER standard class.

In 1946 the assorted numbers of the 'Q1s' (based on the GCR originals) were brought into a single sequence, 9925-37. The new engines proved to be more powerful that the 'J50s', but not as powerful as the big 'S1' 0-8-4Ts or 'T1' 4-8-0Ts (both qv); they were reckoned to be about as strong as an 'O4' 2-8-0, but their use was still restricted by their relatively small water capacity. They were especially successful handling heavy steel trains in the Frodingham and Scunthorpe areas.

The first engine was withdrawn in 1954, and there were still ten at the end of 1957. Thereafter withdrawals came quickly, the last five disappearing in August and September 1959, all Frodingham (36C) residents.

LNER Gresley/Beyer Garratt 'U1' Class 2-8-8-2T

No 69999

Following the opening of the Great Central's Wath concentration yard, coal trains heading west were taken along the freight-only line through Worsborough Dale towards Penistone. Although this avoided congestion in Barnsley, it involved a gruelling 2½-mile-long incline at 1 in 40 (made worse by abrupt slight changes in gradient caused by mining subsidence), hardly suitable for heavy mineral trains! In the early 1920s trains of up to about 1,100 tons were headed by two Robinson 2-8-0s, one of which was transferred to the rear to assist the train up to Wentworth Junction. For the final assault on the bank two further engines were attached at the rear, and even with four engines it might take 20 minutes to ascend the steepest 2 miles of the incline.

The GCR had considered an articulated Beyer Garratt-type locomotive, but it was not until 1925 that Gresley and Beyer Peacock developed the unique three-cylinder 'U1' 2-8-8-2T (there were plans for two engines, but the second was not built). Costing almost £15,000 and built in a matter of weeks, it was equivalent in power to two standard GNR 2-8-0s, and thus provided all the assistance that was required. O. S. Nock recalls being told that Beyer Peacock would have preferred to have had a free hand with the design, but Gresley insisted on being involved (he amended the design to use three cylinders at each end and his own 'derived motion' for the inside cylinders), making the construction process less than harmonious.

The boiler was a massive 7 feet in diameter and 13 feet long, and the firebox was more than 8 feet long, establishing No 2395 as the largest, heaviest and most powerful steam locomotive ever to be built for a British railway. The total weight in working order was 178 tons, and the nominal tractive effort was 72,940lb. The wheels, the six cylinders and the motion were interchangeable with the 'O2' Class 2-8-0s.

The Garratt made its debut in workshop grey at the Stockton & Darlington Centenary celebrations on 1 July 1925, and entered service at Worsborough the following month. Typical trains consisted of 60 or so wagons and arrived with an engine

Introduced 1925	
Designed by Nigel Gresley and Beyer Garratt	
Built by Beyer Peacock	
Number built 1	
Number inherited by BR 1	
Last example withdrawn December 1955	

The unique 'U1' Beyer Garratt 2-8-8-2T No 69999 is seen at Dewsnap, near Guide Bridge, at the Manchester end of the Woodhead route, in 1955 before its final trial on the Lickey Incline. It ascended the Lickey bunker-first, but even so visibility from the cab when buffering up to a train was far from ideal, as can be seen. *E. Oldham*

at both ends; No 2395 then left its siding and coupled up behind the banker. Following arrival at West Silkstone Junction, the Garratt would uncouple and return to Wentworth Junction.

In its heyday the Garratt made about 18 trips up the bank each 24 hours. Near the top were the two short Silkstone Tunnels, and one can only imagine the conditions inside after the passage of four hard-working locomotives. At one time the Garratt was experimentally equipped with respirators for the crew, taking air from near rail-level, until the crews objected to having to share the equipment on hygiene grounds, resorting to the time-honoured practice of wet handkerchiefs over their mouths. The additional work required of a single crew to operate the giant was also not appreciated: 'Twice the work but the same sodding pay' was apparently the general reaction!

In 1946 the engine was renumbered 9999, and gained its BR number, 69999, in November 1948, although the small '2395' cabside numberplates continued to be carried.

By 1949 the engine was in need of a new boiler but, with impending electrification of the Worsborough route, this would be uneconomic unless further work could be found. Thus in 1949-50 the Garratt was reallocated from Mexborough to Bromsgrove shed and tried out as a banker on the Lickey Incline. Visibility from the cab was a problem when buffering up behind a train, especially at night, and an electric headlight was fitted. Returning to storage at Mexborough in November 1950, it was converted to oil-firing at Gorton and was tried again on the Lickey in 1955, but without conspicuous success. Subsequently stored at Bromsgrove, it returned to Gorton at the end of that year, having clocked up just over 425,000 in 30 years. Supposedly the end came through failure of the oil-burning conversion, but the engine was very unpopular with crews, and was slightly out of gauge on the London Midland Region, apparently causing some damage to platform edges. The end came at Doncaster Works in March 1956.

5

British Railways Standard locomotives and 'Austerity' classes

6P5F 'Clan' Class 4-6-2

Nos 72000-09

'Clan' 'Pacific' No 72001 *Clan Cameron* is captured at speed near Brock, on the West Coast Main Line between Lancaster and Preston, in 1961. The similarity to the design of the 'Britannias' is clear. This engine entered traffic on 29 December 1951 and was withdrawn exactly 11 years later, and scrapped at Darlington.
M. Chapman, Colour-Rail

Introduced 1951
Designed by Robert Riddles, at Derby
Built by BR, Crewe
Number built 10
Last example withdrawn May 1966

When the first British Railways 'Standard' steam locomotives appeared in 1951, steam was expected to be around for many years. They were built with an anticipated life expectancy of 30 years, so would probably be around until the 1980s, some into the 1990s. However, the British Railways Modernisation Plan of 1955 changed the landscape, and no more new steam locomotives were to be built after 1956 – although in the event the last was not completed until 1960. The rapidity of the demise of steam was unexpected – evolution rather than revolution had previously been the order of the day, and it was probably assumed that modernisation would follow a similar pattern.

BR inherited about 500 different steam locomotive classes, amounting to about 20,000 machines, and between 1948 and 1960 built just over 2,500 more, comprising 999 Standards and the rest to pre-nationalisation designs. The end of regular steam haulage in August 1968 meant that, of the Standards, the oldest was a mere 17 years old, and the youngest just eight year sold, all withdrawn in working order – a dreadful waste of resources and potential.

The Railway Executive faced much criticism for producing the 12 Standard classes in such short order, but at the time it was felt that dieselisation and electrification – the ideal options, but of which the Executive had little experience in main-line use – would be prohibitively expensive in those post-war austerity years, so were ruled out in the foreseeable future. There was plenty of coal at home, while oil was imported and expensive, and Britain had considerable foreign exchange problems. However, the Modernisation Plan suddenly provided a feast of investment opportunities after

years of famine, and steam was consigned to history as undesirable and obsolete almost overnight.

One positive outcome for the future preservation movement was that there was suddenly available a large number of perfectly serviceable engines, and of the 999 built more than 40 have been preserved, representing eight of the 12 Standard classes. The engines in this section therefore represent the four classes that were lost altogether (together with the two 'Austerity' classes), although all four are currently the subject of 'new-build' projects.

Perhaps the most notable loss was the 'Clan' 'Pacifics'. They were designed at Derby under the overall supervision of Robert A. Riddles, Member for Mechanical and Electrical Engineering at the Railway Executive. As with the other designs, they were largely based on LMS practice, with tapered boilers, high running plates, two cylinders and streamlined cabs.

The 'Clans' were the first Standard Class 6 mixed-traffic engines, and the first was turned out at Crewe Works at the end of 1951, having cost £20,426. Nine more had followed by the spring of 1952, such was the urgent need. It had been planned to build another 15, but an acute steel shortage meant that they were continually postponed until the order was finally cancelled with the publication of the 1955 Modernisation Plan. Had they been built, experience with the hastily constructed first batch might have led to improvements, and a better performance. The 'Clans' had gone effectively straight from the drawing board and into traffic, even missing their slot on the Rugby test plant. Also, it should be borne in mind that four of the Standard classes, including the 'Clans', were almost entirely new designs, so teething problems were to be expected – the other classes were close adaptations of existing proven locomotive designs.

The design of the 'Clans' was based on that of the 'Britannia' 4-6-2s, but with a smaller boiler and other weight-saving measures to increase their route availability in their chosen area of operations, the west of Scotland. The new engines received a mixed response from crews, particularly in comparison with the larger and clearly more powerful Class 7 'Britannias', the principal complaint being poor steaming, which had a distinct 'woolliness', according to E. S. Cox. One of the reasons why the 4-6-2 layout was favoured was that it permitted a wider firebox, able to cope with cheaper imported coal, but the small chimney tended the 'choke' the exhaust, reducing overall efficiency. Later the blastpipe was modified, which improved matters.

It was Cox's suggestion that the engines be named after clans, perpetuating some of the names of the earlier Highland Railway 4-4-0s, the last of which had been withdrawn in 1950. Class leader No 72000 *Clan Buchanan* was named at a special ceremony at Glasgow Central station on 15 January 1952. Had more been built, the first five were to have been destined for the Southern Region, carrying the names *Hengist*, *Horsa*, *Canute*, *Wildfire* and *Firebrand*.

The whole class was based predominantly at Glasgow's Polmadie shed, and Kingmoor in Carlisle. This restricted their area of operation, and opportunities for crews elsewhere to get to know them. Regular crews liked them, but men unfamiliar with them gave the class an undeservedly bad reputation.

Whatever, the 'Clans' did notably good work on Shap and Beattock banks, and on the notorious Settle-Carlisle line. They also handled services from Glasgow and Edinburgh to Crewe, Manchester, Liverpool, Leeds and Bradford, and especially the Stranraer boat trains. One was successfully tried on the West Highland line in 1956, the only 'Pacific' locomotive to have operated on that route. Another worked briefly out of Liverpool Street, but was considered locally to be 'no better than a good "B1"'.

The 'Clans' were hard-working, easily maintained, economical mixed-traffic engines with good availability, but despite their undoubtedly effective (if not spectacular headline-grabbing) work in the right hands, they were generally considered a failure, although falling only slightly short of Riddles's aims.

The first casualties were the Polmadie locos, Nos 72000-04, which were withdrawn en masse in December 1962 and scrapped at Darlington. The Kingmoor allocation were taken out of service between April 1965 and 16 April 1966, when the last example, No 72008 *Clan Macleod*, was dispensed with and scrapped at McWilliams of Shettlestone two months later. Although a mere 14 years 3 months old, it was the longest serving of the class.

The 'Clan' project of the Standard Steam Locomotive Company Ltd aims to build a brand-new member of the class, utilising the original BR design drawings but incorporating many improvements necessary for the modern railway in addition to those intended to have been made had the second batch been built. It will be the 11th of the class, and will take the next number and name in the original Crewe Works inventory, No 72010 *Hengist*. Perhaps when the new 'Clan' is completed, it will be able to prove the potential of this maligned class, just as the restored No 71000 *Duke of Gloucester* was able to vindicate that design.

3MT Class 2-6-0

Nos 77000-19

The BR Standard Class 3 2-6-0 was something of a hybrid design, the chassis being based, as with the Standard 4MT 2-6-0s of the 76xxx Class, on the Ivatt Class 4s of 1947-52, with chassis components also of LMS design, while the boiler was a shortened version of that fitted to the GWR 'Large Prairies' and '5600' Class 0-6-2Ts. This is not surprising, as the design and construction was undertaken by Swindon Works between February and September 1954, at the same time as the 45 3MT 2-6-2Ts, Nos 82000-44 (qv). The motion brackets were based on the design used by the Ivatt Class 2 2-6-0s and 2-6-2Ts. The driving wheels were of the same diameter as those of the 76xxx 'Moguls', but were a different design. The boiler was pressed to 200psi, there were two cylinders, and Walschaerts valve gear. Overall, O. S. Nock described it as 'a very un-Great Western looking design.'

After the 'Clans', these Class 3 'Moguls' were numerically the smallest Standard class, with only 20 built. They were thus hardly 'standard' at all, but proved to be useful, if unspectacular, little engines that were sent to work in the North Eastern and Scottish regions, which required locomotives with a maximum axle loading of 16 tons. However, uniquely No 77014 ended its days on the Southern at Guildford, the last survivor of the class, being withdrawn in July 1967. It had the distinction of being the very last steam loco to run on the Southern when it hauled a parcels train from Poole to Weymouth on the last day of Southern

steam. It was scrapped at Birds in February 1968, but happily its chimney survived and is to be used, together with other components salvaged from scrapyards, by the 82045 Steam Locomotive Trust, which is in the process of building the next member of the extinct 3MT 82xxx tank engine class (see below).

This 'Mogul' class was notable in that it survived intact the longest of the Standards, the first engine not being dispensed with until as late as November 1965. None survived the cutter's torch, but once again the class is the subject of a new-build project. The 77021 Locomotive Group has been formed to fill this preservation gap, and considers that the 3MT 2-6-0, being a relatively lightweight design, will be an ideal heritage line machine, and very much at home on any of the preserved railways in the North East and Scotland. BR standardisation here pays dividends, as significant costs can be saved by using

Introduced 1954
Designed by Robert Riddles, at Swindon
Built by BR, Swindon
Number built 20
Last example withdrawn July 1967

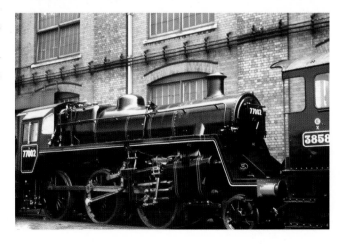

No 77002, resplendent in fresh BR mixed-traffic lined black livery, stands brand-new outside Swindon Works on 14 February 1954. In its short life of just over 13 years it was shedded at Darlington (initially), West Auckland, Hull Dairycoates, Stourton (twice) and Tweedmouth, before moving finally to York in October 1966. It was one of only three of the class to see 1967, being withdrawn in June of that year. *T. B. Owen, Colour-Rail*

patterns held by fellow members of the British Railways Standard Locomotive Owners Group. The new No 77021 will incorporate modern technological and production advances wherever possible, and will be dual-braked. Conforming to the class's original 16-ton maximum axle load, it will be 'a light, go-anywhere locomotive, but with more than ample power for heritage railway use … [and suitable for] … any railway wishing to use a modern, powerful and track-friendly locomotive.' Not unlike the BR originals.

The same locomotive is seen at the end of its brief life in York roundhouse on 10 June 1967. It was cut up the following February. *A. Gray, Colour-Rail*

3MT Class 2-6-2T

Nos 82000-44

These 'Prairie' tanks were the forerunners of the 3MT 2-6-0 tender equivalent of 1954 in the 77xxx series (see above). Again, the chassis was derived from and shared a number of parts with the Ivatt Class 4s of the LMS, with a shortened boiler based on the No 2 boiler as fitted to the GWR 'Large Prairies' and '5600' Class 0-6-2Ts. In general, the design details were the same as for the tender version and, like the 'Moguls', the requirement was for a lightweight engine with a maximum axle loading of 16 tons. It was a brand new design, the 80xxx and 84xxx tanks being based on existing former LMS designs already in use.

Built for light passenger work, the engines emerged from Swindon between 1952 and 1955, the timescale elongated by a national steel shortage. It had been planned to build 63 altogether, but the advent of the Modernisation Plan put paid to any further construction. They were set to work on the Western, Southern, North Eastern and London Midland regions with a design life of 40 years; however, their short lives of no more than 15 years were ended by the widespread introduction of diesel multiple units on branch-line and local passenger services. The engines were outshopped in BR lined mixed-traffic black livery, but after 1957 those on the Western Region

Introduced 1952	
Designed by Robert Riddles, at Swindon	
Built by BR, Swindon	
Number built 45	
Last example withdrawn July 1967	

were given lined green livery (the lining omitted in the early 1960s as an economy measure). These were the only BR Standard tank locomotives to carry more than one livery.

Sceptical at first, Western crews came to like these unfamiliar engines, which proved powerful enough to regularly work seven- or eight-coach trains over the Cambrian Coast route, even being used on pilot duties over Talerddig bank. A disadvantage was their limited water and coal capacity of just 1,500 gallons and 3 tons, although this was increased slightly on later members of the class.

As steam was phased out on other regions, the engines gradually gravitated towards the Southern; at one time Nine Elms had 14 on its books, out of the 32 then remaining. The shortest-lived member of the class was No 82043, withdrawn from Bristol Barrow Road in February 1964 when only 8 years 8 months old. The last two survivors were Nos 82019 and 82029, which lasted at Nine Elms until the end of steam on the Southern in July 1967; No 82029 worked the 7.18am Waterloo-Salisbury train on the final day.

Interestingly, Nos 82000/03/31/34, shedded at Machynlleth and Bangor in 1965, were then moved to Patricroft shed in Manchester for use on local suburban trains. Although not really required for such duties, they were still there when the shed closed in July 1968. One had recently had an overhaul and was in full working order, so was offered for sale at £1,500 – just over £24,000 at today's values, so by no means outlandish compared with present-

At the end of its days, shabby 3MT 2-6-2T No 82029 works what may be empty stock at Clapham Junction on 17 June 1967. It had begun life in the North East, at Darlington, West Hartlepool, Malton (twice), Scarborough and York, before moving south to Guildford in September 1963. It saw out Southern steam at Nine Elms, being one of the last to be withdrawn, in July 1967. *R. Patterson, Colour-Rail*

day new-build costs. However, there were no takers, so the quartet were cut up by Cashmore at Newport, South Wales, in October, two months after the official end of steam on BR.

The fact that not one of these useful engines was able to be spared is to be rectified by the 82045 Steam Locomotive Trust, which is in the process of building the next member of the class, No 82045, intended specifically for heritage line use. The Trust claims that 'batch production' of such a loco – if any other

groups were interested – would bring the price down from the unit cost of between £1,250,000 and £1,500,000, despite being able to use standard patterns common to other new-build Standards (if only £1,500 could have been found in 1968!). The Trust classifies No 82045 as the 1,001st steam locomotive to a BR Standard design, since the commencement of its construction follows that of the new 'Clan', No 72010 *Hengist* (qv). The Trust's patron is, appropriately, HRH the Duke of Gloucester.

2MT Class 2-6-2T

Nos 84000-29

The fourth of the BR Standard classes to have evaded preservation is the 2MT 'Prairie' tank design in the 84xxx number series, the tank engine version of the 2MT 2-6-0 tender engines of the 78xxx series. They were designed at Derby Works, and were a slightly heavier version of the LMS Ivatt Class 2MT 2-6-2T (Nos 41200-329), built between 1946 and 1952, and of which no fewer than four examples have been preserved. These had proved popular across Britain due to their wide route availability, ease of maintenance and efficient performance. Some detail modifications were made to the LMS design, including a lower cab for loading gauge reasons.

All 30 engines were intended to be built in 1952-53, but steel shortages postponed the first 20 until 1953, and the last ten to 1957. The first batch was built at Crewe, destined for the London Midland Region, while the last ten emerged from Darlington, intended for the Southern Region. The livery was BR lined black, and the first 20 carried the early BR 'lion and wheel' logo, while the Darlington batch carried the newer 'lion and crown' emblem introduced in 1956. There was also difference in the size of the cabside numerals between the two batches.

The LMS 2-6-2Ts were all still at work (the first of the 130-strong class was not withdrawn until the summer of 1962), so the LMR batch of the new Standard engines was allocated to replace older pre-Grouping designs on local services.

The engines were fitted with push-pull equipment, and members of the LMR batch were frequently allocated alongside

Introduced 1953	
Designed by Robert Riddles, at Derby	
Built by BR, Crewe (20), BR, Darlington (10)	
Number built 30	
Last example withdrawn September 1966	

their Ivatt sisters. The Southern Region locomotives all initially went to Ashford or Ramsgate for use on several Kent lines. In 1961, following electrification, most were transferred away to the North West, to such places as Llandudno Junction, Bolton and Newton Heath, while a couple found themselves in the East Midlands at Annesley, Leicester and Wellingborough, among others. In 1965 No 84020 moved to Eastleigh to be converted to work on the Isle of Wight, but the plan came to nothing. However, ten of the LMR allocation were reallocated to Eastleigh at the end of 1965 when plans for use on the island were revived. Again the scheme was abandoned, and the engines were all withdrawn in December of that year, following the remaining ten that had still been in service during 1965, rendering the class extinct. Sadly none of these went to Woodham Brothers' famous Barry scrapyard, otherwise the following events might have been different.

The lack of a preserved Standard Class 2 tank is to be made good by yet another new-build plan, but this one has a twist. Four of the Class 2MT 2-6-0 tender versions survive in preservation, and one of them, Darlington-built No 78059, is to be rebuilt into the 'Prairie' tank version to become the next in the numerical series, No 84030. No 78059 was chosen primarily because it lost its tender while at Barry (sold to a steelworks and stripped of its bodywork to be used for carrying heavy steel ingots), so conversion to a tank engine was seen as ideal. Also, the work is being done under the auspices of the Bluebell Railway Trust in Sussex, in an area where the tender engines did not work, but the tanks did. Thus during 2013 No 78059 ceased to exist at it gradually began to morph into No 84030.

2MT 2-6-2Ts Nos 84020-29 were built at Darlington for the Southern Region. In July 1957 the first of the batch, no more than three months old, is seen at the New Romney terminus on the south coast of Kent. Allocated to Ashford at the time, the engine moved north-west to Llandudno Junction in September 1961, and was withdrawn from there in October 1964, aged just 7½ years. *R. Shenton, Colour-Rail*

Ministry of Supply 'WD' 'Austerity' Class 2-8-0

Nos 90000-732
(Nos 90000-100 and 90422-520 were former LNER Nos 63000-199 – qv in LNER section)

The War Department 'Austerity' 2-8-0s were built between 1943 and 1945 for war service, and an enormous total of 935 were built. The design was based Stanier's 8F 2-8-0 for the LMS, a class that also amounted to a significant total of 849 engines, and which up to that point had been the Government's standard design. However, the 8Fs were considered unsuitable for development for further wartime use as they were expensive and labour-intensive to build and used materials that were in short supply. Riddles, then Deputy Director of Royal Engineer Equipment, made various modifications to the design to keep costs low: the boiler was of simpler construction and was not tapered, and the steel (rather than copper) firebox was round-topped instead of the Belpaire flat-topped variety.

Construction was divided between the North British Locomotive Co of Glasgow, which built 251 at its Queen's Park Works and 294 at its Hyde Park Works, and the Vulcan Foundry at Newton-le-Willows, which built the remaining 390. The WD numbers were 800-879, 7000-7509, 8510-8718 and 9177-9312, and all had 70000 added to their numbers before they were shipped abroad (except for those built after 5 September 1944, which had 7xxxx numbers from new). All but three engines saw service with the Army in Europe after D-Day.

Following the cessation of hostilities, the War Department had 930 locomotives to dispose of (it retained two, for use on the Longmoor Military Railway, and three had been scrapped). Although not originally intended for use on home railways, the LNER bought 200, which formed that company's Class 'O7' (qv), while 533 were purchased by the British Transport Commission, having previously been on loan.

In 1948 all 733 engines became BR property and were numbered in a single sequence from 90000 to 90732 (the last engine, a Vulcan Foundry machine of 1945, was named *Vulcan*).

Of the remainder, 184 were acquired by Netherlands Railways (two of which were subsequently resold to Swedish State Railways), 12 went to Hong Kong, and one went to the USA, exchanged for a USATC 'S160' Class engine.

In the ensuing years the engines became familiar to railway enthusiasts as the 'Dub Dees' or 'Austerities', and were easily recognised by the characteristic 'clink-cloink-clink, clink-cloink-clink'

Introduced 1943
Designed by Robert Riddles, for the Ministry of Supply
Built by North British (545), Vulcan Foundry (390)
Number built 935
Number purchased by LNER/BR 733
Last example withdrawn September 1967

End of days: 'WD' No 90721, built by the Vulcan Foundry in 1945 as WD No 79294, was a resident of various West Yorkshire sheds until withdrawn from Normanton in September 1967. Awaiting the cutter's torch, it is seen here still languishing at Wakefield the following January, before being finally cut up in April.
A. Gray, Colour-Rail

of their motion as they hauled long trains of coal, steel, iron ore and general freight around the northern half of England. (Their spartan appearance also gained the somewhat unpleasant nickname of 'Iron Lungs', after the rigid case fitted over a patient's body to provide prolonged artificial respiration, common during the polio outbreaks of the 1940s and 1950s). All but two were still at work at the end of 1961, but four years later only 227 survived. The last 123 were all withdrawn between January and September 1967.

And there the story might have ended, had not a group of Keighley & Worth Valley Railway volunteers found the two 1945 Vulcan-built Swedish examples in a forest clearing at Mallansjo in Sweden in 1972. As Swedish Railways Class 'G11' No 1931, they had been rebuilt to Swedish outline and entered service in 1954, only to be withdrawn two years later and set aside as part of Sweden's strategic reserve of steam locomotives. One of the pair was subsequently purchased and arrived in Yorkshire in 1973 (the other was, sadly, scrapped). It worked until 1976, then in 1993 it was decided to return it to 'as-built' condition, and to give it a British Railways number, 90733, which would have been the next in sequence. Restoration complete, the locomotive finally returned to Haworth on 16 April 2007 and, following a period of testing and running-in, officially re-entered traffic on Monday 23 July.

On 11 April 1962 work-worn Vulcan-built 'WD' 2-8-0 No 90672 comes into the former Stratford-upon-Avon & Midland Junction station at Fenny Compton; it was then shedded at Woodford Halse, where the SMJR connected with the former GCR main line. The down platform of the GWR station at Fenny Compton can be seen beyond the engine. The 'WD' was withdrawn from 1G two years after this picture was taken. *Rob Tibbits, Colour-Rail*

Ministry of Supply 'WD' 'Austerity' Class 2-10-0

Nos 90750-774

The 2-10-0 'Austerities' were developed from the 2-8-0 locomotive (see above), and were similarly provided by the Ministry of Supply for use by the British Army overseas during the Second World War. Apart from the unique and short-lived Great Eastern Railway 'Decapod' 0-10-0 of 1902-06 and the Midland 0-10-0 'Big Bertha' built for banking on the Lickey Incline, they were the first ten-coupled engines to run in Britain, and were precursors of the Standard 9F 2-10-0s, arguably the most versatile and able of all the Standard designs. Their extra pair of wheels would enable them to work over lightly laid track; their axle loading was just 13½ tons, as against the 16½ tons of the 2-8-0s. They were all built by the North British Locomotive Co, in two batches – 100 in 1943-44, and a further 50 in 1945. The boiler was parallel, a rocking grate was fitted in the firebox, and as many parts as possible were common with the 2-8-0s. The central pair of wheels were flangeless, and the next pairs had reduced flanges.

While they were being run in the LNER had 33 from both batches on loan (and had to impose restrictions on their use due to their long wheelbase rendering them out of gauge on curves).

One of the first batch was allocated to the Longmoor Military Railway, and 20 went overseas to the Middle East. The remaining 79 worked on the LMS until shipped to Europe in late 1944. The second batch entered service during 1945, and one of them was also allocated to Longmoor; none worked on the LNER. Those that remained on the continent after the war were bought by Netherlands State Railways in 1946, and 16 of the 20 Middle East engines were moved to Greece.

When the railways were nationalised the British Transport Commission decided to buy 25 of the War Department engines; WD Nos 73774-98 became BR Nos 90750-74. Ownership was transferred in December 1948, but most were kept in store until 1949-50. They were then allocated to former LMS sheds, mainly in Scotland – principally Motherwell and Grangemouth. Two were named, and unusually Nos 90773 and 90774 both carried the same name, *North British*, after their builder!

The class remained intact until July 1961, when Nos 90753 and 90754 were withdrawn from Carstairs and Motherwell

Introduced 1943
Designed by Robert Riddles, for the Ministry of Supply
Built by North British
Number built 150
Number purchased by BR 25
Last example withdrawn December 1962

respectively. By the middle of 1962 another four had been dispensed with, and the whole of the remainder were taken out of service at the end of the year.

The two Longmoor engines were No AD600 *Gordon* (named after General Charles Gordon of Khartoum fame, the second engine to be built, and the last steam loco owned by the Army), and No 601 *Kitchener* – formerly *Sapper* – which was on loan to BR from May 1957 to February 1959, and was scrapped in 1967. *Gordon* was withdrawn in October 1969 when the military railway closed. It was owned by the Ministry of Defence and was on permanent loan to the Severn Valley Railway from 1972 until 2008, when it was formally handed over by the Army to the SVR. It currently awaits overhaul.

Another non-BR survivor carries the fictitious BR number 90775. As No 3652 it was shipped to the Middle East, worked in Egypt until 1945 and was then sold (with 15 others) to Hellenic State Railways. In 1984 a group of Mid Hants Railway volunteers repatriated it, together with a substantial set of spare parts (including some complete fireboxes still in their NBL crates!). It spent some of its preservation years in Longmoor WD livery running as WD No 601 and, after appearing on various heritage lines, it moved on loan to the North Norfolk Railway. In 2006 it was purchased by the Midland & Great Northern Joint Railway Society, and is currently in the last stages of a long and expensive overhaul.

A third loco is privately owned WD No (7)3672, which now carries the name *Dame Vera Lynn*. It, too, is currently awaiting overhaul at Grosmont on the North Yorkshire Moors Railway.

A Dutch 2-10-0, WD No 73755, is on display at the Dutch Railway Museum at Utrecht, named *Longmoor*.

O. S. Nock summed up the 'WD' engines thus: 'In view of the very important part the locomotives played towards the British war effort, and the skill with which such simplification and economy in construction was achieved with so little diminution in their general usefulness, the two types [2-8-0 and 2-10-0] occupy a notable place in British locomotive history.'

WD 2-10-0 No 73779 became No 90755 when purchased by BR following nationalisation. It remained in store until allocated to Grangemouth shed in February 1949, and there it stayed until withdrawal, together with most of its sisters, in December 1962. The locos' simple, austere lines are well shown in this photograph taken at Grangemouth on 11 June 1962. *G. Parry collection, Colour-Rail*

Sources

Books

Adams, William (ed) *Encyclopaedia of the Great Western Railway* (Patrick Stephens Ltd, 1993)

Adley, Robert *Out of Steam: The Beeching years in hindsight* (Patrick Stephens Ltd, 1990)

Awdry, Christopher *Encyclopaedia of British Railway Companies* (Patrick Stephens Ltd, 1990)

Dow, George *Great Central* (3 Vols, Ian Allan, 1959, 1962, 1965)

Griffiths, Denis *Locomotive Engineers of the LMS* (Patrick Stephens Ltd, 1991)

Jackson, Alan A. *The Railway Dictionary: An A-Z of Railway Terminology* (Alan Sutton, 1992)

Longworth, Hugh *British Railways Steam Locomotives, 1948-1968* (Oxford Publishing Co, 2005, 2nd ed 2013; ISBN 978 0 86093 660 2)
BR Steam Locomotives: Complete Allocations History, 1948-1968 (Oxford Publishing Co, 2014; ISBN 978 0 86093 661 9)

Lowe, James W. *British Steam Locomotive Builders* (Tee Publishing, 1975)

Middlemass, Thomas *Steam Locomotive Nicknames* (Silver Link Publishing, 1991)

Nock, O. S. *British Locomotives of the 20th Century* (3 volumes, Patrick Stephens Ltd, 1983-85)
British Locomotives of the 20th Century, Vol 2 (Patrick Stephens Ltd, 1984)
Great Locomotives of the LNER (Patrick Stephens Ltd, 1988)
Great Locomotives of the LMS (Patrick Stephens Ltd, 1989)
Great Locomotives of the Southern Railway (Patrick Stephens Ltd, 1987)

Pike, Jim *Locomotive Names: An Illustrated Dictionary* (Sutton Publishing, 2000)

Simmons, Jack and Biddle, Gordon (eds) *The Oxford Companion to British Railway History* (OUP, 1997)

Tuplin, W. A. *Great Western Steam* (George Allen & Unwin, 1958)

Internet

Among the websites consulted mostly frequently, and which consistently yielded some of the most useful information, are the following:

'A Beginner's Guide to GWR 4-coupled tanks' and 'A Beginner's Guide to Pannier Tanks' by Jim Champ

BR Database: Complete British Locomotive Database 1923-1997 (http://www.brdatabase.info/index.php)

Kent Rail (www.kentrail.org.uk)

London & North Eastern Railway Encyclopaedia (www.lner.info) (Richard Marsden) – a well-organised and comprehensive resource; if only all railway companies had such excellent websites devoted to them!

London & North Western Railway Society (www.lnwrs.org.uk)

Rail UK (www.railuk.info)

Southern Email Group (www.semgonline.com)

SteamIndex (www.steamindex.com), a very useful and comprehensive digest of books and magazine articles

The Great Eastern Railway Society (www.gersociety.org.uk)

www.warwickshirerailways.com

Index